COGNITION AND EMOTION

Cognition and Emotion
From Order to Disorder

Mick Power
University of Edinburgh, Department of Psychiatry, Royal Edinburgh Hospital, Edinburgh, UK

Tim Dalgleish
MRC Applied Psychology Unit, Cambridge, UK

Psychology Press
An imprint of Erlbaum (UK) Taylor & Francis

Copyright © 1997 by Psychology Press, an imprint of
Erlbaum (UK) Taylor & Francis Ltd.

Psychology Press, Publishers
27 Church Road
Hove
East Sussex, BN3 2FA
UK

British Library Cataloguing in Publication Data

A catalogue record for this book is available from the British Library

ISBN 0-86377-738-4 (Hbk)
ISBN 0-86377-739-2 (Pbk)

Printed and bound in the United Kingdom by Biddles Ltd, Guildford and King's Lynn

To Lorna, Liam, and Jack

To Peter and Madeline

Contents

Preface

The idea of writing a book that spanned both the everyday experience of emotion and the emotional disorders seemed like a worthwhile challenge when it occurred to us a few years back. Although there are now many excellent textbooks and monographs on the subject of emotion—they are landing on our desks even as we write this preface—none of them satisfactorily bridges the divide between normal emotions and the emotional disorders. Many books on normal or everyday emotion provide little or no feel for the experience of emotion at its extreme. Equally, none of the books or theories on emotional disorders provide satisfactory accounts for everyday emotion; most take a single emotion as their starting point and few consider other emotional disorders. The challenge therefore was to write a book on emotion that fell straight into the chasm between the normal and the abnormal—and then watch to see if it survived.

We have taken a primarily cognitive approach to emotion in this book, because we believe that this is the best starting point that we have. The cognitive approach is not of course without its limitations and if there is any area that can show up the cracks in the edifice it is the area of emotion. Emotions, *par excellence*, can be viewed at all levels of analysis between the physiological and the cultural levels. In order to understand the role and function of emotion we may need to consider alterations in physiology, the psychological state, the interpersonal signal, and the cultural context. Walking into a hospital in Nigeria and reporting that you are worried because you've got butterflies in your stomach may lead to very different medical procedures than reporting the same symptom in South London. Nevertheless, despite the multiplicity of levels that need to be considered, the psychological level is, we suggest, the crossroads at which all of these influences meet.

The writing of a book, like any other production, involves a cast of thousands. For many years our colleagues and friends have tried to point out our *folies à deux,* sometimes with success, but other times, as will be evident, with no success whatsoever! We apologise in advance therefore to Lorna Champion, Steve Joseph, Marc Lewis, Andy MacLeod, Andrew Mathews, Nicola Morant, Emmanuelle Peters, Charlie Sharp, John Teasdale, and Fraser Watts for the times when we have ignored their better advice, but thank them for their time and effort over the years when we have listened to them. We thank Ann Copeman for help with the typing and Debbie Lawson, who, with great care and dedication, converted scribbles on napkins, backs of envelopes, and rolls of toilet paper into worthy tables and figures. Finally, we would also like to thank Randy Katz who, a couple of years ago, abandoned us in a log cabin in Northern Ontario and left us to write our way out. When we eventually left, we managed to get a cab-driver from Barrie, the local town, to come and collect us. As typical city-dwellers who thought that nothing ever happened in the country, we wondered what it was like to live in Barrie all year round—mightn't it be too *quiet* and *boring* for a young man like himself? "Oh no!" came the instant reply "Why, every summer a hot air balloon lands right down by the side of the lake!" Our hope is that our readers will find our book equally exciting with just the right amount of hot air to make it fly, but enough substance to bring it back to earth when needed. Perhaps, too, we might even send a copy to the cab-drivers of Barrie, Northern Ontario. Wow! That was some year—*two* hot air balloons!

CHAPTER ONE

Introduction

Each venture
Is a new beginning, a raid on the inarticulate
With shabby equipment always deteriorating
In the general mess of imprecision of feeling *(T.S. Eliot)*

PRELIMINARY OBSERVATIONS

The experience of happiness is one that people go to extraordinary lengths to attain, though its pursuit is full of dangers that we consistently and repeatedly ignore. When feeling happy we perceive ourselves to be in control of situations and outcomes that we have little effect on, we believe ourselves to be invulnerable and drive too fast in the outside lane, we are convinced that the attractive person waiting at the bus stop is desperate for our attention, we know that this time we are going to be lucky, that this definitely is the winning set of numbers. Most of the time we "recover" from this unfortunate state, that is, just in time to buy the next lottery ticket with equal portentous certainty, or just in time to pass the next bus stop.

We may prefer to believe that "irrationality" is reserved for the "negative" emotions such as anger or jealousy, as in the concept of "crimes of passion" in which the individual is deemed to have diminished responsibility for his or her own actions. However, as we will argue in subsequent chapters, such "irrationality', in the sense of believing or acting in a way that is contrary to a more appropriate interpretation of reality, can be an aspect of any emotion whatever form it might take. We will consider for example why that common ailment, love, is considered to have such potentially devastating or irrational effects on sufferers as captured in Dryden's phrase "My love's a noble madness". Thus, we may all (hopefully) have at some time experienced "love-sickness" with the whole range of painful emotions that accompanies it. Indeed, the French psychiatrist, Gaetane de Clerambault, has given his name to an extreme form of love-sickness in which the sufferer typically falls in love with a celebrity or a well-known public figure. In their fascinating account of de Clerambault's Syndrome, Franzini and Grossberg (1995, pp.4-5) observe the following:

> There is a long medical tradition, going back to Greek and Roman times, warning of the excesses of carnal love as potentially dangerous to one's physical and mental health. In fact, the Greeks often visited the love-stricken person, bringing gifts and earnest hopes that their friend would soon recover from love and return to his senses. The Roman physician Soranus sternly advised against allowing the mentally ill to indulge in love's pleasures, since such strong emotion would no doubt make them worse ... Cicero went so far as to declare, "Of all the emotions there is none more violent than love. Love is a madness."

Franzini and Grossberg then provide an account of a recent famous American case, John Hinckley Jr., who, after a desperate series of phone calls and letters had failed to attract the attention of the film star, Jodie Foster, decided to shoot the then president of the United States, Ronald Reagan, as a unique love offering to her!

At the other extreme emotions and moods other than happiness and love have long been considered to make us think and act in irrational ways. Many such views often represent cultural or familial beliefs about the permissibility or otherwise of the expression of certain emotions. For example, the view in many cultures including our own that sadness is a "weak" or "feminine" emotion leads to problems in its expression in men; the Ilongot in the Philippines used to prescribe head-hunting as an effective means for their young men to overcome the unmanly feeling of sadness. Notwithstanding these cultural caveats, there is good evidence that emotions do bias our perceptions, beliefs, and actions in characteristic ways, though, as we will argue in our detailed analyses in subsequent chapters, bias does not imply that the outcome is therefore illogical, irrational, or unrealistic. Instead, under appropriate circumstances, a negative bias may lead to more accuracy than a positive bias: we may sometimes be *more* rational and logical when sad or depressed than when we are happy or well (see Chapters 4 and 7). The important point to remember when considering the effects of emotion on our thinking, reasoning, and actions is that under appropriate conditions emotions are adaptive and useful. Contrary to two schools of thought, first, Darwin's (1872/1965) view that emotions are no longer of use but are vestigial like the appendix, and, second, the Platonic and dualist view that emotions are irrational, we will take the view that emotions have crucial short- and long-term functions that enable individuals to adapt to changing social and physical environments. For example, in happiness, seeing the world through rose-tinted spectacles and believing in personal invulnerability gives us the confidence to sail over the edge of the world, climb Everest, and fly to the moon.

Unfortunately, though, the adaptive benefits of emotions can become submerged under the short-cuts that they appear to offer. For example, certainty and the belief in our own invulnerability can threaten our lives and the lives of those around us. In his compelling study of military incompetence, Norman Dixon (1976, pp.398–399) argued that many of the great military disasters were often the consequence of one person's mistaken overconfidence or belief in invulnerability.

> Sunday, December 7th, 1941, had been set aside by Admiral Kimmel (Commander-in-Chief of the Pacific Fleet) for a friendly game of golf with his colleague General Short, ninety-six ships of the American Fleet slept at anchor in the harbour, American planes stood wing-tip to wing-tip on the tarmac, American servicemen were off duty enjoying week-end leave. By the end of the day Pearl Harbor, with its ships, planes and military installations, had been reduced to smoking ruins, 2000 servicemen had been killed and as many more missing or wounded. ...
>
> ... the neglect of intelligence reports and gross underestimation of enemy capabilities, coupled in this instance with an assiduous misinterpretation of warning signals from Washington and amiable dedication to the task of mutual reassurance regarding their invulnerability, Kimmel and his circle of naval and military advisers achieved a state of such supine complacency that they brought upon themselves "the worst disaster in American history.

We are not suggesting that all beliefs in invulnerability arise only from feeling happy nor, of course, do such beliefs afflict only one side during conflicts (Dixon, 1976, p.199):

> So unthinkable was it that Japanese soldiers would ever surrender to the enemy that they were not instructed as to how they should comport themselves if they did. As a consequence Japanese P.O.W.s were a relatively fruitful source of information for Allied interrogators.

Although these military examples may seem extreme and therefore unrelated to everyday life, on the contrary we suggest that they are typical of how certain positive emotions, in interaction with appropriate beliefs and models of the world, can lead to the appearance of irrationality for all of us. A famous example is provided by Winston Churchill who was widely considered to be "doom-mongering" in the 1930s about the build up of military strength in Germany and about the intentions of the Nazis. At the same time it is clear that Churchill was in a period of depression. In his analysis of Winston Churchill's "Black Dog", Anthony Storr (1988, p.15) quoting Churchill's physician, Lord Moran, writes:

> August 14th 1944.
> The P.M. was in a speculative mood today.
> 'When I was young," he ruminated, "for two or three years the light faded out of the picture. I did my work. I sat in the House of Commons, but black depression settled on me. It helped me to talk to Clemmie about it. I don't like standing near the edge of a platform when an express train is passing through. I like to stand right back and if possible to get a pillar between me and the train. I don't like to stand by the side of a ship and look down into the water. A second's action would end everything. A few drops of desperation. And yet I don't want to go out of the world at all in such moments."

As Anthony Storr (1988, pp.16–17) comments perceptively about the role of depression in Churchill's life:

> Many depressives deny themselves rest or relaxation because they cannot afford to stop. If they are forced by circumstances to do so, the black cloud comes down upon them. This happened to Churchill when he left the Admiralty in May 1915, when he was out of office during the thirties,

when he was defeated in the election of 1945, and after his final resignation. He invented various methods of coping with the depression which descended when he was no longer fully occupied by affairs of state, including painting, writing, and bricklaying; but none of these were wholly successful.

In Churchill's case it would appear that the successful pursuit of extremely ambitious political goals gave him some relief from a negative side of his self-concept that otherwise led him into depression. Churchill's famous comment "We are all worms. But I do believe that I am a glow-worm" (cited in Storr, 1988) sums up his self-ambivalence and the role that this must have played in his depression. Indeed, we have argued that such patterns are common in depression in which the pursuit of an overvalued role or goal may hold off depression in a vulnerable individual, but the actual or perceived loss of that role or goal typically leads to depression (Champion & Power, 1995; see Chapter 7). Sometimes, however, the recovery from episodes of emotional disorders need not be so lengthy but can be quite sudden and dramatic. In his account of his personal experience of depression, Stuart Sutherland (1976) tells how after many months of struggle, he overheard a tune that was "Top of the Pops" and his mood suddenly lifted. He also recounts the story of another patient who had been hospitalised for two years with obsessive compulsive problems that were completely disabling. This patient was unexpectedly left a legacy of £30,000 upon which he immediately recovered and discharged himself from hospital! Given the cost of other forms of Health Service treatment, there may be a lesson for us here.

Our intention however is not to write a book about the Second World War, nor about the various possible pathologies of its participants. Our focus will primarily be on the individual and the development of a psychological theory of emotion. In carrying out this task, we do not wish to deny the fact that one of the important characteristics of emotion is its role in communication with others (e.g. Oatley, 1992). This social role has led some theorists to argue that emotion should be viewed *solely* in terms of its social functions. In contrast, our view is that while the social role is important, there are equally important psychological and biological levels at which it is also necessary to understand emotion. If the social role is the tip of the iceberg, then the psychological role forms much of the remainder of the iceberg's bulk. But as we hope to demonstrate throughout this book, all three levels interact in the occurrence and expression of emotion, but the core of emotion in our analysis is at the psychological level.

In order to understand the theoretical framework from which we will approach emotion, there are a number of questions that the passengers on the Clapham Omnibus might ask of themselves and each other in their attempts to understand their emotions. The first of these questions is what exactly is an emotion? We will approach this question through a consideration of the main ways in which other theorists have tackled it and then begin to consider the way in which we propose to tackle the issue.

EMOTION

In this section we will first raise the major question about what an emotion is, about what the cognitive approach to psychology is in general, and about the form that a cognitive approach to emotion might take. We will also return to these questions in more detail in Chapter 2 where a number of subsidiary questions will be considered from a historical viewpoint.

What is an emotion? The question of exactly what an emotion is has been variously addressed by philosophers down the centuries and, in the 20th century by psychologists and neuroscientists also. Two key traditions can be identified. The first stems from Plato's dualistic philosophy that came to dominate Christian theology, and which reached its apogee in Descartes. This approach, in its various forms, came to be known as "feeling theory". In essence, the phenomenal or conscious "feeling" occurs in a psychic or spiritual domain, but it is normally considered to be a by-product of a bodily process. For example, in William James' classic version of feeling theory the bodily process or reaction, such as trembling or running away, is considered to be the *cause* of the conscious feeling of anxiety, not the other way round in contrast to the typical folk psychology belief. The ultimate step in the development of this approach was taken in Watson's Behaviorism in which mental states such as feelings were considered outside the scope of science, which he restricted to objects (stimuli) and to bodily responses (behaviour and physiology). As we will discuss in more detail in Chapter 2, despite feeling theories having dominated the approach to emotion for over two thousand years, there has been a shift away from them in the latter half of the 20th century. Plato's approach has nevertheless left its mark on how we view emotion as "irrational" and in conflict with reason, as in the "wandering uterus" theory that gave its name to hysteria (from *The Timaeus*):

> In men the organ of generation—becoming rebellious and masterful, like an animal disobedient to reason, and maddened with the sting of lust—seeks to gain absolute sway; and the same is the case with the ... womb ... of women; the animal within them is desirous of procreating children, and when remaining unfruitful long beyond its proper time, gets discontented and angry, and wandering in every direction through the body, closes up the passages of the breath, and by obstructing respiration, drives them to extremity, causing all varieties of diseases.

The second major tradition stems from Aristotle, one of Plato's better students in the Athens Academy. Aristotle argued that in order to understand something we must know both its constitution (what it is made of) and its function. In relation to emotion therefore it is insufficient to say that an emotion consists of a set of physiological processes or a sequence of behaviour; one must also state what the function is of the processes or the behavioural sequence. In fact, and this is the essence of modern "functionalism", similar functions may derive from very different physical constituents, just as similar physical constituents may have very different functions. As Karl Popper expressed it in more modern terminology (e.g. Popper & Eccles, 1977), logical form and physical form need not bear any consistent correspondence to each other; this property is especially evident with the modern digital computer in which the "same" physical state of the computer could represent multiple different logical states according to which software program is running, in the same way that the "same" logical state could be implemented on many different physical forms or different types of hardware. In relation to emotion, therefore, any reductionist approach in which the logical form of an emotion is reduced to its physical form is philosophically untenable from this viewpoint. The function of an emotion within a system might be a psychological one, such as to enable the person to switch from one goal to another, or a social one, such as to communicate to another person; the important point is that without knowledge of that function, then we are unable to define emotion (see Chapter 2). A second major aspect of Aristotle's approach to emotion is his observation that different beliefs or, again in more modern terminology, different types of appraisal lead to different emotions; that is, it is not the external object *per se* that is important, but my belief about that object. I believe the knife could kill me and I feel afraid, I believe the knife could cut through the ropes that bind me and I am overwhelmed with joy. Thus, it is my belief about the knife rather than the knife itself that leads to these very different emotions.

Although we have not yet defined what an emotion is, nor, just as importantly, have we attempted to distinguish emotions from related states such as drives (see Chapter 2), we hope that we have provided a map which indicates the direction that we intend to take in our theorising. One point that we do wish to flag up at this early stage, however, is that we will take the view that there are a limited number of basic emotions from which more complex emotions and the emotional disorders can be derived. Although the issue of whether or not there *are* basic emotions is still a controversial one (see Chapter 3), we believe that the approach has many advantages—especially in relation to the emotional disorders—that have not yet been explored. One of the sources of evidence that we will use in favour of this approach will be that basic emotions may be distinguishable from each other at the physiological level (e.g. Levenson, Ekman, & Friesen, 1990). So, the astute reader might point out, would that not be evidence that emotions *can* be reduced to a set of distinct physiological processes? Is that not an argument against the Aristotelian functionalism that we espouse? Well, fortunately for us, the answer to both of these questions is "No!" First, the fact that in Popperian terms logical and physical forms do not correspond one to one but, rather, correspond many to many, does not imply that *any* physical form can have *any* logical function. The physical and logical forms set boundary conditions or limitations on each other, not in a unidirectional way as in reductionistic approaches, but in a mutual or bi-directional way; thus, there need to be "interaction rules" by which the physical and the logical relate to each other. Second, let us imagine that we had a machine that summed together the complete physiological state of an individual and was able, with 99% certainty, to state that the individual was "Angry". How little this wonderful machine would actually tell us! Could it tell us that the person was angry because he could only find one sock and was already late for work, that he had been unfairly accused by his boss of slipshod work, or that his mother had just been insulted by his enemy? Of course not. Instead, we must turn back to Aristotle in order to understand why in one case the individual kicks the wardrobe door, in the second case bites his tongue and keeps quiet, and in the final case takes his gun and shoots his enemy dead.

There are of course many other questions that need to be asked about emotion. We will reserve discussion of these questions until Chapter 2, when the answers will be considered in a philosophical and historical context. Instead, we will next make some preliminary remarks about the cognitive approach to psychology in general and provide some pointers about what an adequate cognitive approach to emotion might look like.

THE COGNITIVE APPROACH IN PSYCHOLOGY

We have already touched on some characteristics of the cognitive approach to emotion in our initial remarks on Aristotle and his current functionalist influence on philosophy and psychology. However, before launching into detailed accounts of cognitive models of emotion and the emotional disorders, it is first necessary to provide some groundwork about the cognitive approach and what we see as its most useful characteristics.

As with any approach, there are a number of distinct churches residing under the same ecumenical roof which offer substantially different approaches to believers and non-believers alike. Even key cognitive psychologists can be followed as they shift churches themselves; for example, Ulric Neisser (1967) wrote one of the key books in cognitive psychology in which he espoused a philosophical idealism known as "constructivism" in which the individual perceives the world based in part on existing mental representations of the world. By 1976 however Neisser had abandoned this extreme constructivism for an approach closer to philosophical realism, which he called "constructive realism". In this approach the individual is seen to be struggling towards mental representations that bear semblance to reality; the testing out of representations and predictions about reality should for most individuals lead to modification of those representations. This constructive realism does, we believe, make sense for approaches to emotion and emotional disorders. Most therapies that address emotional disorders have at some level the idea that individuals may hold rigid inflexible representations of reality that need to be tested out and, potentially, relinquished. In talking about reality, of course, we are not simply referring to physical reality, but also to social reality. In sum, if cognitive approaches can be placed on a continuum from constructivism to realism, approaches to emotions and their disorders might best be placed at the mid-point between the two.

The concept of the unconscious is, as every schoolchild knows, normally associated with Freud. Throughout his life Freud did in fact present several distinct models of the unconscious; surprisingly in some ways, it is now the first model presented by Breuer and Freud (1895/1974) that has most potential for integration with the cognitive tradition (Power & Brewin, 1991). This model was in fact a variant of Janet's dissociationist approach to the unconscious in which an attempt was made to account for dissociations of consciousness seen in fugue states, somnambulism, multiple personality, and so on. The advantage of the concept of dissociationism is that it provides an historical starting point and a conceptual bridge to a number of related concepts, which, at their core, may refer to the same mental phenomenon. These additional concepts include the idea of splitting that the post-Freudian Kleinian and Object Relations Theorists have emphasised, and the recent cognitive focus on modularity (e.g. Fodor, 1983; Gazzaniga, 1988), about which we will have more to say in later chapters. The moral is however that vastly different lines of evidence and different theoretical approaches seem to point to a phenomenon of the mind which has been referred to as the potential for modularity. We propose that in relation to emotional development under the right circumstances basic emotions may develop in a modularised or dissociated way. The failure for these basic emotions to be integrated into the general development of the self can provide an important precursor for the development of emotional disorders, a sequence that we will explore in more detail in the second half of this book (see Chapters 6–10).

We have now briefly discussed several aspects of the cognitive approach. In the process of highlighting even these features of our cognitive model we will have presented at least one feature that almost all of our colleagues would disagree with all of the time and have presented many features that at least some of our colleagues would disagree with some of the time. If psychology ever achieves the Grand Unifying Theory that is currently the Holy Grail of physics, then we will happily abandon those aspects of the model that are untenable. However, we must warn that this promise is unlikely to be worth the paper it is written on, either because of the timescale for such an aim, or because of a philosophical paradox that the quarry is elusive: the modelling of the self by the self may alter the self, and so on, in an infinite regress. We will of course return to all of these features of cognitive models over the next few chapters and add many more features besides. We hope however that this brief overview has at least given enough of a flavour of the main course for this to be awaited with gastronomic anticipation.

SUMMARY OF THE AIMS OF THE BOOK

In order to provide a guiding framework, we will now offer a menu, with comments, about what is to be found in the remaining chapters in this book. This menu will, we hope, provide sufficient information for some selection of the dishes that individual readers might prefer to spend longer over, in addition to those that they might prefer to avoid. The book is divided into two main parts: Part One is mainly theoretical and reviews a range of theories of emotion; Part Two focuses on specific basic emotions and their derivatives.

In our view, it is a sad reflection on many psychological works that there is little or no attempt to provide the historical and philosophical context in which the work resides, nor is there any exploration of the philosophical underpinnings and implications of the models presented. Modern philosophy has of course seen dramatic changes in that the findings of science may be relevant to the choice of one philosophical position over another; philosophers have been forced to abandon their armchairs for laboratory stools. For this reason, Chapter 2 is devoted to the presentation of the philosophical and historical context in which theories of emotion exist. The two key strands mentioned earlier will be presented, one stemming from Plato and leading to the until recently dominant "feeling theories" of emotion, the second stemming from Aristotle and currently resurgent in the form of functionalism in cognitive science. The approaches of William James, Watson's Behaviorism, and further general comments about 20th-century cognitive accounts will also be presented in Chapter 2.

The main aim of Chapter 3 is to provide an account of the major cognitive theories of normal emotions. We begin with an account of associative network theories which historically have provided the starting point for theoretical approaches as diverse as psychoanalysis and behaviorism. The associative network approach was adapted to provide a model of emotion in an influential paper of Gordon Bower's (1981). We point to some weaknesses in the associative network approach, but then raise the question of whether or not the more recent connectionist Parallel Distributed Processing (PDP) theories might have more potential for emotion theory. In the second part of Chapter 3 we consider appraisal theories, beginning with the classic Schachter and Singer (1962) study and the flawed proposal that emotion is the cognitive labelling of an undifferentiated state of physiological arousal. We then consider a number of fully fledged appraisal theories which are not based on physiological arousal. These theories include Richard Lazarus' earlier (1966) and more recent (1991) models and Oatley and Johnson-Laird's (1987) goal-based basic emotion approach from which we have drawn considerably for our own approach.

Theories of normal emotions have often had little to say about emotional disorder, a fault to which the cognitive approaches have been as prone as any other. In Chapter 4 therefore we review an additional set of cognitive theories that have been applied to the emotional disorders. We have included here the various revisions of Seligman's Learned Helplessness Theory, Beck's Cognitive Therapy, the approach presented by Williams, Watts, MacLeod, and Mathews (1988), and Teasdale and Barnard's (1993) Interacting Cognitive Subsystems (ICS) approach. These cognitive models have been included because of their relevance to more than one emotional disorder; cognitive theories that are disorder-specific are discussed in Part Two of the book, in which emotional disorders are covered in detail. In the final part of Chapter 4, we consider the need for purely cognitive theories to take account of social factors, with particular focus on the case of depression. We must reiterate that we see emotion as a complex interaction of biological, psychological, and social factors and although we focus on cognitive theories, it is occasionally necessary to consider the limitations of any purely cognitive approach.

The climax of Part One of the book occurs, we hope, in Chapter 5. In this chapter we draw together the key points from the previous chapters and present our own Schematic Propositional Associative Analogue Representation Systems approach, which, fortunately for all of us, abbreviates to SPAARS. Like Oatley and Johnson-Laird (1987), we adopt a goal-based basic emotion approach. In addition, we argue that there are two main routes to the generation of emotion. The first route we have named the appraisal route and consists of the effortful processing and interpretation of an event as goal relevant. The second route is a direct access or automatic route; initially in development it expresses pre-wired innate emotion programmes, though later in development it also includes automated emotional reactions that no longer require effortful processing. Finally, in Chapter 5 we consider a number of more general aspects of the SPAARS approach.

Part Two of the book is organised around the five basic emotions of fear (Chapter 6), sadness (Chapter 7), anger (Chapter 8), disgust (Chapter 9), and happiness (Chapter 10) on a chapter-by-chapter basis. In each chapter, we consider the basic emotion, complex emotions derived from that basic emotion, and related emotional disorders. For example, in the chapter on disgust, Chapter 9, we consider some general properties of disgust as a basic emotion, theoretical approaches and cross-cultural aspects, complex emotions such as shame and guilt, which we argue are derived from disgust, and the role that disgust plays in a number of disorders including certain phobias and obsessive compulsive disorders, depression, and appetitive disorders such as bulimia and anorexia. In each of the basic emotion chapters we highlight some aspect of the SPAARS approach rather than setting out to provide a full and complete account. For example, in Chapter 6 on Fear we highlight the role of two routes to emotion in relation to panic and phobias; there is also consideration of the significant threat to the configuration of models that can occur in Post-traumatic Stress Disorder. In Chapter 7 on Sadness we examine the importance of different domains of knowledge and experience and the extent to which we invest in them; there is also detailed consideration of the possibility that basic emotions can become "coupled" with each other and thereby lead to emotional disorders such as depression. In Chapter 8 on Anger we highlight the role of cycles of appraisal. In Chapter 9 on Disgust we highlight the role that the application of the emotion to the self, especially in the form of guilt and shame, plays in the generation of a number of disorders. In Chapter 10 on Happiness we are particularly concerned to demonstrate how happiness may also lead to emotional disorders even though Western cultures are biased against seeing such disorders. In the final chapter, Chapter 11, we summarise the SPAARS model in the light of our review of the emotions and their disorders, consider some of the implications for therapeutic practice which can be derived from this approach, and, finally, present a number of novel research ideas based on SPAARS. If, at the end of the day, none of our readers feel like stealing these ideas, then we will have to go back to the drawing board—or join the Foreign Legion!

PART ONE
Philosophy and theory

CHAPTER TWO

The cognitive philosophy of emotion

Those who do not remember the past are condemned to repeat it *(George Santayana)*

INTRODUCTION

The present chapter is something of an express train ride through the historical and philosophical developments in our understanding of emotion and, to some extent, of cognition. Unlike the slow train which stops at every station, no matter how remote the village or infrequent the passengers, the current journey only pauses at the main towns, concerning itself with the major contributions to our appreciation of cognition and emotion. Inevitably, any definition of what constitutes a major contribution is somewhat subjective. Nevertheless, we hope that the work reviewed in this chapter represents some consensus of opinion concerning the central ideas in the literature.

Theories of emotion are almost always sub-texts of much larger theories of mind (Lyons, 1980, 1992). Thus, those who seek to describe and explain the mind as a cognitive system generally subscribe to a cognitive theory of emotions. Similarly, behaviourists advocate a behaviourist theory, dualists a dualist theory, and so on. The majority of the models and theories of emotion outlined in this chapter, and in the two that follow, reflect our belief that the cognitive theory of mind offers the best framework within which to understand emotion phenomena. Consequently, non-cognitive theories of emotion are considered in less detail. This neglect is not meant to imply that these models are the remote villages referred to above, rather they are large towns on altogether different train journeys.

Having said all of this, it remains important for a number of reasons to at least outline the principal non-cognitive theories of emotion which have held sway at various times. First, it is useful to point out the problems with such theories and, consequently, to propose reasons why a cognitive approach can overcome these difficulties. Second, it would be very difficult to communicate a sense of how cognitive theories of emotion have developed historically without some discussion of their critics and opponents.

A problem immediately arises, that of attempting to present a theory of emotion in isolation from the overarching theory of mind under which it resides. For example, any discussion of Descartes' ideas on the subject of the passions has a slightly hollow ring without at least some appreciation of Cartesian dualism and its implications. Perhaps more importantly, many of the criticisms of certain approaches to emotion are, in essentials, criticisms of the philosophy of mind they represent. Whilst not wishing to avoid this particular nettle, it is not easy to grasp it in the space of a single chapter. What we have tried to do is give something of the flavour of the alternative philosophies of mind insofar as they apply to the emotions. In addition, we have noted those criticisms that are directed at philosophies in their entirety, without going into any details or "proofs" of the arguments; instead, we refer the reader to more exhaustive alternative sources.

Having stated a priori that we are principally concerned with a cognitive approach to emotions, it seems incumbent to offer some a priori definition or conceptualisation of what we mean when we use the terms "cognitive" and "emotion" (see Chapter 1). However, we have elected to resist this temptation in the hope that an understanding of these concepts will emerge through the course of this chapter, and to some extent the next; after all, every train journey must have a destination! Similarly, every journey must have a beginning and it seems reasonable at this juncture to consider what sort of questions any comprehensive theory of emotions would need to address.

Some initial questions for the aspiring emotion theorist

1. What distinguishes an emotion from a non-emotion?   As Keith Oatley notes, in the introduction to his book *Best Laid Schemes* (1992, p.9): "Perhaps the most basic observation about emotions in Euro-American culture is that adults report experiences of subjective feelings that they describe as emotional". One might add to this that such individuals also report many other experiences that they would never describe as emotional and, thus, perhaps the most basic question concerns how emotions differ from these other experiences. Another way of putting this question is to ask what underlies the implicit folk psychological understanding of what is an emotion and what is not an emotion.

2. *What are the constituent parts of an emotion? or are emotions irreducible?*   Emotions seem to be characterised by physiological disturbance, changes in facial expression, gestures, behaviours, particular types of thoughts, beliefs, and desires, and a range of other experiences. Which of these are necessary and which are sufficient for something to be called an emotion? or is it not possible or helpful to "deconstruct" emotions in this way?

3. *What distinguishes one emotion from another?*   Few people would disagree that, for example, fear and joy are distinctly different emotions, but can we elucidate exactly where the differences lie. Is it the circumstances of their elicitation, the types of associated bodily feelings, the particular phenomenological feel, the kinds of behaviour to which they give rise? Wherein lies a taxonomy of the emotions?

4. *What is the process of having an emotional experience?*   How do emotional states arise? how are they maintained? and what brings about their termination?

5. *Why do we have emotions?*   It is difficult to imagine what life would be like without the richness and variety of emotional experience, without love and frustration, relief and joy; though anyone who has seen Don Siegal's film *The Invasion of the Body Snatchers* in which the replacement bodies have all the properties of real humans except emotions will have some idea. Furthermore, our emotional reactions to things often seem far more valid and revealing than our rational deliberations. Is it true to say, then, that emotions have some function or purpose and, if so, what might this be?

6. *What is the relationship between emotional states, moods and temperament?*   Imagine that Smith and Jones have a terrible argument at work one day; objectively, neither is in possession of the moral high ground and each gives and receives equal amounts of abuse and intolerance. Smith forgets about the incident as soon as she walks out of the door on her way home; after all, she is not the type of person to get angry about that sort of thing. In contrast, Jones is furious all the way home on the train and even when her anger has died down she is highly irritable for the rest of the evening. Why, in ostensibly the same

circumstances, does Jones get angry whilst Smith does not? What psychological state is Jones in when she is no longer feeling angry but is in an irritable mood?

7. *How many emotions are there? and what is the nature of their relationship with each other?*   William James (1890, p.766) argued famously on the subject of the emotions that: "If one should seek to name each particular one of them ... it is plain that the limit to their number would lie in the introspective vocabulary of the seeker." James' ideas are considered later in this chapter and the issue he alludes to concerning the number of emotions is an important one. Perhaps of even greater import, though, is the relationship of different emotions to each other. Are all emotions equivalent or are some more basic or primitive than others? Are some emotions always violent whilst others are calm? Are some emotions negative whilst others are positive? How is it possible to feel more than one emotion at a time and for those emotions to sometimes be in conflict?

8. *What is the difference between, and the relationship of, the so-called normal emotions and the emotional disorders?*   An answer to this final question facing the aspiring emotion theorist lies at the heart of what we are hoping to achieve in this book. The majority of extant theories are concerned with explaining so-called normal emotions (see this chapter and Chapter 3) or else, present an analysis of a specific emotional "disorder" such as Depression or Generalised Anxiety Disorder (See Chapters 4, 6, and 7). However, we would contend that, just as each human being seems to have the potential for both emotional order and disorder, so it seems that there is the potential for a single theory which can cast some light on both types of experience. With this in mind we consider some of the traditional attempts at answering these eight questions, beginning with the ideas of the Ancient Greeks.

EARLY THEORIES OF EMOTION—
THE GREEK PHILOSOPHERS

The writings of Plato and Aristotle on the subject of the emotions are vastly different, both in terms of extent and in terms of the impact they were to have on subsequent Western philosophy. In this chapter we try to outline both approaches (though with a heavy Aristotelian bias) and endeavour to explain why the clearly articulated ideas of Aristotle were distorted or suppressed, whilst the relatively unformulated opinions of Plato were to exert a strong influence on ways of thinking about emotion for some two thousand years.

The beginnings of an answer to this question are apparent when one considers that Plato's theory of mind was essentially dualist, with an earthly body being inhabited by a divine soul (e.g. *Phaedo*: 64c, 80 a–b, 1977)—an idea with obvious appeal to the Christian and Islamic thinkers who were to follow. In contrast, Aristotle had no time for such notions and was the first to propose a view of the mind which might rightly be called functionalist—an approach which provides the foundation for modern day cognitive science and which gave rise to considerable theological unease.

In retrospect it is clear that, with the works of Plato and Aristotle we have the sources of two rich streams of philosophical discourse and ideas. The first stream runs directly across the surface of the history of Western philosophy and can be traced through the work of René Descartes (1596–1650), John Locke (1632–1704), David Hume (1711–1776) and William James (1842–1910) before drying up in the behaviourist desert. The second stream, with Aristotle as its source, runs a more elusive subterranean course, surfacing at intervals in the writings of the Stoic philosophers, Seneca and Chryssipus (see Rist, 1969), in the work of Thomas Aquinas (1225–1274), and the ideas of Baruch Spinoza (1632–1677), before emerging as a raging torrent in the second half of the 20th century in the work of Magda Arnold, Anthony Kenny, William Lyons, and the numerous theoreticians whose ideas are reviewed in Chapters 3 and 4. This latter cognitive stream is still gaining momentum and the ideas we try to put forward in this volume without doubt "go with the flow".

In the rest of the chapter we trace the courses of both streams of thought. First, we shall consider the writings of Plato and the ideas of the two most influential proponents of dualist philosophy and its derivatives—Descartes and James—and their behaviourist nemesis as illustrated by the work of Watson, Skinner, and Ryle. We shall then turn to a discussion of the development of the cognitive theory of emotions through the writing of Aristotle, Aquinas, Spinoza, and 20th century Anglo-American philosophy.

THE PLATONIC MODEL OF EMOTION AND FEELING THEORY

The Platonic philosophy was essentially dualist with an ethereal soul and an earthly body. There are a number of problems with this approach, which we consider in detail later in our discussion of the flagship of dualist philosophy—the work of René Descartes.

The first choice facing the dualist philosopher is whether to place emotions in the soul or in the body. Plato plumps for the former option. He envisaged the soul as consisting of three parts—reason, desire, and appetite—and at various times linked emotions with all three (though principally with appetite and desire). However, perhaps more important than the exact role of emotions in the arena of the soul, was the Platonic view of them as wild uncontrollable forces continually in opposition to the powers of reason. For example (*The Republic*/1977b, 440):

> What if a man believes himself wronged? I asked. Is the spirit within him not boiling and angry, fighting for what he believes to be just? Will he not endure hunger and cold and such things and carry on till he wins out?

The driving force behind such boiling and angry spirits was something to be despised and fought against in the Platonic world view and his discussion of such conflict has a distinct contemporary ring (*The Republic*/1977b, 604):

> But when there are two opposite attractions in a man at the same time in reference to the same thing, he must, according to our doctrine, be a double man.

The best way forward, Plato argued, is to (*The Republic*/1977b, 604):

> Keep as quiet as possible in misfortunes, and check all feelings of discontent; because we cannot estimate the amount of good and evil contained in these visitations.

We can see here the seeds of some influential modern ideas: first, that emotions are to be contrasted with that which is rational and reasoned (see de Sousa, 1987); and, second, that emotions play a central role in psychological conflict and so there must be processes to defend against the power of the emotions (e.g. Freud, 1917/1984).

It was these views that emotions should be the slaves of reason, and that reason had its home in a divine soul, that made Plato so popular with the Christian and Islamic scholars who were to dominate Western thought throughout the medieval period. As Lyons (1992, p.297) has argued, "A Platonic form was a separated immaterial substance, which being much more like the soul in Christian theology, that it helped make theoretical sense of the Christian eschatology of death, judgement, hell or heaven. A soul was immortal and so perfectly suited to life after death". It was this popularity in part which led to the dominance of the dualist, or what came to be known as the "feeling" theory of emotion up until the late 19th century. There are many more things which could be said about Plato's views on emotions. However, we reserve our comments until our discussion of the more fully formulated versions of the dualist approach, which we turn to next.

The development of the feeling theory of emotions— René Descartes

Descartes presents his theory of emotion in his pamphlet "On the Passions of the Soul" (1649/1989, Article 1), where he kicks off with a dismissal of all previous philosophical discourse on the subject[1]:

> What the ancients taught about them [the passions] is so little, and for the most part so little believable, that I cannot hope to approach the truth unless I forsake the paths they followed. For this reason I shall be obliged to write here as though I were treating a topic which no one before me had ever described.

It is tempting to criticise Descartes for such a cavalier attitude to Greek philosophy; however, because we discuss his ideas with a similar shortage of enthusiasm for the content, it is perhaps wise to resist such temptation!

Having thus wiped the philosophical slate clean, Descartes sets about discussing the concepts of body and soul and their relation to each other. The body, Descartes notes, consists of our blood, bones, muscles, blood vessels, nerves, and so forth and these organs operate as a function of the movements of so-called bodily spirits. With respect to the soul, Descartes (Article 17) argues:

> After having thus taken into consideration all the functions that belong to the body alone, it is easy to understand that there remains nothing in us that we should attribute to our soul but our thoughts, which are principally of two genera— the first, namely, are the actions of the soul; the others are its passions.

According to Descartes, the soul is principally in touch with the movement of the spirits in the body via the pineal gland in the brain through which the spirits always flow. The majority of the experiences in the soul are instances of awareness of such spirit movements. So, the experiences of seeing, hearing, feeling pain, feeling hunger, feeling fear, and being angry are all forms of awareness of the movements of bodily spirits through the pineal gland. In Cartesian terminology these experiences all have the same *immediate cause*, that is, the movement of bodily spirits. The ways in which these experiences differ according to Descartes is: first, in their *exciting cause*, that is, that which caused the movements of the spirits in the first place (what we shall later call events); and, second, in their *objects*, that is, what they are about.

To illustrate these distinctions let us consider an example in the spirit of William James:

> Walking through the woods one day, Susan stumbles across a large Grizzly Bear which then starts running towards her. She is absolutely terrified and turns and runs away. As she is running she remembers that Grizzly Bears cannot climb trees so she scampers up the nearest tree just as the bear catches her. In fact, his paw scratches across her leg causing her to feel a searing pain before she climbs to safety.

The first point to make about this example is that the experience of seeing the bear, the feeling of fear, and the feeling of pain are all, in the Cartesian model, experiences in the soul with the same *immediate* cause—the movement of bodily spirits. However, the experience of seeing has an *exciting* cause outside of the body, namely the bear whose image falls on the retina and excites a movement of the bodily spirits. The *object* of the seeing is also the bear, that is, it is the bear which Susan sees. In contrast, the *exciting* cause of the pain and the *object* of the pain are in the body; that is, the gash on Susan's leg. Finally, the *exciting* cause (event) of the fear is the bear, as in the experience of seeing; however, the *object* of the fear is not the bear and, according to Descartes (1649/1989, Article 25), is not in the body either but in the soul:

> The perceptions that are referred to the soul alone are those whose effects are felt as in the soul itself, and of which no proximate cause to which they may be referred is commonly known. Such are the sensations of joy, anger and others like them.

So, Susan's fear is not about the bear, it is about something in her soul. These differences between seeing, feeling pain, and feeling fear are shown in Table 2.1 (based on de Sousa, 1987).

It is important to elaborate on the claim that the object of emotions such as Susan's fear is in the soul for it is here that Descartes dangles a substantial cognitive carrot.

The essence of the cognitive approach, as we shall see later in our discussion of Aristotle's tripartite theory of emotions, is that the instigation to an emotion such as fear can be a *mental* event—in this case the *belief* that there is danger; that is, it is the belief that there is

TABLE 2.1
Classification of Susan's perceptions according to Descartes
(based on de Sousa, 1987)

Perception	Object	Immediate cause	Exciting cause
Sensory (Seeing)	Outside body (Bear)	Inside body (Spirit movements)	Outside body (Bear)
Proprioceptive (Pain)	Inside body (Gash on leg)	Inside body (Spirit movements)	Inside body (Gash on leg)
Passion (Fear)	Inside soul (?)	Inside body (Spirit movements)	Outside body (Bear)

danger and not the bear which causes Susan to be afraid. Is Descartes, then, trying to argue something like this by suggesting that the object of Susan's fear is not the bear but something "in the soul"? It begins to look that way when he goes on to discuss the emotion of fear in more detail (Article 36):

> Furthermore, if that shape is very unusual and very frightful, that is, if it bears a close resemblance to things that have previously been harmful to the body, this excites the passion of apprehension in the soul, and thereupon, that of boldness or that of fear and terror.

Descartes seems to be implying that fear is somehow a result of something being dangerous or frightful; that is, fear is the result of some form of cognitive assessment of the situation. However, the dualism is lurking in the very next paragraph (Article 36):

> The spirits reflected from the image thus formed on the gland turn to flow in part into the nerves serving to turn the back and move the legs for running away ... these spirits excite a particular movement in this gland [the pineal] which is instituted by nature to make the soul feel this passion.

What Descartes is saying here is that Susan sees the bear and this causes movements of her bodily spirits to her limbs thus causing her to turn and run. In addition, the bodily spirits happen to flow through the pineal gland and so the soul is aware of all these spirit movements and this awareness is the emotion of fear. Fear is merely epiphenomenal. It has no cognitive component and no causal role because the spirits that control the limbs are moved by the image of the bear with no help from the soul (Article 38):

> Simply in virtue of the fact that certain spirits proceed at the same time toward the nerves that move the legs to flee, they cause another movement in the same gland by means of which the soul feels and perceives this flight—which can in this way be excited in the body merely by the disposition of the organs without the soul contributing to it.

Emotions, or more correctly passions, then, are just epiphenomenal feelings without a function. What has happened to the cognitive element now? It seems that Descartes is saying that the movements of bodily spirits that are experienced as fear are excited by an external danger, but he provides no means by which this appraisal of danger can occur. It is just inherent in the exciting cause, in this case the bear. However, bears are not inherently threatening, it is what they mean to us that makes them threatening. Similarly, eating raw liver is not inherently disgusting, we merely appraise it as being so. This difficulty of trying to distinguish emotions on the basis of their exciting causes (or "events" as we shall call them from now on) with no reference to our understanding of those events is one that crops up again and again and we shall refer to it as the *event problem*. So, we are left with the question: what is the object of a Cartesian emotion? All Descartes seems to be saying is that the object is in the soul and we are given no clear indication of what it might be.

This idea of epiphenomenal, non-functional feelings is central to what has come to be termed the feeling theory of emotion, and the feeling theory scheme for anger is illustrated in Figure 2.1.

There are numerous problems with dualism in general and the feeling theory conceptualisation of emotions in particular. For a thorough critique of dualism see Ryle (1949) or, more accessibly, Smith and Jones (1986). Here, we shall confine our discussion to feeling theory. The first problem is that, as we have seen, it is not possible within a feeling theory model for emotions to give rise to behaviour. As Lyons (1980, p.7) argues: "It is not uncommon for someone to say something like 'Jealousy caused Jones to stab his wife outside the bar' ... if we now transcribe the sentence as 'A feeling of throbbing and constriction around the heart caused Jones to stab his wife outside the bar' it becomes more or less absurd. For feelings by themselves don't lead to behaviour." Descartes does attempt to discuss the relationship between the passions and behaviour. He argues that passions cause the soul to will behaviour but that the actual behaviour is caused by the movements of the bodily spirits without any help from the soul. In other words, the passions cause the soul to will behaviour which is *already* happening.

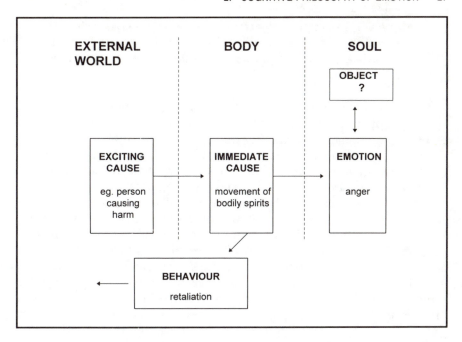

FIG. 2.1. A Cartesian analysis of anger.

The second problem for Descartes is that there is no basis on which to argue that emotions are appropriate or inappropriate. As Bedford (1964, p.91) argues, "if someone were to say 'I felt this pang this afternoon' it would be meaningless to ask whether it was a reasonable or unreasonable pang". However, we clearly do have a sense of the reasonableness of emotional reactions, an issue that has considerable implications for the notion of emotional "disorder"; that is, emotional reactions which are in some sense out of proportion or unjustified.

A third problem for feeling theory is that it makes it difficult to distinguish one emotion from another. Descartes argues that the passions are physiologically distinct because they are based on unique movements of the bodily spirits; so, the soul experiences fear because the movements of the spirits that are being reflected are those of fear. The next question then is how did the fear set of spirit movements start instead of, say, the anger set? Here, Descartes must argue that the different types of spirit movements are associated with different *exciting* causes (events) and once again this leads to the event problem discussed previously. However, Descartes (Article 52) goes further:

Moreover, I note that objects which move the senses do not excite different passions in us in proportion to all of their diversities, but only in proportion to the different ways they can harm or profit us.

Descartes is dangling the cognitive carrot again. Susan's fear in the bear example is a reflection of the movements of bodily spirits caused by her perception of a *frightening* thing—the bear. However, this again raises the further question as to how the bear is appraised as frightening; in other words, where does the cognition reside? It is here, in our view, that Descartes offers no convincing answers.

A fourth problem for feeling theory is that it falls foul of Wittgenstein's private language argument. In *Philosophical Investigations*, Wittgenstein (1958) argues that any word such as "fear", which is purportedly the name of something observable only by introspecting on our inner experience, must acquire its meaning in a purely private and unverifiable way. That is to say, if I use the word "fear" to describe something only I can introspect on, as Descartes argues, then how can I know that this is anything like what anyone else means when they use the word "fear"? Wittgenstein famously illustrates this (1958, p.293) with the example of a beetle:

Suppose everyone had a box with something in it: we call it a "beetle". No one can look into anyone else's box, and everyone says he knows what a beetle is by looking at his beetle. Here it would be quite possible for everyone to have something different in his box.

Wittgenstein goes on to suggest that words only have meaning as part of a language and that language is necessarily public and shared; a view which presents considerable problems for the idea of fear as an epiphenomenal feeling with an audience of one (the private language argument is considerably more complex than this, though we hope that we have accurately presented its essential point; more detailed analysis can be found in Jones, 1971, *The Private Language Argument*). There are numerous other problems for feeling theory which need not concern us here. Fuller expositions can be found in Lyons (1980), de Sousa (1987), and Kenny (1963).

Having, we submit, found Cartesian feeling theory wanting in several respects, it is important to point out that not all is doom and gloom. There are a number of aspects of Descartes' work on the passions that we feel have substantial merit and we shall briefly consider these next.

Descartes was the first to suggest that some emotions might be more basic or primitive than others and this idea is one which has aroused much contemporary interest and heated debate. Descartes listed six primary passions: wonder, joy, sadness, love, hatred, and desire. He argued that the other passions are compounded out of these. So, pride is a mixture of happiness and love. This notion has recently been the subject of considerable empirical investigation and we shall discuss it in detail in Chapter 3.

Descartes also proposed a distinction between those emotions with immediate and exciting causes outside of the soul, as discussed above and exemplified by Susan's fear of the bear, and those emotions: "which are excited in the soul only by the soul itself" (1649/1989, Article 147). Kenny (1963) calls these latter experiences the "intellectual emotions". To illustrate, let us consider Susan's flight from the bear. Although, her immediate reaction is intense fear, it is possible (though admittedly unlikely in this case) that there is a secondary "intellectual" emotion of exhilaration or excitement which, Descartes would argue, is excited in the soul, by the soul. Descartes himself uses the example of a man who mourns his dead wife whilst harbouring a secret joy that she is no longer alive to trouble him. Both of these examples imply secondary or intellectual emotions that are in opposition to the more immediate emotional reactions. However, although Descartes does not discuss this, it seems possible to have secondary emotions which are congruent to the primary ones, e.g. fear of fear, or depression about depression. This idea of "intellectual emotions" is something we shall return to in the chapters to follow.

We have expressed little enthusiasm for Descartes' suggestion that something inherent in an event determines the emotional response to that event in the absence of any cognitive analysis (the event problem). However, while not seeming particularly useful as a theory of all emotional experience, this analysis does seem to fit some types of emotional phenomena—what we shall call automatic emotions—and we return to this in Chapter 5.

Finally, although Wittgenstein may be right to argue that "fear" is necessarily public because it involves a term in natural language, it seems indisputable that emotions do have a distinctive introspective flavour. Philosophy has coined the terms "qualia" and "privacy" to refer to these aspects of phenomenal experience. The question for philosophy and psychology is to try and account for this phenomenology adequately in theoretical structures which rely more and more on "public" criteria.

So, as an aspiring emotion theorist, Descartes does address the eight questions listed at the beginning of the chapter, but his answers are perhaps not wholly convincing. He does outline the process of having an emotional experience (Q.4), he suggests reasons why we have emotions (Q.5) and how one emotion differs from another (Q.3), but his arguments have long since been consigned to the philosophical wilderness. More durable is his analysis of primitive and complex emotions (Q.7) and his analysis of what Kenny called intellectual emotions, so we shall return to these points in more detail later.

The psychologising of feeling theory—William James

Despite the difficulties with feeling theory, it can rank amongst its proponents some of the greatest names in Western philosophy. John Locke's description of pain and pleasure and the emotions they give rise to is thoroughly Cartesian, though less fully articulated. He states that pain and pleasure "cannot be described, nor their names defined; the way of knowing them is, as of the simple ideas of the senses, only by experience" (Locke, 1977, 20; see Kenny, 1963, for a fuller discussion). Similarly, David Hume (1739/1888), in Book II of *A Treatise on Human Nature*, "Of the Passions", presents another version of feeling theory overlaid with his own ideas from his theory of mental activities. He describes emotions as "secondary or reflective impressions" and his elaboration of these arguments is undeniably Cartesian (see Lyons, 1980, 1992 and Kenny, 1963, for a fuller analysis). Some 100 years after Hume, feeling theory was embraced for the first time by the emerging psychology community in the writings of William James.

James began his career as a Cartesian feeling theorist with an article in *Mind* appropriately entitled "What is an Emotion?" (James, 1884); however, the fullest exposition of the Jamesian view is found in his classic work, *Principles of Psychology* (1890). Although James' approach offers nothing substantially new to anyone familiar with the work of Descartes, his emphasis on the physiological aspects of emotions and the potential they provide for an empirical analysis has influenced psychology to the present day. For this reason James' writings merit some discussion.

Let us dispense with the Cartesian core of James' approach first. It is worth quoting James here because his description can hardly be bettered (1890, p.743, original italics):

> Bodily changes follow directly the perception of the exciting fact, and that our feeling of the same changes as they occur *IS* the emotion. Common sense says ... we meet a bear are frightened and run ... The hypothesis here to be defended says that this order of sequence is incorrect, that the one mental state is not immediately induced by the other, that

the bodily manifestations must first be interposed between them, and that the more rational statement is we feel … afraid because we tremble.

So, if we refer back to our Jamesian example of Susan's unfortunate encounter with the bear, James, like Descartes, is saying that we see the bear and this causes the physiological emotional reaction and our perception of this reaction is the emotion of fear—this is undoubtedly a version of feeling theory.

James' next paragraph seems remarkably prescient; he suggests (p.743) that: "Stated in this crude way, the hypothesis is pretty sure to meet with immediate disbelief". We have already discussed our reasons for standing up and being counted among the disbelievers when presenting the original Cartesian version of this approach and we need not reiterate them here.

So the Cartesian core of James' theory renders it, in our view, a philosophical non-starter. However, James' emphasis on the physiological uniqueness of each and every emotion merits some discussion. He suggests (p.743) that:

No shade of emotion, however slight, should be without a bodily reverberation as unique, when taken in its totality, as is the mental mood itself.

and later (p.746):

We immediately see why there is no limit to the number of possible different emotions which may exist, and why the emotions of different individuals may vary indefinitely.

Putting aside the issue of whether James is correct in this assumption, it is clear that this theory is amenable to objective measurement and investigation. That is to say, if each emotion is physiologically distinct then it becomes possible to distinguish and categorise the emotions through detailed physiological experiment and study—an open door to experimental psychology. This is the way forward that James promotes, and here he is heavily influenced by the work of the Danish physiologist Carl Lange.

James' and Lange's assertions that each emotion is specified by a unique physiology and that the emotions do not involve specialised brain centres have indeed motivated an enormous amount of research and debate, most famously an attack by Walter Cannon (1927) in his paper "The James–Lange theory of Emotions: A Critical Examination and an

Alternative Theory". The debate continues to this day with some individuals arguing that certain basic emotions can be distinguished in terms of bodily changes (e.g. Darwin, 1872/1965; Ekman, 1982) whereas others propose a form of generalised physiological arousal which acquires a particular phenomenological flavour by virtue of the cognitive beliefs and evaluations with which it is associated (e.g., Cannon, 1927; Lyons, 1980, 1992; Schachter & Singer, 1962). This issue of physiologically distinct basic emotions is important. However, it is clearly not an issue which can be resolved philosophically and consequently detailed discussion is postponed until Chapter 3.

We argued above in our analysis of Descartes' work that it was difficult to square the notion of emotions as pure feelings with any concept of appropriateness. So, to recap, Bedford (1964) argued that it was absurd to suggest that a pang or any other sensation of a bodily feeling could be unjustified or justified. Furthermore, we suggested that this presented problems for those who wish to use the dimension of appropriateness to propose a distinction between so-called normal and abnormal emotions. Exactly what these problems are becomes apparent in James' discussion of these issues. James (1884, p.749), however, doesn't see it this way:

> One of the chief merits, in fact, of the view which I propose seems to be that we can so easily formulate by its means pathological cases and normal cases under a common scheme.

James illustrates these merits with a discussion (p. 749) of what, we must suppose, are panic attacks:

> If inability to draw deep breath, fluttering of the heart ... with an irresistible tendency to take a somewhat crouching attitude and to sit still ... all spontaneously occur together in a certain person; his feeling of their combination is the emotion of dread.

In this analysis, panic attacks are the feelings of bodily changes which themselves occur spontaneously for no apparent reason. To James' credit this does capture the commonly reported clinical phenomenon (e.g. Dalgleish, 1994a) of feelings of fear and dread seemingly coming "out of the blue". However, the fact that an individual is unaware of any cause of their emotions, whether it be cognitive or external, does not mean that such a cause does not exist. James' analysis of panic and thus of emotional disorder has all the faults of feeling theory in general, compounded with the inability to explain how the bodily changes he describes can originate for no reason. We shall argue later that, in our view, a far more convincing account of panic attacks is offered by a cognitive theory of emotion (see the discussion in Chapter 6).

William James was the first psychologist and the last person to present the feeling theory of emotions in such strong terms; with him the feeling theory stream seems to have dried up. Theoretical analysis of the emotions was soon commandeered by the behaviourists and the psychoanalysts prior to the re-emergence of the cognitive model. It is the behavioural approach that we consider next.

THE BEHAVIOURIST THEORY OF EMOTIONS

We have seen that the feeling theory of emotions regards them as inner states, which can only be known through introspection. It is difficult to think of a greater contrast to this view than that of the behaviourists (Watson, 1913, p.158):

> Psychology as the behaviourist views it is a purely objective experimental branch of natural science. Its theoretical goal is the prediction and control of behavior. Introspection forms no essential part of its methods, nor is the scientific value of its data dependent upon the readiness with which they lend themselves to interpretation in terms of consciousness.

This quote from James Watson sums up what has become known as psychological behaviourism. The official line of the psychological behaviourists makes no epistemological or metaphysical claims—they have nothing to say either way about whether or not mental states exist—they merely argue that we should not study them and that our theories should not rest upon them.

In some contrast, philosophical behaviourism in its various forms (analytical behaviourism, reductive behaviourism, eliminative behaviourism) makes considerable metaphysical claims about the status of mental states.

In this section we shall briefly consider the theories of emotion put forward by two psychological behaviourists, Watson and Skinner, and by one philosophical behaviourist, Gilbert Ryle.

The behaviourist theory of James Watson

Watson's view of emotions sets out its stall in order to repudiate the sort of feeling theory offered by William James. One would therefore imagine, given the meteoric rise of behaviourism, that James' theory would never have been heard of again. However, as we noted previously, James' ideas continue to be influential to the present day. The reason for this becomes clear if we put aside James' discussion of feelings as the sensation of bodily change (because we are unable to investigate them empirically), and concentrate on his arguments that emotions can be differentiated on a physiological basis. It then becomes apparent that Watson's theory and the physiological part of James' theory are identical. The only difference between the two approaches is that James is making some claims about mental states and Watson is saying that we do not have any scientific evidence for such claims so let's not make them.

To proceed, Watson (1919, p.195) presents a formulation which covers some emotions as follows:

> An emotion is an hereditary "pattern-reaction" involving profound changes of the bodily mechanism as a whole, but particularly of the visceral and glandular systems.

In this model, emotions are nothing more than physiological (pattern) reactions (and thus different from instincts, which are more overtly behavioural), which are inherited. Watson goes on to elaborate on this point and is forced to admit that there are only three emotions that can be distinguished in this way, and then only in the newborn infant. According to Watson, these three emotions are fear, rage, and love, though it could be argued that the latter is more akin to a sexual drive than an emotion proper. When it comes to all of the other emotions, Watson (p.197) states:

> When we take into account the whole group of phenomena in which we see emotional manifestations in adults, a pronounced modification is necessary. Apparently the hereditary pattern as a whole gets broken up. At any rate it largely disappears.

In other words, we can distinguish at most three emotions by virtue of their physiology and then only in the newborn. For older humans and for all of the other emotions this criterion is insufficient. This raises a major problem for the Watsonian account: how can we distinguish one emotion from another (Q. 3)? How can we distinguish an emotion from a non-emotion (Q. 1)? Watson tries to clamber out of this philosophical hole but his arguments fail to convince.

It seems then that Watson does not offer a convincing formulation of emotions as responses, so what about the instigating events? Again, there are insurmountable difficulties because the same event can give rise to different emotions in different people. As we argued above, Susan was afraid of the bear because she believed it might kill her; however, Susan's brother, who enjoys hunting and fishing, may have been overjoyed to see the bear striding down the woodland path. So, the same event can lead Susan and her brother to experience different emotions by virtue of differences in their beliefs—Susan believes the bear is dangerous but her brother believes the bear has the potential to be a fine trophy for his study wall. This illustrates the, by now familiar, event problem.

Skinner's operant theory of emotions

Skinner (e.g. Holland & Skinner, 1961; Skinner, 1974) offers us another variety of behaviourist theories of emotions. Skinner discusses emotions within an operant conditioning framework. Within this model emotions serve to put the organism into states in which different sets of event contingencies define the reinforcers (Holland & Skinner, 1961, p.213):

> Under different emotional conditions, different events serve
> as reinforcers, and different groups of operants increase in
> probability of emission. By these predispositions we can (do)
> define a specific emotion.

So in emotion state 1, set of events A will be reinforcing for set of operants A, whereas in emotion state 2, set of events B will be reinforcing for set of operants B. The emotion is defined by the sets of operants and reinforcers that are optimised. In addition, when set of events B is reinforcing for set of operants B, set of events A and set of operants A will be incompatible. For example (p.216):

> Even when deprived of food, an anxious person may not eat.
> The responses which increase in probability during anxiety
> are incompatible with eating.

There is a dangerous circularity lurking in here somewhere as Lyons (1980) has pointed out. If we, once more, consider Susan's lucky escape from the bear then, according to Skinner, Susan is defined as being afraid because she is running away and because the running away is an escape from the bear. However, it is difficult to see how we could be sure that Susan was not afraid if she stood and smiled at the bear (indeed, the US park service recommends standing still in such situations) or scratched her nose, or performed any other behaviour. Skinner is forced to argue that Susan's behaviour is only fear behaviour if it occurs in the the presence of the correct (fearful) event; that is, in the presence of a bear. However, by what means can we decide that the bear is a fearful event (the event problem)? Skinner must resort to saying that it is a fearful event because it gives rise to fear and therein lies the circularity of the Skinnerian theory of emotions.

As well as this circularity which faces the behaviourist, Skinner's ideas invite an extra criticism over and above those directed at Watson. As Lyons (1980, p.22) notes:

> Many instances of some emotions, and most instances of others, exhibit little or no operant behaviour. Grief, especially when it is about something irretrievably lost or dead, does not lead to much, if any, operant behaviour, because no behaviour can bring about any desired results.

Skinner could retort that grief behaviour brings about sympathy from others, but he is on a slippery slope and there is no real answer to Lyons' arguments.

Psychological behaviourism, in our view, seems to offer us little as a framework within which to investigate emotions. Does philosophical behaviourism provide anything substantially different?

The philosophical behaviourism of Gilbert Ryle

Philosophical behaviourism grew out of the psychological behaviourism of Watson, Skinner, et al. and the logical positivism of Russell, Wittgenstein, and Carnap. Perhaps the most influential philosophical behaviourist account of the emotions was presented by Gilbert Ryle in 1949 in *The Concept of Mind*.

The Concept of Mind is a sustained and vicious attack on what Ryle called "The dogma of the ghost in the machine"; namely, Cartesian dualism and variations thereof. In Chapter 4 of this work Ryle sets forth his anti-Cartesian account of emotions.

The first thing Ryle does is to draw out the distinctions between four different uses of the term "emotion". Emotion can be used to refer to inclinations (or motives), moods, agitations (or commotions), or feelings. This goes some way to answering the sixth question posed in the introduction to this chapter—what is the relationship between emotional states, moods, and temperament? Ryle views inclinations, moods, and agitations as various types of disposition. Inclinations are permanent dispositions to behave in certain ways. So, if a person is inclined to be vain, this means nothing more than that he has a disposition to vain behaviour such as boasting. In contrast, if a person is in an irritable mood, this means they have a short-term disposition to display angry behaviour. Agitations are likewise dispositions; in fact, they are merely moods of certain sorts. The only non-dispositional, and thus qualitatively different, category is that of feelings. By these Ryle means things like twinges and pains and butterflies in the stomach. In Ryle's account, such feelings are nothing more than signs of agitations; so, if we have a bodily feeling and we describe it as fear, this is because it is a sign that we are in a fearful mood which itself is nothing more than a disposition for fear-related behaviour.

It can be seen then that Ryle's account offers no more than the other behaviourist accounts already discussed. So, if emotions are defined as dispositions to behaviour then we must distinguish emotions by reference to such behaviour and, as we have seen above, this analysis will not really wash.

An interesting point about behaviourist theories of emotion is how anyone would know whether they were in an emotional state. Somewhat bravely, Ryle (1949, p.99) suggests a possible answer:

> The bored man finds out that he is bored, if he does find this
> out, by finding that among other things he glumly says to
> others and to himself "I am bored" and "How bored I feel".

If this does not seem peculiar to the reader, then perhaps a version of it suggested by Phil Johnson-Laird (1988, p.18) in which two behaviourists are indulging in post-coital pillow talk may have more appeal: "one behaviourist said to another: 'that was fine for you, but how was it for me?' ... "

In summary, neither philosophical nor psychological behaviourist theories of emotion seem able to withstand close scrutiny. In our view, they are unable to address satisfactorily any of the questions posed in the introduction to this chapter, especially those concerning the distinction between different emotions (Q. 3) and between emotions and non-emotions (Q. 1). Ryle does attempt to provide a framework for understanding the relationship between dispositions, moods, and occurrent emotions (Q. 6) but his arguments are so infected with his anti-Cartesian stance that we feel cheated of our own private experience, as illustrated so well by Johnson-Laird. It seems, then, that some notion of an internal state is essential to our understanding of what an emotion is, though we have argued that the feeling theory notion of such internal states is fundamentally flawed. In the next section we develop further another notion of internal states—the cognitive account of emotions, beginning with the pioneering work of Aristotle mentioned at the beginning of the chapter.

THE DEVELOPMENT OF THE COGNITIVE ACCOUNT OF EMOTIONS—ARISTOTLE, AQUINAS, AND SPINOZA

We noted in the Introduction that Aristotle was the first to propose a functionalist model of the mind—an approach that dominates contemporary cognitive science. William Lycan (1987, p.78) has said of functionalism that: "it is the only positive doctrine in all of philosophy that I am prepared (if not licensed) to kill for"; who said that philosophers were quiet and unassuming! It is clear, then, that modern functionalism is a topic capable of arousing passionate feelings. These not only arise between its advocates and opponents but also within the functionalist camp because modern functionalism comes in a variety of flavours: homuncular functionalism; machine functionalism; teleological functionalism, and so on. However, all of these myriad variations can be traced back to the initial ideas of Aristotle and his work still provides one of the best illustrations of the essence of the functionalist approach.

The ideas we develop in this book are embedded within a broadly functionalist framework and for this reason we shall spend some time now in a discussion of functionalism's Aristotelian roots, before considering Aristotle's application of functionalism to the emotions.

The Aristotelian functionalist model of emotion

Aristotle presents his functionalist doctrine of the mind principally in the *De Anima* (1941). The first important distinction he emphasises is between *matter* and *form*. There are two fundamental questions which we can ask about any individual entity: first, what is it made of—what is its matter? and, second, what is it that makes it what it is, rather than something else—what is its form? So, if we take the example of a hamburger, its *matter* is bits of salad, meat, and bread. However, if these were all shredded and placed in a pile on a plate they would not be a hamburger. What is necessary is for the meat and salad to be sandwiched between the bread; this is the *form*. The form of the hamburger is not a question of adding extra ingredients but rather it is a question of arranging things in a certain way.

One could be forgiven for believing, then, that form is just the shape of the matter in some simple geometric sense. However, Aristotle is making a more important point than this. For him, form is that which makes something count as what it is. So, if we take the example of a chair, its matter is what it is made of—wood, or steel, or whatever. However, its form—that by virtue of which it counts as a chair rather than some other thing—concerns its *function* as something that people sit on. Inevitably, this form constrains the simple geometric shape of chairs to some extent but it is still true, as anyone who has recently visited a modern furniture store will testify, that chairs can come in all sorts of different shapes and be no less chairs as a consequence.

There is one other distinction which it is important to grasp before we can apply these ideas to an understanding of emotions, and that is between the capacity that a certain form has and the actual activity of that form. So, if we take once more the example of the chair: it can actively be used by someone as a seat; however, even when it is not being used it still has the capacity to be sat on and is again no less a chair as a consequence.

Within these preliminary ideas we have the main tenets of functionalism. Functionalism is any approach that analyses something in terms of how it functions; that is, in terms of its form. Such an understanding is independent of matter; so, in the strongest version of the argument, if we had a thorough enough grasp of the form of mental processes we could instantiate them not only in biological matter (the nervous system) but also in silicon matter (a computer) and they would be mental processes all the same.

Before moving on to consider the emotions, there is one caveat. This analysis of form and matter cuts through swathes of subtle and complex arguments in Aristotle's discussions and the faint noise in the background is probably the sound of him shifting uneasily in his grave. We can only hope that we have hinted at the richness of his work rather than misrepresented it.

Aristotle's most comprehensive discussion of the emotions is in *The Art of Rhetoric* (1991). However, it is in the *De Anima* (1941, 403, a29–b3) that he draws out the form and matter of the emotions, in this case anger:

> The student of nature and the dialectician would define what anger is differently. For the latter would define it as reaching out for retaliation or something of the sort, the former as the boiling of the blood round the heart. Of these definitions, the first gives the form or defining essence, the other the matter.

So, as an answer to the question, what makes the boiling of the blood around the heart a case of anger? Aristotle proposes something to do with its relationship with retaliation or similar behaviour. This is a functionalist view of emotion: that which makes anger what it is, is its function with respect to retaliation. It is important to note that, in the same way that a chair does not have to be sat upon to have the form of a chair, this retaliation does not actually have to happen for emotion to have the form of anger. It is the capacity for it to happen that gives anger its form. The broad functionalist view of emotions then is that the form of anger is defined with respect to its role or function in the psychological system. As we shall argue later, this function can be considerably more elaborate than Aristotle's disposition to certain types of behaviour such as retaliation.

We can see, then, that already Aristotle has addressed at least one of the questions posed at the beginning of the chapter; namely, why do we have emotions (Q.5)? He proposes that one of the functions of emotions is to give us the capacity to do things such as retaliating. Aristotle also addresses a number of the other questions listed above. To understand how he does this it is necessary to turn to the arguments contained in *The Art of Rhetoric* (1991).

In this handbook for orators Aristotle considers 10 specific emotions. Of these, four are presented as positive (calm, friendship, favour, and pity) and six as negative (anger, fear, shame, indignation, envy, and jealousy). It seems unlikely that Aristotle considered this a finite list of emotions. However, the omissions and inclusions are of secondary significance to the fact that Aristotle presents all of these 10 emotions within the same tripartite scheme. Aristotle argues that for any emotion to arise it is necessary for three conditions to be satisfied: first, the individual must be in an appropriate *state of mind* to experience the emotion; second, there must be a *stimulus* of the correct kind to elicit the emotion; and third, there must be an *object* of the appropriate kind for the emotion to be about (these uses of the terms "stimulus" and "object" are peculiar to Aristotle. He reserves the term stimulus for an internal mental state whereas traditionally it can also refer to an external event. In addition, the term object is reserved for an external event whereas traditionally it is also used to refer to an internal mental state. Aristotle's "object" is Descartes' "exciting cause" and Aristotle's "stimulus" is Descartes' "object". The Cartesian use of the word "object" is more traditional in philosophy. As we have noted, we use the term "event" to refer to Aristotelian objects and Cartesian exciting causes). So, if we consider the case of fear within this scheme, Aristotle (1991, 1382a) invites us to: "Let fear, then, be a kind of pain or disturbance resulting from the imagination of impending danger, either destructive or painful." Here, the *stimulus* for fear is an evaluation of some impending danger. The *event* is whatever causes that evaluation to be made, and thus, that to which the fear is directed; for example, "those able to do wrong to those able to be wronged" or "rivals for advantages that both parties cannot simultaneously enjoy" and so on (Aristotle lists 12 putative events for fear). Finally, such events will only be evaluated as being laden with impending danger if the individual is in the appropriate *state of mind*; that is, possessed by a certain expectation that something dangerous might happen to them at some time. This does not apply to everyone (1991, p.1383a):

> Those in great prosperity or seeming to be would not expect to suffer, nor those who reckon they have already suffered everything terrible and are numbed as regards the future, such as those who are actually being crucified; there must be some hope left of survival from their predicament (1383a)

So, to reiterate, individuals who are of the state of mind that something dangerous could happen to them, when confronted with, say, a rival for something which they want, might evaluate the situation as one of impending danger and this evaluation would be a stimulus to fear. This scheme is illustrated diagrammatically in Fig. 2.2. for the emotion of anger.

Having made some progress, then, with our discussion of the concept of emotion, this seems a timely point to pause and initiate some form of debate about the nature of cognition because Aristotle's is surely the prototypical cognitive theory of emotions. As Rapee (1991, p.194) points out, the term cognition "[has] been used broadly and inconsistently over the years. Few authors tend to define the term[s] and, as a result, a number of arguments have arisen in the literature based largely on a lack of specific definition". Rapee is making two points here: first, that the term cognition is used in a number of different ways; and, second, that much of the confusion is a consequence of a lack of rigorous definition. Both of these points have some truth in them. Sometimes, progress is indeed a relatively straightforward matter of pointing out mere semantic differences as in the early rounds of the Zajonc–Lazarus prize fight over whether cognition or affect is primary (this is discussed in Chapter 3). However, it is also true that the term cognitive has a number of distinct and different uses. In this chapter we endeavour to outline what we consider to be the philosophical definition of "cognitive". In Chapter 3 we go on to consider a number of other uses of the word that have emerged in the psychology literature.

What is the philosophical sense of the word "cognitive"? As we have seen, Aristotle draws an important distinction between what he calls the object of an emotion and the stimulus. So, if someone is a rival for an advantage that only one of us can enjoy, then this situation (object) only arouses fear if I evaluate it as being one of impending danger. On the one hand, we have an event in the world—one of rivalry—whereas on the other we have a mental representation or a belief—that there is impending danger. According to Aristotle, it is this belief about danger

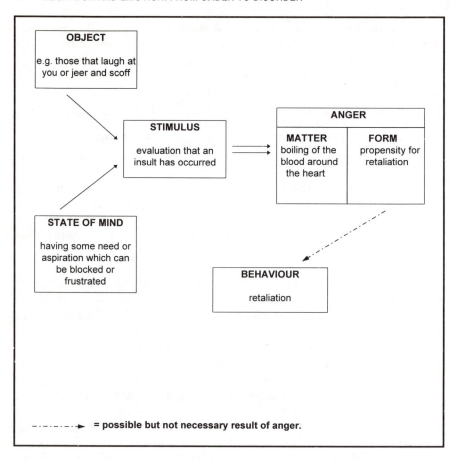

FIG. 2.2. Aristotle's theory of emotions as applied to anger.

that is the stimulus to fear (and thus to the possibility of action), not the rivalry. It is quite possible that on another occasion exactly the same situation of rivalry would not be seen as dangerous and the person would not be afraid. It is equally possible that a situation which objectively does not seem dangerous, such as a trip to the supermarket, could be evaluated as highly threatening (as in the case of agoraphobia), thus leading to intense fear. The (philosophical) use of the term "cognitive", then, is the appeal to mental representations and beliefs about the world in order to describe and explain psychological experiences. So, Aristotle's cognitive theory of emotions sees them as states that are causally dependent on a cognitive belief or evaluation.

At this point we would like to propose another distinction that we feel has important implications for understanding cognitive theories of emotion. Aristotle's theory, as we have shown, views cognitions as essential to emotion. In addition, Aristotle proposes that such cognitions have a causal role; so, in the case of anger, it is the belief (cognition) that an insult has occurred that causes the boiling of the blood around the heart and is causal in the propensity for retaliation. We would like to argue that this is an example of a *strong* cognitive theory of emotions, that is, one in which cognitions are both essential *and* causal. In contrast, a weak cognitive theory of emotions is one in which cognitions are essential but not causal. We shall consider theories of this latter kind (e.g. Spinoza's) later in the chapter.

How does Aristotle fair as an emotion theorist so far? We have already seen that his championing of functionalism provides a partial answer to the question: what are emotions for (Q. 5)? In addition, the tripartite cognitive scheme which we have just considered throws up a few more answers. First, Aristotle has suggested that the constituent parts of an emotional experience (Q. 2) are that it involves an event, a stimulus, a state of mind, and the form and matter of the emotion proper. Furthermore, we have argued that his answers to these two questions make his a strong cognitive, functionalist account of emotions. Second, he has at least made some form of comment concerning the number of emotions (Q. 7), though it is unclear whether he was intending his as a finite list. In addition, he spends some time discussing the relationship of different emotions to each other (e.g. anger is the opposite of calm), though here his analysis is not particularly convincing. Third, he provides us with some insight into how one emotion might be distinguished from another (Q. 3) and it is his answer to this question that we shall consider next.

As already mentioned, Aristotle considers 10 emotions in *The Art of Rhetoric* and he sets out to distinguish between them along all three dimensions of his tripartite scheme. Of these three options we would argue, with the benefit of hindsight, that one is a definite red herring, another has the potential to be a red herring, and a third is a perceptive insight which marks Aristotle out as someone centuries ahead of his time. The definite red herring, we suggest, is a consideration of what Aristotle calls the object and what we have called the event. Although Aristotle goes into some detail as to which events go with which emotions, as we have already stated it is our view that this can at best be an approximation (the event problem). A case of rivalry seems just as likely to be associated with anger, envy, jealousy, or indignation as it is with fear. In addition, one can think of hundreds of putative events for fear which are not included in Aristotle's list of 12 and it would be difficult to tease out what all of these events had in common; for example, fear of heights and fear of forgetting your wedding anniversary.

The possible red herring, we propose, is the consideration of states of mind and we shall return to this when we discuss Oatley and Johnson-Laird's (1987) functional theory of the emotions in Chapter 3. In essence, we would argue that individuals' states of mind *contribute* to their evaluation of danger but do not determine absolutely whether such evaluations take place.

The perceptive insight, we feel, is Aristotle's attempt to distinguish between different emotions on the basis of what he calls the stimulus, and what from now on we shall call the *appraisal*. That is to say, emotions can be distinguished on the basis of the different stimuli or appraisals that elicit them; thus, fear is characterised by an appraisal of impending danger, anger by an appraisal of insult or belittlement, pity by an appraisal that something evil has occurred to one who does not deserve it, and so forth. This proposal immediately provides the makings of an answer to any questions about what two disparate objects (or events) such as heights and forgetting a wedding anniversary have in common—they are both, rightly or wrongly, being appraised as threatening in some way and it this appraisal which makes them instigating events of fear. What we are saying here, then, is that it is the cognitive element in Aristotle's account—the belief or representation—which allows a distinction between one emotion and another and which allows his theory to cut so much psychological and philosophical ice.

Aristotle proffers another dimension along which one emotion can be distinguished from another and this is in terms of function or form. So, anger has the form or function of retaliation, or at least a propensity for it, and fear has the form or function of fight or flight and so on. However, it seems that this boils down to emotions having the function of causing dispositions to correct the circumstances that give rise to the emotion in the first place. This dimension is undoubtedly important but seems insufficiently sturdy to serve as the foundation stone for a distinction between different emotions, as we saw when we discussed behaviourist theories of emotion previously.

To summarise, Aristotle's theory of emotion is both functionalist and cognitive in its conception. The ideas he proposed offer an explanation of the distinctions between different emotions in terms of their antecedent cognitive appraisals and the functions of emotions in terms of the propensity for certain types of behaviour. He also outlines a tripartite framework, which teases out different components of the emotional experience. Many aspects of Aristotle's psychology are remarkably contemporary and are fundamental to the theories of emotion discussed in Chapter 3 and to our own theory which we introduce in Chapter 5. However, the distinctive Aristotelian flavour of these recent approaches reflects a resurgence of interest in his work rather than a culmination of sustained study.

We suggested earlier that the Aristotelian, cognitive stream running through the history of emotion theory was largely a subterranean one, emerging only at one or two points in time prior to the 20th century. The first major emergence subsequent to the somewhat tangential references of the Stoic philosophers was in the work of the 13th century Dominican Friar Thomas Aquinas, a renowned Aristotelian scholar and we consider his work next.

The Thomistic account of emotions

A number of commentators (e.g. Lyons, 1980, 1992) have argued that the Thomistic account of emotions is essentially a non-cognitive one. In fact, Aquinas himself proposes that passions, and therefore emotions, are seated in, what he terms, the orectic rather than in the cognitive part of the soul (*Summa Theologica*, 1266–1273, 1a, 2ae, Q.22, Article 2). In contrast we would like to suggest that the Thomistic model has cognitive elements without being a fully fledged cognitive theory in the Aristotelian vein.

It is useful to reiterate briefly the main points of Aristotle's theory of emotions. Aristotle seems to be saying that, in our tried and trusted example, when Susan sees a bear coming towards her she appraises the situation as one of danger and that it is this appraisal which causes the emotion of fear. Fear includes physiological sensations and a propensity for action, such as running away. In contrast to this, Aquinas suggests that there is an initial non-cognitive *impulse* to approach or avoid an object and that this impulse has an accompanying physiological tone: "every emotion is an approach to or a recoil from good or bad ..." (*Summa Theologica*, 1266–1273, 1a, 2ae, Q.23, Article 4). Impulses are referred to by Aquinas as primary emotions. Subsequent to the initial impulse, a secondary cognitive process comes into play in which the object of the primary impulse is evaluated, thus giving rise to a secondary emotion such as fear or sorrow. So, in the Thomistic model, Susan perceives the bear and this gives rise to an impulse to avoid the bear with an accompanying physiological reaction. The bear is then further evaluated as something which is difficult to avoid and this gives rise to the emotion of fear. The Thomistic scheme for fear is illustrated in Fig. 2.3.

The difficulties for this type of account lie in the non-cognitive nature of the initial impulse or primary emotion. On what basis do certain objects give rise to an impulse to approach or to avoid? and on what basis do some objects lead to impulses and other objects lead to no response at all? This is a similar brick wall to the one with which the behavioural accounts collided, namely the event problem, and the Thomistic model offers no new answers.

Although Aquinas saw himself as someone who built upon and elaborated Aristotle's work, one could argue that the Thomistic account of emotions is considerably weaker that the Aristotelian original. As Lyons (1992, p.298) points out about Aquinas: "Aristotle has not merely been Platonized but, in the area of emotion, de-cognitivized as well."

The cognitive theory of Spinoza

The next significant emergence of the cognitive stream was provided by the Dutch-born philosopher Baruch Benedict Spinoza (1632–1677) in *The Ethics* (1677/1955). Scruton (1986, p.vii) warns:

> Spinoza's greatness and originality are hidden behind a remote, impassive, and often impenetrable style. Few have understood his arguments in their entirety.

This seems to apply particularly to Spinoza's writing on emotions. He sets out in *The Ethics* to provide derivations from first principles of the essential properties of different emotions and the relationship between them. Our account of this task is considerably simplified but hopefully true to the original intention (see Frijda, 1994, for a fuller discussion).

Spinoza's ideas have some similarities with those of Aquinas (and incidentally those of Hume) in that he talks of an initial non-cognitive reaction which is then cognitively elaborated by the presence of "ideas". Spinoza (1677/1955, p.130) states: "By emotion I mean the modifications

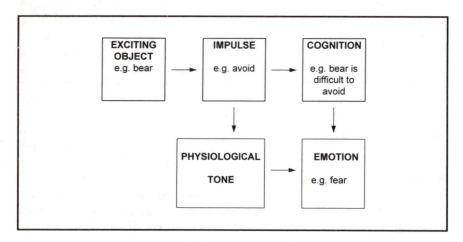

FIG. 2.3. Thomistic account of the emotion of fear.

of the body, whereby the active power of the said body is increased or diminished, aided or constrained, and also the ideas of such modifications." In other words, there is an initial modification, and also the idea of that modification and it is the combination of these two things which makes the emotion.

However, there are a number of important differences between Spinoza's formulation and previous models. Spinoza proposed that the initial emotional reactions were either of desire, pleasure, or pain and that these were responses to external objects in the absence of cognitive evaluation. This contrasts with the Thomistic view that the initial non-cognitive reactions are in the form of impulses. Spinoza's second level emotions such as love, anger, fear, hate, and so on, are the first level emotions *accompanied* by an idea about the causal object. So, love is the experience of pleasure accompanied by the idea that some person is the cause of the pleasure. What is unusual about this model is the fact that the cognitive component (the accompanying idea) has no explicit causal role, it just occurs together with the first-level experience of pleasure, pain, or desire. So, if we once again consider the case of Susan and the bear, in this scenario Spinoza would have to say: that the presence of the bear caused an experience of pain in Susan; that this experience of pain would be accompanied by the idea that the future actions of the bear were uncertain; and that the pain plus the idea are the emotion of fear.

Spinoza's account is clearly a cognitive one, because the belief or idea is essential to emotion. However, it is a theory in which cognitions have no causal role and, thus, Spinoza's theory is an example of what we have called a weak cognitive theory of emotions and, in this respect, it differs from the traditional Aristotelian view.

One problem with non-causal cognitions of this type is that it is never clear how emotions can give rise to behaviour. By what means does Susan come to be running away from the bear? As Lyons (1980, p.40) argues, "Spinoza's emotions cannot of themselves generate behaviour because they are just feelings plus beliefs about their causes." So, not only do the cognitions have no causal role, but the emotion proper has no clear functionality.

A further problem, as with the earlier Thomistic view, concerns the non-cognitive nature of the initial experiences of desire, pain, or pleasure. Again, the aetiological criteria for each of these are unclear and we are left with the event problem. In addition, an initial reaction of pain or pleasure by reference to which the emotion is defined is unable to accommodate the fact that emotions such as love can sometimes be pleasurable and sometimes be painful (see Chapter 10); similarly, for hate and numerous other emotions (Lyons, 1980). A similar charge can be levelled at any of the so-called evaluative theories, which rest on an initial reaction that is either positive or negative (e.g. Hume, Aquinas, Solomon).

Finally, Spinoza's account of emotions seems overinclusive. His idea of an emotion embraces anything which involves pain, pleasure, or desire and an accompanying idea. Emotions therefore include headaches, being tickled, having one's back rubbed, etc. This is clearly at odds with folk psychological views of what is and what is not an emotion (Q.1).

With the benefit of hindsight, Spinoza and Aquinas seem to fare less well than Aristotle as emotion theorists. Nevertheless, their work has considerable merit, if only for the fact that the concepts of emotions described within go against the grain of the philosophical thought of the time. However, the true resurgence of cognitivism in emotion theory occurred in the middle of this century with the work of Anglo-American philosophers such as Anthony Kenny and psychologists such as Magda Arnold.

20TH-CENTURY COGNITIVE ACCOUNTS OF EMOTION

The resurgence of cognitivism was largely a reaction against the stifling effects of behaviourism with its dismissal of all internal psychological states, just as behaviourism itself was a reaction against feeling theory with its overemphasis on private experience. The development of this new cognitivism went hand in hand with advances in computer technology such that, in psychology, the metaphor of the mind as a computer became dominant. In the remainder of this chapter we would like to discuss these recent developments in the philosophy of emotion. The definitions and the development of ideas about what is cognitive and what is a cognitive theory of emotions have tended to take a slightly different, though parallel, course in psychology to that in philosophy, and we consider the arguments in the psychology literature in Chapter 3.

There are a number of seminal papers and books which mark the transformation of the cognitive stream from a trickle that has just emerged from the mountainside to the raging torrent that represents the contemporary philosophical view. Much of this work concentrates on certain aspects of emotion theory and little of it attempts to provide the kind of global view that we have become familiar with in the work of the ancient philosophers. This represents a change in the process of philosophising as a whole. Far reaching, visionary writing has been replaced by detailed analytic dissection, in true Wittgensteinian tradition. For this reason we merely refer to most of the recent work in the philosophy of emotion, reserving the detailed discussion for the writings of William Lyons (1980, 1992), which, in style as well as content, is a throwback to the broader philosophical theories of the past and thus consistent with the spirit of the present volume!

The cognitive revival really began with the work of Magda Arnold culminating in the publication of the book, *Emotion and Personality* in 1960. Arnold's work owes an enormous debt to Thomistic philosophy and as such is concerned with motivation as much as with emotion: "Emotion seems to include not only the appraisal of how this thing or person will affect me but also a definite pull toward or away from it" (1960, Vol. 1, p. 172). At the end of the day, it seems that Arnold's account is yet another victim of the event problem and the chief significance of her work is the part it played in putting cognitive theories of emotion back on the map.

A few more details of this map were filled in by Anthony Kenny's 1963 book, *Action, Emotion and Will.* Kenny is a philosopher in the Wittgensteinian mould and his book is more about how we come to know the meaning of emotion terms rather than a discussion of the concept of emotions. His ideas about what makes something an emotion emerge from the book as opposed to being explicitly stated at any point. For this reason, any brief resumé of his writings is difficult. In a sentence, though, Kenny's "theory" of emotions does provide a central and causal role for cognition in the form of beliefs and appraisals. Indeed, Kenny's model is traditionally Aristotelian in this respect and we can therefore use it as a vehicle to discuss some of the problems with the approach in this simplified form.

To illustrate what we mean, let us return to our example in which Susan is still running away from the bear. Up until now we have argued that Susan holds a belief or has made an appraisal such as "the bear is dangerous" and that this cognition is causal of her emotion of fear. It seems likely, however, that at least two types of cognition are occurring in situations such as this. For example, Susan might interpret that "if the bear catches me it will eat me" and this interpretation will then lead to the appraisal "this situation is dangerous to me and I do not want such danger". In this account it is the appraisal which underlies the fear and not the original interpretation. In an alternative version, Susan might, though we agree it is far-fetched, be seriously into sensation seeking and appraise the interpretation as full of thrills thus leading to the emotion of exhilaration. Lyons (1980) calls the interpretation of the event (e.g. if the bear catches me it will eat me) the "cognition", and the subsequent appraisal (e.g. this situation is dangerous ...) the "evaluation". However, this terminology seems confusing and, because we wish to use the term "cognitive" in a more general sense, we propose the terms *interpretation* and *appraisal* respectively.

To return then to Kenny's book, the central problem is that he does not make it clear whether, in his view, emotions are to be distinguished on the basis of different types of appraisal or on the basis of different types of interpretation. The difficulty with this is that a whole range of different interpretations could be evaluated in the same way and there is no objective criteria by which to argue that any particular one, in and of itself, is directly causal of fear. This, as we have stated many times, is essentially the event problem, except here it is more aptly named the interpretation problem! The conclusion then is that only a theory based on cognitive appraisals can provide a convincing account of emotions and this is the position which we shall try to defend in the remainder of the book.

A number of other influential philosophical accounts of emotion have been provided by Bedford (1964), Peters (1960), Pitcher (1965), and Gordon (1987); however, they only differ in the details to those we have already considered and so we shall pass over them and concentrate on the work of William Lyons (1980, 1992).

The central thesis of Lyons' 1980 book, titled simply *Emotion*, is the traditional Aristotelian model with the addition of the distinction between appraisals and interpretations discussed previously. This framework is presented in Fig. 2.4. for the emotion of fear.

As can be seen in Fig. 2.4, Lyons argues for a causal chain from the instigating event (either external or internal) to interpretation to appraisal (an evaluation of the interpretation along a set of dimensions which differ with respect to the emotion concerned) and, finally, to physiological reaction, desire (that is, what the individual wishes to do about the situation) and possibly behaviour.

We are familiar by now with the components of the standard Aristotelian approach. However, a number of points should be made here about the various fixtures and fittings that Lyons throws in. First, Lyons (1980, p.127) argues that the physiological reactions are not specific to particular emotions, "it is unlikely that there are any particular physiological changes which are to be linked conceptually with any particular emotion", a view clearly opposed to that of William James. This argument immediately raises the question as to whether there is any difference between the physiological changes that occur in the body all of the time and those associated with emotions. Lyons (p.116) tries to get around this by arguing that emotions involve *"unusual"* bodily changes though not physiological disturbance or upset:

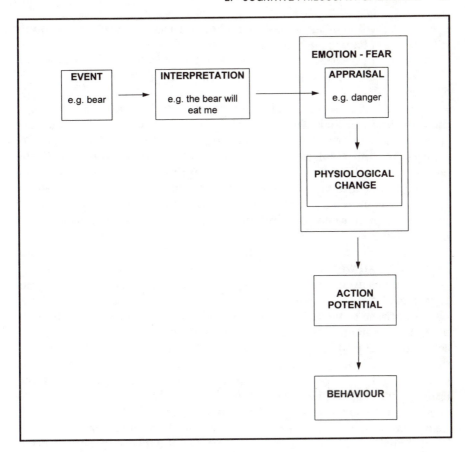

FIG. 2.4. The emotion of fear according to William Lyons.

> Terms such as "disturbance" or "upset" ... may lead one into
> the dual error of thinking that all physiological changes
> associated with emotion are of an alarming or disturbing
> nature and that all bodily changes associated with emotion
> are experienced by the subject of them.

However, there are some empirical problems with this analysis. As
de Sousa (1987) points out, there are still no criteria which allow us to
pick out those physiological changes which count as arousal, and
therefore make up emotion, and those changes which are non-emotional.
In addition, the "relevant physiological states have no naturally salient
boundaries" (de Sousa, 1987, p. 55) and so it is difficult to establish

criteria for what is "unusual". We shall return to these issues in our discussion of basic emotions in Chapter 3.

Another interesting issue is raised by Lyons in his conceptualisation of emotions as consisting of the appraisal and the physiological change. So appraisal is not the antecedent of emotion, it is part of emotion proper and, indeed, it is what enables a distinction to be drawn between one emotion and another. This view of appraisal as a logically necessary ingredient of emotion seems important; however, it has been largely ignored by appraisal theorists in psychology (see Chapter 3). If the concept of emotion does not include the appraisal, and one maintains, as we do, that it is not possible to distinguish different emotions solely on the basis of events, interpretations, physiological changes, or overt behaviour, then it becomes difficult to see how any distinctions between emotions can be drawn.

A further area of debate concerns the role of consciousness. Lyons argues that all we need for something to be an emotion is an appraisal which causes an unusual physiological change. He would not claim (as is evident from the previous quotation) that we need to be conscious of either of these to be in an emotional state. So, if we imagine that Dave is in an important meeting and has to concentrate very hard on the content of the discussion, it would still be possible for him to unconsciously interpret and appraise the situation as insulting, thus giving rise to a physiological reaction—the core components of the emotion of anger. However, according to Lyons, because of his concentration on what people were saying Dave might be unaware that he appeared to be "angry" until his colleagues told him later that he had been shouting and was clearly very angry in the meeting. The question here is: if Dave is unaware of the physiological changes that are occurring in his body caused by an appraisal that he is being insulted, that is, Dave is unaware of "feeling angry", is it legitimate to say that he *is* angry? A simpler, though slightly different way of putting this, is to ask whether it is possible to have an unconscious emotion. There may not be a definitive answer to this question; however, having stated Lyons' position, which is essentially that unconscious emotions *are* possible, it is incumbent on us to at least acknowledge the alternative point of view that unconscious emotions are not possible. In fact, it may be surprising that this view was held by Freud (*The Unconscious*, 1915/1949, p.104):

> It is surely of the essence of an emotion that we should feel it, i.e. that it should enter consciousness. So for emotions, feelings and affects to be unconscious would be quite out of the question.

Lyons, for the most part, discusses what he calls occurrent emotions in his book. These are short-term emotional states (and are the subject of most of the previous discussion in this chapter) as opposed to longer term dispositions. However, Lyons does devote some time to a discussion of these latter conditions. Following in the footsteps of Ryle, Lyons distinguishes two types of dispositions: those focused on something specific; and, those that are unfocused. To give an example, if someone crashes her car she might have a focused angry disposition for a number of days such that any mention of the car causes her to become "occurrently" angry. Alternatively, she might have an unfocused angry disposition; that is, she might just be a generally angry person liable to occurrent outbursts of temper in a wide range of provoking situations. Although appealing, this analysis seems to miss the fact that dispositions caused by crashing one's car can also be unfocused. Anyone who has been around people who have just written off a car will realise that it is not just mentioning cars that will make them occurrently angry, almost anything is a potential trigger!

Another issue which Lyons hints at is the idea of appraisals at different levels of the psychological system. We have already seen that there is no problem with the concept of unconscious appraisal (though it is unclear whether the concept of unconscious emotions is acceptable). However, there seems to be a need for further elaboration. Compare, for example, the case of someone who has a phobia of spiders with the case of Susan's flight from the grizzly bear. In the first instance, the spider phobic can talk about spiders and agree, quite sincerely, that there is really nothing to be afraid of. However, when a spider appears, the conscious appraisal of the situation counts for little and the individual is likely to run away just as quickly as Susan from the bear. In contrast, Susan is unlikely to admit *at any level* that there is nothing scary or dangerous about the bear. In the spider case it seems that the emotional reaction of fear has become so automatised (or, as Lyons and behavioural psychologists would say, Classically Conditioned) that it will always happen in the presence of spiders irrespective of the person's conscious or "higher-level" appraisals of the situation. Lyons (1980, p.77) summarises this as follows:

> In all cases of Pavlovian [classically conditioned] emotions, the person concerned both knows that the conditions which previously caused her to be afraid no longer obtain, but yet still believes against all the evidence, adequate evidence, that they might still hold true. The person simply holds conflicting beliefs.

Here Lyons owes a debt to Descartes for two reasons. First, Descartes paid some lip service to the idea that emotions are associated with those exciting causes (events) that had caused that same emotion in the past; though, as with many of the central struts of his theory, Descartes never elaborated the idea much beyond this. Second, Descartes discussed the idea of what Anthony Kenny has called "intellectual emotions", which can be seen as emotions resulting from higher-level appraisals.

The issue of different levels of appraisal has important implications for considering emotional disorder. As we have already seen, it can shed some light on the nature of simple phobias; furthermore, the notion of appraisals that are in opposition and seemingly occur at different levels of the cognitive system provides a window into the role of conflict which is apparent in so many emotional disorders. We shall discuss the utility of these ideas further in Chapter 5.

Lyons' theory of emotion provides one of the more complete philosophical analyses of the concept and, as such, offers perhaps the most comprehensive attempt at a philosophical reply to the set of questions posed to the aspiring emotion theorist in the introduction to this chapter. For this reason we shall combine our discussion of how Lyons fares as an emotion theorist with an overall summary and review of the chapter and endeavour to draw out how philosophical approaches in general cope with the central questions concerning emotion.

SUMMARY AND CONCLUSIONS

We began the chapter by posing eight questions that any aspiring emotion theorist would need to address. We then considered two main historical strands of philosophical opinion on emotion: the first centres on feeling theory and originated in the writings of Plato and came to rather an abrupt halt following the work of the psychologist, William James; the second cognitive strand originated with Aristotle's analysis of emotions in *The Art of Rhetoric* and is still unravelling itself in contemporary philosophical thought.

In this section we consider again the eight questions listed in the introduction and examine the answers which these two strands, spanning some 2000 years of philosophy, have been able to provide. These answers and our elaborations on them will form the philosophical framework for the rest of the book and will provide both a set of criteria by which to judge the theories reviewed in Chapters 3 and 4 and the philosophical basis of our own model, which we outline in Chapter 5.

Inevitably, the summary we are about to provide reflects our belief that what we have called the strong cognitive theory of emotions is the only approach that has the makings of a truly comprehensive theory. However, we hope that we have been convincing in our claim that the various non-cognitive theories reviewed all suffer from fundamental philosophical flaws. To turn then to the questions that faced our now somewhat world-weary emotion theorist:

1. What distinguishes an emotion from a non-emotion?   As we noted in the introduction there is a considerable folk psychological consensus about which mental states are the emotions, e.g. fear, anger, guilt, and so on. Likewise, there is general agreement that hunger, pain, itches, etc. are not emotions. The challenge for any model of emotion, we suggested, is to produce a conceptual framework from which these accepted distinctions between emotions and non-emotions emerge. The most difficult of these distinctions is that between emotions such as fear and sensations such as pain; if this distinction can be resolved, then the other distinctions should fall into place. In our opinion, this kind of question is one that has received one of the least complete answers from the philosophical models reviewed. Most of these theories provide no conceptual basis for distinguishing emotions and non-emotions. Rather, they provide us with a priori lists of what are and are not emotions with little or no discussion of how the lists were derived. This is a point Lyons makes strongly in his 1980 book so one might expect that the theory contained therein would suggest some form of solution to the problem. Lyons proposes that emotions are physiological changes *caused by* evaluative appraisals of internal or external events. However, at no point is he explicit as to how this differs from an analysis of sensations. One can attempt to make the distinction by proposing that pain is an awareness of a physiological change (the activation of pain receptors) and as such involves no causal cognitive evaluation or appraisal. At first glance this analysis is appealing; however, there are some problems with it in this simplified form.

The major problem is that if we describe pain as the feeling produced by a physiological state, we buy into all the problems of feeling theory we raised in our discussion of Descartes. The principal problems are those outlined by Wittgenstein (1958) in his private language argument. So, according to this line of attack, the word "pain" cannot obtain its meaning as a label for a purely private experience because it is a concept that is only verifiable publicly. If it were such a label, we would have no way of knowing that what we call pain was the same as what someone else would call pain. As we noted earlier, the arguments around this point are immensely drawn out and complicated. We shall content ourselves with providing the functionalist attempt at a solution to the problem. In this analysis, pain is a functional state that alerts us to the possibility of physical damage. However, if we reject the feeling theory idea that pain is merely the label given to our experience of this physical damage, then we need to replace it with something. The standard functionalist line is that the physical damage activates a belief that we are in pain and it is the conscious awareness of this belief which gives pain its distinctive quality. So, there are two components here: the physical stimulus (activation of the pain receptors); and the activated belief. Under most circumstances, this belief will be due to the activation of the pain receptors by an event; for example, the gash in Susan's leg as she flees from the bear. However, the fact that there are two components means that, potentially, they can operate separately and in some cases there will be no such pain receptor activation whilst still being an activated belief that we are in pain. This is psychogenic pain; here the experience of pain is an awareness of the belief that we are in pain, even when there is no corresponding physiological event.

This leaves us with a concept of emotion which is a combined awareness of both a physiological change and an associated appraisal, and a concept of pain (a sensation) which is an awareness of a belief which may or may not have been activated by actual physiological change. The fact that some form of cognitive evaluation or belief state is central to both sensation and emotion in this analysis means that any superficial analysis of the distinctions between emotions and non-emotions along the lines we have referred to above no longer holds any water.

We can perhaps make some progress towards answering this question of the difference between sensations and emotions by reconsidering some of Descartes' ideas. As we saw in Table 2.1, Descartes drew distinctions between sensations such as pain and emotions such as fear by suggesting that the object that they referred to was in the body in the former case and in the soul in the latter case. In our discussion of this framework we tried to point out that the notion of an object of emotions in the soul did not stand scrutiny. However, if we replace the idea of emotions having an object in the soul with the idea that emotions have an object that is cognitive, we have the beginnings of a model in which we can tease apart sensations such as pain and emotions such as fear.

We have so far tried to draw distinctions between: the event (in our familiar example this is the bear); the interpretation (e.g. that the bear will eat Susan); and the appraisal (that there is danger). As we have also seen, these distinctions are central to Lyons' theory of emotion as illustrated in Fig. 2.4. If we think of this in terms of the Cartesian classification system in Table 2.1 presented earlier, we can say that in the case of emotions the appraisal is always about the interpretation; in other words, the object of the appraisal is always something *cognitive*.

In contrast, if we consider the sensation of pain, the appraisal is always a real or imagined bodily stimulus that is believed to be causing the pain. In other words, the object of the appraisal is always *bodily*. This argument is illustrated in Fig. 2.5.

To summarise, it seems that we can begin to answer one aspect of the question as to what the difference is between emotions and non-emotions, namely the aspect which refers to the difference between emotions and sensations. This answer rests on the proposal that the object of appraisal in the case of emotions is always cognitive whereas the object of the appraisal in the case of sensations is always bodily, and hence sensations are always physically localised.

2. What are the constituent parts of an emotion? Or are emotions irreducible?   The first distinction that emerges out of the discussion so far in the chapter is that between emotion as a concept and emotion as a paradigm case. By emotion as a concept we mean those elements that are both necessary and sufficient for something to be called an emotion.

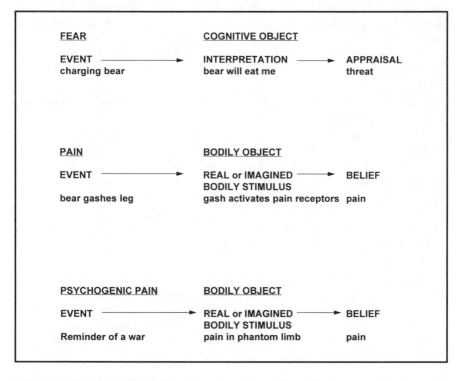

FIG. 2.5. A schematic diagram illustrating the proposed distinction between sensations such as pain and emotions such as fear.

By emotion as a paradigm case we mean the conceptual core plus all of the other aspects of emotion that are neither necessary nor sufficient; for example, shouting and table-thumping behaviour when one is angry.

We saw at the beginning of the chapter that Aristotle proposed that the concept of emotion requires some form of appraisal and some form of physiological change. In addition, he emphasised that emotions must have what he called form and that this was really a propensity for behaviour. The work over the past 2000 years that we have reviewed provides little reason to disagree with the essence of what Aristotle is putting forward. Some fine-tuning is useful, however, and we have tried to show, in accordance with William Lyons, that a distinction between what we have called an interpretation and what we label an appraisal is helpful, especially when it comes to distinguishing emotions from non-emotions (Q.1). Up to this point we have spent very little time elaborating on Aristotle's notion of form or functionality. Nevertheless, we regard this as fundamental to emotions to the extent that we would argue that the potential for action is a conceptually necessary component of emotional experience. We discuss our reasons for this as part of the reply to Q.5 below. This leaves us with a concept of emotion which must include: an event; an interpretation; an appraisal; physiological change; an action potential; and (most probably) conscious awareness. In philosophy this proposal of necessary and sufficient components of emotions is known as an essentialist account. Moving from emotion as a concept to emotion as a paradigm case we can embrace also the notion of overt behaviour.

Within these conceptual and paradigmatic frameworks we have argued for a distinction between a strong cognitive theory of emotions and a weak cognitive theory of emotions. The strong version involves a causal link between appraisal and physiological change and between appraisal and action potential (and thus behaviour, see the reply to Q.5 below), whereas a weak cognitive theory identifies the same constituent elements but makes no claim about their causal relationships. We have suggested that it is the strong cognitive theory that provides the most useful analysis of emotions.

To summarise, the concept of emotions includes an instigating event, an interpretation, and a subsequent appraisal of that interpretation, which is causal of physiological change and a state of potential for action, and the experience of emotion is the conscious experience of some or all of these components. In addition, in the full-blown paradigm case there is an accompanying repertoire of emotional behaviour.

3. *What distinguishes one emotion from another?*   This is probably the question to which the answer provided by the cognitive theory is

most clearly superior to the answers generated by the other approaches we have discussed. The cognitive approach proposes that the distinctions between emotions are a function of the appraisals which are associated with them. So, anger is associated with an appraisal of some form of insult, fear with an appraisal of threat, sadness with an appraisal of loss, and so on.

If we accept this theoretical position, then we are immediately faced with the questions of which appraisal goes with which emotion and, equally as important, how we might determine this. These questions are ones that have received considerable attention from psychologists and we shall discuss them and some of the proposed answers to them in Chapter 3.

4. What is the process of having an emotional experience? The philosophical approaches to emotion, which we have reviewed in the present chapter, have little to say about the underlying processes involved in having an emotional experience. This highlights a fundamental difference between the ambitions of philosophy and psychology. Philosophy is primarily concerned with the construction of a coherent conceptual framework within which to understand emotion, whereas psychology is also concerned with how such a framework might be instantiated in the human mind. This seems to map fairly closely onto what Marr (1982) has suggested is the distinction between the *computational level* and the *algorithmic* level. As we have written elsewhere (Dalgleish, 1994a, p.154):

> The computational level, despite its name, is not concerned with process; rather, it is a description of what the system as a whole is doing, not how it is doing it. It represents an abstract formulation of the task which defines a given psychological ability. The algorithm is a specification of how the task is carried out, the nature of the computational processes involved and the way in which the information these processes use is represented.

So, in the case of emotion, we have suggested, for example, that we need some notion of appraisal. This is a statement at the computational level of analysis. The next questions are:

How would such a process of appraisal work?
What would it need to look like?
Do we need to propose some type of schema or semantic network?
Which appraisals go with which emotions?

These are questions at the algorithmic level of analysis and are the remit of psychology. The present chapter can be seen as providing a computational level analysis, a philosophical analysis, of the nature of emotions. The remainder of the book is concerned with providing a psychological analysis of how these computational level ideas can be instantiated at the algorithmic level.

5. *Why do we have emotions?*   Although we introduced the idea of functionalism in our discussion of the work of Aristotle, we have given the question of why we have emotions little consideration. To recap, the Aristotelian reply to the question is that the function of emotions is related to the propensity they allow for certain types of behaviour. So, the function of fear is to provide a propensity for Susan to run away from the bear. One might even add that the physiological changes associated with such fear, such as increased adrenalin secretion, allow Susan to run that bit faster! Akin to the distinction previously drawn between interpretations and appraisals, we would like to extend this functionalist view further and argue that emotions are associated with potentials for action and also, at times, with overt behaviour. So, having appraised her interpretation that the bear will eat her as one of danger, Susan forms the action potential to run away and, in fact, does run away. The question really then is whether this notion of an action potential is conceptually necessary for a proper understanding of emotion? Recent theorists, such as Lyons, have suggested that the answer to this question is probably no and that action potentials are merely a component of emotion as a paradigm case. To support this claim Lyons (1980, p.96) cites examples of the, so-called, backward-looking emotions such as grief which, he argues, are not associated with any functional desire or potential for action:

> Ultimately, I think that the reason why we would say that grief does not have any desires [action potentials] as part of its concept is that it makes perfectly good sense for us to say "X grieves for Y" and "X has no desires [action potentials] deriving from his grief for Y".

We would like to disagree with this line of argument. It seems to make no sense to suggest that somebody is grieving but has no associated action potential. Part of the essence of grief is surely that of finding it difficult to come to terms with the loss of somebody (or something) who is held in high regard and this loss is reflected by a desire and associated action potential that things had turned out differently and that the person was still present. Lyons would not necessarily disagree with this point. He also notes that grief is associated with desires and potentials for action that things should be otherwise. However, he does not agree that this is always the case.

This is where we beg to differ. We would like to propose that action potentials are a conceptually necessary constituent of the emotional experience and, indeed, help to define the role of emotions in a functional theory of mind. Emotions without action potentials have no functionality. In terms of backward-looking emotions such as grief, we propose that there are action potentials but that the goals to which they are directed either cannot be realised or consist of elicitations of support and sympathy from others or the reassessment of psychological coping resources through internal reflection. These points are expanded on in Chapter 7 on sadness.

Having made these various points, there remains one objection. Why could we not have a system that involves appraisals of say danger and leads to an action potential to avoid the danger without actually having the experience of emotions? This looks suspiciously like the original question: why do we have emotions? And so it seems that we may still have a way to go to find a convincing reply. The answer must be related to the speed of response required in emotion-provoking situations, to the physiological readiness which is necessary to execute that response, and to the need to communicate our evaluations to others; we discuss these issues further in Chapter 3.

6. What is the relationship between emotional states, moods and temperament? As we have seen, perhaps the most lengthy consideration of this question has been provided by the work of Gilbert Ryle in *The Concept of Mind* (1949). However, his account is firmly rooted in the behaviourist tradition and, consequently, has its share of problems. Lyons also provides some discussion but declines to elaborate on the initial distinctions that he draws. We would like to propose a different analysis based on the cognitive theory of emotions. If, as we have argued, the process of appraisal is the central engine of emotion, then the notion of moods and dispositions within the cognitive framework must involve fluctuations in the likelihood of such appraisals taking place. So, within this analysis, an angry mood is a state during which those appraisals that are constituents of anger are more likely to occur or have a lower threshold of occurrence. Similarly, having an angry disposition or being an angry type of person can be viewed as a permanently low threshold for anger appraisals to take place. What a lowered threshold actually means in terms of underlying processes and how such lowering of thresholds comes about is really a question for psychology and we shall consider it in Chapters 3 and 5.

7. How many emotions are there, and what is the nature of their relationship with each other? It seems unlikely that it is possible to answer the question of how many emotions there are or even whether it is meaningful to ask it. Some of the early philosophical analyses of emotion such as those of Aristotle and Descartes did present lists of emotions, but even here it is unclear whether they viewed these lists as illustrative or finite. Within cognitive theory the sensible approach would be that the number of emotions is determined by the number of states which fit the conceptual analysis; that is, include an appraisal which has as its object an interpretation and which causes some form of physiological change concomitant with some form of action potential and conscious awareness. However, this does not help us to come up with numbers. Another way in is to perform some kind of socio-linguistic analysis and look at the number of emotion terms in a given language or culture. This approach has gained considerable currency in recent times (e.g. Johnson-Laird & Oatley, 1989). Perhaps the most important issue to be raised by a consideration of this type of question concerns the relationship of emotions to each other. We have unearthed a variety of ideas about this during our journey through Western philosophy. Descartes was the first to suggest that some emotions may be more basic than others and that more complex emotions were merely elaborations or combinations of the basic few. We consider this idea in some detail in Chapter 3 because it is important in our understanding of emotional order and disorder. It was Plato who floated the idea that we can be in more than one emotional state at a time and that these emotions can sometimes be in conflict. An extension of this is Descartes' proposal that we can have secondary emotions. He gives the example of the man who, although grieving over the death of his wife, feels, in his heart of hearts, great relief that she is no longer there to pester him. We concur with this view of emotions. Within a cognitive theory this is tantamount to saying two things: (1) that the same event and/or interpretation can be appraised in different ways at the same time thus leading to different and even conflicting emotions; (2) that initial emotional reactions can be reappraised and, themselves be the impetus to further emotional experiences, either congruent with the initial emotion (e.g. depression about depression) or in conflict with it (e.g. anger with yourself about being happy at somebody's downfall). These ideas of primary and secondary appraisal or of different levels of appraisal have been considerably fleshed out by empirical and theoretical work in psychology and we consider them in more detail in the section on appraisal theories in Chapter 3.

8. What is the difference between, and the relationship of, the so-called normal emotions and the emotional disorders?   At the outset of the chapter when we introduced this question, and also in Chapter 1, we proposed that what was needed was a theory which could provide an explanation of emotional *order* whilst also shedding some light on the nature of so-called *emotional disorder*. The various philosophical models which we have reviewed have rarely made explicit statements about the nature of this relationship and those comments which we have included in the course of the chapter represent inferences which we have been able to draw from this work.

Through these inferences we have tried to show that the feeling and the behaviourist theories of emotion offer inadequate accounts of emotional disorder. In contrast, we have argued, the cognitive account of emotion does provide a springboard towards an understanding of these complex issues. This rests on the basic idea that emotional responses can be viewed as more or less appropriate reactions to interpretations, which are more or less appropriate analyses of events. So, Susan's fear of the bear seems perfectly appropriate—the general consensus would be that the bear would be likely to eat her if it caught her and that therefore it is dangerous. In contrast, if we consider the example of somebody who has a fear of coffee, then it does not seem outrageous to argue that this fear of coffee is somehow an inappropriate emotional reaction or even an emotional disorder. The important point is that the emotional process is the same in both cases: there is an appraisal of danger which leads to a physiological change and a desire to avoid the dangerous object. These somewhat polarised examples are clearly a gross oversimplification and Part Two of the book is concerned with presenting a considerably more detailed and, hopefully, more thoughtful analysis of these issues.

Hand in hand with notions of emotional disorder goes the issue of therapy. Again, we will consider this in greater detail later; however, it is useful to offer up some preliminary points at this juncture. At the simplest level, and to use a tried and trusted example from cognitive therapy, consider the interpretation that the noise that wakes us up in the middle of the night is that of an armed intruder. We are likely to subsequently appraise this interpretation as one indicative of danger and feel afraid. However, if we then discover that the noise was made by our cat, the fear goes away. Here, then, the process of changing the interpretation and hence the appraisal is enough to dissipate the emotion.

Within the cognitive model of emotions, this is really what therapy may be seen to be trying to achieve. However, most beliefs or interpretations are not as accessible as the noise in the night example and they are often held with far greater conviction. Furthermore, they may be difficult to express in natural language. So, at the other end of the scale from the burglar/cat scenario we might find the case of the individual with a fear of mice. It seems possible that in this instance the "interpretation" that mice are somehow harmful could be so deep-rooted and inaccessible that the person would agree that there is no reason to be afraid of mice and even that she does not explicitly believe that mice are harmful whilst still reacting with fear in the presence of a mouse. In cases of phobia such as this, it is a lot harder to shake the emotional beliefs and appraisals.

In between these two extremes lies a whole range of instances of ordered and disordered beliefs, interpretations, and appraisals and an equally mind-boggling choice of therapies with which to take them on. Some approaches, such as the psychodynamic, involve a process of developing insight into what the underlying beliefs, interpretations, and appraisals might be; the argument being that an understanding of these issues allows the possibility of change. Other processes rely on constructing more "appropriate" beliefs, interpretations, and appraisals either through behavioural demonstration or through reasoned argument. We shall return to all of these issues at points throughout the rest of the book.

To sum up, in the present chapter we have sought to provide an overview of philosophical thought on emotions and to develop a philosophical framework by which to judge the theories of emotion developed in psychology, which we review in Chapters 3 and 4. This framework is illustrated in the answers to the eight questions and reflects our conviction that what we have called a strong cognitive theory of emotions can potentially provide the best model of emotional order and disorder. There are many issues in the philosophy of emotions which we have not touched upon; after all, this is essentially a book about the psychology of emotion. However, we have endeavoured to expose the heart of the philosophy literature in the hope that it can be transplanted successfully into the more psychological discussions that follow.

NOTE

1. Descartes uses the term "passion" in two ways. The first usage incorporates what are traditionally known as perceptions and sensations. The second, narrower usage is the one that Descartes elaborates on and it applies to those perceptions that are referred to the soul alone—namely the emotions.

CHAPTER THREE

Cognitive theories of emotion

My soul is a hidden orchestra; I know not what instruments, what fiddlestrings and harps, drums and tambours I sound and clash inside myself. All I hear is the symphony. *(Fernando Pessoa)*

INTRODUCTION

The purpose of this chapter is to outline some of the major current cognitive theories of emotion in psychology, our focus therefore will be more on the adequacy of these theories than on the empirical data, which will be considered in more detail in the Part Two of the book. We saw in Chapters 1 and 2 that there is a considerable historical tradition for many of the ideas that underpin the cognitive approach, for example, in Aristotle's *The Art of Rhetoric*, in Spinoza, and in cognitive philosophical theories of the 20th century. Two of the key themes that emerge from this background relate to the issues of associationism and of constructivism; thus, the two main groups of theories that we shall examine in this chapter derive either from the associationist tradition and are based on semantic networks, or derive from the constructivist position and have come to be known as appraisal theories. The debate between these two approaches in cognitive science is as strong now as it ever has been; it has been given new impetus with the recent development of connectionism and Parallel Distributed Processing (PDP) models (Rumelhart & McClelland, 1986). Although PDP models have overcome many of the limitations of previous associationist approaches, for example, in their solutions about how networks learn new material, it is yet unclear whether they will provide any advantages for theories of emotion. Nevertheless, we will attempt to gaze into the crystal ball and see whether there could be advantages for emotion theory from this approach.

The starting point for the theories to be presented in this chapter is an attempt to provide a cognitive account of *normal* emotions. A number of important questions were raised in Chapters 1 and 2 that need to be recycled here and, in addition, a number of new ones need to be raised. For example, emotion is an everyday part of human experience, but how do we account for the fact that two people can apparently experience different emotions about the same event? that the same individual can come to feel different things at different times about the same event? why are some emotional experiences more transient than others? why do we sometimes cry with laughter? or feel nothing at all when we *should* feel something? There are dozens of such questions that convey much about our everyday understanding as well as our everyday ignorance about emotion; all of the theories to be presented attempt answers to questions such as these at least some of the time. Of course, a second set of questions relates to how well the theories then account for abnormal or extreme variants of each emotion. Again, we will see that some theories do reasonably well, whereas others pay little or no attention to these extremes.

One of the issues that highlights the question of the role of cognition in emotion is the so-called Zajonc–Lazarus debate. The debate centred on the question of the primacy of affect or the primacy of cognition in the generation of emotion. To summarise, Zajonc (1980) argued that the initial processing of stimuli, that is, within the first few milliseconds following sensory registration, assesses the *affective* tone of the stimulus as positive or negative, safe or threatening, and that "cognitive" processes occur subsequent to this affective processing. Although critics of Zajonc's initial standpoint, such as Lazarus (1982), argued that Zajonc had confused conscious processing with cognitive processing and that he had assumed that any automatic processes were affective processes, Zajonc has subsequently presented a more restricted view. For example, Murphy and Zajonc (1993) now accept that the term "cognitive" can refer to processes that occur outside of awareness, but still maintain their position that the initial processes are qualitatively distinct affective ones; they agree with theorists such as Lazarus that cognitive processes *can* influence the course and type of emotion experienced, but state that this interaction between cognitive and affective processes occurs later. They also state that there are distinct neuroanatomical tracts between the visual system and the limbic system that they interpret as support for the affective primacy hypothesis. That there have been two or more such visual routes has been known for some time (e.g. Luria, 1976). Indeed, the phenomenon of "blindsight" (Weiskrantz, 1986) seems to require such an additional visual route; that is, it has been found possible for a patient without the relevant visual cortex to respond to and avoid objects in the immediate environment and at the same time deny any conscious experience of the objects. The question therefore hinges on whether, contrary to Zajonc, such fast automatic processes should all be labelled "cognitive" in the sense that they involve low-level computations in the perceptual system, one important feature of which is to detect the affective value of the stimulus. By analogy therefore with David Marr's (1982) proposal that there is a fast "primal sketch" of sensory input, we would suggest that there is a fast automatic categorisation of a stimulus, which, as we will discuss later, can for certain innate or automated sequences lead to the rapid generation of emotion: as if "primal sketch" were to meet "primal scream". Even in the case of this automatic or direct route to emotion, we must emphasise that the distinction presupposed in the Zajonc-Lazarus debate between cognition and emotion is a false one, as we argued in Chapter 2. The "emotion" and the "cognition" are integral and inseparable parts of each other and though it is useful to use different names for different aspects of the generation of emotion, the parts are no more separable than are waves from the water on which they occur.

The exact implications of the Zajonc–Lazarus debate for the theories we will consider in this chapter vary considerably. In the case of appraisal theories such as Lazarus' (1966; 1991) or Frijda's (1986), there are clear statements that all preattentive processes are to be called "cognitive"; thus, there has to be some minimal computation of a stimulus's emotional valence and goal-relevance for an automatic generation of emotion to occur. However, it is unclear what the implications of the debate are for a network theory such as Bower's (1981). As will be shown in the next section, in network theories emotions are typically represented as nodes or links in an associative network; they can be directly activated by the appropriate emotion in the environment, or activation can spread from adjoining nodes which could be cognitive *or* physiological. Bower's model therefore would appear to support both possibilities; namely, that under some conditions "affective" processing may be direct and primary, whereas under other conditions "cognitive" processes may be primary. In fact, we will attempt to show that this ambiguity appears to be present in at least one of the recent cognitive appraisal theories (that of Oatley & Johnson-Laird, 1987) that we will also discuss.

One other issue that we will highlight before discussing specific theories is the issue of basic emotions and the number and complexity of emotions that a theory considers. As we will present in detail later in the chapter, on the basis of evidence collected from cross-cultural studies of the facial expression of emotion, from studies of the sequence of development of emotions, from linguistic analyses of emotion terms, from categorisation studies of emotion terms, and from psycho-physiological recording there is strong evidence for the existence of basic emotions, in particular, the emotions of anger, sadness, fear, disgust, and happiness. However, although appraisal theorists generally agree that there has to be some basic categorisation of emotions, there is no agreement about how many such basic emotions there should be and any number from two upwards can be found in one theory or another. Again, the situation with network theories is unclear; as Bower (1992) has himself commented, network theories originally incorporated "lay theories" of emotion, in that beyond being represented as nodes in networks, there was no theory of the relationship between cognition and emotion nor of the types of emotion involved. But if an emotion is no more than a node in a network, it is difficult to see how any distinction between say basic and complex emotions could be incorporated in the original single-level networks that were proposed. Instead, more complex multiple-level networks would seem to be required, which might be better dealt with in connectionist models.

NETWORK THEORIES

Network theories follow in a long tradition that can be traced back to Aristotle and which includes the British Empiricist or Associationist school of philosophy. In psychology, Associationism underpins not only behaviourism and the basis for the laws of learning, but also psychoanalysis and Freud's development of the Free Association technique. Indeed, one of the most detailed and elegant network models of autobiographical memory was presented by Breuer and Freud (1895/1974). Because it bears close resemblance to many current network models, we will begin with an outline of this model.

A modified version of Breuer and Freud's (1895) model of autobiographical memory is presented in Fig. 3.1. Freud argued that one or more early traumatic events, thoughts or wishes can form a "pathogenic nucleus" around which later associated memories become attached according to a number of rules. First, there is a linear

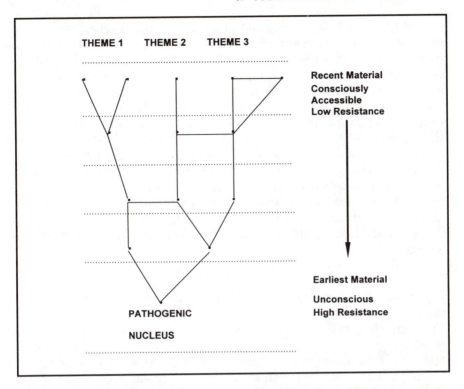

FIG. 3.1. An adaptation of Breuer and Freud's (1895) model of autobiographical memory.

chronological order, with the oldest memories running in sequence to the newer memories. There may however be multiple pathways or themes that can be traced back to the original nuclear memory. Second, the themes are stratified around the nucleus such that the oldest strata are resisted: "near the nucleus we come upon memories which the patient disavows even in reproducing them" (Breuer & Freud, 1895/1974, p.375). Third, logical chains run through the material to the nucleus; these logical linkages meet at memory nodes and may connect across themes as well as within them. Activation of one of the memory nodes leads to a spread of energy through the linkages to the nucleus and one of the ways in which this energy can be discharged is through the subsequent night's dreams (Freud, 1900/1976b). Although Freud's focus was on autobiographical memory, it will be apparent from our review of more recent network models that his account is as elegant as any of the later accounts.

The main impetus for the use of networks within cognitive science came from attempts to model the relationship between linguistic concepts. One of the most influential of these was Quillian's trail-blazing

PhD thesis which was published in 1968. Whereas earlier associative networks had simply assumed that the connections between words in a network consisted of undifferentiated links of varying strength, Quillian proposed that there could be different types of link between the nodes in a network and that these links expressed key features of the semantic relationship between concepts. These labelled links enable the network to capture so-called "intensional" relationships between words in a way that unlabelled links do not. For example, the word "Gooseberry" is associated with "Fruit", with "Fool", and with "Play" (as in "Play Gooseberry"), but the type of semantic or intensional relation is very different in each case; a network that contained only unlabelled links between concepts could not express these different intensional relationships.

The semantic network that Quillian (1968; Collins & Quillian, 1969) presented dealt with the hierarchical arrangement of groups of nouns such as:

$$\text{CANARY} \rightarrow \text{BIRD} \rightarrow \text{ANIMAL}$$

In this network, the nodes represent concepts and the links represent the relation "ISA"; that is, a canary is a bird, and a bird is an animal. The empirical tests of the hierarchically organised nouns initially provided good support for the proposals (Collins & Quillian, 1969). However, it became evident that not all findings were supportive, for example, that sentences such as "A Horse is an Animal" were verified faster than "A Horse is a Mammal" even though the former involved two links in the hierarchy and the latter only one. The problem expressed in this example is that a horse is not a prototypical mammal; amended versions of the network need to be produced to take account of prototypicality (e.g. Collins & Loftus, 1975). Even more problematic was the fact that false statements were found to be rejected faster the *further* two concepts were apart rather than the closer they were together, and the fact that not all word categories can be organised hierarchically anyway (e.g. Johnson-Laird, Herrmann, & Chaffin, 1984). Again, it is possible to produce modifications of networks that can take account of these problems and some of these alternatives will be presented next. However, we hope that this short introduction to some of the features of semantic networks will aid the description of some of the specific network models that have been applied to emotion.

Bower's network theory

The most influential network theory of emotion was proposed by Gordon Bower (Bower, 1981; Bower & Cohen, 1982). Based on the earlier Anderson and Bower (1973) Human Associative Memory (HAM) model, Bower proposed that concepts, events, and emotions can all be represented as nodes within a network. In fact, the type of network originally chosen by Anderson and Bower consisted only of labelled links, the nodes themselves had no semantic labels. However, for ease of explication the network illustrated in Fig. 3.2 uses the system of labelled nodes rather than links; the two approaches are in fact computationally equivalent (see Johnson-Laird et al., 1984).

The network presented in Fig. 3.2 shows that concepts, events, and emotions are all represented as nodes within the network. Activation within the network depends on a number of factors which include the proximity of nodes to each other, the strength of the initial activation, and the time lapse since activation. In the example shown, the Depression Emotion Node, or "DEMON" for short, possesses a wide variety of types of links such as links to phenomenological and physiological characteristics, linguistic labels, and depression-related events and memories; Bower and Cohen (1982) suggest that some of the expressive behaviour and autonomic links may be innate.

Activation of one of the nodes in the network shown in Fig. 3.2 may spread therefore to adjoining nodes; for example, if an individual experiences failure, the experience could activate the DEMON node and spread to a range of adjoining nodes including activating previous events in which the individual experienced failure and activating innate and learned expressive and autonomic patterns. In a passage of purple prose that is more reminiscent of 19th-century science and Freud's early hydraulic model of psychic energy, Bower (1986, p.24) describes this activation as follows:

> The lines represent water pipes, the nodes represent reservoirs, and activation is like water that is pushed down the pipes with more or less pressure, with the water accumulating at the units where the lines come together.

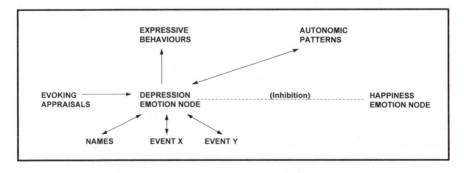

FIG. 3.2. An example of a semantic network (based on Bower & Cohen, 1982).

Bower's network theory initially gave rise to an impressive collection of supportive evidence based primarily on the effects of the temporary induction of happy or sad moods in normal individuals. Bower (1981) reported data that showed that mood induction led to mood state-dependent memory, and that it influenced a range of processes including free association, reported fantasies, social judgements about other people, and perceptual categorisation. For example, in a typical experiment Bower (1981) induced sad or happy moods in a group of hypnotisable subjects and then asked the subjects to recall childhood incidents. The results (see Fig. 3.3) showed that when the subjects were in a happy mood, they recalled significantly more pleasant events from childhood, but when the subjects were in a sad mood, they recalled the same number of unpleasant events. On the assumption therefore that the subjects were in a matching mood at the time of the experience of the events (that is, a happy mood for a pleasant event and a sad mood for an unpleasant event), this study can be interpreted as evidence for mood state-dependent memory.

Problems and subsequent revisions.   Although Bower's theory met with much success, it became apparent that there were a number of empirical and theoretical problems. The theory makes the broad prediction that each mood state should be associated with a range of

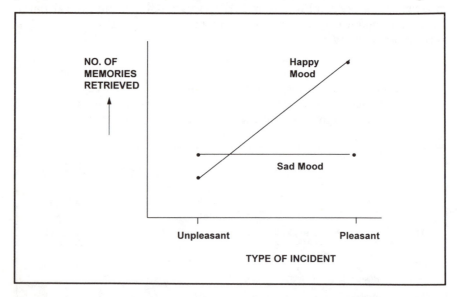

FIG. 3.3. The effect of mood induction on the retrieval of pleasant and unpleasant childhood memories (based on Bower, 1981).

perceptual, attentional, and mnemonic biases. However, it became clear that different types of bias tend to be associated with different mood states; as Williams et al. (1988) have summarised, the evidence to some degree suggests that anxiety is primarily associated with attention-related biases (see Chapter 6), whereas depression may be more associated with memory-related biases (see Chapter 7). Furthermore, even within the comparison of dysphoric versus happy mood states, the results were not as symmetrical as the theory would have predicted. That is, a sad or dysphoric mood tends to *decrease* the accessibility of positive memories more than it increases the accessibility of negative ones, an asymmetry that is in fact illustrated in the data in Fig. 3.3 (see Blaney, 1986, for a summary). Bower (1987, p.451) himself subsequently reported on failures to find effects of mood on perception and even failures to replicate some of the original mood state-dependent retrieval effects originally reported in his 1981 paper:

> The effect seems a will-of-the-wisp that appears or not in different experiments in capricious ways that I do not understand.

In an attempt to patch up this aspect of the theory, Bower (1987) suggested a "causal belonging" hypothesis; namely, that in order for the state-dependent effects to occur, subjects might need to perceive that the material to be learned has some meaningful relation to the mood state that they were experiencing. However, Bower made no suggestions about how the network theory could be adapted to take account of this suggestion.

It may seem unfair to kick a theory when it's already down, but there are also a number of theoretical problems with Bower's network approach, which will prove advantageous to outline in order to help our later discussion of other cognitive theories. The first theoretical problem is that although network theories provide strong accounts of the intensional relations between words or concepts (i.e. the "sense" of words), they provide very poor accounts of extensional relations between words and those things in the world that words refer to (i.e. the "referents" of words). The basic assumption within the network approach is that intensional relations can be analysed separately to extensional ones. However, Johnson-Laird et al. (1984) present a number of examples including the effects of ambiguity and instantiation in which access to referents is essential. For example, in a study by Anderson, Pickert, Goetz, Schallert, Stevens, and Trollip (1976) the subjects were presented with sentences such as "The fish attacked the swimmer". They found in a test of recall that cues such as "shark" were more effective than the original term "fish", a finding that would be difficult to account for in a network approach. Indeed, the fact that the word "fish" tended to be instantiated as a particular Jaws-like variety points to another shortcoming of networks which we will deal with next; namely, that even with sentences presented in a psychology laboratory subjects do not simply store propositional representations in the way that networks suggest, but rather there is a higher level of organisation imposed upon material whenever possible. Before we deal with this point however we might note that Johnson-Laird and his colleagues liken the network account of semantics to an alien that learned the Earth's languages solely from radio transmissions without access to the referents; any such alien might get the wrong opinion of Earthlings if phrases such as "bottoms-up!" and "down the hatch!" reached the airways.

The second theoretical problem therefore with simple networks is that because they were originally designed to represent the relations between individual words, they are inappropriate for representing the structure of other domains such as events, actions, and situations for which more molar forms of representation are useful. The fact that the subjects in the Anderson et al. experiment did not remember the propositional form of "The fish attacked the swimmer", but constructed a more specific form of the sentence, requires a higher-level form of representation such as a schema or a mental model in addition to the initial propositional level of representation. Such a need is even more evident in studies of inference and recall. For example, when presented with sequences such as "The man dropped the bottle. He went to the kitchen to fetch a brush", subjects typically mistakenly recall the bottle breaking even though there was no such statement in the original sequence (e.g. Clark & Clark, 1977). We will argue later (see Chapter 5) that at least two levels of representation, those of propositions and of schematic models, are necessary (cf. Teasdale & Barnard, 1993).

The third theoretical problem we will mention is that, as Woods (1975) originally noted, the links between nodes are treated in an *ad hoc* manner; thus, links between nodes can be unidirectional or bi-directional, they can be excitatory or inhibitory, they have a range of labels (e.g. "has a", "is not a", "name", etc.), and they represent extremely different types of concepts (e.g. "animal", "four legs", "disgust"). Although we acknowledge the usefulness of different types of nodes or links up to a point, a theory that gives emotion the same status as individual words or concepts is theoretically confused (Power & Champion, 1986).

A fourth theoretical problem focuses on the proposal that there is a literal spread of energy along the links between nodes which Bower has variously likened to the flow of water or electricity. As illustrated in Fig. 3.4, there are alternatives to this proposed literal transfer of energy. Figure 3.4(b) illustrates one such system in which a metaphorical transfer of energy is achieved in a network through a signal being sent from one node to another about its current register value which could vary from zero upwards. Note that the signal that passes from one node to another is a signal in the information processing sense rather than the energy sense; that is, the signal to increment a register to a value of "4" need not contain any more energy than a signal to increment by a value of "1". In fact, a signal could be transmitted by a *decrease* in

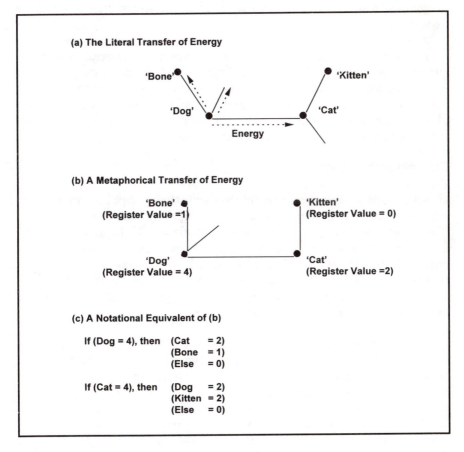

FIG. 3.4. Three ways in which "energy" can be transferred within an associative network: (a) the literal transfer of energy; (b) the re-setting of register values which indicate a metaphorical arousal level; (c) a notational equivalent of (b) in the form of a production system.

energy level, for example, through the interruption of the flow of energy through a link as equally as it might be transmitted through a temporary increase in energy level. To go one step further, Fig. 3.4(c) illustrates a so-called Production System equivalent of the two network models. Production Systems were developed by Newell and Simon (1972) in their classic book *Human Problem Solving* and have had considerable influence in cognitive science. Production Systems consist of condition–action pairs such as in the form shown in Fig. 3.4(c) "If …, Then …"; that is, if the conditions for a particular production system rule are met, then a particular action follows. This example further illustrates the point that networks are not theories in themselves but are one of a number of notational formats in which theories can be expressed.

One final area of complexity in which Bower's network model seems overly simplistic relates to the process of emotion generation that we summarised in Chapter 2. The sequence of event, interpretation/ appraisal, conscious awareness, physiological response, and propensity for action that we derived from cognitive philosophical models has little place within Bower's model, which, therefore is considerably weakened through its failure to offer an alternative account.

Other network theories

There have been a number of other network theories of emotion, some of which are simply variants of Bower's theory applied to specific emotional disorders such as depression (e.g. Ingram, 1984; Teasdale, 1983), aggression (Berkowitz, 1990), and also to Multiple Personality Disorder (Yates & Nasby, 1993), and others that were developed in parallel to Bower's approach (e.g. Lang, 1979; Leventhal, 1984). Because Lang's theory has had a particular impact on the study of fear and anxiety (see Chapter 6), a brief outline will be given of the similarities and differences with Bower's theory.

Lang's network theory.   In Lang's (1979, 1984) network approach propositions are represented in the network through a combination of labelled nodes and links. Following Kintsch's (1974) suggestion that sentences can be represented as combinations of one or more propositions that take the form PREDICATE(ARGUMENT1, ARGUMENT2, …), nodes in a network are taken to represent arguments which are connected by links that are labelled with predicates; thus, in the example shown in Fig. 3.5, the combination of labelled nodes and links would represent a situation along the lines of "You are watching a long, dangerous snake. You feel afraid, your heart pounds, and you run away."

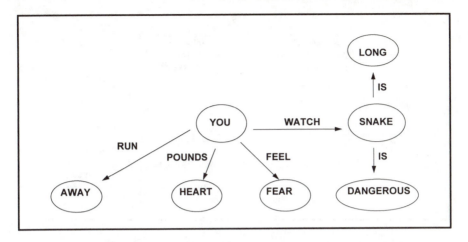

FIG. 3.5. An example of a propositional network (based on Lang, 1979, 1984).

One of Lang's most influential innovations was to suggest that emotions such as fear or anxiety were not single coherent emotional states, but that they were expressed in the three systems of verbal report, behaviour, and physiology. Furthermore, these three systems were only partially synchronised with each other, so that it was possible for an individual to show an emotion-like reaction in one or two of these systems, but not in the remainder. For example, an individual waiting for a job interview might claim to feel relaxed (verbal report) while sweating profusely and pacing up and down; or a soccer manager might look perfectly calm and relaxed to the camera while experiencing utter panic at his team's dreadful performance.

One perhaps common sense objection to Lang's three systems approach might be that there is a single internal emotional state of which the individual need not be aware, but which can be expressed through one or more of the three systems. However, Lang has rejected this possibility on the grounds of parsimony: we will merely note at this point that parsimony is often in the eye of the beholder and we return to the possibility of unconscious emotional states both at the end of this chapter and in Chapter 5.

A further advance that Lang (1979, 1984) offered over Bower's theory is presented in Fig. 3.6. Lang was not only interested in providing an account of normal emotional experience, but was also interested in extreme or disordered forms of emotion. For example, in the case of phobic anxiety Lang argued that three types of propositional networks were closely co-ordinated to form an "emotion prototype" or "emotion schema" (see Fig. 3.6). These three networks consist of a stimulus

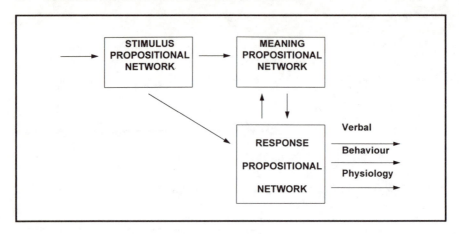

FIG. 3.6. An "emotion prototype" (based on Lang, 1984).

network, a meaning network, and a response network. The stimulus network is directly linked in to the perceptual input and produces a representation of the input irrespective of its modality. In the case of certain "prepared" or "prepotent" stimuli, Lang (1984) suggested that there may be hardwired sensorimotor programmes that provide a direct link from the stimulus network to the response network. Presumably, when our ancestors roamed the plains of Africa, those that were not afraid of snakes picked them up, got bitten and died, leaving behind those that were afraid and whose snake-fearing genes therefore filled the genetic pool. The meaning network can allow our knowledge and experience of the world to play a part in the overall response topology and, therefore, can act to amplify or to inhibit some or all of the three response systems.

Although Lang's network theory falls prey to many of the criticisms that we have already outlined in our commentary on Bower, one of the advantages of the approach is the suggestion that there may be a higher level of organisation of the information. Unfortunately, Lang uses the term "prototype" to name this higher level, which confuses it with the standard use of the term in cognitive psychology; as we saw earlier, one of the criticisms of Quillian's (1968) hierarchical network was that it could not account for some of the effects of prototypicality, a problem that Collins and Loftus (1975) overcame in their associative network, though without recourse to any higher level units of organisation. Nevertheless, it is useful to retain the spirit of Lang's suggestion that emotions may become organised in what we would term a modular fashion (Power & Brewin, 1991); this potential for modular organisation seems to be one of the innate capacities of the human brain, though the form that it takes depends on the many vagaries of development and experience. We return to Lang's ideas in Chapter 6 on Fear.

APPRAISAL THEORIES

The term "appraisal" was first used in relation to emotion by Arnold (e.g. 1960). Whereas some of the earlier emotion theories had equated emotion with physiological or somatic responses (e.g. James, 1890; see Chapter 2), the initial appraisal theories required an additional step, that of cognitive interpretation of a physiological state, for emotion to occur. Perhaps the most famous of these early appraisal theories was that of Schachter and Singer (1962) who presented not only an influential theory, but also carried out one of the classic top 10 psychological experiments to date. This experiment had a considerable influence on a number of areas in psychology including emotion theory and the development of attributional approaches. For these reasons therefore we will start with an account of the arousal-based appraisal theories inspired by and including Schachter and Singer's work and then proceed to more recent appraisal theories.

Arousal- and motivation-based appraisal theories

Schachter and Singer.
The basic proposal of the Schachter and Singer (1962) theory was that emotion involved the cognitive interpretation of a state of bodily arousal (see Figure 3.7). This state of arousal was considered to be a general one in that the same arousal underpinned both positive and negative emotions: the crucial determinant for the type of emotion experienced was how the individual explained the state of arousal. To quote from Schachter and Singer (1962, p.398):

> Precisely the same state of physiological arousal could be labelled "joy" or "fury" or "jealousy" or any of a great diversity of emotional labels depending on the cognitive aspects of the situation.

AROUSAL ·········► INTERPRETATION ·········► EMOTION
(Including situational information)

FIG. 3.7. The theory tested by Schachter and Singer (1962).

In addition, the cognitive interpretation could be based on prior knowledge of a situation; for example, an agoraphobic individual who interprets effects such as rapid breathing during exercise to be anxiety. Alternatively, in situations in which individuals are unclear about why they are aroused, the interpretation may be based on external cues provided by another person; the fact that people can become excessively euphoric or excessively morose while imbibing alcohol illustrates this combination of physiological arousal (at least initially) and attribution based on external cues.

In the actual study carried out by Schachter and Singer (1962), epinephrine (adrenaline) was used to provide the physiological arousal. The subjects in the study were told that they were to be injected with a vitamin compound called "Suproxin" and that they were to carry out visual tasks. In fact, half of the subjects were injected with epinephrine and the other half with a saline placebo. Some of the epinephrine subjects were then informed of its true effects (e.g. increased heart rate and respiration rate), some were misinformed of its effects (told that their feet would feel numb, they would itch, and that they would experience headaches), and some were not told anything. The placebo group were also not told anything. Each subject was then left in a room with one of two stooges, though unknown to the subject they were observed from behind a one-way mirror. One stooge behaved in a euphoric way, for example, he played "basketball" with rolled-up paper, made paper aeroplanes, and found hula hoops and began playing with them. The other stooge behaved in an angry way; thus, in this condition the subject and the stooge were each asked to fill in a lengthy questionnaire that began innocuously but became increasingly personal and asked questions such as "who in your family doesn't wash?", "who needs psychiatric care?", "how many times per week do you have sex?" and, most insulting of all apparently, "how many affairs has your mother had?". The stooge became increasingly angry as he progressed through these questions, finally ripping up the questionnaire and storming out of the room. The rest is now history.

The results from Schachter and Singer's (1962) study gave support to the arousal-interpretation proposal, though a careful re-examination of the original study shows that in the process of mythologisation the results are not as clear-cut as later textbook accounts would have us believe (see Table 3.1). Mythologised accounts tell us correctly that in the euphoria condition, the epinephrine-misinformed and the epinephrine-ignorant groups were more euphoric than the epinephrine-informed group, as predicted by the theory. However, the placebo euphoric group were intermediate and did not differ from any of the epinephrine groups on either the self-report or the behavioural

TABLE 3.1
Summary of the results from Schachter and Singer (1962)

1. In favour of theory

   Euphoria
   Misinformed = Ignorant > Informed

2. Against theory

   (a) Euphoria
   Placebo group no differences to any Epinephrine group

   (b) Anger
   No differences on self-report between groups

measures. Furthermore, in the anger condition, there were no significant differences between any of the groups on the self-report measures, the closest to significance being the comparison between the epinephrine-informed and the epinephrine-ignorant groups ($P=0.08$). Only on the behavioural measure did the epinephrine-ignorant group score significantly higher than the epinephrine-informed and the placebo groups (the epinephrine-misinformed condition not being run in the anger condition, for reasons that were not very convincing).

We suggest therefore that even within the original classic study, there were a sufficient number of problematic findings that meant that the theory would have to be revised. Nevertheless, subsequent studies did provide qualified support for some of the proposals, for example, that unattributed arousal could under some circumstances be influenced by social factors, though not to the degree suggested by the theory (e.g. Reisenzein, 1983). More recent evidence suggests that the concept of an undifferentiated arousal common to all emotions is incorrect, and that there are detectable differences between physiological and bodily characteristics of different emotions (e.g. Ekman, 1992; see later). In addition, the fact that Schachter and Singer limit cognitive interpretation to a minor support role, that of simply labelling the aroused state, provides a simplistic and inadequate cognitive basis in comparison to the lead roles that cognition has been given in more recent appraisal theories and in the philosophical theories that we considered in Chapter 2.

George Mandler.   Mandler (e.g. 1984) has developed a theory over a number of years that bears many similarities to Schachter and Singer's proposals while at the same time presenting a more complex role for cognitive processes. In Mandler's theory, physiological arousal is considered to arise from perceived discrepancy or from the interruption to an ongoing goal or plan. The arousal is seen as an undifferentiated physiological state which underlies both positive and negative emotions;

cognition determines which emotion is actually experienced. As Mandler (1984, p.119) states: "Arousal provides the intensity of the emotional state, and cognition provides its quality". A particular event therefore has a dual function in that on the one hand it triggers the state of arousal and on the other hand it provides input for the cognitive interpretative process. Mandler points out that many environmental stimuli provide automatic responses in the individual; for example, a sudden loss of physical support typically produces a startle response and a subsequent range of negative emotions. However, if the loss of support is under the individual's control such as when diving into a swimming pool, then the experience may be one of pleasure and excitement rather than being negative; thus, interpretation of the arousal determines whether it is experienced positively or negatively.

Mandler argues that many of the discrepancies and interruptions that are experienced are not derived from such hardwired reflex-like mechanisms, but are based on schema-derived expectations that are not fulfilled. For example, a spouse who forgets a wedding anniversary fails to fulfil an important expectation which is likely to lead to negative emotional consequences. In relation to interruptions, while temporary interruptions such as the telephone ringing just as you are sitting down to a meal may be mildly annoying, the "interruption" of a significant life goal such as a woman sacrificing her career for her husband's benefit may contribute to the development of more chronic negative emotional states. Mandler's theory is important therefore in that it provides a transition towards the more recent goal-based approaches to emotion, which we will consider subsequently.

In relation to the experience of positive discrepancies, humour for example often works through the failure to fulfil a schema-driven expectation; to use an example or two from that well-known raconteur, Sigmund Freud (who not only told them, but even went on to tell us why they weren't funny!) (1905/1976d, p.86):

> An impoverished individual borrowed twenty five florins from a prosperous acquaintance, with many asseverations of his necessitous circumstances. The very same day his benefactor met him again in a restaurant with a plate of salmon mayonnaise in front of him. The benefactor reproached him: "What? You borrow money from me and then order yourself salmon mayonnaise? Is that what you've used my money for?" "I don't understand you," replied the object of the attack: "if I haven't any money I *can't* eat salmon mayonnaise, and if I have some money I *mustn't* eat salmon mayonnaise. Well, then, when *am* I to eat salmon mayonnaise?"

Or, in a vein reminiscent of Oscar Wilde's "work is the curse of the drinking classes" (1905/1976a, pp.88–89):

> A man who had taken to drink supported himself by tutoring in a small town. His vice gradually became known, however, and as a result he lost most of his pupils. A friend was commissioned to urge him to mend his ways. "Look, you could get the best tutoring in the town if you would give up drinking. So do give it up!" "Who do you think you are?" was the indignant reply. "I do tutoring so that I can drink. Am I to give up drinking so that I can get tutoring?".

In both of these humorous stories, the normal expectations are explicitly presented by the "straight guys"; the humorous content arises from the creative views which are discrepant to these expectations.

In summary, Mandler's theory bears many similarities to Schachter and Singer's approach, but it has the advantage that cognitive mechanisms have a more elaborate or sophisticated role to play (cf. the discussion of Aquinas and Spinoza in Chapter 2). In addition, whereas physiological arousal seemed to arise from a biological mechanism in Schachter and Singer's approach, the perception of interruption or discrepancy in Mandler's approach requires a preliminary cognitive interpretation of the input; thus, cognitive processes both lead to the initial physiological arousal and then determine the type of emotion that is experienced. However, although Mandler's approach provides a step forward in terms of the cognitive interpretation component, the theory shares the weakness that it is based on a single type of autonomic arousal. As we argued in the case of Schachter and Singer, we believe that there is now sufficient evidence to show that there is no single undifferentiated state of arousal that is the basis for all emotions, but rather there are distinct physiological states associated with different emotions or groups of emotions. In addition, Mandler's suggestion that the interruption causes the emotion may, under many circumstances, put the cart before the horse in that sometimes it may be the emotion that causes the interruption rather than vice versa. We will return to this issue subsequently when we consider recent appraisal theories.

Bernard Weiner. The attribution theory of emotion presented by Weiner (e.g. 1985, 1986) provides one of the transitional theories between the earlier undifferentiated arousal approaches and some of the more recent appraisal approaches that posit two or more differentiated states that are characteristic of emotions. For example, in relation to the Zajonc-initiated debate about the primacy of affect, Weiner (Weiner & Graham, 1984, p.186) sits on the fence:

It is entirely possible that in some instances feelings antedate causal thoughts. For example, in certain situations anger might be a conditioned reaction.

Because Weiner proposes that the occurrence of general or "primitive" emotions may have little or no cognitive involvement, his theory will be included in this section on arousal and motivation based approaches. The fact however that he does consider two different possible routes to the generation of emotion we will flag up for now, though we would argue that a conditioned reaction should be considered as a cognitive rather than non-cognitive route, because of what we now know from modern learning theory (e.g. Dickinson, 1987).

Weiner's attribution approach originally began with his interest in achievement, in particular, success and failure in the classroom. As a consequence of a range of studies of success and failure, Weiner appreciated that affective reactions were intimately connected not only with the experience of success and failure, but also with the attributions or explanations that individuals made for that success or failure.

An outline of Weiner's model is presented in Fig. 3.8. The model assumes that inputs are classified into positive and negative and that the initial affective reactions are therefore of pleasure and displeasure; these initial reactions are described as "outcome-dependent" but "attribution-independent" emotions which are normally triggered immediately and automatically. One of the more contentious proposals the theory makes is that the general positive and negative emotions are separate to the "distinct" or "attribution-dependent" emotions. In contrast therefore to Schachter and Singer's model, undifferentiated physiological arousal is replaced by two different emotional states that have a range of motivational consequences and, in contrast to other appraisal theories, the initial affective state does not provide the input for subsequent cognitive processing (cf. the discussions of Aquinas and Spinoza in Chapter 2).

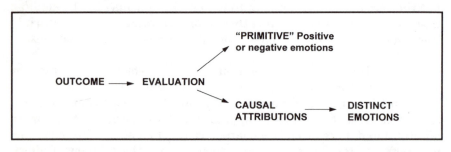

FIG. 3.8. Outline of Weiner's attribution theory of emotion (based on Weiner, 1985).

The type of account or causal explanation that individuals provide for the event or situation then determines which of the so-called "distinct" positive or negative emotions occurs. Over a number of years, Weiner has identified several key dimensions that, he argues, determine which type of emotion is experienced. These dimensions are internal–external, that is, whether the person perceives the cause of an event to be due to factors within the person or to factors within the environment; stable–variable, that is, the extent to which the cause is unchanging over time; and controllable–uncontrollable, that is, whether or not the cause can be influenced by the individual. In their widely known application of Weiner's attribution theory to the study of learned helplessness and depression (see Chapter 4), Abramson, Seligman, and Teasdale (1978) added a fourth dimension to Weiner's list; namely, global–specific, that is, the extent to which the cause has a general effect on all areas of an individual's life or whether it only affects one specific domain. Specific examples of Weiner's three dimensions for an experience of failure are shown in Table 3.2.

The types of attributions that individuals make for success or failure subsequently determine the types of positive and negative emotions that are experienced (e.g. Weiner, Russell, & Lerman, 1978). For example, success that follows from internal controllable factors is likely to lead to pride, success following help from someone else (i.e. an external controllable factor) should lead to gratitude, and so on. In a similar manner, a range of negative emotions depends on the type of attribution made for failure, as illustrated in Table 3.3.

If failure results from internal controllable factors, then guilt is normally experienced, whereas Weiner suggests that shame is more often experienced if the factors are internal but uncontrollable. In contrast, if failure results from external controllable factors such as another individual deliberately bringing about the failure, anger or

TABLE 3.2
Examples of specific attributions for "failure"

| | Controllable | | Uncontrollable | |
	Stable	*Unstable*	*Stable*	*Unstable*
Internal	Need to fail	Lack of effort	Lack of ability	Fatigue
External	Victimisation by another person	Lack of effort of another person	Task difficulty	Luck

TABLE 3.3
Possible emotions associated with different types of attribution for "failure"

	Controllable		Uncontrollable	
	Stable	Unstable	Stable	Unstable
Internal	Resignation	Guilt	Fear	Shame
External	Hatred	Anger	Self-pity?	Surprise Disappointment

aggression is likely to result, whereas bad luck (i.e. an external unstable uncontrollable factor) is likely to lead to surprise and disappointment.

As stated earlier, one of the strengths of Weiner's attributional approach has been its wide applicability to areas other than that of achievement motivation for which it was originally designed. However, this strength is also its weakness because the theory was not developed specifically as a theory of emotion, but rather emotion has been fitted into the Procrustean Bed of attribution theory. For example, although Table 3.3 attempts to show "typical" emotions linked to different types of attributions for failure, these are merely probabilistic associations rather than necessary and sufficient conditions; an attribution of "lack of effort" for failure need not be associated with guilt, but could be associated with anger at the self, with disappointment, or with self-pity. This problem arises in part from the fact that "failure" can be experienced in many different types of situation other than achievement-related ones, and the fact that in other situations the main component need not be failure, but, for example, loss, as in loss of a loved one. It should also be noted that there is no agreed set of attributional dimensions and other dimensions such as intentional–unintentional, personal–universal, and endogenous–exogenous have also been suggested (see e.g. Forsterling, 1988). Indeed, Weiner (1985, p.549) states that "a virtually infinite number of causal ascriptions are available in memory".

Cognitive appraisal theories

Richard Lazarus.   We will begin with a brief discussion of Lazarus' (1966) early theory before going on to consider his more recent revisions (Lazarus, 1991). In the influential 1966 version, emotion was considered to arise from how individuals construed or appraised their ongoing transactions with the world. Cognitive appraisal was considered to occur in two stages. Primary appraisal refers to an initial evaluation of whether an encounter is irrelevant, benign, positive, or stressful; thus, the conclusion that an encounter is stressful occurs in situations in which there is an appraisal of threat, challenge, harm, or loss. Secondary appraisal refers to the individual's subsequent evaluation of coping resources and options that may be available. Primary appraisal and secondary appraisal processes work in conjunction with each other. For example, if coping resources are seen to be adequate for dealing with a threat, then the threat will be seen to be of less significance, whereas if the individual thinks that a threat will overwhelm coping resources, then the threat may become of catastrophic proportions. To give an example, a holidaymaker goes abroad to a hot country and is frightened by large black insects that keep flying at him; he worries that these might be harmful, but then reads in a guidebook: (a) these are a harmless variety of beetle that in fact are a great delicacy amongst the locals and, being of sound constitution and considerable pluckiness, proceeds to attract them in greater numbers; or (b) that these insects can provide a painless harmless bite, therefore he administers insect repellent in order to prevent them biting; or (c) that they carry a dangerous tropical disease for which there is no known cure, and so locks himself in his hotel room and catches the next flight home. In each example therefore the primary appraisal of harm is modified, for better or for worse, by secondary appraisal processes. A summary of these proposals is presented in Fig. 3.9.

Lazarus and his colleagues have also argued (e.g. Folkman & Lazarus, 1980) that secondary appraisal coping processes can be categorised into two main varieties, emotion-focused coping and problem-focused coping. In emotion-focused coping the individual attempts to deal with the resulting emotional state through for example the use of various defence mechanisms. Problem-focused coping is more likely to be used when the situation is appraised as changeable and therefore the individual attempts to alter the problem that is causing the distress rather than simply cope with the stress itself. The distinction between problem- and emotion-focused strategies has proven extremely useful both in the area of coping and in adjoining areas such as social support (e.g. Power, Champion, & Aris, 1988). In research on depression for example it has been found that depressed individuals tend to use more emotion-focused than problem-focused strategies (e.g. Folkman & Lazarus, 1985); furthermore, Nolen-Hoeksema's (1987) suggestion that the higher rates of depression amongst women in comparison to men is due to women's use of "ruminative" strategies (see Chapter 7) may therefore be equivalent to the greater use of this emotion-focused strategy by women.

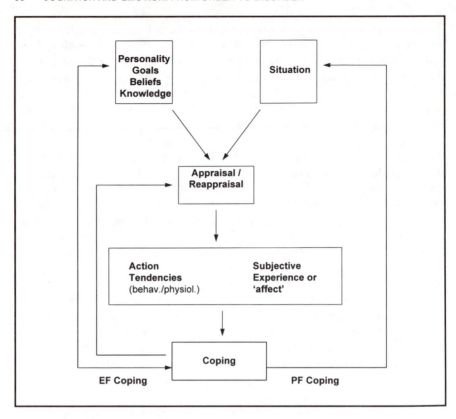

FIG. 3.9. A summary of Lazarus' early appraisal theory.
EF = emotion-focused coping; PF = problem-focused coping.

This early theory of Lazarus's was one of the most influential in highlighting the importance of cognitive appraisal processes. However, its weakness lies in the fact that the theory focuses on stress in general and is not a theory of emotion *per se*; the early theory therefore requires modification for it to become a theory in which specific emotions are linked to specific appraisals. We will now consider Lazarus' own recent modification of the theory to obviate this problem, though as we will see there are alternative modifications that are also viable.

Lazarus (1991) has presented a substantially modified version of his appraisal theory in order to make it a theory of emotion rather than a general theory of stress. First, though, we should note that there are variants of this approach, for example, in collaborative work between Lazarus and some of his colleagues (e.g. Smith & Lazarus, 1990), which Lazarus has now explicitly revised in his latest approach. Lazarus (1991) has termed his new theory a "cognitive-motivational-relational" theory. The main proposal is that each emotion has a specific relational meaning or so-called "core relational theme", that is, the appraisal of a particular person–environment relation is unique to each emotion. There are three revised types of primary appraisal: first, goal relevance which is the assessment of the environment for relevance to an individual's goals; second, goal congruency or incongruency, which is an assessment of enabling versus blocking of a goal; and, third, type of ego-involvement, that is, the extent to which an event has implications for self-esteem, moral values, life goals, and so on. Secondary appraisal consists of an assessment of blame versus credit, coping resources, and expectations for the future. Lazarus, in agreement with other theorists such as Frijda (1986), suggests that there may be some innate mechanisms linked with the appraisal of personal harm or benefit, which are termed "action tendencies"; these action tendencies are not simply innate *behavioural* mechanisms, such as "fight or flight", but rather are the basis for the physiological patterns associated with each emotion (see also Chapter 2). As in his earlier theory, secondary appraisal can enhance, override, or inhibit these innate action tendencies.

An outline of a set of emotions and their core relational themes is presented in Table 3.4. These themes are derived from both Lazarus' and other researchers' conceptual analyses of emotions, though it is as yet unclear how Lazarus' analysis compares with these other analyses (e.g. Frijda, 1986; Johnson-Laird & Oatley, 1989; Ortony, Clore, & Collins, 1988). We might also question whether these supposed core relational themes amount to little more than a dictionary-like definition of the relevant emotion. However, the point at which Lazarus does take his revised theory beyond being a redefinition of each emotion term is in his application of the primary and secondary appraisal components to each emotion; Table 3.5 illustrates the combination of appraisals associated with anger. The table shows that a statement is made about how the primary appraisals (goal relevance, goal congruence or incongruence, and ego-involvement), and how the secondary appraisals of blame or credit, coping resources, and future expectancies all apply in the analysis of anger. In fact, Table 3.5 shows that many of the appraisals are considered to be common to all of the emotions; thus, the initial primary appraisal of goal relevance is linked to any emotion, and the appraisal of goal incongruence is linked to any negative emotion.

Lazarus' (1991) revised theory will undoubtedly be influential, though probably not as influential as the earlier work for the following reasons. First, Lazarus side-steps the issue of the relation between emotions and the possibility that certain primitive or basic emotions provide the basis for more complex ones; thus, each of the emotions shown in Table 3.4 is claimed to stand alone despite the clear overlap

TABLE 3.4
Emotions and their core relational themes (from Lazarus, 1991).

Emotion	Core relational theme
Anger	A demeaning offence against me and mine
Anxiety	Facing uncertain, existential threat
Fright	Facing an immediate, concrete, and overwhelming physical danger
Guilt	Having transgressed a moral imperative
Shame	Having failed to live up to an ego-ideal
Sadness	Having experienced an irrevocable loss
Envy	Wanting what someone else has
Jealousy	Resenting a third party for loss or threat to another's affection
Disgust	Taking in or being too close to an indigestible object or idea (metaphorically speaking)
Happiness	Making reasonable progress toward the realisation of a goal
Pride	Enhancement of one's ego-identity by taking credit for a valued object or achievement, either one's own or that of some group with whom we identify
Relief	A distressing goal-incongruent condition that has changed for the better or gone away
Hope	Fearing the worst but yearning for better
Love	Desiring or participating in affection, usually but not necessarily reciprocated
Compassion	Being moved by another's suffering and wanting to help

that arises from the appraisal components. Lazarus restricts the possibility of "combined" emotions to the simultaneous activation of two or more of the emotions shown in Table 3.4, for example, "bitterness" is considered to combine anger and sadness in the sense that the two relevant sets of appraisals for anger and sadness are said to be evoked at the same time. However, our view is that there is now considerable evidence (e.g. in the work of Ekman, Oatley, and Johnson-Laird, and Plutchik; see later in this chapter) in favour of the proposal that there is a limited set of basic emotions from which more complex emotions are derived through additional cognitive processing of self and self–other relationships.

A second problem is that it is unclear how Lazarus derives the list of emotions shown above in Table 3.4 and why this list should be seen to be exhaustive. For example, the list includes two fear-related emotions, Anxiety and Fright which might parsimoniously be derived from a single basic emotion of fear given the considerable overlap between the two emotions; similar analyses could be applied to other pairs in the table

TABLE 3.5
Appraisals for anger: Components 1–4 are necessary and sufficient
(from Lazarus, 1991)

Anger: Primary appraisal components

1.   If there is goal relevance, then any emotion is possible, including anger. If not, no emotion

2.   If there is goal incongruence, then only negative emotions are possible, including anger

3.   If the type of ego-involvement engaged is to preserve or enhance the self- or social-esteem aspect of one's ego-identity, then the emotion possibilities include anger, anxiety, and pride

Anger: Secondary appraisal components

4.   If there is blame, which derives from the knowledge that someone is accountable for the harmful emotions, and they could have been controlled, then anger occurs. If the blame is to another, the anger is directed externally, if to oneself, the anger is directed internally

5.   If coping potential favours attack as viable, then anger is facilitated

6.   If future expectancy is positive about the environmental response to attack, then anger is facilitated

such as Happiness and Pride, Envy and Jealousy, and Guilt and Shame. In sum, the whole enterprise requires more supporting empirical evidence than is yet available.

Howard Leventhal and Klaus Scherer. In 1987 Leventhal and Scherer combined forces and produced a joint cognitive theory of emotion based on their previously separate ideas. Leventhal and Scherer argue that the operation of cognition and emotion is one of interdependence. They distinguish between emotion and other reflex-like responses, because although reflexes may play important roles as elements of emotional reactions: "Emotional processes decouple automatic, reflex responses from their eliciting stimuli and provide the opportunity for more adaptive reactions" (p.7).

Based on Leventhal's previous work (e.g. 1980), they proposed that there are three main components that constitute the emotion system. These three components are organised hierarchically and are as follows:

1. The Sensory Motor Level. This level includes the basic innate mechanisms that are observable from birth onwards. They respond automatically to both internal and external stimuli; thus, the neonate displays a wide range of facial expressions in response to emotional expression in other individuals and in response to internal gastro-intestinal states.

2. The Schematic Level. This level is also activated automatically; it includes the learned associations that begin from birth onwards which relate to emotional experience. They are said to integrate sensory-motor processes with "image-like prototypes of emotional situations" (Leventhal & Scherer, 1987, p.10). Presumably, these image-like prototypes are similar to Lang's emotion prototypes discussed earlier, but differ in the sense that Lang's prototypes are based on an associative network of propositions rather than on images *per se*. In fact, Leventhal and Scherer propose that it is the highest or conceptual level of processing that is proposition based, a proposal that would appear to run contrary to Lang's.

3. The Conceptual Level. The conceptual level of processing is a volitional level and includes memories about emotion, expectations, conscious goals and plans, and the self concept. It places the current event or situation into a longer-term temporal context in contrast to the shorter-term context offered by the previous two levels. As noted already, Leventhal and Scherer suggest that conceptual processing is propositionally based. However, we would argue that this proposal would make the conceptual level too verbally based; although the content of consciousness *could* be a proposition (just as it could be an individual word or sound or letter), it is normally a schematic model that integrates intensional and extensional information from a number of potential verbal and non-verbal sources (e.g. Teasdale & Barnard, 1993).

The contribution that Scherer has made to this joint theory has primarily been in terms of the so-called Stimulus Evaluation Checks (e.g. Scherer, 1984). These evaluation checks occur in the sequence:

1. Novelty (is the stimulus sudden, intense, or unexpected?)
2. Pleasantness
3. Relevance to goals and plans
4. Coping potential (available energy, power, and ability to deal with event or situation)
5. Compatibility with self-concept and social norms.

One apparent inconsistency between the two parts of Leventhal and Scherer's (1987) joint theory of componential levels and evaluation checks is that whereas the three componential levels by and large are considered to run in parallel to each other, the evaluation checks are considered to run in sequence. Scherer's (e.g. 1984) insistence on the sequential nature of the evaluation checks is based on the false presupposition that because one process may sometimes depend on the outcome of another process, therefore such processes must necessarily run sequentially. In fact, it is clear from developments in connectionism that parallel distributed processing can easily deal with such apparent outcome dependencies through the use of multilayer networks (Rumelhart & McClelland, 1986); thus, at least some of the evaluation checks could occur in parallel to each other with their outputs being fed into a network layer (see Scherer, 1993, for some discussion of the possibility of parallel processing about which he remains unconvinced). The second issue is that Leventhal and Scherer have in Lazarus' (1991) terms incorporated both primary appraisal and secondary appraisal processes into their evaluation checks; thus, coping potential is clearly a secondary appraisal process for Lazarus and would therefore occur after most of the other checks. Finally, there is as yet little empirical evidence or testing of the theory. Nevertheless, the theory provides an important alternative view of what the important appraisals or evaluation checks might be in the occurrence of emotion and we shall attempt to pull these alternative views together in the final section of this chapter. First, though, we will consider the work of Oatley and Johnson-Laird and their contribution to this cognition and emotion endeavour.

Keith Oatley and Phil Johnson-Laird.   The next appraisal theory that we will consider is that of Oatley and Johnson-Laird (1987; see also Oatley, 1992). Oatley and Johnson-Laird propose that in a system engaged in multiple goals and plans there have to be mechanisms by which priority can be assigned because not all active goals and plans can be pursued at once. They argue that one of the important roles for emotion therefore is to provide a possible mechanism by which such priorities can be assigned or altered.

In practice, Oatley and Johnson-Laird (1987) suggest that the effect that emotion has on the assignment of priority to goals and plans occurs through two different mechanisms, one that is evolutionarily older than the other. The older mechanism, they argue, is analogous to the effect of a hormone in that the "emotion signal" is said to have "no internal symbolic structure of significance to the system"; the emotion signal simply sets the whole system into a particular mode. In contrast, the second type of communication is said to be "propositional" in that it is symbolic and has "internal structure" (p.32). To translate these terms into those of other appraisal theorists, the proposal appears to share some overlap with the original Schachter and Singer model that we considered earlier; that is, in Schachter and Singer's model physiological arousal (a "non-propositional emotion signal") occurs and is then cognitively interpreted (i.e. a "propositional" signal is generated). The main differences between the two approaches are (1) that whereas

Schachter and Singer proposed that this sequence occurs *invariably* in the generation of emotion, Oatley and Johnson-Laird propose that emotion can occur through either route, and (2) that Oatley and Johnson-Laird propose that there are several such signals rather than just one (Oatley, 1992, p.64).

> The physiological state associated with each emotion node has a specific neurochemical basis. Associated with this, psychologically active drugs can trigger and maintain the system in a specific mood state, making a person feel happy, frightened, or sad for no semantic reason.

However, the question of whether a distinction between two different types of emotion communication is actually necessary or warranted has not been satisfactorily dealt with by these two theorists.

Oatley and Johnson-Laird (1987) further propose that there is a set of at least five basic emotions which form the foundation for their theory. They base this conclusion on the evidence from, for example, studies of the facial expression of emotion (e.g. Ekman, 1973), studies of emotional development, and so on (see later). In addition, Johnson-Laird and Oatley (1989) carried out a linguistic analysis of emotion terms in which the basic emotions were treated as unanalysable semantic primitives, which in combination with other factors can lead to more complex emotions (see also Ortony et al., 1988, for an alternative approach to the linguistic analysis of emotion terms). The five basic emotions that they derive from these different types of data are captured by the English terms happiness, sadness, fear, anger, and disgust; thus, other emotions are considered to be derived from one of these basic emotions through the inclusion of additional information that relates the basic emotion for example to the self or to some contextual element such as a significant other. Johnson-Laird and Oatley (1989) suggest that derived or complex emotions only involve one of the basic emotions, that is, they offer a *disjunctive* theory. However, we would agree with critics such as Jones and Martin (1992) who demonstrate both conceptually and empirically that many derived and complex emotions are more likely to be derived from two or more basic emotions, that is, contrary to Johnson-Laird and Oatley some complex emotions need to be defined conjunctively rather than disjunctively. In fact, Johnson-Laird and Oatley's proposal that derived emotions must be derived disjunctively does not tally with the analysis of other semantic fields. For example, the word KILL might be analysed in terms of the possible semantic primitives CAUSE, BECOME, and DEAD (Fodor, 1977), that is, KILL would be defined as a conjunction of semantic primitives. Moreover,

Johnson-Laird's own previous excursion into the analysis of semantic fields (Miller & Johnson-Laird, 1976) involves such conjunctive definitions of derived terms. We must note however that this criticism of their linguistic analysis does not detract from the proposal that there are a limited set of basic emotions, a proposal with which we agree entirely.

The final part of Oatley and Johnson-Laird's (1987) theory is that each of the five basic emotions is linked to key junctures in goals and plans, as shown in Table 3.6. The figure shows that happiness is linked to progress being made towards a goal; that sadness is linked to the failure or loss of a goal; that anger results when a goal or plan is blocked or frustrated; that anxiety results from the general goal of self-preservation being threatened; and disgust is considered to result from the violation of a gustatory goal either in the literal sense (e.g. in response to tastes or smells) or in a metaphorical sense (e.g. in response to individuals or ideas).

The links the theory makes between junctures in goals and plans and the experience of emotion is one of the most useful aspects of this theory and is a proposal that we will make much use of subsequently. Nevertheless, we should point out that these junctures are *sufficient* but not *necessary* conditions for the occurrence of emotion: there are numerous examples in which we experience emotion because of what *might* have happened rather than what actually happened (e.g. the car accident that nearly happened); or in which we experience emotion vicariously because another individual is experiencing an emotion (e.g. the laughing policeman); or in the "aesthetic" emotions (e.g. experiencing anxiety while watching a film even though there is no actual threat to self-preservation); or in the recollection of an emotional experience; or in daydreams, nightdreams and fantasies. These examples illustrate that any theory of emotion is necessarily complex and that there is, as yet, no completely adequate theory, though Oatley's

TABLE 3.6
Five basic emotions and their associated junctures in goals and plans
(based on Oatley & Johnson-Laird, 1987)

Basic emotion	Juncture of goal or plan
Happiness	Subgoals or goals being achieved
Sadness	Failure or loss of plan or goal
Anxiety	Self-preservation goal threatened
Anger	Plan or goal frustrated or blocked
Disgust	Gustatory goal violated

(1992) point that many of these examples refer to past, future, or possible goals makes them less of a problem for the theory.

We should also note that the basic emotion of disgust seems to be too narrowly dealt with in the theory, nor is the suggestion of a "violation of a gustatory goal" entirely convincing. First, although the term disgust derives from the same root as gustation, disgust can be elicited automatically and possibly innately by all senses, not just taste; thus, smell also elicits disgust reactions, for example, the smell of tellurium hydride is reputedly the most disgusting smell known and invariably elicits a disgust reaction; certain cold wet slimy tactile sensations can also elicit disgust; and cacophonous sounds and certain experimental works of art have similar effects. Second, it may be disingenuous to claim that a disgust reaction to the smell of rotten eggs involves a juncture in a goal or plan. Instead, an analysis along the lines of Leventhal and Scherer's (1987) multi-component model would seem to provide a better account; that is, sensory-based disgust seems likely to be linked to both innate and learned sensory-motor and schematic based associations, but during development the individual may come to react with disgust to certain physical or psychological aspects of the self and of other individuals (see Chapter 9). In summary, neither version of disgust fits easily into the junctures in goals and plans analysis offered by Oatley and Johnson-Laird. (Oatley & Johnson-Laird, 1990, allude to limitations in their treatment of disgust without presenting the details; Oatley & Jenkins, 1996, focus on contamination but do not provide sufficient detail.)

Despite these and other criticisms, it is still possible to extract the best aspects from theories such as Oatley and Johnson-Laird's in order to specify some of the minimum features of an adequate theory. We will attempt this task in the final section of this chapter in which we review the appraisal theories that we have covered so far. However, we must note that some recent commentators on appraisal theories have criticised the "cognitive imperialism" of earlier theories (Frijda, 1993; Lewis, 1996; Scherer, 1993). For example, Lewis (1996) has argued that positive feedback loops between appraisals and emotions lead to the emergence of complexes in which cognition and emotion interact dynamically. (Cycles of appraisal are further discussed in Chapters 5 and 8.)

The multiple entry memory (MEM) approach.   A general approach to memory and other cognitive skills has been provided by Johnson's Multiple Entry Modular Memory System (MEM), which has recently been applied to the question of emotion (e.g. Johnson & Multhaup, 1992). Johnson has delineated a number of subsystems, which are common to a range of functions. For example, there is a perceptual memory system that underlies both the processes of sensory perception and the recording of sensory information. There is also a reflective memory system which is involved in a wide range of self-generated tasks and activities. The perceptual and reflective systems are each broken down into two further subsystems. Johnson also notes that her use of the term "modularity" is different from Fodor's (1983) use, because she does not consider modular subsystems to be impenetrable, but, instead, they are flexible and may vary from process to process, a view with which we have considerable sympathy.

The four different levels or subsystems are presented in Fig. 3.10. The first main point shown is that some emotions can be generated at all levels within MEM, though Johnson notes that the character of emotions will vary according to the level at which they arise. For example, fear can arise from low-level perceptual processes when an object is detected moving rapidly towards the individual in peripheral vision. However, fear can also arise from high level reflective processes such as imagining oneself being tongue-tied at a job interview. Emotions arising at low-levels are likened to other theorists' basic emotions (see next section). The second main point illustrated in Fig. 3.10 is that some emotions only arise from processes in reflective subsystems; these emotions are "secondary" or "derived" emotions and include examples such as remorse and jealousy.

One of the consequences of the generation of emotions at different levels within MEM is the possibility that conflicting emotions could be generated at the different levels. Johnson notes for example that an individual could feel frightened by noticing a dog at the perceptual level,

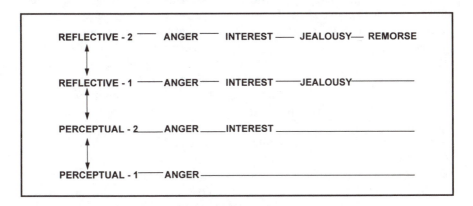

FIG. 3.10. Four levels or subsystems within MEM illustrating the increasing range of emotions arising at higher levels.

but actually feel interested in what the dog is doing because of processes occurring at a more reflective level.

Johnson has provided some interesting evidence in support of the MEM approach, including preliminary evidence in favour of her approach to emotion. The starting point for these studies is as follows (Johnson & Multhaup, 1992, p.50):

> In MEM, emotion may be influenced primarily by perceptual processes or it may be influenced primarily by reflective processes. This suggests one strategy for investigating emotion is studying affect in patient populations who have deficits in either perceptual or reflective processes.

In one study, amnesic patients and controls were asked to rate how much they liked unfamiliar Korean melodies, some of which were repeated. Previous studies with normal controls have shown that repeated stimuli are, on average, preferred over novel stimuli, an effect known as the "mere exposure effect" (Zajonc, 1980). The results showed that the amnesic patients showed the same exposure effect as the controls in that both groups preferred the old melodies to the new, even though on a recognition test the amnesic patients showed the expected deficits. However, in a second study that involved the development of evaluative impressions for vignettes for a good guy and a bad guy, the amnesics showed considerably lowered responses across time than did the controls. Johnson interpreted this effect as due to the impoverished reflective processes in amnesics, because such processes are important in the development of our impressions and preferences for other people.

One potential criticism of Johnson's approach is that the empirical data cited in support of MEM seems to provide evidence for two levels of processing, the perceptual and the reflective, rather than the four levels of processing identified in the model. Unless novel predictions can be derived to differentiate between emotions originating at each level, it is unclear that four levels are needed to account for the generation of emotion via different routes. We reinterpret Johnson's evidence therefore to support two rather than four levels for emotion generation (see Chapter 5).

A second problem stems from the fact that MEM was designed as a general framework for cognitive skills rather than specifically a theory of emotion. Although MEM has advantages because emotion can be integrated with other skills, it also leaves the theory agnostic on too many aspects of emotion and cognition that would need to be specified in an adequate model. For example, Johnson sits on the fence about the theory of emotions that she endorses, saying that it could be basic emotions and derived complex emotions or that it could be some other approach to emotion. Similarly, MEM is indifferent to the types of knowledge representation that are implicated in the model; an adequate cognitive model needs to specify the forms of knowledge representation with which it operates together with the relationships between those forms of representation. Nevertheless, the clear statement that emotion can be generated at more than one level is an important strength of the MEM approach, because it provides a richness for emotion theory with interesting implications that we will pursue further in subsequent chapters.

BASIC EMOTIONS

We have referred at several points throughout the chapter to basic emotions. The issue of whether, amid the breadth and diversity of human emotional experience, there are some emotions that are more fundamental or *basic* than others has exercised the minds of emotion theorists since the time of Aristotle (see Chapter 2). This concept of basicness—the idea that there is a small handful of core human emotions—has considerable purchasing power for theoretical psychology. Potentially it provides a framework within which to divide up, integrate, and organise the confusion of our emotional experience. It provides a way into other important approaches to the emotions such as evolution, biology, and developmental psychology. Finally, it provides the foundations for a bridge between the study of human emotions and research into the emotional experiences of other species. In the face of so much temptation, it would be easy for the emotion theorist to gloss over the issue of whether the concept of basic emotions can be empirically or theoretically justified independently of its obvious heuristic merit. In this section we would like to outline the basic emotion approach and acknowledge its clear advantages. However, more importantly, we would like to address the question of whether the approach is a valid one or whether it is merely "... an unsubstantiated and probably unsubstantiable dogma—an air, earth, fire and water theory of emotion" (Ortony & Turner, 1990, p.329).

The possibility that there is some mileage in the idea of a limited number of basic emotions was first emphasised by Descartes in his pamphlet, *On the Passions of the Soul* (1649/1989; see Chapter 2). However, it was not until the publication of Darwin's "other" book, *On the Expression of the Emotions in Man and Animals* (1872/1965) that serious consideration was paid to the potential importance of basic emotions in biology and psychology (see Russell, 1994, for a more detailed historical account). Since Darwin, the basic emotion debate has shifted in and out of fashion with philosophers and psychologists such as William James, Magda Arnold, Paul Ekman, Jeffrey Gray, and Keith Oatley speaking up in favour of basic emotions and Andrew Ortony, Terence Turner, and James Russell presenting the case against.

In this section we shall endeavour first of all to reformulate the basic emotion debate in terms of the framework developed from the philosophy of emotion literature in Chapter 2. We shall then review briefly in the light of this formulation the empirical evidence that has been cited as support for basic emotions.

A formulation of the basic emotion debate in terms of the philosophy of emotion

In Chapter 2 we argued that the concept of emotion includes an event, an interpretation, an appraisal, physiological change, a propensity for action, and conscious awareness. We further suggested that emotion as a *paradigm case* could also embrace overt behaviour. Within this conceptualisation we suggested that, in philosophical terms, it is only meaningful to distinguish one emotion from another on the basis of the appraisal component. That is to say, an emotion is specified as, for example, one of fear or one of sadness as a function of the nature of its appraisal component. As we noted in Chapter 2, a case can be made for distinguishing emotions on the basis of core components other than appraisal. For example, a number of authors such as William James have suggested that emotions can be distinguished on the basis of physiology (see Levenson, 1988, for a review). In considering this argument it is important to remember that the physiological component of emotion must principally be involved with preparing the system to carry out any behaviour necessary to satisfy the propensity for action component of the emotion. Whilst there may be differences in this behaviour between emotions, we have argued in Chapter 2 that there is also considerable overlap and that it is not possible to distinguish emotions on the basis of their behavioural correlates alone. For example, both fear and anger may be associated with the behaviour of fighting. Of course it is possible that, despite the similarities in associated behaviour, the emotions of fear and anger could still be characterised by distinctive neurophysiological activity. However, unless this is clearly demonstrated by the empirical data, which we review in more detail below, there seems no need to endorse such a strong view. It is more parsimonious to propose that there are a number of distinct autonomic states associated with emotion but that some states may be associated with more than one emotion and hence one cannot distinguish emotions on the basis of physiology alone.

A similar logic can be applied to the other core components of emotion which are cited as candidates for distinguishing emotions from one another, namely propensity for action and interpretation. Different emotions can give rise to similar propensities for action, and similar interpretations can give rise to different emotions. For example, as we noted in Chapter 2, the interpretation that "the bear is going to eat me" can be a component of fear or exhilaration or both.

Having reiterated our proposed conceptualisation of emotions from earlier chapters and underlined the point that emotions can only be meaningfully distinguished on the basis of their appraisal components, we can turn to the concept of a basic emotion. A common criticism of basic emotions is that they are an empirically driven concept with little theoretical justification (Ortony & Turner, 1990). In addition, there are numerous conflicting definitions and proposals about what basic emotions are. At this point we would like to examine the concept of basicness within the theoretical framework presented above, with the aim of providing a more powerful analysis of what it might mean to call an emotion basic. Within the framework that we have proposed, basic emotions would clearly be a small set of core emotions in the form of combinations of the components of event, interpretation, physiological change, appraisal, propensity for action, and conscious awareness. Furthermore, each emotion in this core set would be distinguished on the basis of its own distinct appraisal parameters. For example, threat in the case of fear. This analysis of basic emotions allows for the possibility that different basic emotions could include similar physiological change components or be associated with similar behavioural correlates, including facial expression. So, what do we mean by the term basic in this analysis of basic emotions? What are the inclusion criteria for our small core list? There seem to be two possible replies to these questions; what we might call a strong basic emotion theory and a weak basic emotion theory. A strong version of the basic emotion theory would be to suggest that there is a universal set of appraisal scenarios found in all cultures, that these appraisal scenarios are distinct from each other, and that they cannot be reduced to more fundamental appraisal components. Those emotions which include these core appraisal scenarios as components can rightly be called basic. This line of argument is akin to the traditional type of interpretation of the word basic which suggests pan-cultural, universal facial expressions or physiology associated with different emotions (see later). A weaker form of the basic emotion theory would be to argue that there are a number of common and central appraisal scenarios, distinct from each other, which emerge in human societies and which underlie and shape emotional development. However, the existence and development of these appraisal scenarios will differ slightly across cultures. Within this model, basic emotions would be those emotions which include these most common, central appraisal scenarios in their conceptualisation.

In sum, most researchers in the area of basic emotions have argued for a core set of emotions which can be distinguished by distinct universal or physiological components. We propose that a basic emotion is one which incorporates one of a core set of basic scenarios which may either be distinct and universal or merely distinct, ubiquitous, and subject to minor variation.

Having constructed such an appraisal-driven conceptual framework for basic emotions, it is important to outline the type of empirical data which would be seen as supportive of such a conceptualisation. Clearly the most useful evidence would consist of data in support of the existence of a set of universal appraisal scenarios, each one distinct from each other and a component of a different basic emotion. Unfortunately, there is almost a complete absence of research of this kind (see later). Much of the research cited and carried out under the basic emotion banner concentrates on other components of the emotional experience such as physiological change, behavioural correlates, or stimulus events. There are a number of possible reasons for this; for example, the conceptualis-ations of emotion which drive the research, when there are any, are usually different to the one we have outlined. Also, research which looks at overt behaviour such as facial expression is easier to carry out than research which considers mental concepts such as appraisal scenarios. This means that the search for a core set of basic appraisal scenarios must remain, for the time being at least, largely theoretically driven. However, there remains an important role for evidence of basicness gathered from looking at other components of the emotional experience. The reason for this is that the potential remains that by looking at the question of basicness for a number of the components of the emotional experience including appraisal we will be able to triangulate to a small list of emotions that could be called basic. In the next section we review briefly the various strands of evidence which pertain to this question and consider whether such a list emerges.

The arguments for basic emotions

A host of different writers and researchers have pledged the cause of basic emotions (e.g. Arnold, 1960; Ekman, Friesen, & Ellsworth, 1982; Gray, 1982; Izard, 1971; James, 1884; Mowrer, 1960; Oatley & Johnson-Laird, 1987; Panksepp, 1982; Plutchik, 1980; Watson, 1930; see Table 3.7).

While acknowledging a diversity among proponents of the basic emotion concept, Ekman, Friesen and Ellsworth (1972) have pointed out

TABLE 3.7
A list of the major basic emotion theorists (based on Ortony & Turner, 1990)

Reference	Fundamental emotion	Basis for inclusion
Arnold (1960)	Anger, aversion, courage, dejection, desire, despair, fear, hate, hope, love, sadness	Relation to action tendencies
Ekman, Friesen, & Ellsworth (1982)	Anger, disgust, fear, joy, sadness, surprise	Universal facial expressions
Frijda (personal communication, Sept. 8, 1986)	Desire, happiness, interest, surprise, wonder, sorrow	Forms of action readiness
Gray (1982)	Rage and terror, anxiety, joy	Hardwired
Izard (1971)	Anger, contempt, disgust, distress, fear, guilt, interest, joy, shame, surprise	Hardwired
James (1884)	Fear, grief, love, rage	Bodily involvement
McDougall (1926)	Anger, disgust, elation, fear, subjection, tender-emotion, wonder	Relation to instincts
Mowrer (1960)	Pain, pleasure	Unlearned emotional states
Oatley & Johnson-Laird (1987)	Anger, disgust, anxiety, happiness, sadness	Do not require propositional content
Panksepp (1982)	Expectancy, fear, rage, panic	Hardwired
Plutchik (1980)	Acceptance, anger, anticipation, disgust, joy, fear, sadness, surprise	Relation to adaptive biological processes
Tomkins (1984)	Anger, interest, contempt, disgust, distress, fear, joy, shame, surprise	Density of neural firing
Watson (1930)	Fear, love, rage	Hardwired
Weiner & Graham (1984)	Happiness, sadness	Attribution dependent

that every investigator has obtained evidence for a central list of *six* basic emotions: happiness; surprise; fear; sadness; anger; and disgust/contempt. This point was reiterated by Fridlund, Ekman, and Oster (1987). However, along with Oatley and Johnson-Laird (1987) we question the status of "surprise" because it is a cognitive component that could be present with any emotion, rather than being a unique emotion itself; for example, one might experience "surprise" if Partick Thistle scored six goals against Glasgow Rangers, but only supporters of these teams are likely to experience emotion.

Ekman (e.g. 1992) suggests nine characteristics that distinguish basic emotions: distinctive universals in antecedent events; distinct universal signals; distinctive physiology; presence in other primates;

coherence among emotional response; quick onset; brief duration; automatic appraisal; and unbidden occurrence. In addition, we would also point to supporting evidence from the developmental priority of basic emotions (e.g. Lewis, 1993) and the linguistic analysis of emotion terms (e.g. Johnson-Laird & Oatley, 1989). We will now consider the first three of these categories in more detail.

Distinctive universals in antecedent events. We have argued above and in Chapter 2 that an analysis of appraisal scenarios provides the only meaningful way of distinguishing one emotion from another. Furthermore, we have suggested that the concept of basic emotions can most profitably be reduced to one of basic appraisal scenarios. This view has been most forcefully endorsed by Nancy Stein and her collaborators (see Stein & Trabasso, 1992, for a review). Perhaps the most important point to make about Stein's theory is that the nature of the appraisal associated with each basic emotion is defined functionally (Stein & Trabasso, 1992, p. 227):

> The set of features used to discriminate between each basic emotion category is causally and temporally linked to the status of goals and their outcomes. Goal states reflect either desired or undesired end-states, objects or activities.

This emphasis on functionality provides a set of parameters within which to address the pan-culturality of a core set of appraisal scenarios (p.235):

> We assume that a small number of higher-order goals exist that are related to survival and self-regulation. These common goals guide behaviour and regulate the universal aspects of the appraisal and planning process.

In this analysis then, there exists a small number of core human goals which are shared across cultures. These goals are, in turn, associated with a core set of appraisal, planning, and action processes relating to the attainment, maintenance, and reinstatement of the goals. Basic emotions are seen as those which incorporate appraisal processes linked to these pan-cultural, universal goals.

To date, there is almost no research bearing directly on the issue of the universality of a small set of core appraisal scenarios because much of the work has been carried out with Western adults and children. To summarise its conclusions, it seems that the following list of basic emotions emerges from appraisal research: happiness, fear, disgust, anger, sadness. There is clearly a need for methodologically rigorous cross-cultural data. Despite this, it is our view that the proposal of a small set of core appraisal scenarios offers the best theoretical position for the understanding of basic emotions.

Distinctive universal signals.   Much of the research that has considered whether emotions can be distinguished from each other in terms of the way they are signalled has concentrated on facial expression. That is to say, that there are a small number of core (basic) emotions each of which can be characterised by a unique configuration of facial musculature. This research tradition can be traced back to the writings of Descartes which became the subject for a generation of French artists who depicted facial expressions of the passions on the basis of his treatise (see Fig. 3.11)

Ekman (1992, pp.175–176) offers this summary of the current status of research on facial expression:

> There is robust, consistent evidence of a distinctive, universal facial expression for anger, fear, enjoyment, sadness, and disgust. This evidence is based not just on high agreement across literate and preliterate cultures in the labelling of what these expressions signal, but also from studies of the actual expression of emotion, both deliberate and spontaneous, and the association of expressions with social interactive contexts.

It is beyond the scope of this book to consider the evidence for differential facial expression between emotions in any great detail. A comprehensive review is provided in Ekman's (1982) edited book *Emotion in the Human Face* which is now in its second edition, and in an insightful exchange of articles by Russell (1994), Ekman (1994), and Izard (1994). The empirical core of Ekman's thesis is a series of studies which seem to show that different cultures label emotions in the same way. The majority of these studies have used a forced choice recognition methodology in which subjects have been presented with a series of posed facial expressions and have been asked to choose a suitable label from a small finite list. These studies show a remarkable amount of conformity across many different cultures.

The evidence for distinctive universal signals for a small set of emotions makes compelling reading and, for a number of scholars, the universality thesis as it has been labelled is seemingly carved in stone (see Table 3.8).

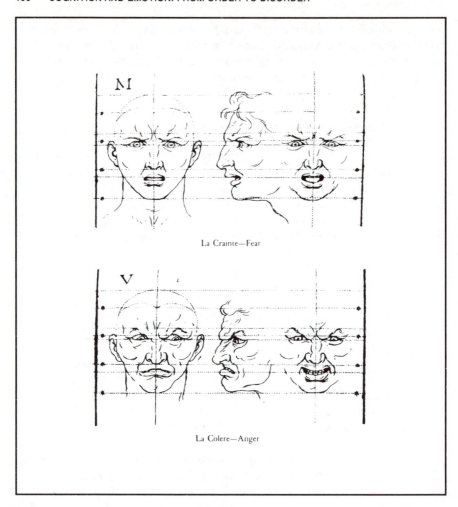

FIG. 3.11. Depiction of emotion by Descartes.

However, as well as the theoretical critiques we have offered above, several other authors (e.g. Ellsworth, 1991; Ortony & Turner, 1990; Russell, 1994; Turner & Ortony, 1992) have questioned the universality thesis. Ortony and Turner (1990) argue that it is not facial expressions that are universal signals but the single muscle actions from which the expressions are compiled. In addition, Russell (1994) has cogently argued that the methodological underpinnings of the research in support of the universality thesis are somewhat shaky. He suggests that the use of a forced choice recognition methodology, for example, serves to elevate the level of agreement in the choice of emotion labels. When

TABLE 3.8

Recent conclusions about the universality of emotion (based on Russell, 1994)

Source	Conclusion
Ekman (1980)	"Are facial expressions of emotion the same for all human beings?" (p.91). "Definitive data are now available on the question of universality" (p.93). "There is conclusive scientific evidence to resolve the question of universality" (p.96). "There are some facial expressions of emotion which are universal" (p.137).
Izard (1980)	"Impressive evidence for the innateness and universality of six of the fundamental emotions: enjoyment (happiness), distress (sadness), anger, disgust, surprise and fear" (p.201). "Since all human beings recognize these expressions and attribute to them the same experiential significance, it is reasonable to infer that they are genetically based or preprogrammed" (p.185).
Frijda (1986)	"Many facial expressions … occur throughout the world in every human race and culture. The expressions appear to represent, in every culture, the same emotions" (p.67).
Fridlund, Ekman, & Oster (1987)	"Observers label certain facial expressions of emotion in the same way regardless of culture" (p.157).
Gudykunst & Ting-Toomey (1988)	"The research cited indicates that facial expressions representing the basic emotions are recognised universally" (p.182).
Buck (1988)	"Research on the communication of emotion via facial expression suggests that certain displays appear and are correctly recognised in widely different cultures" (p.351).
Izard & Saxton (1988)	"The evidence for the innateness and universality of the expressions of the fundamental emotions is sufficiently robust to consider Darwin's hypothesis as an established axiom of behavioural science" (pp.651–652).
Oster, Daily, & Goldenthal (1989)	"Conclusive evidence for the universality of certain facial expressions has come from studies in which observers were asked to identify the emotions shown in photographs of facial expression" (p.114).
Brown (1991)	"The conclusion seems inescapable: There are universal emotional expressions" (p.26).
Mesquita & Frijda (1992)	"Certain facial expressions of emotion appear to be universal across cultures" (p.14). "There appears to exist a universal human set of emotion reaction modes [including] facial expressions" (p.21).
Carlson & Hatfield (1992)	"Ekman and other psychologists have uncovered compelling evidence that six basic emotions are expressed in much the same ways in all cultures" (p.221).

those studies that allowed the subjects to label freely the facial expressions presented to them are considered, the recognition scores are generally lower. Russell also questions the use of posed expressions, the dependence on within-subject designs, the ways in which the stimuli are presented, and the lack of contextual information provided. Furthermore, he raises issues about the ecological validity of much of the research, pointing out that it has mostly been carried out on Westernised subjects. When one considers the handful of studies which have looked at isolated cultures the data are far more equivocal and the methodologies far less satisfactory.

In sum, according to Russell the jury is still out on the question of distinctive universal signals. As Russell concludes (1994, p.136):

> This is a topic on which opinions can differ. The merits of alternative explanations cannot now be decided on the basis of the empirical evidence available and are therefore decided on the basis of a subjective judgement of plausibility ... many readers of this literature might find the universality thesis the most plausible alternative available. On the other hand, those who wait until the evidence compels them to decide must seek further evidence.

To conclude, we have suggested that the search for a concept of basicness within behavioural correlates or signals of emotion such as facial expression is not conclusive. None the less, bearing in mind these theoretical and methodological reservations, the universality evidence has generated a list of basic emotions more or less consisting of: happiness, surprise, fear, sadness, anger, and disgust/contempt.

Emotion-specific physiology.   As we have already noted, a number of writers claim distinctive patterns of autonomic nervous system activity for anger, fear and disgust (Levenson et al., 1990) and possibly also for sadness (Levenson, Cartenson, Friesen, & Ekman, 1991). As we have pointed out, we find it difficult to agree with the logic of this approach. It seems far more parsimonious to think of action- or behaviour-specific physiologies than of emotional ones (see also Davidson, 1992). However, if data exist which illustrate distinctive patterns of physiological activation for different emotions, those data must be taken seriously. So let us consider the evidence.

Many of the data in support of emotion-specific physiology, as with the findings on facial expression, have been provided by Ekman and his colleagues (see Fig. 3.12 for a summary). However, the traffic has not all been one-way. Stemller (1989) has argued that ANS patterning is

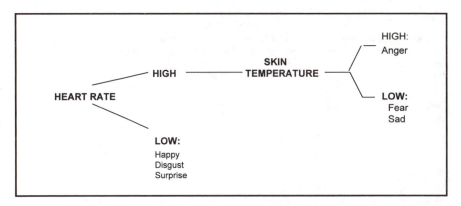

FIG. 3.12. Decision tree for discriminating emotions in direction facial action task.

specific to how a given emotion is elicited, rather than the emotion *per se* (though see Levenson et al., 1990 for a reply to these criticisms). In addition, Davidson (1992) has argued that the variation in underlying physiology between different manifestations of the same emotion can be greater than the differences between emotions.

As with the debate concerning universal signals it seems too early to draw a definitive conclusion about emotion-specific physiology. Theoretical logic would dictate, at least for us, that physiology is specified at the level of the requisite behaviours and it is this view which we feel obliged to endorse until the data on emotion-specific physiology prove incontrovertible. Nevertheless, this body of research claims to distinguish the following basic emotions: anger, fear, disgust, and sadness.

Towards a core set of basic emotions

In this discussion of basic emotions we have tried to argue that the most profitable approach to the question of basicness is in terms of a core set of basic appraisal scenarios which emerge in most, if not all, human societies, and that the emotions that incorporate these appraisal scenarios are the basic emotions. However, analysis of appraisal parameters is still very much a theoretical exercise, so it remains fruitful to examine the conclusions from other lines of investigation of basic emotions such as those looking for distinctive universal signals and distinctive physiology. The motivation for doing this was the hope that we might be able to triangulate from these three areas of research and theorising to come up with a core set of emotions which for our purposes we can describe as basic. The lists of basic emotions which these three approaches have generated are shown in Table 3.9.

TABLE 3.9
Lists of basic emotions derived from theory and research looking at appraisal scenarios, distinctive universal signals, distinctive physiology

Appraisal scenarios	Distinctive universal signals	Distinctive physiology
Happiness	Happiness	Anger
Fear	Fear	Fear
Disgust	Disgust/Contempt	Disgust
Anger	Anger	Sadness
Sadness	Sadness	
	Surprise	

As can be seen from the table, there is considerable agreement between the conclusions of the different approaches. Extrapolating from all three approaches, there is a core list of basic emotions: anger, sadness, fear, and disgust. In terms of the theory of emotions which we propose, these four basic emotions would involve appraisals of stimuli in terms of current goals and plans being in some way compromised. However, there is also a place for an emotional response to goals and plans being successfully maintained. This we (and others, e.g. Oatley & Johnson-Laird, 1987) would argue is the function of happiness and this should also be regarded as a basic emotion.

To conclude, we have arrived at a list of basic emotions as follows: anger, fear, disgust, sadness, and happiness. We have proposed that these emotions reflect basic appraisal scenarios, but there is also considerable support from research on behavioural signals and physiology for such a list. In the Part Two of the book we shall consider each of these emotions in more detail in an attempt to demonstrate the vital role of each to our sense of emotional order and to our understanding of emotional disorder.

SUMMARY

In this final section we would like to replay some of the edited highlights from the theories presented in this chapter. These points along with those from Chapters 2 and 4 will then be carried forward to Chapter 5 where we will attempt an integration of current theories.

Each theory that we have examined has both strengths and weaknesses. Even some of the earlier theories which we now know to be incorrect were influential enough to spawn empirical research that tested basic proposals. We can thereby be informed of what should *not* be included in a theory of emotion, which can often be more useful than information about what *might* be included.

1. The first point we need to make is that the concept of undifferentiated arousal as the basis of emotion would now seem to be in error. The key role given to undifferentiated physiological arousal in the Schachter and Singer (1962) theory and later theories such as Mandler's (e.g. 1984) is mistaken. There seems to be sufficient evidence for a distinction between at least two, if not several, different neurophysiological states. At minimum, it is necessary to distinguish between states that are positive and states that are negative (e.g. Frijda, 1986; Weiner, 1985) on the basis of a range of physiological and psychological evidence; thus, one of the weaknesses of the Schachter and Singer (1962) proposal was that it was much easier to get individuals to interpret physiological arousal negatively rather than positively.

2. Our second point is more contentious because the jury is still out. Nevertheless, we believe there is now sufficient evidence to go one step further than the previous suggestion and come down in favour of the idea of basic emotions. This idea has been central to only one of the appraisal theories that we have considered in this chapter; namely, the Oatley and Johnson-Laird (1987) theory. We considered much of the supporting evidence for this proposal from the pan-cultural recognition of certain facial expressions of emotion (e.g. Ekman, 1973) and the physiological distinctiveness of emotions, also considered in Chapter 2. We also noted in this chapter the additional supporting evidence from the linguistic analysis of emotion terms carried out by Johnson-Laird and Oatley (1989). However, in contrast to Johnson-Laird and Oatley, we would agree both with critics of their approach and with other appraisal theorists (e.g. Lazarus, 1991) that basic emotions can be combined; that is, that more than one basic emotion could underlie both the derivation of complex emotion terms and the actual experience of complex emotions. Indeed, in Chapter 5 and in the subsequent chapters on basic emotions, we will speculate that it may be the coupling of two basic emotions that "locks" the individual into some so-called emotional disorders, for example, disgust and anxiety in obsessional disorders, sadness and disgust in depressive disorders, and so on.

3. We will take an extreme view on the Lazarus–Zajonc debate and come down in favour of Lazarus. As Leventhal and Scherer (1987) have cogently argued, this debate is largely one of semantics (in the pejorative sense) in that it depends on what one terms "cognitive" (see also the discussion in Chapter 2 of what "cognitive" implies). Indeed, in the early debate Zajonc seemed to equate "cognitive" with conscious processes and

affective processes with unconscious processes. However, Zajonc has subsequently clarified his position (e.g. Murphy & Zajonc, 1993) and stated that while cognitive processes can refer to non-conscious processes, nevertheless, the initial processes are qualitatively distinct affective ones. Along with many of the other cognitive appraisal theories that we have discussed here, we would go further and argue that even the initial classification of an input as affectively valent involves a cognitive process; such a process involves a computational decision and approximate matching process and it is irrelevant how "primitive" or evolutionarily old the underlying apparatus is considered to be.

4. A number of theories posit different systems: for example, Lang (e.g. 1979) argued that three systems, the verbal, the behavioural, and the physiological should be considered; in addition, Lang (1984) argued that in the case of anxiety disorders such as phobias three propositional networks, the stimulus network, the meaning network, and the response network should be considered; and Leventhal and Scherer (1987) proposed that three components operate in parallel, the sensory-motor, the schematic, and the conceptual. One might be forgiven for thinking that emotion systems come in threes, but, in contrast, we would like to emphasise the potential desynchrony between two systems, a controlled processing system (variously labelled self-report, phenomenological, etc.) and an automatic processing system (including both physiological and behavioural aspects), which we have discussed in detail elsewhere (Dalgleish, 1994a; Power & Brewin, 1991). Although theorists such as Lang reject the idea of a unifying and underlying emotional state, this alternative seems preferable to Lang's three-headed beast of emotion, the Cerberus who guards psychology from the psychoanalytic underworld! Expressed in simpler terms, we suggest that two systems, one of which is based on controlled appraisal processes, the other of which is based on automatic or direct access processes, may be sufficient to encompass much of the desynchrony that has been emphasised by emotion theorists.

5. Localist varieties of network theories (e.g. Bower, 1981) have too many theoretical limitations and inadequate supporting data. In their place, the emergent properties of massively parallel distributed process networks may be more likely to provide a better framework for the brain and low-level automatic processes, though the types of PDP networks currently available may need to be substantially modified before an adequate theory is achieved. We would however add the possibility that cognitive and cognitive-emotional systems are organised in a modular fashion. Although in their theory Oatley and Johnson-Laird (1987; see also Oatley, 1992) argue in favour of modular organisation, they do not work through its implications for a theory of emotion and of emotional

development. We will therefore leave discussion of this major issue until Chapter 5, while reiterating our earlier statement that different basic emotion modules may become "coupled" in certain emotional disorders, which may make recovery from such disorders extremely difficult (cf. Horowitz, 1988a).

6. The importance of inhibitory as well as facilitatory processes has been emphasised by many different emotion theorists: Bower (1981) argued that many emotions have inhibitory connections such that it is not possible to experience positive and negative emotions at the same time; recent connectionist networks have of necessity incorporated inhibitory connections, for example, from "hidden units", which permit networks to handle logical disjunctives (i.e. the form "either, or, but not both") (e.g. Bechtel & Abrahamsen, 1991); and Frijda (1986) has argued that the control or inhibition of emotion must play a central role in theories of emotion. Overall, therefore, it is necessary to consider inhibitory effects in addition to facilitatory effects at all levels in the emotion system.

7. The importance of junctures in goals and plans (Oatley, 1992; Oatley & Johnson-Laird, 1987) or the general impact of events on the individual's goals (e.g. Lazarus, 1991; Leventhal & Scherer, 1987; Mandler, 1984) has been emphasised by many cognitive theories of emotion. We agree entirely that the impact of an event will vary with the importance of the goal or plan affected by that event and have presented supporting evidence for this proposal (Lam & Power, 1991). However, we argue that junctures in current goals and plans are sufficient but not necessary conditions for emotion and that there are numerous emotional reactions that do not fit easily into this categorisation. Emotion theory requires a more meta-theoretical analysis of the conditions for emotion, which includes influences on current goals and plans as one form of emotion generation. The inclusion of the recall of junctures in past goals and plans, the imagined impact of hypothetical events on current or possible plans, and so on, provides a broader goal-based approach than analyses that focus primarily on current goals or plans.

8. Again, to go one step further and give the punchline first, we present in Table 3.10 the five basic emotions around which we will organise the second part of this book, together with their key appraisals. These appraisals draw on several of the theories that we have reviewed especially those of Oatley and Johnson-Laird (1987) and Lazarus (1991), though we can be sure that none of these theorists would agree with our particular definitions. The appraisal system must provide decisions about the goal relevance, goal compatibility, type of incompatibility (if incompatible), and so on, of any input to the system. These and other

TABLE 3.10
Appraisals for the five basic emotions

Basic emotion	Appraisal
Sadness	Loss or failure (actual or possible) of valued role or goal
Happiness	Successful move towards or completion of a valued role or goal
Anger	Blocking or frustration of a role or goal through perceived agent
Fear	Physical or social threat to self or valued role or goal
Disgust	Elimination or distancing from person, object, or idea repulsive to the self and to valued roles and goals

relevant checks do not have to occur in sequence, but could happen in parallel to each other (e.g. Frijda, 1993; Lewis, 1996).

These points provide the main highlights from the current cognitive theories of emotion, in particular, those theories that have focused on *normal* emotion. Before, however, we attempt to pull these theories together to provide an integrative model of cognition and emotion, we will first examine a number of cognitive theories of emotion that have taken *abnormal* rather than normal emotions as their starting point.

CHAPTER FOUR

Cognitive theories of emotional disorder

In the vast colony of our being there are many different kinds
of people, all thinking and feeling differently.
(Fernando Pessoa)

INTRODUCTION

The cognitive theories presented in Chapter 3 took normal emotions as
their starting point. However, there are a number of influential cognitive
approaches to emotion that have taken their starting points to be
disorders of emotion rather than normal emotions themselves. These
theories will form the focus of the present chapter.

In contrast to theories of normal emotion, cognitive approaches to the
emotional disorders have typically focused on a specific disorder such as
depression rather than attempting broader accounts of a range of
emotional disorders. This carving up of the emotional disorders can lead
to a false sense of disjointedness between the emotions in comparison
to the more over-arching theories that were considered in Chapter 3.
Fortunately there are signs that recent theories may buck this trend,
though for at least two different reasons. First, the sheer success of a
theory in its own domain may lead it, in the tradition of the great empire
builders, to cross into adjoining territories; thus, the success of Beck's
theory of depression has led to its fruitful extension to other areas such

as anxiety and personality disorders. Second, there are signs that the increasing cross-fertilisation between cognitive psychology and clinical psychology may lead to more general theories of emotional disorders rather than theories that are tied to one specific disorder; we will examine the approach of Williams et al. (1988) as an example of this trend. However, we will not examine every specific cognitive theory of every specific emotional disorder, but will leave many of these until the appropriate chapters in the second part of this book. The theories that we will discuss will be chosen for their *potential* to be applied more widely than they may have been so far.

If, in our examination of normal theories of emotion, we detected the possibility of integration for example between cognitive and psychodynamic approaches (e.g. in the increasing interest in unconscious processes) or between cognitive and social approaches, we can also find these integrative forces within recent theories of emotional disorders. For example, an increasing number of approaches to depression look to the interaction of social and cognitive factors to explain its occurrence (e.g. Gotlib & Hammen, 1992); thus, it is now well-recognised that depression is more likely to occur if an individual experiences a severe negative life event, but not every individual who experiences such events becomes depressed. Although the modern interest in the interaction between social factors such as life events and internal cognitive factors such as self-esteem can be traced to the work of researchers such as Brown and Harris (1978), from a broader integrative and historical perspective we should also note Freud's 1917/1984 work, *Mourning and Melancholia*. In this paper, Freud proposed that significant losses (i.e. life events in modern terminology) occur both in the normal state of mourning and in the disorder of melancholia, but in melancholia vulnerable individuals in addition turn their anger against the self (a possible mechanism that would lead to "low self-esteem"). The moral is that, although the wheel may simply have turned full circle in the search for integrative approaches, we should now be in a position to take these approaches further.

One general criticism that we made in Chapter 3 of cognitive theories of normal emotions was that these theories often provided inadequate accounts of how emotional disorders might be explained within their frameworks. However, in relation to theories of emotional disorders, we can identify the opposite problem; namely, how do theories of emotional disorders account for *normal* emotions? Are disordered emotions simply greater amounts of emotion X which last for longer? Or does the disordered variant include some additional factor which is not present in the normal form? In answer to these questions, most of the theories that we will consider are members of the class of so-called diathesis-stress models. That is, many of the theories identify a long-standing vulnerability factor, such as a particular attributional style, a particular group of dysfunctional schemas, particular attentional or mnemonic biases, or whatever, which, in the context of an appropriate stress leads to the emotional disorder in question. It must be noted though that the diathesis-stress accounts have been better worked out for some disorders than others; for example, whereas strong evidence is available for diathesis-stress accounts of depression, the picture is much less clear for the anxiety disorders (e.g. Power, 1993).

THE THEORIES

Seligman's learned helplessness theory

Learned helplessness.   The original Learned Helplessness theory was presented in detail in Seligman's classic book published in 1975. Although the theory has subsequently undergone revisions, the role of perceived non-contingency continues to play an important role. The original proposal began with Seligman's laboratory work with dogs. In the studies, the dogs were placed in a shuttle-box, which was designed so that on some occasions the dog could be allowed to jump from one side of the box to the other, but on other occasions a barrier could be placed across to prevent escape from one side to the other. Seligman found that if the dogs experienced unescapable shock for a number of trials, they failed to escape from subsequent shocks even when it was possible to do so. This condition Seligman termed "learned helplessness" and he suggested that it could also account for a number of conditions in humans, especially that of depression. For example, an individual who may have received reinforcement non-contingently throughout child- hood may come to perceive the world, or important aspects of it, in an uncontrollable way even though in reality control over reinforcement may be possible; the original theory therefore focused on the key features of passivity and helplessness in the face of future events characteristic of depression. There ensued a large number of studies in which students were subjected to unsolvable anagrams and inescapable bursts of noise (e.g. Maier & Seligman, 1976), but unfortunately for the theory the students failed to demonstrate a consistent induction of helplessness; researchers began to realise that the original theory needed alteration to account for the application to humans. Indeed, it was even noticed that dogs began to refuse to become as helpless as consistently as they had done in the earlier experiments (see e.g. Abramson et al., 1978). Alternative biochemical models were also presented to account for the helplessness deficits in which noradrenaline depletion rather than learning was considered to provide a better account for the typically short-term nature of the helplessness deficits (Weiss, Glazer, & Pohorecky, 1976).

In addition to the empirical failures, there were features of depression for which the original theory provided no account. For example, the self-esteem deficit that is common in depression is not predictable from the experience of non-contingency alone, nor would the characteristic depressive emotion of sadness result from, for example, the experience of an unknown well-wisher dropping £100 through your letter-box every week. Even though the experience in this case is non-contingent and likely to be perceived as such, sadness and self-criticism would be extremely unlikely outcomes. This example highlights a problem based on a suggestion that Seligman had made in his 1975 book; namely, that so-called "golden boys" and "golden girls" may have experienced continuous non-contingent positive reinforcement throughout their childhood, but could then become depressed when they left home and found that positive reinforcement was no longer non-contingent, but in fact required active responses on the part of the individual. The possibility of a similar phenomenon of "success depression" has also been disputed by other behavioural researchers on theoretical grounds (e.g. Eastman, 1976), though some of the later social-cognitive models might allow for its occurrence in a particular group of individuals (see later) and we suggest that these concepts might be important in the development of chronic post-traumatic reactions (see Chapter 6).

Reformulated Learned Helplessness.   The original 1975 theory was later reformulated by Abramson, Seligman and Teasdale (1978); an essentially equivalent reformulation was offered independently by Miller and Norman (1979), but, not surprisingly, credit for the reformulation has remained with the theory's originator.

The important features of the reformulation are presented in Fig. 4.1. In short, Abramson et al. added Weiner's attribution theory (see Chapter 3) to the original Learned Helplessness approach; that is, although helplessness continued to be seen to arise from the perception of uncontrollability, the subsequent effects were now seen to depend both on the type and the importance of the event experienced together with the explanation that the individual produced for the cause of the event. The explanatory style dimensions focused on two of Weiner's (e.g. 1972) dimensions as follows: internal–external or "locus", that is, whether the cause is seen to be due to something about the individual (internal) or due to something about other people or circumstances (external); and stable–unstable (or stable–variable in Weiner's terminology), that is,

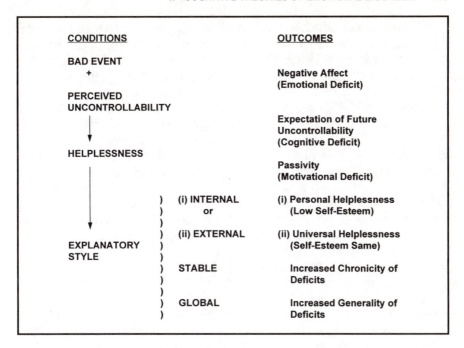

FIG. 4.1. An outline of the reformulated learned helplessness theory.

whether the cause is due to something that would recur for future similar events. In addition, Abramson et al. added a further dimension, global–specific, that is, whether the cause influences only one area of the individual's life or whether it influences many areas. The net combination of these three dimensions led to the proposal that the emotional, motivational, and cognitive deficits seen in depression could be accounted for by a particular set of attributions following the occurrence of a negative event.

The crucial type of attributional style that Abramson et al. (1978) identified as a vulnerability factor for depression was if the individual made internal–stable–global attributions (e.g. due to my personality) for the causes of negative events and external–unstable–specific attributions (e.g. due to luck) for positive events. More specifically, an internal attribution for a negative event was seen to lead to low self-esteem especially if, by social comparison, other individuals were perceived not to be helpless in such a situation (so-called "personal helplessness"). The additional stable and global attributions for negative events were seen to add to the chronicity and the generality of the deficits observed in depressed individuals.

The empirical studies that have been carried out to test the reformulated theory have been summarised, first, to provide overwhelming support for the theory (Peterson & Seligman, 1984), second, to fail to support the theory (Brewin, 1985; Coyne & Gotlib, 1983), and, third, even not to test the theory at all (Abramson, Alloy & Metalsky, 1988)! The problem centres around what is considered to be "support" for the theory (e.g. Power, 1987a, 1987b); thus, questionnaire based correlational studies between levels of depression and type of attributional style tend to support the proposal that internal–stable–global attributions are more commonly associated with higher depression scores, and, possibly, that this type of attributional style may retard recovery from depression (e.g. Hammen, Krantz, & Cochran, 1981). However, the least convincing evidence has been obtained for the proposal that individuals prone to depression have a pre-existing negative attributional style which leads to the onset of depression in the face of negative events (e.g. Coyne & Gotlib, 1983).

Other failures of the Reformulated model include the recognition that evidence for the proposed external–specific–unstable depressive style for positive events has been extremely mixed. For example, in a meta-analysis of 104 studies Sweeney, Anderson, and Bailey (1986) reported reasonable correlations for negative events, but much weaker support for the proposed style for positive events. The theory's excessive focus on the *causes* of events also seems to ignore the fact that a range of other factors including the *consequences* of events are at least equally important in the individual's response (e.g. Hammen & Cochran, 1981); thus, we saw in the discussion in Chapter 3 of Lazarus' (1966, 1991) notion of secondary appraisal or coping that the consequences of events can either be easily dealt with and their impact lessened, or, if the individual perceives that the available coping resources are insufficient, the event may be seen to be overwhelming. Finally, although collections of hypothetical events as measured by the Attributional Style Questionnaire (Peterson, Semmel, von Baeyer, Abramson, Metalsky, & Seligman, 1982) may demonstrate a bias towards a particular attributional pattern, real world events, unless they are sufficiently ambiguous, may completely override an individual's characteristic attributional style. For example, the wife of the man run over by the Clapham Omnibus may well blame the bus rather than herself for her husband's death (i.e. an external attribution), she may well believe or hope that the Clapham Omnibus plays no further role in her life (i.e. an unstable attribution), but, nevertheless, she may still become depressed because of the loss of her husband. The links between style and emotion therefore appear to be weak correlational ones rather than causal ones.

Hopelessness theory. A number of the problems with the Reformulated Learned Helplessness Theory have led at least some of its proponents to offer a second reformulation which they have called Hopelessness Theory (Abramson et al., 1988; Abramson, Metalsky, & Alloy, 1989). Both in terms of name and in terms of content, Hopelessness theory has been placed squarely within the framework of Beck's Cognitive Therapy. Because we will deal with Beck's approach in the next section, the coverage of Hopelessness Theory therefore will be brief and will focus on the differences with the first reformulation.

The Hopelessness reformulation is summarised in Fig. 4.2. This figure illustrates that one of the key differences is that Hopelessness requires only the occurrence of negative events rather than uncontrollable events; thus, it had always been problematic that depressed individuals seemed to blame themselves for events which according to Learned Helplessness theory they should perceive to be uncontrollable (e.g. Peterson, 1979). Hopelessness theory resolved this apparent contradiction through questioning the necessity for perceived uncontrollability. A second key difference is that the main outcome is hopelessness rather than helplessness, a shift that further de-emphasises the role of the lack of control *per se*, but which places the emphasis on perceived negativity instead.

Hopelessness theory also makes some adjustments to the combinations of the attributional dimensions and their consequences;

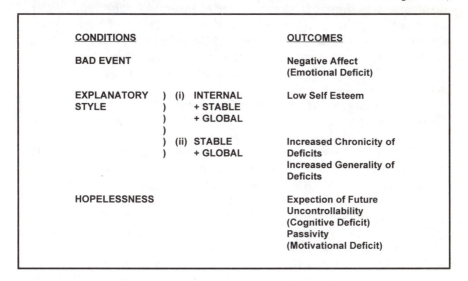

FIG. 4.2. An outline of the revised hopelessness theory.

thus, low self-esteem is now seen to derive from an internal–stable–global attributional style, rather than only from an internal style, and a combination of stability and globality is seen to lead to generality and chronicity of the depressive deficits.

The revised proposal has received some empirical support from within its own framework (e.g. Metalsky, Joiner, Hardin, & Abramson, 1993), though more substantial support for the theory is awaited. Support for the role of hopelessness itself comes primarily from the Cognitive Therapy literature, the approach that we will deal with next.

Beck's cognitive therapy

Beck and his colleagues have developed over a number of years an approach to the emotional disorders known as cognitive therapy. Although Beck's original focus was on depression, this focus has gradually broadened (e.g. Beck, 1976) and now includes substantial contributions to the theory and treatment of anxiety (Beck & Emery, 1985), personality disorders (Beck & Freeman, 1990), and addictions (Wright, Beck, Newman, & Liese, 1993). In the original versions of the theory, there was a simplistic model of the link between cognition and emotion; namely, that cognition causes emotion. However, more recently Beck (e.g. 1987; see also Weishaar, 1993) has stepped back from this strong version and has stated that cognition is not the cause of emotional disorders, but that it is part of a set of interacting mechanisms that include biological, psychological, and social factors. Other cognitive therapists (e.g. Clark, 1986; Teasdale, 1983) have argued for a circular relationship between cognition and emotion rather than a simple linear one; we will examine Clark's approach to panic in more detail in the next section and in Chapter 6.

There are two main components to the theory from which the general therapeutic approach is derived (see Fig. 4.3). The first of these focuses on the types of cognitive structures that underlie the emotional disorders and the second focuses on the types of cognitive processes that are involved in the onset and maintenance of these disorders.

The type of knowledge representation that cognitive therapy focuses on is schemas. These structures have been widely used (and abused) in the history of 20th-century psychology and have appeared in the work of Bartlett and Piaget and in modern cognitive psychology. In Beck's use of the term, schemas are seen to be the units by which memory, thinking and perception are organised; they have been considered by most writers on cognitive-behaviour therapy to be no more than collections of (propositional) beliefs. To quote (Kovacs & Beck, 1978, p.526):

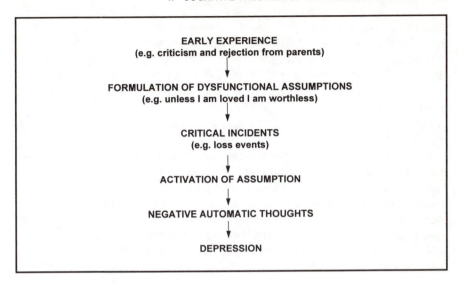

FIG. 4.3. Beck's model of depression.

> Cognitive structures or schemata ... are relatively enduring
> characteristics of a person's cognitive organization. They are
> organized representations of prior experience ... A schema
> allows a person to screen, code, and assess the full range of
> internal or external stimuli and to decide on a subsequent
> course of action ... schemata encompass systems for
> classifying stimuli that range from simple perceptual
> configurations to complex stepwise reasoning processes.

These schemas are in part derived from past experience such as from
the child's relationship with its parents, but they are not seen to be
passive representations of that experience. Instead, they go beyond the
current information; activation of part of the schema leads to activation
of the whole schema, therefore information not represented in the input
will be filled in according to the operative "default" values. To give a
simple example, if you were shown part of a picture or description of a
house, a "house schema" would be activated which would include certain
"default" features such as windows, doors, a chimney, walls, and so on
even though these were not explicitly presented in the original
description. The argument is therefore that schemas that relate to
interpersonal relationships and important roles and goals may also be
activated in a similar manner. The patterning of self schemas and

significant-other schemas, which is based on past experience, will provide the starting point from which current relationships and experiences are viewed; for example, in her biography of Beck, Weishaar (1993) describes how as a young child Beck himself developed a fear of abandonment based, in part, on an experience of being mistakenly left by his family in a large park. Perhaps in its adult form, Beck's fear may manifest itself with the concern that practitioners will one day abandon cognitive therapy!

In relation to specific emotional disorders, Beck has argued that certain groups of dysfunctional schemas are likely to be characteristic. For example, in relation to depression Beck (e.g. Beck, Rush, Shaw, & Emery, 1979) has proposed that these schemas reflect in part a so-called "cognitive triad" that focuses on negative views of the self, of the world, and of the future. That is, the depressed individual is likely to see the self as failed, diseased, or worthless, the world to be full of destructiveness and poverty, and the future to be bleak and hopeless. Haaga, Dyck, and Ernst (1991), however, have pointed out that the cognitive triad really focuses on the self in relation to the negative aspects of the world and the future, rather than the world and the future more generally. Haaga et al. (1991) have summarised the empirical evidence that shows at least some support for the proposed triad, though it may be sufficient for part rather than all of the triad to be present for depression to occur. Beck (1983) has further suggested that depression-prone individuals may be divided into two types; namely, so-called "sociotropic" individuals whose dysfunctional beliefs are centred around issues of dependency on others, in contrast to "autonomous" individuals who are highly goal-oriented and who distance themselves from others. Similar distinctions have been made by Arieti and Bemporad (1978) and Blatt and his colleagues (e.g. Blatt, D'Affliti, & Quinlan, 1976). The data that tests the usefulness of the sociotropy–autonomy distinction has so far been mixed and inconclusive (Weishaar, 1993), though it may be the self-report scale designed to assess the distinction, the Sociotropy–Autonomy Scale (Beck, Epstein, & Harrison, 1983), that is at fault rather than the distinction itself.

In between episodes of emotional disorders such as depression or anxiety, Beck has proposed that dysfunctional schemas are inactive and lie dormant; they become activated only when appropriate matching stressors occur (see Fig. 4.3). Part of the reason for this proposed latency of dysfunctional schemas has been to immunise the theory against the failure to find elevated levels of dysfunctional attitudes and automatic thoughts during recovery; that is, the theory might well have predicted that dysfunctional schemas were active even between episodes of depression and anxiety, but unfortunately the initial empirical research suggested otherwise (e.g. Power, 1990). However, it seems unlikely that such important concerns for the individual become inactive: that, when well, the individual is no longer concerned with issues about failure and rejection. An alternative possibility is that the dysfunctional schemas remain active but that during recovery the individual is able to inhibit the outcomes of such processing. We have also argued that it may be a mistake to focus on global dysfunctionality in assessment and have presented preliminary evidence that at least some core dysfunctional schemas, especially those centred around dependency issues, may remain elevated even during full recovery from depression (Power, Duggan, Lee, & Murray, 1995).

The second main component of Beck's cognitive therapy focuses on cognitive processes. The effect of the activation of dysfunctional schemas is that they produce negative automatic thoughts of the form "I'm a failure" or "I'm unlovable" which the individual believes. Unlike healthy individuals who can dismiss such thoughts, the depression-prone individual may, indeed, seek further evidence in support of these negative thoughts and beliefs. This evidence-seeking includes the so-called logical distortions of thinking which Beck has outlined; these distortions include magnification (e.g. of negative material related to the self), minimisation (e.g. of positive material related to the self), and personalisation (e.g. taking the blame for anything negative). The outcome of these distorted processes, in combination with other biases such as for memory, is that the depressed individual maintains a negative view of the self and thereby remains depressed (see Chapter 7).

Two main points that we would raise about this view of cognitive processes are first that, at least in its original form, the approach implies that normal thinking is logical and rational and, second, that it presents a view of the self-concept in depression that is monolithic and negative. To take the first point, whether or not normal thinking is logical and rational (indeed, whether it can *ever* be truly logical and rational) is a question that remains unresolved (e.g. Evans, 1989); thus, there are numerous demonstrations of the range and types of distortions that affect normal thinking. In one such classic demonstration, Wason and Johnson-Laird (1968) presented subjects with the sequence "2 4 6 ..." and asked them to work out what the underlying rule was. Most subjects set about confirming that the rule was "numbers increasing by two" through the production of additional examples that followed this rule; only after many failed attempts did some subjects appreciate that examples which would falsify their hypotheses rather than confirm them were far more informative. The correct rule "numbers increasing in size" was guessed by very few of the subjects. Oakhill and Johnson-Laird (1985) present examples that are even more relevant to

Beck's proposals in a series of studies in which they showed how prior beliefs interfere with the process of reasoning in normal subjects. They found that erroneous conclusions were more likely to be accepted in a reasoning task if the conclusions agreed with prior beliefs or knowledge (e.g. "some women are not mothers") than if the erroneous conclusions disagreed with prior beliefs or knowledge (e.g. "some athletes are not healthy"). Examples such as these illustrate how *normal* thinking and reasoning reveal many of the distortions that Beck originally attributed to depressed individuals. We propose therefore that the differences between normal and depressive thinking may be less that of logical versus illogical thinking and more that of positively biased versus negatively biased processes. We have further suggested that the so-called findings of "depressive realism" (Alloy & Abramson, 1979), in which, contrary to Beck, it was argued that depressed individuals are *more* rather than less realistic when compared to normal individuals, may be due to the fact that depressed individuals find negatives more congenial as conclusions in thinking and reasoning tasks; therefore, they will appear more realistic when the negatives are true, but less realistic when the negatives are false. That is, we suggest that the issue has been incorrectly presented as one of realism or logic, when it should more correctly be considered one of the acceptance of conclusions that are congenial to the current dominant model of the self (Quelhas & Power, 1991). This shift in emphasis does however appear to be reflected in Beck's more recent work (see Weishaar, 1993).

The second point that was raised about Beck's view of cognitive processes was that it leaves the impression that the self-concept is "monolithically" negative in depressed individuals and "monolithically" positive in normal individuals (Brewin, Smith, Power, & Furnham, 1992). One puzzle that cognitive therapy fails to provide an adequate answer to, therefore, is how the self-concept switches from being negative during an episode of depression to being positive during recovery; if, for example, the proposal is that the negative self-schemas are latent between episodes and only activated during an episode of depression, we must ask: What happens to the positive schemas which are active between episodes? Are they de-activated in some way during an episode of depression? Do they remain active? If the positive schemas remain activated, then the depressive self-concept should demonstrate both positive and negative elements, that is, the depressed individual should show self-ambivalence rather than straightforward negativity. In fact, three separate studies provide supporting evidence for this proposal. Brewin et al. (1992) found that although clinically depressed individuals described themselves in primarily negative terms when asked to describe themselves "right now", they used terms that were equally positive and negative when asked to describe themselves "in general". Wycherley (1995) reported a similar effect when the terms were manipulated from being more global to being more specific; that is, although clinically depressed individuals were largely negative when the terms were global descriptors (e.g. "my life is a failure"), they became more positive the more specific the item (e.g. "I'm a failure in my work"). Finally, in an emotion priming task, Power, Cameron, and Dalgleish (1996) found that positive phrases primed an increase in positivity in clinically depressed individuals, in addition to the expected priming effects of negative phrases. When taken together, studies such as these suggest that a more sophisticated view of the self-concept needs to be incorporated into our views about the emotional disorders.

Before we turn to consider some of the more recent applications of cognitive therapy, it should of course be noted that the great strength of the approach rests on its practical use as a therapy for an increasing range of emotional disorders, whatever limitations one might wish to highlight in the underlying cognitive theory. Because the details of the therapy are beyond the scope of the present account, the interested reader is referred to the many accessible accounts of the practice of cognitive therapy (e.g. Beck & Emery, 1985; Beck et al., 1979; Williams, 1992) and useful summaries of the outcome studies designed to assess the effectiveness of the therapy (e.g. Dobson, 1989). However, as noted previously (e.g. Power & Champion, 1986) evidence of the effectiveness of the therapy is not proof of the correctness of the theory. Witness the various ancient theories such as the doctrine of the four humours and their associated therapies such as blood-letting and trepanning; these treatments undoubtedly helped enough individuals in order to maintain the practices over some thousands of years, though we now know that the underlying theories were somewhat awry.

Clark's adaptation of cognitive therapy for panic

The discussion so far of cognitive therapy has been dominated by reference to depression, but in order to illustrate how the approach can be modified and applied to other emotional disorders we will briefly mention David Clark's (1986) cognitive model of panic, which will be discussed in more detail in Chapter 6.

The key theme in both Beck's general approach to anxiety (Beck & Emery, 1985) and in Clark's (1986) application of the approach to Panic Disorder is that the individual is considered to be prone to the detection of threat or danger in both the external environment and the internal environment. Whereas in generalised anxiety the perception of danger or threat may range across a variety of issues concerned with dependency, competitiveness, and control over self and others, in Panic Disorder the focus is primarily on bodily sensations. The individual interprets normal anxiety symptoms such as breathlessness, increased heartbeat, dizziness, and loss of control in a *catastrophic* manner; for example, a pounding heart may be interpreted as evidence for an imminent heart attack, dizziness may be interpreted to signal a stroke, and a feeling of loss of control or derealisation may be interpreted to mean impending madness. This catastrophic misinterpretation maintains the high level of distress experienced in a panic attack; it may also lead the individual to become hypervigilant for particular bodily sensations and likely to avoid situations or activities (e.g. exercise) that produce similar sensations (e.g. Clark, 1988). Despite the avoidance of certain situations and activities, however, the hypervigilance will still lead the individual to detect small physical sensations due for example to caffeine, excitement, or mild anxiety which push the individual into the vicious circle. In relation to the cognitive treatment derived from the model, again there is initial evidence for the effectiveness of the therapy (Salkovskis, Clark, & Hackmann, 1991).

One of the criticisms that we have raised previously about the cognitive therapy approach was that it focused on a single level of representation, the propositionally based schema (see Chapter 3). We argued instead that in line with the analysis of meaning in psycholinguistics two levels of representation were necessary, one that was propositionally based, and one that reflected a higher level of representation such as that of mental models. We suggested that if cognitive therapy simply focused on the truth-value of propositions in therapy and, if therapeutic practice was primarily the disputation of the truthfulness of such propositions (e.g. "I am a failure"), then the therapist might miss crucial higher-order meanings of such a process. For example, the therapist might persuasively dispute the patient's statement "I am a failure", yet leave the patient feeling worse rather than better! This effect could result from the patient's interpretation of the therapeutic encounter as confirmation of his or her worthlessness because the therapist was so much more intelligent (see later for an extended discussion of this issue). Teasdale (1993) has recently extended these criticisms of the general cognitive therapy model, but has pointed out that one of the strengths of Clark's approach to panic may be that it serendipitously takes the individual's model of the problem as its starting point (rather than the lower level specific propositions) and then offers a new model to the individual for the understanding of panic and anxiety. The hope must be therefore that this serendipitous strength of the specific approach to panic can feed back into the more general cognitive therapy approach.

On the negative side, however, in both Clark's and Beck's approaches the use of terms such as "cognitive" and "automatic" can have somewhat different meanings to how the terms are used in cognitive science (see Chapter 2). For example, although "catastrophic misinterpretations" appear to be conscious interpretations, they seem to be equivalent to "negative automatic thoughts" in the more general theory. The question is therefore to what extent are catastrophic misinterpretations automatic or to what extent can they become automatic if they occur regularly? We must also ask why is one individual likely to misinterpret a threat or a sensation in a catastrophic manner but another individual is not? These questions are of course ones that should help to refine and develop the theory rather than undermine it; they will be considered in greater detail in Chapter 6 when Clark's model is discussed more thoroughly.

Williams, Watts, MacLeod, and Mathews (1988)

The network theories of Bower (see Chapter 3) and the schema theory of Beck predicted that a wide range of cognitive biases should be found in emotional disorders such as anxiety and depression. The failure to find such global biases prompted Williams et al. (1988) to suggest an empirically-based model in which cognitive biases were specific to specific emotional disorders.

Williams et al. (1988) took as their theoretical starting point the distinction made by Graf and Mandler (1984) between "priming" (or "integration") and "elaboration" of stimuli. That is, priming is an automatic stage of processing in which the stimulus may be, for example, linked with its representation in long-term memory, whereas elaboration refers to subsequent strategic or resource-demanding processes. We should note however that this particular distinction between "priming" and "elaboration" is not an ideal one, because of the more general meaning of "priming" in the cognitive literature which can refer to *both* automatic and strategic or controlled processes (e.g. Neely, 1977). This caveat should be borne in mind therefore during the following discussion of the theory.

A summary of the Williams et al. (1988) model is presented in Fig. 4.4. In the case of anxiety disorders Williams et al. propose that automatic priming processes are biased towards the detection of anxiety-relevant stimuli or situations. For example, the individual with a dog phobia may automatically process a stimulus out of focal awareness as if it were a dog, whereas the normal individual would be more likely to perceive the object as a non-threatening four-legged table; thus, the preattentive processes become "tuned" to detect personally-

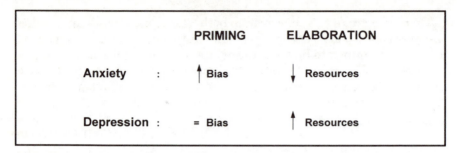

FIG. 4.4. Summary of the Williams et al. (1988) model of anxiety and depression. "Normal" levels of priming and elaboration are taken as the benchmarks for comparisons.

significant stimuli that range from the innocuous such as one's name, to objects with which the individual may have had unpleasant experiences, be it dogs or particular individuals. However, Williams et al. (1988) further propose that although initial priming or automatic processes are biased *towards* the detection of threat in anxiety, subsequent elaborative processes are biased *away from* the processing of threat. This proposal is based primarily on the general failure to find mnemonic biases in anxious individuals despite the fact that they demonstrate pre-attentive biases. Williams et al. state that this shift of strategic resources away from threatening stimuli is evident for example in the Watts, Trezise, and Sharrock (1986; also Watts, 1986) study of spider phobics in which they found poorer free recall of spider-related information in spider phobics despite the same individuals showing biases on a Stroop task, in which spider-related words were found to interfere with the naming of the ink colours in which the words were presented (see Chapter 6).

In contrast to anxiety, Williams et al. (1988) propose that the main cognitive biases evident in depression are resource-demanding elaborative ones that are most apparent in mnemonic tasks. They interpret studies of attentional biases in depression either as direct evidence that there are no such biases (e.g. MacLeod, Mathews, & Tata, 1986) or as evidence that anxiety levels were not accounted for in studies where attentional biases have been reported for depression (e.g. Gotlib & McCann, 1984). However, there is overwhelming evidence that depressed individuals show biases in the recall of emotionally valent material in a range of free recall, cued recall, negative mood induction, and autobiographical memory tasks (e.g. Blaney, 1986). There remains some question though as to whether the mnemonic biases obtained with depressed individuals are mainly due to a "loss of the positive" in that positive self-related material is retrieved more slowly and less readily (cf. Fig. 3.3 and the discussion in Chapter 3 of Bower's studies of positive and negative mood induction), as much as they may be due to a "gain of the negative", a question that we will consider in more detail in Chapter 7.

The great strength of the framework presented by Williams et al. (1988) is that it provided a focus for the dissatisfaction felt by many researchers with the predictions for global cognitive biases from the theories of Beck and Bower. The failures to find biases across a range of tasks and across a range of time periods were drawn together in their empirically driven proposals. However, the Williams et al. approach provides a starting point rather than an aetiological theory; it draws attention to the possibility that certain cognitive biases are more likely to be characteristic of certain emotional disorders than of others. None the less, the evidence, as Williams and his colleagues themselves acknowledge, is by no means as clear-cut as their framework suggests; for example, biased recall for negative material has been found for agoraphobic individuals (Nunn, Stevenson, & Whalan, 1984), and priming effects have been obtained for depressed patients as well as for anxious ones (Dalgleish, Cameron, Power, & Bond, 1995; Power et al., 1996). One of the weaknesses of studies of attentional biases in depression may be that the material used has not been of a sufficiently personally relevant form; thus, studies of specific phobias may typically use stimuli relevant to the phobic object in addition to more general emotionally valent material, whereas studies of depression may need to use more personally relevant material than that used to date—for example material related to the individual's most valued role or goal, or non-verbal material such as facial expressions—before such attentional and pre-attentional biases can be excluded. Equally, failures to find elaborative biases in anxiety may also be a consequence of asking anxious individuals the wrong questions. That is, although the important question in relation to depression may be the processing of material in relation to the self, in anxiety it may be the estimated likelihood of threatening outcomes from which the biases stem; thus, the central role of "worry" in anxiety disorders (e.g. MacLeod, Rose, & Williams, 1993) surely represents the elaborative processing of turning molehills into mountains or, more appropriately, turning moles into cancerous growths. If worry is based on elaborative processes but is not associated with mnemonic biases for worry-related material, then it will be necessary to consider inhibitory effects in retrieval as an alternative to the non-elaboration model of Williams et al. We await the proper test of these ideas, though we will consider more of the relevant empirical data in Chapters 6 and 7 when we discuss anxiety and depression, respectively.

Teasdale and Barnard (1993)

The Interacting Cognitive Sub-systems (ICS) approach (Barnard, 1985; Barnard & Teasdale, 1991; Teasdale & Barnard, 1993) is a recent exemplar of one of a class of multi-level, multi-system approaches (see also Johnson's MEM model in Chapter 3), which, in addition to their potential application to emotion, can provide accounts of a wide variety of cognitive skills and processes (cf. Newell, 1990). As we shall see therefore, the link between cognition and emotion is not easily pinned down in such models, because the relationship is seen as complex and interactive.

There are nine main cognitive sub-systems in Teasdale and Barnard's (1993) ICS approach: the first set of sub-systems is sensory related and includes the Acoustic and Visual sub-systems; the second is Central sub-systems and includes the Morphonolexical, the Propositional, the Implicational, and the Object sub-systems; and the third set is Affector sub-systems and includes the Articulatory, the Body State, and the Limb sub-systems. These sub-systems process information partly in parallel and partly sequentially according to the type of task and other requirements acting on the overall system.

In relation to emotion, the key sub-systems are the so-called Propositional and Implicational, as illustrated in Fig. 4.5. These two systems represent a common distinction made in psycholinguistics because of the need to have both multiple levels and multiple representations in models of the comprehension and production of language (e.g. Johnson-Laird, 1983; Power, 1986). The units of representation in the Propositional subsystem are propositions, which are the smallest semantic units that can have a truth value; thus, the

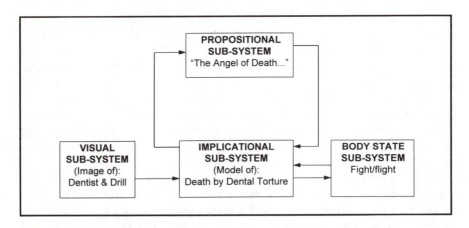

FIG. 4.5. Four of the key sub-systems involved in the occurrence of emotion within Teasdale and Barnard's (1993) ICS framework.

phrases "John Major" or "Ross Perot" do not have truth values in themselves but are merely names about which nothing is asserted. Only when they are included in larger units such as "John Major eats British beef" or "Ross Perot is a fine politician" do the units become propositional because they *are* either true or false.

In contrast, the higher level semantic representations at the Implicational level in ICS are referred to as "schematic models". Like the more commonly used "mental models" approach (e.g. Johnson-Laird, 1983), schematic models combine information from a variety of sources; so, within ICS, they draw upon the whole range of other sub-systems feeding information into the Implicational sub-system. In the simplified example shown in Fig. 4.5, we have highlighted three possible inputs to the Implicational sub-system from the Visual, the Body State, and the Propositional sub-systems. These four sub-systems together are the most important ones in the production of emotion in the ICS approach. For example, a Visual sub-system input of "Dentist approaching with drill", plus Body State input of being tied down in dentist's chair, and Propositional input of the form "The anaesthetic isn't working!" or "The Nazi dentist in the film *Marathon Man* has nothing on this guy!" may all combine at the Implicational level to produce a schematic model of the form "Self About To Die By Dental Torture" together with an experience of total panic. In the ICS approach therefore emotion is treated as a distributed phenomenon that is the result of the combination within the Implicational sub-system of outputs from a number of cognitive sub-systems rather than simply being the output from a specific cognitive appraisal. Although ICS is not alone in considering emotion to be the result of processing in multiple cognitive systems (see, for example, Leventhal & Scherer's, 1987 model and Johnson's MEM approach described in Chapter 3), it provides one of the most detailed and elegant multi-system approaches to the understanding of emotion.

In order to illustrate further the application of the ICS framework to the understanding of emotion, Teasdale and Barnard (1993) compare and contrast ICS with Beck's Cognitive Therapy, presented earlier in this chapter. In Beck's original model (e.g. Beck et al., 1979), it was proposed that emotion was a consequence of thought and that, in particular, the occurrence of Negative Automatic Thoughts caused depression. As shown in Fig, 4.6, the two levels of meaning in ICS provide a more complex picture; thus, in ICS, Negative Automatic Thoughts may be the consequence rather than the cause of a depressive schematic model at the Implicational level, though in turn these negative thoughts may serve to lock the system in a depression-maintaining loop. As noted above, Teasdale and Barnard (1993) also

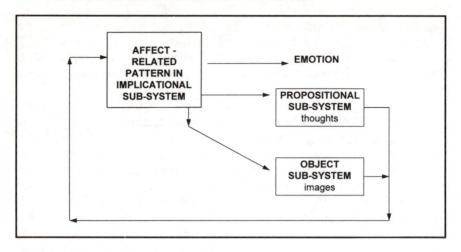

FIG. 4.6. The role of thoughts and images in the maintenance of emotion within the interacting cognitive sub-systems approach.

extend an earlier criticism of Cognitive Therapy made by Power and Champion (1986); namely, that Cognitive Therapy focuses on a single level of meaning, whereas profit might be had from considering two levels of meaning such as propositions and mental models. Teasdale and Barnard argue that much of the challenging of negative thoughts and beliefs in standard Cognitive Therapy occurs at the propositional level and may often ignore the higher level Implicational meaning; the net outcome of such a process can be that the individual is browbeaten into rejecting the negative proposition, but becomes more depressed rather than less depressed because, for example, a higher level model is confirmed in which the individual is always wrong. To give an example of this process, consider the following extract from a therapy session:

Client: You know, I'm really convinced that I'm worthless, that I'm a failure.

Therapist: Well, let's look at this belief that you're a failure. Do you have any evidence for this?

Client: My whole life feels wasted. I'm never going to get anywhere.

Therapist: Perhaps we could take a specific area of your life and have a look at it. How about your work? Do you think you are a failure in your work?

Client: Hm [thinks...] The picture is mixed. There are so many things that I'm never going to achieve.

Therapist: But what about the things you have achieved. You went to university—

Client: —Yes —
Therapist: —Was it a failure to get to university?
Client: No.

[There are several more exchanges in which further specific achievements are discussed.]

Client: I guess you're right, you're right that I'm not a failure in my work. But why couldn't I think of that? I feel worse now rather than better.

This example would illustrate, according to Teasdale and Barnard, the therapist's focus on the Propositional level of meaning because of the attempt to show that the proposition "I'm a failure" is false. Indeed, by the end of the exchange the client has been persuaded that the proposition is false, but has become more depressed in the process! However, a focus on the Implicational level of meaning would suggest that an important issue for this client might be a need to discover things for himself and that a focus on the therapeutic relationship in relation to this and other issues might well be warranted (cf. Beach & Power, 1996).

Teasdale and Barnard also offer the interesting analysis of the difference between "intellectual" beliefs and "emotional" beliefs, as in "I tell myself that I'm a worthwhile person, but underneath I still feel worthless". They propose that intellectual beliefs are meanings at the Propositional level whereas emotional beliefs are propositional articulations of schematic models at the Implicational level. Moreover, the information held at the two levels need not be consistent but can be discrepant (see also the discussion in Chapter 2 of Descartes' ideas about primary and secondary emotions).

Overall, it is too soon to judge the ICS approach, because of its recent development. ICS is of course a general cognitive model that will stand or fall on how useful an account it provides of a wide range of cognitive processes, not just its account of emotion. Because it is in part a framework and in part a theory, then there is a degree to which it is not falsifiable; thus, as we discussed in relation to semantic networks in Chapter 3, there is some flexibility about which particular theory a framework can instantiate. For example, the low level cognitive architecture for ICS could be based on connectionist networks, but it could be based on a viable alternative; the sub-systems could be treated as functional modules within a modular processing system, or, alternatively, if the modular approach goes out of fashion, it could be argued that the cognitive sub-systems were simply a functional description of a set of processes that were instantiated in the brain in a radically different fashion (see Gazzaniga, 1988, for an excellent discussion of this issue in relation to modularity).

In relation to emotion, it remains to be seen how useful the ICS approach is from both the empirical point of view and the clinical point of view. Some interesting preliminary supporting data however have been presented by Teasdale, Taylor, Cooper, Hayhurst, and Paykel (1995) who found that depressed patients completed sentence stems with *positive* words or phrases consistent with high-level schematic models rather than simply offering negative sentence completions as predicted by theories such as Beck's or Bower's. Sheppard and Teasdale (1996) have replicated this finding and have also shown that at two months follow-up, mood-improved patients presented completed sentence stems in a more functional, less positive way. We might note however that the central distinction between the Propositional and the Implicational levels of meaning may not be as clear-cut in practice as it appears, while not disputing that it is advantageous to make *some* distinctions between different levels of meaning. In the extract from the therapy session presented above, Teasdale and Barnard would argue that the focus on the "I'm a failure" statement occurs at the Propositional level of meaning and that the client became more depressed because the Implicational level meaning was ignored. An alternative account is that "I'm a failure" is a proposition derived from a mental model of similar content which is embedded in a higher level mental model along the lines "I must decide things for myself". This alternative retains the importance of different levels of meaning, but it demonstrates that these levels could also be at the Implicational or mental model level and not simply occur between the Implicational and Propositional levels. Teasdale and Barnard do not discuss the possibility of hierarchical organisation of models within the Implicational subsystem.

Ultimately, of course, emotion is generated in ICS via a pattern-matching process, albeit a sophisticated set of such processes. In this manner therefore, ICS appears to swim against the tide of current goal-based appraisal theories of emotion that we highlighted in Chapters 2 and 3. Swimming against the tide is obviously not a criticism in itself and may, indeed, prove to be remarkably percipient. For the present, however, we believe that the tide *is* running in the right direction and will therefore provide the direction that we intend to take.

Social cognitive theories

There now exists a group of so-called social-cognitive theories of psychopathology in which it is argued that vulnerability to emotional disorders cannot solely be located in factors internal to the individual nor in factors that are solely external. Instead, it is proposed that there is a complex interaction between the internal and the external; such theories have probably been best developed in relation to depression, but they have also been considered in relation to anger (see Chapter 8) and anxiety disorders (see Power, 1993, for a summary). For this reason we will briefly look at some of the work on depression, but leave the work on anger and anxiety until the second part of the book.

Social-cognitive theories of depression. The threads of various strands for current cognitive-social theories of depression can be seen, first, in the work on the vulnerability that arises for an individual who overinvests in one particular role (Becker, 1971) or goal (Arieti & Bemporad, 1978); and, second, in the work on life events and depression carried out by Brown and Harris (1978) in which a number of social vulnerability factors were highlighted because of their interaction with adversity to increase an individual's likelihood of developing depression. These earlier ideas have been drawn together more recently by a number of theorists that have included Oatley and Bolton (1985), Power and Champion (1986; Champion & Power, 1995), Brown, Bifulco, and Harris (1987), and Gotlib and Hammen (1992). Although these theories differ in terms of emphasis and detail, they focus on a number of common proposals as follows:

1. The vulnerable individual has a high level of investment in one particular role or goal.
2. The individual may pursue this role or goal, whether it be work-based or interpersonally-based, with considerable success.
3. The occurrence of a severe event which matches the role or goal and which thereby threatens it increases the likelihood of depression.
4. The influence of social-cognitive factors is seen to be strongest for first episodes of unipolar depression, but the repeated experience of adversity and depression may lead to a sense of "defeat" (e.g. Gilbert, 1992) in which the individual disinvests in all domains including those that were previously overinvested.
5. In addition, most theories identify a number of other vulnerability or protective factors. Key factors include whether or not the individual has a close confiding relationship (see Champion, 1990, for a summary), and the balance of positive and negative aspects or "self-ambivalence" of the self-concept (Power, 1987a).

The evidence in favour of *some* form of social-cognitive theory of depression has recently been well summarised by Gotlib and Hammen (1992), who also offer their own potential integration. The data show clearly that depression is not simply the consequence of the occurrence of severe life events, though such events may well be upsetting. As Freud (1917/1984) emphasised in *Mourning and Melancholia*, it is normal to experience sadness over the loss of someone or something important, but it is not normal for this sadness to turn into depression. To give an example, it is well known from the epidemiology of depression that about twice as many women as men develop depression (e.g. Weissman & Klerman, 1977). However, there is no simple biological explanation for this difference, because for example the rates vary dramatically with marital status; thus, the rates are *highest* for married women but *lowest* for married men, with single men and women showing about the same rates (Cochrane, 1983; Nolen-Hoeksema, 1990). We will consider this and other evidence in greater detail in Chapter 7 on Sadness. For the present discussion it must be emphasised that emotions and emotional disorders occur in social contexts. Although we disagree with the extreme viewpoint that emotions are *solely* social constructions (e.g. Harre, 1987), we also believe that many theories of emotion and the emotional disorders have paid insufficient attention to social factors.

In terms of the weak points of social-cognitive theories of depression there are a number of comments that must be made. First, there has been poor agreement over the measurement of social factors whether this be the measurement of social support, the self-concept, or roles and goals. Because of the diversity of measurement, it is often impossible to determine whether a negative result has occurred simply because of the inadequate measurement of a factor, or whether a particular positive finding is artefactual and therefore unique to the idiosyncrasies of a particular measure. The area of social support is probably the best example of this diversity and inconsistency (see e.g. Brugha, 1995, for a recent summary). Second, social-cognitive models often appear to hedge their bets over whether they are models of the onset of disorders, of the maintenance of disorders, of recovery from disorders, or of relapse of disorders. Similarly, even where some attempt is made to untangle for example onset and maintenance the models are developed in an *ad hoc* fashion that may be difficult to replicate. However, one clear exception to this criticism is evident in the work of George Brown and his colleagues. Although their early work focused on the role of adversity and vulnerability in the *onset* of depression (Brown & Harris, 1978), more recent work has extended to longitudinal studies of the maintenance, recovery, relapse, and recurrence of depression. For example, in a study of recovery from depression Brown, Lemyre, and Bifulco (1992) found that recovery is associated with both the occurrence of positive life events that can offer a fresh start for the individual and with the presence of positive evaluations of the self in an interview measure of self-esteem. Third, the models are often poor at explaining how vulnerability factors such as overinvestment in a role or goal arise in the first place; the models tend to be "adultocentric" and apply mainly to the lifestage that the researchers themselves have reached! We must ask therefore how the models apply at other stages in the lifespan. For example, can they account for the fact that although as noted above the female:male depression ratio is approximately 2:1 in adults, up until mid-adolescence the reverse is true and about twice as many boys as girls develop depression (e.g. Nolen-Hoeksema, 1990)? Although such findings lend themselves to psychosocial models, none of the existing models yet provides an adequate account. Finally, on a more general note it must be stated that social-cognitive accounts of depression are well in advance of equivalent accounts of other disorders; this discrepancy could suggest that sadness and its disorders are *par excellence* interpersonal emotional states, but the alternative view that useful psychosocial accounts of disorders of, say, anxiety or disgust have yet to be developed is equally appealing. (See Chapter 7 for a more detailed discussion of these social-cognitive models in relation to depression.)

Miscellaneous theories of emotional disorders

There are a considerable number of specific theories that have been developed to account for specific emotional disorders, many of which will be described in the appropriate chapters in Part Two of this book. There are however one or two theories or proposals that have more general implications for theories of emotion, but which do not fit neatly under the headings that we have considered so far in this chapter. One such proposal is that of "emotional processing" (Rachman, 1980) and various cognate ideas that have implications not only for specific emotional disorders, but also for normal emotional experience.

Emotional processing. The term "emotional processing" was used by Rachman (1980) in reference to how an individual processes stressful events. In fact, there have been a number of related proposals both prior to and subsequent to Rachman's paper which have covered similar ground. For example, in a paper aptly titled *Remembering, Repeating, and Working-through* Freud (1914/1958) first presented the idea of therapy as a working through of repressed material. Although this initial view of working through focused on insight in a more intellectual sense, Freud later recognised that intellectual insight was normally insufficient in itself for change to occur, though it could play an important role in such change. Nevertheless, Freud's famous phrase

"Where id was, there ego shall be" (1933/1971, p.112) captured, as we shall argue, the importance of processing material in relation to the self, especially in which there has been a so-called "primary gain" from avoidance of material that would otherwise cause anxiety or discomfort to the individual.

In Rachman's (1980, 1990) more specific focus on the emotional processing of stressful or traumatic events, the proposal is that it is inevitable that such unpleasant events will occur to an individual at one time or another, but the consequences of such events are normally satisfactorily processed. Evidence of normal emotional processing is provided, first, by the fact that an emotional disturbance has occurred, second, that the disturbance eventually declines in strength, and, third, that there is a return to routine behaviour. For example, a number of theorists and clinicians have studied the stages that individuals pass through following bereavement (e.g. Bowlby, 1980; Horowitz, 1983; see Chapter 7 for a detailed discussion). There are of course a number of variants on the exact stages and on the labels used for each stage, but Horowitz and Reidbord (1992) summarise this sequence of stages as "outcry", "denial", "intrusion", and, finally, "working through". However, in abnormal grief reactions there is a failure in this normal sequence, which, Rachman would argue, could result from a failure of emotional processing.

Rachman (1980, 1990) has listed a number of indices by which these failures in emotional processing can be identified. The indices include the presence of *direct* signs such as obsessions, disturbing dreams, unpleasant intrusive thoughts, inappropriate expressions of emotion (in terms of time and place), behavioural disruptions, pressure of talk, hallucinations (e.g. visual, auditory, and olfactory hallucinations of a loved one following bereavement), and the return of fear after a period of its absence. Additional *indirect* signs include subjective distress, fatigue, insomnia, anorexia, inability to direct constructive thoughts, preoccupations, restlessness, irritability, and resistance to distraction (see Rachman, 1990, p.286, Table 2). Rachman also considers factors which may then promote or impede emotional processing, but we will not present these in detail.

What we do wish to focus on, however, are some of the proposals that consider the mechanisms by which emotional processing might or might not occur. In other words, what types of emotion models are needed to account for the observation that individuals may fail to process stressful events, while at the same time evidence of such failures in emotional processing are still apparent? Can the models that we have considered so far provide an adequate explanation of such phenomena or do these models need to be modified?

One comment that we should make first is about the remnants of Freud's psychic energy model that survive in our metaphors for the repression of traumatic memories. It is now recognised (e.g. Holt, 1967; Power & Brewin, 1991) that in a more cognitive account of the dynamic unconscious there is no need for a literal hydraulic energy model in which dammed-up energy is transformed into symptoms or things that go bump in the night. Instead, we can consider a cognitive conflict model in which the unwanted material is inhibited because it conflicts with, for example, core self beliefs, important goals and plans, or important beliefs about significant others. That is, if the material were to be integrated with other relevant material, it would require significant changes to such important beliefs, goals, or plans, which, not surprisingly, the individual may be reluctant to make. The more dramatic or severe the stressful event then by definition the greater the impact on the individual's beliefs, goals, and plans (see Chapters 6 and 7). For example, the sudden death of a significant other may have a considerable range of effects; thus, in addition to the pain and sadness of the loss, illusory beliefs in the invulnerability of self and others may be shattered; shared goals and plans are no longer viable; and considerable practical hardship may ensue. An individual who had the capacity to deny such a significant loss and its ramifications would not surprisingly cause considerable clinical worry. If we consider the boxing ring as a metaphor for the mind, as Joe Louis said "You can run, but you can't hide". In extreme cases of denial or inhibition, the individual may disown particular emotions, especially emotions that are usually experienced as negative such as anger or fear. Such extreme inhibition is the psychological equivalent of disowning one's legs or arms, because such a self would be constructed on a limited range of acceptable basic emotions such as happiness and sadness while excluding other unwanted basic emotions from the self-concept (a theme that will be expanded upon in Chapter 5 and Part Two of the book).

Does the inhibition or avoidance of painful material "use up energy"? Again, we argue that such energy ideas should not be taken literally, though they have entered common parlance. Instead, in a more cognitive account limited attentional resources may have to be allocated in order to maintain cognitive and behavioural avoidance given the prospect that the more important the stressful event, the greater the likelihood that both internal and external events will prime the conflict-ridden material. Indeed, in Horowitz's (1983) model the individual is considered to oscillate between periods of overcontrolled avoidance and undercontrolled intrusion (see Chapter 6). No matter which model is true however, there is now considerable evidence that the inhibition of traumatic memories is associated with, for example, increased autonomic activity, lowered immune functioning, and an increased risk of physical illness (see e.g. Harber & Pennebaker, 1992, for a summary). Horowitz (e.g. 1983) has suggested that traumatic memories may be held in an "active memory" until they have been worked through, though it is unclear why an additional memory system need be implicated when all that is necessary is the possibility that material can be held functionally separate from core beliefs through inhibition.

In contrast, Foa and Kozak (1986) offer an alternative suggestion; drawing on Lang's (e.g. 1969) proposals about fear networks (see Chapter 3), Foa and Kozak argue that fear reduction requires both activation of the appropriate fear structures and the incorporation of information into these structures that is incompatible with the excessive or pathological information. In evidence, they argue that if there is cognitive avoidance or inattention to a feared object or situation, then failures in emotional processing may occur (see Chapter 6). Rachman (1990) has criticised this proposal on the grounds that fear reduction does not always require fear evocation and because distraction techniques do sometimes work. We return to these issues in more detail in our discussion of trauma in Chapter 6, but suffice it to say that Rachman (1980) has clearly highlighted an important process in the recovery from emotionally significant adversity, a process that has links with features presented in many other models of the emotional disorders.

SUMMARY

There are a number of key points that we wish to highlight and carry forward in the way that we have done in previous chapters. Although many of the theories of emotional disorder that we have reviewed began life specific to a particular disorder, the more successful theories (such as cognitive therapy) have subsequently been applied to a range of other emotional disorders. It is often in the course of such extensions that some of the features of the original model become altered.

1. Several different types of theory (e.g. learned helplessness/ hopelessness, cognitive therapy, and the social-cognitive theories) point to the key role that significant events play in the emotional disorders. However, it is not simply that such events occur, but, rather, the types of explanation that individuals make (see also the discussions in Chapters 2 and 3 about interpretation and appraisal). Dysfunctional explanations are more likely to occur the more negative or severe the event is, and seem to be less important for more trivial events or for

positive events. In contrast to Seligman, however, the focus should not only be on how an individual explains the *causes* of events, but there are a range of other factors that must be considered as part of an overall explanation. Such factors include how an individual perceives the consequences rather than causes of events, how the events impact on important domains or areas of investment, and so on. We would also note that the learned helplessness/ hopelessness approach has often seemed to focus excessively on *conscious* appraisal of events, whereas we would concur with many of the theorists discussed in Chapter 3 that the relevant appraisal processes may primarily occur outside of consciousness.

2. Most of the models that we have reviewed in this chapter have been diathesis-stress models in which a pre-existing vulnerability factor has interacted with subsequent stressors to produce the particular disorder. That is, most models began life as onset models. The slings and arrows of outrageous clinical and experimental data however have frequently led to these models being revised so that they fall somewhere between onset models, maintenance and recovery models, and relapse models, obviously in the hope that enough of the model will survive intact. The problem lies with the fact that the key evidence in favour of a putative vulnerability factor is typically obtained from currently disordered individuals obtaining higher scores on Factor X than non-disordered individuals; thus, the evidence is typically cross-sectional and correlational and the disputes centre around the old statistical chestnut of how to interpret correlations (e.g. Brewin, 1985). It seems more than likely, however, that we will need different models and different weightings of factors to account for the onset of a first episode of an emotional disorder, maintenance and recovery from a first episode, relapse, and future recurrence of subsequent episodes.

3. An adequate cognitive account of emotion requires at least two levels of semantic representation, for example, a propositional level and a mental model level (e.g. Power & Champion, 1986) or Implicational level (Teasdale & Barnard, 1993). In fact, these multiple levels of representation may need to be even more complex (cf. Johnson's MEM approach discussed in Chapter 3) in order for example to account for how the self concept can change so dramatically both within and between episodes of depression. The complex varying hierarchical relationships that exist within the self concept seem to require more than a "monolithic" approach in which the individual is either positive or negative.

4. The age-old problem of the supposed illogicality and irrationality of the emotions is nowhere more strong in evidence than in relation to the emotional disorders. For example, the cognitive therapy approach

initially assumed that normal thinking was logical and rational and that one of the key problems of depression was a breakdown in logical thinking. However, the fact that evidence was obtained for the opposite proposal, namely, that depressed individuals were *more* rational or realistic than their non-depressed counterparts highlights the problems with these two opposite proposals; namely, how can we explain the fact that there is evidence for both? Our interpretation is that the proposals for depressive distortion and depressive realism present only one view of the proverbial elephant (Power, 1991) and that both proposals are true though under different circumstances. Indeed, the same arguments can be applied to normal thinking which can be shown to be accurate and realistic under certain circumstances but considerably distorted under others. Of course, the demonstration that both normal thinking and "emotional thinking" can be rational or can be distorted still leaves open the question of whether there is an inherent mental logic in which distortions arise from say performance limitations, or whether the mind's achievements are at best quasi-logical but there is no inherent mental logic (e.g. Evans, 1989). The jury is still out on this issue. What is clear though is that "emotional" thinking should not be equated with "irrational" thinking; thinking can short-cut rationality under numerous different circumstances.

5.   Theories that have predicted global cognitive biases or that have searched for global vulnerability factors in the emotional disorders need to be revised, because the evidence suggests that more specific biases are implicated. This evidence converges from a number of directions. For example, predictions from Beck's and from Bower's models were that biases should occur in a wide range of cognitive processes, whereas the evidence now points more strongly to mnemonic biases being implicated in depression and attentional biases in anxiety. In a similar manner global measures of attributional style, dysfunctional beliefs, and self-esteem also need to address more specific content domains, because for example the global scores are often too contaminated with symptom measures.

6.   The idea of loops and locked systems has become more evident in models of the emotional disorders. Whereas the initial cognitive therapy model had a simplistic linear model of cognition causing emotion, there have been a number of subsequent qualifications of this idea (Clark, 1986; Greenberg & Safran, 1987; Teasdale, 1983) in which circular causal models of the cognition–emotion link have been considered. Indeed, as noted in Chapters 2 and 3, it should now be noted that cognition does not cause emotion, nor vice versa, because the cognition is *part* of the emotion. We also note with interest an additional type of loop included within Teasdale and Barnard's (1993) ICS framework in

which two different levels of representation, the Implicational and the Propositional sub-systems, may serve to maintain a disorder through becoming locked in a loop. In the next chapter, we will consider an extension of this idea; namely, the possibility that basic emotions may become coupled under appropriate circumstances and that the continued reactivation of one emotion by another may serve to maintain an emotional disorder.

7. The cognitive and the social-cognitive theories have all highlighted the importance of social factors in the emotional disorders, though to varying degrees. For example, in Beck's and Seligman's theories there are key roles for the occurrence of stressful events many of which will be social in nature, and also the key role of the early caretaker–child relationship for the development of a depressogenic attributional style or underlying dysfunctional assumptions. By definition, the social-cognitive theories have focused on the importance of interpersonal roles and goals and the possibility for example that overinvestment in one particular role or goal will leave the individual vulnerable in the face of adversity. We must emphasise, however, that we would disagree with an extreme social constructionist position (e.g. Harre, 1987), which argues that emotions *are* the enactment of certain interpersonal roles.

8. Again we must emphasise that an adequate model of mental functioning must be able to account for a range of inhibitory phenomena in relation to emotion. For example, it has been clear from Freud and Janet onwards that individuals may inhibit certain traumatic memories or relationships and that these may remain in a form that is not integrated into the core belief system. These unintegrated traumatic memories may, in Freud's words, form a "pathogenic nucleus" (Breuer & Freud, 1895/1974) around which subsequent related material is organised. The more recent interest in "emotional processing" has rejuvenated this issue, because of its importance for understanding the emotional disorders. In this respect, we should emphasise that it may not simply be traumatic memories that are inhibited, but also particular emotional states that the individual may attempt to inhibit or which may be experienced as a "loss of self" if inhibition fails. This possibility will form one of the key points that will be included in the integrative model to be presented in Chapter 5.

CHAPTER FIVE

Towards an integrated cognitive theory of emotion: The SPAARS approach

An analogous issue is the relationship of emotion, feeling, and affect to cognition. Despite recent stirrings and a long history within psychology ... no satisfactory integration yet exists of these phenomena into cognitive science. *(Newell, Rosenbloom, & Laird, 1989, p.885).*

OVERVIEW

The present chapter is the fulcrum of the book. In it we draw together the ideas from the first four chapters and carry over the central points to develop an outline for a cognitive model of "normal" emotional experience—of emotional order. We then illustrate how this framework has the potential to embrace the variety of "abnormal" emotional experiences—emotional disorder. We expand on this analysis of emotional order and disorder in the chapters that follow in which we focus on the basic emotions of fear, sadness, anger, disgust, and happiness.

The present chapter is divided into several sections. First, we endeavour to draw together the main theoretical threads from Chapters 2, 3, and 4 with the aim of providing a summary of the philosophical and psychological constraints, culled from an analysis of normal emotions and emotional disorders, within which any theory of emotion must exist.

Such a resumé provides a working sketch for a theory of mind; however, this requires some expansion. Consequently, in the second section we develop this theory of mind to provide a framework for the discussion of emotions that follows. Finally, we present a model of emotional order and disorder based on this theory of mind.

The picture so far—a resumé of Chapters 2, 3 and 4

In Chapter 2 we reviewed the development of philosophical ideas about emotions. We finished the chapter by setting out a number of philosophical ground rules to which, we suggested, any theory of emotion must adhere if it is to make philosophical sense. These ground rules provide us with some of the main components of emotional experiences within a broadly functional theory of mind. What the rules do not do is to say very much about the *psychological* processes underlying emotional experience and we presented a review of this psychological literature, with respect to normal, everyday emotions, in Chapter 3. Again, we ended Chapter 3 by listing a number of psychological ground rules which, we felt, should constrain any given theory of emotions. A worrying truth about the psychology of emotion literature is that the majority of theories of normal, everyday emotions make little or no reference to emotional disorder. Similarly, there are a host of theories of emotional disorder, which are only loosely anchored, if indeed they are anchored at all, to theories of emotional order. Consequently, we reviewed the principal theories of emotional disorder (restricting ourselves to those theories which seek to explain more than one "type" of emotional disturbance such as both anxiety disorders and depression) in Chapter 4 (we consider a number of other theories of emotional disorder, namely those which concentrate primarily on only one specific type of emotional disturbance, in Chapters 6–10). Once more we sought to extract a number of key points from this literature at the end of that chapter. In this section we summarise and integrate the key points that these chapters have generated in an attempt to paint the first broad brush strokes of a theory.

In Chapter 2 on the cognitive philosophy of emotion we introduced the idea of Aristotelian functionalism which, when applied to emotions, requires that they be defined with respect to the functional role that they perform. So, for example, in *De Anima* Aristotle argues that a central defining characteristic of anger is its function with respect to retaliation for some wrong that the individual has suffered. That is, anger has the function of motivating the individual to retaliatory behaviour. This functional role of emotions is echoed in many of the psychological theories of emotion reviewed in Chapters 3 and 4, either explicitly (e.g. Oatley & Johnson-Laird, 1987) or implicitly (e.g. in the work of Beck). Although, as we noted in Chapter 2, philosophical functionalism comes in many guises, it is the broad notion that emotions and indeed all mental states are most usefully conceptualised in terms of the functions they perform in the individual's psychology and the causal attributes they posses that we endorse here. This endorsement of functionalism does not mean that we necessarily agree with Aristotle's analysis that particular emotions can be *defined* with respect to certain behaviours or dispositions to behave, such as retaliation. In contrast, and to anticipate slightly, we take the line that the functionality of emotions is best understood in the light of the plans individuals are pursuing (cf. Oatley & Johnson-Laird, 1987) to achieve certain active goals that they hold. So, to summarise, the first broad brush stroke on our canvas is that the mind is best conceptualised as a functional, goal-directed system.

In addition to this endorsement of functionality, we proposed in Chapter 2 that emotional experiences can be divided into what we have called emotional states, moods, and dispositions (after Ryle, 1949). To clarify these distinctions it is helpful to consider what we mean by emotional states in more detail. We suggested in Chapter 2 that emotional states consisted of the following defining components (see Fig. 5.1): an event; an interpretation; an appraisal; physiological change; a propensity for action; and conscious awareness. In addition, we proposed that emotional states often included reference to certain patterns of behaviour or action.

To illustrate, consider the example of Adam who wants to start a relationship with his neighbour Eve. One day Adam bumps into Eve in the street and she tells him that her new partner is moving in with her the next day. This event leads to the interpretation that Adam will never now achieve his goal of having a relationship with Eve. This interpretation will then be appraised in terms of the loss of an important goal, a component of the emotion of sadness (see Table 5.1). This

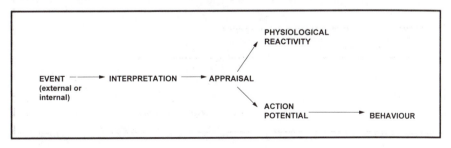

FIG. 5.1. Components of an emotional state.

TABLE 5.1
Appraisal components of basic emotions

Basic emotion	Appraisal
Sadness	Loss or failure (actual or possible) of valued role or goal
Happiness	Successful move towards or completion of a valued role or goal
Anger	Blocking or frustration of a role or goal through perceived other agent
Fear	Physical or social threat to self or valued role or goal
Disgust	Elimination or distancing from person, object, or idea repulsive to the self and to valued roles and goals

appraisal may be accompanied by physiological change and, most likely, some conscious awareness of being in an emotional state—Adam will feel sad. Adam may even behave in certain ways such as keeping out of Eve's way or moping around the house. This example illustrates what we consider to be the core components of *all* emotional states and Adam's plight is summarised in Fig. 5.2.

As well as deriving these core components of emotions, we also suggested in Chapter 2 that it is only really possible, at least in the light of our current knowledge, to reliably distinguish one emotion from another on the basis of the appraisal component. For example, fear is associated with an appraisal of physical or psychological threat, sadness, as we saw in the case of Adam, with an appraisal of loss, and so on. This idea was substantially elaborated in Chapter 3 where we reviewed appraisal theories of emotion in some detail and concluded that there are various levels or cycles of appraisal involved in the generation of emotion. We present these points in Table 5.1. To summarise, the second and third brush strokes on our canvas are that

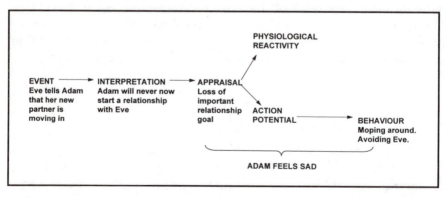

FIG. 5.2. Adam's sadness at the loss of Eve.

there is a set of components which make up all emotional states (event, interpretation, appraisal, action potential, physiological change, conscious awareness) and that one emotional state can be distinguished from another on the basis of the appraisal component.

Let us return to moods and dispositions. We argued in Chapter 2 that moods are states in which particular emotion-related appraisals are more likely to take place; that is, they are temporary shifts in outlook which alter the likelihood or threshold for emotion-related appraisals. Similarly, dispositions reflect a more *permanent* readiness to make appraisals pertaining to a given emotion. So, a sad mood reflects a temporarily enhanced readiness to appraise interpretations about events in a loss-related way, such that the individual feels sad. Likewise, a dispositionally sad person is someone who has a permanent tendency to appraise interpretations in a loss-related fashion such that he or she often feels sad. This broad distinction between occurrent emotional states, moods, and dispositions is the fourth brush stroke on our emotion canvas and the final one that we want to carry forward from the philosophy of emotion chapter.

A number of further key points arose from the discussion of theories of normal, everyday emotions in Chapter 3. The first of these points concerns the issue of basic emotions. In Chapter 3 we proposed (after Stein and her colleagues) that there are certain universal appraisal scenarios corresponding to emotions, which are represented by the English emotion terms, Happiness, Sadness, Disgust, Anger, and Fear, and that these emotions can rightly be called basic. We also devoted some space to what we might mean by the term basic in this context. In Chapter 3 we summarised the characteristics of these core universal appraisals (see Table 5.1). One of the central proposals of the book is that basic emotions and their associated appraisal scenarios shape and organise our emotional development and emotional existence. We endorse the view that all emotional experience is derived from the different basic emotions, either alone, combined with each other, or as components along with social and cultural factors of more complex emotions. For example, one can experience sadness at the loss of a valued self-related goal, or a combination of sadness and happiness as in nostalgia, or sadness with respect to another's loss of goals as in empathy. As well as the suggestion that basic emotions are the building blocks of emotional order, we also propose that emotionally disordered states are best understood in terms of basic emotions and that the same model of emotions can be used to understand both emotional order and disorder. Consequently the second half of the book is given over to a detailed discussion of each of the five basic emotions listed above and the order and disorder associated with them.

The second important point to arise out of Chapter 3 was an emphasis on the distinctions between unconscious and conscious psychological systems. Although, we have argued, albeit somewhat tentatively, that conscious awareness is a characteristic of emotions, it remains possible to be unaware of the interpretations and appraisals that constitute emotional experiences. Furthermore, we propose that it is possible to be conscious of one interpretation of an event whilst also holding an unconscious and contradictory interpretation. Similarly, interpretations can be appraised consciously in terms of one emotion and unconsciously in terms of another; for example, a bereaved wife who is conscious of appraising the death of her husband in a sadness-related way reflecting the magnitude of her loss, whilst being unconscious of appraising his death in terms of freedom to pursue her long dreamed of goals, that is, in a joy-related way. Clearly, this example is somewhat simplistic. However, we would argue that the notion of conscious and unconscious psychological systems goes some way towards accounting for the variety of desynchronous and conflictual phenomena that characterise emotions and which need to be considered in any comprehensive model of emotional life. It will be possible to paint a far richer picture of these dynamics when we have outlined more of the theory later in the chapter.

Consistent with this notion of conscious and unconscious systems, is the proposal from Chapter 3 that a certain amount of processing is carried out by some form of associative cognitive architecture. Furthermore, we proposed that the representations and processes, both conscious and unconscious, which are involved in emotions might be organised in a functionally modular fashion (e.g. Gazzaniga, 1988). Both of these points were presented with minimal elaboration in Chapter 3 and we expand on them in the present chapter.

The final point to be carried forward from Chapter 3 is that a further key to understanding how emotional processes operate is the notion of multiple levels and types of representation of emotion-related concepts in the mind. Indeed, it was clear from our review of theories of normal emotion that multi-level approaches such as Interacting Cognitive Sub-systems (ICS; Teasdale & Barnard, 1993) and the Multiple Entry Memory System (MEMS; Johnson & Multhaup, 1992) had by far the greatest explanatory power of the theories on offer. We are indebted to and strongly endorse this type of approach and we also propose that there are multiple and often conflicting representations of emotion-related information which influence processing both consciously and unconsciously. We shall further argue that such representations exist at different levels of the psychological system; some are present as simple concrete beliefs which can readily be translated into natural language (propositional representations); other types of representation exist at higher levels and reflect generalised, abstracted views of the world and the self which cannot be readily expressed in natural language (schematic model representations; cf. Teasdale & Barnard, 1993); while others have become instantiated in the associative architecture which we referred to previously. Once more, we expand considerably upon these ideas concerning multiple formats and levels of representation in the sections which follow and illustrate how they are influenced by and build upon previous work.

To summarise, the review of theories of normal everyday emotions from Chapter 3 allows us to paint some more brush strokes on the emotion canvas with the notions of conscious and unconscious systems, multiple levels and formats of representation, the notion of modularity and an emphasis on a core set of basic emotions and related appraisal scenarios.

Finally, the review of theories of emotional disorder in Chapter 4 raised a number of core points, which any model that seeks to provide an understanding of emotional problems must take into account. The first of these points concerns the issue of life events. A number of theories highlight the importance of key events in the development of emotional disorder (e.g. Brown & Harris, 1978). It is our intention to show that the reason such events are important is a function of the individuals' models, goals, and appraisals about themselves, the world, and others, rather than anything inherent in the events themselves (Ellsworth, 1991). This links to the second point to arise out of the discussions in Chapter 4, that of vulnerability. Again, a common feature of a number of models of emotional disorder (those known as diathesis-stress models; e.g. Beck et al., 1979) is the notion that certain individuals are more vulnerable than others to the onset and development of certain types of emotional problem. We shall argue that the concept of vulnerability, as with life events, can best be understood in terms of the models, appraisal systems, roles, and goals which the individual uses in interacting with and interpreting the world.

In the brief tour of the highlights of Chapter 3, we stressed the importance of multiple levels and formats of representation in the mind allied to the existence of conscious and unconscious systems. The centrality of these ideas in any attempt to understand the conflictual and contradictory nature of emotional experience is most evident in the area of emotional disorder. For that reason we would like to stress two further, related points that emerge from the review in Chapter 4. The first of these concerns the process of inhibition. The notion that certain ideas or beliefs are so disturbing that they have to be prevented from entering conscious awareness in an undiluted or unaltered form is obviously not new—it is one of the cornerstones of the psychodynamic model of psychology. However, within cognitive theories of emotion and of mind the idea that such inhibitory processes might have an important role has gained little currency. As Erdelyi (1988, p.84) points out: "It is almost as if the literature, imitating a Zen master, were conveying the profound essence of the repression process through inexplicable acts (and omissions of acts) rather than through formal verbal exposition." We shall argue that the concept of inhibition, not only between conscious and unconscious systems but also between and within different levels and formats of representation, is important in any attempt to understand emotional order and disorder. The second related point from Chapter 4 is the broad idea that different sub-systems of the mind may become interlocked or coupled (cf. Teasdale & Barnard, 1993) in a pathological way which serves to maintain and exacerbate emotional difficulties.

To summarise, our analysis of theories of emotional disorder in Chapter 4 allows us to add the final broad brush strokes to our canvas. These concern the importance of life events, the concept of vulnerability, the process of cognitive inhibition, and the idea of interlock or coupling between different psychological components and systems.

A summary of the important points from Chapters 2-4.   The principal points from Chapters 2–4 on: the cognitive philosophy of emotion; theories of normal emotion; and theories of abnormal emotion are summarised in Table 5.2.

These ideas are carried forward in the sections which follow where we shall present some of the details of the model. First, we shall endeavour to sketch briefly a theory of mind and, second, we shall seek to apply it to the domain of emotional experience.

SOME THEORETICAL REMARKS CONCERNING A THEORY OF MIND

As we have seen above, in our review of psychological theories of emotional order and disorder in Chapters 3 and 4, we introduced a number of important topics from cognitive psychology, such as modularity, multiple representations, and so forth. These ideas were presented very much on a "need to know" basis with only those details necessary to understand the theory under discussion being addressed. This has left us with a somewhat heterogeneous collection of cognitive processes and principles (see Table 5.2), which we have argued are important to an understanding of emotion. In the present section we shall endeavour to tie all of these various strands together into a more

TABLE 5.2
Principal points derived from Chapters 2–4, which any comprehensive model of emotions would need to account for

CHAPTER 2 *The cognitive philosophy of emotion*	CHAPTER 3 *Cognitive theories of emotion*	CHAPTER 4 *Cognitive theories of emotional disorder*
The mind is a functional system	The notion of conscious and unconscious emotional systems	The importance of life events
All emotional states comprise: an event; an appraisal; an interpretation; a physiological change; and conscious awareness	Multiple levels and formats of representation Modular architecture	The concept of vulnerability The processes of inhibition The concept of emotional interlock and/or coupling
Emotional states can only meaningfully be distinguished one from the other on the basis of the appraisal component	One set of basic appraisal scenarios Idea of levels or cycles of appraisal leading to increasingly sophisticated emotional responses	
Broad distinctions can be drawn between emotional states, moods, and dispositions		

comprehensive theory of mind which we can then use as a framework for the discussion of emotions which forms the main part of the chapter.

Presenting a theory of mind, however briefly, is an ambitious undertaking and it is important to emphasise that our reasons for doing so arise from the need for such a theoretical outline when approaching the subject of the emotions. We shall side-step many important philosophical and psychological issues along the way because they are beyond the scope of our rather focused ambitions and we have no wish to squander the reader's hard-won attention on them. We shall also draw distinctions between different types of knowledge or between different cognitive systems because we believe they are useful in understanding emotional phenomena. Some of these distinctions will cut across the more familiar divisions which are established in philosophy and psychology. However, there is little convincing evidence that the cake should be sliced in one way as opposed to another and we make no apologies for the size, shape, or taste of our particular slices.

It is useful at this point to preview briefly how this section of the chapter is organised. The first area that we tackle concerns what we shall bravely call the *contents of the mind*; that is, how the subject matter of the representations that people hold might be organised. We then move on to discuss how those representations are instantiated in the mind; that is, the *format* of the representations that people hold and their relationship to each other. Finally, we discuss the *processes* which seem to act on these representations.

These distinctions between the content of representations, the type and format of representations and the processes which act on representations are inevitably somewhat artificial. Contemporary cognitive science with its appetite for connectionist approaches has often dispensed with any meaningful content/process distinction (e.g. Posner, 1989). However, as will become clear, although we envisage an important role for connectionist or associative representations in a model of emotions, we also acknowledge the importance of other types of representational architecture. For this reason, a distinction between format, content, and process remains heuristically useful and is implemented throughout the rest of the book.

The content of mental representations as it pertains to emotions

In Chapter 2 on the cognitive philosophy of emotion we stressed that an important component of emotions is appraisal and that it is only by virtue of this component that one emotion can be reliably distinguished from another. Any appraisal that an individual makes has to be with respect to something. So, if we take a simple example, we have suggested that the emotion of fear is characterised by appraisals of unwanted psychological or physical threat. This begs the question of what we mean when we use the term threat here. There are a number of ways that this question can be answered but the reply which is most representative of the cognitive functionalist position, is that threat is defined in terms of the individual's active goal structure. So, in a simple case, threat would be appraised in any situation in which the completion of an important goal such as, in the most extreme case, personal survival, was challenged. However, this analysis does not tell the whole story. A further question is raised as to how a given situation comes to be viewed as likely to challenge the continuation or completion of an important goal such as personal survival. Why, for example, would the ubiquitous bear running out of the woods (see Chapter 2) be seen as something that might endanger personal survival? The somewhat obvious but none the less important reply is that situations are appraised in terms of the content of the individual's mind; that is, the individual's knowledge of the world, of themselves, of previously similar occasions, and so forth. Susan, our heroine from Chapter 2, faced with the charging bear undoubtedly knows that bears can, and do, kill people, that she is unlikely to be able to outrun the bear or fight it off, and that she has heard that three people were killed in these very woods only last year by vicious woman-eating bears. This knowledge leads Susan to interpret the charging bear as a situation likely to endanger her personal survival; that is, as a threatening situation. Consequently, Susan's cognitive system makes a threat-related appraisal and Susan feels afraid. The first important question to consider in our brief theory of mind is that, if appraisals are made with respect to mind content as we have suggested, what types of "mind content" might be important?

Traditional research (for detailed reviews see Baddeley, 1990; Eysenck & Keane, 1990; Hampton, 1990; Schank, 1986) has conceptualised the content of the mind in ways which are primarily heuristically useful; for example representations in short-term and in long-term memory. Sometimes these divisions appear to have no reality outside of the theorist's own imagination and are merely convenient ways to organise the data. This is not always the case; some theoretical divisions have considerable empirical support; for example, the distinction between procedural and declarative memory (e.g. Ryle, 1949). However, generally speaking, our present level of psychological understanding does not permit too many statements about how the content of mental representations is organised in reality (although with the rise of cognitive neuropsychology the ground is beginning to shift. See Ellis & Young, 1988, for a review). For this reason we shall propose a way of organising mind content that we have found useful in understanding emotions, while acknowledging that this is largely a heuristic exercise rather than necessarily a reflection of the actual subject matter.

In Fig. 5.3. we illustrate schematically the main domains of mind content, which we feel are important for understanding the emotions.

These domains consist of:

1. Knowledge and models of the world. This domain comprises: semantic knowledge about the world, such as the fact that Paris is the capital of France or that English people tend to be reserved; knowledge of the physical world and its objects and their inter-relations, what Schank and Abelson (1977) have called a "naive physics"; and abstracted "models" of the individual's views of the world which can be partially captured in statements such as; "the world is a reasonably safe place" (Janoff-Bulman, 1985) or "the world is just".

2. Knowledge and models of the self. This domain includes semantic knowledge of ourselves and our capabilities; for example, my name, the fact that I am a passable pasta cook, and so on. This domain also incorporates episodic memory information about the self: for example, the memory of last year's holiday in Timbuktu. Finally, the domain

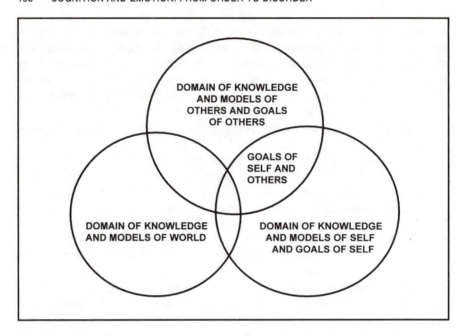

FIG. 5.3. Domains of mind content.

includes abstracted models of the self, which might be partially captured
by statements such as "I am a successful person", or "I am an angry
person".

3.   Knowledge and models of others. This content domain incorporates
knowledge of other individuals in our world. This includes
straightforward semantic knowledge such as the fact that Harry is my
grandfather and also episodic memories about others such as the
memory of how pleased Harry was with his Christmas present last year.
In addition, as with the other domains, more abstracted "models" of
others are represented. These might be partially captured by natural
language statements such as "Harry is a complicated man". Finally, this
domain includes prototype and stereotype information about other types
of individual in our world. These allow us to construct models of new
people we meet. This information is a combination of data about people
we already know, with information reflecting social representations (e.g.
Moscovici, 1976) about what different types of people are like, derived
from the media and social discourse. So, for example in England, where
the class system remains an important social factor, the belief that, for
example, James is middle class engenders a set of assumptions about
what James would be like, his tastes, his clothes, his type of job, and so
forth. These representations of "middle classness" will be an amalgam

of information about middle-class people whom we know, combined with social and cultural information about what it is to be middle class.

Goals

We propose that, subsumed within the domains of knowledge and models of the self and of others, is information concerning what we shall call "goals". This term is intended as a linguistic heuristic to convey the principle of functionality. Goals are a way of talking about the temporal dimension of representations and plans which the individual operates with. This kind of idea, as we stressed earlier, is central to any functional theory of mind and of emotions. Further, we have suggested that the appraisal process, a component of all emotional experience, is carried out with respect to the individual's extant goals. It is envisaged that in the present framework information about goals is hierarchically arranged, with major goals such as self-preservation having some overarching status with respect to much more minor goals such as wishing to watch a certain film at the cinema on Friday evening. Although goal compatibility is an ideal functional state of affairs, it is clear that goals often contradict each other both at similar levels of a hierarchy (e.g. also wanting to go to a party on that same Friday night) and at different levels of the hierarchy (e.g. having the goal of fighting for one's country which clearly increases the chances of not maintaining the goal of self-preservation). Those who have thought about and written on the subject of internal goal structure have emphasised these facilitatory and inhibitory relationships between goals (Ortony et al., 1988; Ravlin, 1987). In addition, they have utilised the concept of necessary and sufficient links between goals to capture the fact that the completion of, for example, goal p is sometimes a necessary requirement for the completion of goal q or that completion of goals a, b, or c would be sufficient for the completion of goal d, but that neither one of a, b, or c is necessary. These types of relationships between goals are schematically illustrated in Fig. 5.4, which represents the virtual goal structure of someone who aspires to be a secret agent but, alas, is heading for a less glamorous academic career.

It is beyond the scope of this book to elaborate on the nature of internal goal structures; a more detailed review can be found in Ortony et al. (1988). The point we would like to emphasise is that it is the conflicts between goals and/or the various types of other problems involved in attaining them which are central to a functional understanding of the role of emotions.

In addition to information about the individual's own goals in the self domain, the other domain includes information about the goals of others. These representations of the goals of others are essential in the

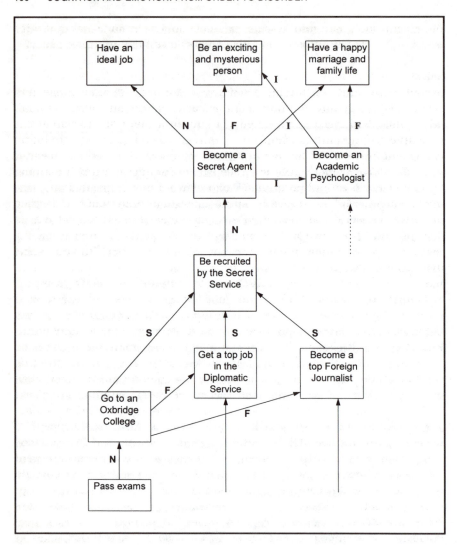

FIG. 5.4. Imaginary example of part of a virtual goal structure of an aspiring secret agent (based on Ravlin, 1987).
F = facilitatory link to achieve goals; S = sufficient link to achieve goals; N = necessary link to achieve goals; I = inhibitory link to achieve goals.

construction of the "models" of others used during social interaction. For example, I might avoid talking to somebody because I have a model of her which says that she does not want to speak to me and that she has the goal of avoiding contact with me. I might then utilise this model in my social interactions by keeping out of her way.

Finally, the domains of self and other include information about goals which are shared by the self and by others. This information represents what might be thought of as social standards and incorporates many of the things which are traditionally associated with the Freudian idea of a superego. For example, most of us, though clearly not all, share the goal of not stealing each other's possessions.

In concluding this section on the content of the mind, there are two points which we would like to emphasise. First, as we have stated above, these divisions between various domains of mind content are not intended as statements about distinctions within the actual subject matter; rather, they are heuristic divisions, which we feel are of use when one comes to formulate a model of emotion. The reader might well question why we need divisions at all. The answer to this, we hope, will become clearer in the chapters that follow when we try to show that the overinvestment of resources in one domain (e.g. the self) or in one set of goals at the expense of others is one of the pathways from emotional order to emotional disorder. Furthermore, we shall suggest (in Chapter 10) that the emotion of happiness is a function of goal status across multiple knowledge domains. The second point that we wish to highlight is that in all three domains of mind content we have not only referred to information of a factual kind such as one's name or the capital of France but also to more abstract models about the self, others, or the world. As we have pointed out earlier, this distinction between different types of representation is important to an understanding of emotions and is discussed in some detail in the next section on the format of mental representations.

The format of mental representations

Having introduced briefly some broad divisions in the content of mental representations, we shall now turn to a consideration of the nature or format of those representations. In the resumé of Chapters 2, 3, and 4 we indicated a number of important points which bear on the format of mental representations including conscious vs. unconscious systems; connectionist vs. symbolic architecture; and multiple levels of meaning (see Table 5.2). In this section we look at the ways in which these different concepts relate to each other and to other concepts in mental representation theory; for example, the analogical vs. propositional debate, which is where we begin.

The analogical–propositional debate.   The debate between proponents of analogical and propositional mental representations is one of the oldest in cognitive psychology. Theoreticians such as Paivio (see e.g. 1971, 1986) have argued that both forms of representation are essential to any understanding of human cognition. In contrast, psychologists such as Pylyshyn (e.g. 1973, 1979, 1981, 1984) have proposed that all mental knowledge can be represented in propositional terms. What then do we mean by the terms analogical and propositional?

The prototypical example of an analogue representation is a picture. If we consider a colour photograph of the Taj Mahal, it is clear that it structurally resembles the real Taj Mahal. The colour of the marble is the same, as is the spatial configuration of the dome and of the minarets. In the picture we can see that the dome is in the centre of the four minarets. Such structural resemblance means that this image of the Taj Mahal is analogous to the real building. In contrast, if we consider the English sentence "The dome of the Taj Mahal is in the centre of its four minarets" we are clearly dealing with a non-analogical representation. In the sentence there is no reason why the configuration of letters "T-A-J M-A-H-A-L" should represent the famous building in India; indeed, in the original Hindi language the building is obviously represented by a completely different set of symbols. A further difference between analogical and non-analogical representations is revealed when we consider the relation between the position of the dome of the Taj Mahal and the minarets. The relation between these architectural features requires an explicit sequence of symbols in the non-analogical sentence; namely, the phrase "in the centre of". In contrast, the relative positions of the minarets and dome is implicit in the picture—no explicit symbol for the relation is necessary. A further difference between the two types of representation is that the sentence can be broken down into words which in turn can be broken down into letters. Further deconstruction is not possible if one wants to retain meaning in the language, as a fraction of a letter means nothing in English. In contrast, pictures have no such discrete symbols; there is no smallest unit in the image of the Taj Mahal. Finally, the non-analogical sentence has clear rules of combination, in the form of English grammar, for the symbols it includes. Pictures, on the other hand, do not posses clear rules of combination.

Clearly we have not been talking about the format of mental representations in the preceding section but of external representations —pictures and written sentences. However, the crux of the analogical vs. propositional debate amongst mental representation theorists is contained in this discussion of external representations. The differences between analogical and non-analogical external representations above are paralleled by the distinctions drawn by theorists such as Paivio between analogical and propositional mental representations. In contrast, other mental representation theorists such as Pylyshyn, as we have noted previously, deny the validity of this distinction and propose that there are no analogue mental representations and that the external world is represented mentally by propositions. It is beyond the scope of this chapter to enter into the intricacies of the debate between these two schools of thought. An excellent blow by blow account is provided by Eysenck and Keane (1990) and a number of the important source articles are reproduced in Collins and Smith (1988). The line we shall take in this chapter and those that follow is that a concept of analogical mental representations is both useful and valid when we come to try and understand emotion-related phenomena. Such representations, as we have indicated, have similar properties to the colour photograph of the Taj Mahal. That is to say, they are non-discrete, they represent things implicitly, and they have loose rules of combination. Finally, analogous representations are tied to a particular sense modality (e.g. vision in the example of the Taj Mahal). This last point is important because we endorse the view that there are several modalities of analogical mental representation which are important in understanding emotions. These are olfactory, auditory, gustatory, visual, proprioceptive, and tactile. The importance of these different forms of analogical representation is highlighted to some extent in the discussion that follows. However, the main advantages of endorsing a role for analogical representations in the emotional system are more fully explored in the chapters in Part Two of the book.

So, where does this leave propositional representations? In contrast to analogical representations, propositional representations are considered to be explicit, discrete, and abstract entities. They represent beliefs, ideas, objects, and concepts and the relations between them in a form which is not specific to any language. In other words, propositions are a kind of language of thought (e.g. Fodor, 1987), a mental lingua franca, in which different components of the mind communicate. However, an essential point about propositional representations is that although they are language-free, their entire semantic or meaning context can be captured by statements in natural language. So, for example, the propositional information that the capital of France is Paris, although not represented in the mind in English or French, is entirely captured by sentences in either language; namely, "Paris is the capital of France" or "Paris est la capitale de France". Both sentences have the same propositional content. Given this, cognitive scientists are then faced with the problem of how to characterise these non-language-specific representations. This problem has traditionally been side-stepped by presenting propositions in the form of the logical system of predicate calculus. So, for example, the natural language sentence in English, "the writing is on the wall", can be characterised in propositional terms using predicate calculus as:

ON (WRITING, THE WALL)

It is not necessary to enter into the intricacies of predicate calculus here. The essential point is the postulation of a form of mental representation—the propositional—which is able to represent ideational content in a non-language-specific way but for which the meaning can be totally captured by sentences in natural language.

So far we have talked about two forms of mental representation: analogical which includes visual, olfactory, auditory, gustatory, proprioceptive, and tactile images; and propositional which is a non-language-specific representation of beliefs, ideas, and concepts (N.B. the term "proposition" is occasionally used in cognitive psychology to represent ideational content which is of a higher-order than natural language and which can be only be expressed in natural language with a corresponding loss of meaning. It is important to emphasise that for our purposes, the former usage of the term proposition is employed throughout). Earlier in our summary of the important points to arise from Chapter 3, we emphasised the advantages of multiple levels of meaning in any analysis of mind. Consequently, because propositions refer to thoughts and beliefs that can be expressed in natural language without any corresponding loss of content, there remains a need to propose a structure which can represent higher-order ideational content that cannot be expressed in natural language; for example, the models of the self, the world, and others to which we referred in the previous section on the content of the mind. In cognitive psychology concepts such as Schemas (e.g. Bartlett, 1932; Rumelhart & Ortony, 1977), Scripts (Schank & Abelson, 1977), Frames (Minsky, 1975), Memory Organisation Packets (MOPS) and Thematic Organisation Packets (TOPS) (Schank, 1982), Mental Models (Johnson-Laird, 1983), the Implicational Level of Interacting Cognitive Sub-systems (ICS; Barnard, 1985; Teasdale & Barnard, 1993; see Chapter 3) and Thematic Abstraction Units (TAU; Dyer, 1983) are all concerned with the representation of knowledge at higher levels than that of verbally expressible propositional concepts. Again, it is beyond the scope of this chapter to discuss the pros and cons of these varieties of higher-level meaning representations. For our purposes we shall borrow a term from Teasdale and Barnard and refer to these higher-order representations of ideational content generically as "schematic models".

We have discussed briefly the distinction between propositional representations and these schematic model (or implicational) representations in our discussion of ICS (Teasdale & Barnard, 1993) in Chapter 3. Teasdale and Barnard captured some of the essence of the two levels of meaning by comparing the following two passages:

Passage one (poetic version: Implicational meaning):

O what can ail thee, knight-at-arms,
  Alone and palely loitering?
The sedge has wither'd from the lake,
  And no birds sing

Passage two (prose version: Propositional meaning):

What is the matter, armed old-fashioned soldier,
Standing by yourself and doing nothing with a pallid expression?
The reed-like plants have decomposed by the lake
And there are not any birds singing.

As Teasdale and Barnard note (1993, p.73): "The implicational meaning or 'sense' conveyed by the two versions is very different. The poetic form conveys a sense of melancholy, emptiness, and abandonment that is largely lost in the much more 'matter of fact' tone of the prose version." This example from Teasdale and Barnard captures the sense of evoked feelings and understanding which are carried by schematic model information. The second passage contains little more than straightforward propositional information. In contrast, the first passage unlocks whole areas of higher-order meaning.

A less poetic and slightly different illustration of the schematic model level of representation is provided by Schank and Abelson (1977) in their discussion of restaurant "Scripts". Schank and Abelson argue that for commonly encountered situations such as going to a restaurant we have schematic representations, or "Scripts" as they call them, of the order and type of events which might happen. These Scripts help us to organise and process the information with which we come into contact in the restaurant situation (see Table 5.3).

Schank and Abelson suggest that the restaurant "script" is constructed by abstracting large amounts of propositional information and combining it to form a schematic whole larger than its constituent propositional parts. However, it could be argued that a more sophisticated schematic model (or script) of restaurants would include analogical information about visual appearance, smells, sounds, and also the feelings associated with going to a restaurant, and so on. This would give the schematic model of the restaurant more of the properties of the poem in the example from Teasdale and Barnard (1993). On these lines, it is important to emphasise that schematic models are not mere collections of propositional beliefs. Rather they are abstracted across all levels of the system including the analogical. In this sense, schematic

TABLE 5.3
The components and actions of the restaurant script
(based on Schank & Abelson, 1977)

Script name	Component	Specific action
Eating at a restaurant	Entering	Walk into restaurant
		Search for table
		Decide where to sit down
		Go to table
		Sit down
	Ordering	Get menu
		Look at menu
		Waiter arrives
		Order drinks
		Choose food
		Waiter arrives
		Give orders to waiter
		Waiter takes order to cook
		Wait, talk
		Cook prepares food
	Eating	Waiter delivers drinks
		Cook gives food to waiter
		Waiter delivers food
		Customer eats
		Talk
	Leaving	Waiter writes bill
		Waiter delivers bill
		Customer examines bill
		Calculate tip
		Leave tip
		Gather belongings
		Pay bill
		Leave restaurant

models differ from, for example, Beck's schemas (see Chapter 4), which Beck refers to as integrated collections of propositional beliefs.

The two examples we have borrowed in order to illustrate the distinction between the propositional level of meaning and the schematic model level have an important difference. In the poetry example of Teasdale and Barnard we are constructing a schematic model "on line" as we read the poem and our awareness of this schematic model is what provides us with the feelings of poignancy and sadness which the poem evokes. In contrast, Schank and Abelson's restaurant script describes a schematic representation in long-term memory. This script is activated and utilised whenever restaurant-related information is encountered. Clearly, the schematic model level of meaning usually functions in a combination of these two ways. Stored *schematic* representations in long-term memory are called up and combined with analogue and propositional information to build an on-line *model* of the current situation.

It is becoming increasingly clear that such schematic models are central to an understanding of emotions and, as with propositional representations, it is important to decide on a notational system to represent them in the discussions which follow. Any notational system in natural language, will, by definition, suffer from a significant loss of schematic level meaning. However, with this caveat in mind, we propose the following notation:

{REASONABLY-SAFE WORLD—
BAD THINGS DON'T HAPPEN TO ME}

to represent the schematic models of the world as reasonably safe and as one in which bad things generally do not happen to me, rather than a propositional belief that this is the case.

To sum up, in this section we have discussed three formats of mental representation: analogical representations including visual, olfactory, gustatory, proprioceptive, tactile, and auditory "images"; propositional representations, which represent the ideational content of the mind in a non-language-specific way but which can be directly translated into natural language; and schematic models, which contain higher-order abstracted information about the self, world, and others that cannot be fully expressed in natural language. Later in the chapter we discuss one further representational format—the associative. However, in the next section we address briefly how the content of the mind is captured in the three different representational formats that we have introduced so far before describing the first of two proposed routes to the generation of emotions which utilises this representational scheme.

EMOTION GENERATION VIA SCHEMATIC MODELS

We now have a significant part of the main framework of the theory of emotion which is the centrepiece of this volume. So far in this chapter we have reiterated the argument that the components of the emotion process always involve: event, interpretation, appraisal, action potential, physiological change, and conscious awareness. We then sketched out the principal divisions in the content of the mind, which we feel it is useful to adopt in an understanding of emotions. Finally, we have described three formats of representational architecture within which these other constraints and processes can be instantiated. In this section we shall endeavour to bring about some kind of *rapprochement* between these aspects of the theory to illustrate the first of two proposed ways in which emotions are generated; in this case via the activation of the schematic model level of meaning. First, it will be useful to illustrate how the three main domains of information represented in the mind (knowledge and models of the world, knowledge and models of the self, knowledge and models of others) are captured by the analogical, propositional, and schematic model representation formats. More importantly, it is necessary to return to the question of goals because it is the relationship between schematic models and goals which provides the functionality within our proposed model of emotion.

Mind content revisited

We propose that the three domains of knowledge are represented across the various representational formats in similar ways. If we consider knowledge of the world as an example; we propose that abstract models of the world such as the world as a safe place would be represented at the schematic model level {WORLD—SAFE PLACE}. However, less abstracted information about the world such as the fact that the chances of being mugged alone in Central Park at night are high would be represented at the propositional level. Other forms of knowledge of the world might be represented analogically such as the shape and form of visual objects, sounds, smells, or visual memories of places and events. The first important point is that representations of information in memory are possible in all three representational formats for all content types. Furthermore, as the examples illustrate, it is possible for information at one level to contradict information at other levels.

We have proposed that cutting across the domains of information about the self and information about others there is information concerning goals both of the self and of others in our lives. This suggestion of a virtual goal structure provides the model with functionaility. However, it is important to reiterate that we are putting forward the idea of goals as an heuristic concept. Goals, essentially, are a way of talking about the temporal dimension of schematic models. Goals about the self, for example, are a function of schematic models of the self projected into the future. In this analysis, emotions are psychological processes which configure the system in order to resolve goal-related issues. The pattern of an individual's virtual goal hierarchy is a reflection of the pattern of schematic model information "in place" within the system. So, if we consider the goal of being a good father, what we are referring to is a configuration of schematic model information about "good fatherness" and individuals' self-concepts. So, the use of the concept of goals provides a *language of functionality* to describe the configuration of schematic model information in place. The highest goal in the system within this analysis is to preserve the current configuration of dominant schematic models of world, self, and other. These models provide individuals with their sense of self and their sense of reality. The massive impact of events that threaten these highest level goals (namely, traumatic events) is discussed in detail in Chapter 6 on Fear.

Although goals are therefore primarily a function of schematic models, they can also be represented propositionally. We all have a number of goals and aims we can articulate clearly such as the goal of trying to finish this book. Other goals are less accessible to such propositional articulation.

As we have discussed earlier, goals are hierarchically arranged. So, achieving the goal of being a good father requires the attainment of goals relating to various subsumed qualities. For example, achieving the goal of being around on Sunday afternoons to take the children to the park would, perhaps, *facilitate* the goal of being a good father. At other times goals are clearly *inhibitory*, so the goal of going to make a cup of coffee inhibits the short-term achievement of finishing this paragraph in the next 10 minutes. As with self-related goals, our representations of the goals of others can be mutually facilitative or inhibitory. In addition, the representations of goals of self and others may be either facilitatory or inhibitory. So, the woman who decides to leave her loving husband for another woman is pursuing her own goal in a way which inhibits the achievement of her husband's goal of a long and happy marriage but most likely facilitates the achievement of her lover's goal to be together with her. We shall return to the question of goals at various points later in the chapter in order to discuss their importance in understanding emotions.

AUTOMATIC GENERATION OF EMOTIONS

Having finished our rather lengthy introduction by indicating how the various domains of knowledge including goals are accommodated within the representational structure we have outlined, we can now return at last to a discussion of the emotions. In this section we shall outline the first of two ways in which the various components of the emotion process might operate within the framework that we have sketched so far.

The most instructive way to demonstrate the generation of emotions via the activation of schematic meaning is to use a familiar example and what better than the case of Susan's encounter with the bear in the wood which pervaded the discussion in Chapter 2.

If we remember, it was suggested that the process of Susan stumbling across a bear in the woods, feeling afraid, and running away and climbing a tree could be understood in terms of the following seven components of the emotion process:

1. an event—the bear
2. an interpretation—the bear is going to eat me
3. an appraisal—survival goal is threatened
4. a physiological change—emotion system activity associated with fear
5. a propensity for action—to run away
6. conscious awareness—feeling afraid
7. overt behaviour—running like mad!

In terms of the model we have described, the bear would be perceived and recognised via visual analogical representations. Information from this level would feed into the propositional level where knowledge about bears and their likely behaviour would be activated. This interaction between events, their analogical representation (if applicable), and propositional information, we conceive of as an interpretation; for example, that the bear is probably hungry. This interpretation would be relevant to a number of Susan's goals such as that of finishing the leisurely walk through the woods. However, the most important goal that would be involved would be her goal of personal survival. At this point we need to make the first theoretical proposal concerning the generation of emotions; that is, that events and interpretations can only be appraised with respect to the individual's goals, such that emotions are generated at the schematic model level of meaning. In other words, although goals can be represented propositionally they can only be the subjects of an *emotion-related appraisal* process at the schematic model level. The reason for this is that, in order for the implications of a given event for an individual's goals to be appraised, a schematic model of how the individual's situation will change needs to be constructed. It is this process which leads to the generation of emotion. We are not suggesting that new information cannot be processed with respect to goals at the propositional level; rather, we are claiming that such propositional processing will be merely semantic—it will be cold and non-emotional. Let us consider an example: if someone wanted to give up smoking they could reason propositionally along the lines that evidence indicates that smoking can kill, that they have a goal to live a long and fruitful life, and, therefore, that they will give up smoking. We submit that such reasoning can occur in the absence of any emotion by being carried out at the propositional level of representation. In contrast, many anti-smoking advertising campaigns endeavour to access schematic model meaning by providing material to encourage the individual to construct a schematic model of the implications of the fact that smoking can kill. This proves very distressing and, the argument goes, ensures a higher probability of someone kicking the habit. However, on a final note, a friend of a friend, having been subjected to a particularly gruesome example of such an anti-smoking campaign, was heard to say: "It was so distressing, I had to have three cigarettes before I even began to calm down."

So, to return to our bear, in the analysis we have just presented, appraisal is the processing of the interpretation (e.g. the bear is going to eat me) with respect to the individual's extant goal structure (e.g. personal survival) at the schematic model level of meaning. The relationship between the interpretation and the extant goal structure, as we have stated previously, determines which emotion is experienced (see Table 5.1). So, for example, if the interpretation means that important goals run the risk of future non-completion, an appraisal of threat occurs at the schematic level and the individual begins to experience fear. If we return to the woods, the interpretation "the bear is going to eat me" is appraised with respect to the individual's extant goal structure at the schematic model level. This interpretation means that the goal of personal survival runs the risk of future non-completion and an appraisal of threat occurs. The appraisal of threat serves to activate physiological systems associated with fear and gives rise to an action potential to run away. Finally, the combined awareness of the appraisal of threat and the physiological changes constitute the phenomenal experience of fear (see Fig. 5.5).

We can see in this example of Susan and the bear how the different domains of knowledge (of self, the world, and others, and their subsumed goals) are utilised in the experience of emotion. Recognising the danger represented by the bear is a function of knowledge of the world; specifically, knowledge of what bears are capable of. Forming the interpretation that the bear is going to eat her utilises Susan's representation of the bear's goal structure. That is, that the bear, on seeing Susan walking along the path, would form the goal of devouring her to satisfy a survival-related goal of finding something to eat. The action potential and subsequent decision to run draws upon information about the self to the effect that there would be little point in Susan stopping to fight the bear because she would not be strong enough to succeed. These somewhat straightforward points only give a flavour of the complex cognitive interactions that occur in a situation like this.

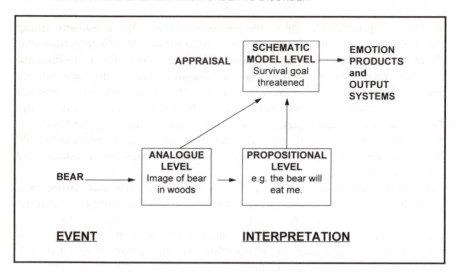

FIG. 5.5. Components of the model involved in the generation of the emotion of fear via schematic models for the event of a bear in the woods.

Once Susan starts running, for example, her schematic model of the situation leads to a whole new set of goals (and plans to realise them) being created and put into operation such as getting to a nearby tree. Success or failure of these plans and goals leads to further emotion-related interpretations and appraisals at the schematic level. Susan might also experience other emotions such as anger. She might have taken a gun with her on every previous walk in the wood but had not done so that morning because the gun needed cleaning and she could not be bothered to clean it. The interpretation of having been negligent with the knowledge that the negligence was perpetrated by the self would be appraised with respect to the goal of being prepared and thorough. This would lead to appraisals associated with self-directed anger. Furthermore, the generation of a given emotion will serve to bias the system in favour of information congruent with that emotion. So, once afraid, Susan is likely to attend to threat in the environment and the interpretations she makes of the event are likely to be biased in a threat-related direction (see Dalgleish & Watts, 1990; Eysenck, 1992; Williams et al., 1988).

An important question raised by this example is the content of Susan's conscious awareness. She will doubtless be aware of the presence of the bear. However, her conscious awareness may include little or no bear-related propositional information. So, Susan will experience fear and this experience will be a function of an awareness that the goal of personal survival has been challenged, combined with an awareness of the physiological changes occurring in the body. The awareness of the schematic level appraisal process might, however, be devoid of propositional content and would then be experienced as a sense, albeit a strong sense, of threat or danger. Susan may not be conscious of the process of forming an interpretation such as "the bear is going to eat me"; as we have said, this is as much a way of talking about the interaction of the analogical representation of events with propositional representations as it is a valid reflection of thought content. In addition, Susan may or may not be conscious of a propensity for action or even an explicit desire to run and may just find herself hotfooting it in the opposite direction. All that is required by the model we have outlined is that Susan is aware of being in an emotional state, which is subsumed by a combination of the appraisal process and the physiological changes. There may be no awareness of the event, the interpretation, or the action potential.

Cycles of appraisal

In the example above of Susan and the bear, we presented a simplified discussion of the appraisal processes involved. In fact, as we have pointed out in Chapter 3, we proposed that appraisals occur in levels or cycles with each cycle leading the event to be appraised in a more sophisticated way. To illustrate, let us consider Susan and the bear again; the appraisals are likely to consist of the following: (1) goal relevance/irrelevance; (2) goal compatability/incompatability; (3) threat to future completion of valued goals; (4) inappropriate resources to fight, and so on. Each cycle provides a more sophisticated analysis of the situation (cf. Leventhal & Scherer, 1987) and, after the third cycle, the appraisal process becomes part of the generation of fear. In addition, the emotions themselves can feed back into the appraisal process (Lewis, 1996); so, for example, we might get angry with someone, and then feel guilty as we appraise that the anger was inappropriate.

To summarise, we have described an architecture involving analogical, propositional, and schematic model representational formats. Within this framework we have illustrated the first of two proposed routes to emotion generation; in this case via the schematic model level of meaning. However, as we noted earlier, central to the model of emotions we are proposing is the existence of a further type of associative representation which provides the machinery for a second route to emotion generation. It is this route to emotion generation that we consider next.

The automatic generation of emotions via the associative level of representation—some preliminary remarks

In Chapter 3 we reviewed associative network theories of emotion. We began with a discussion of Bower's theory (e.g. Bower, 1981) in which emotions are represented by single nodes in a localised network. Having illustrated the numerous empirical and theoretical problems with this type of model (see Chapter 3, for a fuller discussion) we speculated on the advantages of a distributed network or parallel distributed processing architecture for the modelling of emotions. We concluded that the most likely role for such an architecture was in the representation of low-level or automatised processes in the generation of emotion and it is this point we wish to pick up and expand upon here. The main thesis is that:

1. A useful distinction can be made between controlled and automatic cognitive processes (Shiffrin and Schneider, 1977).
2. Automatised processes of emotion generation are both possible and frequent.
3. Such automatised emotion generation occurs via an associative level of representation and does not require concurrent access to the schematic model level of representation.

We shall tackle these points one by one.

Automatic and controlled processing.   It is a widely held view amongst cognitive psychologists that some processes, through repetition or practice, cease to make demands on executive resources or attention; that is to say, they become automatic. The first theoretical analysis of this distinction between automatic and controlled processes was promoted by Shiffrin and Schneider (1977) in one of the seminal papers in cognitive psychology. They suggested a number of distinctions between automatic and controlled processing, which have been elaborated upon by many others (e.g. Jonides, Naveh-Benjamin, & Palmer, 1985; Logan, 1980; 1988; Norman & Shallice, 1980; Shiffrin, Dumais, & Schneider, 1981) and we have summarised these elsewhere (Power & Brewin, 1991; see Table 5.4).

Paralleling the emergence of a consensus amongst theorists of the main differences between automatic and controlled processing has been the development of increasingly sophisticated theories of what happens during the automatisation process (Anderson, 1982, 1987; Logan, 1980, 1988; Rosenbloom & Newell, 1986). It is beyond the scope of the present book to do justice to the many remarks and points of dispute in the automaticity debate and we shall confine ourselves to making a number of key points pertaining to the current analysis of the emotion domain:

TABLE 5.4
Some characteristics of automatic and controlled processes
(based on Power & Brewin, 1991)

Automatic processes	Controlled processes
Parallel	Sequential
Modular	Dependent/Interactive
Fast	Slow
Effortless	Effortful
Low awareness	High awareness
No central resources required	Central resources required
Low subsequent LTM storage	High LTM storage
Attention not required	Attention required
Inflexible	Flexible
Difficult to modify	Easy to modify

1. A black and white distinction between automatic and controlled processing is clearly invalid and unwieldy. Instead, it seems clear that on the path from novice (controlled) processes to fully automated processes there are meaningful intermediate positions. However, it is heuristically useful to employ the terms automatic and controlled to refer to the end points of this continuum.

2. Theories vary as to whether the passage from controlled processing to automatic processing involves the freeing up of limited attentional resources (e.g. Shiffrin & Schneider, 1977) or whether it rests on an increase in memory representations associated with the process in question. Whilst acknowledging that these two positions are not mutually exclusive, we broadly endorse the latter view as stated by, amongst others, Logan (1988, p.493):

> Automaticity is memory retrieval: Performance is automatic when it is based on single step direct-access retrieval of past solutions from memory. The theory assumes that novices begin with a general algorithm that is sufficient to perform the task. As they gain experience, they learn specific solutions to specific problems, which they retrieve when they encounter the same problems again. Then, they can respond with the solution retrieved from memory or the one computed by the algorithm ... Automization reflects a transition from algorithm-based performance to memory-based performance..

3. Almost all cognitive and social cognitive processes (e.g. attitude activation; Bargh & Gollwitzer, 1995) have the potential to become automatised including those involved in the generation of emotions.

Automatically generated emotions. Before we discuss how emotions might be generated automatically in terms of our proposed model, it is important to illustrate the kind of phenomenon we are referring to. Consider the following two examples:

Example 1
Peter had experienced a difficult childhood. His father had conducted a reign of terror over him and his siblings. His father was always shouting at him even when he had done nothing wrong. Peter's memories of his childhood are shrouded by the sense of fear he always felt with his father and, as an adult, Peter harbours a lot of anger and resentment towards the way his father treated him as a child and indeed continues to treat him. He is also very intolerant of anybody shouting at him. The very act of someone shouting immediately makes him angry. Peter and his father remain in contact, though their relationship is somewhat fraught. Often Peter's father will shout at him over something inconsequential, treating him as a child again. When this occurs Peter immediately experiences two very strong emotions at the sound of his father's raised voice: the fear that permeated so much of his childhood; and intense anger that somebody is shouting at him. Peter also feels angry at the content of his father's exclamations and the fact that he is not being given the credence he deserves as an adult.

Example 2
For as long as she can remember Julie has been frightened of birds. If you get her on to the subject she will say, in a somewhat embarrassed way, that she can see that there is nothing about birds to be afraid of and, indeed, she genuinely believes that birds are not really dangerous. However, as soon as she has to go anywhere near a bird feelings of intense fear sweep over her, which are completely outside of her control and she has to leave the situation as quickly as possible.

We suggest that these somewhat different examples illustrate two important points about the generation of emotions: First, that certain events lead to an automatic generation of emotions in contrast to the generation via schematic level meaning we described above. So, the event of Peter's father shouting at him in Example 1 leads to the automatic generation of fear and also of anger. In Example 2, the presence of birds for Julie leads to the automatic generation of fear.

The second point is that automatically generated emotions can conflict with either: (1) emotions generated via access to schematic models; (2) other automatically generated emotions; or (3) non-emotional rationalisations of an event. So, in the first example, Peter experiences a conflict between his experience of the automatic generation of fear at the sound of his father shouting and his experience of the schematic generation of anger, at the content and style of his father's exclamations. In addition, there is some conflict between the experience of the automatic generation of fear to the fact that it is *father* who is shouting, and the automatic generation of anger to the fact that he is in the situation of being shouted at (see Fig. 5.6).

In the second example Julie experiences the automatic generation of fear to the presence of the bird with no rational understanding of what it is she is afraid of. Again, there is a conflict caused by the automatic generation of an emotion.

In sum, the proposal is that there is a second, *automatic* route to emotion generation which differs from the generation of emotions via the schematic model level of meaning which we described earlier. How this automatic generation of emotion occurs in terms of the proposed model is discussed next.

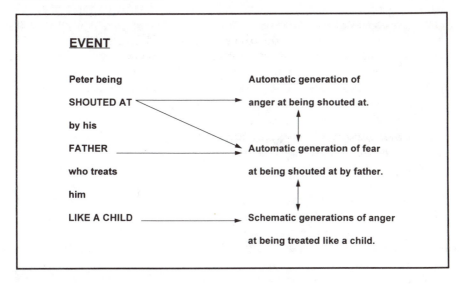

FIG. 5.6. Some of the types of emotion conflict experienced by Peter on being shouted at by his father
↔ = conflict.

The automatic generation of emotions via the associative level of representation.   In addition to the representation architecture we have discussed so far (namely, schematic models, propositional, and analogical representations) and which is outlined in Fig. 5.5, we suggest a further associative level of representation, which is responsible for automatised cognitive processes. Figure 5.7 represents the central components in the model of emotion we are proposing. From this point onwards we shall refer to this architecture as the SPAARS approach (Schematic, Propositional, Analogical, and Associative Representation Systems) to reflect the levels of meaning that are utilised.

We propose that within SPAARS emotions can be generated directly, via an associative level, without concurrent access to the schematic model level of meaning. To understand what we mean by this statement in more detail, it is useful to return once again to the components of the emotional experience, which we outlined following the philosophical analysis in Chapter 2. These were: an event, an interpretation, an appraisal, physiological change, an action potential, and conscious awareness.

In our discussion of emotion generation via schematic models we argued that the process of appraisal consists of an analysis of the interpretation of the event in terms of the individual's extant goals at the schematic model level. The point we wish to make here is that,

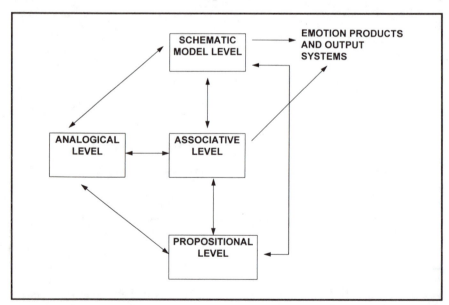

FIG. 5.7. The SPAARS model of emotions showing the four representational systems.

within SPAARS, emotions can be generated without this appraisal process occurring at the time of the event's occurrence. The appraisal only needs to have occurred at some time in the emotional history of the individual's experience of that event or, for a small circumscribed set of events, in the evolutionary history of the species. That is to say, the process of emotion generation can become automatised so that it appears as if a concurrent process of appraisal is occurring even though it is not and has in fact occurred at some time in the emotional past. In other words, the accessing of the schematic model level of meaning is "short-circuited".

Let us illustrate further by returning to the example of Peter and his father. During Peter's childhood, his father's tendency to shout at him about inconsequential things would initially have been appraised at the schematic model level and Peter would have felt afraid. Peter never knew how his father was going to react next. For example, an evening with friends could easily be ruined by a tirade from his father, resulting in his friends being asked to leave. After many repetitions of similar events the generation of fear via schematic level meaning gradually became *automatised*. The emotion of fear was then generated *as if* a concurrent appraisal was occurring (that is, as if schematic-level meaning was being considered) even though it was being short-circuited.

As we have already mentioned, we propose that this second route to the generation of emotions occurs via a separate associative level of representation. In proposing such an additional representation system, two important questions need to be addressed: First, why is it not possible for part of the schematic model level to be the vehicle for automatically generated emotions? And, second, if such a process does occur outside of the schematic model level, why is there a need to posit a separate representational system? Would it not be possible to have direct links between events and emotional output?

As we have noted, we endorse Logan's suggestion that automatic processes represent single-step, direct access to past solutions in memory. These solutions, we submit, are not mere input–output connections but are representations of interrelationships between events and, in this case, emotion products. In a straightforward input–output model the idea of an emotion is lost. How would phobic individuals, for example, "know" that they were afraid, as opposed to angry, or even simply aroused, if their phenomenal experience derived merely from an awareness of the phobic object and any concurrent physiological changes that the object activated? Such an argument might be tenable if it was agreed that emotions can be distinguished reliably on the basis of physiology alone. However, it is not clear that this is the case and we have argued in Chapters 2 and 3 that the physiological systems recruited by the different emotions overlap considerably. An automatically generated emotion obtains its distinctive "feel", we propose, because it is an awareness of both a physiological change and the *content* of an associative representation of the interrelationships of the event with the emotion products at hand.

Granted that automatically generated emotions require more than simple input–output connections, it is incumbent on us to justify why a separate representational system is necessary. It would be functionally equivalent to locate automatically generated emotions in the schematic model level by proposing a "direct" route through that system, as it is to propose a separate associative level of representation. Indeed, the former instantiation is the architectural solution in Interacting Cognitive Sub-systems (ICS; Teasdale & Barnard, 1993; see Chapter 4).

The principal argument for describing automatically generated emotions as a function of a separate associative system is the clear dissociation between them and schematically generated emotions, especially in the clinical domain. Again, phobias are the clearest example; the phobic individual will experience fear or disgust at the phobic object whilst being able to recognise no rationale for such emotions. Furthermore, the fear reaction is invariable in the presence of the phobic object and cannot be modified by cognitive techniques—the phobic individual can talk at length about how there is no reason to be fearful, but be afraid none the less in the presence of the phobic stimulus.

As a final note it is useful to emphasise again the functional equivalence of the choices of placing automatically generated emotions in either the same or in a different system to emotions generated via schematic models. In the final analysis, we are endeavouring to provide a theoretical *framework* that has heuristic value in understanding emotion phenomena. It is our contention that there are clearly two routes to the generation of emotion, that this helps us to understand many aspects of the psychology of emotion, and, finally, that this understanding is *facilitated* by proposing separate representational systems to mediate the two routes. Clearly, the dynamics of emotional life would result from a combination of schematically driven and automatic emotional experience.

There are two further points we would like to make about the automatic generation of emotions within SPAARS before summarising the ideas we have put forward so far. These are, first, to clarify the role of the propositional level of meaning and, second, to outline the conditions under which automatisation occurs.

The role of the propositional level of meaning in the automatic generation of emotions in SPAARS

Earlier in this chapter we noted that the interpretation of an event, that is, the initial analysis of its meaning, can occur at either the propositional or schematic model level and is most usually a function of the two levels interacting. The concept of an interpretation is therefore a way of articulating the interaction of an event with representations of semantic information in memory. So, in the example we have used throughout the book of Susan and the bear, we proposed that essentially a propositional interpretation (e.g. "the bear is going to eat me") occurred and that this was appraised with respect to Susan's extant goals at the schematic model level. Within SPAARS the generation of such propositional interpretations can become automatised in the same way as access to schematic model information. In this case is it *as if* a concurrent interpretation is being made even though it is not. So, if we consider again the example of Julie and her bird phobia it is as if Julie is making interpretations such as "the bird is going to attack me", even though the process of interpretation has in fact become short-circuited. A second function of propositional representations in automatised emotion generation within SPAARS is where an event leads to a propositional interpretation which itself automatically generates emotions. This means that any number of events, if *interpreted* in the same way, could lead to the automatic generation of emotion. Consider the example of David who is a somewhat paranoid individual. For David, a whole series of external events give rise to an interpretation which can be expressed as "I am being cheated". This interpretation has come to generate automatically the emotion of anger through repetition. Finally, the event itself might be a proposition; for example, the thought "I am a failure" might automatically (via the associative level) generate components of the emotions of sadness or disgust (see Chapters 7 and 8). That is to say, at one time in the individual's emotional history the event consisting of the propositional thought "I am a failure" was appraised at the schematic level and the emotions of sadness and/or disgust were generated. Through repetition this process becomes automatised such that the thought "I am a failure" comes to automatically generate those emotions via the associative level. Figure 5.8 illustrates the different ways the propositional level of meaning can be involved in the automatic generation of emotions.

The conditions under which automatisation of emotion generation occurs in SPAARS

Whether or not an emotional response to an event or to an interpretation of an event becomes automatised within SPAARS is not merely a

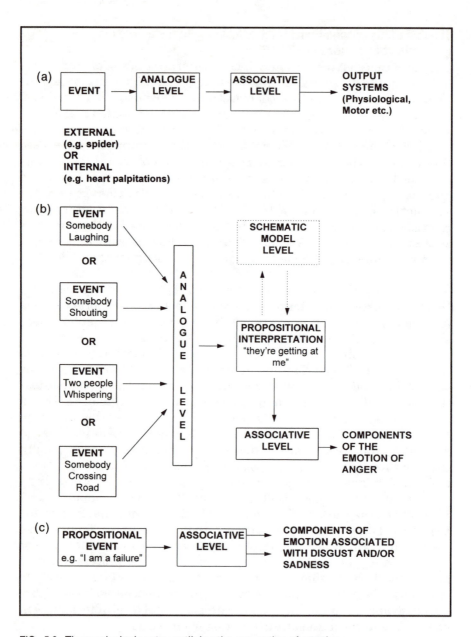

FIG. 5.8. Three principal routes outlining the generation of emotions.
(a) Fully automated emotion generation with no propositional information. (b) Schematised diagram showing how a number of different events can lead to the same propositional interpretation, which then automatically generates anger. (c) Propositional level meaning as an event that automatically leads to emotion generation.

function of repetition, although this is an important consideration. A number of other factors must also be taken into account. We propose that these other factors centre on the salience of the event to the individual's psychological or physical survival during the evolutionary history of the species. Events which throughout evolutionary history have had a high probability of leading to psychological or physical harm are liable to evoke strong emotions and the pathways between the event and these emotional reactions are likely to become automatised more readily. Let us again consider a couple of examples:

Example 1
A couple of hours after finishing a delicious meal of steak in pepper sauce, James felt very sick and in fact was awake all night being ill. The next day he found that even the thought of pepper steak generated strong feelings of disgust. This disgust reaction to peppered steak persisted for a number of years.

Example 2
Five-year-old Julia went to put her cup in the kitchen sink when a large house spider which had been basking near the plug hole ran across her hand and up the side of the sink. Julia screamed and dropped the cup. From that day onwards Julia was terrified of spiders.

These two examples illustrate a number of factors that are important in the automatisation of emotion generation within SPAARS. The first example illustrates the development of the phenomenon of taste aversion (e.g. Garcia & Koelling, 1966); that is, the ability of the system rapidly to learn about foodstuffs that lead to illness. In terms of emotion, it is suggested that emotional reactions to such foodstuffs can become automatised very rapidly such that after a single encounter, the foodstuff in question acquires the ability automatically to evoke feelings such as disgust (this issue is dealt with more fully in Chapter 9 on disgust). The second example illustrates the fact that a number of events seem to mesh with genetically programmed sensitivities for the automatisation of fear responses. This is known as the preparedness hypothesis (Seligman, 1971; see Ohman, Dimberg, & Ost, 1985, for a review)—the events are evolutionarily "prepared" in some way. What is distinctive about these events is that they reflect potential dangers to the survival of prehistoric humans and/or their ancestors such as through predation or disease. Such "events" include, for example, spiders, snakes, heights, enclosed spaces, and blood. Finally, it is possible that some automatic event–emotion pathways are hard-wired; for example, fear in response to large, fast-moving objects (LeDoux, 1993).

Automatic generation of emotions via the associative level within SPAARS—a summary

In this section we have proposed that there is a second method of emotion generation, which occurs automatically via an associative level of representation within SPAARS. This type of emotion generation happens in the absence of any concurrent appraisal process via the schematic model level. With emotions generated in this way it is *as if* a concurrent appraisal is occurring when in fact it has occurred at some point in the emotional past. Essentially, this automatic generation of emotion is a function of frequently occurring aspects of the individual's emotional life being efficiently "handed down" by the schematic model level to a lower level of the system. Emotions can become automatised to external or internal events, to propositional/schematic interpretations, and/or to propositional events. Automatisation of emotion generation within SPAARS is most usually a function of the repetition of event–emotion combinations. However, a number of factors such as taste aversion conditioning or the preparedness of the events can facilitate the automatisation process. Finally, we propose that automatised emotions happen invariably in the presence of the event, are difficult to modify, and are inflexible.

ADDITIONAL CONSTRAINTS AND PROCESSES WITHIN SPAARS

So far in this chapter we have outlined the SPAARS model of emotion with its four basic levels/formats of representation; analogical; propositional; schematic model; and associative. Within this architecture we have proposed two routes to emotion which we have discussed in some detail: (1) via appraisal at the schematic model level; and (2) automatically via the associative level. In this section we elaborate on some of the details of the SPAARS approach by turning to some of the other points generated by our review of theories of emotional order in Chapter 3. These issues are those of consciousness, inhibition, and modularity. Finally, we shall also touch on some of the points generated by the review of theories of emotional disorder in Chapter 4 such as the role of life events, the issue of vulnerability, and the idea of coupling.

First of all, however, having now presented the model in its entirety, we must return to a discussion of schematic models because it is these representations that are the organising principles of the whole SPAARS system.

Schematic models revisited

At different points in the chapter we have underlined the central importance of the schematic model level of representation for an understanding of emotions within SPAARS. We have described how schematic models represent higher-order meaning abstracted from information at other levels of the system (cf. Teasdale & Barnard, 1993). In addition, we have discussed the interactive relationship between schematic models and goals, with the content and structure of the schematic model delineating the sorts of goals generated as well as, itself, being a function of the individual's goal history. Finally, we have proposed that the paradigmatic route to the generation of emotions within SPAARS is via appraisal at the schematic model level of representation.

There remains one further piece to the schematic model jigsaw: their organising role with respect to the rest of SPAARS because SPAARS is conceived of as a self-organising system. The representations which are active at any one time across the different levels are a function of the schematic models which are currently dominant. So, if, for example, generally positive schematic models of the self are dominant, the positive, self-related information will be more active and accessible at the propositional and analogical levels. Furthermore, other aspects of the cognitive system such as attention, perception, and memory may be biased in favour of information congruent with the dominant schematic models. This final aspect of schematic models is elaborated in various ways in the next sections on consciousness, inhibition, and modularity.

The role of consciousness in SPAARS.   In Chapter 3 we stressed the importance of both conscious and unconscious systems in any understanding of emotion. Clearly it is beyond our ambitions to provide anything like a comprehensive discussion of consciousness and the problems it poses for psychology and philosophy. Instead, we shall restrict ourselves to a few necessarily inadequate remarks about the role and place of consciousness within SPAARS.

In SPAARS the content of conscious awareness is a product of the various levels and formats of the system (schematic model, propositional, associative, and analogical). The individual can be aware of images, smells, sounds, and tastes (analogical), of thoughts and language (propositional), and finally of the higher-order schematic meaning these things evoke. In addition, one can be aware of the products of associative level processes; for example, Peter's awareness of his fear at his father's shouting.

Whether or not someone is conscious of the content of these various representational systems depends on both the extent of the person's attention to the information in question, the level of activation of that information in the system, the current configuration of schematic models, and the influence of any inhibitory processes within the system (see later). So, for example, it is possible to close your eyes and concentrate on the sounds you can hear or the sensations in the body or the flow of thoughts, whereas usually most of these sounds or sensations or thoughts may impinge very little on conscious awareness. However, if there is a loud unexpected noise or a sharp bodily twinge or a persistent worry, then we become immediately conscious of it. The information available to consciousness is also a function of the schematic model that currently dominates the system. Incompatible information is often inhibited (see later). Once information is brought into consciousness it can be restructured and re-organised. This executive ability of consciousness extends from manipulation of visual images (e.g. Shepard, 1978) to reconstructing schematic models of the world.

Inhibition

We have touched on the concept of inhibition at various points in the book. In our discussion of networks in Chapter 3 we noted the importance of both inhibitory and facilitatory connections between nodes in a network. We also noted that some of an individual's extant goals will be in an inhibitory relationship with other goals. So, for example, Sally cannot fulfil the goal of staying in and revising for her exams *and* of going out and seeing her partner. This inhibition between goals, as we noted above, applies both within the same level of representation and across different levels of representation.

There are a large number of other phenomena in the psychology of emotion, especially in the clinical domain, which point to the existence of one or more processes of inhibition. These include, for example: the psychodynamic concept of defence processes such as repression and suppression; the experience of emotional numbing; psychogenic amnesia; dissociative states; hysterical blindness; fugue states; alexythymia; psychosomatic conditions; and many others. If one considers defence processes alone, Horowitz (1988b) lists some 28 phenomena which he argues can be viewed as distinctive psychological states (see Table 5.5).

Furthermore, as well as its importance at the level of cognitive architecture (e.g. connectionism) and at the psychological level (e.g.

TABLE 5.5
List of defence mechanisms (based on Horowitz, 1990)

Altruism
Conversion of passive to active
Denial
Devaluation
Disavowal
Displacement
Dissociation
Distortion
Exaggeration
Humour
Idealisation
Intellectualisation
Generalisation
Isolation
Minimisation
Omnipotent control
Passive aggression
Projection
Projective identification
Rationalisation
Reaction formation
Regression
Repression
Somatisation
Splitting
Sublimation
Turning against the self
Undoing

repression), inhibition also operates culturally. So, for example, in certain Malay societies it is seen as inappropriate to express anger (see Chapter 9) and there is "social" inhibition of anger expression. In this section we shall try to draw together a number of ideas concerning inhibition and present them in the context of the SPAARS framework.

First, it is important to distinguish between two uses of the term inhibition in the psychological literature (Bjork, 1989; Dalgleish, 1991). One usage, the term "passive" inhibition, is a description of the strengthening or activating of incompatible or alternative representations to the one that is being inhibited. So, for example, Fiona, who is having a bad time at work, might wish to forget about her job whilst on holiday. As a result, whenever anybody mentions work or whenever she finds herself thinking about work, she changes the subject or distracts herself by thinking about something else. Information about work is passively inhibited by virtue of Fiona attending to other things. A more controversial formulation of the inhibition process is what might be called "active" inhibition. In this case representations are again rendered less accessible; however, this lack of processing is not the result of attending to incompatible or alternative information but is a function of some direct inhibitory process. So, for example, John may have been abused as a child but have no memory of the abuse. One analysis of this situation utilises the concept of direct active inhibition of the abuse memories which prevent their entry into awareness.

Passive inhibition is an accepted phenomenon in the clinical and cognitive literature (e.g. Bower, 1990). In contrast, the process of active inhibition has so far gained little currency (though some of the literature on directed forgetting and negative priming is an exception e.g. Geiselman, Bjork, & Fishman, 1983). Bjork (1989) offers several explanations for this lack of enthusiasm for active inhibition. He argues that the standard computer metaphor, which has motivated cognitive research since the late 1950s, is incompatible with notions such as inhibition and suppression. He also states (1989, p.310) that: "notions of inhibition or suppression in human memory have an unappealing association to certain poorly understood clinical phenomena, such as repression". Despite the paucity of theoretical debate within cognitive psychology concerning the existence and role of inhibitory processes in memory, we propose that there is a clear role for both active and passive inhibitory processes within SPAARS and in this section we embroider upon this initial distinction.

The pattern of inhibition within SPAARS is dictated by the individuals' dominant schematic models (see above) which are mirrored in their active goal structures. So, for example, an individual could have dominant schematic models representing the world as a safe place {WORLD—SAFE}, themselves as reasonably successful likeable people {LIKEABLE—SELF—SUCCESSFUL}, their friends as loyal dependable people {LOYAL—FRIENDS—DEPENDABLE}, and so on. All incoming information will be interpreted in terms of these dominant models of the world, self, and others. The system as a whole will seek to integrate new information with the existing models. This process of bringing the old and the new into some kind of harmony has been termed the completion process by Horowitz (e.g. 1986), or achieving Gestalt, without which the system would tend towards chaos. Information which is incompatible with an individual's dominant schematic models and thus resists such integration can either be ignored or reinterpreted. For example, most of us have experienced the truth of the saying "love is blind" when we have ignored or explained away faults in those with whom we are besotted. These faults are incompatible with our schematic model of that person as perfect for us. Some information, however, cannot be ignored or explained away in this fashion because it is too significant. For example, somebody who suffered the trauma of being raped by a friend would have experienced too serious a challenge to her abstracted schematic models such as {WORLD—SAFE} or {FRIENDS—DEPENDABLE} to "ignore" the new incompatible information concerning the rape. In this case something must give; either the models will be rejected or "shattered" (Janoff-Bulman, 1985), or the new information might be inhibited both passively and actively in order to try to preserve the extant models (see Chapter 6).

In addition to this inhibition of salient information that is incompatible with an individual's active schematic representations, it is proposed that within SPAARS whole alternative schematic models of the world, the self, and others can become established, which are inhibited most of the time but have the potential to dominate the system, for example, in times of stress or in particular emotional states (e.g. Power, 1987a). The establishment of these alternative models of the self, the world, and others is most likely to occur during childhood when the dominant models are themselves becoming established. The existence of inhibited alternative models of self, world, and others, which are incompatible with the dominant models makes such individuals vulnerable (see Chapter 4) to the onset of emotional disorder when events occur which mesh with the normally inhibited models, thus allowing them to dominate the system. To illustrate, let us consider a familiar example from the depression literature:

> Joan was always criticised by her parents as a child. However hard she tried, nothing she did ever seemed good enough. Her parents always seemed to think she could do better. Perhaps not surprisingly, Joan did very well at school and won a place at a top university where she excelled. She turned out to be a confident and successful career woman. Joan's parents were exceedingly proud of her achievements and they told her that they had always pushed her as a child for her own good in order that she could realise the success she now had. Inevitably Joan had the odd setback or life event and it was remarkable how even the slightest sign that she had failed in some way could send her tailspinning into a depressed state in which everything looked gloomy.

Within SPAARS one would account for Joan's plight by proposing that, as a child, Joan had developed schematic models of herself as a failure and as never being good enough {FAILURE—SELF—NEVER GOOD ENOUGH}. Later, as she grew older, Joan developed healthier models centred on her success and developing confidence—the old models became inhibited. However, as soon as events conspired against her and meshed with these old inhibited models of {FAILURE—

SELF—NEVER GOOD ENOUGH} the models became reactivated and dominated the system. It is as if Joan is putting on the opposite of a pair of rose-tinted spectacles, that is, a pair of spectacles that make everything look black and gloomy, and she suddenly sees everything through these new lenses—these reawakened models of the self (Power, 1987a). Similar ideas have been put forward in other theories of emotional disorder. For example, in our review of Beck's work in Chapter 4 we discussed his idea of latent schemata, which are formed in childhood and reactivated in later life following some form of congruent life event.

It is proposed that groups of active schematic models are organised together within SPAARS in a coherent fashion within the different domains of knowledge we have discussed. So, for example, models of the self might be organised around a central theme of the self as an individual with many broadly positive aspects. Models of the self that are incompatible with this organising theme are those most likely to be inhibited. Similarly, models of the world are organised in a coherent fashion. A model of the world as a generally safe place is likely to coexist with a model of the world as a just place and so on. Compatible schematic models such as these mutually activate each other and serve to inhibit incompatible models.

The inhibition of alternative incompatible schematic models has a knock-on effect throughout the different levels of SPAARS. At the propositional level, activated representations of past events and the generation of current thoughts will normally be congruent with the dominant schematic models. Thoughts and memories which are incongruent with the dominant models and/or congruent with the inhibited models may either be inhibited from coming into awareness or dismissed if they do enter awareness. Similarly, analogue representations of visual memories which are incompatible with the dominant models will be inhibited. However, if and when inhibited models come to dominate the system, these thoughts and images quickly become available to consciousness.

The extent of the inhibition of either new information which is incompatible with an individual's active models or of alternative schematic models can vary considerably. In the most extreme case the individual might experience dissociative states or even multiple personality disorder. Consider an example offered by Spiegel and Cardena (1990, pp.25–26):

> A young man's car broke down on a heavily travelled freeway. As he was trying to examine the car, he was struck by an intoxicated motorcyclist attempting to escape the pursuing

highway patrol. He was severely injured, both legs were broken, and one later required amputation. He lay injured on the freeway in the midst of oncoming traffic. His friends were begging him to get off the road, and at first he protested that he could not move, but at the suggestion of a friend he started to think about one of his favourite places, a fishing lodge where he and his father went. He found himself concentrating almost entirely on the experience of fishing, got up, and walked off the freeway on his badly injured legs. He experienced no pain at all until several hours later when his leg was being manipulated for X-ray.

As the authors argue (p.26): "This unfortunate young man had clearly separated, or dissociated, himself from the traumatic experience while it was occurring, keeping his shock, pain, and fear out of conscious awareness, even though he at no time lost consciousness." In instances such as these, there seems to be strong active inhibition separating one existential space from another.

The interaction of inhibition and emotion within SPAARS—emotion modules and the inhibition of emotional experience. We have proposed in the preceding two sections that the configuration of the SPAARS system is a function of the dominant schematic models and is maintained by a combination of facilitation and inhibition throughout the system. What is the interaction between these processes and emotion?

We have stressed throughout that emotions have functionality and we have proposed a cognitive theory of emotions in the present chapter which employs the concept of roles and goals to provide a language for the functionality of emotions. The basic emotions of anger, fear, sadness, disgust, and happiness are functional processes, which operate when valued goal states are affected in different ways. So, for example, fear operates when a valued goal is threatened. The functionality of these emotion processes is manifested in the emotion "taking over" the SPAARS system which is reconfigured such that all of the constituent parts are employed in resolving the goal-related events that instigated the emotion (cf. Oatley & Johnson-Laird, 1987; see Chapter 3). So, in the case of fear, for example, the system will be configured to deal with the current threat and the environment will be monitored for future threat. This emotional imperialism—the reconfiguration of the system as a function of the generated emotion—can perhaps best be conceptualised as the activation of an emotion module. Once the emotion module is activated, the system is configured in a certain way and other configurations of the system are inhibited. We use the term module here in its functional sense (Gazzaniga, 1988), rather than as a label for distinct systems of the brain. That is, we are adopting the notion of software modularity as opposed to hardware modularity.

In most circumstances, we suggest, emotion modules cease to dominate the system when the instigating event circumstances are altered. So, in the case of fear, when the event which acts as a threat to the individual's goal has passed or has been reconceptualised as non-threatening, then the fear module will cease to be active. However, there are a number of circumstances in which this relatively smooth functional transition in and out of emotional states and their corresponding SPAARS configurations does not take place.

Individuals can become "locked" into a particular emotion module such that it becomes very difficult to revert back to previous functioning. This idea has been expressed in different ways in a number of other models of emotional order and disorder. For example, Beck and Emery (1985) put forward the idea of danger schemata in their discussion of anxiety disorders (see Chapter 3). Within Beck's model, anxiety-prone individuals possess latent danger schemata which contain information about danger and fear and can lead the individual to view and interpret the world in a distorted, danger-related way. In the presence of a stressor, such danger schemata can become activated and the individual is seemingly locked within this distorted, anxiety-laden conception of existence. Within SPAARS a characteristic of being stuck within a particular emotion module is that this state is maintained by the different components of SPAARS reciprocally activating each other, or becoming *interlocked* (cf. Teasdale & Barnard, 1993). For example, a given set of events might lead to the automatic generation of fear via the associative level. This is in turn may lead to propositional and schematic interpretations which trigger the generation of fear via the schematic model route. This in turn may automatically generate more fear via the associative level and so on. An excellent account of this type of interlock is provided by Teasdale and Barnard (1993) for the case of depression. Here higher-order models such as "self as failure" lead to propositional thoughts such as "I am a failure" or "the future is hopeless". These thoughts in turn strengthen the higher-order model, and so on.

The final circumstance in which the activation and deactivation of emotion modules can become dysfunctional is when the experience and expression of one or more emotions becomes inhibited as a function of the individual's learning history. For example, in Albert Camus' (1958) novel *L'Etranger*, the anti-hero is so emotionally disconnected from his world that he feels nothing but indifference to his own mother's death.

This inaccessibility of one or more basic emotions is commonly encountered in the clinic. Consider the following example:

> Ann was referred for therapy because she kept experiencing intrusive and disturbing thoughts and images in which her husband was killed or horribly mutilated in a car or plane crash. It emerged that Ann's husband spent a lot of time travelling away from home and that even when he was home he often seemed distant. A year earlier Ann had discovered that her husband was having an affair which was now over. Ann was very upset by the content of her intrusions; she loved her husband very much and was very happy as they had a comfortable life due to the money his job brought in. During the course of therapy Ann started to become angry with her husband, culminating in a series of angry outbursts which felt alien and ego-dystonic to her. She had never been an angry person and could not remember having lost her temper before.

This quasi-dissociation of one or more basic emotion modules and the subsequent feeling of ego dystonia when the emotion is experienced is, we propose, a result of the individual's developmental history in which the expression of certain, or indeed any, emotions was prevented or discouraged; for example, because it was considered inappropriate. We propose that within SPAARS, an event which satisfies the core appraisal parameters for an emotion, for example a blocked goal with an attribution of agency for anger, will lead simultaneously to the activation of in this case anger-related products, but also to the activation of schematic models which immediately inhibit the experience of the emotion. In this analysis, the individual will undergo physiological changes associated with emotion but will not experience that emotion. The schematic models that act to repress the experience, we suggest, are essentially the internalisation of a developmental history that socialised against the experience of such emotions.

The coupling of emotions

The final process within SPAARS we wish to discuss is the proposal that emotion modules themselves can become coupled. Emotions can become coupled within SPAARS in two ways: first, the generation of one emotion can initiate the generation of a second emotion which, in turn, initiates the generation of the first emotion and so on; second, the same event can lead to the simultaneous generation of two or more emotions. Let us illustrate with some examples:

Example 1:
Anna gets very anxious about things in her life. Her feelings of fear and anxiety always make her feel sad and depressed as she dwells on what she has missed out on as a result of her problems. Such feelings of sadness in turn make her anxious that things will never change and she becomes caught in a self-perpetuating cycle of emotions of anxiety, fear, and sadness.

Example 2:
Looking back over events from when he was a young student, Ed becomes nostalgic. He feels happy as he remembers the good times he had but, at the same time, sad as he dwells on the fact that those times are in the past.

The first example, then, illustrates the cyclical coupling of two basic emotion states which reciprocally activate each other. Such coupling can also occur when an emotion module activates itself as in fear of fear or depression about depression. So, for example, as we shall see in our discussion of panic in Chapter 6, it is possible for the experience of fear to become the object of fear such that the individual becomes locked in a vicious circle in which fear activates fear. In contrast, the second example illustrates how two emotions can be generated by the same event; often giving rise to a complex emotion such as, in this case, nostalgia.

A note on complex emotions

For ease of explication, we have restricted the examples we have used in this chapter to basic emotions such as fear or anger. It is therefore useful to clarify the ways in which so-called complex emotions can be derived from the basic five. We propose three routes to the generation of complex emotions within SPAARS:

1. A coupling of two basic emotions: for example, sadness and happiness can become coupled to generate the emotion of nostalgia.
2. Further appraisal cycles which embroider on those necessary for the generation of the basic emotion: for example, the emotion of indignation would be an experience of anger combined with an appraisal that the object of the anger is a social inferior.
3. The integration of appraisals relating to the goals of others: for example, empathy can be derived from the emotion of sadness combined with an appreciation of another's lost goals.

CONCLUSIONS

In this chapter we have drawn together the summary points from Chapters 2, 3, and 4 and used them as the starting point for the construction of a multi-level model of emotion, an approach which we have labelled SPAARS (Schematic, Propositional, Analogical, and Associative Representational Systems).

We have described the model in three broad sections: the content of the mental representations involved; the various formats these representations take; and the processes which act on the representations. The basic architecture of the model is a multi-representational one and has much in common with other multi-representational approaches to emotion, particularly, MEMs (e.g. Johnson & Multhaup, 1992) and ICS (e.g. Teasdale & Barnard, 1993) which both include sub-systems or levels representing higher-order meaning and ones which reflect basic propositional and analogical properties of the information space. It is this class of approaches which we believe offers the most powerful framework within which to consider emotions. In addition to the basic architecture, SPAARS has a number of properties which are an extension of existing multi-level models. In SPAARS, emotions are primarily appraisal-based and appraisals are a function of goals; thus, within SPAARS, emotions are explicitly functional and the model is couched in functional language. Furthermore, goals are a function of separate domains of mind content involving the self, the world, and others. Within SPAARS there are two routes to the generation of emotion: the paradigmatic schematic model route and an associatively driven automatic route. Emotions generated via either route are seen as modules which act as reconfigurations of the SPAARS system. Such reconfigurations are partly maintained via processes of inhibition which are a central feature of the SPAARS approach and inhibition processes are also implicated in other ways within the model. Finally, the SPAARS approach uses the five basic emotions of Happiness, Disgust, Fear, Sadness, and Anger as building blocks and the proposal is that emotional order and emotional disorder can be derived from these basic components.

None of these ideas is completely new and we have devoted Part One of the book to tracing their origins and development. However, we hope that the SPAARS framework that we have presented in this chapter combines the strengths of a number of different approaches to emotion while avoiding some of the weaknesses.

The second part of the book is organised into five chapters, each concentrating on one of the five basic emotions mentioned above and discussed in Chapter 3; namely, Fear, Sadness, Anger, Disgust, and

Happiness. In each chapter we discuss the literature on the normal variant of the emotion. We shall then discuss so-called abnormal manifestations of the emotion and the theories that have been proposed to account for these emotional disorders. We also consider complex emotions derived from the basic emotions.

We shall use these chapters not only to provide comprehensive reviews of the literature concerning each basic emotion but to illustrate some of the strengths of the SPAARS approach. This does not mean that we shall attempt an analysis of all aspects of emotional experience within the SPAARS model. Rather, we shall expand on different aspects of the model at different points in Part Two of the book in the hope that the SPAARS approach will offer a new take on some familiar and some less familiar aspects of emotional order and disorder. So, for example, we concentrate on a discussion of cycles of appraisal in Chapter 8 on Anger, on the coupling of basic emotion modules in Chapter 7 on Sadness, and on the explanatory power of two routes to emotion in Chapter 6 on Fear. However, for some aspects of emotional order and disorder we do present a more complete analysis within the SPAARS approach; for example, the section on post-traumatic stress in Chapter 6.

A final chapter presents an overall summary and discusses some of the clinical and research implications of the SPAARS model as well as some considerations of the future direction of work in the cognition and emotion field.

PART TWO

Basic emotions and their disorders

CHAPTER SIX

Fear

Life is made of fear. Some people eat fear soup three times a day. Some people eat fear soup all the meals there are. I eat it sometimes. When they bring me fear soup to eat, I try not to eat it, I try to send it back. But sometimes I'm too afraid to and have to eat it anyway.
Don't eat fear soup. Send it back.
(Other People, *Martin Amis, 1981*)

INTRODUCTION

A pregnant woman feels terrified that she will give birth to a monster; a man shopping in a supermarket suddenly panics and, throwing people out of the way, runs from the shop; a young girl never goes to parties or out for a drink because she is afraid that everybody will laugh at her; a veteran of the Vietnam war dives for cover in his local high street when a car backfires; a middle-aged married woman spends her days and most of her nights worrying about her relationship, her job, and her personal finances; a young man is anxious before being interviewed for his first job; Susan is terrified and runs away when she comes across a bear in the woods; an old lady is frightened when she hears a noise in her house in the middle of the night. These are all examples of the order and disorder of fear. Fear is the emotion theorist's favourite emotion because it seems so vital and functional when it works and so dysfunctional and disabling when it goes awry. Normal, healthy fear is functional in that it prepares and empowers the individual for fight or flight in the presence of appraised danger. Furthermore, the different components of the fear experience are clear: physiological arousal such as butterflies in the stomach, tension in the muscles, perspiration, dry mouth, and so on; cognitions such as thoughts about being in danger or of dying; and behavioural components such as avoiding the feared stimulus, running away, or fighting. For these reasons, fear is the prototypical example of emotional order. However, the divide between emotional order and emotional disorder can be breached in so many ways in the case of fear: phobias, panic attacks, post-traumatic stress disorder (PTSD), obsessions, pathological worry; these are all labels for types of disordered fear or anxiety.

Throughout the book, we have frequently used the emotion of everyday fear as an example to illustrate the philosophical and psychological issues that arise from the study of emotions. In addition, we took fear as the prototypical emotion in our development of the SPAARS model in Chapter 5. Consequently, we shall do little more than review these issues here, before going on to discuss the varieties of abnormal fear in some detail.

NORMAL FEAR AND ANXIETY

To review the conceptualisation of fear within the SPAARS framework it might be useful to consider a new example; after all, Susan has been running from the bear for so long now that she is almost certainly exhausted. Let us consider a common example from the cognitive therapy literature (e.g. Beck et al., 1979). Imagine the event of a loud noise in your house (in which you are alone) in the middle of the night. There are a number of interpretations of such an event; for example, one might interpret the noise as evidence of an intruder—"There is an intruder in the house—he might come up the stairs—he might kill me ...". Such an interpretation is likely to be appraised at the schematic model level within SPAARS as one pertaining to threat and to lead to the generation of the physiological arousal components associated with fear and, thus, the experience of the emotion of fear. A schematic diagram of this process within SPAARS is presented in Fig. 6.1.

The reason that the example of the noise in the night is used in cognitive therapy is that there are, of course, *alternative* interpretations of such an event. For example, the noise may merely be the cat patrolling its territory downstairs. Such a feline interpretation is unlikely to lead

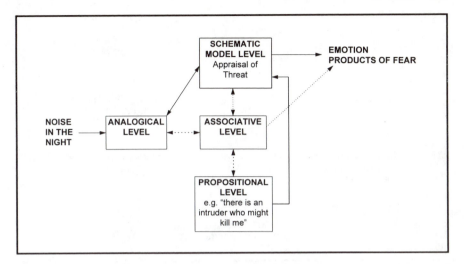

FIG. 6.1. Generation of fear within SPAARS following a noise in the night.

to the generation of fear. Hypothetical scenarios such as the intruder/cat example are used to indicate to the client that the way we think about (or interpret) things determines the way we feel about them. However, having used this example to illustrate to a client this very point, one of us (TD) was presented with an alternative illustrating that things are never quite that simple (see Fig. 6.2).

The cat/intruder example, we suggest, illustrates the generation of fear via the schematic model level of meaning within SPAARS. However, as we have discussed in Chapter 5, there are two routes to emotion within SPAARS and it is possible for fear to be generated automatically via the associative level. For example, in Chapter 5 we presented the case of Peter who throughout his childhood had been shouted at and bullied by his father. As an adult, Peter experienced the automatic generation of both anger and fear at the sound of the father's raised voice. In this case, we have argued, the repetition of the appraisal-based generation of fear had become automatised during Peter's development and became part of the emotional baggage he carried as an adult.

For most of us the automatic generation of fear is a frequent occurrence. In our everyday lives we continually encounter events and stimuli that send a shiver down our spine because of the automatic fear reaction they induce. A number of these automatic fear responses will be the result of repeated experiences of events as in the case of Peter. Yet others will be reactions to stimuli that may be biologically prepared in some way (Seligman, 1971) such that we only need one bad encounter with them or to see someone else react fearfully to become afraid

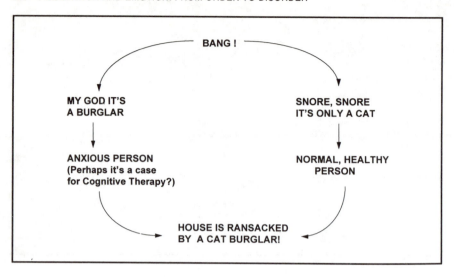

FIG. 6.2. The perils of cognitive therapy.

ourselves. Such stimuli include spiders, snakes, rats, mice, heights, and so on. Finally, some event attributes such as "fast-moving" or "approaching" seem to induce innate fear reactions.

Such automatically generated fear often leads to feelings of conflict. Feeling afraid of things which we think we should not be afraid of or which society deems as non-threatening, is a common occurrence and individuals often go to some lengths to avoid embarrassing situations such as finding themselves screaming because of the harmless mouse nibbling crumbs on the kitchen worktop. Sometimes such avoidance can become disabling and the fear can become disordered; we consider this later in this chapter and in Chapter 9 when we discuss phobias.

So, what sorts of things most commonly elicit normal fear? One of the first truly systematic studies to address this question and survey the types and extent of fear in the normal population was carried out by Agras, Sylvester, and Oliveau (1969) who interviewed randomly chosen residents of Burlington, Vermont about their fears. There are a number of methodological difficulties with the study; however, the principle findings are as follows: the most commonly reported fear was one of snakes, with 25% of the sample expressing intense levels of such fear; the second most common fear was that of heights; also high on the list were fears of public places and transport, fear of injury, and fear of illness. A larger community study was carried out by Costello (1982) with a sample of 449 women. The results indicated that animal fears were again most prevalent, followed by fears of tunnels, heights, and enclosed spaces. Next came social fears, fears of mutilation, and fears of separation. As a rider to this, it is important to note that studies in children (e.g. Rutter, 1984) reveal a slightly different fear taxonomy and that many childhood fears such as fear of the dark disappear with age.

These data generate a number of interesting issues regarding the relationship of normal, common fears and abnormal fears or anxiety. First, some of the most common fears appear to be of the "irrational" type we considered previously, in that the feared event or object is neither dangerous nor consciously thought to be so by the individual concerned (e.g. house spiders). Second, a number of such common fears, whether rational or not, differ from those most commonly seen in clinical settings (for example, animal fears are rarely seen in the clinic). So, although these fears might meet some psychiatric definition of phobia (e.g. the *Diagnostic and Statistical Manual of Mental Disorders*, 4th edition [DSM-IV]; American Psychiatric Association, 1994), they are in fact quite normal and non-pathological. Third, fears of events or objects that reason would demand are fearful or threatening are relatively uncommon; for example, driving at speed (Rachman, 1990) is hardly ever cited as a cause of fear in the normal population. Finally, as we have suggested above, the distribution of human fears appears to be non-random—some fears (for example, the fear of snakes) are very common whilst others are extremely rare. This confirms that a number of common fears, at least, are biologically "prepared" in some way (Seligman, 1971) and, as a consequence, the things of which we are most afraid are those most likely presenting the greatst danger to our primitive ancestors rather than those most threatening in contemporary society.

Components of the emotion of fear

In line with our discussion of the components of emotion throughout the book, we see fear as comprising: an event; an interpretation; an appraisal; physiological arousal; conscious awareness; and, in the paradigm case, overt behaviour (see Chapter 2). However, before considering some of these components in detail, it is important to review briefly other deconstructions of the fear response; most notably the work of Peter Lang, which we have considered more fully in Chapter 3.

Lang (e.g. 1977, 1979, 1984, 1985) argues that the data of anxiety, as distinct from what he describes (1985; p.131) as the "feeling state, i.e., a direct experience or internal apprehension, requiring no further definition", are: (1) verbal reports of distress; (2) fear-related behavioural acts such as avoidance or hypervigilance; and (3) patterns of visceral and somatic activation. Lang's analysis of fear has been highly influential in research on anxiety and so-called anxiety disorders (see, for example, the work of Foa in the later section on PTSD) and has received considerable empirical and theoretical support. For example, one of the empirical foundation stones of Lang's tripartite analysis is evidence showing the desynchrony of the three components (e.g. Rachman & Hodgson, 1974). That is, the finding that therapeutic intervention can modulate the three sub-systems at different rates so that, for example, an individual with an animal phobia might show a reduction in behavioural aspects of fear such as avoidance but with no reduction in reported fear or symptoms of physiological arousal (Lang, 1964, 1968).

Lang's deconstruction of the emotion of fear has much in common with the philosophical analysis of emotions derived in Chapter 2. The principal difference is that Lang seems most concerned with the available data of fear—that which the clinician or researcher is able to work with in understanding the phenomenon. In contrast, the analysis outlined in Chapter 2, and employed throughout the rest of the book, is principally concerned with what the components of a given emotion might be, irrespective of their accessibility to behavioural investigation. Despite this, both Lang's analysis and the one used here broadly recognise phenomenological, behavioural, cognitive ("verbal"), and physiological components of the fear response and in this section we consider these factors in more detail.

Appraisals involved in the emotion of fear.   In the emotion of fear, we propose that the first analysis by the appraisal system within SPAARS, as for all negative emotions (see Chapter 5), is that the event/interpretation is appraised as incompatible in some way with existing goals and/or models of the self, world, and other. The second cycle of the appraisal system, and the first specific to the emotion of fear, is the appraisal of threat; that is, the appraisal that there is a chance of future non-completion of valued goals. Further levels of appraisal might concern whether the threat is unwanted, whether or not the threat can be successfully avoided, and so on. These levels of appraisal are illustrated in Fig. 6.3.

That fear can be a function of the first two levels of appraisal alone seems evident to us all the time. When we sit strapped in to the roller coaster before it starts, we cannot help feeling a tingle of fear, even though we have chosen to be there. The appraisal that the threat is "wanted" makes no difference.

Physiological components of the fear response.   We all know what it's like to feel afraid; we may sweat more, feel flushed, experience changes in our breathing, increases in heart rate, intestinal discomfort,

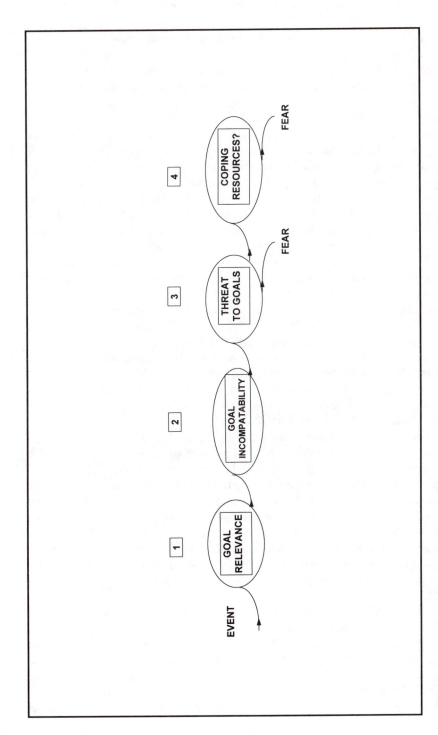

FIG. 6.3. Cycles of appraisal involved in the generation of fear.

muscular tension, dry mouth, butterflies in the stomach, and so on. There has been an enormous amount of research and theoretical discussion on the physiological subsystems which subsume these experiences of fear and a number of excellent reviews are provided in Tuma and Maser's (1985) encyclopaedic, book *Anxiety and the Anxiety Disorders*. The important point which we would like to emphasise here about the physiological components of fear is that the majority of factor analytic work, on both observed and self-reported symptoms of fear or anxiety, suggests a clear distinction between such physiological or somatic reactivity and cognitive or psychic components of fear or anxiety; for example, intrusive and unwanted thoughts, worries, and ruminations (Buss, 1962; Fenz & Epstein, 1965; Schalling, Cronholm, & Asberg, 1975). This distinction mirrors Lang's tripartite analysis of fear which we discussed earlier and, as we shall see, also has clear implications for an understanding of fear order and fear disorder.

We suggest that physiological changes are but one component of what we have called the fear module (see Chapter 5). When fear is generated, either via the appraisal route or automatically via the associative route, then the fear module "takes over" the SPAARS system which reconfigures to deal with the appraised threat. Such reconfiguration serves to bias associated attention systems to the detection of further threat (Dalgleish & Watts, 1990; Eysenck, 1992; Williams et al., 1988) and prepares the individual for action—the fight or flight response.

A note on anxiety and its relationship with fear

The relationship between the emotion of fear and the experience of anxiety rouses considerable debate within the psychology literature. For example, *DSM-IV* (American Psychiatric Association, 1994, p.392) proposes that the term anxiety denotes "apprehension, tension or uneasiness that stems from the anticipation of danger, which may be internal or external", a definition, we suggest, which could just as readily apply to fear. One possible difference, it is argued, (e.g. see Ohman, 1993) between anxiety and fear is that the former lacks a recognisable external source of threat. However, an alternative analysis has been proposed by, amongst others Epstein (1972), that external stimuli are insufficient to distinguish fear and anxiety. Epstein submits that fear is related to action (particularly escape and avoidance) in a way that anxiety is not. Anxiety, he suggests, is what happens when fear-related action (namely flight) is blocked or thwarted. In other words, anxiety is unresolved fear or, as Ohman (1993) has suggested, anxiety is "a state of undirected arousal following the perception of threat". It is this latter definition, in our view, which has the most mileage and, for the purposes of this chapter, anxiety is conceptualised as a state in which the individual is unable to instigate a clear pattern of behaviour to remove or alter the event/object/interpretation that is threatening an existing goal.

This discussion of anxiety inevitably brings us to the question of worry—the ruminative process we indulge in, in order to deal with threats which do not seem to go away. In this respect, worry is clearly a functional process. It allows us to review options, construct schematic models of possible outcomes and to make suitable plans. Despite this common and adaptive role of worry, most theories of worry focus on the pathological form whereby individuals become overwhelmed by concerns in various domains. Consequently, we leave discussion of the main theories of worry until later in the chapter when we consider generalised anxiety states.

In summary, in this first part of the chapter we have considered normal fear and anxiety. As we have noted, fear has been the emotion we have turned to most often to illustrate various philosophical and psychological points in the previous five chapters and we have chosen not to reiterate those points here. Consequently, the balance of the present chapter tilts somewhat towards fear disorder. However, we must emphasise that this is not to imply that fear is necessarily any more pathological than the other basic emotions.

DISORDERED FEAR AND ANXIETY

Fear and anxiety can become disordered in a variety of ways. We can experience excessive fear to relatively harmless objects or we can develop beliefs that certain things are threatening or harmful when they are not. In other situations fear or anxiety can seem appropriate but overgeneralised such as in post-traumatic reactions or chronic worry. The challenge for any theory which seeks to explain both fear order and fear disorder is to account for these varieties of abnormal fear without making them seem like discrete pathological entities. Balancing this is the need to integrate new ideas with the existing literature on disordered fear, which is centred around the so-called anxiety disorders. In this second half of the chapter we have elected to use the anxiety disorder categories to organise our discussion of fear disorder. We must emphasise, however, that this by no means reflects a belief on our part that anxiety disorders are qualitatively different from normal fear reactions.

Within psychiatric classification systems such as *DSM-IV* (American Psychiatric Association, 1994), disorders of fear are labelled something like: Phobias, Post-traumatic Stress Disorder, Panic Disorder, and

Generalised Anxiety Disorder. The symptoms of each of these disorders of fear can be listed as follows (based on Ohman, 1993):

Phobias. Feeling panicky; sweating; tachycardia; difficulty breathing.

Post-traumatic stress disorder. Difficulty falling or staying asleep; irritability or outbursts of anger; difficulty concentrating; hyper-vigilance; exaggerated startle; enhanced physiological reactivity to relevant stimuli.

Panic disorder. Shortness of breath; dizziness, unsteady feeling, or faintness; palpitations or tachycardia; trembling and shaking; sweating; choking; nausea or abdominal distress; depersonalisation or derealisation; numbness or tingling sensation; flushes (hot flashes) or chills; chest pain or discomfort; fear of dying; fear of going crazy or doing something uncontrolled.

Generalised anxiety disorder. Trembling, twitching, or feeling shaky; muscle tension, aches, or soreness; restlessness; easily fatigued; shortness of breath; palpitations or tachycardia; sweating or cold, clammy hands; dry mouth; dizziness or lightheadedness; nausea or abdominal distress; flushes or chills; frequent urination; trouble swallowing ("lump in throat"); feeling keyed up or on edge; exaggerated startle response; difficulty concentrating or blank mind; trouble falling or staying asleep; irritability.

So, if individuals experience frequent, recurrent, unexpected panic attacks combined with concern about such attacks and worry about the implications of such attacks, then they are considered to be suffering from a panic disorder. Phobias, in contrast to panic attacks where the nosological focus is on the symptoms of fear or anxiety, are defined with respect to the avoided situations. So, social phobics exhibit excessive and inappropriate fear of situations involving putative scrutiny by others or situations in which there is a perceived risk of embarrassment or humiliation. Specific phobias involve fear that is focused on specific, discrete stimuli such as small animals, heights, blood, receiving an injection, etc. The individual with the specific phobia recognises that the fear is excessive or unreasonable and avoids the fear-provoking stimulus.

When the fear reaction is a result of exposure to a traumatic, possibly life-threatening event, then the individual may be thought of as suffering from post-traumatic stress disorder (PTSD) in which: the traumatic event is persistently "re-experienced" (for example in the form of nightmares); stimuli or events associated with the trauma are persistently avoided (for example, via emotional numbing); and the individual experiences symptoms of hyperarousal (for example, irritability).

In manifestations of disordered fear in which the emotional response is not a discrete episode, as in panic disorder, or is not instigated by a specific event or situation, as in phobias or PTSD, then disordered fear can take the form of generalised anxiety disorder (GAD). In GAD, the individual is bothered by excessive anxiety and worry about life circumstances such as financial problems, health, relationships, and so on. Such worry is accompanied by symptoms of fear.

The final so-called anxiety disorder within psychiatric classification systems is Obsessive Compulsive Disorder (OCD). However, no fear symptoms are usually listed for this disorder and a detailed consideration of OCD is, therefore, outside the scope of our ambitions within this chapter. Instead, we present a brief analysis of those obsessions we believe to be fear based and offer further discussion in Chapter 9, in which we suggest that some types of OCD can be considered as the coupling of disgust and fear, rather than being derived from fear alone.

When the symptoms of fear/anxiety characteristic of each of the different so-called anxiety disorders are listed side by side as above, as Ohman (1993, p.514) notes:

> There is a striking overlap among them. It is clear that these clinical symptoms can easily be subsumed under the headings of "Somatic Overactivity" versus "Cognitive/ Psychic Activity" ... The somatic symptoms seem to be dominant in panic and in phobic responses, whereas cognitive symptoms are more prevalent in PTSD and particularly in generalised anxiety disorder.

We broadly concur with Ohman's analysis; however, we shall argue in this chapter that different anxiety disorders represent disordered processing involving either the interpretation, the appraisal, or the physiological activity components within the SPAARS framework with the disorder focusing on either the automatic, direct access generation of fear of the appraisal-based, schematic model route. In illustration, we consider in some detail panic disorder, generalised anxiety disorder and post-traumatic stress disorder, offering first a description of the characteristics of the disorder, then a review of extant cognitive theories and research , and finally, in the case of panic disorder, a brief re-analysis in terms of the two routes to emotion in SPAARS, and, in the case of PTSD, a much more detailed analysis of the disorder within the SPAARS framework. The remaining so-called anxiety disorders (simple phobias, social phobia, and some types of OCD) are considered only briefly here and are revisited in Chapter 9 on Disgust.

Panic

> Mary was a 23-year-old woman with a family history of schizophrenia. At the age of 18, Mary suffered a bad viral complaint and one evening when she was feeling particularly under the weather, she started to become very anxious about her blocked throat, her headache, and her fuzzy thinking. The anxiety seemed to build and build until Mary went into a complete panic where she felt unable to breathe and thought she was going to faint. When asked about it afterwards, Mary reported that she had been convinced that she was going mad.

As we have mentioned above, panic disorder is usually characterised by recurrent unexpected panic attacks, such as Mary's, followed by persistent concern about having additional attacks, worry about the implications of the attack, and/or a significant change in behaviour relating to the attacks. Individuals experiencing such panic attacks may begin to avoid situations or scenarios in which a panic would prove incapacitating or humiliating. Often such avoidance becomes widespread and the individual presents with agoraphobic symptoms.

Panic disorder is a relatively common condition. Studies investigating six-month prevalence estimate it to range from 0.6% to 1% for panic disorder without agoraphobia and between 2.7% and 5.8% for panic disorder with agoraphobia (e.g. Weissman, 1986). Some 75% of agoraphobics with panic attacks are female (e.g. Bourdon, Boyd, Rae, Burns, Thompson, & Locke, 1988) and the disorder usually develops during early adulthood, especially in association with negative life events (for example, bereavement; e.g. Pollard, Pollard, & Corn, 1989). Panic disorder is characterised by a variable, usually chronic course (Breier, Charney, & Heninger, 1986).

Panic was first claimed as a discrete anxiety presentation in response to the work of Klein (1981). His research in psychobiology led him to propose that panic attacks and non-panic-related anxiety are two distinct pathophysiological syndromes. Klein's work has inspired a whole body of theoretical and empirical research focusing on the idea that panic disorder originates from a genetically transmitted neurochemical abnormality which presents as a sudden surge of autonomic arousal and fear symptoms. However, more recently, theoretical work in psychology (e.g. Clark, 1986) has suggested that such biological hypotheses represent inadequate explanations of the phenomenology of panic. Consequently, a number of psychological theories of panic have been proposed, alternatively emphasising personality, conditioning and information processing analyses of the disorder. Furthermore, a considerable body of psychological research into the processes underlying panic has been carried out (see McNally, 1990, for a review).

Cognitive theoretical approaches to panic disorder

Psychological approaches to understanding panic disorder have revolved around the idea that the panic is in some way a "fear of fear" (e.g. Foa, Steketee, & Young, 1984; Goldstein & Chambless, 1978). that is, people panic because they are threatened by the presence or potential presence of fear-related phenomenal states. There are a number of variations of the fear of fear hypothesis: Pavlovian interoceptive conditioning (Goldstein & Chambless, 1978; Mineka, 1985; Seligman, 1988; Wolpe & Rowan, 1988); catastrophic misinterpretation of bodily sensations (Clark, 1986, 1988; Clark & Beck, 1988; Clark, Salkovskis, Gelder, Koehler, Martin, Anastasiades, Hackman, Middleton, & Jeavons, 1988); and anxiety sensitivity (see, McNally, 1990). In this section we shall concentrate on the work of Clark because this is the only fully blown cognitive account of panic disorder in existence; however, we shall also discuss some of the research on anxiety sensitivity where relevant.

Clark's cognitive model of panic.   Clark's model of panic owes much to the ideas of Beck (e.g. 1976), which are discussed in detail in Chapter 4. According to Clark's (1986, 1988) model of panic, "catastrophic misinterpretations of certain bodily sensations are a necessary condition for the production of a panic attack" . Thus, a panic attack may originate from the misinterpretation that an increase in heart rate signals an impending heart attack, or that the onset of feeling slightly dizzy or flushed is a sign that the individual is about to faint. Although such bodily sensations are symptoms of fear, and consequently Clark's model can be thought of as an extension of the fear of fear hypothesis, such sensations are not uniquely associated with fear. So, for example, heart palpitations may result from excessive caffeine intake rather than any interpretation or appraisal related to threat. The point, then, is that Clark's model is about the catastrophic misinterpretation of bodily sensations whatever their cause; that is, it does not restrict itself to a fear of fear analysis.

The specific sequence of events that Clark suggests occurs in a panic attack is illustrated in Fig. 6.4.

So, as can be seen from Fig. 6.4, panickers are spiralling down a vicious circle—the more afraid they become, the more intense the feared bodily sensations and, thus, the greater the fear and so on. According to Clark, two further processes contribute to the maintenance of panic disorder once the individual has developed the tendency to catastrophically misinterpret bodily sensations. First, panickers become hypervigilant and repeatedly scan the body for evidence of bodily sensations that might be signals of impending catastrophe. This leads them to notice sensations, of which many other people would be unaware and these sensations are taken as further evidence of the presence of some serious physical or mental disorder. Second, panickers develop a series of avoidance strategies. Clark (1989) cites the example of a patient who was preoccupied with the idea that he had some form of cardiac disease; he thus began to avoid exercise or sex whenever he noticed palpitations. Such avoidance, he believed, helped to prevent the onset of cardiac arrest. However, as Clark points out, because the patient did not actually have cardiac disease, the effect of the avoidance was to prevent him from learning that the palpitations he was experiencing were innocuous.

In line with Clark's ideas, panic patients report that thoughts of imminent catastrophe accompany their panic attacks (e.g. Beck, Laude, & Bohnert, 1974; Hibbert, 1984; Ottaviani & Beck, 1987). Furthermore, these thoughts most usually occur following detection of identifiable bodily sensations (e.g. Hibbert, 1984; Ley, 1985). According to Clark

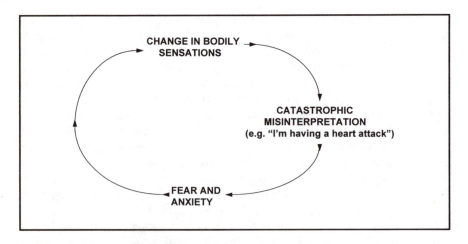

FIG. 6.4. Clark's cognitive model of panic (based on Clark, 1986).

(1988, p.76), the catastrophic misinterpretation of bodily sensations need not be accessible to awareness: "in patients who experience recurrent attacks, catastrophic misinterpretations may be so fast and automatic that patients may not always be aware of the interpretive process". This provides a possible explanation for panic attacks that either begin when the subject is asleep or which come "out of the blue".

There have been a number of critiques of Clark's work. Seligman (1988), for example, questioned the persistence of panic attacks which were the result of misinterpretations by the subjects that they were becoming insane or about to have a heart attack. Such individuals, Seligman argued, would be immediately presented with information which illustrates that the instigating bodily sensations did not lead to catastrophe. To accommodate this problem, Seligman suggested that panic may be a response to certain biologically "prepared" bodily sensations (Seligman, 1971). However, as we have already noted, Clark does not need to resort to such theoretical gymnastics in order to explain the maintenance of panic attacks in the face of seemingly contradictory information, because patients routinely avoid situations that might arouse fear and so never test out whether the predicted catastrophes have any basis in reality. Indeed, within the cognitive therapeutic approach to panic, behavioural experiments carried out by the client involve putting aside these avoidance strategies in order to allow the hypothesis that a catastrophe will occur to be refuted (e.g. Clark & Beck, 1988). However, as McNally (1990, p.407) points out "it still remains a mystery why some individuals require such rigorous demonstrations for them to abandon their pathological beliefs, whereas others are immediately convinced that their symptoms are harmless when provided corrective information by their family physician". We shall consider this comment by McNally when we look at the analysis of panic within SPAARS.

A second criticism of Clark's cognitive model of panic revolves around the issue of whether all panic attacks are proceeded by catastrophic misinterpretations. As Teasdale (1988) has argued, just because a catastrophic misinterpretation of a bodily sensation can lead to a panic attack, it does not mean that all spontaneously occurring panic attacks are the result of catastrophic misinterpretations. In support of this, a number of studies have shown that panic patients insist that they do not catastrophically misinterpret bodily sensations (e.g. Rachman, Lopatka, & Levitt, 1988). However, as we have stated, Clark has submitted that such catastrophic interpretations need not be conscious and it is perfectly consistent with his arguments that the individual would be unaware, and thus unable to report, any precipitating catastrophic cognitions. McNally (1990, p.407) rejects this assumption on intuitive grounds: "it seems implausible that thoughts of imminent disaster do not at some point enter consciousness either during or immediately after an attack. If patients think, however momentarily, that they are having a heart attack it seems they would remember having had this thought". Intuition, though, is a dangerous ally when it comes to theoretical refutation; this seems compounded by McNally's confusion of the term interpretation with the idea of a thought. Again, these issues are discussed in more detail when we come to consider panic disorder within the SPAARS framework.

Anxiety sensitivity research in panic

An additional factor which has been put forward to try to explain individual differences in the vulnerability to panic is anxiety sensitivity. The research on anxiety sensitivity revolves around the issue that not everybody is equally likely to misinterpret bodily sensations as catastrophic (see McNally, 1990, for a review). The central thesis of much of this work is the suggestion that a set of pre-existing beliefs about the harmfulness of certain bodily sensations predisposes individuals to misinterpret those sensations in a catastrophic manner, thus leading to panic experiences. This has been termed the Anxiety Sensitivity Hypothesis (Reiss & McNally, 1985). A considerable body of research has focused on the establishment of a measure of anxiety sensitivity—the Anxiety Sensitivity Index (ASI; Reiss, Peterson, Gursky, & McNally, 1986). This is a self-report measure of fear of fear and has been shown to be distinct from trait-anxiety (e.g. McNally & Lorenz, 1987); the latter denoting the tendency to respond fearfully to stress in general, whereas the former denotes the tendency to respond fearfully to symptoms of fear. A number of studies have indicated that high scores on the ASI are associated with a predisposition to develop panic disorder (e.g. Rapee, Ancis, & Barlow, 1988) and this raises the possibility that anxiety sensitivity may be a cognitive risk factor for the development of panic disorder (McNally & Lorenz, 1987).

Research suggests that anxiety sensitivity can be acquired in various ways, similar to the acquisition of common fears (e.g. Rachman, 1977). As McNally (1990, p.408) suggests "hearing misinformation about heart disease, or watching someone die of a heart attack following complaints of cardiac distress, may establish a fear of cardiac sensations".

A re-analysis of Clark's theory of panic disorder within the SPAARS framework

David Clark's theoretical work on panic has been extremely influential, especially within the clinical domain, and an analysis of panic phenomena within SPAARS has much in common with Clark's ideas.

Enshrined within the SPAARS approach is the proposal (see Chapters 2 and 5) that emotions consist of an event, an interpretation, an appraisal, physiological arousal, an action potential, conscious awareness (and behaviour). We can see that these components are clearly delineated within Clark's model: bodily sensations are the event; catastrophic misinterpretations are the interpretation; and there is an implicit assumption that these interpretations will be appraised in a fear-related way leading to the physiological activation of fear-related bodily systems. Furthermore, Clark argues that the catastrophic misinterpretations of bodily sensations need not be conscious, and we have made this suggestion in Chapter 5 with respect to all emotion-related interpretations. In addition, Clark argues that the pathway from bodily sensation to emotion generation can become relatively automatic and, hence, outside of the individual's control; this suggestion is loudly echoed by the proposed second route to emotion generation, the automatic generation of emotions, via the associative level of meaning within the SPAARS model.

So what might the SPAARS framework offer in addition to Clark's work? We propose that the greater theoretical power provided by a multilevel approach can perhaps go some way to answering the criticisms of Clark's work mentioned above The key to this lies in the automatic generation of fear within SPAARS. Such automatisation, we have suggested, is a function of the repeated activation of the pathway between bodily sensation via interpretation to appraisal of threat at the schematic model level (see Fig. 6.5). However, this automatisation can take two different forms within panic disorder. First, it is possible that the interpretation of a bodily sensation (for example, "I am feeling dizzy and that means I am likely to faint") could come to instigate the automatic generation of fear via the associative level of representation. Alternatively, it is possible that the bodily sensation itself, in the absence of any interpretation of its putative consequences, could come to automatically instigate the emotion of fear via the associative level of meaning within SPAARS (see Fig. 6.5).

With this state of affairs, the individual is likely to experience some panic attacks which seem to arise out of a clear awareness of bodily sensations and a clear awareness of catastrophic misinterpretations of those sensations (schematic model route). Other panic attacks, however, would seemingly come "out of the blue" or may even arise during sleep; in these cases it is possible that the individual is catastrophically misinterpreting bodily sensations but that these interpretations are inaccessible to conscious awareness (cf. Clark). One might then expect that, within the therapeutic context, such interpretations would become more and more accessible and become more and more under the

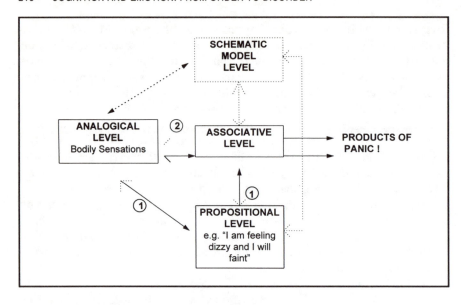

FIG. 6.5. Automatic routes to panic in SPAARS.
1 = propositional misinterpretation route; 2 = direct analogical route

individual's control. Alternatively, it is possible that no interpretations are being made and that the panic attack is being automatically generated via the associative level of meaning as a result of the onset of bodily sensations. In these situations, it seems unlikely that the individual would be able to report any misinterpretations of the bodily sensations even within the therapeutic milieu.

Let us return, then, to the two points raised by McNally (1990) as possible problems with Clark's approach. McNally suggested: first (p.407), that "it remains a mystery why some individuals require such rigorous demonstrations [that is behavioural experiments within cognitive therapy] for them to abandon their pathological beliefs"; second, the concern that, if interpretations of imminent disaster are always extant in the onset of panic symptoms, it would seem unlikely that the client would never be able to bring these interpretations into conscious awareness. With respect to the first point, it is inherent in the SPAARS approach that the automatic generation of emotions is a relatively inflexible and uncontrollable process. Thus, in a situation in which the emotion of fear is automatically generated via the associative level by a catastrophic misinterpretation then, although the individual may be fully aware of the interpretation that is being made, it would be very difficult to interrupt or control the generation of emotion which is a result of that interpretation. In this analysis, some individuals will "recover" from panic disorder following a few well-chosen words from their doctor because, for them, panic is entirely schematically driven. Others will require more intensive therapeutic work to overcome associatively driven panic. With respect to McNally's second point, within SPAARS it is possible, as we have said, for the automatic generation of fear with no concurrent catastrophic interpretations; consequently, it would be expected that for some individuals, access to catastrophic misinterpretations prior to the onset of panic would not be possible. Finally, it is important to note that, although an explicit specification of two routes to emotion clarifies some of the issues associated with panic, it seems likely that for most sufferers, panic disorder is driven by a combination of both routes.

Research into information processing biases associated with panic

In recent years, psychologists with an interest in clinical issues have applied the ideas and experimental paradigms of cognitive psychology in an attempt to understand any information processing biases which might underpin the clinical phenomenology of anxiety and depressive disorders (see Dalgleish & Watts, 1990; Eysenck, 1992; Williams et al., 1988 for reviews). This experimental approach enables the researcher to side-step a number of the methodological problems involved in the more traditional self-report studies; for example, self-report studies reveal only conscious, verbally accessible aspects of mental processes (Lang's verbal data). In addition, self-report studies are subject to the intentions and whims of the individual involved (Nisbett & Wilson, 1977). In contrast, information-processing paradigms, at their best, are potentially able to shed some light on the nature of non-conscious, non-verbalisable psychological processing and are also less susceptible to response biases.

Research which has applied information-processing paradigms to the area of emotional order and disorder includes a number of highly innovative and compelling prototypical studies. However, there are also a host of studies which are either: minor variations of the original experiments; applications of the paradigms to new subject populations; or poorly thought-out applications of new paradigms. It is beyond the scope of our ambitions in this book to even begin to review this literature. Instead, we have chosen one or two key studies to illustrate this approach to cognition and emotion. For the case of panic, we have chosen the interpretation paradigm and the interoceptive paradigm.

Interpretation paradigms and panic. Having extolled the virtues of information-processing paradigms to examine basic cognitive processes associated with emotion, we shall nevertheless begin with a brief look at some self-report data. As we have seen in our discussion of theoretical approaches to panic, the idea that individuals suffering from panic disorder catastrophically misinterpret bodily sensations is a central claim within the literature (e.g. Clark, 1988). To examine such biases in interpretation, McNally and Foa (1987), inspired by the work of Butler and Mathews (1983, see below), studied agoraphobics with panic attacks, recovered agoraphobics, and "healthy" controls using a series of ambiguous scenarios involving either internal or external stimuli (e.g., "you feel discomfort in your chest area. Why?"). Subjects were required to write down the first explanation that came to mind for each scenario and then to rank order three candidate explanations of the scenarios provided by the experimenter. In each case, only one of these candidate explanations was threat-related. The results revealed that agoraphobia with panic subjects, in contrast to the other two groups, tended to interpret the ambiguous scenarios as threat-related. This was the case for interpretations of both internal stimuli (that is, bodily sensations) and external stimuli.

A similar study was carried out by Clark and his colleagues (cited in Clark, 1988), this time investigating panic patients without agoraphobia. These subjects did not provide threatening interpretations for scenarios involving external stimuli, or even for bodily stimuli which would not indicate sudden changes in bodily state (for example, a new spot on the back of one's hand). However, for scenarios involving sudden changes in internal stimuli, there was threat-related interpretation bias in the panic subjects. These two studies show that panic patients, whether or not they have agoraphobia, seem to interpret ambiguous scenarios involving internal bodily sensations in a threat-related way; however, only those patients with concomitant agoraphobic symptoms interpret more general scenarios in a threat-related fashion.

Interoceptive biases in panic.   Interoception is the perception of bodily cues and Shands and Schor (1982, p.108) have suggested that panic patients "are interoceptive experts, being able to describe significant changes in almost every organ system and region of the body". This issue was investigated in a series of studies by Ehlers and her colleagues. In the first two studies, Ehlers, Margraf, Davies, and Roth (1988) and Ehlers, Margraf, Roth, Taylor, and Birbaumer (1988) did not find that panic disorder patients were more accurate in their cardiac perceptual abilities, compared to controls, in a task in which they had to match the frequency of a train of audible pips to their own heart rate. There are a number of problems with this methodology; for example, the subject is required to monitor both an internal and an external signal. That is, the task requires abilities over and above those involved in interoception. This is particularly important because interoception is known to be impaired under conditions of external stimulation (e.g. Pennebaker, 1982). In a further study, therefore, Ehlers and Breuer (1992), employed a revised methodology using patients with panic disorder, infrequent panickers, patients with other anxiety disorders, and normal controls. Subjects were required to count their heartbeats silently during signalled intervals without taking their pulse or using any other strategies such as holding their breath. In the second of three experiments, panic disorder patients showed better performance on the heartbeat tracking task than the other groups. In the third study patients with panic disorder and patients with generalised anxiety disorder showed better heart-rate perception than depressed controls.

The research we have chosen concerning information-processing biases in panic disorder raises a number of points. First, panic patients interpret ambiguous stimuli as threat related; however, in patients without any agoraphobic symptomatology, this bias is specific to ambiguous bodily sensations. Second, panic patients, along with other anxiety groups, appear to have greater interoceptive acuity relative to normal controls. Both of these sets of studies imply the existence of a dominant schematic model in panic disorder subjects. As we have suggested in Chapter 5, such models will serve to facilitate the processing of congruent information and inhibit the processing of incongruent information within the SPAARS system. Consequently, ambiguous material is likely to be interpreted in a panic-related way and attentional resources are likely to be focused on interoceptive changes. In line with this, other information-processing research indicates that, first, there is some evidence that the relationship between representations of bodily sensations and putative catastrophic interpretations of those sensations is a strong one within the memory structures of individuals with panic disorder (e.g. Clark et al., 1988). Second, panic patients exhibit memory biases for panic-related material (e.g. McNally, Foa, & Donnell, 1989); and, finally, that panic patients exhibit attention biases for panic-related material on a number of attention-related tasks (Asmundsen, Sandler, Wilson, & Walker, 1992).

Generalised anxiety and worry

Generalised anxiety problems involve excessive worry about several lifestyle domains such as health, finances, relationships, and so on. Such worrying usually takes up most of the individual's time and becomes highly disabling, both for the individuals concerned and for their partners, friends, and families. This so-called pathological worry is associated with a number of physiological/somatic symptoms of fear or anxiety; though, for diagnostic purposes, it is not usually regarded as including among its domains of concern the sorts of stimuli which are associated with the other so-called anxiety disorders (for example, a specific aetiological trauma as in PTSD, the phobic object in phobias, etc.).

Such generalised worry has been labelled Generalised Anxiety Disorder (GAD) in psychiatric classification systems such as *DSM-IV* (American Psychiatric Association, 1994). There are a variety of nosological issues involved in the conceptualisation of GAD. These concern: first, the relationship between GAD, a so-called clinical disorder, and sub-clinical levels of chronic anxiety as measured by concepts such as trait anxiety (e.g. Spielberger, Gorsuch, & Lushene, 1970); second, the relationship of GAD with depression and with mixed anxiety-depression disorders; and, third, the relationship of the type of anxiety-related problems found in someone with GAD with the type of anxiety-related problems which epitomise panic disorder (Barlow, Vermilyea, Blanchard, Vermilyea, Di Nardo, & Cerny, 1985). An excellent overview of the debates can be found in Rapee and Barlow's (1991) edited book, *Chronic Anxiety: Generalised Anxiety Disorder and Mixed Anxiety Depression*. For the purposes of the present chapter we confine ourselves to highlighting two points: (1) that most individuals who meet the criteria for a diagnosis of GAD are also somewhat depressed and that this has implications for much of the research which we shall discuss; (2) there is clearly a relationship between sub-clinical chronic anxiety as measured by constructs such as trait anxiety and the clinical problem of GAD and it does not seem unreasonable to suggest that high levels of trait-anxiety represent a vulnerability factor for the onset of GAD (e.g. Eysenck, 1992). Rather than discuss either of these two points at any length we shall return to them at the appropriate points in the chapter.

Worry

As we indicated in the introduction to this chapter, worry is most usually a functional state which allows us to plan options and review possibilities concerning threatening situations. However, worry is also the central psychological process implicated in generalised anxiety problems and so we have postponed our review of the worry literature until now. Precise definitions of worry have been few; an example is Borkovec, Robinson, Pruzinsky, and DePree's (1983, p.9) suggestion that: "Worry is a chain of thoughts and images, negatively affect-laden and relatively uncontrollable. The worry process represents an attempt to engage in mental problem-solving on an issue whose outcome is uncertain but contains the possibility of one or more negative outcomes.

Consequently, worry relates closely to fear processes." A more functional definition is offered by Tallis, Eysenck, and Mathews (1991b) who argue that worry is an involuntary process—initiated by a subjective appraisal of imminent threat—whereby negative thoughts and images repeatedly gain entry into awareness. The primary function of the worry process is to prompt active coping, directed at reducing negative uncertaincies.

A crucial distinction between these two definitions, and one which is borne out by the respective theoretical models of the sets of authors, is that Borkovec et al. (1983) suggest that worry is designed to solve problems which the individual faces; in contrast, Tallis et al. (1991b) argue that worry is some kind of "alarm system", which makes the individual aware of an appraised future threat. The activation of such an alarm system, according to Tallis, may or may not result in consequent problem-solving behaviour.

In this section, we review some of the research which has considered what the domains of worry might be; that is, what areas of life do people worry about. We shall then discuss some examples of the information-processing research which has been carried out on worry. Finally, we shall discuss the principal theoretical models of worry. More detailed discussions of the literature on worry are to be found in Davey and Tallis' (1994) edited book *Worrying: Perspectives on Theory, Assessment and Treatment*.

Domains of worry

Considering its history of neglect by researchers, the area of worry can boast a surprisingly large number of questionnaire intruments designed to tap the various domains or concerns that individuals worry about. These include the Penn State Worry Questionnaire (PSWQ; Meyer, Miller, Metzger, & Borkovec,1990), the Worry Domains Questionnaire (WDQ; Tallis, Eysenck, & Mathews, 1992); the Worry Questionnaire (Eysenck & Van Banberkun, cited in Eysenck, 1992); and the Anxious Thoughts Inventory (AnTI: Wells, 1987, 1994).

So, for example, Tallis et al.'s 30-item WDQ focuses on six clusters of concern to potential worriers: relationships; lack of confidence; aimless future; work incompetence; financial concerns; and sociopolitical concerns. Interestingly, the initial study using the WDQ indicated that the most important domain of concern was the sociopolitical; however, as Eysenck (1992, p.103) indicates "It appears improbable that most people actually worry more about issues such as the starving millions in the Third World or violations of human rights, than about themselves and their future. It seems likely that social desirability bias affected responding within the sociopolitical domain." Nevertheless, other studies by Tallis and his colleagues (e.g. Tallis et al., 1991b) provide some further support for the psychological validity of five or six different principal worry domains.

Elevated evidence requirements and worry.   Tallis and Eysenck (cited in Eysenck, 1992) have suggested that worriers have elevated evidence requirements; that is, in order to make a decision, a worrier must spend more time weighing up the relevant information in memory and in the environment. As Tallis et al. (1991b, p.22) suggest "a worrier has to be absolutely sure that he or she is doing 'the right thing', before a decision can be made". Tallis (1989), cites a study by Zaslow (1950) in which worriers, when shown a continuum of geometric figures, are less likely than non-worriers to accept imperfect exemplars. Furthermore, the number of ambiguous figures rejected (the elevated evidence requirement measure) was significantly correlated with a worry frequency measure. In a similar experiment, Tallis, Eysenck, and Mathews (1991a) presented subjects with the alphabet randomly distributed on a computer screen. Subjects had to generate a reaction time response to the presence or absence of a target letter. There was no difference between individuals on target-present trials; however, on target-absent trials high worriers showed a significant response delay which the authors interpreted as support for explanation in terms of elevated evidence requirements. That is, when the target did not "pop out", according to the authors, the worrier continued to search for the target for longer than the non-worrier to ensure it really was absent.

Theoretical approaches to worry

Borkovec's theory.   The three theoreticians, Borkovec, Metzger, and Pruzinsky (1986), combined to propose a tripartite theory of worry and anxiety. The three tiers reflect their three predominant areas of interest: learning theory, cognitive psychology, and self-theory. However, the foundation of the model is Borkovec's work on learning theory and we shall concentrate on that in our brief review of this approach. Borkovec et al. (1986, p.240), inspired by Mowrer's (1947) two-stage theory of fear, suggested that worry "can be viewed as a cognitive attempt to anticipate and avoid a myriad of possible, future outcomes". Thus, the individual anticipates a series of desired goals; however, due to a learning history of frustrated non-reward, the individual, when presented with cues associated with these goals, begins to feel increasingly anxious and thus attempts to avoid such cues. Worry, then, is viewed as an attempt to avoid negative outcomes by anticipating and contemplating all possibilities; Borkovec transfers Mowrer's concepts of frustrated non-reward and avoidance into the cognitive domain.

This initial theoretical formulation of Borkovec et al. has been developed (e.g. Borkovec, 1994; Borkovec, Shadick, & Hopkins, 1990). The reformulation emphasises that worry primarily involves a verbal-linguistic activity; however, they go further, and suggest that such verbal-linguistic worry processes have a function of reducing the generation of threat-related imagery and subsequent physiological activity; "We are positing an actual suppression of physiological/ affective process as a direct consequence of worrisome conceptual activity" (Borkovec et al., 1990, p.453). It is this negatively reinforcing function which, Borkovec suggests, maintains the worry process.

Barlow's (1988) theory.   Barlow (1988) conceptualises worry as the end process in a series of causally linked events. These events are schematically illustrated in Fig. 6.6.

Barlow's theory is impressive in that it incorporates psychological processes which are clearly important in worry such as memory, attention, and self-evaluation. Furthermore, there are a number of studies which seem to support some of Barlow's proposals; for example, there is a body of research emphasising the importance of uncontrollability and unpredictability in the maintenance and onset of anxiety states (e.g. see Mineka & Kihlstrom, 1978 for a review). Barlow goes some way towards explaining why intense worrying is so pervasive and difficult to bring to a halt, in that an internal focus of attention and a narrowing of attentional focus make it difficult for attentional resources to be directed to non-worry relevant stimuli. However, as Eysenck (1992) points out there are a number of problems with Barlow's approach: first, he is focusing almost exclusively on intense worrying as experienced by anxious patients; second, he argues that high arousal is a necessary antecedent of worry; and, third, that worry is always a dysfunctional state. As Eysenck (1992, p.114) notes "These contentions may be largely correct when applied to clinical worries, but seem implausible with respect to the everyday worries of normal individuals."

Tallis and Eysenck's theory (cited in Eysenck, 1992).   Tallis and Eysenck (as cited in Eysenck, 1992), building on the theoretical work of both Borkovec and Barlow, have proposed a new theoretical approach to worry which sees worry as a process which fulfils several major functions: first, worry serves an alarm function in that it introduces information concerning threat-related material into consciousness; second, "worry serves a prompt function" in that threat-related information in memory is continually re-presented to awareness so that the cognitive system might resolve it in some way; and third, worry serves a preparation function, in that it allows the worrier to anticipate

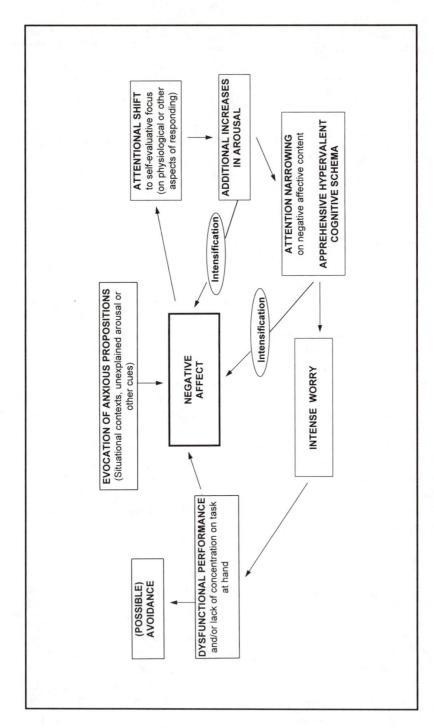

FIG. 6.6 Barlow's theory of worry (based on Barlow, 1988).

future situations and conceptualise possible solutions and dangers involved in them.

Eysenck and his colleagues incorporate the functions of worry, as they see them, into the theoretical framework illustrated in Fig. 6.7.

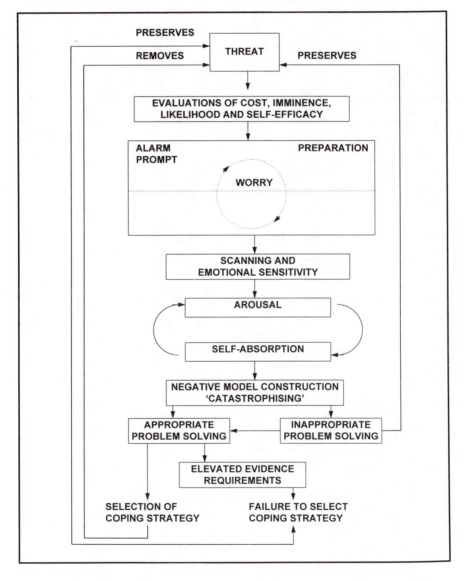

FIG. 6.7. Schematic diagram of the theory of worry (based on Tallis & Eysenck, 1994).

As is clear from Fig. 6.7, external stimuli are appraised in terms of their threat value and threat is seen by Eysenck et al. as a function of the putative cost, imminent likelihood, and self-efficacy associated with the event. Events which are appraised in this way as highly threatening initiate the process of worry which serves to prompt the individual, ring alarm bells that something threatening is in the internal or external environment, and help prepare the individual for possible future situations. Such worrying increases hypervigilant scanning of the environment and emotional sensitivity to worry-congruent material. This in turn increases arousal and self-focused attention, which operate in a vicious circle. Becoming lost in the vicious circle of worrying, increased arousal, and increased self-focused attention leads the individual to construct negative, catastrophic models of future events. The individual can then appropriately problem solve the issue surrounding these events in which case either the initial threat is diminished and the worry process recedes, or the individual can enter into inappropriate problem-solving strategies in which case the threat is preserved and the worry processes maintained.

Information-processing biases in generally anxious individuals

The study of various information-processing biases in generally anxious subjects has mushroomed even more prolifically than in the case of panic. Again, in this section we endeavour to describe a few of the more innovative studies in the various domains of cognition whilst referring the reader to more exhaustive sources for detailed reviews (Dalgleish & Watts, 1990; Eysenck, 1992; Wells & Mathews, 1994; Williams et al., 1988). Most studies have used individuals meeting criteria for a diagnosis of GAD (American Psychiatric Association, 1994).

The attentional deployment task.   The attentional deployment task is an ingenious methodology which involves subjects giving a neutral response to a neutral stimulus. Subjects are first presented with two words on a computer screen, one above the other, for a fixed period of time. The task is to read aloud the top word, while ignoring the lower one. After the screen clears, one of two things happens; either there is a pause and the next trial begins with two more words being presented, or a small dot appears in the space vacated by either the top or the bottom word. If this is the case the subjects have to respond as rapidly as possible by pressing a button. The latency to detect this dot probe is used to assess the location of attentional deployment; the rationale being that subjects will be faster to respond to a dot probe appearing in a screen location to which they are currently attending.

The prototypical study using the attentional deployment paradigm with GADs was carried out by MacLeod, Mathews, and Tata (1986). MacLeod et al. (1986) presented the task to groups of GADs, clinically depressed subjects and normal controls. The results showed (p.15) that: "clinically anxious, but not clinically depressed, subjects consistently shifted attention towards threat words, resulting in reduced detection latencies for probes appearing in the vicinity of such stimuli. Normal control subjects, on the other hand tended to shift attention away from such material."

Interpretations of such data as these tend to emphasise shifts in attention. However, there are some potential problems with this approach because by the time the probe stimulus appears (after 525ms), there has been ample scope for several shifts of attention. Consequently, all we can really say about the results from this task is that subjects are more likely to be attending to a screen location where a threat word appeared 525ms earlier. On this basis an alternative interpretation offers itself; that is, that all subjects immediately shifted attention to the location of the threat word but that anxious subjects did not shift their attention away again because they continued to attend to it.

The emotional Stroop task. The Stroop task uses stimuli consisting of two dimensions. One dimension is a word and the other is a physical attribute such as colour, form, pitch of voice, etc. Frequently, the physical dimension is a necessary attribute of the word, for example, the colour of the ink used to print the name of the colour as in the standard Stroop (1935) task. The essential variable is the degree of congruence between word and colour. In the congruent condition both dimensions match (e.g. the word RED printed in red); in the incongruent condition they mismatch (e.g. the word RED printed in green). The subjects' task is to name the colour or to read the word while ignoring the other dimension. The reaction times (RTs) to congruent and incongruent stimuli are usually evaluated by comparing them with a control condition that lacks one dimension. Traditionally the difference between the RTs for naming incongruent stimuli and for naming control stimuli is called the Stroop phenomenon.

In the emotional Stroop paradigm the incongruent stimuli are emotional words and the control stimuli are neutral words. The emotional Stroop effect is the difference in RT to name the ink colours of the emotional stimuli and the control stimuli. Research using the emotional Stroop task has used two different types of presentation. The words are either presented singularly on a computer screen (with the subjects' RT being recorded with a voice key or a button press) or the stimuli are presented in sets of up to 100 words, drawn from the same category, on large cards with the subjects' RT being the time to name the ink colours of all of the words on the card.

The emotional Stroop task has been used in countless studies (e.g. Mathews & MacLeod, 1985) to illustrate retardations in colour-naming for threat-related material in anxious subjects. However, there have been relatively few innovative variations of the methodology. An exception is a study by MacLeod and Hagan (1992) who examined the emotional Stroop effect in a longitudinal design. Women awaiting colposcopy investigation (a test for cervical cancer) were screened on both traditional questionnaire measures of emotional vulnerability and on an emotional Stroop task. A two-month follow-up was carried out of those women who had been given a diagnosis of cervical pathology (about half of the sample, all of whom by this time had received their laser surgery). These subjects were asked to complete a post-diagnostic mood questionnaire designed by the authors. MacLeod and Hagan found that anxiety, as measured by the questionnaires, was associated with a selective slowing on the threat-related stimuli in the Stroop task, but only in a masked exposure condition (in which subjects were unable to accurately report the words). In terms of the longitudinal analysis the best predictor of a subject's emotional response to a diagnosis of cervical pathology was again the masked Stroop effect—those subjects who showed the greatest degree of colour-naming interference from masked threat words, compared to non-masked threat words, experienced the most negative emotional reactions to this life event. Similar findings were reported by MacLeod and Rutherford (1992) with subjects about to take an examination.

The ambiguous sentence task.   Interpretation biases in anxiety were investigated by Eysenck, Mogg, May, Richards, and Mathews (1991). They presented GADs, recovered anxious, and control subjects with a series of sentences. Some of the sentences were ambiguous, with both threatening and non-threatening interpretations (e.g. "The two men watched as the chest was opened."). After presentation of the sentences the subjects were given an unexpected recognition memory test, in which they had to decide whether each sentence corresponded in meaning to one of the sentences presented previously. The memory test items were unambiguous, reworded versions of the original sentences which captured the meaning of either the threatening or non-threatening interpretation. The results showed that the GADs recognised more of the threatening interpretations and fewer of the neutral interpretations than the other two groups. There were no significant differences in the memory performance of the recovered anxious group and the normal controls. In a short additional study,

Eysenck et al. (1991) applied signal detection analyses to the recognition of ambiguous, threatening, and neutral sentences, and concluded that GADs did not differ from controls in terms of response bias.

The judgemental bias task.   Research into the investigation of risk has suggested that individuals make use of the availability heuristic (Tversky & Kahneman, 1974) when rating the likelihood of future events. According to this heuristic, the frequency of a class of events is estimated as a function of the ease with which instances of such events can be brought to mind. For example, in the judgement of likely causes of death, risk estimations were disproportionately increased by prior exposure to information about lethal events (Lichtenstein, Slovic, Fischoff, Layman, & Combs, 1978). This leads to the hypothesis that anxious individuals will find it easier to bring to mind instances of danger-related events and will subsequently show inflated risk estimates for those events relative to control subjects.

Butler and Mathews (1983) gave groups of GADs, clinically depressed subjects, and normal controls a set of three questionnaires concerned with estimating risk. The first questionnaire consisted of brief ambiguous scenarios (e.g. "you wake with a start in the middle of the night, thinking you heard a noise, but all is quiet"). Subjects were first required to provide an explanation for why they thought they might have woken up, and then to rank order three possible explanations, one of which was threatening (e.g., "it could be a burglar"). The second questionnaire was concerned with subjective cost and subjects were asked to rate 20 threatening items on a scale in answer to the question "how bad would it be for you ... ?" The final questionnaire was concerned with subjective probability. Subjects had to rate the probability that positive, neutral, or negative events would happen, first, to themselves and, second, to a significant other. The results indicated that both anxious and depressed subjects were significantly more likely than controls to interpret ambiguous situations as threatening, and both groups placed significantly higher subjective cost than controls on the occurrence of threatening events. Similarly, both anxious and depressed groups rated negative events (but not positive) as significantly more likely to happen than did the control subjects. Finally, ratings of negative events by the two patient groups for themselves were significantly higher than ratings of the same items when made for another person.

Recall, recognition, and implicit memory tasks.   Mathews, Mogg, May, and Eysenck (1988) investigated explicit and implicit memory in groups of GADs, recovered anxious subjects, and controls. The explicit memory task was a free recall paradigm and, in line with previous findings with GADs (e.g. Mogg, Mathews, & Weinman, 1987), there were no significant effects. The implicit memory paradigm was a word completion task. Subjects were simply instructed to complete a word stem with the first word that came to mind. The extent to which the previous presentation of list words increased the tendency to produce those words as completions was the measure of implicit memory. The results showed that the currently anxious patients produced more word completions that corresponded to threat-related list words, but fewer corresponding to non-threatening list words, than did the normal control subjects. The performance of the recovered anxious group was closer to that of the normal controls than that of the currently anxious patients

Summary and implications of the findings from information-processing research in generally anxious subjects

In this section we have been able to give no more than a flavour of the large body of information processing research in anxious individuals. We have illustrated that individuals with generalised anxiety problems show biases in favour of threat-related material on attention type tasks such as the attentional deployment paradigm and the modified Stroop paradigm (other attention paradigms include: the dichotic listening task, e.g. Mathews & MacLeod, 1986; a two-string lexical decision task, e.g. MacLeod & Mathews, 1991; an attentional search task, e.g. Mathews, May, Mogg, & Eysenck, 1990; and numerous studies of self-focused attention, e.g. Slapion & Carver, 1981). Similar threat-related biases have also been shown on interpretation paradigms such as the ambiguous sentences task (Eysenck et al., 1991. Other interpretation paradigms include the homophone task, e.g. Mathews, Richards, & Eysenck, 1989; the anagram task, e.g. Dalgleish, 1994b; and judgement tasks, e.g. Butler & Mathews, 1983). Finally, we presented evidence that generally anxious individuals do not exhibit biases for threat-related material on tests of explicit memory such as recall and recognition; though there is some evidence of such a bias on an implicit memory task (Mathews et al., 1989).

So, what are we to make of this enormous body of research on information-processing biases in generally anxious subjects? The findings of processing biases for personally relevant emotional (usually threat-related) material on attentional tasks, judgement tasks and tasks which require the interpretation of ambiguous stimuli are in line with theoretical predictions from a range of models of anxiety (see Chapter 3) including our own SPAARS approach, and we have discussed these arguments in the previous section on panic.

However, the surprising finding is that of an absence of explicit memory biases in generally anxious subjects for threat-related material. This contrasts markedly with the state of affairs in depression (see Chapter 7) and in other so-called anxiety disorders such as PTSD and panic states (see the relevant sections in this chapter). We propose that there are two reasons which may help explain this profile of results in generally anxious subjects. The first is methodological in that many of the studies which have investigated memory for threat in generally anxious individuals have not chosen words that are specific to the subject's exact domain of concern. In contrast, in such research with more circumscribed anxiety states such as panic the stimuli have meshed much more closely with the preoccupations of the participants. It is possible therefore that mnemonic biases are a function of generally anxious states but that they have yet to be properly tested for. However, it seems unlikely that such methodological inadequacies can account for the wealth of negative findings in this area and for this reason we are sympathetic to Williams et al.'s (1988) suggestion that depression is characterised by biases at the elaborative stages in processes, whereas anxiety is characterised by biases at the preattentive stage (see Chapter 4). We would couch it somewhat differently in the SPAARS model and suggest that the configuration of the SPAARS system in the sadness module is such as to direct the system to reflect on lost goals and to assess resources in order to compensate for the lost goals. In contrast, the configuration of SPAARS in the fear module serves to focus resources on detected and possible future threat.

Are there any clinical implications of this information processing research? Perhaps the biggest potential for this area of research is that it can shed new light on issues of vulnerability. Several extant theories of emotional disorder (e.g. Beck et al., 1979; see Chapter 3) argue for cognitive differences between those individuals who are vulnerable to the disorder and those who are not. Self-report measures do not seem good at detecting such differences and researchers have looked to cognitive paradigms to provide some answers. The preliminary evidence does not provide any clear indications as to the causal relationship between processing biases, anxious state, and anxiety disorder; for this a larger scale prospective study would be the optimal methodology. A compromise has been to use groups of recovered individuals and the few studies which have done this have produced equivocal findings with the recovered subjects performing in a manner intermediate to both clinical and control groups or showing no differences to the controls. As a result, the jury is still out on this issue with respect to anxiety; however, work on cognitive vulnerability in depression (e.g. Teasdale, 1988) indicates that the approach has considerable potential. There are several ways in which processing biases of the type discussed earlier could operate as diathesis factors. Individuals could be biased towards selective processing of threat-related information; this would increase the probability of an anxious appraisal of that information and the onset of an anxious state which in turn could increase the extent of the bias towards threat-related information, and so on. The vulnerable individual would thus be caught in a vicious circle similar to that proposed as a maintaining factor in depression (e.g. Teasdale, 1983). Alternatively, in terms of appraisal processes, vulnerable individuals could be conceptualised as those whose criteria for an appraisal related to the onset of anxiety are very low, such that a whole range of stimuli which are ordinarily regarded as having little emotive value act as anxiety triggers.

So far there has been relatively little research on the use of cognitive paradigms in assessment and treatment evaluation. Perhaps the most interesting development is the work of MacLeod and Hagan (1992) described previously, in which the masked emotional Stroop test showed an ability to predict subjects' reactions to a diagnosis of cancer better than a range of self-report measures. This has potential for use in screening individuals at risk for psychopathology either prior to a potentially traumatic event (e.g. colposcopy as in the study) or immediately following a traumatic event (such as a natural disaster). However, this research needs further replication.

In summary, generalised anxiety has proved the focus of an enormous amount of attention from cognition and emotion researchers. This is not because it is inherently more enthralling than other so-called anxiety disorders but because it involves such a clear cognitive component in the form of worry and overlaps extensively with the preoccupations of healthy individuals as regards the domains of concern involved. Such research interest has reaped dividends, principally in the greater understanding of the various information-processing biases involved in anxiety, and this research has clearly been highly influential to progress in work with other anxiety disorders, not least PTSD, which we consider next.

Post-traumatic stress disorder (PTSD)

Geoff was a policeman who had served on the streets for over 10 years; in that time he had won two commendations for bravery. Geoff was a popular guy, who was respected, trusted and liked. He had a reputation for being the life and soul of the party. While on escort duty one day in the back of a police van, the prisoner whom Geoff was in charge of became extremely violent. He managed to throw Geoff against the side of the van and smashed Geoff's head through the window before being overcome by the other policemen. The incident lasted less than a minute in total. Following that day, Geoff underwent profound changes. He had nightmares about the event and kept thinking he saw the prisoner amongst crowds on the street. He felt very vulnerable and it became such that his colleagues could no longer trust him to back them up in a tight situation. At home, Geoff became withdrawn and irritable and his marriage started to suffer. Twelve years later, Geoff came for help. He had been thrown out of the police, his wife had left him, and he worked in an office job where he had taken care to get the office in the centre of the building where no one could "get to him". On describing that minute of his life 12 years earlier, Geoff broke down in tears, saying "I always thought that whatever happened, I would be able to handle it; now I'm frightened of my own shadow".

Since its inclusion in *DSM-III* (American Psychiatric Association, 1980), post-traumatic stress disorder (PTSD) has been the subject of a great deal of empirical and theoretical work. A number of well thought-out psychological models of PTSD have been proposed, many within a cognitive framework (e.g. Foa, Steketee, & Rothbaum, 1989; Foa, Zinbarg, & Rothbaum, 1992; Horowitz, 1979; Litz & Keane, 1989). In this section we review briefly existing empirical and cognitive theoretical work in PTSD before outlining in some detail how PTSD might be conceptualised within the SPAARS framework.

According to *DSM-IV* (American Psychiatric Association, 1994), PTSD can follow traumatic events in which individuals experience a threat to their own life or the lives of others or a threat to their own or others' physical integrity. Although such attempts at objectively defining the aetiological events in PTSD are useful, we suggest that it is the impact of the event or events on individual's current models of self, world and other that is central. For some this might indeed be the life-threatening car crash or the tour of duty in Vietnam; for others, however, being shouted at by their previously calm and supportive boss at work might be sufficient.

The clinical features of PTSD following such events include: (1) re-experiencing symptoms, such as intrusive memories, thoughts or images, and nightmares; (2) avoidance reactions such as emotional numbing where the individual is unable to feel a range of emotions or is able to describe the trauma in a dispassionate way, amnesia for all or part of the event, behavioural avoidance where individuals go to great lengths to avoid stimuli which will remind them of the trauma, and cognitive avoidance such as the use of distraction techniques to get rid of unwanted thoughts; and, (3) arousal symptoms such as an exaggerated startle response, irritability, and hypervigilance for trauma-related information. In addition, PTSD is commonly accompanied by a wide range of negative emotions such as sadness, anger, and guilt. A distinctive feature is that in many cases the intrusive memories consist of images accompanied by high levels of fear or are re-enactments of the original trauma ("flashbacks"). Herman (1992) has referred to flashbacks as "frozen memories", a term that captures their repetitive, unchanging quality.

In psychiatric terms, around 70–80% of PTSD sufferers usually receive an additional diagnosis (McFarlane, 1992). Epidemiological surveys indicate that rates of somatisation disorder, psychosis, anxiety disorder, and depression are substantially elevated in PTSD sufferers (e.g. Shore, Vollmer, & Tatum, 1989) and studies of combat veterans indicate that depression, GAD, and substance abuse are the most frequent co-diagnoses (e.g. Davidson & Foa, 1991).

Rates of PTSD, following exposure to a traumatic event, average around 25–30% in the general population; although certain events such as rape seem to be associated with much higher rates (Green, 1994). Prevalence rates tend to decrease over time although up to 50% of individuals may develop chronic PTSD. Indeed, studies have shown PTSD up to 40 years on in World War II veterans (e.g. Davidson, Kudler, Saunders, & Smith, 1990) and survivors of the Holocaust (e.g. Kuch & Cox, 1992). The course of PTSD can be intermittent (e.g. Zeiss & Dickman, 1989) and onset may be delayed by many years (e.g. Blank, 1993; McFarlane, 1988) though reliable estimates of the rates of delayed-onset PTSD are not yet available.

A number of event variables have been found to be important in PTSD such as bereavement (e.g. Joseph, Yule, Williams, & Hodgkinson, 1994) and personal injury and life-threat (e.g. Fontana, Rosenheck, & Brett, 1992). In addition, a premorbid history of psychological or behavioural problems is predictive of PTSD following a subsequent trauma (e.g. Atkeson, Calhoun, Resick, & Ellis, 1982; Breslau, Davis, Andreski, & Peterson, 1991; Burgess & Holmstrom, 1978; McFarlane, 1989). However, other research has not found prior clinical history to be associated with outcome (e.g. Solkoff et al., 1986). The important role of prior experience of traumatic events in general has been confirmed in numerous studies (e.g. Breslau et al., 1991; Burgess & Holmstom, 1974) and it may be that rates of prior traumatisationcanaccountfortheassociationbetweenpreviousclinical history and the severity of PTSD.

Higher levels of social support have been found to be protective against the development of PTSD (e.g. Kilpatrick, Veronen, & Best, 1985). Work with combat veterans has shown an association between better outcome and a more internal locus of control (e.g. Frye & Stockton, 1982) and a more internal and controllable attributional style for positive events (e.g. Mikulincer & Solomon, 1988). Furthermore, internal and controllable attributions for disaster-related events seem to be associated with poorer outcome (e.g. Joseph, Brewin, Yule, & Williams, 1991, 1993).

Information processing biases in PTSD

There have been a number of studies of PTSD using information processing methodologies derived from the cognitive psychology literature. Again, as with panic and generalised anxiety, we can only consider a selection of this research here.

The most direct investigation of attention in PTSD used the dichotic listening task with a group of Vietnam veterans with PTSD (Trandel & McNally, 1987). Subjects repeated a message presented to one ear while ignoring an (unattended) message relayed simultaneously to the other ear. The variable of interest was the amount of processing which items in the unattended message received. This reflects the degree of attentional bias to those items. Trandel and McNally found no evidence of attentional bias for seven PTSD-related target items in the unattended message. However, given the error variance associated with this paradigm, it is possible that the number of target stimuli was too small to pick up any attentional effects.

Other studies of attentional processing in PTSD have used a modified Stroop colour-naming paradigm (see the previous section on GAD for a description of this methodology). Research indicates that individuals who have PTSD following a traumatic event show greater Stroop interference to words related to the trauma whereas traumatised individuals without PTSD show no such interference effects (e.g. Thrasher, Dalgleish, & Yule, 1994).

Memory biases have also been found on an autobiographical memory task with both Vietnam war veterans and adult survivors of childhood incest (McNally, Lasko, Macklin, & Pitman, in press; McNally, Litz, Prassas, Shin, & Weathers, 1994). Both groups exhibited deficits in retrieving specific autobiographical memories to a set of cue words. The effect is especially pronounced in veterans with PTSD who wear combat regalia in daily life.

This finding of memory biases for threat-related material contrasts with the lack of effects found with more generally anxious subjects (e.g. Mogg et al., 1987; see previous section on generalised anxiety). We have suggested earlier that the lack of a bias in GAD subjects may, in part, be because the stimuli used in the tasks did not mesh closely enough with the concerns of the subjects. This sort of interpretation is given extra weight by the findings of memory biases in PTSD using material specifically related to their trauma.

Finally, Dalgleish (1993) examined judgemental bias in survivors of a major disaster with and without PTSD. It was shown that only those survivors with PTSD generated elevated judgements of the probability of a range of negative events happening in the future.

Cognitive theoretical models of PTSD

A number of psychological paradigms provide frameworks for understanding PTSD, for example the psychodynamic (e.g. Freud, 1919), learning theory (e.g. Keane, Zimmering, & Caddell, 1985), and cognitive (e.g. Horowitz, 1986). While all of these paradigms encompass theories which offer interesting insights into the nature of the disorder, it is the cognitive approach which, we feel, is the most fully developed and offers the greatest explanatory and predictive power.

Cognitive theories of PTSD have a certain theoretical family resemblance. They propose that individuals bring to the traumatic experience a set of pre-existing beliefs and models of the world and of themselves. The experience of trauma provides information which is on the one hand highly salient and on the other incompatible with these pre-existing meaning structures. The attempt to integrate this new trauma-related information with the existing models leads, it is argued, to the various phenomena which characterise post-traumatic reactions. Successful resolution of the trauma occurs when the new information is integrated into the existing set of beliefs or models (often by virtue of changes in those same beliefs or models). Unsuccessful resolution occurs when individuals are unable to bring the new trauma-related information into accord with their pre-existing beliefs or models of the world. This can lead to chronic post-traumatic reactions. In this section we review briefly a number of social-cognitive and information-processing theories of PTSD before discussing how the SPAARS model might account for post-traumatic emotional experiences.

Horowitz's theory.   Horowitz's (1973, 1976, 1979, 1986; Horowitz & Reidbord, 1992; Horowitz, Wilner, Kaltreider, & Alvarez, 1980) formulation of stress response syndromes offers perhaps the most far-reaching and influential social-cognitive model of reactions to trauma. Although inspired by classical psychodynamic psychology (notably Freud, 1920), Horowitz's theory is principally concerned with discussing such ideas in terms of the cognitive processing of traumatic information (i.e. ideas, thoughts, images, affects, and so on). Horowitz has argued that the main impetus within the cognitive system for the processing of trauma-related information comes from a completion tendency (Horowitz, 1976): the psychological "need" for new information to be integrated with existing cognitive world models or schemata (Horowitz, 1986).

Horowitz (1986) proposed that, subsequent to the experience of trauma, there is an initial "crying out" or stunned reaction followed by a period of information overload in which the thoughts, memories, and images of the trauma cannot be reconciled with current meaning structures. As a result, Horowitz suggests, a number of psychological defence mechanisms come into operation to keep the traumatic information in the unconscious and the individual then experiences a period of numbing and denial. However, the completion tendency maintains the trauma-related information in what Horowitz calls "active memory", causing it to break through these defences and intrude into consciousness in the form of flashbacks, nightmares, and unwanted thoughts as the individual endeavours to merge the new information with pre-existing models. According to Horowitz, this tension between the completion tendency on the one hand and the psychological defence mechanisms on the other causes individuals to oscillate between phases of intrusion and denial-numbing as they gradually integrate the traumatic material with long-term meaning representations. Failures of such processing can mean that the partially processed traumatic information remains in active memory without ever being fully assimilated, thus leading to chronic post-traumatic reactions.

Horowitz's discussion of the processes underlying completion, intrusion, and denial has considerable explanatory power for PTSD phenomenology. His theory indicates clearly the ways in which normal reactions to trauma can become chronic (see Fig. 6.8 for a schematic summary of Horowitz's model).

However, Horowitz's model has a number of limitations which it is important to highlight. First, there is little discussion of the six million dollar question in trauma research—why some individuals develop PTSD while others, after ostensibly similar traumatic experiences, show little or no outward signs of being traumatised. Indeed, there is little

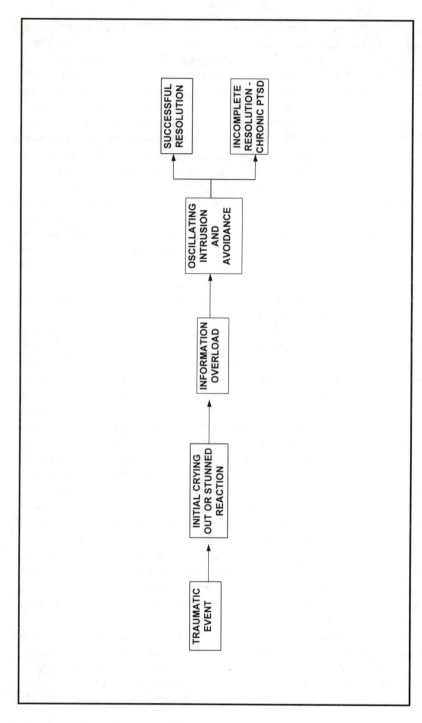

FIG. 6.8. Schematic summary of Horowitz's theory of PTSD.

detail in Horowitz's writings concerning the nature of the existing schema structure and the exact ways in which it fails to accommodate new information from the traumatic experience. Second, Horowitz's formulation seems to struggle to account for epidemiological data regarding the frequency of late-onset PTSD (though, this might be ascribed to a long period of denial which later breaks down). Third, while Horowitz provides a clear description of the time course of post-traumatic reactions, it seems uncertain that all individuals do experience an initial period of denial, or later oscillations between denial and intrusion. In fact, Creamer, Burgess, and Pattison (1992), in complete contrast, argue for an initial episode of intrusive symptoms. Fourth, although Horowitz highlights processes such as social support, which, as we have seen above, are clearly important, there is little explanation of how such factors might operate and interact with processes such as completion. Finally, little credit is given to the power of the individual's attributions and interpretations of the traumatic experience and the effect that these have on outcome.

Janoff-Bulman's cognitive appraisal theory. The cognitive-appraisal model of Janoff-Bulman (1985, 1989; Janoff-Bulman & Frieze, 1983) focuses almost exclusively on the nature of the pre-existing beliefs about the world which the individual carries into a traumatic situation. Janoff-Bulman argues that PTSD is the result of certain basic assumptions about the world being "shattered" as reflected in the title of her (1992) book which outlines the approach in detail: *Shattered Assumptions: Towards a New Psychology of Trauma.* The assumptions which Janoff-Bulman highlights are: the assumption of personal invulnerability; the perception of the world as meaningful or comprehensible; and the view of the self in a positive light. The suggestion, then, is that these assumptions provide structure and meaning in the individual's life but that they cannot be maintained in the face of a traumatic experience and, therefore, "shatter". Once shattered, the individual is plunged into a confusion of intrusion, avoidance, and hyperarousal.

Janoff-Bulman's work is important in that it describes the ways in which trauma-related information is incongruent with the usual assumptions people possess about the world. There is little attempt, however, to explain how such assumptions are represented or what processes are involved when they are shattered. An additional problem is the ubiquitous finding (e.g. Kilpatrick et al., 1985) that individuals with a pre-morbid psychiatric history are more likely to develop PTSD following a trauma. Such individuals would presumably be characterised by assumptions of personal vulnerability and views of the self in a negative light. Such pre-morbid negative assumptions are unlikely to be shattered by a traumatic experience (in fact, they are more likely to be confirmed) and the high incidence of PTSD in this population has yet to be addressed by cognitive-appraisal models such as that of Janoff-Bulman.

Foa's theory. Applying Lang's (1977, 1985) concept of fear structures (see the introduction to the present chapter and Chapter 3), Foa and her colleagues (Foa & Kozak, 1986; Foa & Riggs, 1993; Foa et al., 1989, 1992) have put forward an information-processing theory of PTSD which centres on the formation of a so-called fear network in long-term memory. This fear network (cf. Lang) encompasses: stimulus information about the traumatic event; information about cognitive, behavioural and physiological reactions to the trauma; and interoceptive information which links these stimulus and response elements together. Activation of the trauma-related fear network by triggering stimuli (i.e. reminders of the trauma), according to Foa et al., causes information in the network to enter conscious awareness (the intrusion symptoms of PTSD). Attempts to avoid and suppress such activation of the network lead to the cluster of avoidance symptoms of PTSD. Foa et al. argue that successful resolution of the trauma can only occur by integrating the information in the fear network with existing memory structures. Such assimilation requires, first, the activation of the fear network so that it becomes accessible for modification and, second, the availability of information that is incompatible with the fear network so that the overall memory structure can be modified. A number of factors mediate the course of such integration; for example, Foa et al. argue that the unpredictability and uncontrollability of the traumatic event can make it very difficult to assimilate into existing models in which the world is controllable and predictable. In addition, factors such as the severity of the event disrupt the cognitive processes of attention and memory at the time of the trauma and Foa et al. argue that this disruption can lead to the formation of a disjointed and fragmented fear network which is consequently difficult to integrate with existing, more organised models. See Fig. 6.9 for a diagrammatic summary of Foa et al.'s (1989) approach.

By outlining an information processing architecture within which some of Horowitz's and Janoff-Bulman's social cognitive ideas can be instantiated, Foa et al. have made considerable progress towards a greater understanding of how the processes underlying PTSD might operate within a cognitive system. Furthermore, in stressing factors such as the predictability and controllability of the trauma, Foa et al. highlight one important role of the individual's attributions and

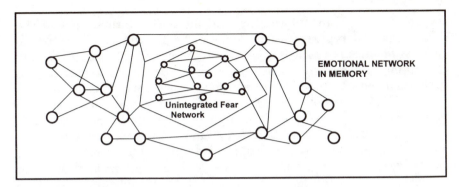

FIG. 6.9. Unintegrated fear networks in memory (Foa et al., 1989).

interpretations of the traumatic event. The suggestion that the availability of information incompatible with the trauma is necessary for successful processing provides a framework for understanding both the role of social support as a vehicle for the provision of such incompatible information and also the processes underlying the success of exposure-based interventions for PTSD (Foa et al., 1991). What is less clear, however, is whether network theory provides an architecture powerful enough to cope with the range of PTSD phenomenology. We have discussed the criticisms of network approaches to emotional order and disorder in Chapter 3 and we shall not reiterate them here; suffice to say that a network with a single level of representation struggles to explain how the existing meaning structures and models of the world which are such a feature of the social-cognitive models (Foa & Riggs, 1993) are represented and how integration of the trauma-related information with such models might take place, nor of why fear networks develop in some individuals and not others.

Brewin's dual representation theory.   Brewin, Dalgleish, and Joseph (in press) have applied Brewin's (1989) dual representation theory (DRT) to post-traumatic stress reactions in general and to PTSD in particular. This approach endeavours to circumvent some of the difficulties of single level theories such as Foa et al.'s (see above) by proposing two levels in memory at which trauma-related information can be represented. The first level of representation is of the individual's conscious experience of the traumatic event. This forms what Brewin et al. (in press) have called Verbally Accessible Memories (VAMs), characterised by their ability to be deliberately retrieved and progressively edited by the traumatised individual. VAM representations, it is argued, as with Foa et al.'s fear network, comprise sensory, response and meaning information centred on the traumatic event. The second level of representation proposed by Brewin et al. (in press) consists of what are called Situationally Accessible Memories (SAMs), containing information which cannot be deliberately accessed by the individual and which is not available for progressive editing in the same way as VAM information. In fact, SAMs, as the name suggests, are accessed only when aspects of the original traumatic situation cue their activation. DRT proposes that VAM and SAM representations are encoded in parallel at the time of the trauma and between them have the power to account for the range of PTSD phenomenology. For example, holistic, dissociative memories or "flashbacks" would be considered to be the result of the activation of SAM representations, whereas the person's ability to recount the trauma, for example in a therapeutic situation, would be a function of the accessibility of VAM representations. See Fig. 6.10 for a schematic illustration of DRT.

Brewin et al. (in press) propose that the emotional processing of trauma needs to proceed on both the VAM and SAM fronts in order to be successful. It is argued that individuals need to consciously integrate the verbally accessible information in VAM with their pre-existing beliefs and models of the world and "the end point of this process is to reduce negative affect by restoring a sense of safety and control, and by making appropriate adjustments to expectations about the self and the world". The second emotional processing element, it is suggested, is the activation of information in SAM through exposure to cues concerning the event. In fact, as Brewin et al. point out, this would usually happen automatically when the individual begins to progressively edit VAM information. Alterations in SAM representations can then occur via the integration of new, non-threatening information into the SAMs (cf. Foa)

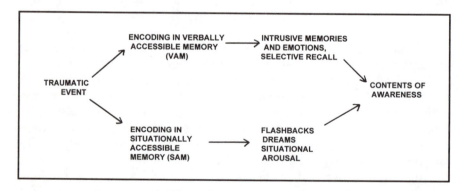

FIG. 6.10. A schematic illustration of dual representation theory applied to PTSD (based on Brewin et al., in press).

or by the creation of new SAMs (Brewin, 1989). These two proposed routes to successful emotional processing are derived from the theoretical ideas reviewed earlier. The editing of VAM information to bring it into accord with pre-existing models of the world owes much to the work of Horowitz and Janoff-Bulman, while the requirement of activation and the subsequent integration of new information into SAMs is reminiscent of Foa et al.'s implementation of fear networks.

It is proposed that successful emotional processing of VAM and SAM information concerning the trauma may not always be possible. Brewin et al. suggest that in some circumstances, for example when the discrepancy between the trauma and prior assumptions is too great, emotional processing of trauma information will become chronic. Alternatively, emotional processing may be prematurely inhibited due to sustained efforts to avoid the reactivation of highly distressing information stored in VAM and SAM. In this situation, Brewin et al. suggest, there may be no active emotional processing but the SAM information should still be accessible under certain circumstances and the individual is hence vulnerable to delayed onset PTSD when those circumstances arise.

DRT offers a coherent account of the phenomenology of PTSD, and makes particularly clear statements concerning the more distinctive experiences such as flashbacks which traumatised individuals report. There is also considerable discussion of the various courses post-trauma, what Brewin et al. call the three endpoints of emotional processing, and the *modi operandi* of both cognitive- and behaviour-based treatments are outlined in some detail. Finally, important processes such as attributions, social support, and attitudes to emotional expression are considered in tandem with the three endpoints of processing. One strength of Brewin et al.'s approach is the application of a coherent cognitive architecture which was developed as a general framework for understanding therapeutic processes (Brewin, 1989) to PTSD. However, it is perhaps too early to judge how much mileage the concepts of VAM and SAM will turn out to have. Some problems are immediately apparent; first, although credit is due to Brewin et al. for moving away from the single-level theories such as Foa et al.'s, the proposal of dual representations still leaves it unclear how higher-order models and assumptions about the world and the self might be represented. Are these just one part of the VAM system? If so, then is it really true to say that the contents of such models are verbally accessible in their entirety? Furthermore, exactly how does the integration of information concerning the trauma into pre-existing VAM representations take place? and what functions do VAMs and SAMs serve in memory generally or are they merely systems for dealing with memory for emotional material? Overall, Brewin et al.'s ideas make considerable progress towards a coherent theory of mind which can account for the known variables of interest in PTSD; however, a number of important puzzles remain to be addressed.

In summary, there are a number of good, useful models of post-traumatic stress, within both the social-cognitive and information-processing approaches. However, each model, while being able to account for some aspects of the psychology of trauma very well, seems to struggle with one or more important questions central to an understanding of PTSD and associated conditions. We have tried to argue that a multi-level theory of emotion such as DRT (Brewin et al., in press) is able to offer greater explanatory power when applied to post-traumatic stress and in the next section we examine in some detail how the SPAARS approach attempts to account for PTSD and related conditions.

PTSD within SPAARS

In this section we shall consider how the SPAARS model of emotion accounts for the processing of trauma-related information at the time of the traumatic event and also how that information and the individual's reactions to it are processed subsequent to the traumatic event.

At the time of the trauma, we propose that information about a traumatic event is appraised at the schematic model level of meaning in a threat-related way as part of the individual's experience of intense fear. In addition, trauma-related information is encoded and represented at the analogical, propositional and schematic model levels of meaning.

So, if we consider an example: John is involved in a terrible road traffic accident (RTA). As the RTA is happening, John's interpretation of the sequence of events (e.g. cars colliding, people being injured) is appraised at the schematic model level of meaning within SPAARS as highly threatening with respect to valued goals such as personal survival and also to the highest goal of all (see Chapter 5), which is the maintenance of the existing configuration of dominant schematic models; that is, the maintenance of a sense of reality and of how the world "should" be. Perhaps not surprisingly, therefore, John experiences intense fear as the trauma occurs. Furthermore, information concerning the trauma—the images, sounds, what John was thinking, the sense of danger—is encoded within SPAARS at the various levels of the model (analogical, propositional, and schematic model). See Fig. 6.11.

Such trauma-related information is highly incompatible with the individuals' schematic models of themselves, the world, and others. This very incompatability, we have suggested, means that the trauma-

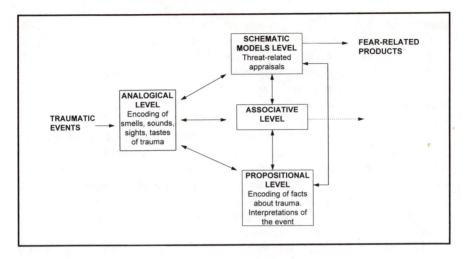

FIG. 6.11. Experience of a traumatic event within SPAARS.

related material threatens the person's very sense of self and reality which are a function of these models. Consequently, trauma-related information is poorly integrated into existing representations at encoding.

In sum, then, the information associated with the traumatic event is incompatible with the individual's extant goals, is threatening, and is appraised as such at the time of the trauma. Furthermore, it is information that cannot be readily integrated with the schematic models of the self, world, and other.

Following a traumatic event, the individual possesses representations of trauma-related information in memory at the analogical, propositional, and schematic model levels. Within SPAARS, however, this information is unintegrated with the individual's dominant models of the self, world, and other. We submit that this pattern of representation within SPAARS accounts for the constellation of symptoms characterising PTSD and related problems following the trauma and we turn to a discussion of these issues next.

Intrusion symptoms. We propose that the representations of unintegrated information at the different levels of SPAARS leads to a constellation of intrusion phenomena via two principal routes. First, the appraisal systems at the schematic model level of meaning will continue to process the unintegrated information and this information will continually be appraised as incompatible and as a threat to the existing configuration of schematic models (the first levels of appraisal in the generation of fear). This process is similar to Horowitz's completion tendency; however, in this instance it is the schematic models of self, world, and other which organise and provide a meaning structure for the information represented in memory at the different levels within SPAARS. This continual appraisal of the incompatibility and threatening nature of the trauma-related information in memory occurs on every appraisal cycle and means that the individual experiences constant activation and reactivation of the fear module. This ensures that traumatised individuals are in an almost continuous existential state of "being in danger", even though they will not always be explicitly experiencing intrusive thoughts or images. In addition, information related to the trauma which is the object of such appraisals will intrude, by virtue of its activated state, into consciousness in a variety of ways ranging from intrusive thoughts to nightmares.

The second of the two routes to the generation of intrusion phenomena depends on the fact that the chronic activation of the fear module will mean that the traumatised individual will exhibit a number of cognitive processing biases for information related to the trauma (see the earlier brief review) as that information is represented in memory as: (1) danger-related; and (2) related to current concerns because it has not been successfully integrated into the individual's models of the self, world, and other. This means that any cues in the environment which are related to the traumatic information are likely to be selectively processed and will themselves activate the trauma-related information in memory, thereby increasing the probability of intrusions.

We propose that because the trauma-related information across the different levels of representation within SPAARS remains unintegrated it retains high levels of internal cohesion within memory. In other words, the representational links between different aspects of the traumatic memory are far stronger than the links between the traumatic memory representations and pre-existing memory structures. Furthermore, the representations of the trauma are very "true to life" as there has been little assimilation or blending with other information in memory. As a result of this high level of cohesion, we propose that external cues are able to activate the entire trauma memory much more easily than if the trauma-related information had been intermeshed with existing information in memory. This results in such phenomena as flashbacks in which stimuli which represent fragments of the traumatic experience are able to trigger intrusive phenomena which involve re-experiencing the whole. Finally, as well as experiencing the generation of fear via repeated appraisal in these ways at the abstracted level of meaning, the individual who has been traumatised will experience the automatic activation of fear via the associative level of meaning as a function of the repetition during intrusions of the link between trauma-related information and fear. Consequently, external or internal trauma-related cues will lead to the generation of fear "out of the blue" and this, we suggest, is a characteristic of chronic post-traumatic stress states.

Avoidance phenomena.   The magnitude of the intrusive phenomena leads individuals to recruit a number of protective mechanisms and processes. They are likely consciously to endeavour to avoid any reminders of the trauma and will try not to think about the trauma or talk about it. In addition, individuals may minimise their interaction with the world generally by socially withdrawing in order to reduce the number of putative triggering stimuli. Other extreme avoidance symptoms of PTSD such as psychogenic amnesia are considered later.

Hyperarousal.   The process of dealing with the existence of unintegrated traumatic information in memory can lead to the various manifestations of hyperarousal in different ways. First, as we have suggested previously, the fear module within SPAARS is continuously being activated and reactivated by both the direct appraisal of the unintegrated representations of trauma-related information within memory and also via multiple cueing from the environment; second, such continual appraisals utilise executive processing resources and the resultant lack of available resources means that the more sophisticated levels of appraisal, which would normally be used in the mediation of emotions via the schematic model level, are less likely to operate. So, for example, in the case of anger we have suggested (see Chapters 5 and 8) that three principal levels of appraisal are involved:

1. The interpretation of the event is appraised as incompatible with existing goal structures (the first level of appraisal in all negative emotions).
2. The interpretation of the event is appraised as a violation of valued goals with an identifiable agent behind the violation.
3. The interpretation of the event is subject to the "moral" appraisal that the agent intended the event—that is, an appraisal of deliberation, avoidability, or negligence.

The first two levels, we have suggested, are necessary and sufficient for the generation of anger. However, in most situations individuals also make further moral appraisals (level 3). We propose that when processing resources are limited, the higher level of moral appraisal is less likely to be invoked and the individual will experience anger and annoyance at any interpretations of events which are appraised in the first two ways only. Consequently, individuals whose processing resources are continually being utilised by appraising the incompatibility of unintegrated trauma-related information in memory are likely to be irritable and to get angry at events which were not deliberate or could not be helped. Similarly, there will be less processing resources for appraisal elaboration and individuals with post-traumatic stress, we submit, are likely to experience fewer complex emotions unassociated with the trauma.

Individual differences at the schematic model level.   It is important to elaborate on the types of models of self, world, and other, which we propose that the individual holds at the schematic model level of meaning within SPAARS and how they relate to the individual's prior emotional and developmental history in order to try to understand the enormous range of individual differences in the way people respond to traumatic events. An individual's models of the self, world, and others seem to vary considerably along the dimensions highlighted by authors such as Janoff-Bulman; for example, how safe the world is, how meaningful events in the world are, how vulnerable the individual is, how positive the view of the self is, and so on. So, some individuals might hold schematic models such as {WORLD—REASONABLY SAFE} or {SELF—GENERALLY INVULNERABLE} whereas others might hold models such as {SELF—COMPLETELY INVULNERABLE}. In addition to these variations in the models of self, world, and other, we propose that individuals will have developed very different ways of dealing with information which is incompatible with these models thoughout their emotional histories. Some people may have become highly practised at repressing or denying such incompatible information in the past such that it has rarely actually been integrated with the models of the self, world, and other but instead has been fenced off in memory—swept under the emotional carpet (see Chapter 10 for a discussion of the repressive coping style). Other individuals will have learnt to deal with information incompatible with their models of the world, self, and other and to emotionally process it (Rachman, 1980) such that there is a *rapprochement* between the models and the information.

If we consider these two broad issues together, namely individual differences in the content of the models of self, world, and other and the different histories of dealing with incompatible information, several combinations emerge which seem important in the understanding of trauma and in particular the three pathways highlighted by Brewin et al. (in press).

Most individuals, we submit, will possess models of the world, self, and others at the schematic model level in which the world is a reasonably safe place, the individual is reasonably safe, and in which there is a high concordance between the individual's actions in the world and their consequences. In most cases, such models are not overvalued in the sense that, for example, the individual holds an assumption of complete invulnerability. Furthermore, such models are not rigid and inflexible because they are usually the product of a learning history in which the individual has had to process information which is at odds with extant models and has had to integrate that information in adapting those same models; for example, when goals have not been fulfilled. Consequently, these individuals' models of the self, world, and other—the structures which provide the sense of meaning and reality— have a certain flexibility and potential to adapt to incorporate disparate information. We propose that individuals such as these, namely the majority, will most usually experience an initial period of post-traumatic reactions (though some will be able to integrate the trauma-related information almost immediately) but would normally be able to integrate the traumatic information into their models of the self, world, and others within weeks or months, either within therapy or within their social support networks (and we discuss these processes later). Such individuals would be unlikely to develop chronic PTSD reactions.

Other people will possess what we shall call overvalued models and assumptions about the self, world, and others at the schematic model level. These models can be expressed as propositional beliefs such as the world is completely safe, nothing really bad will ever happen to me, and so on. An individual might hold such models of the world for two very different reasons: they may have led very predictable, controllable, safe lives in which things have rarely gone wrong and goals have invariably been fulfilled; that is, the schematic models of self, world, and other might be a reasonable reflection of the lives that they have experienced. Alternatively, they may have evolved a way of dealing with emotional events which has involved the repression and denial of any information which is incompatible with the overvalued models which they hold in order to maintain those models (see Singer, 1990, and Chapter 10). We propose that a characteristic of the models of the self, world, and other of such individuals, whether the models are maintained through repression and denial or are a function of the individual's relatively unscathed past, is that they are likely to be inflexible. In neither case will such individuals have a history of adapting their schematic models in order to accommodate incongruent information.

We suggest that both of these types of supposedly invulnerable individual *are* highly vulnerable to extreme emotional distress following a traumatic event but in different ways. The individuals whose pre-trauma life has been safe, controllable, and predictable will have no way of beginning to integrate the trauma-related information into their relatively inflexible models of the self, world, and other; furthermore, they will have no way of defending against its impact. Consequently they are likely to be most at risk of suffering severe and chronic PTSD. This is unlike individuals who over a period of months are able to adapt their schematic models to eventually assimilate the trauma-related information through "emotional processing" (Rachman, 1980) in therapy or within their social support network, those with inflexible models will be unable to resolve this tension and are likely to *abandon* their models of self, world, and other. It is really only these individuals who experience Janoff-Bulman's "shattered assumptions". Most other trauma survivors seem to cling desperately to the models of self, world, and other in order to retain some sense of meaning and some grasp of reality in the face of what has happened. Such abandonment of the models of self and reality which, until the trauma, had served so well, we suggest can lead to severe and chronic personality change which proves destructive for the individuals and their families. Furthermore, the chronic fear reactions can become coupled with sadness at the loss of so much and disgust at the self's inability to cope. Finally, we submit that chronic post-traumatic stress is characterised by increasingly automated emotion generation. In contrast, those individuals who have employed a repressive coping style in order to maintain their overvalued models are likely to be able to continue to employ these coping processes fairly effectively in dealing with the new trauma-related information. In these people, then, there will be few outward signs of post-traumatic reactions in most cases (although in the extreme case they may suffer severe dissociative reactions and psychogenic amnesia). Most usually, we suggest, they will be able to lock the trauma-related information away in memory and throw away the key. Such individuals are likely to be vulnerable to late onset PTSD when, either, later life changes shift the way that their schematic models of self, world, and other are organised, or, when situations similar to the original trauma occur. For example, in Kuwait a number of individuals developed late-onset PTSD when the Iraqi troops amassed once again at the border between the two countries some two years after the original invasion (Dalgleish & Power, 1995). Life events such as these may be sufficient to overwhelm the system, which is already trying to repress the information related to the previous trauma; late-onset PTSD is then likely to occur.

Finally, there are individuals who have premorbidly damaged models of the self, world, and others; that is, they already have schematic model representations that the world is not safe, they are vulnerable, and so on. Such individuals may even have a premorbid psychiatric history. These people, we would speculate, are either (1) likely to have their models confirmed by the new traumatic information in which case we propose that they are likely to experience increases in their associated feelings of anxiety and depression concerning the trauma rather than severe PTSD symptomatology; or (2) their premorbid models of the world are more threat-related with respect to minor negative events, but extremely positive with respect to the kind of low-probability, high-cost events which usually constitute traumas.

Emotional processing and treatment

We have suggested above that, following a traumatic event, the majority of people are able to integrate the trauma-related information over time into their schematic models of self, world, and other. In this section, we discuss how this assimilation might occur.

The integration of trauma-related information, or emotional processing as Rachman (1980) has called it, normally occurs as a function of exposure to the information either within a therapeutic context or within a supportive social network. Such exposure can take many forms; for example, systematically recounting the event, returning to the place that it happened, or just talking about it in more general ways. We propose that this exposure serves to reduce post-traumatic symptomatology in two main ways. First, it allows the individual to re-experience the trauma-related information, information which is incompatible with higher-order models, in a safe context—an environment in which the higher-order models of safety, controllability, predictability, and so on, to which the person clings, do still hold. This process allows the individual to begin to conceptualise the event as something anomalous and unusual in a world where the models of meaning and reality which had served for so long do still have a significant place. Foa and her colleagues talk of this process as an integration of non-danger-related information into the fear network (see above). However, we would argue that it is more readily understood at the higher level of meaning represented by schematic models.

The second means by which various forms of exposure to the trauma-related information operate, we propose, is by weakening the links between that information and the automatic generation of fear via the associative level within SPAARS. This is the same principle we have proposed for the success of exposure-based treatments of phobias (see Chapter 11) and depends on the individual experiencing a reduction in fear during the exposure session. Such exposure-based emotional processing, as we have suggested, serves to enable the individual to integrate the trauma-related information in memory. Consequently, we would argue, this approach is likely to have little benefit for those individuals with chronic PTSD as a consequence of their very inflexible models of the self, world, and others as they are unlikely to be able to modify those models to integrate the trauma-related information, regardless of how many times that information is re-presented through exposure. For these individuals, their sense of reality and meaning have been "shattered" (Janoff-Bulman, 1985) and it seems likely that cognitive-oriented treatment would be more efficacious in replacing the abandoned, overvalued, inflexible models with more adaptable, functional ones.

In this section of the chapter we have reviewed the constellation of difficulties experienced by people with PTSD and discussed the various extant theoretical models of the disorder. We have then sketched an analysis of PTSD within the SPAARS model developed in Chapter 5. We have paid particular attention to the issues of chronicity and late onset within PTSD and have discussed briefly the mechanisms by which treatment effects might operate. In sum, we submit that the complexity of post-traumatic reactions can be explained more effectively within multiple level theories such as DRT and SPAARS than within the simpler single-level theories which exist in the literature.

Phobias and obsessions

We have concentrated in this chapter on panic, generalised anxiety and PTSD in order to illustrate several ways in which fear can become disordered. Two further traditional categories of so-called anxiety disorders—phobias and obsessions—can also be derived from fear. However, we propose that some phobias and obsessions can perhaps be more usefully derived from the basic emotion of disgust and there may be little or no role for fear responses in these cases. Consequently, we talk briefly about fear-derived phobias and obsessions here and continue the discussion in Chapter 9 on disgust.

Phobias

Phobias are usually defined as irrational fears of objects or situations. Simple phobias involve fear of, for example, snakes or spiders combined with an ability to see that there is no reason to be afraid. Agoraphobia is somewhat different and is characterised by fear of leaving the home or safe environment. Agoraphobia is highly co-morbid with panic problems and we have touched upon it briefly in the section on panic. Finally, social phobia involves anxiety about social situations and a fear of embarrassment.

We have argued in the introduction to this chapter that phobic problems, particularly simple phobias, are extremely common and that it is in our view a mistake to assume that, just because indivduals meet criteria for a clinical diagnosis of phobia, it means that they are pathological, abnormal or disordered in any way. This issue of distinguishing normal fears from phobias is a factor in epidemiolgical studies which, nevertheless, reveal an average of about six per 100 in community surveys for mild phobias with approximately two per 1000 being viewed as disabling (Myers, Weissman, & Tischler, 1984). Phobias tend to have their origins in childhood in the case of simple phobias (e.g. Rutter, 1984), though as we noted in the Introduction a large number of childhood fears disappear as the individual matures. Social phobia and agoraphobia have a later onset (Ost, 1987). Phobias are more usually reported by women, with estimates as high as 95% for simple phobias (Marks, 1969).

In this section we shall consider simple fear-derived phobias. Social phobia and certain other simple phobias, we propose, are more usefully derived from the basic emotion of disgust and we consider them in Chapter 9.

Fear-derived simple phobias are characterised by extreme fear and anxiety in the presence of the phobic stimulus, an uncontrollable desire to leave the feared situation, and, outside of the feared situation, an ability to see that the fear is unfounded. Theoretical work suggests that there are three main routes to the acquistion of such phobias (Rachman, 1990). The first is through a two-process conditioning sequence in which the phobic stimulus becomes classically conditioned to elicit fear, and is then instrumentally reinforced by the subject avoiding the feared stimulus (Mowrer, 1960). The second route is through vicarious conditioning or modelling in which the individual witnesses another person's fear reaction. Finally, phobias may become acquired through the dissemination of information about the phobic object. Support for these three putative routes has been through simple self-report surveys (e.g. Hekmat, 1987). However, as we shall argue in Chapter 9, it is by no means clear that the intial emotional reactions, particularly in the vicarious route, were ones of fear. A final point, one we made in the Introduction, is that some phobias are more common than others and this seems to reflect some form of evolutionary preparedness (Seligman, 1971) where we have a propensity to develop fear reactions quickly to objects and situations that were genuinely threatening to our forebears. Unfortunately, there have been few experiments on prehistoric humans to test this hypothesis!

Within SPAARS, the proposal of two routes to emotion generation seems to offer a ready account for the phenomenology of simple phobic states. The SPAARS analysis would propose that the phobic object was initially appraised at the schematic model level as threatening. This would not have to involve an actual encounter with the object; fear-related appraisals could result from a vicarious experience of the phobic stimulus or from some form of instruction. The next stage in the development of the phobia would be the automatisation of this fear response. In the case of prepared stimuli, we have suggested that this can occur after one distressing encounter; other non-prepared stimuli would come to elicit fear automatically as a result of repeated fear-related appraisals at the schematic model level. As the individual develops, the schematic model appraisals of the phobic object will not be fear-related and the individual will be able to see no reason to be afraid. However, we propose that the automatic generation of fear within SPAARS via the associative level will persist each time the person encounters the phobic stimulus. This automatic generation will activate the fear module which will reconfigure the SPAARS system in order to deal with threat. The associated action potential to flee the situation is, thus, likely to be extremely strong and difficult to resist.

In sum, in this section we have presented a brief review of fear-derived phobias and indicated how they can be explained within the SPAARS framework. However, not all phobias are characterised by a fear reaction; for many, the spider is more disgusting than fearful and the role of disgust in these cases is considered in more detail in Chapter 9.

A note on obsessions

Obsessional states are immensely complex phenomena. In some ways the fear or anxiety components involved in some obsessions are the easiest aspect of the disorder to account for. Individuals might be afraid that if they do not check the gas tap then the house will blow up and people may be killed. Such anxiety is reduced by checking that the tap is switched off. What is much more difficult to account for is why the obsessional individual has to check again and again and again that the gas is turned off. It is beyond the scope of our ambitions to provide a comprehensive empirical and theoretical review of fear-based obsessional states here as it does not seem clear that the emotional component is central to the disorder. Others have done this job more than adequately (e.g. Rachman & Hodgson, 1980; Tallis, 1995a,b). What we do wish to spend some time on, however, is the suggestion that some obsessional states can best be conceived of as disorders of disgust; particularly those involving washing compulsions and contamination-related intrusions. The role of disgust has been sadly neglected in such cases and we present an analysis of disgust-based obsessions in Chapter 9.

CONCLUSIONS

In this chapter we have considered normal fear and its disorders. The balance in the chapter does not reflect the balance in nature. We spent relatively little time discussing normal fear even though it is ever present in our lives; this is mainly because we have used and abused the example of fear throughout the rest of the book and have assumed that the reader is aware by now of the parameters of normal fear reactions. Similarly, we have spent considerable time discussing three so-called anxiety disorders: panic, generalised anxiety, and PTSD; and relatively little time on phobias, which are far more common. This reflects our belief that the three disorders we have focused on are theoretically more compelling and offer challenges to our own model, SPAARS, which simple phobias do not. Finally, although we have used standard psychiatric labels to refer to varities of disordered fear, it is our contention that what is needed is a taxonomy of emotional disorders that is theoretically derived and not based on surface features. Consequently, we have provided a number of pointers as to how such an analysis within the SPAARS model might depart from the traditional psychiatric classificaion; for example, a number of simple phobias would be derived from the basic emotion of disgust, as would some obsessional states. In other chapters we consider how disorders of more complex emotions might be derived from fear; for example morbid jealousy (see Chapter 8).

CHAPTER SEVEN

Sadness

When sorrows come, they come not single spies, but in battalions. *(Hamlet)*

INTRODUCTION

Sadness is little studied in psychology. This failure is surprising given its widespread portrayal in art, the cinema, music, and literature. Instead, the more extreme variants of sadness such as grief, bereavement and mourning, or disorders derived from sadness such as depression have dominated psychological study (cf. Stearns, 1993). The focus on the extreme and the abnormal may perhaps represent something of our cultural ambivalence towards sadness and its expression, though we will try to hold back from such wild interpretations, at least until later. We must note though that much of what we think about as sadness should more correctly be viewed as sadness combined with other basic emotions such as fear, anger, or disgust. For example, a common procedure used to study "sadness" in the psychology laboratory is to use a mood induction procedure such as the Velten card technique (Velten, 1968) in which the subject reads through a list of statements along the lines of "I'm worthless", "I'm a failure", and so on. Such lists encourage a state of self-criticism which, as Freud emphasised in his classic work *Mourning and Melancholia*

(1917), is a feature that *distinguishes* melancholia from mourning rather than represents a defining feature of it. Much mood induction work therefore may have studied sadness combined with disgust (directed towards the self) rather than sadness itself.

A second point that we must note is that sadness, like many other so-called "negative" emotions, is not inherently negative; thus, even though we associate sadness with predominantly negative phenomenological states, we may watch films such as *Brief Encounter because* they are "good weepies", or remain unconvinced by "bad weepies" because they fail to induce a persuasive state of sadness. As Shelley wrote "Our sweetest songs are those that tell of saddest thought." We will also argue later, when we consider combinations of basic emotions, that sadness and the "opposite" emotion of happiness may combine for example in complex emotional states such as nostalgia. Rapid oscillations between sadness and happiness can be seen in some cases of mania which may often be more of a disinhibited or emotionally labile condition rather than simply an abnormal and extreme variant of happiness (see Chapter 10).

So what is sadness? The sense that this question is similar to asking for a definition of the colour "red" perhaps adds weight to the proposal that sadness is basic, as we discussed in Chapter 3 in the section on basic emotions. Part of the definition of sadness emphasises the possible contexts in which it occurs; thus, it could be defined as that state appropriate to being in a graveyard in which one is reminded both of one's own mortality and of the loss of the people we love. But is the gravedigger in a constant state of sadness? Presumably not. Again, we think of continuing or unchanging states as associated with abnormality and disorder; thus, even in extreme though normal grief reactions one may laugh, cry, and get angry with the lost person rather than remain in a constant state of sadness. We must define sadness therefore in terms of a number of features (cf. Lazarus, 1991), which in Chapters 2 and 5 we have identified as the key external or internal event, an interpretation, an appraisal, a physiological state, an action potential, conscious awareness, and overt behaviour. To elaborate on these and other points:

1. There is an appraisal of loss or failure, in which the lost object or goal varies in degree of importance and type; it could be a person, a place ("Oh to be in England, now that April's here"), an ambition that has not been attained, an object of personal value (e.g. a special pen, an important gift), or a loss of an ideal or moral value. The focus of sadness is therefore on the appraisal of loss of one or more goals across one or more domains.

2. The loss need not be permanent, but could be a temporary separation from a loved one or a loved place or even a sadness experienced at the return to a loved one or a loved place following a period of separation. We would disagree therefore with analyses of loss that suggest that the loss need be permanent or irrevocable (e.g. Lazarus, 1991; Oatley & Johnson-Laird, 1987).

3. The focus of the loss may be on a significant other rather than oneself, for example, one's child failing an exam or being ill or injured. Indeed, the loss may be communal rather than personal as in the loss of a Head of State, a favourite film star, or a failure by one's National team. In David Lean's film *Brief Encounter*, the focus of the loss is on two film stars acting a part that was filmed 50 years ago; we are capable of setting aside these aspects of "reality" therefore in our experience of sadness and other emotions.

4. The temporal frame of the loss may vary from past to present to future. One may reminisce and feel sad about the loss of childhood or of schooldays, just as one may feel sad about a current loss. However, the loss could be an imagined one that has not yet happened as in the imagined future loss of one's parents, or, indeed, it might never happen except in a dream or a daydream. Some of the most poignant experiences of basic emotions may be in dream states during which complex cognitive appraisals may be absent and the emotion may be activated by the direct route, as outlined in Chapter 5.

5. The phenomenological experience thereby differs considerably both in intensity and in duration according to these and other factors and relates to our earlier discussion of emotions, moods, and dispositions (see Chapter 2). Sadness can be mild and last a few seconds as in the mention of an emotion-laden name in passing in conversation; it can last minutes when the hero dies at the end of a novel; it can last hours because of breaking a favourite ornament; and, in a sense, it can last a lifetime because of the loss of a homeland or of a parent or of a child if the person is always remembered with sadness. Our vocabulary reflects these variations in the intensity and the focus of the loss or failure, as illustrated in Fig. 7.1.

In relation to the key question that we have addressed to all of the emotions, we must ask what might be the functions of sadness and what are its adaptive features? The fact that we have to ask this question with a hint of surprise reflects something of the bad press that sadness receives in our culture. In many cultures, sadness is not considered to be inherently negative, because sadness, or states akin to sadness, are more valued (e.g. Kleinman & Good, 1985; Lutz, 1985); for example, a state of sad reflectiveness may be considered a step along the road to

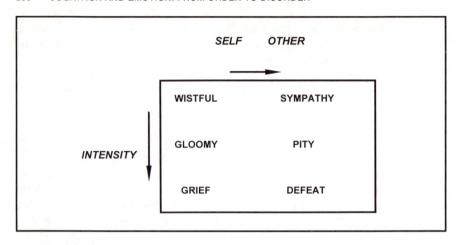

FIG. 7.1. Examples of terms used to describe the basic emotion of sadness according to variations in intensity and focus.

salvation in many Asian societies. These schematic level goals therefore are both culturally inspired and culturally maintained and may be shared goals between the self and significant others. As Stearns (1993) emphasises, the variation across cultures in the approach to sadness reflects a culture's view of the perceived lack of self-mastery, and the perceived "demands" that may thereby be placed on others in the social network as a consequence of sadness. Both lack of self-mastery and demandingness on others are viewed negatively in those cultures which emphasise individuality rather than collectivity and activity rather than passivity. In Western cultures, when a soccer player sheds tears in public, he becomes headline news. One important social function of sadness therefore is that it may lead the individual to make emotional and practical demands on others; it can thereby strengthen social bonds and lead to altruism in which others feel sympathy or pity (Izard, 1993).

In addition to its social functions, sadness also serves a more personal function, though this may be over-emphasised in our culture because of the emphasis on the active individual. This personal function is the increase in self focus that may (though not necessarily) occur in sadness; in such a state of self-focused sadness the individual may review priorities given to important goals and roles in the light of an experienced loss or the possibility of such loss. Such reviews may enable individuals to alter the balance of their lives, for example, to reassess the overvaluing of one goal such as work at the expense of others such as personal relationships. Following an irrevocable loss such as that of a partner, the implications for shared goals and plans may be so widespread that the individual may take a considerable length of time to realise the extent of the loss (e.g. the first holiday or the first Christmas without that person) let alone to replace both the person and any mutual plans.

Definitions of emotion that emphasise an "action tendency" (e.g. Frijda, 1986; Lazarus, 1991) associated with each emotion often express a puzzlement because sadness is not associated with an obvious action tendency. This apparent absence even leads Lazarus (1991, p.251) to question whether or not sadness is an emotion!

> In sadness there seems to be no clear action tendency— except inaction, or withdrawal into oneself—that seems consistent with the concept of a mood.

Furthermore (1991, p.251):

> If we treat sadness as a mood, then we are relieved of having to resolve certain difficult issues such as specifying an action tendency.

Along with others we have included "propensities for action" as defining features of emotion (see Chapters 2 and 3). However, we do not experience Lazarus' problem which leads him to query whether or not sadness is an emotion because it does not fit the Procrustean Bed of his definition. An alternative approach may be to question his definition instead. At the same time, we suggest that there probably is a "propensity for action" in sadness; as outlined above, sadness prompts the individual to make demands for help from members of the social network especially in cultures in which help-seeking is a cultural norm. Indeed, when considered developmentally (e.g. Harris, 1989) it is hard to see what function the accompaniments of sadness such as tears and crying might have in the pre-linguistic infant other than to communicate information about an internal state to the infant's caretakers. This social "propensity for action" is typically inhibited in our culture because we value stoicism in the face of adversity. In fact, in the face of extreme disasters such laudable "strength" has been shown to increase the risk of developing elevated post traumatic stress symptomatology in the longer term (e.g. Joseph et al., 1996; see Chapter 6). In the Ifaluk, a group of Pacific Islanders studied by Lutz (e.g. 1988), who seem to focus primarily on the interpersonal implications of emotion, the nearest term for sadness is "fago", a type of sadness-compassion felt for someone else who is in need or who has lost someone and who therefore needs help from others. As a tailnote, it should be remarked that the Ifaluk treat happiness as a "negative" emotion and disapprove of it because the "sufferer" may as a consequence come to disregard others.

Another indirect way of inhibiting a culturally unacceptable emotion is to convert it into another more acceptable one. In Western cultures males are not meant to express fear and sadness, so these emotions may be "converted" into more acceptable ones such as anger and excitement. A dramatic example of such a conversion culture is the Ilongot in the Philippines (Rosaldo, 1980). The Ilongot encourage the expression of anger in their young men, because it is seen as a positive emotion. Emotions such as sadness or grief, however, are not so highly valued and the practice of head-hunting was traditionally used as a means of transforming an extreme and unwanted emotion such as sadness into a positive one such as anger. Fortunately for anthropologists, the practice of head-hunting has apparently now stopped.

SADNESS —SOME THEORETICAL CONSIDERATIONS

Following the outline general model presented in Chapter 5 of the SPAARS approach to emotion, we will now consider the application of the model to sadness. The focus will initially be on all forms of sadness, but in subsequent sections we will examine how the model applies to the extreme forms of sadness seen in grief, and to the sadness-based disorder of depression.

Three of the key points we proposed in Chapter 5 were that basic emotions have the potential to develop in a modular fashion, that multiple levels of meaning must be considered especially in relation to important roles and goals across the domains of self, world, and other, and that we must take account of the considerable range of inhibitory and facilitatory processes that occur both within and between different levels of processing. The application of some of these points is presented in Fig. 7.2, which takes as its starting point an appraisal of loss or the potential for loss. As the figure shows, the generation of sadness can occur either as a function of the appraisal (schematic model) route or the automatic (associative) route. For example, sadness might be generated by the automatic route because of an innate aspect of sadness linked to the loss of any key attachment figure (see later), or because of an automated sequence in which for example a particular place becomes associated with a loss.

It is likely that low level activation of emotion modules occurs continually throughout both our waking and our sleeping lives, the large part of which goes unnoticed except perhaps in research on videotaping and psychophysiological recording of emotional responses (e.g. Ekman & Friesen, 1978).

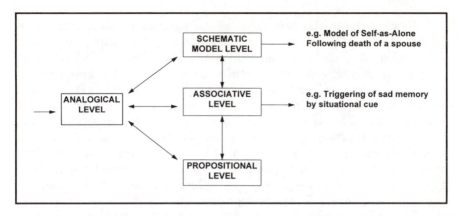

FIG. 7.2. Different levels of activation of the sadness emotion module.

A second level of possible initial activation of the emotion module is through the propositional level of input, though as we have argued in Chapter 5, propositional input could lead to the generation of emotion through either the appraisal or the automatic route. Many of the aesthetic emotions are likely to be experienced through this level because they are encoded in propositional form; the novel, play or film causes some transient experience of sadness in us because of its propositional content, which is then coded into a schematic model:

> He felt an overwhelming sense of loss invade his being, a terrible sense of life's impermanence and transience, a sudden understanding of the meaning that this vision held. He crossed the road to the sea wall and sat down on it ... unobserved, alone, he put his head in his hands and wept. (*William Boyd*, The Blue Afternoon, *1993, p.200*).

A third level of activation occurs at the schematic model level. At this level a whole variety of sources of information both external and internal to the individual may be combined into a holistic representation; thus, a schematic model associated with sadness could incorporate propositional material, body-state input, and mnemonic material none of which in themselves might be sufficient to activate a schematic model associated with sadness, yet their combination could be the opposite of the apparent sum of their parts. For example, as the widow sits back in her armchair to watch her favourite television programme, she might suddenly be reminded of how her husband too used to sit in that particular armchair; even though the memory in itself might be a happy one, she might nevertheless feel sad *because* it was something that was in the past.

Following the initial activation of the sadness module, a range of possible facilitatory or inhibitory processes may then come into effect. The activated module includes physiological change, the biasing of processing at different levels within the system, and a potential for action associated with sadness. Figure 7.3 presents examples of possible facilitatory effects within a module. A series of positive feedback loops may maintain and even enhance the activation of the sadness module; thus, stored representations at the associative level may trigger off sadness related propositions which, in turn, can serve to maintain the activation of the schematic model of being in a state of sadness. In fact, as we shall present subsequently, one of the problems with extreme grief reactions and severe forms of depression is that the individual feels unable to shift to a different state or to a different emotion; these positive feedback loops can maintain the activation of the module for months or even years at a time under certain conditions (see later).

In normal individuals mild activation of the sadness module is typically very transient; thus, in mood induction studies subjects may begin to recall mood incongruent happy memories and generate positive self-related propositions in order to inhibit the unwanted mood and replace it with a more positive one (e.g. Isen, 1984; Parrott & Sabini, 1990). Under normal circumstances individuals may use a variety of

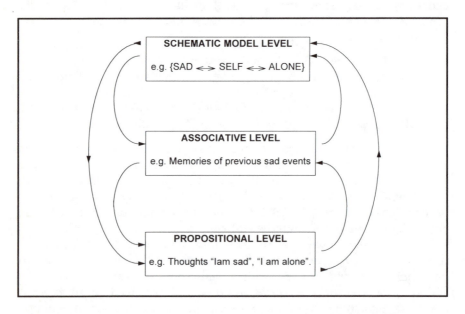

FIG. 7.3. Some possible feedback loops by which activation of the sadness module can be maintained.

strategies that operate at one or more levels. For example, one of us (MP) finds that eating hot chilli food is dysphoria-relieving. These strategies can operate at an associative level such as recalling something pleasant; at the propositional level by having positive thoughts about oneself; or at the schematic level by generating a different emotional self-model (see Figure 7.3). Of course, in practice an effective strategy will operate at all levels, for example, a pleasant memory may generate a series of positive propositions, and include the recollection of the self with a different schematic model. We are merely focusing on the starting point at which the inhibitory or facilitatory processes begin.

In some individuals the inhibitory processes may be so strong that they have great difficulty in experiencing an emotion such as sadness even when it is appropriate to do so. One such group are so-called repressors who may recall little if anything negative from their past, endorse few negative trait adjectives, and show poor retention of self-related negative material (e.g. Myers, Brewin, & Power, 1992; see Chapter 10).

Although we have focused on facilitatory and inhibitory processes occurring primarily *within* the sadness module, as we argued in Chapter 5, it is also important to consider facilitatory and inhibitory processes that can occur *between* emotion modules; here may lie the royal road to emotional disorder, which will provide a key focus for the remainder of this chapter. We turn next therefore to a consideration of how sadness may interact with other basic emotions.

COMBINATIONS OF SADNESS AND OTHER BASIC EMOTIONS

One of the possibilities that we suggested in Chapter 5 was that two or more basic emotions could, under certain circumstances, continuously activate each other. This "coupling" between emotion modules can be considered to work in a similar way to the within-module activation that was outlined in the previous section. The proposal does of course run counter to a number of emotion theories such as that of Oatley and Johnson-Laird (1987), in which it is argued that even complex emotions are derived from only one basic underlying emotion. We hope, however, to demonstrate that there is much to be gained from taking a different line; namely, that the coupling of two or more basic emotions may lock the individual into a complex emotional state from which it may be difficult to escape.

The fact that even under normal circumstances sadness can readily be experienced together with other basic emotions is illustrated by the examples presented in Table 7.1. By "experienced together" we literally mean simultaneously, rather than in succession. All emotion theorists acknowledge that one emotion can be replaced by a succession of others as circumstances or appraisals change; for example, the student who feels disappointed at getting a lower mark than hoped for on a test may subsequently feel overjoyed on finding out that she actually came top of the class. The first example in Table 7.1 shows a combination of Sadness and Disgust and an example under which such a combination might occur; namely, someone feeling self-disgust following the break-up of a relationship. Such a combination may be central to the experience of depression, so we will return to the pairing of Sadness and Disgust in the subsequent section on depression. The second example is that of the combination of Sadness and Anger, a pairing that used to be thought pathological in the experience of bereavement, but which, from the work of Bowlby (e.g. 1980) and others, is now known to be a common experience in both children and adults following temporary or permanent breaks in attachment relationships. The third example is that of Sadness and Anxiety which, again, may be a common combination following a loss in which the individual feels depleted of resources and therefore fears for their capacity to deal with future demands. The final combination, that of Sadness and Happiness, is probably best known to us in forms such as nostalgia, homesickness, and love-sickness, and at the end of Hollywood movies. For example, in the film *It's a Wonderful Life* the hero, Jimmy Stewart, tries to kill himself because he concludes that his life has been a failure, but is then given a dramatic view of how much he *has* contributed and he finally decides that he wants to live.

In addition to our own anecdotal experience of combined basic emotions, there is empirical evidence of the types of combinations that may occur. Keith Oatley has recently carried out a number of diary

TABLE 7.1
Pairings of sadness with other basic emotions together with some typical examples

	Example
Sadness – Disgust	He left me because I am such an awful person
Sadness – Anger	Why did he leave me, the *******?!
Sadness – Anxiety	How will I cope now that he's gone?
Sadness – Happiness	Oh, how I miss the good times we had

studies in which individuals were asked to make detailed recordings of emotions that they experienced over a number of days (Oatley & Duncan, 1992). Despite having claimed in earlier theoretical work cited peviously that basic emotions cannot be combined, Oatley and Duncan reported that more than a third of everyday experiences of the basic emotions of fear, anger, sadness, and love were found to be simultaneously accompanied by the experience of one of the other basic emotions. In fact, sadness was found to be the emotion that was most likely to occur in combination, providing 77% of all such examples. Furthermore, where emotions were found to change over the course of an incident, the commonest change was found to occur between sadness and anger (with 33% of such changes being accounted for by this pairing). The predilection for sadness to combine with other basic emotions may provide some clue as to why conditions such as grief and depression can be so long-standing.

It seems therefore that the combination or coupling of basic emotions is a common everyday experience and that sadness in particular is more likely than any of the other basic emotions to be involved in such combinations. We will proceed to examine therefore two particularly insidious combinations, those of Sadness–Anger and Sadness–Disgust which, we suggest, may underlie atypical grief reactions and some forms of depression, respectively. Before doing so, however, we must reiterate that, because combinations of basic emotions occur so readily within the bounds of normal experience, our approach emphasises that the emotional disorders are extreme variants of normal experience rather than being qualitatively different.

Grief

Queen Victoria was 42 years old when her husband, Prince Albert, died of typhoid in Windsor Castle. She went into seclusion for many years after his death and went through a period of considerable unpopularity with her subjects. She wore black for the rest of her life, refused to wear the crown or robes of state, but wore a humble bonnet that symbolised widowhood. She kept a picture of her husband at her bedside, and constantly grieved his loss. On her own death some 40 years later, she was buried along with his dressing gown, photographs, and a plaster cast of his hand.

In this section we will examine an extreme though normal variant of sadness that almost everybody will experience at some time, that is, grief. In fact, it may be the individual's *failure* to show emotion following a major loss or trauma that is the key to an atypical outcome (e.g. Parkes, 1972). The importance of sadness and grief both in childhood and adulthood can probably best be understood in terms of attachment theory (e.g. Bowlby, 1988), though it must be noted that recent work has broadened this focus to emphasise more general aspects of stress and coping (e.g. Stroebe, Stroebe, & Hansson, 1993).

One of the key innate systems is that of attachment to the primary caretaker; threats to this relationship are experienced with considerable distress by the child. There is also evidence that problems can develop early on in attachment style and that these problems may be associated with later psychopathology; thus, so-called anxious attachment and avoidant attachment styles may be associated with a range of later adult attachment problems. We can certainly predict that longitudinal studies from early childhood onwards of attachment style and adult studies with the so-called adult attachment interview (e.g. Main, 1991) should greatly increase our understanding of a range of problems including both normal and abnormal reactions to grief.

In an attempt to understand both the lengthy nature of the normal grief reaction and the even lengthier nature of abnormal reactions, studies of children's separations from their primary caretakers provide a wealth of information. Bowlby's (1980) excellent summary of this work showed that the child initially goes through stages of protest and despair because of the separation, but, eventually, if the mother (or other primary caretaker) returns, the child may treat her as if she were a stranger. In contrast, a non-primary caretaker (perhaps the father) may be greeted with warmth and relief over the same length of separation. Bowlby's interpretation of these different reactions is that the child reacts to the separation or loss of the mother eventually by "defensively excluding" or inhibiting the negative emotions. Even with very short separations of a few minutes studied in the laboratory, for example, with the Strange Situation Test (Ainsworth, Blehar, Waters, & Wall, 1978), a proportion of children as young as 12 months show ambivalent positive and negative reactions to the mother's return.

A second related area from work with children focuses not so much on whether children *express* ambivalent feelings, but on whether they can *conceptualise* such ambivalence. Harter (1977), for example, noticed that many children she saw clinically were unable to admit to ambivalent feelings particularly towards primary caretakers. In her subsequent work with normal children, she found that only at about 10 years of age can children acknowledge and describe these ambivalent feelings (Harter & Buddin, 1987). The following quote from Bowlby (1980, pp.70–71)) captures the same idea:

> In therapeutic work it is not uncommon to find that a person
> (child, adolescent or adult) maintains, consciously, a wholly
> favourable image of a parent, but that at a less conscious

level he nurses a contrasting image in which his parent is represented as neglectful, or rejecting, or as ill-treating him. In such persons the two images are kept apart, out of communication with each other; and any information that may be at variance with the established image is excluded.

The conclusion that we draw from these findings and our previous proposals is that the loss of the main attachment figure whether in childhood or adulthood leads to not only the emotion of sadness, but frequently also to anger at that person for abandoning the individual to an uncertain fate. However, the expression and conceptualisation of such ambivalence requires a developmentally sophisticated level of maturity that many individuals may fail to negotiate or may only partially do so; thus, the individual may feel sadness following such a loss, but feel extreme guilt about feelings of anger, or, psychologically, go one step further and idealise the lost person so that no feelings of anger could even be imaginable towards such a perfect individual. In addition, as noted above, the combination of pressures on an individual in Western and other cultures to inhibit the expression of both sadness and anger following loss may all lead to the result that grief runs an atypical course.

In terms of our general SPAARS model presented in Chapter 5, the experience of extreme grief consequent on the loss of an attachment figure can be seen as the major loss of mutual goals, roles, and plans that the loss of attachment figures entails. Because of the evolutionary base to attachment, the universal experience of grief across cultures must in part have an innate basis and must therefore involve operation of the direct access route to emotion within SPAARS. However, the impact of the loss of a significant other is so wide-ranging on the individual's life that multiple and continued appraisals will accompany any automatic reactions. For example, studies of the impact of bereavement in our culture show that the nature of the impact and its consequences may differ for widows and widowers; Wortman, Silver, and Kessler (1993) reported that widowers were particularly vulnerable to limited social relationships and problems with taking on tasks that their wives had handled, whereas widows were more vulnerable to financial strain following the death of their husbands. The net effect of these and other problems is that bereaved individuals may make appraisals that they will be unable to cope with the practical and emotional burden that they have been left with. In addition, if the bereaved appraise the grief reaction itself as weak or not allowed, because of a more general rejection of negative emotions, then a more atypical course may be likely for grief.

This atypical course may be more likely to occur, we would speculate, if the coupling of the basic emotions of sadness and anger occurs, as shown in Figure 7.4, given that many grief reactions have in addition to the primary emotion of sadness other appraisals that lead to anger. The anger may be directed at the lost individuals themselves, be directed at others who caused the loss or did not offer enough to prevent the loss; anger is more likely to occur where deaths are sudden and unexpected (e.g. Vargas, Loye, & Hodde-Vargas, 1989) and may thereby explain in part why sudden and unexpected deaths may lead to more chronic or difficult grief reactions. We argued earlier and in Chapter 5 that once such couplings of activated basic emotions occur, they may reciprocally activate each other and thereby prolong the emotional state. In the case of grief, however, we must also emphasise the internal and external pressures to inhibit not only the expression of sadness, but especially the expression of anger towards the lost individual. The greater the attempts to inhibit one or both of the emotions of sadness and anger involved in grief therefore, the longer the course that the grief reaction will run. The loss of the main attachment figure whether in childhood or in adulthood involves nothing less than a redefinition of the self; an individual who prevents, whether consciously or

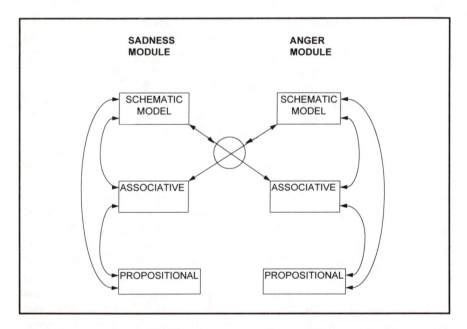

FIG. 7.4. The coupling of the sadness and anger modules in grief showing some of the main intra- and inter-module feedback loops.

unconsciously, such a process from occurring, who attempts to deny the loss of the key other, will be left with a model of the self that is maladaptive, inaccurate, and out of date.

In summary, we propose that the experience of grief can run a number of possible courses depending on a variety of factors. First, the cultural and familial pressures that inhibit the expression of sadness in men ("Boys don't cry"), and anger in both men and women ("Don't speak ill of the dead"). Second, the developmental history of the individual in which early childhood ambivalence towards the primary caretaker may have been outlawed, because the adult was, for example, unable to contain the child's anger. Third, the nature of the relationship with the lost individual, that is, the degree to which the relationship was secure or ambivalent. Fourth, the type and suddenness of the loss, for example, the degree to which an individual has been able to prepare for the loss of an ageing parent, versus at the other extreme the premature and unexpected loss of a healthy child. And, fifth, the quality and the nature of the support from significant others in the individual's network ("We don't mention her, so as not to upset him"). We will now briefly examine some of the empirical studies of bereavement in order to see in more detail how these factors influence outcome.

Most studies of bereavement show that it is a long process and that even after 12 months only approximately half show reasonable recovery (e.g. Glick, Weiss, & Parkes, 1974; Parkes, 1972), with two to three years being the more typical timescale to recovery. The Glick et al. (1974) study included both widows and widowers and demonstrated that the emotional reactions such as yearning for the lost person, intense sadness, emotional isolation, and anger were similar in both groups, as was the rate of recovery. More widowers, however, were found attempting to exert control over their sad and angry feelings, though they also evidenced more self-reproach initially and found their energy and ability at work considerably reduced. Stroebe and Stroebe (1993) in a study of younger bereaved adults reported that at four to seven months after the loss 42% of their sample met Beck Depression Inventory criteria for at least mild depression; two years after the loss this figure had fallen to 27%, a value considerably greater than would normally be expected. Indeed, Rubin (1990) found that the especially painful loss, that of a parent losing a child, may lead to sadness being unabated some 13 years after the loss. Rubin also found that it may be harder for older parents to come to terms with loss than it is for younger parents. Whereas the younger parents may eventually come to develop new plans and goals, older parents have fewer options, for example, to have additional children to replace the lost child, or to come to value some other role or goal in the place of the lost child.

Not all losses of course involve loss through death, but losses also happen through separation and divorce both of which have their own psychological costs. Losses can also be less tangible when, for example, they involve the loss of an ideal, nor do they necessarily involve another person when, for example, they involve the loss of a limb, or the loss of capacities through chronic illness. Such examples highlight the fact that although we have emphasised the interpersonal context in which losses occur, reactions to losses that are not interpersonal must also be considered.

To consider first a complex case that involved the loss of an ideal, though in the context of key interpersonal losses:

Maria was the fourth born of six children, all close together in age. Her father died suddenly and unexpectedly when she was five years of age, though she remembered her childhood as extremely happy. Her mother however had had little time for her after her father's death and had clearly endured considerable hardship in raising six children on her own.

Maria met and married her husband when she was eighteen. Although he had not been her first steady relationship, she was soon sure that he was her ideal match. They had two daughters within the first few years of marriage and Maria stayed at home and devoted herself to her husband and her children. She described herself during this time as a completely happy person, great fun to be with, with the ideal family. She was unable to understand why her friends' relationships were never as good as hers and, equally, that she and her husband were the envy of everyone they knew.

Maria came into therapy with her "ideals shattered". She had discovered about 15 months previously that her husband had slept with her best friend, once by his account in a moment of temptation. So she forgave him. However, a year later she arrived unexpected at her friend's flat to find her husband there also. Her friend and her husband had carried on an affair for well over a year.

Maria felt overwhelmed by emotions "that weren't hers". She found herself in absolute rages, even though she was someone who had never become angry "even in situations where other people did". She would burst into uncontrollable floods of tears, and so now avoided seeing her other friends or going out, because of her "complete personality change".

The thing that she was the most furious about was that he
had taken away the perfect relationship and destroyed the
perfect family. Needless to say, they were still living together.

Maria provides a dramatic example of someone who to all intents and
purposes was going through a double bereavement, even though her
husband still lived with her and her former friend still lived in the same
town. What she had lost though was the idealised relationship and the
idealised family that she had created for herself, repeating the pattern
of the early loss and subsequent idealisation of her father. The child who
had to hide her own grief and be strong and care for others might well
never have had to face up to such, but for the failure of others to play
their parts in her melodrama. All of Maria's major goals and plans were
mutual ones that she believed she shared with her husband and her best
friend. In many ways therefore the affair violated her basic assumptions
about the world (Janoff-Bulman, 1992; Wortman, Silver, & Kessler,
1993), and about the roles that loving partners and best friends should
play in that world. Maria's continuing air of shocked disbelief at what
her husband and her friend had done to her world, demonstrated the
strength of the schematic models that she had created, presumably
partly in response to the early loss of her father and her consequent
caring for her mother at the expense of her own needs. The price of her
devoted caring was not returned by her spouse or her best friend. (See
also the trauma section in Chapter 6 for more detailed discussion of
"shattered assumptions" about the world.)

In conclusion, grief is a powerful and universal reaction to the loss of
attachment figures in particular. The experience of loss leads to
overwhelming sadness and, in addition, a myriad of accompanying
appraisals that revolve around the loss of mutual goals, roles, and plans,
together with bereaved individuals' appraisals of whether or not they
will be able to cope without the lost person. Theorists such as Bowlby
(e.g. 1980) who have proposed that the grief reaction follows a series of
stages have also emphasised the angry protests that the bereaved
individual typically goes through. Although recent theorists present
more flexible models with, for example, the possibility that stages
overlap (e.g. Shuchter & Zisook, 1993), nevertheless anger is a very
frequent accompaniment of grief. We have speculated therefore that, in
terms of the SPAARS model, the duration and outcome of grief will
depend on whether basic emotions such as sadness and anger become
coupled together and thereby sustain each other. In order to explore
speculations such as these, it will be necessary to consider pre-existing
characteristics of individuals and their typical styles of coping with

emotion. It will also be necessary for bereavement researchers to distinguish more carefully between bereavement and depression rather than treat one as if it might be the same as the other. As Clayton (1990) found, bereavement depressions show lower levels of hopelessness, worthlessness, and loss of interest in friendships, which would be expected if the basic emotion of disgust is an essential part of depression, but not of bereavement. Moreover, Clayton's comparison of a group of recently bereaved individuals and a group of matched community controls showed near identical levels of worthlessness with 14% in the bereaved and 15% in the controls, even though the overall rates of "depression" were 47% for the bereaved versus 8% for controls. We will examine these differences in more detail in the next section.

Depression: Preliminary remarks

The term melancholia was first used in the fifth century BC by Hippocrates. Based on the ancient doctrine of the four elements, four humours were identified in blood, each of which in excess could lead to problems; thus, the melancholic type suffered an excess of black bile. Whichever type you were though, the treatment was usually the same, namely, bloodletting. Over the subsequent 1000 years and more a lot of melancholic individuals lost an awful lot of blood. Galen in the first century AD added further to our knowledge of melancholia, emphasising the occurrence of, in his term, hypochondriacal symptoms in the disorder. He also recorded the first case successfully treated by electricity, an individual who recovered from melancholia after being shocked by an electrical fish. Descriptions of individuals who were clearly depressed can be found for example in the Bible. One such famous account is in the Book of Job, in which Job is robbed by Satan of all his children, his possessions, and his health. These losses lead Job into a state of severe depression (Job, 17:1–2):

My spirit is broken, my days are extinct,
the grave is ready for me ...
He has made me a byword of the peoples,
and I am one before whom men spit.

There is even a classic painting by Lucas Cranach the Elder entitled *Melancholie* which depicts a depressed woman harangued by three young children at home while her husband is out hunting with his friends, pre-dating the now well-known Brown and Harris (1978) vulnerability factors for depression by several hundred years!

So what is depression? The diagnostic approach to this question, as represented in the World Health Organization's (1992) *International Classification of Diseases—Version 10* (ICD–10) and the American Psychiatric Association's (1994) *Diagnostic and Statistical Manual— Version IV* (DSM–IV), typically demand a certain number of symptoms lasting for at least a particular length of time, in the absence of certain other symptoms or conditions. For example, the individual might be required to have something like the following:

1. Depressed mood lasting for at least two weeks

Plus at least three of the following:

2. Loss of interest in pleasurable activities
3. Low self-esteem
4. Feelings of guilt
5. Thoughts and/or attempts of suicide
6. Decreased energy
7. Agitation or retardation
8. Sleep disturbance
9. Increase or decrease in appetite
10. Problems with thinking and concentration.

However, while this diagnostic approach might seem eminently reasonable so far (apart from a little arbitrariness about exact numbers and duration of symptoms), the few attractions of the approach are then lost under an avalanche of further distinctions: for example, organic mood disorders, schizoaffective disorder depressive type, bipolar affective disorder, recurrent depressive disorder, persistent mood disorder, and adjustment disorders—to name but some of the distinctions made in *ICD-10*. The major problem of these systems is that they are deliberately designed to reflect fashion and practice rather than inherent order within nature. Linnaeus' classification of living things and Mendeleev's Periodic Table of the elements *are* designed to reflect such inherent order, not "Well, I think we'll call a tomato a type of vegetable this year, because it doesn't really taste like a fruit, now does it!" or "Whales have always looked like fish to me ...". The upshot is that diagnostic distinctions should be kept to a minimum and that while there may be some evidence in support of rare conditions such as manic-depressive disorder (see Chapter 10), such distinctions should only be offered because they have an aetiology and course that is clearly different to the common disorder such as depression that is under consideration.

Our view therefore as we have stated in Chapters 5 and 6 is that a psychological classification system of the emotional disorders needs to be theoretically based; that the range of such disorders needs to be derived from a shared underlying framework; and that at no point should sight be lost of the fact that emotions lie on dimensions of strength or severity. The definition of disorder therefore may be provided by individuals themselves because they have labelled their experience as such (e.g. Thoits, 1985) or by an expert working with a replicable algorithm. The catch however is that the experts' definition will cast its net wide over the majority of people in the community who do not define themselves as emotionally disordered even though they may be "depressed", have panic attacks, or whatever. One of the powerful messages from epidemiology is that there is a considerable amount of "caseness" out there that never comes into contact with any professional service (e.g. Weissman, 1987) and that the "filters" that lead a small minority to seek professional help are many and various, but only one of which is the severity of the symptoms experienced.

The epidemiology of depression, as we have noted in earlier chapters, provides such a puzzling picture that almost any simple model can be eliminated by one or other of the statistics. One of the most cited and replicated findings is that there is a 2:1 ratio of women to men who experience the disorder (e.g. Weissman & Klerman, 1977), a ratio that holds for both clinical samples and untreated community cases (Cochrane, 1983). However, any simplistic biological explanation can be discounted by the fact that the ratio differs significantly according to marital status such that the rates for *single* men and women are about the same, whereas the rates for married women are highest and those for married men lowest (e.g. Champion, 1992). Additional problems include the following observations: first, that prior to mid-adolescence there is more depression in boys than in girls (Rutter, 1984), with twice as many boys as girls being treated for depression (Cochrane, 1983); that the rates of depression appear to be increasing in younger as compared to older age groups, especially for men, and that the rates for depression appear to even out for older adults (Nolen-Hoeksema, 1990). In addition, cross-cultural studies further demonstrate that the 2:1 ratio is not obtained consistently either between or within cultures; for example, Jenkins, Kleinman, and Good (1991) reported a number of studies that have found higher rates of depression for women in cultures where the female role is devalued, but significantly lower rates amongst women in the same culture who reject the traditional roles.

With these issues in mind therefore we turn now to some theoretical considerations of how the SPAARS approach to emotion and emotional disorder might illuminate a number of the problems posed by depression.

Depression: Some theoretical comments

The main cognitive models of depression were presented in Chapter 4 because Seligman's Learned Helplessness and Beck's Cognitive Therapy models have also been applied to other psychological disorders. Rather than repeat these presentations therefore we will simply highlight some of the conclusions that we reached.

First, there is no convincing evidence that attributional style is a vulnerability factor for the *onset* of depression, whatever its role in maintenance and recovery might be. For example, although researchers have been at pains to demonstrate that depression *can* result from the impact of independent or uncontrollable life events (e.g. Brown & Harris, 1978), as Champion (1990; Champion, Goodall, & Rutter, 1995) has clearly shown, there is normally a more complex interaction such that vulnerable individuals may experience more of both uncontrollable (independent) and controllable (dependent) events. In sum, uncontrollability of events is not a necessary feature for the onset of depression.

Second, the cognitive models of Beck (1976) and Bower (1981) sent researchers off in pursuit of global cognitive biases in a range of cognitive domains. As in Lewis Carroll's classic tale of such pursuits, the Snark turned out to be something of a Boojum. The failure to find global biases led some critics to reject the cognitive approach (Coyne & Gotlib, 1983), it led others to consider a more refined approach to the question of cognitive bias (e.g. Williams, et al., 1988), and, at the other extreme, yet others claimed that bias was a feature of being normal whereas "realism" was a feature of depression (Alloy & Abramson, 1979). We pitch our tent somewhere in the middle ground on this issue and argue that bias is as much of a feature of normal thinking as it is of depressed thinking, though the biases may operate in different ways. The question of bias however remains an important one, so we will return to it later in the chapter.

Third, in Chapter 4 we also presented some of the key points from the more recent integrative social-cognitive theories of depression (Gotlib & Hammen, 1992; Oatley & Bolton, 1985; Power & Champion, 1986). At the forefront of these theories have been some of the puzzling epidemiological findings mentioned in the previous section. These and other puzzles have contributed to the belief that an adequate model of depression will require the integration of a range of social, psychological, and biological factors, and that no theory pitched at a single level is likely to be successful. We will examine in more detail therefore the account of depression presented by Champion and Power (1995), which attempts to integrate a range of social and psychological factors.

The key points from the Champion and Power (1995) model are presented in Fig. 7.5. Along with a number of social and social-cognitive

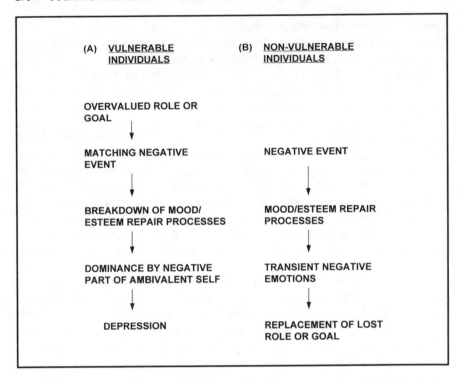

FIG. 7.5. A summary of the model of depression presented by Champion and Power (1995).

accounts of depression, one of the key components of the model relates to the roles and goals that are available to the individual. Unlike purely social accounts (e.g. Becker, 1964; Thoits, 1986), however, the theory focuses on the perceived value of roles and goals and not simply their availability or mere existence. It is proposed that vulnerable individuals typically overinvest in one role or goal, but underinvest and do not value other areas of their lives. When things go wrong therefore, for example, when a relationship with "the only person in the world who understands" breaks up, or when the adored child proves fallible, or when the longed-for promotion does not occur, the matching negative event leads to a breakdown in the defensive processes that normally protect the individual during successful pursuit of the role or goal (see also the discussion in Chapter 5 of roles and goals in different domains). Lam and Power (1991) reported supporting evidence for this proposal using the Roles and Goals questionnaire which was in part designed to test the model. They found as predicted that the proposed pattern of over- and under-investment was more typical of depressed than non-depressed adult and elderly community samples. The studies were however cross-sectional so it was unclear whether the pattern was a cause or a consequence of depression. Lam, Green, Power, and Checkley (1994, 1996) have more recently reported evidence in a longitudinal study of outpatient depressives that the further occurrence of negative events in the most invested domain delays recovery from depression or increases the likelihood of relapse in someone who has already recovered. Additional evidence in support of this part of the model is presented in Champion and Power (1995).

A second key component of the model presented in Figure 7.5 is highlighted in the contrast between vulnerable and non-vulnerable individuals and concerns the self-protective function that the overvalued role or goal provides. The proposal is that while the overvalued role or goal is being successfully pursued, the vulnerable individual may stave off self-negativity. However, if the role or goal is threatened or subsequently lost, the consequent combination of sadness and self-negativity (primarily, that is, the predominance of self-disgust) will lead to depression. Although, as highlighted in Figure 7.5, non-vulnerable individuals also experience a range of emotions at the loss of important roles and goals (see the earlier section on grief), such individuals are less likely to experience self-disgust or self-negativity and are more likely to replace the lost role or goal from a range of other valued roles and goals.

> John was a 35-year-old man who had become depressed for the first time when his current girlfriend, whom he had known for a year, suddenly and unexpectedly walked out on him one morning. Never before had he experienced such loathing of himself and a constant preoccupation with wanting to kill himself.
>
> He remembered little of his childhood before the age of eight, only that he had a constant longing to be an adult so as to escape a feeling of desolation. His first clear memories were of being sent away to boarding school, because, as he thought at the time, his parents wanted him out of the way. Unlike other boys who got upset and ran away from school, he knew there was no point in giving in to such "weak emotions". However, he did little work at school and left at 16 without qualifications to go and work in a factory. Even now he took pleasure in the fact that he had been such a disappointment to his parents and turned out "the opposite of what they wanted".

His mother died after a long illness a few years later, but his father had never allowed anyone to talk of her illness, nor to express any emotion after her death. Shortly afterwards John married. It was an "ideal match", they were "completely suited to each other" and during the eight or so years of the marriage John gradually "got his life together" and gained some qualifications and eventually they set up their own small business together. Unfortunately, however, for John, this idyllic period in his life was suddenly brought to an end when his wife was tragically killed in a car accident. The news, he said, sent him into a not-unpleasant "numbed state" which lasted for three months. Again, he had little or no memory for what happened at that time, and when he looked back at his diary it suddenly went from being crammed full to being completely empty.

John is now recovering from his first episode of depression, he says, "because his girlfriend unexpectedly returned one day". His main worry now though is how to avoid "ever feeling so bleak and suicidal again" and how to forget all that has happened to him.

John's case draws together much of what we have said in this chapter about both grief and depression. The familial pressure not to express emotion had been internalised to the extent that he had been unable to grieve the earlier deaths of his mother and of his wife. Instead, these losses had left John in a state of numbness in which not only did he not experience emotion, but nor was he able to achieve much else either. In relation to the SPAARS model one possibility in John's case was that the direct emotion route was being continually reactivated in the types of emotion cycles that we considered earlier in the chapter (see also Chapter 5), but that the emotion generated via this route was under such strong inhibition that the inhibition affected most other things in his life as well and produced a state of numbness. It was only the subsequent event of his new girlfriend walking out on him that led to him finally experiencing both depression and grief, a sequence that has been observed in other inhibited grief reactions (e.g. Parkes, 1993).

There are two further points that we should make about the loss of a valued role or goal. First, the loss may of course occur late in life: the individual may have pursued a highly successful career or have been involved in a long and satisfying relationship, before tragedy in one form or another strikes. Indeed, the very fortunate though vulnerable individual may skate on thin ice for a lifetime and be lucky enough to escape depression. Nevertheless, there is a substantial amount of first onset depression in later life (e.g. Murphy, 1982), which can come as a particular shock to an individual who may have taken pride in a belief in his or her emotional strength.

> George was the son of a docker and, indeed, had himself worked as a docker all his life. He had never had time for "soppiness", that was women's stuff, as his father used to say. He couldn't ever remember having cried throughout his adult years, that is until the last few months when, at the age of 64, he had become "deeply depressed" for the first time in his life and now couldn't stop crying. He felt totally ashamed of himself at this weakness and, even though his father had been dead for over thirty years, he could hear him laughing at him and making fun of him for being "such a sissie"
>
> George had worked hard and been a devoted, if somewhat reserved husband. His wife had been "his first real love" and they had met and married when they were both 18. His dream had been to retire early and buy a small cottage by the sea, where he and his wife would blissfully pass their twilight years. Indeed, he had just taken early retirement and they were about to move into a cottage they had just bought when his wife had a stroke and was rushed into hospital. She died two days later.
>
> George had put the cottage up for sale and hidden himself away from everyone "for fear that someone might see him in the dreadful state that he was in".

The second point that we would like to make is that the apparent "loss" of a role or goal can also occur because of its successful completion (e.g. Champion, 1992) in addition to the more commonplace meaning of loss that we have used until now. For example, the famous painter and sculptor Michelangelo Buonarroti (1475–1564) became depressed and often lost interest in his work as it was nearing completion and many of his most famous sculptures remained incomplete. The philosopher John Stuart Mill reported in his autobiography (1853/1991) on an episode of depression. He was already in a low mood, but he then imagined the following:

> In the frame of mind it occurred to me to put the question directly to myself, "Suppose that all your objects in life were realized; that all the changes in institutions and opinions which you are looking forward to, could be completely

effected at this very instant: would this be a great joy and happiness to you?" And an irrepressible self-consciousness distinctly answered, "No!" At this my heart sank within me: the whole foundation on which my life was constructed fell down.

In Mill's case therefore merely imagining the successful completion of his goals and plans was sufficient to lead to a severe episode of depression. Although the evidence for so-called "success depression" is primarily anecdotal and clinical and its existence has been disputed on theoretical grounds by behavioural theorists (Eastman, 1976), one area deserving of further research is that of the "Golden Boy" and "Golden Girl" syndrome identified by Seligman (1975) in his classic book on learned helplessness (see Chapter 4). Seligman's proposal was that so-called Golden Boys and Golden Girls had experienced non-contingent *positive* reinforcement throughout their lives, because their parents had indulged them completely, but without ever requiring anything of them. When they then entered the "real world", however, they were unable to cope with the fact that rewards were no longer non-contingent, but, instead, were very much contingent on their own actions, and as a consequence became depressed. However, an alternative interpretation is suggested by Lorna Champion's proposals about the importance of lifestage transitions in relation to roles and goals (Champion et al., 1995; Champion & Power, 1995; Maughan & Champion, 1990); namely, that the transition from adored-child-cum-adolescent may require the individual to relinquish the role in which they starred and, hence, to abandon the role that gave them most satisfaction. Many such individuals may therefore attempt to delay the transition rather than face up to it, rather like Hilde Bruch's (1978) "golden cage" interpretation of anorexia as an attempt to prevent or delay the onset of maturity and adulthood. To return though to the possibility of "success depression" we recount the story of Martha. We hope that her story provides at least some clinical support for the proposal that the pursuit of an overvalued role or goal may provide a crucial self-protective or defensive function for the individual, a proposal, therefore, that runs counter to any straightforward cognitive account of emotion which equates happiness with the achievement of goals and sadness with their loss (e.g. Oatley & Johnson-Laird, 1987); occasionally, the reverse may be true.

Martha was an extremely successful and competitive individual. She had until shortly before entering therapy been the deputy director of a well-known charity. Her rise through the ranks had been fast and predictable and had followed an equally successful time as a student in which she had done a degree in Russian "simply as a challenge".

She lived alone, though occasionally picked up men at parties to satisfy her sexual needs. If ever any such man attempted to get close, she ended the relationship. She very much resented these times of weakness when she needed other people and wished she could be completely self-sufficient.

The reason for her depression was that she had been promoted to Acting Director and, subsequently, to her extreme surprise, actually been appointed Director of the charity. However, the circumstances in which these promotions took place proved to be excessively disturbing to her mental calm. She had come to suspect the previous Director of the charity to be purloining money that was donated to the charity. He realised that she was on his trail and had tried to get her sacked by the Trustees of the charity on the grounds of incompetence. She had confided her concerns to one of the Trustees and, eventually, was completely vindicated.

Martha had no comprehension of why she felt so depressed having reached the height of her ambition.

Martha's story also illustrates a third key part of the Champion and Power model, that is of the role of self-ambivalence in depression. Some of the characteristics of Martha's self-ambivalence are presented in Figure 7.6. The figure illustrates that as long as Martha remained in pursuit of a work- or achievement-based goal this maintained the positive sense of self and the avoidance of negativity in relation to the self and significant others. In addition to the ambition to run the charity, Martha thought for example that one day she would write a great novel that would make her famous, though she had not yet embarked on this task. However, she had achieved her current main goal which was to head the charity, and her success had left her feeling "completely empty". Perhaps, too, the fact that this success had been marred by personal antipathy in which she had competed with and subsequently triumphed over a man in authority had also helped to prime some of the more personal relationship issues that were held at bay during the blinkered pursuit of her dominant goal. Whatever the truth, by the time she entered therapy those aspects of her self-concept that she experienced as negative were now completely dominant; in contrast to how she had been, she now felt unable to put any energy or effort into her work, and

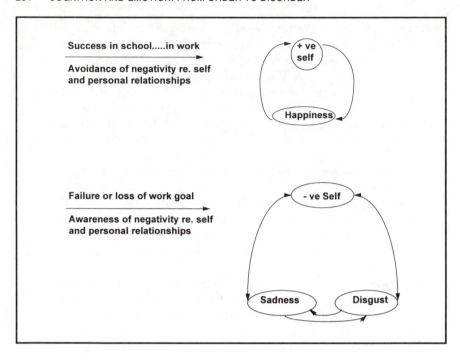

FIG. 7.6. An example of the ambivalent self based on Martha.

was worried that the considerable amount of time that she was off sick would lead to her dismissal. Moreover, three basic emotions were now predominant; namely, the emotions of sadness and disgust as shown in Fig. 7.5, but also considerable amounts of anger that she did not normally experience (the opposite in fact of retroflective anger). She felt sadness because her life was empty and meaningless. She lived alone and had no close relationships with either sex; weekends were particularly painful because she now did not have the pretence of too much work to have time to see people. She felt self-disgust because of her physical appearance, because of her weakness in needing other people, particularly men, and because of her current "wallowing in emotion". She felt angry with everybody, but especially with her mother who never allowed Martha to have any needs, because her mother's needs were always greater than everybody else's. It was clear from Martha's history that she was only acceptable to her mother when she was good and did not need anything; her negative self was unacceptable and remained unintegrated with her positive self. The negative self therefore contained everything that was disgusting and unacceptable, everything about herself that Martha now wanted to get rid of, and that her mother had originally instructed her to get rid of. The attempt to "eliminate" emotions and needs that are labelled as "weak" and as "negative" is a common feature of depression and other emotional disorders, as revealed, for example, by the endorsement of such attitudes on the "Self-Control" sub-scale of the 24-item Dysfunctional Attitude Scale (Power, Katz, McGuffin, Duggan, Lam, & Beck, 1994). The expression of disgust by significant others therefore towards aspects of the child's self, needs, and expression of emotion seems a crucial area for research in relation to disorder. Indeed, in extremely vulnerable adults such expression by significant others has been shown to lead to relapse in both depression and in schizophrenia; thus, in the work on Expressed Emotion (EE) Vaughn and Leff (1976) originally reported that the occurrence of "critical comments" by significant others greatly increased the chance of relapse in both depression and in schizophrenia. Although most of the subsequent work has focused on schizophrenia (e.g. Lam, 1991), the important point is that many of the critical comments are expressions of disgust by a significant other directed at the vulnerable person.

On a more general level it should also be noted that a positive self that is unfettered by negativity is as pathological as a negative self unfettered by positivity. Such extreme positive selves may for example be seen in some manic conditions in which the self can become grandiose, powerful,. and invulnerable (see Chapter 10). Although there is a psychoanalytic clinical tradition (e.g. Lewin, 1951) and some empirical data (Winters & Neale, 1985) that such states are a "manic defence" against depression, the argument here is that, sure, the positive state inhibits the negative state, but the obverse is also true in that the negative state inhibits the positive state. Both the positive and the negative states have "validity" therefore, but they inhibit the expression of the other state because they are unintegrated and work antagonistically, rather than the positive state being simply a defence against the "true" state of depression.

In contrast to grief, therefore, which we derived from the basic emotions of sadness and anger, we argue that depression may be derivable primarily from the basic emotions of sadness and disgust. This proposal offers an alternative to that for example suggested by Freud in *Mourning and Melancholia* (1917/1984), in which mourning was derived from sadness whereas depression was derived from sadness in conjunction with anger that was turned against the self. The key rejection of Freud's proposal for retroflective anger occurred in Bibring's (1953) classic ego psychoanalytic reanalysis of depression, a paper that anticipated all of the major cognitive approaches to the disorder (see Chapter 4). Nevertheless, our proposal does hold some similarities to

Freud's in that we emphasise self-condemnation and guilt as defining characteristics of depression, the crucial difference being that we derive them from the basic emotion of disgust rather than from anger. We would also point out that, since Bibring's paper, most cognitive models have focused on the role of low self-esteem in depression; thus, in both Beck's (1976) cognitive therapy and in Abramson et al.'s (1978) Learned Helplessness Reformulation, the self is seen as culpable for negative events, and is considered to be worthless, failed, or bad. All of these aspects of the self can be derived from the turning of the basic emotion of disgust against the self, such that aspects of the self are seen as bad and have to be eliminated or rejected from the self.

Another basic emotion that is frequently observed along with depression is that of anxiety; thus, self-report measures of depression and anxiety typically correlate at about 0.7 across a range of populations (Clark & Watson, 1991; Goldberg & Huxley, 1993). Indeed, the so-called "tripartite model" proposed by Clark and Watson (1991) argues that there is a common core of "negative affect" that forms the major component of a range of emotions including depression and anxiety. While there is much to be commended in such analyses, we take issue with the basic underlying model: first, because so-called "negative affects" are not necessarily experienced as negative, as we have argued earlier; second, because most of the results are based on student populations or, even in their latest tests of the model, patient groups such as those with drug problems that do not directly test the model (Watson, Clark, Weber, Assenheimer, Strauss, & McCormick, 1995; Watson, Weber, Assenheimer, Clark, Strauss, & McCormick, 1995); and, third, because individuals may show *less* anxiety rather than more as they become increasingly depressed (Peterson, Maier, & Seligman, 1993). We would therefore concur for once with the DSM-IV (American Psychiatric Association, 1994) in their decision that more evidence is necessary before the putative category of mixed anxiety-depression can be introduced. These points do not in any way deny the high comorbidity of depression and anxiety, particularly for less severe depression, and, indeed, there is every likelihood that the coupling together of the basic emotions involved in depression together with anxiety will undoubtedly lead to a prolongation of this distressing state. The proposal is however that anxiety is not a defining feature of depression, nor depression of anxiety. What we do wish to emphasise is that severe life events often unfold over time rather than occur suddenly and out of the blue, they often occur in the context of long-term related difficulties (e.g. Brown, Harris, & Hepworth, 1995), and, as we shall subsequently provide evidence, in depression-prone individuals they can occur in an over-invested domain about which there is already considerable worry.

In addition, the threat of loss may subsequently turn into an actual loss (Finlay-Jones & Brown, 1981), and so a state of anxiety in which the individual remains hopeful may turn into a state of depression in which the individual feels hopeless (Peterson et al., 1993).

The key coupling of the basic emotions of sadness and disgust that we argue is the basis of some presentations of depression is shown in Fig. 7.7. So why have we given disgust such a central role? For this choice we offer a number of reasons, some of which are more speculative than others, though we accept that the overall proposal requires direct empirical testing. Nevertheless, we are persuaded by ideas from a number of different areas that the role of disgust has largely been unrecognised in the development of emotional and other disorders (see Chapter 9).

In support of the proposal we should note first that the basic emotions of sadness, disgust, and happiness appear within the first three months of infancy, with sadness appearing for example at the withdrawal of positive stimuli, disgust in relation to unpleasant foodstuffs, and happiness for example in reaction to familiar faces (e.g. Fischer, Shaver,

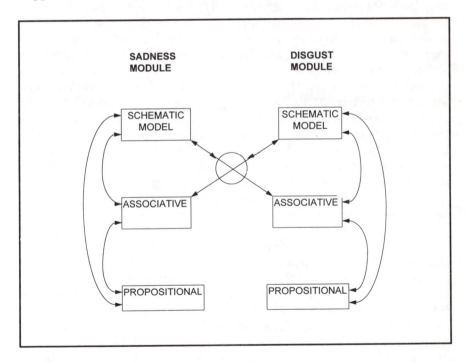

FIG. 7.7. The coupling of the basic emotions of sadness and disgust that form the core of depression.

& Carnochan, 1990; Lewis, 1993). As Fischer et al. (1990) argue, the early appearance of the basic emotions in the first year of life indicates that they provide important guiding principles around which development is organised, in particular, the development of the self and interpersonal relationships. However, it is a mistake to focus on disgust primarily as a reaction to food or excrement in the way that some analyses of the term suggest (e.g. Rozin & Fallon, 1987; see Chapter 9). Disgust is used by significant others to socialise the developing child in a range of permissible expressions and activities, not simply those related to food and the contents of nappies. The gradual development of self-disgust in relation to bodily activities and emotional expression provides the basis for a number of disorders in addition to depression (see Chapter 9).

The second point in support of this proposal is that there are a number of complex emotions such as shame, guilt, and embarrassment whose role in psychopathology has been highlighted in the psychoanalytic literature, all of which may be derived from the basic emotion of disgust (e.g. Johnson-Laird & Oatley, 1989). Although Freud (1910/1957) proposed that guilt did not appear until five or six years of age following the resolution of the Oedipus Complex, it is now clear that even by the age of two children show considerable individual differences in the expression of shame and guilt; for example, in Western cultures girls are more likely to show shame and boys to show guilt in relation to an apparent transgression (Barrett, Zahn-Waxler, & Cole, 1993). Shame was defined by Barrett and her colleagues to be disgust towards the self, and guilt to be disgust towards some action carried out by the self rather than towards the self *per se*. Because guilt led to more active attempts to obviate the transgression ("Amenders" in the researchers' terms) whereas shame led to more passive withdrawal ("Avoiders"), one can therefore identify even at two years of age strategies that are successful in repairing mood and self-esteem in contrast to strategies which maintain a negative self-state. Indeed, one is reminded of the distinction made by Nolen-Hoeksema (1987; 1990) between "Ruminators" and "Distractors", the former individuals being more likely to maintain a negative self-state through a comparatively passive preoccupation with that state and the events that led to it, the latter being more active and using other activities to escape from the aversive feelings. Moreover, Nolen-Hoeksema has found that Ruminators are both more likely to be women and more likely to become depressed. Recent evidence that shame and humiliation may provide important factors in the onset of depression has come from two separate studies of the same population in Islington, North London. In the first study, Brown et al. (1995) have reported that life events that lead to feelings of humiliation and entrapment in addition to loss or danger were more predictive of depression onset than loss or danger events that did not include humiliation and entrapment. In the second study, Andrews (1995) found that a strong link between childhood physical and sexual abuse and the later occurrence of depression was mediated by the experience of bodily shame which typically developed in the teenage years, presumably in response to the teenagers' own physical and sexual development. Andrews interpreted her findings as evidence for Gilbert's (1989) proposal that shame relates to the experience of defeat and inferiority, implicit in the experience of abuse.

Our third line of argument is a definitional one, though it also draws on the phenomenology of depression. It is clear that the phenomenological "taste" of dysphoric mood or of depression is not one of sadness, though sadness is there as a component. Nor, as we have argued above, is it anxiety that adds the missing ingredient. The additional ingredient is in fact a loathing of the self, a loathing of relationships and ambitions, that colours the world grey. In a state of dysphoria this additional flavouring is there just as a soupçon, just enough to add its unique taste, though in severe depression the taste may be completely overwhelming. We suggest therefore that the core phenomenological state is a combination of sadness and self-disgust.

Cognitive biases and depression

The question of cognitive biases and distortions has long held interest in the study of depression with, for example, the emphasis on logical distortions and irrational beliefs in the early work of Beck (e.g. 1976) and of Ellis (e.g. 1962) (see also Chapter 6). However, as Haaga et al. (1991) have pointed out, the terms "bias" and "distortion" were not distinguished in this early work, and it has only been recently that care has been taken with this distinction. A bias is a proclivity to take one direction over another which under some conditions will lead to accuracy or realism, but under other conditions will lead to inaccuracy or distortion (see Power, 1991). In contrast, distortion is invariably wrong. For example, if a group of depressed and a group of normal individuals are given a set of positive and negative adjectives to recall, then the depressed are typically found to recall more negative adjectives and the normal controls more positive adjectives (e.g. Derry & Kuiper, 1981). Neither group is *distorting* reality, but, rather, the depressed group are showing a negative bias and the normal group a positive bias (see also Chapter 4): they are presenting different views of the *same* reality in what has been called a Rashomon Effect in reference to Akira Kurosawa's film masterpiece in which four witnesses recount contrasting views of the same event, a murder in a forest. As we shall expand upon in more detail below, the debate between proponents of the so-called "depressive realism" position versus cognitive therapy's proposed "depressive distortion" view has been an artificial one in which oranges have been compared with apples: both positions are "true", but under appropriate conditions. Nevertheless, even if it is now accepted that emotional disorders such as depression and anxiety are associated with cognitive biases rather than distortions, the question remains of the extent of such biases. For example, as discussed in Chapter 4, the network theories of Bower and the schema theories of Beck lead to predictions for pervasive biases in a range of cognitive processes in emotional disorders which, unfortunately for the theories, have not been supported; thus, in their summary of the evidence, Williams et al. (1988) argued that the biases most apparent in anxiety were those concerned with automatic preattentive processes (see Chapter 6), whereas those most apparent in depression were controlled mnemonic processes. Again we argue that these discrepant theories may have approached the problem of bias from the wrong angle: that whether or not bias is evident in a pre-attentive, mnemonic, or other cognitive process depends in part on the content and the appraised relevance of that content as we have outlined in Chapter 5.

A further key problem that has arisen with the cognitive bias approach is whether observed cognitive biases are merely state-dependent consequences of depression or whether they are vulnerability factors that are causal antecedents in the development of depression. As with many national economies, this area has been through a number of boom-and-bust cycles. Much of the initial work focused on global self-report measures such as of dysfunctional attitudes, automatic thoughts, and hopelessness and reported that depressed individuals scored significantly higher than normal controls. Unfortunately, subsequent studies which followed up depressed individuals until they were fully recovered showed, as stated above, that levels of global self-reported attitudes and automatic thoughts return to those shown by normal controls. Such findings have led some (e.g. Coyne & Gotlib, 1983) to question the whole basis of the cognitive approach, but has led others (e.g. Power, 1987a; Williams et al., 1988) to call for the use of more sophisticated measures of cognitive vulnerability that can assess automatic as well as controlled processes. The results that have been obtained so far from this enterprise suggest a more complex view of vulnerability than the results from the self-report measures would suggest. We will first, however, summarise the evidence for biases from a range of cognitive processes before returning to the theoretical implications.

Biases of attention.   A number of paradigms have been employed to test for possible biases in attentional processes in both anxiety and depression. The most widely applied task has been the emotional Stroop (see Chapter 6 for a detailed discussion of this task) in which disorder-relevant words are tested for their degree of interference with colour-naming the ink in which such words are presented. Gotlib and McCann (1984) reported Stroop interference effects that distinguished dysphoric students from controls. Gotlib and Cane (1987) repeated this study with clinically depressed individuals and again found an interference effect with the naming of negative content words. However, when the task was repeated on recovery no effect was found. These studies can be criticised however for not partialling out the effects of anxiety levels which are often higher in depression and, as Mogg, Mathews, May, Grove, Eysenck, and Weinman (1991) found, may well be the source of the effects reported in Gotlib's studies. Thus, MacLeod et al. (1986) used their dot probe task with groups of both depressed and anxious individuals (see also Chapter 6). In this task, the individual is presented with a pair of words one of which may be threatening; on the critical trials the threat word is replaced with a dot to which the subject must respond as quickly as possible, the reaction time being used as an indicator of the focus of attention. MacLeod and colleagues found an attentional bias towards threatening words in anxious subjects, but no such bias in depressed subjects. Because this study is one of the few in which both clinically depressed and clinically anxious subjects have been compared on the same task, the results have had more impact on views about attentional bias than is warranted. Major problems, also noted in Chapter 6, that limit the interpretation of the study are: that the delay of over 500msec between word presentation and the dot probe could allow two or more changes of attentional focus; that the key words themselves were threat-related rather than depression-related; and that the overall reaction times for the depressed group were considerably slower than those for the anxious patients.

In a variant on the dot probe task, Gotlib, McLachlan, and Katz (1988) found with more appropriate negative and positive words that normal subjects attended more to positive words than to negative words whereas mildy depressed subjects attended equally to both. Gotlib and his colleagues interpret these findings as evidence that normal individuals show a positive bias, but no bias is shown by mildly depressed individuals who are therefore "realistic". This interpretation runs of course headlong into the problems faced by the "depressive realists" which we have mentioned above and which we will cover in detail in the subsequent section on judgement and reasoning. Overall, though, the findings emphasise that attentional biases can be found in depression with carefully chosen depression-related content. These findings concur with results obtained from the Emotional Priming Paradigm with clinically depressed patients (Power et al., 1996) in which depression-related primes were found to increase the speed of endorsement of negative adjectives by depressed patients. Such results emphasise the need for careful selection of appropriate materials and suggest, for example, why Clark, Teasdale, Broadbent, and Martin (1983) failed to find effects of depressed mood on lexical decision times for negative words.

Other tasks that have been used to assess attentional biases include the dichotic listening task and an eye fixation task. For example, McCabe and Gotlib (1993) reported that depressed subjects were distracted by depression-relevant words occurring on the non-attended channel in a dichotic listening task, though following recovery this effect no longer occurred. The recovered subjects were, however, more distracted by *positive* words on recovery, though the effect just failed to reach significance. Interestingly, the depressed subjects in the Power et al. (1996) priming study were found to show positive priming effects for positive adjectives. The possibility therefore that recovered depressives may be *more* positive on some tasks needs further exploration. Preliminary results with an eye fixation task reported by Matthews and Antes (1992) showed that dysphoric students made more eye fixations towards sad visual material than did normal students.

Biases of memory.   One of the most heavily researched areas of bias in the emotional disorders has been the area of mnemonic biases in depression. For example, an influential study by Lloyd and Lishman (1975) reported that depressed patients were faster to recall unpleasant than pleasant memories in response to neutral cue words. In a cleverly designed application of this procedure, Clark and Teasdale (1982) tested a group of depressed patients who showed considerable diurnal variation in their mood and found that more unhappy memories were retrieved when subjects were at their most depressed, but a greater proportion of positive memories were recalled when depression was at its lowest. Williams (e.g. 1992) has further shown that not only do the recollections of depressed and suicidal patients differ in terms of valence from the recollections of normal controls, but they also tend to be general rather than specific memories, for example, recollections along the lines of "I always used to be unhappy" rather than "I was unhappy on that particular occasion".

In addition to studies of variations in autobiographical memory, there have also been a considerable number of studies that have investigated verbal learning. Derry and Kuiper (1981) found that from a list of words depressed subjects recalled more self-related negative words than positive words whereas normal controls recalled more self-related positive words. Bradley and Mathews (1983) found that this effect was limited to negative words that were endorsed for the self but that their depressed subjects recalled more positive words that they had endorsed as descriptive of other people. This study demonstrated therefore that the negative recall bias is not a general response bias, but, rather, may be a feature of particularly salient information such as that related to the self. A subsequent study, however, showed that the negative bias was no longer present once the depressed individuals had recovered (Bradley & Mathews, 1988). Dobson and Shaw (1987) reported similar findings in which currently depressed individuals showed a negative recall bias on the self-reference encoding task, but this effect was no longer present following recovery.

These and related findings suggest that there is a significant mood congruency effect in depression in that material that is congruent with the depressed mood is better learned and better recalled, but there is less evidence for state dependent learning which would require better recall of material, irrespective of its valence, that was learned when depressed (see Blaney, 1986, for a summary). The effects are stronger for recall than recognition (see Dalgleish & Watts, 1990), which points to the fact that mood has an important influence on retrieval. However, the effects are in part a decrease in the positive biases shown in normal individuals who have been found to forget more negative than positive self-descriptive adjectives in a directed forgetting task (Power, Dalgleish, Claudio, Kentish, & Tata, submitted). There is also evidence that recall of to-be-learned material is improved if the structure is inherent in the material rather than if it has to be provided by the subject (Dalgleish & Watts, 1990). Finally, most of the research on mnemonic biases has focused on so-called explicit or strategic memory tasks. Indeed, theorists such as Williams et al. (1988) have proposed that the memory biases evident in depression are restricted to explicit or strategic memory. However, there has been recent interest in the question of whether implicit memory biases are evident in the emotional disorders and Tobias, Kihlstrom, and Schachter (1992) have summarised preliminary data showing that under carefully designed conditions induced sad mood may also lead to retrieval biases. The fact that the data on implicit memory biases in depression are contradictory with some studies reporting no implicit memory effects (e.g. Denny & Hunt, 1992; Hertel & Hardin, 1990), but other studies obtaining such biases (e.g. Elliott & Greene, 1992; Ruiz-Caballero & Gonzalez, 1994) emphasises that the effects are subtle and may be easily swamped by other retrieval factors (Tobias et al., 1992). We will, however, have to wait to see if these findings can be replicated both in further mood induction studies and in clinically significant depression in order to provide a resolution for the currently contradictory data.

The work on mood incongruent memory and mood regulation provides some support for our suggestion that the basic emotions modules may be more difficult to alter in individuals prone to emotional disorders. For example, studies of mood incongruent memory show that the induction of a sad or depressed mood in normal individuals leads to the retrieval of mood incongruent positive memories as part of mood-regulation (e.g. Parrott & Sabini, 1990). Wegner (1994) has proposed that this effortful control over mental states will be more successful where more working memory capacity is available, but where there is a reduction in such capacity, control is more likely to backfire and lead to the opposite; thus, the more that depressed individuals attempt to rid themselves of the depressed mood, the more the depressed mood predominates, because of the loading of working memory with preoccupations about the lost role or goal and its implications for the self. In addition, however, we are suggesting that the modular or near-modular organisation of the basic emotions of sadness and disgust in depression leads to their autonomous operation. That is, once a state of sadness–disgust has been entered, the fact that in depressed individuals there is no integration with the positive aspects of the self means that the emotional state is difficult to alter or regulate; thus, the mood-regulation strategies in which normal individuals can retrieve positive memories of the self or focus on other valued goals or roles are less available in a state of depression.

Biases of reasoning and judgement.   A number of earlier studies of judgement in depression showed that although depressed individuals were clearly more negative than their non-depressed counterparts (e.g. DeMonbreun & Craighead, 1977), nevertheless, they were often found to be more realistic or accurate on such tasks (Lewinsohn, Mischel, Chaplin, & Barton, 1980). The classic statement of this position was by Alloy and Abramson (1979), who, from a series of judgement of contingency studies with depressed and normal students, concluded that normal individuals show illusory biases of control over positive outcomes and of no control over negative outcomes, whereas depressed individuals are more "even-handed" and show "depressive realism". In the Alloy and Abramson study, the subjects' task was either to press or not press a button following which the outcome was the onset of a green light. However, the degree of contingency was varied across a number of studies that were carried out. Alloy and Abramson found that dysphoric students tended to be more accurate in judging the degree of control in comparison to normal subjects who overestimated control when the outcome was associated with success (winning money), but underestimated their degree of conrol for failure (losing money). As we noted earlier, Alloy and Abramson's depressive realism proposal contrasts directly with Beck's cognitive therapy in which the emphasis is on depressive distortions that are considered characteristic of depressive perception, reasoning, and judgement (see Chapter 4). However, there have more recently been a number of restrictions placed on the original proposals for depressive realism; thus, Vazquez (1987) reported that the effect was dependent on a number of effects such as whether the information was self- or other-related. Dykman, Abramson, Alloy, and Hartlage (1989) have shown that whether a positive or negative bias is found will depend on the beliefs held by the individual.

There have been a wide range of other tasks designed to assess biases in judgement, expectancies, predictions, attributions, and perception of feedback. For example, Golin, Terrell, and Johnson (1977) found that in a dice game dysphoric students' predictions were more accurate when they rolled the dice themselves, but normal students were more accurate when the experimenter rolled the dice. Alloy and Ahrens (1987) found that dysphoric students were more negative about the likelihood of future academic success, whereas normal students overestimated their chances of success. Rozensky, Rehm, Pry, and Roth (1977) found that depressed patients rewarded themselves less and punished themselves more than did normal controls or non-depressed patients on a reinforcement task. However, the depressed patients were more accurate, whereas the other two groups over-rewarded themselves. Alloy and Abramson (1988) provide a useful overview of these and other related studies in an attempt to interpret them in relation to their depressive realism position. However, it is clear from these and from subsequent studies that the depressive realism and the cognitive distortion proposals reflect differing views of the proverbial elephant.

Power (1991) has suggested that a more sophisticated account of this literature needs to take account of a number of factors including the truth value and the valence of the information together with the degree of positive or negative bias (see also Chapter 4). As shown in Fig. 7.8, with a negative bias "depressive realism" should be found for True Negatives and False Positives whereas "depressive distortion" should be found for True Positives and False Negatives. In contrast, normal individuals showing a positive bias should be "realistic" for True Positives and False Negatives, but show "illusory biases" for True Negatives and False Positives. The empirical studies of Vazquez (1987) provide some support for these proposals. We have also modified a linear syllogism reasoning task, the preliminary results from which have

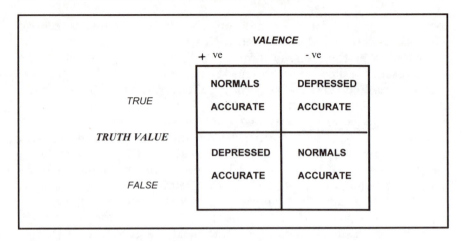

FIG. 7.8. Conditions under which normal positively biased individuals are more likely to be accurate, versus those under which negatively biased individuals should be more accurate.

shown the presence of positive reasoning biases in normal students and an absence of positive bias in dysphoric students (Quelhas & Power, 1991). In addition, there are a range of social judgements that are affected by positive and negative moods, including the liking of other people, ratings of life satisfaction, partner choice, and optimism about the future (see Fiske & Taylor, 1991; Forgas, 1995).

General comments on bias research. The findings from studies of cognitive biases in depressed and normal moods show that there are a number of effects. Perhaps the strongest evidence for bias in depression comes from work on explicit memory including word-list and autobiographical memory tasks. These studies, however, emphasise that the clearest biases are obtained in the processing of self-related negative material rather than *any* negative material. The fact that findings for biases in implicit memory tasks have been less consistent probably indicates that the mechanisms involved in such biases are more poorly understood, in particular, in the way in which mood and other factors combine. This problem also seems to be have been evident in studies of attentional biases in depression, where there is evidence both for and against bias. Again, it must be emphasised that factors such as the personal relevance of the materials have not been properly taken into account in many of the studies. The problem also arises of whether evidence of a positive bias in normals and of apparent "even-handedness" in depressed individuals should be interpreted as evidence for depressive realism or for depressive negative bias. As we argued previously, under certain circumstances biases lead to accurate or realistic responses; thus, conclusions of even-handedness in depression and positive bias in normal individuals should, in our view, be seen as evidence for a negative bias in depression. This recommendation applies not only to the contingency judgement studies of Alloy, Abramson, and colleagues, but also to studies of attentional bias (e.g. Gotlib, McLachlan, & Katz, 1988).

Postnatal depression

The experience of postnatal depression occurs for approximately 10–15% of women within the first few weeks post-partum. Although often thought of as a biological depression, presumably because of the significant hormonal changes accompanying childbirth, postnatal depression is not characterised by so-called "endogenous" features, and there is lower suicidal ideation than in other types of depression (Bhugra & Gregoire, 1993). From what little research that has been carried out, there appears to be a pattern emerging of a complex interaction of a number of factors.

Childbirth itself is a significant life event, which can range from being completely unwanted and being seen as a tragedy, to the opposite extreme of being something wanted desperately and therefore being extremely positive. Without knowing the circumstances therefore it would be possible, in theory, for the event to increase the likelihood of depression for some women, but considerably decrease the likelihood for other women. However, even when a pregnancy is planned or wanted, there are additional factors that may come into play including the impact of the transition to parenthood on other valued roles and goals and the degree to which the members of the mother's close social network provide good support with the extreme emotional and practical demands that follow. In terms of other roles and goals, if parenthood leads to the loss of ones that are valued, or leads to perceived conflict with these roles and goals, then depression is more likely to follow (e.g. Simon, 1992). In addition, the mother may approach the role of motherhood with high expectations of being the perfect mother, even, perhaps with the intention of making up for perceived weaknesses in how she herself had been parented. Moreover, as a mother there may be particular emotions that are not allowed towards the newborn baby, which, if they are experienced, may lead the mother to conclude that she is bad or for her to feel frightened of being left alone with the baby. In such cases, the spouse or partner plays a significant role; thus, as in other types of depression discussed previously, a poor marital relationship and low levels of social support have been the two factors most consistently found to be associated with the occurrence of postnatal depression (Bhugra & Gregoire, 1993; Kumar & Robson, 1984).

In relation to the model that we have presented in this chapter, although there is much less research to draw on, nevertheless, there seems to be some support for the SPAARS approach. If the occurrence of pregnancy and childbirth leads to the loss of or conflict with other valued roles and goals, then the mother will experience sadness because of those losses. This reaction will be exacerbated by a poor marital relationship. In addition, the ambivalent mother is likely to experience negative feelings towards the newborn child and towards her own reactions to motherhood. The physical and mental stresses involved in supporting a newborn child with little or no other support, will make the direct route to emotion more likely, as tiredness and exhaustion reduces the capacity for appraisal-based emotional responses. The mother may "catch herself" reacting in completely ego-alien ways, such as shouting at the newborn. These shame–disgust based reactions to herself and to her child may provide the final part of the jigsaw that leads to postnatal depression.

One of the factors that makes parenting more problematic is of course the quality of parenting that the new mother and father themselves received as children. For example, in an interesting study of the partners of women with postnatal depression, Lovestone and Kumar (1993) reported that these men also had high rates of depression and other disorders themselves. The two factors that were predictive for depression in the men were, first, a past history of psychiatric problems, and, more interestingly, a poor relationship reported with their own fathers, but not with their mothers or with their wives. This finding was obtained on two different measures, one the Parental Bonding Instrument that retrospectively assesses childhood parental support, the other being the Significant Others Scale which measures current levels of support. One can only speculate, as did Lovestone and Kumar, that if the schematic model of one's same-sexed parent is deficient as a parent, when plunged into that role oneself, extreme feelings of self-inadequacy may result.

Two other disorders that are observed following childbirth are the "maternity blues" and the puerperal psychoses. Maternity blues are common within the first 10 days postpartum, typically lasting for one to two days. They occur in 50–70% of women and they seem to occur irrespective of the cultural practices surrounding childbirth (Bhugra & Gregoire, 1993). The frequency and timing of the problem suggests that it may be of hormonal origin and Kennerley and Gath (1989) have also shown that it is related to severe premenstrual tension. However, in their prospective study, Kennerley and Gath also found that the blues were related to anxiety and depression occurring during pregnancy, to anxieties about labour, and to the ubiquitous poor family and marital relationships. Although, therefore, there is a clear biological foundation for the problem, psychological and social factors are also significant. There does not seem to be any clear relationship between the occurrence of maternity blues and the occurrence of postnatal depression (e.g. Kumar & Robson, 1984).

The puerperal psychoses are much rarer than the maternity blues or postnatal depression, with a prevalence of about one per 1000 births. From their large case register study, Kendell, Chalmers and Platz (1987) found that the highest risk was during the first 30 days postpartum, though some risk continued even after several months. Factors that increased the risk were being primiparous, a family history of affective disorder, obstetric complications, and, of course, a poor marital relationship. Kendell et al. (1987) did in fact conclude that most puerperal psychoses were actually bipolar disorders that had been triggered by childbirth. If true, then it is interesting evidence again that even in the most apparently biological of disorders one must examine the interplay with psychological and social factors as well.

Other affective disorders

Other rarer affective disorders include the Bipolar Disorders and the Seasonal Affective Disorders. Because of the important role of mania and hypomania in the diagnosis of Bipolar Disorders, we will hold the discussion of these disorders until Chapter 10 when we discuss disorders of the basic emotion of happiness.

The key paper on Seasonal Affective Disorder (SAD) was by Rosenthal, Sack, Gillin, Lewy, Goodwin, Davenport, Mueller, Newsome, and Wehr (1984). Rosenthal and his colleagues described a seasonal pattern for a sample of 29 individuals in which there was a regular occurrence of autumn or winter depression followed by spring or summer normal, hypomanic, or manic mood. An extremely high proportion of this first sample had a bipolar affective disorder (93%); this high figure has been found in some other samples, for example, Blehar and Lewy (1990) summarised figures of 90% bipolar disorders from a number of studies totalling 246 individuals, though, for example, Thompson (1989) reported lower rates of 71% in an English sample. Whatever the true rates, *DSM-IV* has taken the view that the seasonal pattern can occur for both unipolar and bipolar disorders. We do caution, however, that the continued finding of any association with bipolar affective disorders could lead to views turning full circle to the original proposal that they may be a variant of the bipolar disorders.

The main features of SAD include low mood, increased appetite and weight, hypersomnia, and low energy. Because of the seasonality of the disorder, most theories have examined biological hypotheses especially in relation to the light-sensitive hormone melatonin. Despite early enthusiasm however, the melatonin hypothesis has not been supported by the available data (Rosenthal & Wehr, 1992). There are a number of more recent biological hypotheses (see Dalgleish, Rosen, & Marks, 1996, for a summary), but there is as yet no clear support for any of them.

FURTHER COMMENTS AND CONCLUSIONS

In relation to the more general SPAARS theory presented earlier in this chapter and in Chapter 5, we suggest that in depression-prone individuals there is a preoccupation with an overinvested role or goal. A major threat to or loss of this dominant role or goal leads the individual to focus on the aspects of the self-concept that are normally rejected and the lost role or goal that was central to self-worth (Champion & Power, 1995). This preoccupation with the lost role or goal leads to working memory resources being allocated primarily to working through the loss and, therefore an apparent emphasis on the past. The individual may therefore allocate fewer resources to non-goal relevant tasks, in part because of reduced capacity (Ellis & Ashbrook, 1988; Hasher & Zacks, 1988), but also because of the depressed individual's proclivity to under-value non-goal relevant tasks or information; this combination leads to an appearance of reduced initiative for allocating resources to other tasks (Hertel & Hardin, 1990) as well as reduced working memory capacity.

One of the more interesting predictions from our proposal about the modularisation of basic emotions in depression-prone individuals concerns the processing of self-related positive material in recovered depressives. Following, for example, our demonstration of priming effects for positive material in depression (Power et al., 1996), our prediction would be that recovered depressives should be "too positive" and, should, for example, find it more difficult to moderate a positive mood, under conditions in which such a mood would interfere with a cognitively demanding task; thus, normal individuals may use mood incongruent recall under such conditions in order to modify positive distractions (Erber & Erber, 1994). If however there is a failure of integration of positive and negative aspects of the self in depression, then during recovery when the positive aspects of the self predominate, there should be less regulation of the positive state because negative aspects of the self may be unavailable or excluded at such time. At their most extreme, such uncontrollable positive mood states are, as we have noted, present in mania and hypomania, but we will leave further discussion of these until Chapter 10 when we consider happiness and its disorders.

Finally, we reiterate that the emotional disorders related to sadness often run a long and complicated course. These disorders, in particular grief and depression, reflect the fact that sadness is a response to the failure of our most important goals and our most cherished relationships. In addition, however, these losses leave the vulnerable individual prone to feelings of anger or self-disgust which, we suggest, may prolong grief and depression when they become coupled with sadness.

CHAPTER EIGHT

Anger

Anyone can get angry—that is easy; ... but to do this to the right person, to the right extent, at the right time, with the right motive, and in the right way, that is not for everyone nor is it easy; wherefore goodness is both rare and laudable and noble. *(Aristotle,* Nicomachean Ethics, 1947, *1109a25)*.

INTRODUCTION

Anger is a profoundly uncomfortable emotion. Its association with sometimes uncontrollable aggression and violence and, moreover, the attributions of blame and intent which always lurk beneath the surface ensure that, for many of us, giving vent to our anger is something rarely indulged. It can be argued that such emotional conservatism has its place; however, folk theories of anger also suggest that it's good to let it all out, to rant and rave for a while—there's no real calm unless you've had the storm. This line between too much anger or too little is difficult to tread and in this chapter we shall explore some of these tensions between appropriate and inappropriate anger. Along the way we shall review the existing theoretical models of anger in the literature before attempting to use anger to illustrate the utility of the idea of cycles of appraisal within the SPAARS model developed in Chapter 5. Finally, we shall consider disordered anger and emotions related to anger.

To illustrate some of the complexities and the sheer force of anger, there is no better place to start than with the cinema:

> DANNY: "There's a passage I've learned by heart—Ezekial 25:17: The path of the righteous man is beset on all sides by the inequities of the selfish and the tyranny of evil men. Blessed is he who in the name of charity and good will shepherds the meek through the valley of darkness for he is truly his brother's keeper and the finder of lost children. [INCREASED ANGER] And I will strike down upon these with great vengeance and furious anger those who attempt to poison and destroy my brothers and you will know my name is the Lord when I lay my vengeance upon thee."
> VICTIM: screams
> [SOUNDS OF GUNFIRE AS VINCENT AND DANNY SHOOT THE VICTIM]

In this memorable scene from Quentin Tarantino's cult film *Pulp Fiction*, the hitman's ritual recitation of the passage from Ezekiel prior to shooting his victims reveals a number of the issues which have dominated the psychology of anger both historically and cross-culturally for almost 2000 years. Anger is, in the first place, a moral emotion. Danny's victim has seemingly plumbed such depths of moral depravity that Danny is surely doing him a favour by killing him. Second, anger is a passion; having worked himself into such a temper, Danny not only finds it easier to carry out his unsavoury profession but would probably find it hard to stop. Third, the appropriateness of anger varies both within and across cultures. In Danny's eyes his victim has clearly broken the code of the criminal underworld by which both operate. However, whether such a transgression would be viewed as an appropriate instigation to such anger by the rest of society is questionable. In this first part of the chapter we consider in detail some of these aspects of anger.

THE MORAL NATURE OF ANGER

There is an oft-voiced contention that anger is most usually what we might call a "moral" emotion—a response to personal offence. Consequently, for a thorough understanding of anger we need to appreciate the judgements of blame and the attributions of intent which are involved. The fact that anger usually involves these moral judgements emphasises, of course, the role of the cognitive processes of appraisal and interpretation as integral parts of the anger experience. There is considerable historical agreement as to the exact ways in which these interpretations and appraisals are involved in the generation of anger: Plato, Aristotle, Seneca, Lactantius, Aquinas, and Descartes (see Chapter 2) all suggest that anger is the result of an appraisal of some deliberate, negligent, or at least avoidable, slight or wrongdoing; that the anger is most usually directed at another person (though clearly it can be directed at the self or inanimate objects); and that the desires (or action potentials) associated with anger concern punishment for, or correction of, the wrong that has been carried out. This analysis clearly raises questions concerning what constitutes a deliberate wrongdoing and under what conditions it is therefore appropriate to feel anger and so on—the issues, in fact, which were raised by Aristotle in the quote with which we opened the chapter.

As a rider to this, most of the ancient philosophers have also endorsed the suggestion that anger is a singularly adult and a uniquely human emotion, as subhuman animals (and human infants) lack the cognitive processes necessary to form judgements about whether events are unjustified, deliberate or arise through negligence. As Seneca (*De Ira*, p.115) argued: "Beasts and all animals, except man, are not subject to anger; for while it is the foe of reason, it is nevertheless born only where reason dwells." Furthermore, historical teachings on anger suggest that the wrongdoing or slight will have been committed by another human being; again, because only human actions can be judged in moral terms.

In sum, there is considerable historical and philosophical consensus that anger is a moral emotion involving attributions of intent to a recognisable, usually human, agent for a personal offence. In the next section we consider some of the research in contemporary psychology which has sought to examine these issues.

THE EVENTS, AGENTS, INTERPRETATIONS, AND APPRAISALS INVOLVED IN ANGER

Research shows that there is considerable agreement within a given society on what exactly the events, agents, interpretations, and appraisals which appropriately lead to anger might be (Averill, 1982; Ben-Zur & Breznitz, 1991; Snell, McDonald, & Koch, 1991). This is far from being a trivial point as is clear from an analysis of the homicide law in the United States (Averill, 1982; Oatley, 1992). To summarise, in the US legal system it is possible for a verdict of (voluntary) manslaughter, based on anger, rather than one of murder to be given if the killing was done in the heat of that passion and not in cold blood and if it is shown that there was adequate provocation which caused the defendant to be angry and which would have roused any reasonable person to anger (in contrast, in the United Kingdom if it is judged that the homicide was voluntary, a verdict of murder is mandatory). It could be argued then, that, in this instance anger (temporary insanity) is viewed by society as sufficiently appropriate that it can be weighed against the value of human life in the eyes of American law. At the very least, anger here is sufficient vindication for the taking of human life.

Homicide apart, there have been numerous studies and surveys of the more everyday experience of anger and the events, agents, interpretations, and appraisals associated with them. Early studies were carried out by Gates (1926), Meltzer (1933), Anastasi, Cohen, and Spatz (1948) and McKellar (1949, 1950) (see Table 8.1 for a summary). However, the findings of all these surveys are mirrored in the work of James Averill (e.g. 1979, 1982, 1983) and we shall devote much of our space in this section to a consideration of his research.

Averill (1982) reports a series of five questionnaire and diary studies looking at individuals' experiences of their own anger, individuals' experiences of another person's anger, differences between the experiences of anger and of annoyance, temporal dimensions of anger, and, finally, the differences between men and women in the everyday experience of anger. We shall concentrate here on the data pertaining to anger as experienced by the angry person; however, we shall examine the data on the differences between anger and annoyance in the section on anger-related emotions at the end of the chapter.

Averill's main study included 160 subjects; 80 were randomly chosen from the community, were aged between 21 and 60, and were married; the other 80 were single, under 21 years old, and were volunteers from a university. Averill's questionnaires comprised 88 items and required subjects to estimate the number of anger episodes they had experienced and to provide detailed descriptions of instances that had made them most angry over a given time period. Such anger episodes were almost invariably perceived as having been instigated by another human being (88%) or a human institution (7%). In only 6% of episodes was the anger directed at inanimate objects; however, as Averill points out, even in these cases there was a large amount of anthropomorphism or indirect reference to human agency.

Averill (1982, p.166) provides a number of illustrative examples of anger towards inanimate objects: one woman became angry at being seriously ill and actually envisioned a little man (personifying her illness) to whom she could direct her anger. A plumber became angry at a trap he had installed (after it developed a hair-line leak) and described his response as follows: "I made the hole in the trap bigger, as if to

TABLE 8.1

Instigations to anger as classified in early studies (based on Averill, 1979)

Study	Sample	No. of incidents reported	Nature of the instigation	Percentage of incidents
Gates (1926)	51 college students; female	All incidents during 1 week; total = 145	Frustration of routine activities Frustration of self-assertive activities: a) defensive reactions to persons (36%) b) assertive reactions to persons (7%) c) defensive reactions to things (21%)	37 64
Meltzer (1933)	93 college students; male and female	All incidents during 1 week; total = 393	Frustration of routine activities Frustration of self-assertive activities: a) defensive reactions to persons (38%) b) assertive reactions to persons (13%) c) defensive reactions to things (35%)	14 86
Anastasi, Cohen, & Spatz (1948)	38 college students; female	All incidents during 1 week; total = 598	Thwarted plans Inferiority and loss of prestige Schoolwork Family relationships Abstract problems	52 21 13 10 5
McKellar (1949)	200 adult education students; male and female	1 or 2 recent incidents, total = 379	Need situations Personality situations	47 53

say—'That's what you should look like if you are going to leak.'" When describing his motives, he added: "Silly, but if I am doing my job, why can't the trap do its job?" The agents of anger were most often individuals whom the subject knew well and liked such as parents, friends, partners, or children.

In Averill's study the agents or individuals provoking the anger were most usually perceived as doing something voluntarily which they had no right to do, or as doing something avoidable. Relatively few incidents involved behaviour that was perceived as voluntary and justified or unavoidable (see Table 8.2).

Turning to anger inducing events, the majority were perceived as frustrating or as interrupting some ongoing, planned activity. However, frustration or interruption was rarely the sole cause. Over 90% of the subjects in the study who mentioned frustration as a factor also invoked: violation of important personal expectation; a loss of personal pride; violation of socially accepted rules; possible or actual property damage; or personal injury. Nineteen percent of subjects did not mention frustration. The reasons they provided for their experience of anger were: loss of self-esteem; violation of personal wishes or expectations; or violation of socially accepted rules.

Averill summarises his findings by compiling a table of a partial list of the rules and norms related to anger. These are partly reproduced in Table 8.3.

Recent studies largely confirm the findings from Averill's more comprehensive analysis. Snell et al. (1991) examined the nature of anger-provoking experiences in psychology students. Responding to the question "What makes you feel angry?", subjects revealed 48 categories

TABLE 8.2
Instigation to anger in terms of justification

	Justification	Percentage of incidents (N = 160)
1.	Voluntary and unjustified: the instigators knew what they were doing and they had no right to do it.	51
2.	Potentially avoidable accident or event: the results of negligence, carelessness, or lack of foresight.	31
3.	Voluntary and justified: the instigators knew what they were doing and that they had no right to do it.	11
4.	Unavoidable accident or event: it could not have been foreseen or was beyond anyone's control.	7

TABLE 8.3
A partial list of the rules and norms related to appraisals, events, and agents of anger (based on Averill, 1982)

A	*With respect to the events and appraisals*

1. Prescriptive
(a) We have the right (duty) to become angry at intentional wrongdoing, including an affront to our honour, freedom, property, or other rights.
(b) We have the right (duty) to become angry at the unintentional misdeeds of certain others if those misdeeds are due to negligence, carelessness, oversight, and so forth.

2. Proscriptive
(a) We should not become angry at events which are beyond our influence.
(b) We should not become angry at events which can be remedied in more standard ways.

B	*With respect to the perceived agent*

1. Prescriptive
(a) Anger should be directed only at persons, and by extension, other entities (the self, human institutions) that can be held responsible for their actions.
(b) Anger is more appropriately directed at a peer or subordinate than at a superior.
(c) Anger is more appropriately directed at someone who is well known than a stranger or mere acquaintance.
(d) Among strangers, anger is more appropriately directed at men than at women.

2. Proscriptive
(a) Anger should not be directed at those who cannot be held responsible for their actions (e.g. because of age or ignorance).
(b) Anger should not be directed at those who cannot profit from the experience (e.g. because of infirmity).

---

of anger-eliciting experiences characterised by three dimensions: (1) individual inadequacies and failures related to unattained pursuits and goals; (2) frustrating events associated with the public, social aspects of the self; and (3) incidents associated with interpersonal exploitation. Similarly, Ben-Zur and Breznitz (1991) carried out three studies with university students and concluded that anger was affected by three basic aspects of a harmful event: the extent of damage; the causes of the damaging act; and the likelihood of damage occurrence.

In summary, systematic diary studies in psychology have given flesh to the philosophical analysis we presented in the previous section. According to Averill's work, anger is most usually directed at another person who is perceived to have deliberately or negligently caused personal offence. There do appear to be exceptions to this normative case and we discuss these exceptions in more detail in our analysis of anger within the SPAARS model later in the chapter.

OTHER FACTORS WHICH CONTRIBUTE TO
THE EXPERIENCE OF ANGER

In the excerpt from *Pulp Fiction* with which we began this chapter, Samuel L. Jackson's character becomes enraged through his recitation of the passage from Ezekiel. This contribution of what Averill (1982) calls "non-normative factors" to the experience of anger is considered here. Although we are using the emotion of anger as an illustrative case, the conclusions from this type of research can broadly be extended to other basic emotions. We shall begin by examining the contribution of physiological arousal.

Physiological arousal

A whole series of studies, particularly those of Zillmann, has examined the suggestion that physiological arousal from different sources may combine to enhance whatever emotional experience might occur in a given situation (Dienstbier, 1979; Schachter, 1971; Zillmann, 1971, 1978, 1979). The main findings of this research are as follows:

1. Arousal from another source only influences the individual experience of anger when anger has been independently provoked. For example, Konecni (1975) found that auditory stimulation which increased arousal had little effect on anger-related behaviour unless the subject had been insulted and reported themselves to be angry.
2. The "transfer" of extraneous arousal, to quote Zillmann's phrase (e.g. 1971), to enhance the experience of anger is strongest when the individual is unaware of the source of the extraneous arousal and misattributes it to the event which has instigated the anger. For example, Zillmann, Johnson, and Day (1974) showed that the subjects who could attribute their arousal to exercise showed little or no increases in anger-related behaviour, whereas subjects who were unable to make such an attribution showed good "transfer of arousal" and a subsequent increase in the experience of anger.
3. Even if subjects do make the connection between an extraneous stimulus and the resultant arousal, the nature of the stimulus may still influence the development of an anger episode. For example, Geen and Stonner (1974) induced physiological arousal in their subjects by showing them a boxing match on film. Subjects were informed that the fighting was motivated either by (a) a desire for revenge, (b) by professionalism, or (c) by altruism. Subjects who had been informed that the fight was motivated by revenge (that is, an action-potential associated with anger) showed the most anger-related behaviour. In sum, if the arousing event is itself irritating, causes the person to

contemplate perceived wrongs or slights, or suggests that revenge or retaliation is in some way appropriate, then the experience of anger may be enhanced. In contrast, if the arousing event is pleasant, or induces any incompatible response tendencies, then the experience of anger may be reduced.

Facial expression and posture

Both Darwin (1872/1965) and James (1884) have suggested that the experience of an emotion is at least partly a product of the facial changes that occur during an emotion episode. Modern counterparts of these ideas have been encapsulated in the facial feedback hypothesis (see Laird, 1974, for a review). Winton (1986) identified two versions of the facial feedback hypothesis. In the categorical version, adopting the facial expression associated with a particular emotion enhances the experience of that emotion and that emotion only. In the dimensional model, facial expressions affect a single emotion-related dimension, probably that of pleasantness–unpleasantness. Much of the existing research is unable to distinguish between these two approaches, as subjects are most usually required to only adopt one positive and one negative facial expression. The arguments for and against the facial feedback hypothesis are many and complex and are somewhat reminiscent of the debates we reviewed in Chapter 3 concerning the evidence for universal facial expressions corresponding to basic emotions. While having no wish to oversimplify the issues, we shall restrict ourselves to the suggestion that the evidence for some form of facial feedback which enhances the individual's experience of emotions is, in our view, convincing. Let us consider one example in support of this claim. Duclos, Laird, Schneider, Sexter, Stern, and Van Lighten (1989) carried out a series of two experiments examining Winton's categorical version of the facial feedback hypothesis. In Experiment 1, subjects had to adopt facial expressions related to fear, anger, disgust, and sadness. The subjects were informed that the facial expressions were part of a study looking at brain lateralisation and were not explicitly informed that they were emotion-related. Subjects then had to complete emotion rating-scales and the results indicated that each expression increased the self-reported experience of the corresponding emotion significantly, over and above at least two of the other expression conditions.

If the evidence in support of the facial feedback hypothesis does stand up to scrutiny, the question is then begged as to what mechanism underlies feedback. Zajonc, Murphy, and Inglehart (1989), in their Vascular Theory of Emotional Efference (VTEE), have suggested that facial muscular movement, via its action on the cavernous sinus, restricts venous flow and thereby influences the cooling of the arterial blood supply to the brain. Independent studies suggest that such cooling produces changes in the phenomenal experience of emotions. Such theories are clearly speculative and the jury is still out on the mechanism that facial feedback might use.

In addition to the research looking at facial feedback, there are several studies which examine the effects of posture on the experience of emotion (Duclos et al., 1989; Riskind, 1984; Riskind & Gotay, 1982). Work in this area is still very preliminary; however, there does appear to be some evidence to suggest that posture as well as facial feedback can influence or mediate an individual's experience of emotions.

Aggressive stimuli

There are a number of studies which suggest that aspects of a person's appearance or the situation in which an event occurs can enhance an individual's experience of anger (see Averill, 1982, for a review) and again this basic thesis would apply to all emotions. For example, Berkowitz and LePage (1967) found that subjects who had been provoked to anger exhibited more intensive anger-related behaviour when a gun, rather than a neutral object such as a tennis racquet, was present in the room. The design of the study was such that the subjects had no reason to relate the gun or neutral object to any events occurring in the experiment. This effect has been replicated in several other studies (e.g. Fraczek & Macaulay, 1971; Frodi, 1975). However, there have also been numerous failures to replicate (e.g. Page & Scheidt, 1971; Turner, Layton, & Simons, 1975). In discussing the difficulties in replicating this "weapons effect", Berkowitz (1974) has suggested that an extraneous stimulus such as a gun will only facilitate anger-related behaviour if the person has already been provoked to anger and if the weapon is not considered to be so dangerous as to have an inhibitory effect.

A note on social-cognitive and cognitive biases associated with anger

Related to this discussion of additional factors involved in anger are the effects of being in an angry state on the cognitive and social cognitive system (Bodenhausen, Sheppard, & Kramer, 1994; Keltner, Ellsworth, & Edwards, 1993). For example, Keltner et al. (1993) carried out five experiments which examined angry subjects' and sad subjects' perceived causes for certain events. Angry subjects judged events caused by human beings (that is, recognisable agents) as more likely than events caused by situations; in addition, angry subjects interpreted ambiguous events as more likely to be caused by human forces than situational forces. Studies such as these indicate that the experience of the emotion of anger leads individuals to interpret new events in terms of the appraisal parameters involved in the emotion they are experiencing and we return to this issue in our discussion of SPAARS later in the chapter.

TOO MUCH ANGER VERSUS TOO LITTLE

We headed this chapter with a quotation from Aristotle's *Nicomachean Ethics* (1947) in which he suggests that the trick with anger is not to be angry but to be angry in the right way; that is, anger should be an appropriate response to events in their social and psychological context. As with much of the discussion in this chapter, this is true not just for anger but for all emotions. Consider Aristotle (*Nicomachean Ethics*, 1106e20) again:

> For instance, both fear and confidence and appetite and anger and pity and in general pleasure and pain may be felt both too much and too little, and in both cases not well; but to feel them at the right times, with reference to the right objects, towards the right people, with the right motive, and in the right way, is what is both intermediate and best, and this is characteristic of virtue.

In Aristotle's view, it is as bad to show little or no emotion when the situation requires it as it is to show too much emotion in that situation. By seemingly quantifying emotions in this way, Aristotle is not suggesting that there is some objective amount of emotion which is desirable and that deviations from this amount are unacceptable. Rather, he is suggesting that, within the social and interpersonal context within which events occur, one can formulate the concept of an appropriate emotional response and, consequently, of either excessive or understated emotion responses. What this appropriate emotional response should be will vary considerably as a function of the social and interpersonal context in which the individual's find themselves.

Earlier in the chapter we considered research investigating the sort of circumstances in which anger was seen as appropriate. Clearly the implication is that anger in other circumstances is somehow inappropriate. In most such cases the situation is self-correcting— people realise that they have over-reacted to a situation, or that their anger was not justified because the events to which it was a reaction were perhaps not deliberate, or were unavoidable, or were not due to negligence. However, sometimes this self-correction procedure is absent and anger slides down the slope from order to disorder. Implicit in all of this analysis is the suggestion that, although anger can sometimes be excessive or misplaced, it has a genuine and important function in our psychological and social existence. Indeed, this is the Aristotelian line which we have taken throughout this volume; emotions are functional states which enable individuals to deal with events which conflict with, interrupt, or facilitate their active goals. This suggests that, as well there being potential problems with excessive or misplaced anger, there may also be difficulties with too little anger. Again, this is far from being a trivial point, both philosophically, and also in terms of the consequences for an individual's health from failures to experience or express anger. In this section we endeavour to provide a brief historical and cross-cultural analysis of some of these issues.

A review of the historical teachings on anger reveals that the Stoic philosophers were alone in suggesting that anger is *never* appropriate in any situation and that any expression of anger is excessive. The Stoic flag was carried principally by the philosopher Seneca and in *De Ira* (p.107), he presents the case that anger has no value and in fact, is: "the most hideous and frenzied of all the emotions". An excellent review of Seneca's ideas is provided by Averill (1982), and we shall supply only the briefest of summaries here. Seneca's principal thesis was that no provocation adequately justifies anger, no situation permits it, and no benefit is ever gained by it. Once individuals allow themselves to become angry, that anger entirely consumes its possessors and prevents them from controlling their own behaviour, dulls their capacity for reasoning and sensible action, and harbours the potential to provoke people to the most terrible crimes on both the individual and the state level. Consider, in illustration, the following story which Seneca told of Cambyses, the King of Persia, who was much addicted to wine. At a banquet one of Cambyses' closest friends, Praexaspes, urged him to drink more sparingly, declaring that drunkenness was unbecoming to someone in his high position. Cambyses was insulted and consequently drank even more heavily than he had before. When he was sufficiently intoxicated he asked his servants to bring before him Praexaspes' son. Then, in order to show to the father that the enormous amount of wine that he had drunk did not affect his performance, he unerringly shot the son through the heart with an arrow. Seneca uses this story to illustrate the supreme irrationality of acts carried out in anger. However, an alternative argument (Averill, 1982) might be that if Cambyses' purpose had been to silence and intimidate his critic as well as to demonstrate the steadiness of his hand there would be few better ways of doing so!

As we have noted, Seneca's arguments go considerably against the grain of the philosophical teachings of his time. Consequently, he endeavoured to pre-empt his critics by suggesting a number of problems with his ideas; for example:

Should not a man become angry in defence of others, for example if his father is murdered or his mother outraged before his eyes?

Certainly not! retorts Seneca. Such anger is a sign of weakness not of loyalty; it is far better for an individual to defend and seek retribution for such wrongs merely by using his or her sense of duty, acting with complete volition, using rational judgement, and moved neither by impulse nor fury. Here Seneca is not denying the psychological imperative to feel angry. What Seneca is suggesting is that this initial prompting need not be yielded to. The individual should control his anger and make decisions in a rational and sensible way as to what punishment is required.

What are we to make of Seneca's ideas? The principal problem, in our view, is Seneca's understanding of the concept of anger as a passion. Seneca is content to argue that it is the passionate nature of anger which makes it dangerous; anger, once generated, can overwhelm the individual and become responsible for heinous crimes. However, in the same breath Seneca suggests that such compelling passion can be brought under volitional control such that it is eliminated from our psychological life; the psychological imperative can be resisted. Such idealism seems to ignore two fundamental points about the psychology of emotion and, indeed, the human condition: first, anger is a passion and, in some situations or in some individuals, it will be uncontrollable and outside of the influence of volitional power (see below); second, attempts to control or master such passion are liable to have "costs" in other parts of the system and it is possible that these costs will outweigh the gains of replacing anger with rational deliberate decision making (e.g. Breuer & Freud, 1895/1974). It is this latter point to which we next turn.

The area of emotion, inhibition, and health is an empirical and theoretical minefield; however, an excellent review is provided in Trauer and Pennebaker's edited book *Emotion, Inhibition and Health* (1993). We shall restrict ourselves to considering briefly the question of whether individuals who suppress their expression of anger suffer greater cardiovascular reactivity and related problems. In research which directly tries to establish links between the expression of anger and cardiovascular reactivity (CVR), individuals are most usually classified as "anger in" (suppression of anger) or "anger out" (expression of anger) on the basis of self-report measures (e.g. Spielberger, Johnson, Russell, Crane, Jacobs, & Worden, 1985). A typical finding is that of Dimsdale, Pierce, Schoenfeld, Brown, Zusman, and Graham (1986) who found a significant relationship between higher levels of systolic blood pressure and suppressed anger for white men, a trend in black men, and no relationship in women.

However, the picture is considerably more confused than this (see Siegman, 1993; Siegman & Wolfe, 1994) with the evidence for associations between suppressed anger and diastolic blood pressure being weaker, and between heart rate and suppressed anger often turning out to be negative (e.g. Lawler, Harralson, Armstead, & Schmied, 1993). The bottom line seems to be one which Aristotle would heartily endorse: that suppression of anger and the chronic full-blown expression of anger are both significant risk factors for cardiovascular disease (Siegman, 1993).

In this section we are in good company in arguing that, although anger often goes wrong thereby causing great misery and distress, it serves important and necessary psychological, social, and possibly health functions. Furthermore, even if we dispute this functional argument, we have suggested that it would be very difficult if not impossible to eliminate anger completely from our emotional lives due to the psychological imperatives which drive its generation.

A consideration of the role of anger in other cultures and societies does reveal some groups in which anger is rare (though interestingly none in which it is absent). Briggs (1970, cited by Averill, 1982) in his book, *Never in Anger*, examines the society of Utku, a small group of Canadian Inuit. Amongst the Utku there are no situations or events in which anger is considered a justifiable or appropriate reaction. There is an Utku term which can be loosely translated as anger ("Ningaq") but this really refers to aggressive tendencies. This word is seldom used in the first person, but most usually in reference to others. Briggs reports that, when provoked by events including the behaviour of others, a member of the Utku is more likely to experience amusement ("Tiphi") or depression ("Hujwjaq") than anger. This, then, is surely exactly the kind of utopia that Seneca was hoping for; however, as Averill (1982, p. 340) notes, there are several qualifications:

> The number of Utkus varies from about 20 to 35 individuals, and they are the sole inhabitants of an area of about 35,000 square miles. Considering the smallness of the group and the harshness of the environment, it is imperative that social conflict be kept at a minimum. Anything resembling anger, at least in its more aggressive aspects, is therefore discouraged; but so too is any deviation from established custom that might provoke anger. One might also ask when a provocation does occur, is amusement and/or depression a more appropriate response than anger?

THEORIES OF ANGER

In the first half of this chapter we have covered some of the basic research concerning anger. We have illustrated how anger is most usually a moral emotion, depending on attributions of intent to recognisable agents for perceived wrongdoings. We have also discussed the influence of non-normative factors such as extraneous physiological arousal on the experience of anger. Finally, we have considered the question, which is not unique to anger, of the balance between too much of a given emotion and too little. Much of this discussion has been relatively atheoretical. In the second half of the chapter we examine theories of anger, including the issue of cycles of appraisal in our own SPAARS model, before considering varities of anger disorder and other anger-related emotions.

Four theories of anger are considered in detail: the reformulated frustration–aggression hypothesis of Berkowitz; his later re-reformulation into a neo-associationist model; the cognitive-clinical theory of Novaco (e.g. 1979); and the SPAARS approach. Other cognitive theorists have considered the emotion of anger (Beck, 1976; Ellis, 1977); however, in neither of these approaches is anger analysed in great detail and we shall not dwell on them here.

The reformulated frustration–aggression hypothesis (e.g. Berkowitz, 1962)

In 1939 an eminent group of psychologists, sociologists, and anthropologists published a small book in which they set out a theoretical framework for understanding frustration and aggression (Dollard, Doob, Miller, Mowrer, & Sears, 1939). Their basic thesis was as follows: (1) The occurrence of aggression presupposes the existence of frustration; and (2) the existence of frustration always leads to some form of aggression.

Dollard et al. (1939, p.7) defined frustration as "an interference with the occurrence of an instigated goal-response at its proper time in the behaviour sequence". Aggression was defined (p.9) as any behaviour for which the goal "is the injury of the person to whom it is directed". This original formulation of the frustration–aggression hypothesis had very little to say about anger. However, in a major reformulation Berkowitz (e.g. 1962) placed anger centre-stage. According to Berkowitz, frustration leads to anger which acts as a drive and heightens the probability of aggressive behaviour. That is to say, frustration is not the immediate cause of aggression; rather, it is mediated by anger. This reformulation represents a considerable departure from the initial arguments of Dollard et al. In this reanalysis, frustration need not necessarily lead to aggression, merely to anger. Berkowitz's first pass at the frustration–aggression hypothesis (1962) is represented schematically in Fig. 8.1

In these early theoretical writings, Berkowitz leads an attack on what he considers traditional attributional/appraisal views of anger (as revealed by the normative research reviewed in the first part of the chapter), by providing evidence that anger can be provoked when the action of an agent in thwarting or interrupting a goal is *neither* deliberate, avoidable, nor due to negligence. Furthermore, he cites evidence where the frustration of the goal has *no* recognisable human agent. As fully paid-up subscribers to the appraisal theory approach (see Chapter 5), we concur with Berkowitz that the evidence he cites does indeed knock over the straw man of a *strong* version of the appraisal theory of anger in which anger can *only* result from an appraisal of a thwarted or interrupted goal with a recognisable agent and a judgement of deliberation, avoidability, or negligence. However, there are very few adherents to this strong appraisal view and the majority of people who find an appraisal approach useful in their understanding of anger would tend to endorse a much weaker version of the argument as exemplified by the partial analysis within SPAARS presented later. In this case, then, one could argue that Berkowitz is concentrating on the exceptions rather than the norms and we shall try to argue that this does not provide the most useful model of either anger order or anger disorder. More could be said about Berkowitz's early ideas; however, as he himself has revamped them, it seems more sensible to pass on.

Berkowitz's reformulation of his reformulation— the neo-associationist model of anger (e.g. Berkowitz, 1990)

In more recent work, Berkowitz has taken the themes which run through his theoretical writings on anger in the 1960s and provided a new framework for understanding anger episodes. This neo-associationist model of anger is represented schematically in Fig. 8.2.

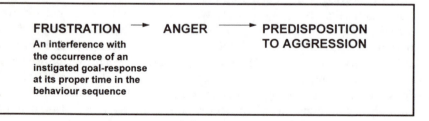

FRUSTRATION → **ANGER** → **PREDISPOSITION TO AGGRESSION**

An interference with the occurrence of an instigated goal-response at its proper time in the behaviour sequence

FIG. 8.1. A schematic diagram illustrating Berkowitz's original (1962) reformulation of the frustration–aggression hypothesis.

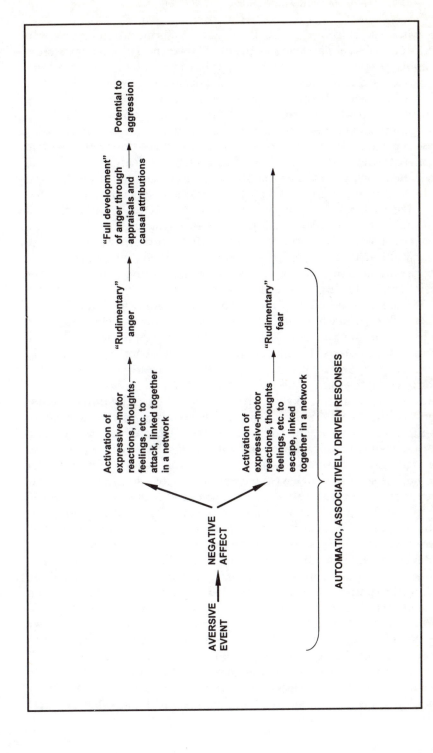

FIG. 8.2. Berkowitz's cognitive neo-associationist model of anger.

319

As can be seen from Fig. 8.2, Berkowitz's reformulation begins with what he describes as "an aversive event". This term is all-encompassing; it includes people who feel bad because they have a toothache, are very hot, are exposed to foul smells or unpleasant noises, or who are just very sad or depressed. Berkowitz argues that a process of preliminary cognitive appraisal labels these events as "aversive" and that this leads to the generation of "negative affect". This negative affect generated by the aversive event's occurrence "automatically gives rise to at least two sets of reactions at the same time: bodily changes, feelings, ideas, and memories associated with escape from the unpleasant stimulation and also to bodily reactions, feelings, thoughts, and memories associated with aggression. A variety of factors—genetic, learned, and situational—supposedly determine the relative strengths of these two 'response classes' " (Berkowitz, 1990, p.496). In Berkowitz's model these two sets of reactions (aggressive, escape) are mediated by associative networks in memory and give rise to rudimentary fear and anger experiences. Following the onset of these rudimentary emotional states (p.497): "the affected person makes appraisals and causal attributions and considers what feelings and actions are appropriate under the particular circumstances. This additional thought leads to the differentiation, intensification, suppression, or elaboration of the early rudimentary experiences".

Berkowitz cites numerous research findings in support of his model and many of these seek to show that the presence of "aversive events" of various kinds—loud noises, heat, toothache, having your arm in an uncomfortable position, and so on—increase the thoughts, feelings, and motor reactions, usually associated with anger. Berkowitz's model can account for much of these research data as well as other findings. For example, the studies which we have reviewed above suggesting that the presence of extraneous aggressive stimuli or extraneous physiological arousal can enhance the individual's experience of anger would be accounted for in Berkowitz's model by reference to an associative network which is the mediator of the transition from negative affect to the development of rudimentary anger (see Fig. 8.2). A strength of Berkowitz's Neo-Associationist approach, in our view, is its emphasis on an initial rudimentary anger-related appraisal which is then supplemented by a more sophisticated level of appraisal. However, it is regarding the nature of these two appraisal components where we disagree somewhat with the Neo-Associationist approach. In Berkowitz's model the initial appraisal is one of an "aversive event", which Berkowitz (p.496) talks about as something which "makes someone feel bad for one reason or another". As we have said, this, may include toothache, foul smells, loud noises, uncomfortable physical positions, and so on. However, we have argued in Chapter 2 that there is no such thing, in our view, as inherent "badness" in the world. We have suggested that something is bad because it is appraised with respect to models of the self, world, and other, and more importantly as a function of goal structures. It seems that Berkowitz's ideas may be in danger of lapsing into circularity: an event is aversive if it makes somebody feel bad for one reason or another, and people feel bad for one reason or another following aversive events.

According to Berkowitz, the first pass of the cognitive appraisal system, on detecting an aversive event, leads to the generation of what he has called "negative affect" (cf. Watson & Clark, 1992). This negative affect is essentially affect related to anger and affect related to fear. The question is begged as to why, if the affect is generally negative, there is no place for sadness or disgust or a whole host of other more complex "negative" emotions? Also, it seems unparsimonious for "aversive events" to lead to the generation of *both* fear and anger. We would propose again that it is more useful to think of events as being appraised as aversive with respect to the individuals' extant goal structures and thus to their models of world, self, and others. Given this, the event in question will have a particular meaning with respect to those goal structures. Then, if the event involves the interruption or thwarting of goals with an attribution of agency, the emotion which will be generated will be one of anger; whereas if the event suggests the *future* disruption or removal of a valued goal, then the emotion will be one of fear, and so on. More sophisticated levels of appraisal will then embroider on these initial processes.

In sum, Berkowitz's most recent analysis of anger has several strong features and his approach has generated an enormous amount of interesting and highly useful research investigating the role of physiological arousal, extraneous stimuli, and expressive-motor reactions in the onset and development of anger and our current understanding of the area owes much to his efforts. However, we have suggested that there are potential problems with the emphasis on an initial generalised appraisal of "aversion" and the subsequent generation of generalised negative affect.

Novaco's cognitive-clinical approach to anger

Novaco's (e.g.1975, 1979) model of anger is the most influential in the clinical context. A schematic flow diagram of Novaco's formulation is presented in Fig. 8.3.

In Novaco's model, external events are "cognitively processed" and may lead to a state of emotional arousal. This arousal is a general physiological response, which may be labelled differently by the individual

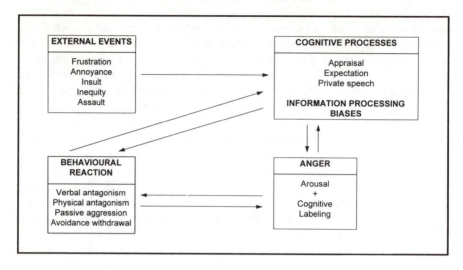

FIG. 8.3. Determinants of anger arousal according to Novaco.

depending upon the contextual cues and his/her interpretation of the eliciting events. Once anger has been aroused there are four main behavioural reactions which may follow: physical or verbal antagonism; passive aggression; and/or avoidance withdrawal. Which of these responses is most liable to develop is a function of how the event is viewed, as well as the individual's past experience and the predicted outcome.

In many ways Novaco's model of anger is a description of the processes which we have identified throughout the chapter. While it perhaps lacks explanatory power, it does provide a framework for understanding the interaction of external events, internal cognitive processes, behavioural reactions, and physiological reactions. Again, as with Berkowitz's model, we would disagree with Novaco's claim that the first pass of cognitive appraisal leads to generalised physiological arousal which is then labelled by the individual in an anger-related fashion. This view echoes Schacter and Singer's (1962) original formulations of the generation of emotions, which we reviewed in Chapter 3 and we will not reiterate the objections to this approach here.

In sum, Novaco's model provides a good descriptive framework within which to understand the main processes involved in anger and represents the most influential theoretical description of anger in the clinical domain. In line with this, the focus of Novaco's work has principally been on the development of treatment programmes for individuals experiencing significant difficulties with anger and Novaco's anger control training system (Novaco, 1975, 1979) is the most comprehensive and systematic therapy package for anger problems to date.

Other researchers in the field of aggression have put forward theoretical models which are relevant to an understanding of anger (e.g. Geen, 1990). However, they are broadly similar to the work we have already reviewed and we shall not consider them here.

The SPAARS model of anger

We have outlined the SPAARS model of emotion in detail in Chapter 5 and in the present chapter we endeavour to use the case of anger to illustrate the potential utility of the concept of cycles of appraisal within SPAARS.

Appraisal-based generation of anger within SPAARS. Within SPAARS the core appraisal parameters which make the emotion one of anger reflect the research reviewed in the first part of the chapter and consist of the interruption or thwarting of an active goal, combined with an appraisal of agency. Within the SPAARS framework, the satisfaction of these two parameters is both necessary and sufficient for the generation of anger. However, as we have discussed in Chapter 5, the core appraisal parameters involved in a given basic emotion become refined through the processes of development and socialisation such that the appraisal parameters most usually implicated in the generation of that emotion—the paradigm case—might well be more elaborate. So, in the case of anger, although an appraisal of goal interruption/ thwarting by a recognisable agent is sufficient for the generation of anger, the most usual or paradigm case also involves the further *moral* appraisal that the instigating event was deliberate, avoidable, or arose through negligence.

This conceptualisation of different levels of appraisal involved in the generation of emotions within SPAARS may provide a number of refinements over previous philosophical and psychological theorising with respect to anger. First, anger may be fully experienced following satisfaction of the core appraisal parameters alone when the cognitive system as a whole is placed under stress or load such that the resources necessary for the more elaborate, moral appraisal components involving deliberation and intent are unavailable. So, for example, someone who is very stressed or busy at work might be more likely to get angry regardless of whether or not the instigating event had been appraised as deliberate, avoidable, or due to negligence. Similarly, an empirical prediction might be that individuals who are placed under a task load (for example rehearsing a set of numbers) would be more likely to experience the generation of anger on the basis of the core appraisal parameters alone.

Second, there will be frequent occasions when individuals experience the onset of anger following the core appraisal of a goal being thwarted or interrupted by a recognisable agent and then have to suppress or terminate the generation of anger when more sophisticated appraisal indicates that anger is inappropriate. For example, I (TD) lent a car to a friend whilst I was travelling for several months. During my absence, the car was stolen from outside the friend's house. This theft was unavoidable and involved no deliberation or negligence on the part of my friend but, despite this, I felt angry towards him, and had to struggle to suppress this anger due to the knowledge that no attribution of blame could be put on him for the theft of the car.

The appraisal system within SPAARS, then, as we have discussed in Chapter 5, is working in cycles. So to take the above example: first, the event is appraised as incompatible with existing goals implicating a negative emotion; second, the event is appraised as interrupting/thwarting an existing goal with a recognisable agent, this initiates the generation of anger; third, the event is appraised as not deliberate, avoidable, or due to negligence, the generation of anger is blocked and there are perhaps feelings of sadness/disappointment (see Fig. 8.4).

The third point concerns the existence of anger in human infants or even sub-human animals. We are not going to quibble too much with Seneca's (1963) suggestion that "While it [anger] is the foe of reason, it is nevertheless born only where reason dwells"; however, we would contend that perhaps human infants and sub-human animals possess enough "reason" for the rudimentary generation of anger (that is, as a function of the core appraisal parameters) but that what they do lack are the more sophisticated processes of cognition involved in the higher levels of appraisal which contribute to the paradigmatic expression of anger in the adult human. So, a child can become angry and that anger will be directed at a perceived wrongdoing; however, what will be lacking is any sophisticated appraisal that the wrongdoing could have been avoided, was deliberate, or was carried out through negligence. The child's anger is indiscriminate in these respects; indeed, when adults fail to take into account the fact that actions which prevent the realisation of their extant goals are sometimes unavoidable, we tend to describe their anger as childish or petulant.

The fourth point we wish to highlight is illustrated by non-paradigmatic cases in which adult anger is generated when the instigating event was clearly not deliberate or unjustified or due to negligence; the type of anger which we have suggested is sometimes labelled as childish or petulant. However, let us consider two examples of such a scenario in which the experienced anger is anything but childish: the anger which individuals feel during periods of

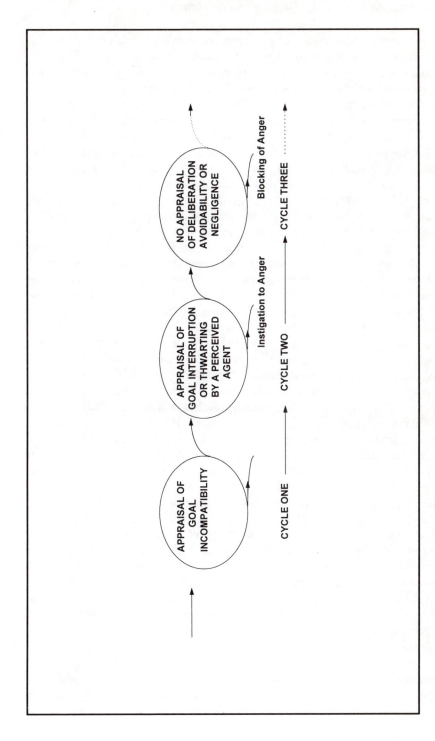

FIG. 8.4. Example of the sequence of appraisal cycles involved in anger.

bereavement; and emotional reactions of mental health workers who work with individuals with challenging behaviours.

Following a death it is very common for individuals close to the deceased to experience anger towards him/her for having abandoned them or for having died. The phenomenal experience of anger is, understandably, often very hard to deal with for the bereaved person; it seems wrong to feel angry towards somebody who was loved and who did not die or abandon anybody intentionally. This experience of anger in the absence of an avoidable, deliberate, or negligent instigating event often leaves the angry individual feeling bewildered and/or guilty. In this case, it seems that the shared goals which have been thwarted are so major that the imperative for the generation of anger on the basis of core appraisal components alone is sufficiently powerful to override the suppressing effects of any more sophisticated appraisals which take place. All the sophisticated levels of appraisal do in this case, we contest, is contribute towards the individual's experience of the anger as inappropriate, thus enhancing feelings of guilt and bewilderment. The role of anger and its combination with sadness in bereavement reactions is considered in greater detail in Chapter 7.

The second example of anger in the absence of an unavoidable, deliberate or negligent instigating event sometimes arises on wards for individuals with learning disabilities or challenging behaviours. These behaviours are often violent, disruptive, and unpredictable and would fulfil many of the criteria for events which would normally lead to the generation of anger (as discussed earlier). However, an appropriate psychological understanding of these behaviours and indeed the mental health philosophy on such wards, is normally along the lines that the individuals cannot help behaving in this way and that the behaviours are neither deliberate nor negligent according to the normal understanding of these terms. Despite such heuristic models of mind, members of staff who work with challenging clients occasionally find themselves experiencing strong feelings of anger and vindictiveness towards the individuals under their care following behaviours which are violent, disruptive, or unpredictable. Again, as with the bereaved person's experience of anger, it seems inappropriate to describe the mental health workers' emotional reactions as childish or petulant. In this situation it is as if the interelated sets of social and cultural rules and norms by which individuals make judgements of intent (and which are instantiated within SPAARS as models of self, world, and other at the schematic model level of meaning) are extremely difficult to replace consistently with "working" models of the individuals with challenging behaviours and the worlds in which they exist; consequently, the mental health workers' own, socially derived, models will sometimes override the working models they are trying to apply to the individuals in their care and they will feel angry.

A final issue is the potential for anger to be directed towards inanimate objects. The notion that the paradigmatic instigation of anger requires an event that is avoidable, deliberate, or negligent implies the ability of the agent to form some kind of intent. However, if we refine our analysis of anger such that, in its most basic form, it does not require such intent, it becomes clear that one can potentially feel anger towards objects or "agents" which are unable to form intent. For example, most of us would have experienced feelings of anger towards the hammer that hit our thumb or the car that wouldn't start. In fact, it is likely that many of us will have exhibited quite vindictive or punishing behaviour towards these objects. Following such incidents, we tend to feel pretty foolish as we realise that our anger is directed toward an object which could not have intended to provoke us.

Other aspects of anger within SPAARS. In instances of the automatic generation of anger within SPAARS it is proposed that there will have been anger-related appraisals of an event at some time in the emotional history of the individual which, through a process of repetition of that event (see Chapter 5), have become automatised such that eventually there is no longer a need for access to the schematic model level of meaning for the emotion of anger to be generated following that event.

To illustrate, let us return to the example of Peter and his shouting father from Chapter 5 (see Fig. 5.6). If we remember, Peter's childhood was overshadowed by the constant fear that his father would shout at him and be angry with him about inconsequential things or about things for which Peter was not to blame. As a child, we suggested, the father's behaviour was appraised at the schematic model level as an (avoidable or deliberate) wrongdoing which thwarted Peter's goal of having, for example, an enjoyable afternoon with friends. Such repeated appraisal of his father's shouting led to the automatisation of the generation of Peter's anger such that, eventually, at the event of his father's shouting, Peter experienced anger which had been generated automatically via the associative level of meaning in SPAARS with no access to the schematic model level which mediates appraisal. As a result of these childhood experiences, whenever Peter was shouted at in later life as an adult, he experienced the automatic generation of anger even when the shouting was done in humour or when the shouting was entirely appropriate as a response to Peter's behaviour.

A summary of the generation of anger, either via the schematic model level or via the associative level in SPAARS, is presented in Fig. 8.5.

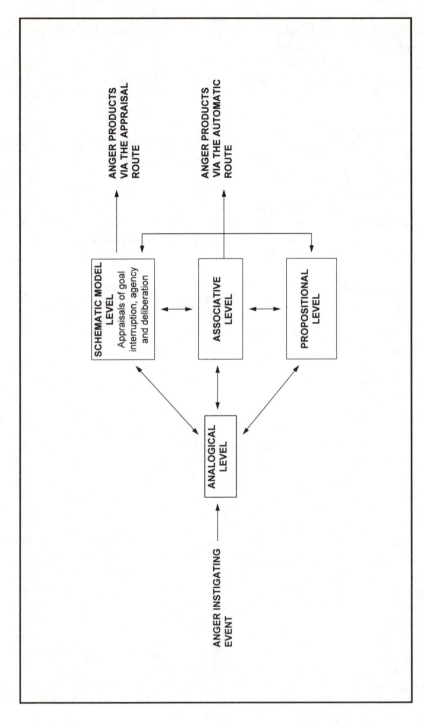

FIG. 8.5. Schematic diagram illustrating the routes to anger in SPAARS.

So far we have endeavoured to illustrate how the SPAARS model can provide an account of anger which is able to explain not only the normative, morally driven experience of anger but also the exceptions to this paradigm case. It remains, however, to consider a number of other issues which arose in the literature review in the first part of the chapter; namely, the influence of non-normative factors, the passionate nature of anger, and too little versus too much anger. This last point will serve as a good introduction to our discussion of so-called anger disorder.

Non-normative factors are seen as feeding into the experience of anger in different ways within SPAARS. We propose that facial feedback (and possibly postural feedback) would operate via the associative level of representation. Body state information, such as the status of the facial musculature, would be processed at the analogical level of representation and would then serve to initiate the generation of the congruent emotion via associative links between body state representations and emotion generation (see Fig. 8.6).

In contrast, we suggest that the presence of aggressive stimuli is most likely to feed into the experience of anger via the schematic model level within SPAARS. For example, the presence of a gun might be appraised in a fear-related way and the associated physiological activation would then enhance the experience of anger.

At various points so far in the chapter we have referred to anger as a passion. As we have touched on in Chapter 5, the passionate nature of emotions within SPAARS can be a function of several processes. First, when schematic-based, emotion-related appraisals occur, we have argued that there is an imperative for the generation of the emotion. So, if an event is appraised at the schematic model level as intentional, carried out by a recognisable agent, and as harmful to active goals, then anger will always be instigated. A second sense in which emotions can be thought of as passionate within SPAARS concerns the concept of emotion modules discussed in Chapter 5. Once a given emotion is generated, the emotion module will "take over" the SPAARS system and SPAARS will be reconfigured in order to deal with the instigating events. Such reconfiguration not only biases the system in favour of information congruent to the emotion module and its associated appraisal characteristics (for example, the cognitive and social cognitive biases implicated in anger) but also activates the related action potentials. For an emotion such as fear the passionate experience may be so strong that the individual cannot help but succumb to the related action potentials and avoid the feared situation by, say, running off. However, for an emotion such as anger where the action potentials involve retaliation and aggression, the consequences of succumbing to passion can be far more severe. As we have already seen, the homicide

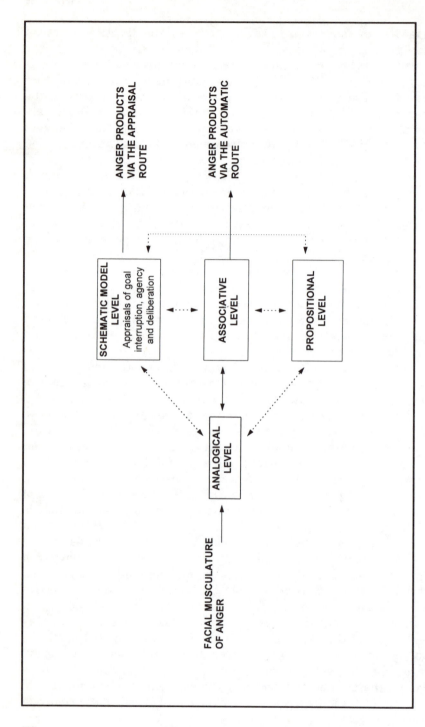

FIG. 8.6. Schematic diagram illustrating the operation of facial feedback in SPAARS.

law in the United States takes into account the fact that anger can so overwhelm someone that he will kill another. For this reason, the implications of too much or too little anger, especially the social ramifications, are perhaps more pressing than the similar cases of say, too much or too little disgust or too much or too little fear. Finally, an emotion can be experienced as a passion when it is generated automatically via the associative route within SPAARS. In this situation, real-time appraisals at the schematic model level may not be anger-related but the event still leads to a feeling of anger in the individual.

Too little anger, as we have seen, does seem to have a number of health-related consequences. Within SPAARS we have suggested that the failure to experience an emotion when it would be considered appropriate to do so can occur in two ways, both of which are discussed in Chapter 5. To take the case of anger, first, the core appraisals related to anger can simultaneosly lead to anger-related products and also to the activation of schematic models which block the experience of those products. So the individual would not feel angry, even though anger-related appraisals have occurred. We considered an example of this in Chapter 5 in which Ann had rarely experienced anger in her life as she had learnt as a child that it was inappropriate. However, in later life, a course of therapy for intrusive obsessional ruminations released a lot of anger towards her unfaithful husband. Experiencing this anger was very painful and ego dystonic for Ann.

A second way in which anger might not be felt, even when it is appropriate, is for the relevant event information to be blocked from entering the schematic model level. In this case, an event can be viewed as a personal offence, carried out by a recognisable agent entirely at the propositional level with no appraisal-based, schematically generated anger at all.

NOTES ON THE RELATIONSHIP OF ANGER TO OTHER EMOTIONS

The main focus of the present chapter is an analysis of the basic emotion of anger. However, anger, we submit, is the building block of several more complex emotional states and we present some brief thoughts on these here for the sake of completion.

Annoyance

The most complete study of annoyance and its similarities and differences to anger was performed by Averill (1982) in his series of diary studies that we referred to earlier in this chapter. Subjects were encouraged to keep a diary record of incidences of both anger and annoyance; in addition, subjects were asked to perform a content analysis on their own diary entries. Specifically, they were asked "On the basis of these experiences [incidences of anger and annoyance], what do you believe are the main differences between anger and annoyance? If you can, list three dimensions or distinguishing features, indicating how anger differs from annoyance on each dimension." The results based on the first half of the study and derived from the diary records are shown in Table 8.4.

The differences between anger and annoyance based on content analyses of the features which subjects identified is shown in Table 8.5.

Averill (1982, p.248) summarises a number of features which can be derived from these data and which capture the main differences in anger and annoyance; to quote:

> Anger is a relatively more intense, interpersonal emotion, and is more likely to involve attribution of blame and desire for revenge. Anger is typically provoked by instances regarded as serious and/or personally threatening; and it is accompanied by a strong desire for direct action, this in spite of the fact that normal coping resources may seem inadequate. Moreover, since anger is cognitively and socially more complex than annoyance, it is affected differently by changes in the mood of the individual.

TABLE 8.4
Differences between anger and annoyance (based on Averill's 1982 diary records)

1. Anger is more likely than annoyance to be directed at another person (as opposed to an inanimate object, institution, etc.)

2. Anger occurs less frequently than annoyance.

3. Anger lasts longer than annoyance.

4. Anger is experienced as more difficult to control than annoyance.

5. Anger is more likely than annoyance to be occasioned by an act that is appraised as unjustified; annoyance is more likely than anger to be occasioned by acts that are appraised as either justified or unavoidable.

6. Anger is more often accompanied than annoyance by verbal aggression and/or expressive reactions.

7. Anger is more often motivated than annoyance by a desire to get even for past wrongs and/or gain revenge for the present incident.

8. Anger is more likely than annoyance to effect a change in the situation.

TABLE 8.5
Differences between anger and annoyance (derived from content analyses of the distinguishing features mentioned by subjects; based on Averill, 1982)

1. Anger involves greater physical expression.
   e.g. "Usually when I am annoyed I keep it to myself unless it bugs me for a long time. When I'm angry I let it be known—passively (calmly) or violently."

2. Anger is more intense than annoyance.
   e.g. "Annoyance—the feeling is less vivid, less intense (though certainly it can be equally upsetting."

3. Anger lasts longer.
   e.g. "For me there is definitely a time factor involved. If something affects me just at a certain moment, it's usually annoyance. If it's a long-term affect (plans, feeling) it's usually anger."

4. Anger is caused by more serious incidents.
   e.g. "Annoyance occurs over trivial incidents; things one usually wouldn't think twice about (unless writing them down in a journal). Anger occurs over a major issue."

5. In anger the precipitating incident is taken personally.
   e.g. "Anger is more personalised than annoyance. To make me angry, the incident must be intense but also it must be directed at me."

6. Anger is more difficult to control.
   e.g. "Anger is an explosion of emotions while annoyance is controlled, restrained emotions."

7. Annoyance, if repeated or sustained, may lead to anger.
   e.g. "Being annoyed is being bothered somewhat yet not really being concerned about it, while anger is the 'last straw' of annoyance where emotions come into play."

8. Anger is less frequent than annoyance.
   e.g. "Anger is a lot harder to arouse than annoyance. Please get annoyed often, and angry less often."

9. Anger is more often directed at people.
   e.g. "In proportion I get more angry at people, and more annoyed at objects, weather, etc.."

10. One's mood at the time helps determine the emotion.
    e.g. "It depends on the mood of the person at the time, sometimes you're quicker to anger."

Indignation, hatred, and wrath
Solomon (1993), in his book *The Passions*, has argued that indignation differs from anger in that its criteria are more "authoritative"—that is, they are more strongly moral than in the case of anger, and consequently the individual experiencing indignation is more self-righteous. Solomon proposes that these fundamental differences lead to others (the person or institution towards whom anger is directed) to be viewed as inferior and that this further increases the indignant individual's own sense of self-righteousness and innocence. Furthermore, this leads to an emphasis on the differences between the individual experiencing the

emotion and the individual who has caused the emotion. Solomon's views are summarised in Table 8.6.

We have already discussed above (albeit briefly) the emotion of indignation within SPAARS. We suggested that the sophisticated moral appraisals which Soloman highlights as implicated in indignation occur subsequently to appraisals of deliberation, avoidability and negligence at the schematic model level of meaning—they represent advanced cycles of the appraisal system.

Anger at an agent, an institution, the self, or even inanimate objects can generalise such that the object or agent becomes imbued with the negative. It is then that we can say that the person or object is hated. In a sense, then, hatred seems to be generalised anger. It is a strong negative emotion which has ceased to be about one event or one thwarted goal and has broadened to embrace parts of, or indeed all, aspects of the person or object. Some authors have analysed hatred in terms of disgust (e.g. Oatley, 1992) and we concur with this to some extent; any person (including parts of the self) or thing in which we

TABLE 8.6
The attributes of indignation (based on Solomon, 1993)

1. Direction	Outwards (but with implicit contrast between the immorality of the other and one's own innocence)
2. Scope/focus	Another agency
3. Object	Human action
4. Criteria	Highly moral
5. Status	Self as superior; other as inferior
6. Evaluations	Extremely negative evaluation of other's (others') action. May generalise to global negative evaluation of the person or persons committing that action
7. Responsibility	Other(s)
8. Intersubjectivity	Very defensive
9. Distance	Tends to be impersonal, may even approach indifference
10. Mythology	The offended moralist, personally outraged but not for any personal reasons; rather for reasons of principle. (If you insult me, I will be angry; but if you insult my race/religion/country/occupation, etc., I will be morally indignant because of the "principle of the thing")
11. Desire	To punish
12. Power	Indignation without power merges with resentment; indignation with power tends to satisfy itself through effective action (like anger)
13. Strategy	To attend to the moral frailties and offences of others, thus setting oneself up by way of contrast as comparatively moral, good, etc.

invest so much negative feeling must, in a sense, feel strongly "not self"—an object of disgust (see Chapter 9). However, we would want to argue that hatred is primarily derived from anger—it is a moral judgement of agency in instigating events. We have suggested throughout the chapter that the moral nature of anger is a function of attributions of intent, deliberation, or negligence regarding a wrongdoing. It is, we suggest, the further attribution that such intent was a function of permanent aspects of the person or object that may transform the anger into hatred.

As with anger, which can seemingly arise in the absence of higher-level, moral appraisals, so can hatred. It is a common occurrence for us to hate certain things about people we are close to, even though it is clear that no deliberation or intent on their part is involved; for example, hating the fact that someone eats noisily even though we know it is because of their false teeth.

It may be somewhat surprising to the reader that we include the emotion of wrath in this chapter as it has surely gone out of common usage in the English language. However, the experience of the emotion of wrath is theoretically interesting because of the emphasis on the action-potential component. Wrath we would suggest is essentially the emotion of anger where the desire for revenge (action potential) is of extreme intensity and extended duration. Wrath is all about the desire for getting even as enshrined in *lex talionis*—eye for eye, tooth for tooth (Exodus, 21:24). The desire for vengeance in the emotion of wrath seems to be concerned with actions that are not necessarily intended to right the suffered wrong and are quite often incited by wrongs that cannot be put right. Furthermore, the wrathful individual has full insight into these facts. Two excellent and recent analyses of wrath and its corollary vengeance have been written by Nico Frijda (1994) and Robert Solomon (1994).

Jealousy and envy

The green ey'd monster of jealousy is a highly complex beast. However, as Neu (1980, p.426) points out "That [jealousy] has such rich surroundings, that we make such a wealth of fine discriminations in the area of jealousy (envy, resentement, indignation, *schadenfreude*, begrudging, malice, spite, ill will, hatred, ingratitude, revenge, hostility, and so on indefinitely) is itself a sign of its interest and importance". Comprehensive reviews of these "rich surroundings" can be found in two recent books on the subject: *Jealousy: Theory, Research and Clinical Strategies* (White & Mullen, 1989) and *The Psychology of Jealousy and Envy* (Salovey, 1991). What we shall do here is provide some brief speculations concerning the core features of jealousy.

Jealousy, we propose, is not only about anger but also about fear. To some extent this is the fear of losing someone, but, more importantly, it is perhaps the fear of losing our place in that person's affections and, consequently, aspects of our self-worth which depend on those affections. Finally, jealousy requires a rival, real or imagined, who competes for the person we are jealous over and for their affections. The suggestion that these ingredients are necessary and sufficient for jealousy may seem more compelling after a couple of thought experiments. First, we do not feel jealous if we fear losing someone or their affections without a rival. The fading of love in a relationship can lead to feelings of regret, disappoint- ment and nostalgia but does not alone invoke jealousy. Jealousy may rear its head with respect to future rivals—people our departing lover has not yet met but may come to love in the future—but without such a sense of rivalry, then the green ey'd monster will remain slumbering. Similarly, we can fear losing a valued object to a rival. A colleague at work might be pushing hard for our job. In such circum- stances we may feel anger, resentment, sadness, or even envy (see later) but not jealousy over the job. What jealousy there may be will concern the loss of our place in our boss's esteem. So, jealousy cannot exist, we submit, over objects or things only over people because the real fear is the loss of others' feeling for us, not the the loss of the individuals themselves.

We have claimed that the above components of the fear of loss com- bined with real or imagined rivalry are enough for jealousy. So, what of anger? Others have suggested that anger, often in the form of hatred, is essential to jealousy. Consider Spinoza (*Ethics*, 1955, Part III, Prop. XXXV):

> If I imagine that an object beloved by me is united to another person by the same or by a close bond of friendship than that by which I myself alone held the object, I shall be affected with hatred toward the beloved object itself, and shall envy that other person ... This hatred toward a beloved object when joined with envy is called "jealousy".

In contrast, we suggest that angry jealousy is perhaps only one form—one of several reactions to the severe fear of loss and threat to the self. In other circumstances jealous individuals may become depressed or withdrawn, may intensify their original attachment or intellectualise the situation (Tov-Ruach, 1980).

Jealousy is an extremely common emotion. In many relationships it is not destructive and, indeed, is often functional in serving to improve communication and understanding, or by enabling individuals to recognise the strength of their feelings. However, jealousy is always in danger of becoming intense and pathological and we consider some examples of so-called disordered jealousy later in the chapter.

Envy, we suggest, differs from jealousy in two important ways. First, envy is about things that others possess, whether it be good looks, a fast car or a beautiful partner; in contrast, jealousy is about individuals that we "possess". Second, envy can extend to objects whereas jealousy, as we have argued above, primarily concerns other people. The core of envy is the rivalry with another; the envied object or quality may itself be non-transferable (for example, good looks) or even if the envied object is magnanimously transferred by the rival, this may be met with ingratitude or even greater envy.

As with the case of jealousy, we would suggest that it is not immediately clear that envy is derived from anger. However, envy does seem to be a response to others achieving goals we ourselves wish to obtain and it is a small appraisal step to the idea that our rivals are somehow *blocking* our goal fulfilment by virtue of their own achievements. Some authors argue that this step is always taken, albeit unconsciously. This is mainly true of the psychoanalytic literature as in the work of Melanie Klein (1957) on destructive impulses. Max Scheler (*Ressentiment*, 1972, p.52) sums up the flavour of these ideas:

> This tension between desire and nonfulfillment does not lead
> to envy until it flares up into hatred against the owner, until
> the latter is falsely considered to be the cause of our
> privation.

Even if we agree that envy is always a function of anger or hatred towards the rival, it seems clear that the conscious manifestations can be quite different. Neu (1980) usefully distinguishes between malicious envy, a state where the anger and hatred are manifest and where we wish to lower our rival to our level, and admiring envy, a state in which we wish to raise ourselves to the level of the rival. The latter seems more clearly to be a functional emotional state, whereas the former seems more destructive. Klein would of course smile knowingly and point out that admiring envy may be a mere mask for the destructive, unconscious envy which lurks beneath the surface; a debate which we are unlikely to be able to resolve here.

ANGER DISORDER

We discussed earlier in the chapter the idea that an individual might feel too little anger. Although such experiences are theoretically interesting and, in some cases, can be regarded as pathological, the essence of the so-called anger disorders is really about too much anger or anger which is inappropriate. In this section we consider these reactions and also the case of morbid jealousy.

Anger can slide down the slippery slope from order to disorder in a number of ways. First, individuals can become angry at events in a way which most of society would regard as inappropriate. Second, anger can be directed at or displaced onto inappropriate agents. Third, anger can be an appropriate reaction to the circumstances whilst being excessive in its intensity. Finally, anger can be extrinsically motivated. We consider each of these possibilities in turn.

Non-normative events, agents, interpretations, and appraisals implicated in anger. When the schematic models of self, world, and other differ from those which can be inferred from the diary studies discussed earlier—that is, when they are non-normative—then the generation and expression of anger in those individuals can appear abnormal. Averill (1982, p.336) calls this "anger gone awry"; to quote:

> Inappropriate behaviour, especially of a violent nature, may also result from a failure of an individual to internalise appropriate regulative rules. Of course, what is considered "appropriate" in this sense depends on the group making the valuation, namely, the dominant culture. Subgroups within the culture, whilst sharing many of the norms or values that help constitute anger, may nevertheless regulate their behaviour differently.

Detailed discussion of the rules and regulations of such sub-cultures may be found in Wolfgang and Ferracuti (1967) who examine the Vendetta Barbaricina in Sardinia and the Mafia in Sicily, and in Wolfgang (1979) who has worked with populations of street boys in Philadelphia. Such "anger gone awry" is clearly illustrated by the assassination scene from *Pulp Fiction* at the start of the chapter.

In addition to the failure to adopt normative social rules in particular sub-groups of society, there are individual differences in the make-up of the domains of knowledge of the world, self, and other. In their most extreme form such variations begin to take on clinical characteristics; for example, certain forms of paranoid personality disorder are likely to be characterised by appraisals of deliberation, avoidability, and negligence which fall outside the range of social normality.

Anger with inappropriate attributions of agency. Consider the example of Peter:

> Peter is a 13-year-old boy with severe kidney problems which are being treated with regular and prolonged dialysis requiring frequent hospitalisation. Peter gets on reasonably well with his parents and friends but has a very bad relationship with his slightly older sister, Julie. Whenever Julie is around, Peter is always bullying her and shouting at her and sometimes her very presence seems to rouse him to uncontrollable rages.

Peter is clearly and understandably angry at the world or fate for singling him out as someone to have a highly disabling illness, for making him different and an object of pity. However, it seems that all of this anger is displaced onto Julie even though it is clearly not her fault that Peter is ill. Such displacement of anger is an everyday occurrence; no doubt we have all "taken it out" on someone close. However, the displacement of anger can also become disordered and disabling to relationships and social groups.

Anger can also be directed at and displaced onto the self. The research we reviewed in the first half of the chapter, despite its breadth of sampling and methodological rigour, says little about such self-directed anger. This is perhaps surprising as no doubt all of us have at some time or other felt angry with ourselves for being negligent or behaving inappropriately in a way which could have been avoided. An understanding of anger directed toward the self seems especially important in considering emotional order and disorder; indeed, during the earlier part of this century, self-directed anger and rage were central to a number of theories of depression, especially those from the psychoanalytic school (e.g. Freud, 1917/1984). The pioneering work which proposed a role for self-directed anger in depression was Freud's *Mourning and Melancholia*, published in 1917 when Freud was in his 60s and had his own personal experiences of being depressed to draw upon. We discussed Freud's ideas of the involvement in depression of anger turned inwards towards the ego in greater detail in Chapter 7 so we will spend no more time on this aspect of anger here.

Disproportionate anger.   A third way in which anger can become disordered is when individuals experience and express anger in ways entirely out of proportion to the precipitating circumstances. In these scenarios, the fact that anger is an appropriate reaction to the precipitating events and interpretations is not in question; what seems disordered is the extent and force of the individual's anger reactions. In the American television series *The Incredible Hulk*, the mild-mannered Bruce Banner often warned his would-be protagonists: "Don't make me angry, you won't like me when I'm angry." Those who foolishly ignored this warning then had to deal with a raging, towering green monster who was prepared to tear them limb from limb. While this is clearly an extreme example, we all know individuals with whom we feel the need to tip-toe around their sensibilities in the fear that the slightest provocation will elicit "Hulk-like" behaviour. Some have argued that "anger attacks"—extreme examples of the inability to control one's anger—may represent a discrete clinical syndrome (e.g. Fava, Anderson, & Rosenbaum, 1993). Whether or not one agrees with this, there is a widespread consensus that inability to control one's anger frequently presents as a problem at the clinic (e.g. Novaco, 1979) and this has led to the development of systematic therapeutic procedures to develop anger control.

As we have noted, the principal problem with disproportionate, uncontrollable anger lies in the related action potentials to retaliate and aggress. A famous example from the Maudsley Hospital in London, which was the subject of a television documentary, illustrates this point:

> John [real name changed] was a man with a violent history. He had several criminal convictions for bodily harm and can recount times when he has nearly killed people in uncontrollable rages. At the time that John came into contact with mental health services he would only rarely leave his home and then he would be accompanied by several bodyguards—not to protect him from others, but to protect others from him.

In cases such as John's it seems clear that there are few holds on the full-blown expression of anger. Such behaviour seems most likely to be the result of a troubled, violent development in which anger and aggression are socialised as appropriate and acceptable responses to events.

Clearly, the problems of anger and aggression are not merely interpersonal ones. At social and cultural levels they lead to large-scale war and violence. An excellent discussion of these issues is provided by Anthony Storr (1988), aspects of which we refer to in Chapter 1.

Anger with an extrinsic motivation. There are a number of situations in which the motives behind episodes of anger are extrinsic ones; that is, they do not depend on the interruption or thwarting of a valued goal with an attribution of agency. Anger which is extrinsically motivated in this way is a recurring issue in the mental health clinic; Averill (1982, p.338) provides the following example:

A man is frustrated at work because he cannot complete a project as anticipated, due to an unavoidable delay in securing needed material. While driving home from work in heavy traffic, he is involved in a near accident. Although outwardly calm by the time he arrives home, he retains a residue of physiological arousal. The man has promised to take his son to a school function that evening, and would very much like to get out of it. He goes to his son's room, where the boy is playing a war game, with a variety of toy weapons lying around the room. The man becomes quite angry at his son, ostensibly because the boy has not done certain chores; and as punishment he refuses the boy permission to leave the house that evening.

In this example, the man is ostensibly angry because his son has not performed the household tasks which he should have done. However, it seems clear that even if the son had been exemplary in his domestic duties, the father would have found something to get angry about in order that he did not have to take his son out that evening. In this scenario there is an anger-provoking event (the son's failure to perform his chores); however, there is also a clear indication that the father's anger is motivated by his extrinsic desire to have an evening at home. Examples such as this are common and often relatively unproblematic; however, again the slope from emotional order to emotional disorder is a slippery one and many therapeutic hours are spent in understanding and intervening in situations where not just anger but other emotions are employed for instrumental gain. Anger can be used to exert control, to gain attention, to maintain fear in loved ones, as a barrier to intimacy, and as a way of justifying behaviour that would not otherwise be committed.

Morbid jealousy

Examples of pathological jealousy are common in the cinema and literature. In the film *L'Enfer*, for example, Daniel Auteuil's character experiences angry, violent jealousy over his innocent and beautiful wife. In the denouement, the wife is shackled to the couple's bed whilst the husband stalks the room wielding a cut-throat razor. The camera shifts suddenly to the view from the window where ambulance men from the nearby psychiatric hospital can be seen approaching the house. Similarly, in Paul Sayer's novel *Howling at the Moon*, the anti-hero becomes obsessively jealous of his, again innocent, wife and, resigning his job, sets off to work each day as usual only to inhabit the house opposite from where he observes his wife's every move through binoculars, recording the details minutely.

Examples such as these are not merely flights of fictitious fancy. Consider the following case study (De Silva, 1994, p.176):

> X, a woman in her twenties, and Y, her partner who was also in his twenties, were referred for help. The problem was morbid jealousy on the part of X. They had a close passionate relationship. She developed strong feelings of jealousy within a short period, a few months prior to referral. There was no clear reason for the onset of the jealousy, except that Y had been particularly busy in his job for several months. She became increasingly unhappy about his association with his female colleagues and secretaries etc. and began to accuse him of flirting with them. She interrogated him every day, and searched his briefcase and pockets for evidence of his involvement with other women. She also verbally abused him and physically attacked him at times, in the context of quarrels related to this. She was quite distressed at her own behaviour, and said she "could not help" acting in this way.

What is it that makes jealousy pathological in all of these cases? Clearly, the extreme nature of the different types of behaviour involved is important. However, perhaps more central is the fact that in each case the jealousy is a function of beliefs which are unfounded. It is important to note that the truth value of the beliefs is not what is at issue. The belief may be a false one but understandable given the circumstances. For example, Othello's jealousy was a function of false beliefs; however, these beliefs were not unfounded as they were grounded in Iago's deception and manipulation of the situation. Interestingly, morbid jealousy is sometimes referred to as Othello Syndrome, a label which, in this analysis, seems wholly unfair. A consequence of the ungrounded nature of morbid jealousy is the jealous person's attempt to provide a basis of reality to the feelings. As we saw in the novel, *Howling at the Moon*, this can often lead to an obsessional attention to the minutiae of the other's life.

How can morbid jealousy be explained? The traditional Freudian view is that such unfounded jealousy is a projection of individuals' doubts about maintaining their own fidelity and ability to resist temptation. As Freud (1920, p.241) so neatly summarises, "A man who doubts his own love may, or rather must, doubt every lesser thing". Beyond this generalisation perhaps each case will require separate explication.

Finally, Neu (1980, p.451) notes another form of disordered jealousy:

> Consider the swaggering bully who goes in a jealous rage if
> someone so much as looks at his woman ... whilst such a man
> may fear loss, the loss he fears is not of affections. What he
> values is his domination or appearance of domination ...

Such proprietorial jealousy is pathological in that, although it involves a fear of loss and, indeed, a fear of loss of others' regard, it is not the feelings of the woman that the man fears losing but the macho esteem that he receives by exhibiting such dominance.

SOME CONCLUDING REMARKS

In this chapter we have tried to do three things. First, to provide a broad review of the myriad interrelationships of the components of anger and to illustrate how some progress towards understanding these relationships can be achieved by a consideration of anger within a variety of theoretical models including a discussion of appraisal cycles within the SPAARS framework. Second, we have selected a handful of issues to discuss, which have particular relevance beyond the case of anger to other emotional states: the passionate nature of emotions; the effects of non-normative variables; and the idea of too little emotion versus too much. Third, we have attempted to illustrate the fine line between anger order and anger disorder. In addressing these issues we have chosen to sample widely from the theoretical and research literature on offer, both in psychology and philosophy. However, we hope we have conveyed, not just this breadth, but also something of the complexity of anger.

CHAPTER NINE

Disgust

I don't want to belong to any club that will accept me as a member. *(Groucho Marx)*

INTRODUCTION

The temptation when beginning a chapter on disgust is to launch into a series of bathroom-style jokes in an attempt to induce sufficient levels of disgust in the reader. Although we will refrain from such temptation, at least temporarily, we must note that sensitivity to disgust induction is a largely unexplored though potentially fruitful topic for psychopathology research. In fact, we must thank Paul Rozin and his colleagues for having produced one such trail-blazing measure, the Disgust Sensitivity Scale, from which the following items are taken (Rozin, Fallon, & Mandell, 1984): "You discover that a friend of yours changes underwear only once a week"; "You are walking barefoot on concrete, and you step on an earthworm"; and, "You are asked to wear Adolf Hitler's sweater", the latter item being apparently one of the most disgusting questionnaire items ever invented. It is clear both from these examples and from one's own experience that the range of objects, situations, and actions to which disgust is applied must make it the most generalisable of the basic emotions. When, as we shall argue, disgust comes to be applied to the self or some important aspect of the self, then the foundations for many emotional and other related disorders may be laid. However, the lack of research on the emotion of disgust means that the present chapter will be one of the most speculative in the book. Nevertheless, we will argue that perhaps more research has been carried out than realised, because the complex emotions of guilt and shame, together with some forms of embarrassment, will be derived from the basic emotion of disgust.

Darwin (1872/1965, p.256) noted that the term "disgust" referred, in its simplest sense to "something offensive to the taste"; thus, we may presume that the evolutionary origins of disgust are concerned with the rejection of noxious substances from within the organism together with attempts to prevent potentially noxious substances from entering the organism. At least one theorist (Tomkins, 1963) however, has argued that the so-called reactions of "distaste" and "dissmell" should be distinguished from disgust, but we will concur with the more widely held view that these gustatory reactions form the *origins* of the basic disgust emotion rather than provide alternatives to it. For example, in one of the early classic papers on disgust Angyal (1941, p.399) proposed that:

> The [disgust] reaction is mainly against ingestion, even in cases where there is no apparent danger of the disgusting materials reaching the mouth.

Angyal noted also that occasionally attempts are made to overcome disgust reactions, as in an apparent "epidemic" in 1938 amongst American university students of swallowing live goldfish. More recently one can detect a trend in Hollywood horror movies and Japanese game shows of inviting the audience to wallow primarily in disgust as much as in any other emotional reaction. Rozin, Lowery, and Ebert (1994) have also pointed to one of the great advantages of studying disgust:

> Disgust has a particular advantage for research in that it is easy to elicit in the laboratory in a realistic way without presenting serious ethical problems.

Could disgust be *the* basic emotion for the 21st century?

In relation to the question of the definition of disgust, an omnibus definition has been offered by Davey (1994a, p.135):

> A type of rejection response characterized by a specific facial expression, a desire to distance oneself from the object of disgust, a physiological manifestation of mild nausea, a fear of oral incorporation of the object of disgust, and a feeling of "revulsion".

Davey's definition provides a number of the key components that form part of the definition of basic emotions that we reviewed in Chapter 2, summarised as follows:

1. There is an object or event which may be external, as in the reaction to particular foodstuffs or to faeces, or internal, as in the reaction to particular thoughts or images.
2. The object or event is interpreted to be noxious in either a literal sense or in a symbolic sense.
3. The interpretation leads to an appraisal that the object or event should be eliminated or excluded from the organism, because it violates a goal of maintaining a state of non-contamination.
4. The appraisal leads to a propensity for action to distance oneself, either literally or symbolically, from the object or event.
5. Characteristic physiological reactions include a feeling of nausea together with a characteristic facial expression that is universally recognisable (Ekman et al., 1987).
6. There is a characteristic conscious feeling of "revulsion" together with an awareness of other reactions.
7. The reaction of disgust may be accompanied by characteristic behavioural reactions such as removing oneself from the object of disgust.

In relation to the behavioural component of disgust it is worth noting that the avoidance of disgust-related objects and situations can often be confused with fear-based avoidance; for example, Davey (e.g. 1994a) has argued that a number of specific animal phobias such as those that involve spiders and snakes may be based more on disgust reactions than on fear reactions, a point that we will return to later.

Apart from the evidence on specific physiology and universal recognition of the accompanying facial expression, other evidence that disgust is a basic emotion comes from studies of the development of disgust. The reaction of distaste, from which it is proposed the reaction of disgust derives, can be observed in the newborn infant within two hours of birth (Rosenstein & Oster, 1988). Indeed, the facial expression for distaste in the newborn is identical to that for disgust in adults. The first item to acquire disgust properties is typically faeces which occurs at about two years of age. The importance of this point was not lost on Freud (1910/1957) who argued that the primary role of disgust was to prevent childhood coprophagia. Of course, from the age of two onwards the range of potential items that may become associated with disgust depends on a complex interaction of personal, familial, and cultural factors. For example, at the cultural level there are numerous variations about whether it is permissible to eat the pet dog, McDonald's hamburgers, your grandmother, or the visiting missionary. Indeed, our reactions to other cultures can often be grounded in our disgust reactions to foods acceptable in that culture which are not acceptable in our own, in part because of a quasi-magical belief that "you are what you eat" (e.g. Rozin & Fallon, 1987). These cross-cultural studies of disgust can of course provide interesting insights into the range of culturally acceptable activities, though even we have to confess our own surprise at a study reported in Haidt, McCauley, and Rozin (1994), which compared the reactions of North Americans and Brazilians to items such as "eating one's dead pets", but which also included the item "eating a chicken one has just had sex with"!

Recent evidence on the perception of emotion in Huntington's disease has shown that such individuals show deficits in the perception of anger, fear, and disgust, with the most marked problem being with disgust (Sprengelmeyer et al., in press). These deficits were apparent with tests of both the facial expression and the vocal expression of disgust. The authors argue on the basis of these and other neuropsychological deficits that a number of basic emotions including disgust may have dedicated neural substrates.

Much of our discussion so far has focused on the food-related aspects of disgust. However, we believe that this aspect has been over-emphasised at the expense of potentially more interesting characteristics which relate to the application of disgust to the self and to other people. In their seminal review of the topic, Rozin and Fallon (1987) noted that disgust is one of the most powerful ways of transmitting cultural values not only in relation to acceptable and unacceptable foodstuffs, but also in relation to moral values. The Hindu caste system for example is in part based on the possibility of interpersonal contamination through contact with particular social groups. As Akhtar, Wig, Varma, Pershad, and Verma (1975) remarked in their study of the form and content of a group of Hindu obsessive-compulsive patients, the largest proportion of cases (46%) were directly connected with dirt and contamination issues. Akhtar et al. (1975, p.347) suggest that:

> The Hindu code of ethics provides a great variety of purification rituals ... The scriptures regard the human body as basically dirty and an object of disgust.

Rozin, Haidt, and McCauley (1993) state that in their studies of the perception of contamination from a range of human and animal products, one of the most powerful stimuli they have found is, as we have already noted, Adolf Hitler's sweater. These examples illustrate that the disgust reaction expands during development to cover non-food related characteristics of the self and of others. In fact, much of the remainder of the chapter will focus on an analysis of self-disgust and its role in complex emotions such as shame, guilt, and embarrassment, together with a discussion of the role of these disgust-derived emotions in fears and phobias, obsessive-compulsive disorders, and depression. Although the focus of the book is on emotional disorders, we will briefly examine the potential role of disgust in appetitive disorders such as bulimia, anorexia, and certain sexual disorders. First, however, we will review in a little more detail some of the theoretical analyses that have been offered for the role of disgust.

SOME THEORETICAL COMMENTS

Darwin's (1872/1965) views on the role of emotion were considered briefly in Chapter 3. We noted that although Darwin considered many aspects of emotion to be evolutionarily "vestigial", he drew attention to the importance of the facial expression of emotions and how these were apparent in different cultures. He noted too that cultural variation also occurred; in the case of disgust, he recorded numerous instances in his diaries of *The Voyage of The Beagle* (1839/1988) of cultural practices that evoked disgust in himself but meant something very different in the culture he was visiting. For example, he tells the following story of an incident that occurred during one of the many opportunities that he took during the years of the voyage to explore South America on horseback and during which he sometimes received the hospitality of the local inhabitants. On one such occasion he noted (1988, p.157) his feeling of disgust towards something intended as a compliment:

> One of the greatest inconveniences ... is the quantity you are obliged to eat. Time after time they pile heaps of meat on your plate; having [eaten] a great deal too much ... a charming Signorita will perhaps present you with a choice piece from her own plate with her own fork; this you must eat, let the consequence be what it may, for it is high compliment. Oh the difficulty of smiling sweet thanks, with the horrid and vast mouthful in view!

Darwin emphasised that disgust related to "something offensive to the taste" and he thereby started a tradition in the analysis of disgust that emphasised the aspect of it being a reaction to bad taste. As we noted above, Freud (1910/1957) proposed a specific variant on this proposal in which he emphasised the role of disgust in the child's overcoming coprophilic tendencies at about two or so years of age. Subsequent cross-cultural work has shown that faeces are almost invariably the first objects to which the disgust reaction develops (Rozin & Fallon, 1987), though there is some minor variation; for example, Eskimos will eat the gut contents of herbivorous mammals. There does, however, appear to be universal rejection of the gut contents of carnivores.

The traditions of Darwin and Freud were continued in Angyal's (1941, p.394) classic paper:

> The nucleus of the disgust reaction ... is the oral incorpora-
> tion of certain substances.

Angyal again emphasised disgust as a reaction to foodstuffs, with animal-derived meat products being considered one of the main categories of disgust-related objects; thus, even within the narrow range of acceptable meats within a culture, many of the processes for the presentation of meat are concerned with disguising the fact that meat is part of a dead animal.

As noted above, Tomkins (1963) argued that disgust as such should be distinguished from two sense-based reactions, that of distaste which is the reaction to bad tastes, and dissmell which is the reaction to bad smells. Although we have argued that all of these reactions are disgust based, Tomkins made an important early contribution in his emphasis on cognitive factors in disgust and in other emotional responses. His analysis of disgust had a considerable impact on the work of Rozin and colleagues (e.g. Rozin & Fallon, 1987), who have provided the fullest analyses of disgust to date.

One of the important contributions that Rozin and his colleagues have made is an emphasis not only on the food-based aspects of disgust, but also on its under-explored role in the transmission of cultural values. In relation to food, Rozin et al. (1993) note that all cultures have prohibitions about particular foods, whether it be particular animals or parts of animals. They have emphasised that ideas of contamination or disease often form important aspects of these prohibitions; later in the chapter we will examine the importance of contamination reactions in obsessional disorders. On the basis of their considerations, Rozin et al. (1993, p.584) offer a broader conception of disgust in their proposal:

> Anything that reminds us that we are animals elicits
> disgust.

This conception includes therefore the earlier proposals about food and about faeces, but, in addition, provides a more interesting point from which to examine the role of disgust in emotional disorders as well as in the more obvious examples of eating disorders. Rozin et al. note, for example, that the one body product that does not elicit disgust is tears, because tears are seen as uniquely human. (Although crying may be prohibited for men in Western culture, it is the act of crying rather than the tear itself that is treated with disgust.)

Rozin et al. (1993) identified four key components of disgust. First, there is a behavioural component in which there is an attempt to distance oneself from the object, event, or situation. Second, there is a characteristic physiology, which includes a combination of nausea, increased Galvanic Skin Response, bradycardia, and increased salivation. Third, there are expressive features that centre in particular around the face and the nose and which may reflect an attempt both to exclude obnoxious smells from entering the nose and to eliminate obnoxious material from the mouth. Fourth, there are characteristic qualia which relate to the other components and which centre around feelings of revulsion. The components identified by Rozin and colleagues map well onto the response components of the model that we presented in Chapter 5, the main difference being the absence of the interpretive-appraisal processes that we include in order to explain the initial occurrence of emotions such as disgust. Nevertheless, despite this difference, Rozin and his colleagues have contributed substantially to our understanding of disgust in relation to both food and animal products and in relation to cultural norms and values. As Rozin et al. (1993, p.590) themselves state:

> Our analysis suggests a cultural evolution of disgust that brings it to the heart of what it means to be human.

In the cognitive theory presented by Oatley and Johnson-Laird (1987) disgust was also given a central role as one of their five basic emotions (see Chapter 3). The core of the theory is that emotions occur primarily at junctures in goals and plans; the important juncture for disgust being a "gustatory goal violated" which leads the individual to reject the substance or withdraw. In addition, the infant emotion is seen to develop into adult forms as seen in loathing and distaste. Although Oatley and Johnson-Laird (1987) say little further about disgust, Johnson-Laird and Oatley (1989) in their semantic analysis of emotion terms, show how a number of complex emotions such as guilt, shame, contempt, and loathing are derived from the basic emotion of disgust. In his more recent book, Oatley (1992) further emphasises the interpersonal functions of disgust and disgust-based emotions. Oatley states that the complex emotions of hatred, loathing, and contempt have the interpersonal function of withdrawing from other people and of disengaging from joint or mutual plans. However, we must observe that we do not share Oatley and Johnson-Laird's view that the complex emotions of hatred and contempt are solely disgust-based emotions, and, indeed, in our own personal semantics we would derive hatred primarily from anger (see Chapter 8). Because, however, Oatley and Johnson-Laird theorised that complex emotions could be derived from only one basic emotion, it is possible that they have been overly restricted by this aspect of their theory; thus, emotions such as contempt and loathing may be best derived from a combination of disgust and anger and instead of having to argue that embarrassment has two or more different forms derived from different basic emotions, it would seem more parsimonious to derive embarrassment from a combination of primarily fear and disgust (especially as shame). Keith Oatley himself (1992, p.60) has recently commented that "the basis for Oatley and Johnson-Laird's treatment of disgust and contempt is less satisfactory than for happiness, sadness, anger, and fear" so perhaps we should not rub their noses in it any further!

Additional theoretical comments

One of the things that we emphasised in our analysis of basic emotions presented in Chapter 5 was the importance of two different routes to emotion (see Fig. 9.1). In relation to disgust, the direct access route will be most familiar in the automatic reactions to food and smell, which presumably have an innate basis such as shown in the neonate's disgust reaction to bitter tastes. However, a whole range of foods, objects, and smells soon come to elicit associatively based disgust reactions through

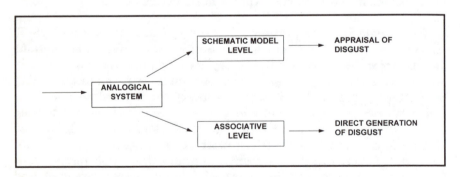

FIG. 9.1. Two routes to disgust within the SPAARS approach.

the direct access route. To give a personal example, one of us (MP) was determined to eat an oyster for the first time ever. However, try as hard as I might, I was completely unable to overcome the automatic retching reaction that the combination of taste and texture evoked. Nor have I tried to swallow one since!

The development of taste aversions through associative learning has of course long provided a challenge to the traditional laws of learning enumerated by Pavlov and Skinner (e.g. Dickinson, 1987). Whereas Pavlovian and Skinnerian conditioning are based on the temporal contiguity of stimulus and response, so-called long-delay conditioning does not require such contiguity but may span several hours (e.g. Revusky & Garcia, 1970). It seems likely, however, that we are witnessing different patterns of learning in relation to the different basic emotions implicated; that is, work on Pavlovian and Skinnerian conditioning primarily focused on the basic emotions of happiness and fear (in the form of reward and punishment), whereas taste aversions are based on disgust. More specifically, Pavlov's dogs and Skinner's pigeons were typically either in a state of hunger and showed happiness at the delivery of dinner, or were in a constant state of anxiety in anticipation of the next aversive experience. In contrast, Revusky's rats were nauseous because of something the experimenter had cooked up several hours before. We might speculate therefore that well-designed studies that examine learning in the context of different basic emotions may find significantly different learning patterns both for the temporal relationships between the elements and for the content of the elements themselves; thus, where cognitive biases have been studied in relation to fear and sadness important differences appear (see Chapters 6 and 7).

The automatic reactions shown in Fig. 9.1, however, are not limited to foodstuffs, but may happen at the sight of a tramp, to things that the cat brought in, and at the memory of what one did at that drunken New Year's Eve party. It is in fact this last category, the disgust-based reactions to the self, that provides a potential starting point for much of the pathology in the emotional disorders. That is, the innate taste-based disgust reaction may be turned on the developing self especially, as we will show, when factors such as culture, religion, and the views of significant others combine. The chronic activation of this self-disgust may provide one of the bases of mood disorders such as that found in depression in which the automatic processing of material is biased in a negative way (e.g. Haaga et al., 1991; see Chapter 7).

The second route shown in Fig. 9.1 is the interpretive-appraisal route to disgust and disgust-based complex emotions such as guilt, shame, and embarrassment (see next section) and is perhaps most obvious when one subsequently reinterprets or reappraises one's own or another's actions. Again to give an example, having moved house some time before, I (MP) was unable to find a particular object and became convinced that one of the removal men had taken it. Whenever I thought about this object I became angry with the removal men and even mentioned the presumed theft to a number of others. Imagine my shame, however, when the object turned up and it had been my fault all along for not having unpacked properly! In this case, my appraisal that I had been wronged in some way and consequent feelings of anger turned to feelings of shame when I realised that I had falsely accused the removals firm. This example emphasises how reappraisal of an event can take place over considerable time periods. In more extreme cases, such reappraisals may form one of the cornerstones of therapy (see Chapter 11) in which the existence of apparently contradictory emotions or the clear inhibition of emotion may signal that the interpretive-appraisal route is being used for one emotion but a direct access route exists for another. For example, the physically abusive parent may attempt to inhibit the abused child's anger by statements such as "I'm doing this because I love you" or "I'm doing this for your own benefit": the child's "joy" at such loving attention may be tempered by anger because of the pain inflicted by physical abuse. However, the repeated experience of contradictory parental messages has long been considered by theorists such as Bateson, Jackson, Haley, and Weakland (1956), Bowlby (1973), and others to be an important developmental influence on psychopathology. One of the roles of therapy may therefore include the re-examination of assumptions such as necessarily being loved by one's parents.

> John was the adopted son of a highly successful barrister. However, nothing he ever did was good enough for either of his parents. He had, for example, wanted to be a teacher, but his father's dismissal of this profession with "Those that can't do, teach" forever echoed in his ears. When John came into therapy he loathed himself and had been unable to work for over a year. Needless to say, he worshipped his father.

For the child, completely dependent on his or her parents, it may be preferable to believe in being loved by one's parents at the price of hating oneself. However, the adult who is no longer dependent on his or her parents may need to reinterpret such relationships with all the consequent emotions that this process entails.

COMPLEX EMOTIONS DERIVED FROM DISGUST

The complex emotions of guilt, shame and embarrassment are part of the group known as self-conscious emotions (e.g. Lewis, 1993) in that they require an internal evaluation of the self against a set of rules, standards, or goals and in which the self or some aspect of the self is seen to have failed (see Fig. 9.2). There is now agreement that guilt refers in particular to specific aspects or acts which fall short of some standard, whereas in shame it is the self rather than some specific act or aspect that is at fault (e.g. Johnson-Laird & Oatley, 1989). The more global nature of shame typically leads the individual to desire to avoid the painful person or situation whereas the more specific nature of guilt means that it is more associated with attempts at reparation (e.g. Niedenthal, Tangney, & Gavanski, 1994). There is interesting evidence that girls may be more prone to shame but boys more prone to guilt even in the face of the same problem. In one particularly devious set of psychology experiments (Barrett et al., 1993), when a toy apparently collapses because of the child's action, girls were found to be more likely to show shame reactions in which they avoided the owner of the toy, whereas boys were more likely to show guilt and try to make reparation. This sex difference is also present in adulthood in that women on average score higher on disgust sensitivity scales than do men (Rozin et al., 1993). Given that shame-proneness is now thought to be more associated with psychopathology than is guilt-proneness (e.g. Niedenthal et al., 1994), this sex difference may relate to the higher

	SUCCESS	FAILURE
GLOBAL	HUBRIS	SHAME
SPECIFIC	PRIDE	GUILT/ REGRET

FIG. 9.2. The relationship of self-conscious emotions to success–failure and global–specific characteristics (based on Lewis, 1993).

rates observed for particular emotional disorders in women, as we will argue subsequently (see also Chapter 7).

The recent focus on the role of shame in psychopathology breaks with the traditional psychoanalytic focus on guilt. This focus stemmed largely from Freud's (1917/1984) analysis of Melancholia in which he highlighted the operation of a "critical agency" (later called the superego) whose standards the individual fails to meet. We noted in Chapter 7 that most diagnostic systems for depression such as the American DSM system and the World Health Organization's ICD system identify guilt as a core symptom of depression. However, we share the views of recent theoreticians (e.g. Tangney, 1992) who argue instead that shame is the key emotion in depression in the sense that we define shame as disgust directed towards the self in which we judge ourselves to have fallen short of the standards set by a real or imaginary significant other. The point that we wish to emphasise, however, is that, although both shame and guilt are derived from the basic emotion of disgust, in shame it is the self rather than an act carried out by the self that becomes the object of that disgust.

The recent increase in interest in the self-conscious emotions (e.g. see the edited book by Tangney & Fischer, 1995) has provided new impetus to the study of shame and guilt and the question of their role in development, normal functioning, and psychopathology. Whereas an analysis of the function of disgust begins within the individual, an analysis of the function of shame and guilt is best begun with a consideration of their interpersonal characteristics. Recent analyses of shame emphasise its role in social dominance hierarchies in which submission and defeat versus dominance and triumph may be frequent consequences (e.g. Barrett, 1995; Gilbert, 1992). In an account of shame and guilt that, allowing for differences in terminology and minor points of emphasis, runs similar to the present SPAARS approach, Barrett (1995) has proposed seven principles, as outlined in the following points.

1. Shame and guilt are primarily social emotions that develop from early social interactions, and that primarily occur in the context of real or imagined social interactions.

2. Shame and guilt have important functions; for example, shame typically functions to distance the individual from others, whereas guilt leads the individual to make reparation to others.

3. Particular "appreciations" (i.e. "appraisals" in more common usage) are associated with shame and guilt. Barrett proposes that the key appraisal in shame is of both self and other seeing the self as bad, whereas guilt involves a failure to meet one's standards which may have led to the other being harmed by this failure.

4. Shame and guilt are associated with particular action tendencies (or what we have called propensities for action); as stated above, shame tends to lead to distancing whereas guilt tends towards reparation.

5. Shame and guilt aid in the development of the self. The experience of shame and guilt during development provides models for the child of acceptable and unacceptable behaviour and, in addition, provides the child with important feedback about how the self is viewed by significant others, which, in turn, guides the development of the self.

6. Shame and guilt do not require particular cognitive stages of development for their occurrence, but are observable early on in development. Although this proposal appears to contradict the notion that shame and guilt are therefore "self-conscious", Barrett's view is consistent with our own in the sense that early applications of disgust towards the self can be observed in the child, which, although not fully developed in the form of being self-conscious, provide the foundations on which the self-conscious forms of shame and guilt (in e.g. Lewis's, 1993, sense considered earlier) may subsequently develop.

7. Shame and guilt therefore have crucial socialisation roles because the child wants to follow social standards and cares about the opinions of others.

An additional aspect of Barrett's theory that takes it even closer to the SPAARS approach, is her endorsement of the fact that emotion is not only generated by "appreciations" (appraisals), but may also occur in their absence, that is, by means of what we have termed the direct route (Barrett, 1995, p.36):

> [Appraisals] are typically involved in an emotion process, but, like any other aspect of the emotion process, [they] are not viewed as necessary for an emotion to unfold. Brain stimulation, emotion communication from a conspecific, or other such stimuli may initiate an emotion process. The emotion process elicited without an [appraisal] often differs phenomenologically from that elicited by an [appraisal], but it is still recognisable as a member of the same emotion "family".

In the SPAARS approach we have grouped these non-appraisal possibilities together in our direct access route, whereas Barrett does not clarify whether the different non-appraisal examples that she cites are separate routes to emotion or whether they feed into a common mechanism. Other emphases within the SPAARS approach that are not considered by Barrett include the proposal that the basic emotions and their derivatives may become modularly organised; that the emotion state can be maintained via internal feedback between the associative, propositional, and schematic model levels of representation; that the emotions may become coupled with each other and thereby lead to more chronic domination of working memory. Perhaps the most important difference of all is that in the SPAARS approach the complex emotions of shame and guilt are derived from the basic emotion of disgust whereas there is no such conceptual model within Barrett's approach.

In comparison to shame and guilt, embarrassment may be even more complex in that it can be derived from either fear or disgust (Johnson-Laird & Oatley, 1989) or perhaps, as we suggested earlier, some combination of the two. Embarrassment though is normally less intense than the experience of shame and, indeed, it can to some degree be positive when it occurs for example in the context of being praised by someone else in public; thus, blushing can accompany either the positive or the negative versions of embarrassment.

Contempt is another disgust-related emotion though the object of contempt is typically another person rather than the self; conceptually it seems to represent a combination of both disgust and anger. In fact, in a scaling analysis of ratings of facial emotion, Rozin et al. (1994) reported that contempt was closer to anger than to disgust in multidimensional space. Contempt therefore is discussed in more detail in Chapter 8 on anger.

Overall, therefore, we propose that there are a number of complex emotions that are derived from the basic emotion of disgust. These emotions include guilt, shame, embarrassment, and contempt; they primarily involve disgust being focused in varying degrees on the self or on aspects of the self and, as a consequence, it can be argued that they form the basis of a number of emotional and appetitive disorders that will be considered next.

DISORDERS OF DISGUST

Fears and phobias

It has long been the tradition to derive the anxiety disorders from the basic emotion of fear (see Chapter 6) and, of course, we do not dispute that many fears and phobias have their origins in fear-based responses. However, there are a number of early onset specific phobias that do not conform to the original Mowrer (e.g. 1939) two-factor theory of phobias (see Chapter 6). In an attempt to deal with some of these problems, more recent theorists such as Rachman (e.g. 1990) have proposed that in addition to the classical or traumatic conditioning route to the acquisition of phobia, there are two further routes that consist of observational learning and of information transmission. However, these additional routes also fail, we believe, to explain the onset and characteristics of a number of specific phobias. Instead, as we hope to show, many of these phobias appear to be disgust-based rather than fear-based.

As discussed in Chapter 6, the majority of simple phobias such as animal, blood, and dental phobias begin in childhood, with the animal phobias typically arising earliest. Of course, it is clear that emotional problems are very common in childhood, though the majority tend to be transient and show only modest continuity across time (Rutter, 1984). When emotional problems do continue into adulthood, they tend to be homotypic, that is, they are consistent in their presentation; thus, many individuals presenting in adulthood with specific phobias report that the problems started in childhood. The majority of such individuals tend to be women even though the ratios for fears in childhood are similar for boys and girls (Power, 1993).

> Jane had been frightened of dogs from about the age of five or six. She could not recall any specific incident that had occurred to start the phobia, only that she had always disliked dogs, but had managed to cope with her phobia for nearly 30 years. She had worked as a nurse for many years on an inpatient psychiatric ward so had easily avoided dogs both at home and at work. The problem, however, that finally brought her to seek help was the proposed closure of the psychiatric ward. Her new post was going to be community based, part of which would involve home visits and, therefore, the risk of coming across dogs in situations from which she could not escape. Her only choice, she thought, was that she would have to give up work altogether. As well as finding large dogs frightening, Jane reported that all dogs were disgusting, because of the things she had witnessed them doing in public such as soiling the pavements and sniffing and mounting each other. Her reactions therefore seemed to contain both fear-based and disgust-based elements.

Data reported by Hekmat (1987) based on the retrospective reports of people with phobias showed that only 22.5% of a group of animal phobics reported aversive encounters with the animal in question. A further 36% reported that they had been "teased" with the appropriate animal, for example, by an older sibling; we would speculate that such teasing would more than likely involve a disgust reaction on the part of the child which could encourage the propagator of the teasing even more, though this possibility remains to be tested. Hekmat also reported that 57% of his animal phobics attributed onset either to information given to them about the animal in question or to watching someone else reacting negatively in the presence of the animal; the child's mother was the most common source of such information or observation. Again, we suggest that this information is just as likely to be about disgust-related aspects of the particular animal, for example, because of the animal's potential to cause disease or contamination (e.g. dogs, cats, rats, mice, spiders, wasps, flies) or because of its similarity to mucus and faeces (e.g. worms, snakes), a possibility that could be tested in future retrospective studies.

The so-called blood phobia has always provided a puzzle because of its clear differences to other phobias. For example, Ost, Sterner, and Lindahl (1984) reported that blood phobics show bradycardia and lowered blood pressure in contrast to other phobics who tend to show an increase in heart rate and in blood pressure. The pattern of lowered heart rate has, notably, also been found to be characteristic of the basic emotion of disgust, in contrast to fear which is associated with an increase in heart rate (Ekman, Levenson, & Friesen, 1983). It is possible to speculate therefore that blood phobia may be primarily a disgust-based rather than a fear-based disorder, but, moreover, future studies of the physiology of the specific phobias should distinguish for example between predator- and contamination-based animal phobias, rather include all of these in a single animal phobia category.

Social phobia is typically of later onset than the animal, blood, and dental phobias; thus, Ost (1987) reported a mean age of onset of 16.3 years. Although one or two studies have reported a slightly higher rate for women (e.g. Marks, 1969), the different rates for men and women are probably not significant (e.g. Bourdon et al., 1988). Because social phobia tends to be less debilitating than conditions such as agoraphobia, it is less commonly seen in the clinic (Mannuzza, Fyer, Liebowitz, & Klein, 1990). The *DSM-IV* criteria for social phobia are presented in Table 9.1 (American Psychiatric Association, 1994) and show a clear emphasis on fear. We suggest however that the social phobic's reactions may be as much disgust-based as they are fear-based, in that the central theme in social phobia is an imagined negative evaluation or rejection of the self by other people (e.g. Butler, 1989). As Beck and Emery (1985, p.156) state:

> The experience of shame is important in discussions of social anxiety because the socially anxious person is fearful of being shamed in many situations.

TABLE 9.1
***DSM-IV* criteria for social phobia**

Diagnostic criteria

(a) A marked persistent fear of one or more social or performance situations in which the person is exposed to unfamiliar people or to possible scrutiny by others. The individual fears that he or she will act in a way (or show anxiety symptoms) that will be humiliating or embarrassing. Note: In children, there must be evidence of the capacity for age-appropriate social relationships with familiar people and the anxiety must occur in peer settings, not just in interactions with adults.

(b) Exposure to the feared social situation almost invariably provokes anxiety, which may take the form of a situationally bound or situationally predisposed panic attack. Note: In children the anxiety may be expressed by crying, tantrums, freezing, or shrinking from social situations with unfamiliar people.

(c) The person recognises that the fear is excessive or unreasonable. Note: In children this feature may be absent.

(d) The feared social or performance situations are avoided or else are endured with intense anxiety or distress.

(e) The avoidance, anxious anticipation, or distress in the feared social or performance situation(s) interferes significantly with the person's normal routine, occupational (academic) functioning, or social activities or relationships, or there is marked distress about having the phobia.

(f) In individuals under the age of 18 years, the duration is at least six months.

(g) The fear or avoidance is not due to the direct physiological effects of a substance (a drug abuse, a medication) or a general medical condition and is not better accounted for by another mental disorder (e.g. Panic Disorder With or Without Agoraphobia, Separation Anxiety Disorder, Body Dysmorphic Disorder, a Pervasive Developmental Disorder, or Schizoid Personality Disorder).

(h) If a general medical condition or another mental disorder is present, the fear in Criterion (a) is unrelated to it, e.g. the fear is not of stuttering, trembling in Parkinson's disease, or exhibiting abnormal eating behaviour in Anorexia Nervosa or Bulimia Nervosa.

Specify if: Generalised: if the fears include most social situations.

Beck and Emery (p.157) further state:

> In his mind, the antidote for shame is to vanish from the shameful situation. A person will say, for example, "I should like to fade away," or, "I felt like merging into the woodwork." In contrast, anxiety is generally accompanied by the inclination to flee or by passive immobility.

It is apparent from these quotes that Beck and Emery (1985) identify the importance of a disgust/shame-based response in socially anxious individuals in which the label "anxiety" may be misleading. Of course, prior to entering a social situation the social phobic may feel an anticipatory anxiety, but the key emotion in the situation itself may be shame. The more severe and disabling the social phobia therefore the more likely it would seem that the basic emotions of disgust and fear become coupled, in the sense outlined in Chapter 5, and thereby continually reactivate each other. We await with interest therefore studies of disgust and disgust sensitivity in social phobics.

One further point we would make about studies of cognitive biases in anxiety (discussed in detail in Chapter 6) relates to the distinction made between materials based on physical threat versus those based on social threat (e.g. MacLeod, Mathews, & Tata, 1986). On closer examination, the social threat words in these studies seem to fall into two categories, the first being a group of social anxiety terms (e.g. Ignored, Insecure, Indecisive) and the second being a group of shame terms (e.g. Humiliated, Ashamed, Despised). These studies unwittingly have made the distinction between true social anxiety and shame, but have failed to analyse these two groups of materials separately. We would recommend therefore that future studies of cognitive biases should analyse the fear-based and the disgust-based materials separately, because there may be important individual differences in the extent to which so-called anxiety disorders may be disgust-based rather than fear-based.

To return to the issue of simple phobias and disgust, Graham Davey and his colleagues (e.g. Davey, Forster, & Mayhew, 1993) have carried out a number of studies that demonstrate the importance of disgust reactions rather than fear reactions for these disorders. Davey has argued that many of the animal phobias are not simply fear-based reactions to predatory animals, but are disgust-based reactions to, for example, associations with disease, contamination, mucus, and faeces. Davey (1994b) reported from a fear survey that the number of fears was positively correlated with disgust sensitivity levels and that females had higher disgust sensitivity levels and higher rates of fears than did males. In an experimental manipulation, Webb and Davey (1992) found that if subjects were primed with either a violent film or with a disgust-based film, the violent film was found to increase subsequent fear ratings for predatory animals but not for "revulsion" animals, whereas the disgust film increased the ratings for non-predatory revulsion animals, but not for predatory animals. In a further correlational study, Ware, Jain, Burgess, and Davey (1994) found significant correlations between disgust sensitivity, "fear" ratings towards revulsion animals, and the Washing sub-scale of the Maudsley Obsessive-Compulsive Inventory (MOCI; Hodgson & Rachman, 1977). Taken together, these studies provide some empirical support for the proposal that disgust sensitivity provides a factor of crucial importance in the development of many simple animal phobias and that the three pathways to fear model (e.g. Rachman, 1976) needs to be revised to take account of one or more additional disgust pathways that, so far, have received little attention. We also suggest that there may be important treatment differences for disgust-based as opposed to fear-based phobias, though we will discuss the treatment implications of the current approach in more detail in the final chapter (Chapter 11).

Obsessive-compulsive disorders

The obsessive-compulsive disorders (OCDs) have long been derived from anxiety in the main classification systems. This tradition follows in part the early analysis of OCD and other disorders by Freud who proposed, amongst many other things, that consciously experienced anxiety is a consequence of the transformation of repressed libido (e.g. Breuer & Freud, 1895/1974). Thus, the most recent American (*DSM-IV*) and World Health Organization (*ICD-10*) classification systems both include obsessive compulsive disorders as sub-types of anxiety disorders. For example, *DSM-IV* (American Psychiatric Association, 1994) criteria for obsessions include the following:

1. Recurrent and persistent thoughts, impulses, or images that are experienced, at some time during the disturbance, as intrusive and inappropriate and that cause marked anxiety or distress.
2. The thoughts, impulses, or images are not simply excessive worries about real-life problems.
3. The person attempts to ignore or suppress such thoughts, impulses, or images, or to neutralize them with some other thought or action.
4. The person recognises that the obsessional thoughts, impulses, or images are a product of his or her own mind.

Both the general approach to classification of obsessions and compulsions and their specific defining criteria emphasise therefore an anxiety-based origin for such problems.

In contrast to the traditional and current classification systems, and in parallel to our analysis of specific phobias, we propose that certain types of OCD may be primarily derived from the basic emotion of disgust rather than the basic emotion of fear or anxiety. Although much less is known about OCD than about phobic disorders, epidemiological studies have suggested that the incidence in the community is higher than would be expected on the basis of attendance at psychiatric services; thus, Myers et al. (1984) reported that mild obsessional problems showed a prevalence of between one and two per 100, though less than 1% of the psychiatric outpatient population present with an obsessive compulsive disorder. Even on epidemiological grounds however there appears to be a case to be made for two different groups of obsessional disorders. Minichiello, Baer, Jenike, and Holland (1990) found that the onset of obsessional checking disorders tended to occur at about 18–19 years and that this group contains relatively more males than the second group of cleaning obsessionals who have a later age of onset at about 27 years and who tend to be female. Studies of the content of obsessional disorders also suggest that there may be at least two groups. A study by Akhtar et al. (1975) showed that 46% of their sample reported dirt/contamination obsessions. A more recent study by van Oppen, Hoekstra, and Emmelkamp (1995) of 206 obsessional patients showed that a factor analytic derived measure of "Washing" correlated significantly with measures of depression and with interpersonal sensitivity, but did not correlate significantly with measures of anxiety or hostility. This study provides good evidence therefore that there is a sub-group of obsessional patients whose problems are not related to anxiety, but which may be disgust-based.

The general two-factor theory of learning originally applied to anxiety disorders (Mowrer, 1939; see Chapter 6) was applied to obsessive-compulsive disorders by Dollard and Miller (1950). In this model, escape or avoidance from an anxiety-provoking conditioned stimulus is maintained through anxiety-reduction. Rachman and Hodgson (1980) and other researchers have noted however that the negative emotional state in OCD is best characterised by the term "discomfort" rather than just anxiety, in that a range of unpleasant emotions may be experienced in the presence of the crucial stimulus. The main treatment method for dealing with OCD has been exposure to the avoided stimulus together with response prevention. Whereas exposure on its own may be sufficient to overcome the passive avoidance present in specific phobias, the characteristic active avoidance associated with OCD in which the individual typically experiences an urge to carry out a compulsive action, is normally prevented during behavioural treatment of the disorder. To date, the outcome literature has shown that exposure plus response prevention is the most effective form of treatment for OCD (e.g. Emmelkamp, 1994). However, it is apparent that the treatment may be more successful for those with cleaning disorders than for those with checking disorders. In an insightful analysis of this problem, Watts (1995) has suggested that in compulsive washers the contamination-anxiety may be effectively reduced by compulsive washing whereas in compulsive checking there is less apparent anxiety reduction. In terms of treatment, therefore, Watts suggests that instead of preventing checking altogether, the checker should be allowed a single high quality check that is carried out consciously, rather than being allowed to enter a sequence of repetitive checks that may be carried out automatically. In terms of our current analyses however we should emphasise that "contamination-anxiety" or "discomfort" may reflect a combination of disgust and anxiety. If true, then higher levels of depression should be reported for cleaning rather than checking disorders, if our proposal that disgust is common to some forms of OCD and depression has any validity. The treatment results may also indicate that more active avoidance strategies may be a feature of disgust-based obsessions and phobias, because of attempts to rid the body of presumed contamination, in contrast to the more passive avoidance in anxiety-based phobias in which avoidance of the object or situation (e.g. in fear of flying) is sufficient.

The probable type of onset for the two groups also tends to be different, though again the evidence is sparse. Rachman and Hodgson (1980) reported that the later onset of cleaning disorders in women tends to be sudden and is sometimes associated with pregnancy and the transition to motherhood. However, the earlier onset of checking disorders in men tends to be more gradual and to be associated with increases in responsibility in both work-related and social settings. Ware et al. (1994), as we have noted earlier, have also found significant correlations between levels of disgust sensitivity, reported fears towards disgust-relevant animals, and the washing sub-scale of the Maudsley Obsessive Compulsive Inventory (MOCI). We might hypothesise therefore that cleaning disorders are more likely to arise because of disease/contamination concerns which are of particular biological and evolutionary importance around pregnancy and childbirth. In contrast, checking disorders are more likely to reflect the anxiety-based appraisal that the individual's coping resources will be insufficient to meet increasing demands. We must emphasise, however, that it would be an error to equate all cleaning disorders with disgust and all checking disorders with fear, because the symptoms merely reflect a final common pathway which could be reached by a variety of routes. Hence, a number of exceptions to these rules were noted by Rachman and Hodgson (1980), one of our own favourites being the patient who reported the gradual onset of a cleaning compulsion in relation to any word or photograph or object associated with the City of Birmingham.

In relation to current and recent theoretical models of OCD, there is little as yet that might identify two different groups of individuals. Reed's (1985) influential cognitive model focused on so-called "underinclusion" in that obsessionals were considered to pay too much attention to detail in a variety of cognitive tasks. Although some empirical support has been found for Reed's underinclusion hypothesis, there are a number of methodological and conceptual problems with the supporting studies (see Tallis, 1995a,b). In addition, the theory is cognitive in a narrow sense, because it fails to account for the emotional and motivational features of OCD; this problem can be likened to the problems encountered by Seligman's original Learned Helplessness theory (1975) which, though appealing in its simplicity, unfortunately failed to account for the emotional concomitants of depression (see Chapter 4).

A potentially more promising line of theorising in work on OCD has been offered by Salkovskis (e.g. 1985) and by Rachman (e.g. 1993) in their focus on responsibility and guilt in obsessional disorders. For example, Rachman (1993) has summarised four key elements that relate to the attachment of excessive significance to intrusive thoughts, images, and impulses:

1. A high level of responsibility is taken for intrusions
2. Intrusions are given heightened significance
3. Thoughts and actions are more likely to be fused ("the thought is the deed")
4. There may be continuous attempts to "neutralise" the intrusions, for example, through the use of mental or behavioural compulsions.

Some preliminary evidence in favour of the increased responsibility hypothesis has now been reported. For example, Rheaume, Ladouceur, Freeston, and Letarte (1995) found increased ratings for both danger and responsibility in students rating scenarios relevant to OCD. Rachman (1993) has also reported that if OCD sufferers become inpatients, their symptom levels at first reduce dramatically. He suggested that this initial reduction may be due to a temporary sharing of the burden of responsibility with the ward staff. Of particular importance to us, however, is the fact that Rachman and Salkovskis have highlighted the role of responsibility and guilt; thus, we have derived the complex emotion of guilt from the basic emotion of disgust and would therefore concur with these theorists on the role of a disgust-derived emotion in OCD. However, whereas Rachman and Salkovskis have pointed to the role of *guilt*, in parallel to our previous analysis of depression (see Chapter 7), we would argue instead that *shame* as a more extreme disgust-based reaction to the self may be more appropriate. Although it can be difficult to distinguish shame and guilt with self-report measures, some evidence in favour of a shame-based rather than guilt-based analysis for obsessive-compulsive disorders has been summarised by Harder (1995). Harder found that self-report measures of shame and obsessive-compulsive problems remain significantly correlated when the effects of guilt are partialled out, but the significant correlations with guilt are no longer significant when the effects of shame are partialled out. It is possible, however, that Rachman and Salkovskis have simply used the term "guilt" in a looser sense than is defined in the emotion literature. Nevertheless, their approach suggests the possibility that disgust may play a role not only in the more obvious cleaning and washing disorders that we have focused on, but also in checking disorders because of a disgust-based reaction towards particular intrusions.

Turning briefly to studies of cognitive processes and cognitive biases in OCD, the same issues arise that we encountered earlier in our discussion of phobias; namely, that although the materials used in these studies are treated as if they were *anxiety-related*, in fact, they are often disgust-related. For example, studies by Foa and McNally (1986), Foa, Ilai, McCarthy, Shoyer, and Murdock (1993), and Lavy, van Oppen, and van den Hout (1994) provide data on dichotic listening and Stroop tasks (see Chapter 6) carried out with OCD patients. However, in each of the studies the researchers used a mix of anxiety-relevant and disgust-relevant materials, yet they consider their results only in relation to fear. To consider one of the studies in more detail, Foa et al. (1993) carried out a primed Stroop task in which the prime words "danger", ·"disturb", and "fruit" were used to prime a series of contamination, threat, and neutral words. The results reported from three groups of "washers", "nonwasher OCD" and "control" subjects showed clear support for our proposals; thus, washers showed significant Stroop interference with contamination words, but not threat words, whereas nonwasher OCD subjects showed Stroop interference from threat words but not from contamination words. The researchers were puzzled, however, by the fact that the prime word "danger" failed to have a priming effect on contamination words for the washer OCD group. Our proposals suggest that this failure occurred because "danger" is primarily fear-related rather than disgust-related; thus, if there is an effect to be found in the Foa et al. primed Stroop task, it should occur with a disgust-derived prime such as "dirt" or "contamination" rather than with a fear-derived prime. A recent study by Tata, Leibowitz, Prunty, Cameron, and Pickering (1996) reported results from the dot-probe task (see Chapters 4 and 6 for details of this task) in a group of OCD patients with contamination concerns and groups of High and Low Trait Anxiety controls. The results showed that the OCD group were vigilant for the contamination-related words, but not for the social threat words, thereby offering further support for the proposal that at least some types of OCD may be primarily disgust-based rather than anxiety-based disorders.

To conclude, there is preliminary evidence from a number of sources that some obsessive-compulsive disorders may be primarily disgust-based rather than anxiety-based, contrary to current diagnostic and classificatory systems. Although the distinction between so-called washing and checking obsessionals may, at least superficially, provide a possible boundary between these two varieties, in practice, we suspect that the distinction will not map on to the form or content of the disorders so neatly. The recent focus on responsibility and guilt in relation to OCD seems to present a move in the right direction, though we suggest that shame rather than guilt should be the disgust-based emotion given more prominence. Even in cases that are primarily anxiety-based however, there still appears to be a secondary role for disgust in relation to the individual's attempts to eliminate a thought, image, or impulse that is experienced as ego-alien. In the process of feeling distressed about such thoughts, images, or impulses, the individual attempts to rid the self of this unacceptable material in a manner analogous to the gut eliminating its own unacceptable contents. We suggest too that some of the empirical and experimental studies of OCD will be more readily interpretable and provide more revealing data once the distinction between disgust and anxiety is explicitly acknowledged in the design of future studies.

Depression, parasuicide, and suicide

The putative relationship between depression and disgust has been dealt with in detail in Chapter 7. We argued for an analysis of depression in which the basic emotions of sadness and disgust may become coupled together and thereby maintain the individual in a painful emotional state which may prove difficult to alter or regulate. Instead of covering the same ground again, therefore, we will focus on the related problems of suicide and parasuicide. We will, however, make a brief comment on the increasing recognition of the role that shame may play in depression. For example, Gilbert (1992) has cogently argued that one of the important aspects for the development of the self is that children should come to see themselves as people with value and status in relationships. If, however, children experience parental devaluing, such as being put down and being shamed, this may lead to the internalisation of a sense of self which is of low status and low value to others. The recent work by Andrews (1995) on the links between childhood abuse, bodily shame, and adult depression provided evidence for the important role of shame in depression (see Chapter 7 for a further account of this study). Gilbert, Allan, and Goss (in press) have also recently reported preliminary evidence from a group of students that early experience of being shamed by parents and of being a non-favourite child is associated with later interpersonal problems and symptomatology. The net effect of these recent studies is to strengthen our view that there is considerable mileage to be had with the proposal that some forms of depression may result from the coupling of sadness and disgust.

To turn to the question of suicide and parasuicide, the first point to make is that not all suicide and parasuicide individuals are depressed, just as not all depressed individuals are suicidal; thus, we do not wish to suggest that *all* suicide is based on disgust towards the self, only that it is a major component that has failed to be investigated. The figures however suggest that 35–79% of parasuicide cases are depressed (Weissman, 1974), and, even with clinical assessment rather than self-report, the figures are between 30 and 66% (Ennis, Barnes, Kennedy, & Trachtenberg, 1989). Population estimates of the prevalence of suicide and parasuicide are beset with difficulties not least because until recently suicide was illegal in the UK and because of religious sanctions; thus, official suicide figures necessarily underestimate the true rates because of these and other factors. Nevertheless, in the USA there are more than 25,000 suicides per year, and upwards of 200,000 cases of parasuicide. Kreitman (1990) estimated that in Edinburgh there were 1.67 cases of parasuicide serious enough to warrant treatment per 1000. The suicide rate is of course higher in some diagnostic groups than in others; thus, the rate for manic-depressive disorder is estimated to be between 10 and 30%, with suicide being associated with the depressive rather than the manic symptomatology (e.g. Linehan, 1993).

Having now identified some links between depression, suicide, and parasuicide, we should note that there are a wide range of terms in use, especially those that refer to Kreitman's (1977) so-called parasuicide category. Such terms include "self-wounding", "self-mutilation", "self injurious behaviour", "deliberate self-harm", and "cry for help". The terms "parasuicide" and "deliberate self-harm" avoid many of the assumptions that other terms imply and should therefore be preferred. That is not to say though, that there are no useful sub-categories. For example, Tantam and Whittaker (1992) provide a useful overview of the category of "self-mutilation" for which there are diverse cultural practices; thus, there is widespread evidence from archaeological sites that trepanning occurred in many ancient groups, and practices such as foot-binding, ear-piercing, and finger mutilation have been carried out in more recent times for the purpose of fashion or status. However, there are a number of widespread culturally prescribed practices that can be interpreted as disgust-based and which may target certain parts of the body as a consequence. To quote from Tantam and Whittaker (1992, p.452):

> The stated intention of self-mutilation is often to rid oneself of an offending organ or body part ... common targets are the eye (the evil eye, the roving eye), the genitalia (John Thomas), or the tongue (the filthy tongue, the tongue that runs away with you).

In this type of self-mutilation therefore the individual attempts to rid the self of badness which has come to be identified with a particular part of the body. However, in so-called self-injurious behaviour or deliberate self-harm the pain or injury may even more clearly be an attempt to purge the individual of an unwanted aversive feeling. As MacLeod, Williams, and Linehan (1992) and others have argued, the suicidal individual may have problems with the regulation of negative affective states, so feelings of being unreal or depersonalised are commonly reported prior to parasuicidal acts (e.g. Van de Kolk, Perry, & Herman, 1991).

> Sheila felt unreal whenever she became very anxious or became angry. She would do anything to avoid these feelings and, on various occasions, had been hospitalised because of overdosing or because of wrist-cutting. Her mother had spent long periods in hospital when Sheila was a child and Sheila had been sexually abused as a young teenager by a friend of her father's.

As in Sheila's case, there is a high likelihood that neglect or abuse may occur in childhood in cases in which the individual resorts to self-harm; thus, Van Egmond and Jonker (1988) reported that 52% of first-time self-harm cases and 77% of repeat episode cases had either been sexually or physically abused in childhood. Such childhood abuse or neglect leads to an individual with poor self-esteem and, particularly in the case of abuse, with a feeling of disgust towards the self or the body, as noted above. In extreme cases, repeated abuse may lead to severe dissociative disorders (e.g. Terr, 1991), the dissociative states being triggered off by a range of emotion and drive-related experiences. Even in individuals without obvious abuse or neglect, the presence of self-derogatory views predicts an increased likelihood of suicidal ideation and parasuicide; Kaplan and Pokorny (1976) followed up a group of teenage school children over 12 months and found that those with self-derogatory views at the first assessment reported more suicidal ideation and parasuicide over the ensuing 12 months when compared to those children without self-derogatory views.

Theoretical approaches to parasuicide and suicide have focused on a range of psychological and social factors, beginning with Durkheim's classic sociological analysis of "social anomie". The epidemiology of suicide and parasuicide provides at least some evidence in favour of social and cultural factors. For example, the suicide rates are higher for groups with lower social status such as immigrants. Similarly, suicide rates for whites and blacks are inversely related to the proportions of whites and blacks in a given population (Davis, 1979); that is, the rates amongst whites are highest when they form the minority group and, equally, the rates amongst blacks are highest when they form the minority group. It seems likely, therefore, that cultural disgust-based values which have as their target particular social or ethnic minorities contribute to the greater incidence of suicidal behaviour in these groups. However, it is not sufficient to look only at sociological factors, because, for example, suicide still occurs in high status groups.

Psychological accounts of parasuicide and suicide initially focused on anger, but more recently have focused on hopelessness as key factors. The early focus on anger derived from Freud's (1917/1984) proposal that depression (melancholia) was, in part, due to anger turned against the self. As we summarised in Chapter 7, Bibring (1953) disputed the central role that Freud gave to retroflective anger in the occurrence of depression. He proposed, instead, that narcissistic defeats (i.e. the failure or loss of significant goals and plans, in cognitive terminology) lead to feelings of helplessness and hopelessness in the individual. Furthermore, in parasuicide cases, as in individuals who are depressed, there may be *more* aggression towards other people rather than less, contrary to the early psychoanalytic model. More recent views of suicide and parasuicide have therefore focused on the central role of hopelessness rather than anger, though, as MacLeod et al. (1992) pointed out, the expression of anger may be more relevant to parasuicide than to suicide.

Recent studies of hopelessness have shown that it may have a mediating role between depression and parasuicide. Beck, Brown, and Steer (1989) reported that high levels of hopelessness predicted completed suicide up to 10 years later. However, MacLeod et al. (1992) have argued that, as a concept, hopelessness needs to be better defined; for example, MacLeod's own work suggests that hopelessness may be more related to an absence of positive events in the future than it is to the expectation of increased numbers of negative events. MacLeod et al. (1992) also argue that the focus on hopelessness may simplify a far more complicated picture; thus, in Linehan's (e.g. 1993) development of

Dialectical Behaviour Therapy for the treatment of parasuicidal individuals, parasuicide is treated more often as a desperate attempt to escape from painful emotional states as much as it is about longer term feelings of hopelessness which may provide a context in which painful affects are even less tolerable and more exaggerated.

In summary, we propose that there is a significant role for disgust-based emotions in the occurrence of suicide and parasuicide. The effects of disgust are evident both at the cultural level and at the individual level in that groups who are perceived to be of lower status show higher rates of suicide and parasuicide. In a similar manner, individuals who have experienced abuse or neglect in childhood are vulnerable to poor self-esteem and the viewing of aspects of the self and the body in a disgust- or shame-based way. Certain emotional states may be particularly aversive for such individuals, for example, the experience of anger, fear, or sadness and, in the attempt to eliminate these unwanted affects from the self, parasuicide or suicide may follow. However, we are not suggesting that all acts of deliberate self-harm are based on disgust towards the self or towards certain minority groups. In the case of certain types of self-mutilation for example, such as the Chinese practice of foot-binding, there is an attempt to increase the perceived status of the individual. Equally, certain suicides may be carried out for noble reasons, as Albert Camus (1955) argued, such as in the case of Japanese kamikaze pilots who gained status through suicide. The majority of everyday suicides and parasuicides are not, however, the consequence of pursuing lofty or noble causes but are, in large part, desperate attempts by unhappy individuals to escape overwhelmingly painful emotions and circumstances.

Miscellaneous disgust-related disorders
The focus of this book is primarily on normal emotions and their associated disorders. However, there are a number of appetitive and drive-related disorders which may be based, in part, on a particular drive becoming the focus of a disgust-based reaction either as a primary part of the disorder, or as a secondary feature in which some other motive is primary. Two groups of disorders to which this approach may usefully be applied are the eating disorders and the sexual disorders. The role of disgust in these groups of disorders can often be glimpsed indirectly through reports of high comorbidity of certain eating and sexual disorders with depression. Our analysis would suggest however that such comorbidity is likely in part to be more due to the disgust-based aspects of depression, especially in relation to the experience of shame and guilt, rather than depression in the sense that we have defined it in Chapter 6 as the coupling of the basic emotions of sadness and disgust.

It is an open empirical question however as to whether the apparent comorbidity with depression is primarily because of the association between depression and disgust.

In relation to eating disorders, rates of major depression of between 40 and 60% have been identified in underweight patients with anorexia (Patton, 1988). High rates of affective disorders have also been observed in the relatives of individuals with anorexia. In the case of bulimia, the rates of depression have been estimated at between 24 and 79% (Patton, 1988). Two disgust-based reactions provide defining features of anorexia (Mitchell & Fensome, 1992). First, there is a disgust-based avoidance of foods that are considered to be fattening. And, second, there is a disgust-based reaction towards the body or certain parts of the body which are either perceived to be fat or prone to becoming fat. Our emphasis on disgust and disgust-based avoidance contrasts with the normal fear-based definitions, such as Russell's (1970) widely cited one which emphasises a "morbid fear" of becoming fat (cf. the discussion of specific phobias earlier). In contrast to anorexia, individuals with bulimia may be normal weight or even overweight. Bulimics are also less likely to come from middle- or upper-class backgrounds, tend to be older, and are more likely to engage in anti-social behaviour, drug abuse, and deliberate self-harm (Mitchell & Fensome, 1992). Again, Russell (1979) in the first definition of the disorder focused on a "morbid fear" of becoming fat, which, following periods of overeating up to 27 times the normal calorific intake, leads the individual to vomit or abuse laxatives.

> Sandra was a 30-year-old woman from a religious background. Over the past four or five years she had come to see her thighs as disgusting because they always seemed to be fat. She had periods however of feeling extremely alone and miserable, in which she felt loathsome and believed that everyone else found her loathsome too. During these times, she increasingly comforted herself by eating large quantities of cakes and chocolate, foods that she reacted with disgust towards at other times. After these binges she felt ashamed of herself and worried that her thighs would get fatter; therefore, she would either vomit or take large quantities of laxatives, or even on "bad days" do both.

As noted in the discussion of suicide and parasuicide, there are important cultural factors that need to be taken into account in the role of disgust in eating disorders in addition to disgust reactions in the individuals themselves. For example, the fact that 90–95% of anorexics are female (Bemis, 1978) and are teenagers highlights the role of such cultural factors. Indeed, the "ideal" body size for women shows considerable variation across cultures and across time within the same culture; thus, in the interests of science Garfinkel and Garner (1982) carried out a taxing study of the magazine, *Playboy*, and discovered that over a period of 20 years the ideal size for female Centrefolds had decreased substantially. The societal pressure to diet and be thin provides a context therefore in which overeating and being overweight is viewed with disgust; the majority of American women for example report being dissatisfied with their weight and approximately 56% diet on a regular basis (Vitousek & Ewald, 1993). Finally, there is also some evidence that there may be higher rates of a history of sexual abuse amongst women with eating disorders. Oppenheimer, Howells, Palmer, and Chaloner (1985) reported that 64% of a sample of anorexic and bulimic patients had experienced sexual abuse, commenting that (p.359) "frequently the sexually molested subject has feelings of inferiority or disgust about her own femininity and sexuality". Waller (1992) has reported that sexual abuse may be more common in bulimia than in anorexia and, furthermore, that the amount of reported vomiting and bingeing was greater when the abuse was by family members rather than non-family and involved more force.

In relation to sexual disorders again there is a clear role for disgust at a number of individual and social levels. Kaufman (1989, p.115) states:

> In sexual dysfunction syndromes ... the sexual drive has become fused with shame, either by itself or in combination with disgust and fear.

Unlike Kaufman, we would not of course derive shame and disgust separately to each other, but we would concur with his statement that "fear" has been overemphasised in sexual dysfunction at the expense of disgust and shame, though it is clearly possible that the anticipation of shame could lead to excessive anxiety being experienced in certain situations. For example, as Kaufman (1989, p.146) argues, so-called "performance anxiety" is more likely to be based on feelings of shame than it is on fear.

> Early fusion of sexuality with shame ... is a developmental precursor of adult sexual dysfunction. The patterning of affect with drive is a process spanning years. Sex-shame binds create the nuclei of eventual dysfunction in the sexual life.

The range of sexual disorders in which disgust may play a major part includes, in women, vaginismus, dyspareunia, and orgasmic dysfunction; in men it includes premature ejaculation, retarded ejaculation, and erectile dysfunction (see Dring & Kingston, 1992, for an overview). A more general impairment of interest in sex, termed Disorders of Sexual Desire by Helen Singer Kaplan (1979), rather than specific impairments may also occur in both men and women. As with many of the disorders discussed in this chapter, the occurrence of childhood sexual abuse often leads to adult sexual dysfunction. Jehu (1988) reported that 94% of a group of women who had been sexually abused in childhood experienced sexual dysfunction in adulthood. However, traumatic experiences in adulthood, for example, following the experience of rape or following childbirth, can also lead to sexual problems in which the individual may react with fear and disgust in subsequent sexual situations.

SUMMARY AND CONCLUSIONS

The basic emotion of disgust has been probably one of the least studied of the emotions, in part, it would seem, because its role in a number of emotional disorders has been minimised if not overlooked altogether. We hope that we have demonstrated that the SPAARS approach to disgust and the disgust-based complex emotions such as guilt and shame has much to offer. We hope too that we have drawn enough evidence together to suggest that certain phobias and obsessive-compulsive disorders may be disgust-based rather than fear-based. If true, then current diagnostic and classification systems have incorrectly labelled them as anxiety disorders. We have noted also that the failure to distinguish fear from disgust may have led to mistaken assumptions in a number of information-processing studies of anxiety and obsessive-compulsive disorders. We hope therefore that the future will hold great things for disgust and that disgust will be given the position that it rightly deserves!

CHAPTER TEN

Happiness

All happy families are more or less like one or another; every
unhappy family is unhappy in its own particular ways.
(Anna Karenina, *Leo Tolstoy*)

INTRODUCTION

Despite an almost unhealthy interest in the negative emotions such as
anger, fear, or disgust, emotion theorists rarely address the subject of
happiness. There may be many reasons for this; as Tolstoy articulates
so well in the opening line of *Anna Karenina*, there appear to be many
more ways to not be happy than there are ways to be happy. Similarly,
in the clinic, people present with a range of emotional disorders but
these can rarely be conceptualised as "disorders of happiness". Indeed,
in Johnson-Laird and Oatley's (1989) linguistic analysis of emotion
terms, of the 590 English words reviewed, there was a predominance of
terms for the usually negative emotions and the pervasiveness of this
imbalance has led Frijda (1986) to adopt the term "hedonic asymmetry".
A second reason for the comparative scarcity of happiness research may
be that, as Averill and Moore (1993, p.617) point out, happiness seems
to have a much broader scope than more circumscribed emotions such
as anger or sadness and "has depth of meaning that seems to mock
analysis". Belying this lack of precedent, we shall take a few deep

breaths and attempt to tackle the subject of happiness with the eventual aim of providing some theoretical remarks within the framework we have been developing throughout the book.

So, what is happiness? Attempts to define happiness within the psychology literature generally reflect the breadth of scope which, according to Averill and Moore, is so mocking of analysis. For example, Wessman and Ricks (1966, pp.240–241) proposed that happiness:

> Appears as an overall evaluation of a quality of the individuals own experience in the conduct of his vital affairs. As such, happiness represents a conception abstracted from the flux of affective life indicating a decided balance of positive affectivity over long periods of time.

Similarly, Veenhoven (1984, p.4) suggests that happiness is "the degree to which an individual judges the overall quality of his life-as-a-whole favourably" and is "not a simple sum of pleasures, but rather a cognitive construction which the individual puts together from his various experiences".

It seems clear that broad conceptualisations of happiness such as these are referring to a different type of emotional experience to those of anger, sadness, fear, and so on, which we have focused on in the previous four chapters. These emotions, we have argued, are functional, modular responses to information which is incompatible with a particular active goal. In contrast, the above definitions of happiness seem to refer to an emotional state which is a conflation across numerous goals in different domains in the individual's life. Clearly there are positive emotions which are circumscribed in the same way as the ones which we have discussed; the emotions of joy, exhilaration, ecstasy, and so on are most usually about the achievement of a particular valued goal and, indeed, the term happiness is also frequently used in this way. In this chapter we will begin by briefly examining circumscribed positive emotions such as joy before proceeding to a more detailed discussion of happiness as defined above by authors such as Veenhoven and Wessman and Ricks. We shall reserve the term happiness for this latter usage whilst acknowledging that it can also be used to refer to a more circumscribed reaction to the achievement of a specific goal.

JOY AND OTHER CIRCUMSCRIBED
POSITIVE EMOTIONS

Joy may be conceptualised as the emotional state related to an appraisal that a valued goal has been achieved, or that movement towards such an achievement has occurred. So, for example, somebody might feel joy when she is able to go and book her summer holiday. Such an analysis of joy clearly distinguishes it from what we shall call happiness. Joy is very much an emotional reaction to a specific goal in a specific domain, whereas happiness, it seems, casts its appraisal net much wider than this. It seems perfectly feasible for an individual to experience joy with respect to a specific goal whilst not being generally happy when all goals in all domains are considered together; similarly, it seems possible for an individual to be happy whilst also feeling some fear, anger, or sadness as a result of appraisals concerning specific goals in specific domains.

Clearly a conceptualisation of joy as an emotional response to the achievement of a valued goal is an insufficient analysis. The same set of constraints could be used to talk about quiet satisfaction or exhilaration or ecstasy; it seems that there is something about the type of goal and the individual's expectations of fulfilling that goal which are important in defining the emotional state the individual will experience once the goal has been achieved. Having acknowledged this, it is less clear what it is about these goals which serves to define an emotion as ecstasy or joy or quiet satisfaction; perhaps the more invested an individual is in a particular goal then the stronger the feeling of positive emotion when that goal is achieved. Alternatively, perhaps the less expected such an achievement is, the stronger the feeling of positive emotion when that achievement does come about.

As the antithesis of the negative emotions, the circumscribed positive emotion of joy seems to contribute to an enormous amount of emotional conflict. As we noted in Chapter 2, Descartes recounts the tale of the man who, whilst being sad at his wife's death, was also unable to contain his joy at his new-found freedom. Such conflict between feelings of joy at the achievement of goals which we may feel uncomfortable with and negative emotions to those goals is frequently the subject of therapeutic work. Much of this conflict not only incorporates our own goals but also those of others. The state of *schadenfreude*, which is almost the opposite of envy (see Chapter 8), and which involves joy at another's misfortune, can often prove distressing. Whether it involves being secretly pleased that our friend did not succeed in getting a distinction in her exams or feeling a surge of exhilaration when someone's perfect relationship seems to break down, feelings of *schadenfreude* can disturb us as they reveal wants, needs, and goals which we perhaps did not realise we had and which feel uncomfortable and incongruent with our idealised models of self.

Happiness as a non-circumscribed emotional state

In the Introduction to this chapter we noted several definitions of the broad emotional state of happiness. Although these attempts at definition capture some of the breadth of the concept of happiness, research into the nature of happiness has, for the most part, been conducted outside of such definitional guidelines or theoretical frameworks. Such research has tended either to ask people what they feel makes them happy or has examined the correlates of happiness in people who claim to be happy. The findings from these approaches have revealed a number of issues and paradoxes which, in our view, underline the need for a thought-out, theoretical framework before we can achieve any measure of understanding of the concept of happiness. In the section that follows we consider some of this research and some of the issues that it has generated.

TRADITIONAL APPROACHES
TO THE STUDY OF HAPPINESS

In order to assess whether or not individuals are happy, or, if they *are* happy, what makes them so, researchers have devised a number of self-report measures. It is not always happiness that these inventories purportedly measure; there exist questionnaires which look at "positive affect", "emotional well-being", "satisfaction with life", and a number of other constructs. Although there are clearly debates about the relationship of these different concepts to each other, it is our broad assumption in this chapter that they are all more or less intended as synonyms for the concept of happiness.

On the prototypical happiness questionnaire, the respondent is asked, on a single or multiple item scale, how happy he or she is (for example, the Satisfaction with Life Scale, Diener, Emmons, Larsen, & Griffin, 1985; The Depression–Happiness Scale, McGreal & Joseph 1993; The Memorial University of Newfoundland Scale of Happiness, Kozma & Stones, 1980; see Andrews & Robinson, 1991 and Larsen, Diener, & Emmons, 1985 for reviews). Convergent validity for such measures is surprisingly good. For example, Sandvik, Diener, and Seidlitz (1993) found a strong relationship between self-reports of emotional well-being and interview ratings, peer ratings, reports of the average ratio of pleasant to unpleasant moods, and an index of a memory for pleasant and unpleasant events. Furthermore, such measures are purportedly uncontaminated by social desirability (Diener, Sandvik, & Pavot, 1991), and show structural invariance across time and cultural group (e.g. Balatsky & Diener, 1991).

Correlates of happiness

There exists a plethora of research findings concerning the covariation between measures of happiness on scales such as those described above and a variety of demographic and resource variables. This research is comprehensively reviewed by Argyle (1987) and Eysenck (1990). To overview briefly, age and education show only small correlations with subjective reports of happiness (Diener, 1984). It has been found that income is related to well-being, but that this relationship is only significant below a minimal level of income (e.g. Freedman, 1978) and is consequently much stronger in poorer countries (Diener & Larsen, 1993). Okun and George (1984) found a surprisingly small correlation between health and reports of happiness when objective measures of health are employed. Similarly, Wolsic and Diener (cited in Diener & Larsen, 1993) found that physical attractiveness correlates very weakly with subjective reports of happiness as does intelligence (e.g. Emmons & Diener, 1985). Finally, unemployment has been a predictor of unhappiness in some studies (e.g. Diener, 1984) and marriage has been a consistent but weak positive predictor of subjective reports of happiness with married individuals being reportedly more happy than single individuals (e.g. Tran, Wright, & Chatters, 1991).

Even putting aside basic methodological issues, for example, that perhaps it is happy people who get married, rather than married people who are happy, the general lack of positive correlational findings between what objectively might be thought of as desirable resources or qualities and subjective reports of happiness requires explanation. It seems that objective life situations and resources are not good predictors of happiness. Indeed this has been starkly illustrated in some comparative studies; for example, Easterlin (1974) found that poor people are often happier than rich people, and Brickman, Coates, and Janoff-Bulman (1978) found that recent lottery winners are often no happier than control subjects, only slightly happier than recently paralysed accident victims, and no happier than they were before they won the lottery. Overall, Andrews and Withey (1976) found that age, sex, race, education, income, religion, occupation, employment status, and size of city only accounted for approximately 11% of the total variance in subjective judgements of happiness. Similarly Kammann (1982) concluded that objective life circumstances routinely account for less than 5% of the variance in subjective judgements of happiness.

Happiness as the sum of positive experiences

Ed Diener and his colleagues have taken a somewhat different tack in the search for what makes people happy. They (e.g. Diener et al., 1991) have proposed that self-reports of happiness are primarily a function of frequently experienced pleasant or positive affect and infrequently experienced unpleasant affect. In a number of studies they have shown that people who differ in their reports of happiness invariably differ in the amount of time in their lives in which they experience pleasant affect. It is important to note that Diener and his colleagues are talking principally about the frequency of experiences of positive emotions and not the intensity. In fact they claim that intensity is almost unrelated to subjective reports of well-being (e.g. Larsen & Diener, 1985, 1987).

Diener's work is interesting and important in that it reveals a relationship between global concepts such as happiness and more circumscribed positive emotions such as joy, exhilaration, and others which come under the umbrella of positive affect. Furthermore, his work clarifies the relationship between the frequency of emotional states, the intensity of those states, and longer-term constructs such as happiness. However, a number of questions remain; for example, it is unclear how happiness relates exactly to more circumscribed experiences of positive affect. In addition, there remains the possibility that self-reports of global happiness and the experience of circumscribed episodes of positive affect may themselves both be functions of a similar set of underlying psychological processes.

"Gap" accounts of happiness

The research we have considered above on the affective and resource correlates of self-reported happiness has taken the subjects' avowed happiness as a starting point and systematically invested aspects of the individual's life which might be related to feeling happy. In contrast, gap theories are concerned with the processes which might underlie self-reports of happiness; that is, what determines whether individuals will report that they are happy.

Such gap theories of happiness (e.g. Michalos, 1986; Parducci, 1968; Smith, Diener, & Wedell, 1989; Wills, 1981) have proposed that individuals judge their own happiness by making a comparison between their actual conditions of life or performance or view of themselves versus some standard. If the comparison is favourable, happiness is increased; if the comparison is unfavourable, happiness is compromised.

There are a variety of different gap theories of happiness. For example, Michalos (1985, 1986) describes six which reflect discrepancies between: (1) what one wants and what one has; (2) actual and ideal conditions; (3) actual conditions and expectations; (4) actual conditions and best past conditions; (5) what one has and what others have (upward and downward social comparison); and (6) personal attributes and environmental attributes.

Studies have found that these gap theory variables account for considerable amounts of variance in self-reported happiness (e.g. Emmons & Diener, 1985; Michalos, 1985). Furthermore, a range of studies has indicated the efficacy of this type of theoretical approach. Indeed, Michalos (1986) reviewed 41 such studies and over 90% of these supported gap theory explanations. Despite such a supposed wealth of positive evidence, a number of authors have strongly criticised gap theory approaches and Veenhoven (1991) suggests that the process of comparison may not have a causal role in everyday happiness judgements. Averill and Moore (1993) note a number of other problems with gap theories which might account for Veenhoven's scepticism. First, they suggest it is not clear which way a comparison would have to go in order to make a person happier. For example, thinking that there are many people worse off than oneself may make someone happier under one set of conditions but thinking that if others can succeed so can I may make someone happier under another set of conditions. Second, gap theories have little explanatory power. They are merely ways of describing a state of affairs. As Averill and Moore (1993, p.625) question: "Why should personal satisfaction be increased by a favourable contrast between oneself and others who are less fortunate?" Third, if we consider that there are at least six gaps which may be important (cf. Michalos, 1985, 1986), the possible combinations and interactions between them become uninterpretable. In illustration, Averill and Moore cite the example of the gap between what one wants and what one has, being either exacerbated or mitigated by the gap between what one has and what others have. Finally, even if gap theories do have some validity, they are merely one mechanism which might account for some of the variance in happiness judgements. Simple biological pleasures, for example, clearly do not always need the existence of some prior discrepancy to be enjoyable. The same is true of many other constituents of happiness; for example, laughing at a good joke.

To summarise, in this section we have looked at research investigating avowed happiness and the reasons people are able to generate for that happiness. It is clear that such research, whilst often illuminating and provoking, suffers from the lack of an overarching theoretical framework within which to approach the numerous issues which are generated. In addition, there seems a clear need to move away from self-reports of happiness to a more objective theoretical approach. There is considerable evidence, for example, that people are influenced by culturally shared theories rather than their own phenomenal experience of cause and effect when generating self-report data (e.g. Nisbett & Wilson, 1977) and this work is reviewed by McIntosh and Martin (1991) with respect to happiness. Perhaps even more illuminating, with respect to the need to shift away from the self-report approach, is the anecdotal description by Freedman (1978) of the problems involved in researching happiness using interview techniques. Apparently, in Freedman's research, when interviewed in small groups, people joked and made light of the topic of happiness; in contrast, when interviewed on an individual basis, they became very serious and found it difficult to talk at all about the topic. Freedman's research assistant concluded that it would be easier to ask people about intimate details of their sexual lives than about what makes them happy. Discussing these anecdotal points, Averill and Moore (1993) suggest that the fact that happiness involves an evaluation of life as a whole and touches upon an individual's deepest goals and ideals means that, to talk about the subject seriously, it is necessary to drop all pretences and admit to shortcomings as well as successes. This, they suggest, makes happiness difficult to discuss not just for the individual in a research study but for the emotion theorist as well. A related point concerns the difference between happiness and more *circumscribed* emotions such as sadness, anger, or disgust. The circumscribed nature of the latter examples means that it is easier for subjects to translate how they are feeling into answers to questionnaire items such as "Are you feeling sad?" or "Are you currently angry?". In contrast, the broad scope and elusive nature of happiness ensures that simple inventory measures will always suffer from problems of validity.

TOWARDS A THEORETICAL ACCOUNT OF HAPPINESS

As we have stated above, for the purposes of the present chapter, whether or not an individual is happy conflates across many goals in different domains and at different levels of the system. In the domain of positive emotion, experiences such as joy or exhilaration, then, are responses to the achievement of single active goals and are more akin to the states of anger, fear, sadness, and disgust. We are not presenting anything new here; this understanding of happiness has been around for thousands of years. To quote Aristotle in the *Nicomachean Ethics* (1177a5):

> Any chance person—even a slave—can enjoy the bodily pleasures no less than the best man; but no-one assigns to a slave showing happiness.

Recently, a number of authors (e.g. Averill & Moore, 1993; Carver & Scheier, 1990; Ortony et al., 1988) have suggested that happiness is a function of individuals' fulfilment in various domains of their life (for example, self, social, biological, and so on) and across different levels of goals (for example, the high-level goal of being a good person, or the low-level goal of buying nice food). The exact nature of the proposed domains and levels across which happiness conflates varies from one researcher to another; for example, Averill and Moore (1993) suggest that three systemic domains are important in the understanding of happiness: the biological system; the psychological system; and the social system. In this section we outline a slightly different systemic theoretical account of happiness.

In Chapter 5 we developed two points which, we suggest, are important in an understanding of happiness. First, that information within the SPAARS model at the schematic model, propositional, analogical, and associative levels can be heuristically grouped into three domains: the self, the world, and others. It is important to reiterate that we view these systems as abstractions which can be distinguished in theory but rarely in practice. At the end of the day, they are heuristics for understanding aspects of our emotional life and one might easily take Averill and Moore's biological, psychological, and social systems. Second, we proposed that the generation of emotion within SPAARS occurs initially via the schematic model level of meaning and involves an appraisal of interpretations of events in the world with respect to goals. Each goal, we suggested, is part of a virtual goal hierarchy towards the top of which are goals of the highest order such as personal survival, and at the bottom of which are more short-term pragmatic goals such as reaching out to pick up a cup of coffee. A possible goal hierarchy was illustrated in Fig. 5.4. By integrating the idea of three domains of knowledge, with the concept of virtual goal hierarchies, it seems that there are three classes of goal which are potentially important in the understanding of emotion: self-related goals; our perceptions of the goals of others; and goals shared by self and others (for example, social standards). Within this framework, we would like to propose an analysis of happiness which is a function of five premises (cf. Averill and Moore). We shall discuss each premise in turn and use these discussions to illuminate and, hopefully, move towards resolving some of the issues which have been generated by our review of basic happiness research above.

Happiness is the result of optimal levels of goal fulfilment across different domains.   In order to claim that happiness is a function of optimal levels of goal fulfilment across the different domains of self, others, and self plus others, we need to make the a priori assumption that for most individuals all three of these goal domains are important. That is to say, most of us perceive the need to pay attention, not only to self-related goals but also to the goals and needs of others and the shared goals of self and others. Granted this starting assumption, we propose that if an individual neglects goals which are perceived to be important in one or other of the three domains, then it seems likely that the individual will not be happy. For example, if we have to endure an extended period in which we are so concerned with the goals of various others (e.g. colleagues, family, friends) that we are unable to find time and/or space in which to pay attention to the self, we are unlikely to be happy. Clearly not all individuals have to have an investment in all three goal domains. Some people seem almost entirely invested in one domain at the expense of others and we consider such cases below and in the section on so-called "disordered happiness".

Happiness is a function of the fulfilment of both lower- and higher-level goals. In his *Nicomachean Ethics*, Aristotle makes the point that, just as slaves cannot be happy if they are denied the opportunity to pursue virtuous activities (higher-order goal fulfilment), neither can the victim of torture be happy merely by virtue of being a good person (that is, because of the lack of fulfilment of lower-order biological goals). These are contentious points, the first seems to be an argument against any form of hedonism whilst the latter seems to provide objections to certain forms of spiritualism or religious happiness.

The principal objection to taking an entirely bottom-up approach to happiness (that is, that happiness can derive from the fulfilment of low-level goals in the various goal domains) is that individuals seem to habituate fairly rapidly to such events (e.g. McIntosh & Martin, 1991). So, events that at one time seem very positive come to be perceived as less positive when people get used to experiencing those events. For example, the brand new Saab in the driveway can be a source of great joy; however, after a few months the owner will become used to seeing the car parked outside and it will no longer be a source of such positive affect. This habituation suggests that the path to happiness does not lie with increasingly indulgent satisfaction of low-level goals, but requires also the satisfaction of higher-level, less materially dependent goals and needs.

What about the possibility of happiness when there is no fulfilment of low-level goals? It seems unlikely that the biological and psychological systems with their evolutionary imperative to satisfy basic goals and needs such as hunger, thirst, and physical comfort could be continually short-circuited such that the absence of satisfaction of these needs was not an impediment to the individual's overall happiness.

As Aristotle retorts (*Nicomachean Ethics*, 1947, 1153b, 19):

> Those who say that the victim on the rack or the man who falls into great misfortune is happy if he is good are ... talking nonsense".

This notion of the fulfilment of basic needs prior to the achievement of higher-order aims is central to a number of theories in humanistic psychology (e.g. Maslow, 1968).

The problems of optimal goal fulfilment lead to a weighting of investment in one goal domain at the expense of others. If, as is suggested, happiness is a function of the optimal fulfilment of goals of both a higher order and a lower order and across all goal domains, then being happy is clearly a considerable achievement. Such optimal levels of goal fulfilment would probably be very rare indeed; one method of coming to terms with this difficulty would be for each individual to invest more heavily in one goal domain than others. For that individual, happiness will be more dependent on goal fulfilment in one domain at the expense of the other goal domains. On these lines, Averill and Moore (1993) argue that happiness is principally a function of goal fulfilment within what they term the "social system" of behaviour which translates within SPAARS as a combination of the domains of the goals of others and of self plus others. This, they suggest, accounts for the close link, so often emphasised by philosophers and writers on ethics, between happiness and virtue. However, as the individualist philosopher Bertrand Russell (1945, p.173, see also 1950) retorts: such a proposal "appeals to the respectable middle-aged, and has been used by them.... to repress the ardours and enthusiasms of the young". Clearly Russell has a point here; we all know rebellious individuals who reject social values, and thus the goal domains of self plus others and of others, in favour of self-related goals and needs. Furthermore, there are clear cross-cultural differences in goal domain investment. Western society is more individualistic than, say, Japanese society in which shared social goals are more prominent.

Finally, we have argued elsewhere (e.g. Champion & Power, 1995) and in Chapter 7 on sadness that perhaps over-investment in one goal domain at the expense of others can make the individual vulnerable to depression when those over-invested goals are compromised. We address this issue further in the later section on so-called disordered happiness.

The proposal that happiness is a function of goal fulfilment across various domains and levels, even allowing for the fact that individuals can invest more heavily in one domain or another, entails that happiness is necessarily a fleeting and elusive emotional state. A sense of happiness lasting minutes, hours, days, weeks, or months will arise out of a process of psychological negotiation in which the goals and needs in one domain are pursued and realised at the expense of goals and needs in other domains.

The importance of goal setting for happiness.   So far we have talked about different goal domains and different levels of virtual goal structures as if they are static entities. Clearly, this is not the case. As human beings we continually create new goals for ourselves and continually shift our profile of investment from one domain to another or from one level of a domain to another.

Kekes (1982, p.361) proposed that "a man is extremely unlikely to have a happy life without having a more or less clearly formed view about what his life should be" and such a claim is supported by psychological research (Emmons, 1986; Maslow, 1968; Ryff, 1989); furthermore, as Averill and Moore (1993) point out, goal-setting strategies are also important parts of happiness enhancement programmes (e.g. Fordyce, 1981). Such programmes often advise individuals to shift away from setting long-term grandiose goals to setting short-term realisable goals. Although this advice has some face validity, it seems likely that happiness is a function of both short-term and long-term goal-setting abilities; an emphasis on short-term goals alone is likely to lead to a foreshortened sense of future and possibly an impoverished sense of self (Averill & Moore, 1993).

The relativity of happiness.   Recently this year in Britain the newspapers carried a report of a man who committed suicide when he realised he had not won the National Lottery. The situation was this: the man in question had selected a set of numbers which he entered into the lottery each week, subscribing six or seven weeks in advance. Eventually, he hit lucky and his numbers matched those drawn out of the hat. However, on checking the following day after a night of celebration, he found that his lottery entry was not valid as his advance subscriptions had lapsed a week earlier. Unable to cope with the fact that, having thought he had won millions of pounds he had now won nothing, he committed suicide. What is perhaps most illuminating about this case is the fact that, prior to his false lottery win, the man concerned was reportedly happy. Following his discovery that he had not won the lottery, the objective circumstances of his life which had previously made him very happy were no different; however, it seems that the man's goals and dreams in various domains of his life had shifted in line with his supposedly new-found fortune and the inability to attain or approximate these new goals and needs is likely to have led to desperate unhappiness and eventual suicide. Paradoxically, the need to be able to set new goals and project our goals into the future in order to be happy is probably part of the process which makes happiness such an elusive state of affairs. When people do achieve optimal levels of goal fulfilment, one reaction is to set new goals and higher standards and the pathway to happiness is thus redefined.

The relationship between goal structures and schematic models within SPAARS

In Chapter 5 we developed the idea that, at the schematic model level of representation within SPAARS, individuals possess a variety of models of the world, self, and other which form the basis of their "reality". For most of us, there is a sense that the world is a reasonably safe place, that we have more or less control over what goes on in our world, the actions of other people are pretty much predictable, that bad things don't usually happen to us, and so on. These models act as organising and guiding principles throughout our daily lives and are fundamental to the goals we set for ourselves and the ways in which we try to fulfil them. The maintenance of schematic models also represents the highest level on the goal hierarchy. For example, the "goal" of maintaining a sense of self or a sense of reality.

Within this kind of analysis, schematic models develop as a function of the individual's learning history. This learning history, in turn, is essentially a history of the success at achieving goals and the various obstacles to those goals which the individual has encountered. A learning history in which the individual has been reasonably successful in fulfilling goals or has been able to negotiate the obstacles to those goals is likely to lead to a set of schematic models about the self, world, and others which is generally positive. We are not suggesting that this is a one-way relationship; as we have stated above, the goals individuals set either implicitly or explicitly are a function of the schematic models which individuals bring to bear on their circumstances. An individual is only likely to set goals which are viewed as more or less attainable within the parameters of the schematic models which are being applied. Such goals, clearly, are consequently more likely to be attained and the positive nature of the schematic models is thereby strengthened. What we have, then, is a proposed interactive system involving schematic models of the self, world, and other, and the achievement and setting of goals at different levels and in different domains of the individual's life such that the system as a whole functions in a generally positive way.

An interactive system of this kind would have several implications: (1) That the schematic models of normal healthy individuals are generally positive and self-serving; (2) that, consequently, such individuals will show processing biases on a number of cognitive and social cognitive tasks (Alloy, 1988) and a number of such positive biases are discussed in the section on depressive realism in Chapter 7 on Sadness and also below; (3) the current state of the interactive goal-model system is reflected in trait constructs such as optimism/pessimism (see Scheier & Carver, 1987).

Cognitive processing biases and positive affect

In Chapter 6 on Fear and Chapter 7 on Sadness we saw that there is a growing body of research into processing biases associated with these emotions, particularly when the material to be processed is affectively valenced in one way or another. The line we have taken in those chapters (and elsewhere, see Champion & Power, 1995; Dalgleish, 1994a; Power & Champion, 1986) is that processing biases are not exclusively the preserve of mood-disordered individuals but, rather, are present as ways of selecting and ordering personally relevant information for everybody. We have further suggested that different emotional states seem to be associated with different profiles of processing biases across a range of tasks (cf. Williams et al., 1988). So, for example, anxiety seems to be associated with attentional biases and sad mood with mnemonic biases. These particular profiles of processing bias for different emotions, we argued in Chapter 5, are a constituent of being in that particular emotion module; that is, they are a function of the reconfiguration of the entire SPAARS system.

The majority of research with sad and anxious moods has focused on fundamental cognitive processes such as memory, attention, and perception. In contrast to this, much of the research on cognitive processing and positive affect has looked at higher-order processes such as decision making and judgements. We have reviewed the literature on mood biases and memory and attention in earlier chapters. Here we shall concentrate on the effects of positive mood on higher-order processes. We shall first consider some of the factors which interact with positive mood to influence an individual's performance on such higher-order processing tasks, we shall then look at some examples of research which have used such tasks to elucidate the role of positive affect in information processing. We have been somewhat selective in this process and the reader is referred to an excellent review by Alice Isen (1993) for a more comprehensive discussion of these issues.

There are four factors which it seems important to consider in any analysis of the effects of positive mood on processing tasks. These are: (1) a basic memory bias for positive material (see Chapter 7); (2) the interest level and importance of the task at hand; (3) the tendency of the cognitive system to maintain positive affect (see above); and (4) the association between the use of heuristics and stereotypes in processing and the existence of positive affect.

A number of studies have indicated that the presence of positive feelings is likely to cue positive items in memory, thus making access to such material easier, (e.g. Isen, Shalker, Clark, & Karp, 1978; MacLeod, Andersen, & Davies, 1994; Nasby & Yando, 1982; Teasdale & Fogarty, 1979). For example, MacLeod et al. (1994) asked subjects to provide self-ratings of positive and negative affect terms and to retrieve personal memories associated with those terms. Self-rated positive affect was associated with the latency to retrieve positive affect memories but not negative affect memories. Similarly self-rated negative affect was associated with the latency to retrieve negative but not positive affect-related memories. This dissociation of the effects of positive and negative affect on memory has been a ubiquitous finding. Furthermore, a number of studies have also noted an asymmetry between the two types of emotional state; that is, although positive affect is an effective retrieval cue for positive material in memory, negative affect is not always found to be an effective cue for negative material (see the review of depressive realism research in Chapter 7). This memory bias is clearly likely to be an important factor when trying to understand any research involving the effect of positive mood on higher-order processes such as thinking and reasoning, especially when those tasks involve valenced material. A related factor to this, according to Isen (e.g. 1993), is that because positive material is more extensive and diverse than other material in memory in healthy subjects (e.g. Cramer, 1968) then "the cognitive context is more complex when a person is feeling happy as a broader range of ideas is cued" (Isen, 1994, p.262). Consequently, positive affect may influence the context within which any information-processing task is carried out and there is clear evidence that such context is also a factor which influences thinking and decision making (e.g. Bransford, 1979; Kahneman & Tversky, 1979).

The second factor which is important when considering the influence of positive affect on information processing is that the precise effect that such feelings have seems to be a function of how interesting or important the task is to the individual subject. Individuals in whom positive affect has been induced show a number of information processing differences to controls, but usually only on tasks or with material which is relatively interesting or important to them (e.g. Isen, Johnson, Mertz, & Robinson,

1985; Isen & Patrick, 1983; Isen, Rosenzweig, & Young, 1991; Kraiger, Billings & Isen, 1989).

The third factor, and one which we have discussed above in the section on the relationship between schematic models and goals, is the configuration of the emotion system to maintain positive affect in healthy individuals. Consequently, individuals who are experiencing positive affect may avoid difficult or unpleasant tasks or materials, and may opt to work with more pleasant items instead (e.g. Isen & Reeve, 1992; Isen & Simmonds, 1978).

The final factor to consider when analysing the effects of positive affect on cognitive processes is the increasing body of evidence which suggests that individuals experiencing positive affect are more likely to recruit heuristics than stereotypes when faced with task demands, as opposed to systematically processing the various options available. For example, Bodenhausen et al. (1994) report four experiments examining the effects of happiness on the tendency to use stereotypes in social judgement. In each experiment, subjects in the induced happy mood rendered more stereotypical judgements than those in a neutral mood. However, when the subjects were told that they would have to be held accountable for their judgements, the stereotypic thinking bias disappeared. This finding that, although there is some evidence for the use of stereotypes and heuristics in individuals with positive affect, they can nevertheless still engage in more systematic processing of the material when required has been repeated in a number of other studies (see Isen, 1993, for a review).

Having considered a number of important factors which bear on an understanding of the influence of positive affect or happiness on processing tasks, it is useful to look at one or two examples of experiments from the literature which implicate these factors in various ways.

Isen, Niedenthal, and Cantor (1992) carried out a series of studies to examine the influence of positive affect on categorisation. Subjects were requested to rate the degree to which atypical examples of positive or negative categories of people (e.g. "bartender" as a member of the category "nurturant people") fit as members of that category. Positive affect subjects rated atypical members of positive categories as fitting better in the category than controls; however, this effect was not present for the negative person categories (e.g. "genius" as a member of a negative category "unstable people"). Isen et al.'s explanation of these findings indicates the ways in which the various factors we have discussed above might interact. She argues that (Isen, 1993, p.265):

> Although an underlying process (increased elaboration) is
> postulated to occur, this process is expected to be different

for different kinds of material in the situation described. Since positive affect cues positive material, the elaborative process would be expected to occur with positive material (for all subjects) or for positive-affect subjects working with neutral material.

Furthermore, as suggested above, the positive-affect subjects may make a choice not to deal with the negative material.

Finally, a number of studies have investigated the influence of positive affect on complex decision making. Briefly, the studies suggest that individuals who are experiencing positive affect are both more efficient in decision making, but at the same time are also able to be more thorough if the task demands require such increased effort. For example, Isen, Rosenzweig, and Young (1991) asked medical students to choose the patient most likely to have a diagnosis of lung cancer from six descriptions of patients varying with respect to each of nine health-relevant labels (e.g. cough, chest X-ray, and so on). Subjects were assigned to one of two groups—a positive affect group or a control group. Both groups performed similarly with respect to their ability to make the correct choice of patient. However, the positive affect subjects made the choice significantly earlier in their protocols. Of additional interest, the positive-affect subjects went on to do much more with the materials they were presented with; they proposed working diagnoses for the other (control) patients in the study and started to make suggestions concerning treatment plans.

In summary, in this section we have presented some examples of a large body of research examining the effects of positive mood or happiness on various types of cognitive processing. We have reviewed the arguments that the pattern of performance on a variety of processing tasks and in a variety of situations is a function, not just of the person's affective state, but also of the parameters of the task itself; for example, whether the task is intrinsically interesting, whether it involves positive material, whether it can be solved using stereotypic thinking or requires more systematic processing.

THE REPRESSIVE COPING STYLE

Another topic which deserves inclusion in any chapter on Happiness concerns the question of individuals who maintain their self-esteem or happiness by denying the existence of negative material in their lives. Much of this research comes under the umbrella of the term "repressive coping style" and it is this series of studies which we turn to now.

The term *verdrängt* (repressed) is forever associated with the work of Freud and was first employed by him in *Studies on Hysteria* (Breuer & Freud, 1895/1974). From this point on, Freud's use of the term repression was varied and sometimes contradictory. The consensus of opinion is that Freud's conceptualisation of repression varied throughout his writings from a narrow view of a single defence mechanism to a broader definition of many types of defence mechanism. As Singer and Sincoff in their own chapter in the excellent edited book *Repression and Dissociation: Implications for Personality Theory, Psychopathology and Health* (Singer, 1990, p.474) have stated:

> Freud began by describing repression as motivated forgetting, as an intentional failure to access information stored in memory. As his theory of the defences developed, the concept of repression absorbed these developments and began to represent defence mechanisms in general rather than forgetting in particular ... Repression eventually came to denote the systematic avoidance, through any variety of mechanisms, of potentially threatening material in thought or social experience.

This confusion as to the exact meaning of the term repression in Freud's writings is compounded by Freud's refusal to be explicit about whether repression is an unconscious or a conscious psychological process. Indeed, Freud used terms such as suppression (a conscious process) and repression (either a conscious or an unconscious process) interchangeably throughout his career (see Erdelyi, 1990). Despite these sources of confusion, it is clear that by using the term repression Freud was broadly referring to psychological processes involved in keeping disturbing material at a distance from the conscious; for example (Freud, 1915/1949, p.153), "the motive and purpose of repression was nothing else than the avoidance of unpleasure ... If a repression does not succeed in preventing feelings of unpleasure or anxiety from arising, we may say that it has failed".

More recently, there have been numerous attempts to operationalise the concept of repression and to treat it as an individual difference variable. Furthermore, a number of self-report and questionnaire measures have been developed to measure an individual's tendency to employ a so-called repressive coping style. The basic premise behind most of these scales (e.g. the Byrne Repression–Sensitization Scale, Byrne 1964; Weinberger Adjustment Inventory [WAI], Weinberger, Schwartz, & Davidson, 1979) has been to conceptualise individuals as high in repressive coping style if they show elevated scores on a measure of social desirability and low scores on a measure of anxiety. There is an enormous amount of debate in the literature concerning the relative merits and intercorrelations of the different scales; for example, Weinberger et al. (1979) argued that the Byrne Repression–Sensitization Scale does not discriminate between truly low-anxious individuals and repressors. However Turvey and Salovey (1994) compared six common measures of repression and found that all of them were highly intercorrelated and, furthermore, all loaded on a single factor. This psychometric literature is reviewed in detail by Myers (1993).

This definition of repression as a function of the pattern of scores obtained from self-report measures of anxiety and defensiveness (social desirability) suggests that, for some individuals at least, a sense of happiness and high self-esteem may be maintained through the denial and defence of distressing information. Furthermore, it suggests that these individuals are likely to differ in a number of ways from individuals who are happy without seeking to deny the existence of distressing information. In this section we shall review selectively some of the research which has looked at the type of information that repressors might deny, the type of emotion ruled out, the information-processing research using repressors and controls, and finally we shall attempt to conceptualise the concept of repression within the SPAARS framework developed in Chapter 5.

Weinberger et al. (1979) have suggested a fourfold classification of individuals with respect to their scores on measures of anxiety and defensiveness: low anxious (low anxiety–low defensiveness); repressor (low anxiety–high defensiveness); high anxious (high anxiety–low defensiveness); and, defensive high anxious (high anxiety–high defensiveness). Initial attempts at a validation of this system indicated that repressors reported the lowest level of subjective distress, even though a variety of physiological measures (heart rate, spontaneous skin resistence, and forehead muscle tension) and behavioural measures (reaction times, content avoidance, verbal interference) revealed that they were more stressed than the low anxious group. Weinberger et al. (1979, p.378) concluded that repressors employ a coping style that involves:

> An avoidance of disturbing cognitions ... supported by ... denial of cognitive (relative to somatic) anxiety and ... decreased trait anxiety following a stressful experiment ... [the] repressors claim of having less trait anxiety than the lowest group is contradicted by three measures of their behaviour for three of their physiology.

These findings were replicated by Gudjonsson (1981), Asendorpf and Scherer (1983), Jamner and Schwartz (1986), Schwartz (1990), and Newton and Contrada (1992).

Deception of self and others by repressors

Integral to the concept of the repressive coping style and a clearer link to the emotion of happiness is the fact that repressors, by psychometric definition, score high on measures of social desirability. High scores on such measures imply that repressors, either consciously or unconsciously, are employing processes of "self-deception". However, research findings also suggest that repressors are attempting to deceive others. For example, Jensen (1987) administered the Self Deception Questionnaire (SDQ) and the Other Deception Questionnaire (ODQ; Sackeim & Gur, 1978) to groups of repressors and non-repressors. The repressors, relative to the non-repressors, reported significantly more self-deception *and* other-deception. There are clear limitations to the conclusions which can be drawn from simple self-report studies such as this and a far more innovative study was employed by Baumeister and Cairns (1992) in a series of two experiments. The first experiment employed two conditions: public and private. In the private condition, subjects were anonymous and in the public condition subjects were asked for their names and other personal details. Subjects were required to complete a number of computer-administered tests. The computer then generated a personality profile, either good or bad, reportedly based on the results of the tests. Subjects in the private condition received reassurance that nobody would ever see the profile and it was just data to investigate broad population trends. In contrast, subjects in the public condition were informed that the personality profile would be shown to their partner. All subjects were left alone to read the profile at their leisure.

Repressors who received a negative profile in the private condition spent the least amount of time reading it, whereas repressors who received a negative profile in the public condition spent the longest amount of time reading it. Furthermore, repressors overall spent less time reading the unfavourable profile in relation to the favourable profile. The non-repressor subjects were unaffected by the favourability or the public nature of the situation.

In the second experiment, only the public condition was employed but the methodology was extended to ask subjects their thoughts whilst reading the personality feedback. The results of Experiment 1 were replicated; in addition, the repressor subjects showed an elevated tendency to think about how their partner might use the personality profile to form an impression of them. Overall, the data suggested that repressors spent a long time reading their feedback in both experiments because they were trying to think of ways to refute the personality profile, as opposed to worrying about any impression they were making on others.

In summary, the authors concluded that the results of the two experiments suggested that repressors are able to avoid distressing information in private by ignoring it but are unable to employ this technique in public. In this latter condition, repressors will attend closely to the negative information, conceptualise the impression which their partner will form of them, and generate ways to refute the negative information about themselves. Similar results have been reported by Newton and Contrada (1992).

Secondary emotions and the intensity of emotions in repressors

Numerous research findings (e.g. Davis, 1987) have indicated that repressors do not differ from non-repressors in terms of the self-reported intensity of emotional experience for primary, dominant emotions in response to memories or events. However, significant group differences are found for non-dominant or secondary emotions to such events on memories. For example, Weinberger and Schwartz (reported in Schwartz, 1982) asked groups of repressors and non-repressors to rate the levels of emotional intensity to hypothetical scenarios such as discovering that their car had been broken into. Repressors reported similar levels of intensity for anger (the primary, dominant emotion) to the low anxious subjects; however, with respect to secondary constellations of emotions such as depression, the repressors reported experiencing less intense affect than the low anxious controls. Similar results have been found by Hansen (Hansen & Hansen, 1988; Hansen, Hansen, & Shantz, 1992). Furthermore, Sincoff (1992), using groups of school children and undergraduates, showed that repressors at all educational grades reported lower levels of mixed feelings and significantly greater certainty about their feelings than control groups.

Cognitive processing biases and repressors

As we have discussed above, in definitional terms repressors do not differ from low anxious subjects on scores on anxiety measures (e.g. the Speilberger State Trait Anxiety Inventory; Speilberger et al., 1970). This has clear implications for the research on information processing biases and anxiety discussed in Chapter 6 on Fear; namely that the supposed low-anxious subjects in those research studies, because they are selected on the basis of questionnaire measures, are likely to include individuals who are not genuinely low anxious but are in fact so-called repressors. These implications are few if there are no information processing or cognitive processing differences between repressors and genuine low-anxious individuals; however, a number of experimental investigations have shown that this is not the case.

Research in this area was pioneered by Penny Davis and her colleagues (e.g. Davis, 1987, 1990; Davis & Schwartz, 1987; Davis, Singer, Bonanno, & Schwartz, 1988). In the first of these studies (Davis & Schwartz, 1987) subjects were asked to free-recall personal experiences from childhood. Repressors recalled fewer negative memories than controls. Furthermore, the age of the subject at the time of the first negative memory recalled was substantially greater in the repressor group. Similar findings in studies in which response bias has been ruled out in various ways have been reported by Davis (1987), Davis et al. (1988), and by Myers (Myers, 1993; Myers & Brewin, 1994).

As with all autobiographical memory tasks, the question arises as to whether the repressors actually experienced fewer negative events in childhood or are merely failing to remember them. Lynn Myers (Myers, 1993; Myers & Brewin, 1994) examined this question by using semi-structured interviews with groups of repressors and controls in which subjects were asked detailed questions about their childhood. She found that repressors' accounts of their childhood were more likely to be characterised by paternal antipathy and indifference and that the repressors were less likely to record an emotionally or physically close relationship with their fathers. It seems, then, that repressors do have negative events in their autobiographical past, but that access to those events is difficult in simple recall scenarios.

In addition to research investigating mnemonic biases in repressors, there are a number of studies which have looked at attentional processes. For example, Fox (1993) used the attentional deployment paradigm of MacLeod et al. (1986) to investigate the allocation of attention in groups of repressors and controls. This paradigm is described in detail in Chapter 6. Fox's results showed that high anxious subjects seem to shift their attention towards socially threatening words whereas repressors shifted their attention away from such words and the low anxious subjects showed no consistent biases.

Similar results were reported using a dichotic listening methodology (Bonanno, Davis, Singer, & Schwartz, 1991), the modified Stroop task (Dawkins & Furnham, 1989), and a negative priming task (Fox, 1994). Taken together, these studies suggest that repressors are able to orientate their attention actively away from unwanted material and, furthermore, that there is an automatic attentional bias which serves to screen out socially-threatening material.

The concept of repression within SPAARS

We have speculated about the various roles of inhibition processes within SPAARS in detail in Chapter 5. Within the analysis which we presented there, repression would be a clear example of dominant schematic models of the world, self, and others configuring the system in such a way that incongruent information at other levels (propositional, analogical, associative) becomes inaccessible. In the case of repressors it seems that the dominant schematic models may be such that *any* disturbing information is incompatible. The overvalued nature of such models would be a function of the individual's developmental history in which disturbing information and the congruent expression of emotions might well have been regarded as unacceptable and weak. There is tentative support for this suggestion in Myers' work which reveals a certain amount of emotional aridity and paternal indifference in the childhood of repressors (Myers, 1993).

The psychology of repressors seems a clear illustration of the role of inhibition processes within a SPAARS analysis. As we have discussed in Chapter 5, we propose that for some individuals the fulfilment of core appraisal criteria for certain emotions leads to a simultaneous imperative for the generation of emotion-related products such as physiological change, action potential, and conscious awareness on the one hand and an inhibition of the experience of that emotion as a function of dominant schematic models which have become established during the individuals' development on the other hand. In the case of repressors this would mean that physiological concomitants of emotion would be present but the individual have no experience of that emotion and this is what the research data suggest (e.g. Weinberger et al., 1979). A further suggestion in Chapter 5 was that such emotional inhibition utilises processing resources and consequently less resources are available for the more sophisticated appraisals necessary as part of the generation of more complex emotional states. Again, the research which indicates restricted experience of mixed and secondary emotions in repressors provides partial support for this hypothesis (e.g. Sincoff, 1992). Finally, the suggestion that there is still an imperative for the generation of emotion products and the consequent modular reconfigur-ation of SPAARS, following the fulfilment of core appraisal criteria in repressors would predict that repressors should exhibit processing biases for emotion-congruent information and again the available evidence is broadly consistent with this suggestion (e.g. Davis, 1987).

A note on happiness and personality

Contemporary research into personality focuses more and more on the "big five" personality traits: introversion–extraversion, neuroticism (or negative affectivity), openness to experience, agreeableness, and conscientiousness (e.g. Digman, 1990; McCrae, 1992). A host of studies indicate that individuals who score highly on extraversion and/or low on neuroticism tend to report greater happiness (e.g. Costa & McCrae, 1980; Emmons & Diener, 1985; Larsen & Ketelaar, 1989). Similarly, openness to experience, agreeableness, and conscientiousness also make contributions to self-reported happiness over and above the contributions of the other big five dimensions. Indeed, McCrae and Costa (1991) found that the five factors accounted together for some 25% of the variance of avowed happiness.

Other researchers have delved more deeply into the processes that relate personality characteristics to emotional well-being or happiness. For example, Pavot, Diener, and Fujita (1990) and Diener, Sandvik, Pavot, and Fujita (1992) showed that extraverts report being happier even when alone, and were happier than introverts regardless of whether or not they worked in a social or non-social job. Furthermore, Larsen and Ketelaar (1989, 1991) showed that extraverts were more susceptible than introverts to experimentally induced positive affect whereas high-neuroticism subjects were more susceptible than stable subjects to negative mood inductions.

At the present time, the jury is still out as to what the processes which link personality characteristics and happiness might be. Averill and Moore (1993) suggest that similar mechanisms may facilitate both a particular personality trait and the emotion of happiness, thus explaining the relation between the two. For example, with the case of extraversion they suggest that extraverts may be inherently less sensitive to negative reinforcement or punishment or that extraverts may be more engaged in convivial activities, or, finally, that they may be more likely to make favourable comparisons between the self and others.

EMOTIONAL STATES RELATED TO HAPPINESS

Throughout this chapter we have conceptualised happiness as an emotional state which conflates across a number of different dimensions and levels of the cognitive system. We also noted at the start of the chapter that there is a host of other positive emotional states which seem much more specific than what we have called happiness; for example joy, gladness, being pleased, satisfaction, delight, exhilaration, ecstasy, and so on. In addition, there are a number of quite complex emotional states which clearly have one of these positive emotions as an ingredient; for example, nostalgia, homesickness, love. In this section we shall discuss a *selection* of these aspects of emotional life and their relationship to happiness. Our analyses are by no means comprehensive; rather, the intention is to provide some pointers to the more complex emotions which we think are derived from or related to the basic emotion which is the focus of the chapter.

Love

It would be unforgiveable to write a book on the psychology of emotions without spending some time talking about perhaps the most compelling and sought after emotional state of all. An excellent overall review is provided in Hatfield and Rapson's (1993) book *Love, Sex, and Intimacy: Their Psychology, Biology, and History* and so we shall limit our discussion to a number of selected points.

Any trip to the popular psychology shelves of the local bookshop will reveal the central place that love, intimacy, and attachment have in our emotional lives. However, along with a host of books on how to fall in love and how to love the same person for the whole of your life, we are also invited to browse books on women who love too much or pathological love or erotomania or a whole range of what we might conceive of as "love disorders". Such a cursory content analysis of the book shelves raises a number of interesting questions: is there just one type of love? Is the love which we feel when we love someone for the whole of our lives the same as the love we yearn for when we are trying to fall in love? Is the person who is seen as "loving too much", or loves "pathologically" just choosing the "wrong" partners or is he somehow loving in the "wrong" way? We shall endeavour to delve into some of these mysteries of love and offer some thoughts as to how different aspects of love might be conceptualised. Embarking on such an exercise, it is well to bear in mind Valéry's caveat (cited in Rilke, 1986) to aspiring poets: "that in the making of a work an act comes into contact with the indefinable".

Several researchers have proposed typologies for the varieties of love. For example, Hatfield and Rapson contend that two kinds of love can be distinguished: passionate love (sometimes called obsessive love, infatuation, love sickness, or being in love) and companionate love (sometimes called fondness). Other researchers have been more elaborate; for example, Lee (e.g. 1976) described six love styles: Eros (romantic love), Ludus (game-playing love), Storge (friendship love), Mania (possessive love), Pragma (logical love), and Agape (selfless love). In tandem with these taxonomies, a number of questionnaire measures of love have been developed; for example, the Passionate Love Scale (Hatfield & Sprecher, 1986) and the Love Style Questionnaire (e.g. Mallandain & Davies, 1994). In this section we shall talk briefly about passionate love which we equate with Lee's concept of Eros and in more detail about companionate love which we equate with Lee's concept of Storge. Finally, we shall touch on varieties of so-called pathological love, some of which are related to Lee's other love styles.

Some remarks on passionate love.   Hatfield and Rapson (1993, p.5) have defined passionate love as follows:

> A state of intense longing for union with another. Reciprocated love (union with the other) is associated with fulfilment and ecstasy. Unrequited love (separation) is associated with emptiness, anxiety, or despair. Passionate love is a complex functional whole including appraisals or appreciations, subjective feelings, expressions, patterned physiological processes, action tendencies, and instrumental behaviours.

It is clear from this attempt at a definition that Hatfield and Rapson conceptualise passionate love as consisting of the same types of components which we and others have argued constitute all emotional states: appraisals, subjective feelings, physiological change, action tendencies, and interpretations. But what type of emotion is passionate love? The problematic nature of such a question is well illustrated by a cross-cultural study carried out by Shaver, Wu, and Schwartz (1991). They interviewed students in the United States, Italy, and the Peoples Republic of China about a variety of emotional experiences including happiness, love, fear, anger, and sadness. There was a remarkable level of cross-cultural agreement concerning all of these emotions except for one—love. The subjects from the United States and Italy tended to equate love with happiness and other positive affective states. The Chinese students, on the other hand, had a far bleaker view of love. In Chinese there are few idiographs which correspond to the happy love words found in Western languages; instead love is associated with sadness and other negative emotions. The Chinese subjects associated passionate love with idiographs which translate as "infatuation", "unrequited love", "nostalgia", and "sorrow love". When informed about the views of love of other cultures, both the Eastern and Western Groups regarded each other's visions of love as "unrealistic".

Perhaps both groups are correct. Is not passionate love a combination of exhilaration and despair, joy and sadness, with healthy doses of shyness, jealousy, anger, ecstasy, and insecurity thrown in? Indeed, Tennov (1979), who interviewed more than 500 lovers, concluded that almost all of them took it for granted that passionate love is a bitter-sweet experience—the biggest and most frightening emotional roller coaster of them all!

An important point which Hatfield and Rapson miss in their attempt at definition is the very passionate nature of passionate love. Like anger (see Chapter 9), the ability of passionate love to overwhelm individuals provides a vehicle by which they can be absolved of the responsibility for their behaviour. Such passions, it is argued (e.g. Averill, 1985, 1990; Oatley, 1992), enable the individual to take on a role in which they can do things that are out of the ordinary. Oatley cites the example of Anna Karenina, with which we opened the chapter. By falling passionately in love, Anna left her albeit suffocating marriage, was separated from her child, rejected by her friends, and lost all of the support offered by her previous way of living. This excommunication eventually led to Anna's suicide.

In an evolutionary sense, falling passionately in love clearly has functionality. It provides the momentum for binding two people together to form a relationship, to have children, and to raise their children. One can even go further than this; Oatley suggests that often emotions function when rational solutions are unavailable. The implication being that the only way you could find yourself entering into a mutual plan as momentus as a long-term relationship, is if you are carried there by the overwhelming passion of an emotion.

Companionate love.   Companionate or conjugal love seems a far less intense emotion than passionate love, though it involves feelings of deep attachment, commitment, sharing, and intimacy. As with passionate love, Hatfield and Rapson (1993, p.9) have attempted a definition. Companionate love is:

> The affection and tenderness we feel for those with whom our lives are deeply entwined, companionate love is a complex functional whole including appraisals or appreciations, subjective feelings, expressions, patterned physiological processes, action tendencies, and instrumental behaviours.

Again, this definition is perhaps not quite adequate. Much of the definitions of passionate love and companionate love are word for word the same and there is very little explication of how one differs from the other. Is companionate love, in Hatfield and Rapsons' eyes, merely passionate love which has lost its intensity? Certainly, companionate love seems more approachable in theoretical terms than its passionate counterpart. It seems that companionate love can be conceptualised in a similar way to the analysis of happiness presented earlier. The crucial difference being that the goal domains and levels which drive the emotion of happiness are essentially those of the individual, whereas for the emotion of companionate love it is necessary to apply a dyadic framework. Companionate love is a function of not only having an investment in one's own goals but also an investment in the goals of our partner in the various domains of self, other, and self plus other. Furthermore, requited companionate love involves the sense that our own goals across various domains are shared by our partner. This sharing of goals leads to the sense of feeling understood and accepted, of sharing a sense of union, and at feeling secure and safe, which characterise companionate love.

Perhaps discovering the potential for such sharing of goals across different domains is what occurs in passionate love. One can speculate that passionate love is the enthralling, desperate, exciting, whirlwind of emotions which arises from the discovery that here is someone with whom I can potentially share goals and needs and who can share his or hers with me. Perhaps, as Oatley (1992) suggests, such monumental mutual planning is so daunting a prospect that we need something like passionate love to blind us to all the possible pitfalls!

A note on nostalgia and homesickness

The combination of the emotion of joy with the emotion of sadness we suggest gives rise to the two complex emotional states of homesickness and nostalgia. Homesick individuals reflect on the home they have left behind with a mixture of sadness at the loss (albeit sometimes temporarily) of home life and joy at the memories of the many rewarding things which are incorporated in the idea of the home. Similarly, nostalgia involves looking back at aspects of our personal past, or sometimes even the historical past of our country or family, with the same mixture of sadness that those times are no more, and happiness at the rewards and fulfilment that those times brought. Both of these complex emotions, we propose, would be a result of coupling within SPAARS (see Chapter 5), so that the same event (the home or an aspect of the past) leads to simultaneous appraisals at the schematic model level related to joy and sadness. One or both of these appraisal-based emotion pathways can also, we suggest, become automatised, such that reminders of the past or home can automatically lead to pangs of sadness, joy or the complex states of nostalgia or homesickness. In some cases it is as though everything is a reminder of what used to be.

Recently, there has been increased interest in the effects of homesickness on the performance of workers and students who are away from home. Shirley Fisher (e.g. Fisher & Hood, 1988) has suggested, for example, that homesickness decreases individuals' ability to attend to the task at hand and that this may lead to decrements in their performance. However, other researchers (e.g. Burt, 1993) whilst agreeing that homesickness can affect concentration, dispute the fact that alone it can account for any marked loss in academic or work performance.

HAPPINESS DISORDER

The concept of happiness "disorder" is one which is rarely discussed in the emotion literature. Perhaps it is because, in Western society, we are more tolerant of variations and extremes within the parameters, both cognitive and physiological, which define a particular individual's positive emotions and are thus less likely to "label" the emotion as disordered than in the case of extreme variants of negative emotions such as anger, fear, or sadness. In other, non-Western cultures happiness or joy are regarded are far less socially acceptable than in the West. For example, the Ifaluk, whom we discussed previously, equate happiness with a tendency for the individual to disregard others and the needs of the social group. For the Ifaluk, then, happiness is a negative emotion, whereas sadness is encouraged as a positive emotional state. Despite the paucity of discussion in the literature on abnormal happiness, we propose that extreme variations in the cognitive or physiological parameters which contribute to the emotion of happiness may be usefully conceptualised as types of "happiness disorder". It is these varieties of happiness disorder which we discuss in the present section and again the aim is to provide some pointers rather than any comprehensive analysis.

Hypomania and mania

Mrs Evans had been diagnosed by the junior psychiatrist as suffering from mania. She had been brought into the emergency referral clinic by her son who had come home to find her sitting in the living room surrounded by new, expensive commodities she had purchased with her cheque book, even though there was not enough money in the bank to cover the outgoings. Mrs Evans was extremely happy about her new acquisitions but, when her son pointed out that she had done something wrong, she very quickly became petulant and started throwing things at him. In the ward round, after the junior psychiatrist had presented Mrs

Evans' case, she was invited in to talk to the team. She immediately tried to sit on the consultant's lap and flirted with him outrageously throughout their short chat. The consultant tried to ask Mrs Evans how she was feeling and to talk to her about medication, but she seemed unable to concentrate on his words and her conversation leapt, seemingly at random, from one topic to another, each sentence ended by her characteristic giggle.

Perhaps the disorders which seem most clearly ones of happiness or positive mood are Hypomania and Mania. The central features are elevation of mood, hyperactivity, and grandiose ideas about the self. Manic individuals often seem cheerful and optimistic when their mood is elevated and have an infectious gaiety. However, other individuals can be irritable rather than euphoric and their emotions are extremely labile so that this irritability can easily translate into anger. There is often diurnal variation in the individual's mood, whether it be irritable or euphoric. However, this variation does not normally conform to the regular patterns of other depressive disorders (see Chapter 7). Even in patients who are elated, it is not unusual for their periods of elevated mood to be interrupted by brief episodes of depression.

The manic individual's choice of clothing often reflects the prevailing mood—there is an emphasis on bright colours and ill-matching garments. In more severe cases of mania, individuals often appear untidy and dishevelled. Manic persons are highly active, often leading to physical exhaustion. Furthermore, many activities are started but seldom finished as new activities become more tempting; speech is often rapid and copious and, in more severe cases, there is marked flight of ideas such that it is difficult to follow the train of thought of the manic person's discourse. Sleep is often impoverished or absent with early morning waking, appetite is increased as are sexual desires; indeed, sexual behaviour may be uninhibited.

Finally, manic individuals commonly experience expansive ideas. They believe that their thoughts and ideas are original, their opinions important, and their work of the most outstanding quality. Occasionally these expansive themes merge into grandiose delusions in which the individual believes he or she is a religious prophet or a famous person. Such grandiosity and expansiveness also manifests in extravagant behaviour; manic individuals often spend more than they can afford, and make reckless decisions, give up good jobs, or embark on schemes and ventures which have little chance of success. Such problems are compounded by impaired insight in most cases. Manic individuals will often see no reason why their grandiose plans should be reined in or their extravagant expenditure curtailed. Manic individuals rarely think of themselves as having an emotional problem or needing any kind of help (see Kay Jamison's, 1995, autobiography for a vivid account of these characteristics).

In mania and hypomania, it appears that the individuals' dominant schematic models of self are highly self-serving, leading to the settting of unrealistic and optimistic goals. The achievement of these goals, or the belief that they have been achieved, is a source of joy and elation. There seems to be little or no access to the representations of the goals of others and, most notably, the shared goals of self and others—the social standards which are so important on setting limits on behaviour. Allied with this is the manic person's tendency to switch from periods of extreme gaiety to periods of intense anger or depression. It seems that different configurations of self-related schematic models come to dominate and regulate the system, such that at one moment everything is all rosy and the next it is all black. The tendency for mania and hypomania to co-occur with depression provides a difficult challenge that no biological or psychological theory has effectively accounted for (see also Chapter 7 on sadness). One might speculate that, first, if the self becomes predominantly organised around issues of success versus failure, appraisals of goal attainment versus goal failure for a highly invested domain are very likely to occur at different points, so the person may swing between the emotions of joy, sadness, and self-disgust accordingly. Second, one of the findings that distinguishes bipolar disorders from other disorders of depression is the substantial genetic component in the bipolar disorders (McGuffin & Katz, 1989); perhaps this genetic component influences the development of the basic emotions early on, so that they are more likely to be unintegrated with each other. This proposal would suggest that this would be true not only for the basic emotions of sadness and happiness, but for the other basic emotions as well.

Personality disorders

We have suggested above that individuals' sense of happiness conflates across a number of domains of their life (self, others, and self plus others) and across higher-order and lower-order goals within those domains. We have also discussed, albeit briefly, Averill's suggestion that, for most of us, even in supposedly individualistic societies, there is an investment weighting towards the shared domain of self and others—at the end of the day, we are all essentially social beings. Within this framework, individuals whose sense of happiness is a result of over-investment in the self domain might be thought of as struggling with "disordered happiness".

We all know individuals whom we consider to be arrogant, selfish, self-absorbed or insensitive to the needs of others. However, these patterns can also be found in the diagnostic profiles of a number of the so-called personality disorders (American Psychiatric Association, 1994). For example, the criteria for Antisocial Personality Disorder include something like the following: a failure to conform to social norms with respect to lawful behaviour; deceitfulness; reckless disregard for the safety of others; consistent irresponsibility, and lack of remorse as indicated by being indifferent to the concerns of others:

> Jack was a builders' labourer and married with two children. As a child he had been fostered after he was repeatedly beaten by his natural father. Jack had a childhood history of conduct disorder and behavioural problems and he started small-scale criminal activities at the age of 14. He had served two prison sentences for robbery and violent assault. Jack reluctantly entered therapy after an incident in which he had assaulted his wife and felt like he was going to kill her. Jack regarded his irritability and anger control problems as the things he would most like to change. However, he showed little motivation as it was his wife who had insisted that he come for help and he was only doing it to "shut her up". Jack was a heavy drinker and had used illicit drugs in the past.

It seems that through his development Jack had not internalised the need to facilitate the fulfilment of others' goals and needs. All that was important to Jack was his own goals and wants. This led to a lifestyle in which his disregard for others led him into trouble and eventually into therapy.

The psychiatric criteria for so-called narcissistic personality disorder include symptoms such as an unwillingness to recognise or identify with the feelings or needs of others and the expression of arrogant, haughty behaviours or attitudes:

> Angela was a successful journalist. She wrote a regular weekly column for a major national newspaper and did a lot of lucrative freelance work. Angela believed that this was no less than she deserved as she was different—more talented, more special, more enthralling than anyone she knew. Angela was very engaging on first meeting; she came over as thoughtful and understanding and people used to seek her company again. After a while, however, the façade seemed to crack and people began to feel manipulated by

Angela. At work she had a reputation for absorbing other people's ideas and making them her own. She had a talent for understanding how the world of journalism worked and this brought her considerable success; however, she was generally regarded as having little creative ability. Angela herself would never have tolerated such criticism. It was her view that she enhanced the lives of those around her and the slightest sign of criticism used to lead her to cruel and vicious acts of revenge. Yes, she would agree, that she did take advantage of people but, if they were stupid enough to let her, then what was the problem? Angela knew that one day she would be famous and would leave such petty individuals behind.

Again, as with the case of Jack, Angela seems to show scant regard for the goals and needs of others. She is entirely invested in goals in the self domain. Unlike Jack, who seems unaware of others' needs, Angela seems all too aware, she simply feels that her needs are far more important.

A note on "disorders" of love

It was inevitable: the scent of bitter almonds always reminded him of the fate of unrequited love. (Love in the Time of Cholera, *Gabriel García Márquez*, 1989)

The smell of almonds, of course, is the aroma of the poison cyanide and it is testament to the power of passionate love that, when it goes unrequited, the rejected individual can be driven to suicide and more. This is one way in which love can go off the rails; we can fall in love with people who seem to be inappropriate in that they are either unlikely to return our love or that somehow they would not make good companions in a relationship. It seems possible, then, for love to be "disordered" with respect to who we love. However, it is not just who we love but the way we love that is fraught with danger for are not the "women who love too much" of bookshelf fame also viewed as exhibiting "disordered love"?

Both of these aspects of love, it has been argued, can be understood more clearly in terms of attachment theory (e.g. Bowlby, 1969, 1973, 1980). Bowlby proposed three styles of attachment in infancy: avoidant, secure, and anxious/ambivalent. Recently, Hazan and Shaver (1987) have proposed that these infant attachment styles manifest themselves in adulthood in the way that the adult attaches in the loving relationship. They proposed that children with secure infant attachments who are allowed to be both affectionate towards, and independent of, their mothers are likely to mature into secure adults who are able to engage in comfortable intimate relationships with trust and a healthy level of dependence on their partners. Children with anxious/ambivalent attachment relationships to their mothers have learned to be clinging and dependent, or fearful of being smothered or both. Such children, Shaver and Hazan suggest, are likely to become anxious/ambivalent adults. They will fall in love easily, they will seek extremely high levels of closeness and intimacy, and they will be terrified that they will be abandoned. The love affairs they have are thus likely to be very short-lived. Finally, the avoidant child who has been abandoned early on in infancy is likely, it is suggested, to become an avoidant adult. He or she will be uncomfortable getting too close and will have difficulty depending on others. Shaver and Hazan (1988) have amassed considerable support in favour of this formulation and similar formulations have been proposed by other authors (e.g. Bartholomew, 1990).

The idea that our "choice" of lover is also somehow a function of our attachment processes is clearly not a new one. It is a fundamental concept in psychodynamic psychology. For many people, this choice is likely to be a functional one. The potential lover often has qualities which would also make them a good partner in a loving relationship over the long term. However, for other individuals the people who rouse their passions are exactly the sort of people whom their rational thoughts tell them should be avoided. Furthermore, as we have mentioned above, for the majority of individuals the choice of lover is partly a function of the likelihood that the chosen person will reciprocate our feelings. However, for others, there is often a pattern of falling in love with people with whom the chances of a reciprocated loving relationship are small or non-existent. This is manifest, in its most extreme form, in the disorder of erotomania or De Clerambault's syndrome in which individuals fall in love with public figures or famous personages whom they are unlikely even to meet. The sobering example of this is the case of John Hinckley, mentioned in Chapter 1, who attempted to assassinate Ronald Reagan in 1981 as a last ditch attempt to impress the actress Jody Foster with whom he reported being desperately in love.

In summary, we have ended the last of our chapters on specific basic emotions with some remarks on the nature of love. We have tried to indicate that it is possible (if not necessarily forgiveable) to make some interesting theoretical remarks about love without destroying its essence and it is our hope that this philosophy is true of all the aspects of emotional life we have sought to explain throughout the book.

CONCLUDING REMARKS

In this final chapter on the basic emotions we have made two important shifts in the focus of our theoretical analysis. The first is from the consideration of negative emotions to the consideration of positive ones; the second is from an analysis of emotions related to the fate of specific goals to the consideration of an emotional state, which for the present purposes we have labelled Happiness, which reflects the goal status of the whole system.

Our analysis of happiness is intended to show how the whole of the SPAARS model of emotion can function over and above the workings of its constituent parts. Being happy does not preclude ever being sad, angry, disgusted, or afraid and, indeed, if this were the case then you would have to question the status of such happiness (see the section on repressors).

In the final chapter we continue this attempt to draw together the constituent parts of the SPAARS approach and endeavour to give a sense of the whole and the implications of this account for the clinic and for future research.

CHAPTER ELEVEN

Overview and conclusions

You can't fool me, there ain't no Sanity Clause. *(Chico Marx)*

INTRODUCTION

The aims of this final chapter are, first, to draw together the key components of the model that we have presented over the previous chapters and, second, to present some of the therapeutic and research implications that result from this framework. One of the key tests for any model is of course its usefulness, whether it ultimately turns out to be true or false. We hope to demonstrate therefore that the SPAARS approach has within it a number of non-trivial implications for therapeutic practice together with a number of non-trivial research predictions that, we believe, should help to distinguish it from competitor models.

In Chapter 1 and in subsequent chapters we raised a number of questions about what an emotion is and how emotion should be best approached and understood. We identified two main approaches that can be tracked historically to the present day. The first approach, stemming from Plato and reaching its height in the philosophy of Descartes and the psychology of William James, identified emotion with conscious "feelings", which did not play a causal role in behaviour. The second approach, which has only recently gained precedence, stemmed from Aristotle and has provided the starting point for a number of functionalist models of emotion. The key distinction made by Aristotle was between matter and function; thus, although it is possible to describe an emotion in terms of its physical nature, such as its physiology and behaviour, it is necessary to know the biological, psychological, and social *functions* of an emotion otherwise it cannot be adequately described or modelled.

On the basis of more recent philosophical and psychological models (see especially Chapters 2 and 3), the following components of emotion can be identified; these are an initiating event (external or internal), an interpretation, an appraisal of the interpretation especially in relation to goal relevance, physiological reaction, an action potential, conscious awareness, and overt behaviour. Probably all of these components are necessary for emotion, with the possible exception of conscious awareness; we argued that the concept of "emotion" is a holistic one that covered all of these potential components, but it was not identifiable with any one component in particular. This holistic approach is contrary to prior theories that have equated emotion for example with the conscious feeling, or with the physiology and overt behaviour.

We also reviewed other aspects of the range of cognitive models, both philosophical and psychological, and summarised their strengths and weaknesses as models of emotion. One of the starting points that we then took for our own SPAARS approach is the proposal that there are five basic emotions—not three, not eight, not 57—but five, which can be distinguished in terms of their basic appraisals. How can we be so sure of this number when other basic emotion theorists are criticised for failing to agree on any precise number (e.g. Russell, 1994)? There is little doubt that the evidence from studies of child development, universal recognition of facial expression, physiological distinctiveness, linguistic analyses, and emotion concept analyses suggest different numbers of potential emotions (see Chapter 3). This conflict does not imply that the evidence is contradictory but, rather, that these systems also serve functions other than those related to emotions. For example, facial expression serves to communicate a wide range of drive-related, non-emotional cognitive and interpersonal states such as pain, hunger, interest, and surprise; physiology too reflects a vast array of non-emotional states. Part of the confusion therefore about the exact number of basic emotions reflects the misidentification of emotion with one particular expressive system. Because of this multi-functional nature of expression systems, it is necessary to take each as a triangulation point rather than the definite location; in statistical terms, taking a multi-trait multi-method approach may be necessary in order to determine the true number of latent traits (or basic emotions) within the data.

In relation to the question of the number of basic emotions, there is one piece of further crucial evidence that has generally failed to be taken account of in the debate; namely, how many basic emotions need to be posited in order to account for the range of emotional disorders? Indeed, here lies the weakness in a number of theoretical approaches to emotional disorders: many fail to offer generic models applicable to all disorders, but, instead, focus on one or two disorders typically related to anxiety and depression (e.g. Gray, 1982; Watson & Clark, 1992). A further problem (see Chapter 4) is that some generic theories of emotional disorders such as Beck's (1976) cognitive therapy are agnostic in relation to basic emotions and any number of such emotions could be accommodated within the models in an *ad hoc* fashion. As we have demonstrated in the previous chapters and will summarise in this one, we believe that the range of so-called emotional disorders can be derived from the five basic emotions of fear, anger, sadness, disgust, and happiness operating either singly or in combination. The fact that this derivation is possible is, we believe, powerful evidence that these form *the* five basic emotions.

SUMMARY OF THE SPAARS MODEL

The cognitive model of emotion that has been presented throughout this book is summarised in Fig. 11.1. The model is multi-level and includes four different levels of representation. The initial processing of stimuli occurs through a number of mode-specific or sensory-specific systems such as the visual, the auditory, the tactile, the proprioceptive, and the olfactory which we have grouped together as the analogical representation system; the importance of such systems in emotions and emotional disorders is clearly evident for example in post traumatic stress disorder (see Chapter 6) in which certain sights, sounds or smells may become inherent parts of the traumatic event. The output from analogical processing may then feed into three semantic representation systems operating in parallel. At the lower level there is an associative system which, in terms of current possible architectures, may take the form of a number of potentially modularised connectionist networks.

The intermediate level of semantic representation within SPAARS is the Propositional. This is the most language-like level of representation, though, as explained in Chapter 5, propositions are not language specific: most propositional representations are expressed in the form of one or more arguments linked by a predicate as in the example

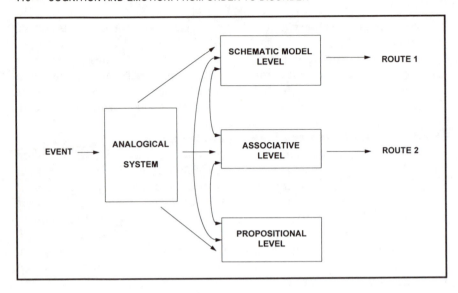

FIG. 11.1. Two routes to emotion within the SPAARS multi-level representation system. Route 1 includes the appraisal of a goal-relevant event; Route 2 is a direct access route of which the person may not be aware.

IS(SPAARS, USEFUL), which we leave to the reader to interpret! Although such propositional representations have played a key role in the generation of emotion in a number of theories, such as the role of propositional level automatic thoughts in Beck's (e.g. 1976) Cognitive Therapy (see Chapter 4), we propose that there is no direct route from propositions to emotion, but that they feed either through appraisals at the schematic model level (see later) or directly through the associative route. For example, particular words or phrases may become directly linked to emotion for certain individuals; thus, swear words come in a whole range of culture-specific forms. These words and phrases are normally designed to elicit an emotional reaction in the recipient, which, we suggest, is typically through the direct access route. Indeed, the fact that such words seem to be retained longest even in the lexical access problems seen with extreme alcoholic Korsakoff's conditions suggests that they may be stored separately to non-emotion laden words and phrases. In addition, of course, each individual will collect a set of unique words and phrases which may also directly access emotion through the associative route: significant names and significant places provide two such examples (cf. the classic "cocktail party phenomenon", Cherry, 1953).

The highest level of semantic representation, as illustrated in Fig. 11.1, we have labelled the Schematic Model level. The term is taken from

Teasdale and Barnard (1993); it is designed to capture the advantages of a mental models level of representation (Johnson-Laird, 1983), a level that is designed to integrate intensional and extensional information in a flexible and dynamic fashion, in combination with the advantages of the more traditional schema approach, which provides a good account of repetitive and invariant relationships between concepts but which is weakest therefore where more flexible representations are needed (Kahneman & Miller, 1986). In relation to emotion, the Schematic Model level is extremely important because it is at this level that the generation of emotion occurs through the process of appraisal (shown as Route 1 in Figure 11.1). The key processes through this route include therefore the interpretation and appraisal of any relevant input, whether of external or internal origin, according to the basic appraisal processes considered in the previous chapters. Table 11.1 presents a summary of these core appraisals for each of the five basic emotions.

The core appraisal for Fear involves the interpretation of threat to the individual, for example, to the individual's physical safety, or to the individual's goals or plans (in addition to the goal of physical safety), or of threat to something or someone valued by the individual. Sadness involves an appraisal of loss or failure, again of something or someone valued by the individual. Anger consists of the frustration or attempted blocking of a goal or plan where there is a perceived agent that has caused the frustration or blocking. The agent, however, while typically taking a human form need not necessarily do so, be it the lamp-post that shouldn't have been there, the glass of milk that shouldn't have spilled, or fate that shouldn't have been against you. Happiness (in the sense of "joy") on the other hand is the achievement of a goal or plan or of movement towards a goal or plan. Finally, disgust is the rejection of something, whether concrete or abstract, that is repulsive to the individual's goals because it is seen to lead to physical or psychological contamination; our definition therefore goes beyond the traditional

TABLE 11.1
The key appraisals for each of the five basic emotions

Basic emotion	Appraisal
Sadness	Loss or failure (actual or possible) of valued role or goal
Happiness	Successful move towards or completion of a valued role or goal
Anger	Blocking or frustration of a role or goal through perceived agent
Fear	Physical or social threat to self or valued role or goal
Disgust	Elimination or distancing from person, object, or idea repulsive to the self and to valued roles and goals

association of disgust with food or faeces to include a range of psychological and interpersonal states that may become repulsive to the individual.

The appraisals outlined in Table 11.1 provide the starting points from which a wide range of more complex emotions are derived, or from which a sequence of emotions may emerge. The idea that complex emotions can be derived from a set of basic emotions has been considered by a number of previous theorists, whether in the form of blends of two or more emotions (e.g. Plutchik, 1980) or in the form of linguistic analyses of complex emotion terms (e.g. Johnson-Laird & Oatley, 1989). Examples of complex emotions and their underlying basic emotions are shown in Table 11.2. Each of the complex emotions listed would typically be derived from the basic emotion with the addition of cognitive complexity including subsequent cycles of appraisal, the involvement of the self, an additional basic emotion, or an interpersonal context. For example, Worry normally takes the form of ruminative anxiety about an unwanted outcome that *might* happen in the future and that might be realistic or unrealistic. Envy typically takes the form of anger towards someone who has something of which the individual feels more deserving. Shame is a feeling of disgust directed towards the self or towards something or someone with which the self identifies and which occurs because of a perceived failing of the self or of the identified-with other. In each of these examples, therefore, complexity is added to the basic emotion through additional cognitive information.

In sequences of different emotions the occurrence of a particular emotion, for example, may itself come to be appraised as the starting point for another emotion; thus, in the discussion of bereavement in

TABLE11.2
Examples of complex emotions derived from each basic emotion

Basic emotion	Examples of complex emotions
Fear	Embarrassment
	Worry
Sadness	Grief
Anger	Envy
	Jealousy
	Contempt
Happiness	Joy
	Love
	Nostalgia
Disgust	Guilt
	Shame

Chapter 7, we noted that some individuals feel guilty whenever they begin to feel angry with the lost person, a repeated sequence that may become automated and thereby block the normal grieving process. Alternatively, sequences of events may unfold which lead to a series of emotions; the tragic case of the man who thought he had won the National Lottery (see Chapter 10), subsequently realised that his ticket had run out the week before, then killed himself the following day reflected the loss of a brief period of ecstatic joy for a life that he might have had rather than the loss of anything that he actually did have. Fortunately, most events do not unfold in such a dramatic fashion, but reflect a sequence of new appraisals as more information becomes available to the individual.

One of the main arguments of this book has been not only that complex emotions can be derived from the underlying set of five basic emotions but also that the emotional disorders can be derived from this same set. As illustrated in Table 11.3, in order to make these derivations some alterations are needed to the normal classifications of emotional disorders. The disorders associated with Fear include some phobias, some obsessional compulsive disorders, generalised anxiety disorder,

TABLE 11.3

Emotional disorders linked to basic emotions. Some apparently unitary disorders have been divided up (labelled as "1" or "2"), whereas other disorders have been derived from the coupling of two basic emotions

Basic emotion	Coupled emotion	Emotional "disorder"
Fear		Panic
		Phobias (1)
		OCD (1)
		GAD
		PTSD (1)
	? Disgust	PTSD (2)
Sadness	Anger	Pathological grief
	Disgust	Depression
Anger		Pathological anger
		Morbid jealousy
Happiness		Polyannaism/pathological optimism
		Hypomania/mania
		Love sickness
		De Clerambault's syndrome
Disgust	? Fear	Phobias (2)
	? Fear	OCD (2)
		Suicide
		Eating disorders, etc.

panic, and post traumatic stress disorder. However, as we argued in Chapter 6 and Chapter 9, there are certain types of phobias and obsessional disorders which do not seem to be predominantly Fear-based, but, instead, appear to be Disgust-based. Phobias of certain insects and animals appear to be based on associations with dirt and contamination rather than fear: if fear were the only component why are there so few lion phobics and car phobics in the world? Of course, not all insect and animal phobias are therefore disgust-based, because traumatic experiences genuinely do occur with, for example, dogs and bees thereby leading to the generation of fear-based phobias.

In the case of obsessional disorders there seems to be a prima facie case for a set of disgust-based disorders; thus, many OCD cases present with concerns about disease, dirt, or contamination which the individual may prevent or obviate through rituals such as washing or through careful avoidance. Other disgust-based reactions may occur in relation to thoughts or impulses which are considered to be dirty in a moral sense and which may reflect unwanted or disowned aspects of the self; for example, impulses to harm or threaten others, and sexual thoughts or impulses. The possible consequences of this process of trying to rid the self of physical or psychological "dirtiness" have been well-expressed by Daniel Wegner in his book *White Bears and Other Unwanted Thoughts* (1989, p.ix):

> Attempts to concentrate, to be happy, to relax, to be good or fair, or even just to hold still, create ironic mental processes that make us do just the opposite of these things— particularly when we are under stress or have a lot on our minds.

We have also highlighted the possibility in Table 11.3 that disgust-based reactions in some post traumatic stress disorders may play an important role. Such disgust reactions can occur towards the self because of the nature of the trauma such as in rape, or, alternatively, the individual may feel shame or guilt because of a perceived role in the cause of the trauma: "if only I hadn't deviated from my usual route ...", "I should have died, not them", "I should have foreseen what was going to happen", and so on. Joseph et al. (1994) have shown that these internal attributions for the causes of traumatic events are more likely to lead to a chronic course for the disorder.

A second important feature of the emotional disorders listed in Table 11.3 is the proposal that some of the disorders may be derived from the coupling of two or more basic emotions, or may involve the "interlocking" of different semantic levels within an emotion module. As argued in

Chapter 6, some forms of depression seem to occur from the coupling of Sadness and Disgust in which the individual feels both sad because of some actual or imagined loss, but, in addition, turns disgust against the self because of perceived inadequacy or culpability. Although previous theorists have derived depression from other combinations, for example, Freud derived Melancholia from Sadness and Anger, and more recent theorists have proposed that the comorbidity of depression and anxiety has theoretical implications (Watson & Clark, 1992), we believe that disgust has been swept under the carpet for too long and that its crucial role, especially in the form of self-disgust (shame), has gone largely unrecognised in relation to both the emotional disorders and a number of other drive-related disorders (see Chapter 9).

Another emotional state which can lead to disorder is that of grief, because of the possible coupling of Sadness with Anger that is typical of this state. Most of the studies show that the loss of something or someone extremely important to the individual involves not only the reaction of sadness, but also anger because of feeling abandoned or whatever (e.g. Bowlby, 1980). The failure to express the anger or the sadness again may lead to atypical grief reactions in which the individual presents in an emotionally disordered way.

Two routes to emotion

One of the distinctive characteristics of the SPAARS model is the fact that emotion can occur through either of two possible routes (see Fig. 11.1 above). The first route is one that is shared with other appraisal theories of emotion and has been sketched in the previous section. The second route, however, requires further comment, both in terms of its operation, and in terms of its relationship to the interpretive–appraisal route.

The need for two routes to emotion is based in part on the fact that the basic emotions have an innate prewired component and, in addition, on the proposal that certain emotions may come to be elicited automatically. For example, Seligman's (1971) proposal that in relation to phobias certain stimuli may be "prepared" stated that people are more likely to develop phobias towards snakes, rats, and spiders, than they are to cars, public transport, and kitchen sinks (despite frequent unpleasant experiences with the latter group). Seligman argued that such biological preparedness made sense on evolutionary grounds, even if individuals had little or no direct experience of these stimuli in modern society. Although Seligman's proposal has had a somewhat chequered history (e.g. Rachman, 1990), it forms part of a more general recognition that genetics provides us with a psychological starting point and a set of maturational tasks, albeit that these paths may ultimately take different courses because of the interaction of cultural, familial and personal factors. The evidence now amassed on the universal expression and recognition of basic emotions, their physiological distinctiveness, and their developmental sequence (see Chapter 3) provides persuasive evidence of an innate component that underlies emotion. The infant's early experience of the emotions of happiness, disgust, anger, fear, and sadness will therefore have an innate starting point, though the subsequent developmental pathways may be dramatically different from individual to individual, just as the objects of these emotional states will also vary dramatically.

An additional way in which emotion might come to be generated through a direct route is from the repeated pairing of certain event–emotion sequences which could eventually lead to the automatisation of the sequence. That is, in a manner akin to the learning of a skill such as swimming or cycling which eventually becomes automatic, it is possible that certain repeated event–emotion experiences could come to be automated. In other words, the repetition eventually bypasses the need for an interpretative appraisal that the event has important implications for one's plans or goals, but the event becomes directly associated with the emotion. There is clear evidence for example from work we reviewed in Chapters 6 and 7 that learning can be implicit as well as explicit and that the subsequent implicit memories can have a wide variety of effects on other processes (e.g. Power & Brewin, 1991; Tobias et al., 1992). It might also be speculated that prewired or prepared innate emotion reactions reflect repeated event–emotion sequences important in the survival of the species that have come to be coded genetically. We should note, however, that although we have presented the two routes as completely separate within SPAARS, many skills are likely to be performed in a semi-automatic way and there are gradations in the process of automatisation (e.g. Logan, 1988). Nevertheless, it is still useful to distinguish the endpoints of this dimension from each other as we have done in emphasising the two separate routes.

Examples of the direct route to emotion seem to be particularly evident in the emotional disorders, such as in the phobic individual's automatic processing of an object or event as anxiety provoking even though the appraisal route is processing the object or event as non-threatening. Such automatic reactions are of course very likely to be developed in childhood as for example in the teaching of disgust responses to young children towards a range of objects, foodstuffs, ideas, and beliefs (see Chapter 9). These automatic disgust reactions can be innocuous if they merely prevent the individual from eating oysters or snails, or they can be life-threatening if they leave individuals with disgust towards their own bodies, for example, to the extent that they view themselves as fat even in extreme anorexic states.

One of the extreme forms of the possible automatisations of emotion that we considered earlier was that, under certain circumstances, the development of one or more basic emotion modules could become particularly rigid or autonomous. In such cases the module for example would become difficult to alter because the positive feedback between the different levels would cause the module to lock in place (cf. Teasdale & Barnard, 1993). That is, if early in emotional development there is a consistent set of instructions about, for example, the unacceptability of one or more of the basic emotions, then the development of that basic emotion module may become separated from the rest of development. As we have argued elsewhere (Power & Brewin, 1991), one of the important functional properties of the developing nervous system is its potential for modular organisation whether in the area of motor skills development, cognitive skills such as reading and writing, or, we suggest, in the consistent experience of the basic emotions. Again, some of the strongest evidence for the possibility of modularisation of emotion comes from the clinical data in relation to emotional disorders. For example, the typical experience of a dissociated basic emotion module is that the individual experiences the emotion as a dystonic state in which the sense of self may be lost, because the emotional experience is excluded from the definition of the self. The individual may engage in desperate attempts to rid the self of this state, but, paradoxically, the lack of integration of the state into the self means that it is harder to change the state itself once it occurs. Of course, as we argued earlier, even in normal healthy adults, a traumatic experience may initially be held in a quasi-dissociative state because of its pervasive implications for the self and important roles and goals; eventually, however, the healthy though traumatised individual is able to work through the experience and integrate it into the self, altering or developing key goals and plans in the process. In contrast, the young child or the vulnerable adult may hold the traumatic experience in a form that is dissociated or separate from the self (see Chapter 6), and, in addition, may attempt to maintain the experience permanently in this dissociated state in order to protect the self and important goals and plans from the unwanted implications of the traumatic experience. This capacity for dissociation was recognised by Freud in his early book with Breuer, *Studies on Hysteria* (1895), but never developed by Freud presumably because of the lifelong antagonism between Freud and Janet (Perry & Laurence, 1984). Only with the advent of the Object Relations Theorists (e.g. Fairbairn, 1952) and their recognition of the importance of so-called "splitting" does psychoanalysis seem to have regained the important insight that dissociation may be a far more universal characteristic of the mind than is repression, with repression arguably being a sub-type of the former. From the point of view of the experience of emotion in individuals with emotional disorders, the problem is not simply that some individuals fail to experience emotion, but rather that many individuals are overwhelmed by emotional states which feel alien to them because they lead to a loss of the sense of self.

Other theorists have also raised the possibility that emotion can be automatically generated by drugs or hormones, that is, by a direct physiological route in contrast to the direct psychological route that we have suggested. For example, Keith Oatley (1992) has argued that this physiological route is necessary to account for the effects of psychotropic drugs or hormones on emotional states (see Chapter 3). Although the general proposal, which we endorsed above, that there are innately coded aspects of basic emotions might appear to make such a physiological route a possibility, we would caution against drawing such a conclusion. It is clear for example from the study of alcohol and drug dependence that many of the apparent physiological responses to alcohol and drugs come to be associatively conditioned to the objects and situations in which drug use occurs and which may be evident therefore in the absence of the drugs themselves (e.g. Powell, 1992). Such a process would be identical to the automatisation process that we have just considered and would not therefore require a separate direct physiological route to emotion. Nor is it clear that the initial responses to drugs or hormones before any associative learning might have taken place are sufficiently consistent to argue for a prewired physiological route, though there may be some alteration at the analogical level of physiological thresholds. Indeed, there is the history of the various arousal and arousal-appraisal theories of emotion that we considered in Chapter 3 that would argue against Keith Oatley's proposal. Instead, our model would suggest that the physiological state induced by a drug or hormone becomes the object of the interpretative-appraisal process from which consequently an emotional state may result. A drug or hormone that consistently induces a state that is appraised in a positive way may, therefore, eventually give rise to a positive emotion through the direct route because of associative learning, whereas one that consistently induces a physiological state that is appraised negatively is likely to lead to an emotion such as fear in the way that Clark's (1986) cognitive model of panic includes physiological symptoms that are interpreted in a catastrophic manner (see Chapter 4 and Chapter 6).

One final comment that must be reiterated about the existence of two routes to emotion is that *conflicting* emotions may be generated via the two routes. It is clear from the work of Harter (e.g. 1977) onwards that both the experience and the acknowledgement of conflicting emotions is a developmentally sophisticated task and that the failure to achieve this ability is more often seen in children and adolescents with emotional disorders. We also noted in Chapter 10 that repressors also rarely report experiencing mixed emotions (Sincoff, 1992). One source of this problem may be that the parent too is unable to acknowledge conflicting emotions towards the child, and that the parent emphasises love while often demonstrating the opposite (e.g. Bowlby, 1980). For example, much of the evidence showing that high Expressed Emotion leads to relapse in depression and schizophrenia (Vaughn & Leff, 1976; see also Lam, 1991, for a recent summary) may reflect the fact that the individual may be the target for overinvolved care plus hostility. The upshot of these and other studies is that two conflicting emotions may be expressed simultaneously; for example, the individual may appraise a situation in a Happy way while a different emotion is generated through the direct route. The fact that a conflicting emotion occurs via the direct route may be obvious to others (even though denied by the individual) through, for example, fleeting facial expressions, and observable changes in physiology and body posture. The existence of a conflict between verbal report and non-verbal responses provides important clues in therapy about problems that the client may be denying or inhibiting, an aspect of the model that we will consider next.

Inhibition and facilitation

In a number of chapters we have highlighted the roles that inhibition and facilitation play in the expression of emotion. It was pointed out, for example, that many cultures have preferences for which of the basic emotions are permissible and which are not; thus, the Ifaluk treat happiness as a negative emotion because it makes the "sufferer" blind to the needs of others and full of pride for the self. As the bible also reminds us:

> Pride goeth before destruction, and a haughty spirit before
> a fall ...

We know too from studies of the nervous system that the current states represent subtle balances between inhibitory and facilitatory processes at all levels of complexity. In sum, inhibition and facilitation need to be considered at all levels of explanation in relation to emotion, from the neurone up to the level of culture.

There are a number of points within the SPAARS model at which inhibitory forces might operate from the initial interpretation-appraisal, to the expression of the emotion, to subsequent cycles of appraisal. Route 1, the appraisal route (see Fig. 11.1), can be blocked temporarily because it may be inappropriate to express the emotion in a particular situation, for example, to laugh in church or to get angry with your boss. The capacity to temporarily suppress an emotion but express it later appears to be healthy. Vaillant (e.g. 1990) reported from a 50-year follow-up study of college men, that use of the defence of suppression was predictive of good mental and physical health and stable relationships over that time period. In contrast, Vaillant found that use of the defence mechanisms of repression, reaction formation, and dissociation was less healthy. These defence mechanisms represent different types of inhibition within the SPAARS model. We have considered dissociation at length and noted that it can range from an emotion of which the individual is aware but excludes from the self temporarily, to the extremes of fugue states and multiple personality disorder for which the individual has no recollection. In these extreme cases both routes to the unwanted emotions are strongly inhibited, but when these inhibitory forces break down, the autonomous nature of the emotion modules makes them difficult for the individual to escape from.

One of the most powerful ways in which facilitatory processes may operate in the emotional disorders is when two basic emotions become "coupled", that is, they become locked in a facilitatory loop in which the activation from one emotion continually reactivates the other. Teasdale and Barnard (1993) have presented a within-module variant of this process in which propositional output such as Negative Automatic Thoughts feeds back into the Schematic Model. We would add an equally important within-module loop which is between the appraisal route and the direct route and which, again in extreme, would be apparent in the forms of fear of fear, depression about depression, and so on, in which the individual might appraise a small amount of fear or depression that may have arisen automatically as a sign that the downward slope is happening again and thereby making the thing most feared more likely to happen! To take the case of depression however, our argument is that depression can be seen as the coupling of the two basic emotions of sadness and disgust (see Chapter 7), with the disgust being focused on the self in the form of shame. The loss or failure of an important role or goal is a key appraisal for sadness in all individuals, but in those individuals whose self-worth is overinvested in the lost role or goal and underinvested in other domains (Champion & Power, 1995), the loss is also appraised to mean that the self is disgusting and worthless, and at the extreme the outcome may be suicide or parasuicide. The length of time for which the individual will remain in this Sadness–Disgust coupled state will depend on a number of other factors, for example, the extent to which the basic emotions are modularised and therefore unfettered by other emotions, the occurrence of further losses or failures some of which may be brought about by the individual, and through changes in physiology which may also be appraised in a depressogenic manner.

Rationality, irrationality, and the function of emotions

When given a choice, people are less likely to choose an operation if told they have a 7% chance of dying than if they are told that they have a 93% chance of survival (e.g. Sutherland, 1994). These and a whole range of similar observations have come to question the long-cherished belief of the rationality of the Western male; at best it would seem that we can approximate to logic or rationality in our thinking, but there are a host of circumstances under which logic and rationality disappear in the face of something more important. From at least Plato onwards, emotions have had a bad press: there has arisen a Western view that the "passions" circumvent the state of sanguine rationality to which we all should aim (see Chapter 2). Such views of course fail to recognise that the limits on rationality and logic are numerous and that emotions present merely one amongst many short-cuts that thinking may take because of necessity.

The ideas of Keith Oatley and Phil Johnson-Laird have been particularly important in underscoring the role of emotions in thinking (e.g. Johnson-Laird, 1988; Oatley, 1992; Oatley & Johnson-Laird, 1987). In a modular system with multiple goals and plans, it is crucial to have mechanisms which can put a current goal or plan rapidly on hold while another more immediate goal is given priority. There is little point in solving relativity if you are about to be run over by a bus. Occasionally, though, our preoccupations *can* get in the way of our survival, as when the atheist philosopher David Hume almost drowned in a marsh and was only saved when an old woman spotted him and forced him to recite the Lord's Prayer before being saved. Most of the time, however, our lofty preoccupations are quickly supplanted by a range of survival needs; Oatley and Johnson-Laird's (1987) argument that emotions provide one such rapid switching mechanism at junctures in goals and plans provides an important understanding of one of the primary roles of emotion (see Chapter 3).

As we reviewed in the chapters on the basic emotions, the short-cuts that each emotion provides vary considerably. Although Happiness is normally thought in our culture to be closer to rationality than the other "negative" basic emotions, it is clear that there are a range of self-serving biases associated with happiness that lead "sufferers" to overestimate their contribution to the positive things in the world and underestimate their contribution to the negative (see Chapter 1 and Chapter 10).

Although we come to tolerate mild levels of grandiosity in our friends and colleagues, we know of course that really they have borrowed their best ideas from us, and that we are far superior to them but are careful not to point this out. Unfortunately, in some individuals the normal state of mild self-grandiosity can become completely out of control and the individual can believe in complete invulnerability, special powers, and that one is a special person (see Chapter 10). Such beliefs in invulnerability do not only happen at an individual level but also occur throughout history in groups and cultures, whether it be the Charge of the Light Brigade, or the Japanese entering the Second World War. In *The Psychology of Military Incompetence*, Norman Dixon (1976) catalogued a host of battles that have been lost due to, amongst other things, individual and group illusions of invulnerability (see Chapter 1).

Each of the other basic emotions also provide short-cuts in thinking as a function of the modular reconfiguration of the SPAARS system. Fear permits the individual to switch rapidly to a threatened survival goal. Sadness in the face of failure or loss provides the opportunity to reassess important goals and plans and assign new priorities. Anger motivates the individual to overcome an obstacle that is blocking the path towards a desired goal. And disgust allows individuals to rid themselves of something unwanted, whether concrete or abstract, or to distance themselves literally or psychologically from something repulsive in the outside world and thereby maintain the model of the self. All of these emotions therefore provide a useful set of biases relevant to their functions. These biases are, by-and-large, adaptive and useful, and can lead to "depressive realism", "anxious realism", "angry realism", and "disgust realism". At the same time however they run the risk of generalising beyond their range of applicability and in doing so lead to "depressive distortion", "anxious distortion", and so on, especially when the temporary emotional states become long-standing and chronic disorders.

THERAPEUTIC IMPLICATIONS

In his book, *Jokes and Their Relation to the Unconscious*, Freud (1905/1976a, p.100) recounts the following tale:

> A borrowed a copper kettle from B and after he had returned it was sued by B because the kettle now had a big hole in it which made it unusable. His defence was "First, I never borrowed a kettle from B at all; secondly, the kettle had a

hole in it already when I got it from him; and thirdly, I gave him back the kettle undamaged".

This comic story illustrates the extraordinary lengths to which individuals will go in order to protect the self from unwelcome or unwanted information. One theme that we will discuss (see later) therefore in relation to therapeutic interventions for the emotional disorders is how to overcome the pervasive need to reject unwanted aspects of the self, be this in terms of unwanted experiences, unwanted impulses, or unwanted emotional states. A second major theme that we will explore is the proposal that there are two main routes to emotion; what are the therapeutic implications of such a model and how might it relate to the processes of therapeutic change? First, however, we will consider the question of the exclusion of unwanted information from the self.

Disbelief, dissociation, and modularisation

> The first thing I would do if I were returning to teaching and practising psychotherapy is remind myself that the *modularity* of emotions is central to understanding and treating a number of human problems. The principle of modularity means that each emotion exists as a relatively *independent* and *dissociable* module with powers for organising and motivating specific sorts of cognition and action. (Izard, 1994, p.149, original italics)

Izard's advice to himself is completely in tune with the message that we have argued for in this book; namely, that many of the current therapeutic approaches work with an inadequate theory of emotion (see Chapter 4), an inadequacy which, in turn, will invariably lead to problems in therapeutic practice. The first principle to remember in the development of emotion is, like with any other cognitive skill, the tendency towards modular organisation, which is an inherent characteristic of the functional organisation of the brain (Fodor, 1983; Gazzaniga, 1988; Power & Brewin, 1991), that is, we are emphasising a potential for the equivalent of software modularity rather than hardware modularity. The tendency towards modularisation, and perhaps therefore of dissociation, remains an inherent capacity of the functional architecture throughout life, though the capacity clearly decreases with age. This capacity, we suggest, is evident in the initial responses in all individuals to severe losses, traumatic events, and even to extreme positive events such as winning the National Lottery until the event "sinks in". As we saw in the discussion of bereavement (Chapter 7) and of post traumatic stress disorder (Chapter 6), the initial experience is of shock and disbelief to these extreme losses or life-threatening events: the disbelieved experience is held separate to the self in a mildly dissociated form, because of the extent of the impact on the individual's important goals and plans. The individual may remain in this state of disbelief for some time, and continue with normal activities in a trance-like state (cf. Hilgard, 1986). However, the initial phase of disbelief subsequently recedes as the normal individual begins to integrate the loss or trauma, and its implications, into the self. This process is an extremely painful one in which the individual feels overwhelmed by a range of emotions, in particular, sadness and anger in the case of loss (see Chapter 7), and fear, anger, and disgust in the case of trauma; these are not the only emotions, but, rather, the ones that are most commonly experienced (e.g. many traumatic experiences may involve multiple losses). Many individuals seek professional help at a point where the mix of disbelief and overwhelming emotion feels too great a burden. The seeking of help at this point may reflect a mix of intra- and inter-personal factors; as we discussed in relation to sadness and loss, one of the socially cohesive actions associated with sadness is to seek out and express one's feelings to others within one's social network. If, however, the lost person was the individual's key confidant, the individual may feel too ashamed to burden other members of the network and, equally, other members of the network may feel unable to support the individual through the grieving process. The key components of therapy in such cases are: first, to provide a supportive relationship in which the client can work through and integrate the trauma or loss into the self; second, to help the client to experience and express emotions that may feel overwhelming and not to reject these emotions as in some way abnormal; eventually, to encourage the individual to develop new plans and goals that can replace those that have been lost in order to develop a new sense of value and purpose in life. These points are of course simple, straightforward ones and, we hope, they should seem self-evident to most therapists!

The more difficult clinical cases are those in which the initial disbelief strengthens into a dissociative exclusion of the material from the self; for example, Vaillant's (e.g. 1990) study of college men followed up for half a century that we noted earlier showed the use of dissociation was the strongest predictor of a wide range of mental and physical health problems, unstable relationships, and alcohol abuse. The use of such extreme denial means also that these individuals are less likely to seek help early on in response to loss or trauma, but, instead, if they appear in therapy, it will be much later and with a variety of diffuse physical, psychological, and social problems which typically leave the individual perplexed (see e.g. Kihlstrom, 1994, for an overview of a range of dissociative and related conversion disorders that may result).

The most difficult cases are those in which the experience or expression of one or more of the modularised emotions is either completely inhibited or only ever experienced as a terrifying ego-alien dissociated state. This early developmental pathway can occur for a variety of reasons, including the experience of childhood trauma (though as Tillman, Nash, & Lerner, 1994 emphasise, trauma does not invariably lead to dissociative disorders), childhood neglect, and the combination of parental and cultural attitudes towards "acceptable emotions". One of the most extreme of the dissociative disorders, multiple personality disorder, has been shown to be associated with the highest rates of physical and sexual abuse in comparison to any other psychiatric disorder (e.g. Ross, Joshi, & Currie, 1990).

There are now a wide range of cognitive, cognitive-behavioural, psychoanalytic, and other therapies that have been developed to deal with dissociative disorders (e.g. see Lynn & Rhue, 1994). In addition, we propose that a number of more common emotional disorders, such as those relating to anxiety and depression, may reflect the modularisation of basic emotions. For example, the early experience that emotions such as sadness, anger, or fear are not acceptable, or that they are shameful and need to be eliminated from the self, means that when these emotions *are* experienced in later life, the consequent autonomous nature of the emotion modules puts the individual in an emotional state that is difficult to escape from, especially, as we have argued, when the emotion modules become coupled and continually activate each other. We have shown that disgust, in particular, may become coupled not only with other emotions in this way, but also with basic drives such as those related to food in anorexia and bulimia, and those related to sex in a number of sexual disorders. Again, we would argue that the basic principles that should be followed in any successful therapy, of whatever form, should be the same: namely, that the therapist needs to establish a safe therapeutic relationship with the client; that the client begins to re-experience the rejected emotions and memories in this safe environment; and that the client is gradually encouraged to integrate these memories and emotions back into the self. The more damaged the client then, of course, the more difficult the process of therapeutic change and the longer it may take. In addition to these basic principles, however, there are a number of other implications of the SPAARS approach which need to be considered in relation to the theory and practice of therapy.

Two routes revisited: Fast versus slow change processes in therapy

> The evidence clearly shows that emotion responses can be learned and activated without benefit of neocortex and thought processes ... This makes them difficult to access and treat through interventions that are strictly cognitive in nature. Emotions acquired through subcortical pathways are difficult to extinguish by any technique. (Izard, 1994, p.151)

In Izard's further advice to himself and other would-be therapists, he points to the danger of assuming that there is only one route to emotion and that this is modifiable by cognitive psychotherapeutic techniques. Although we may differ about the details of the routes to emotions, we fully concur with Izard that not only must therapists be aware of the potential modular organisation of emotions, but they must also be aware of the fact that there are two different routes to emotion and, therefore, that the therapeutic techniques for working successfully with emotional disorders may vary according to the primary route involved in the disorder.

As a powerful example of the role of the two routes, we considered David Clark's (1986) model of panic in Chapters 4 and 6. In this model, the person with panic disorder is seen to misinterpret catastrophically certain physiological changes such as a faster beating heart, dizziness, or shortness of breath, as indicative of impending death or madness. That is, the individual appraises one or more internal signs in a threat-related manner; the high-level schematic model produces extreme fear or panic in the individual. The successful cognitive treatment developed by David Clark in essence provides the individual with an alternative schematic model for the internal signs (cf. Teasdale & Barnard, 1993). Once the more appropriate model has been both accepted and applied, then recovery can occur quickly. Such changes provide an example of the Fast Change processes that can occur in therapy, in which, for example, it is the appraisal of an internal or external event that provides the primary problem in the disorder. However, the panic disorder patient will still continue to experience the previously threatening internal signs in the same situations; these are likely to represent the direct activation of threat and will change much more slowly and gradually, that is, they reflect Slow Change processes in therapy.

The two routes to emotion therefore can be linked with a number of features of automatic versus controlled processes (Dalgleish, 1994a;

Power & Brewin, 1991), one of which relates to associative learning versus rule-learning processes (e.g. Holyoak, Koh, & Nisbett, 1989) and the fact that associative learning is typically slow, but conscious rule-learning is typically fast. Cognitive therapy techniques which address Schematic Models will be successful to the extent that the Schematic Models are the primary source of the emotional disorder. However, as has been pointed out (Power & Champion, 1986; Teasdale & Barnard, 1993), if the cognitive therapy technique merely focuses on Propositional Level representations as in the technique of challenging Negative Automatic Thoughts, it may fail to address the higher order Schematic Models and, indeed, in some unfortunate circumstances may serve to confirm them. Examples of such problems were given in Chapter 4; thus, if the therapist robustly challenges the patient's statement "I am a failure", this may serve to reinforce the Schematic Model, because the patient now believes that he or she was incapable of carrying out such a task and is inferior to the therapist. The first conclusion therefore is that cognitive therapy needs to address high level Schematic Models rather than focus on lower level Propositional Representations. The second conclusion however is that this focus will not work if the source of the problem is via the automatic route to emotion.

How therefore should one work with emotional disorders in which the direct route to emotion is primarily indicated? In these cases, we suggest, the process of therapeutic change will be slower, because the problems are based on associative learning mechanisms. This proposition suggests that there are some individuals who, for example, should be more likely to benefit from behavioural exposure techniques in the treatment of anxiety and obsessional disorders. For example, in the case of post-traumatic stress disorder (PTSD), we noted (cf. Brewin et al., in press) that it was important to distinguish different types of individuals including, first, those individuals with extreme beliefs in invulnerability whose schematic models may be "shattered" by the traumatic experience (Janoff-Bulman, 1985) and, second, those individuals in whom extreme cognitive and behavioural avoidance may initially lead to an apparent stoicism in coping with the trauma, but who are more likely to develop late onset PTSD. Individuals with shattered schematic models should, we predict, benefit more from a cognitive therapy approach, whereas those individuals whose primary problem is the avoidance of automatically generated aversive emotions should do better with exposure techniques. This division is of course somewhat crude and there are many cases in which a combination of cognitive and exposure-based approaches is indicated. Nevertheless, the different challenges in PTSD, in particular, shattered high-level models versus unpleasant low-level intrusions, provide dramatic examples of the different effects of the two routes to emotion in the emotional disorders.

The examples of therapy that we have provided so far have contrasted cognitive versus exposure-based techniques, but we do not in any way mean to imply that Slow Change processes only occur in the exposure-based treatments. The complexity of therapeutic relationships and the many routes to effective change demonstrate that Slow Change processes may be set in motion in any form of therapy; for example, the adoption of a new and more appropriate Schematic Model for panic (a Fast Change process) should eventually lead to Slow Change processes, as noted above. A problem is more likely to arise when the therapist aims for Schematic Model change but the patient wants only lower level (e.g. symptom) change. Part of the assessment for therapy should consist therefore of the degree to which the patient is satisfied or dissatisfied with self-related Schematic Models; short-term therapies will have little or no hope of altering Schematic Models that patients are completely satisfied with and even long-term therapies are well aware of the limited amount of change possible for ego-syntonic aspects of the self.

Finally, we should note that the existence of two routes for emotion generation provides an account for a number of puzzles that arise in therapy. The first of these is the issue of "intellectual" versus "emotional" change. The SPAARS model would suggest that an "intellectual belief" is likely to be represented at the Propositional level, and that change may follow an alteration of one's appraisal of a particular event or situation and no longer lead to the generation of emotion a particular propositional belief. In contrast, if the automatic route still leads to the generation of emotion, the individual will be left with an awareness of a dissociation between the "intellectual" and the "emotional": the two systems are operating in conflict with each other and the individual is aware of the difference between their outputs. The existence of the two routes also provides an explanation for a related problem that people report; namely, that they experience their emotional reactions as "irrational", but, nevertheless, the reactions continue to happen out of the individual's control. Again, the SPAARS explanation would be that in such cases no emotion is generated via the appraisal route, only via the direct route; for example, the individual appraises the butterfly to be non-threatening, yet still experiences "irrational" anxiety, that is, anxiety generated by the direct route and, most likely, acquired through an associative learning mechanism. In relation to recommendations for therapeutic practice, we suggest that the presentation of information booklets to patients with emotional disorders should include an amended model of the relation between cognition and emotion. One of the strengths of the cognitive approach has been the educational component which provides the patient with, in Jerome Frank's (e.g. 1982) terms, a strong rationale for the therapeutic approach. However, an amendment of that model would seem warranted, even as presented in handouts to patients.

Roles, goals, and plans

One of the important features of the SPAARS approach with important therapeutic implications is the centrality of the individual's roles and goals and the ways in which events are appraised in relation to these goals and plans. For example, the extent to which an individual will experience happiness, anger, depression, or whatever, will depend to a considerable degree, on the nature of that person's roles and goals, the extent to which roles and goals are achievable and realistic, the extent to which the focus on a particular role or goal serves an inhibitory function in relation to domains of potential conflict, and the extent to which life is fair or unfair.

In the areas of depression and happiness for example, we have argued that there is a tendency for some individuals both to overinvest in one particular role or goal and underinvest in other roles and goals (Champion & Power, 1995). The individual vulnerable to depression may possibly experience success in the chosen domain and never become depressed while continuing to remain vulnerable; there is no doubt that many high-achieving individuals are motivated in this way. However, the vulnerable individual is more than likely to experience a negative event that impacts on the overinvested domain (e.g. Lam & Power, 1991), in part, because the overinvestment itself is likely to lead to events in the critical domain, in the way that Lorna Champion has shown that the vulnerability factors themselves lead to increased rates of events (Champion, 1990; Champion et al., 1995). Perhaps, too, more goals are likely to be set in an overinvested domain which, therefore, increase the possibility of going wrong. One of the functions of this pattern of overinvestment plus underinvestment is that it may protect the individual from conflict-ridden areas of life that may be riddled with emotions that are experienced negatively. The overinvested role or goal provides a compensation therefore for these other perceived inadequacies (cf. Arieti & Bemporad, 1978).

By the time the depressed individual enters therapy, however, there may be a number of possible scenarios. For example, the individual may have recently experienced a loss or failure in relation to the major role or goal; the patient's wish is for the therapist to help the patient get back on course once the loss or failure has been overcome. Therapists may well decide to concur with this wish while being aware that the person may run a risk of the same repeating pattern when the next negative event occurs which impacts on the critical domain. A more preventative strategy however is to explore the range of underinvested roles and goals, to discover something of why these domains are valued so little, and thereby help the individual to lead a more broadly satisfying life. Of course, the therapist may well fall foul of the issue raised above that it is more difficult for patients to change Schematic Models that they are happy with. However, one of the positive functions of depression may be that it gives the individual access to split off aspects of the self, it can provide the opportunity to work through painful experiences that have been avoided, and it can provide the opportunity to reassess one's purpose and meaning in life. Indeed, depressed patients can often be harder to work with in therapy once they have recovered, because the old high-level Schematic Models seem to be working again, so there is no perceived need for change. One of the positive functions of depression therefore may be similar to Freud's (1926/1979) proposed "signal anxiety" which can be used by the individual or the individual's therapist as a warning that something is amiss; that is, "signal depression" may also provide a dire warning to the individual.

A more general way in which roles and goals are important in therapy relates to the observation that the majority of emotions are experienced in the context of relationships, a fact that is evident for example from diary studies of emotion (e.g. Oatley & Duncan, 1992). The therapeutic relationship may become a very significant relationship for the patient therefore and one in which extreme emotions are likely to be experienced. Studies of therapy process have shown that the expression of negative emotions are often very poorly dealt with by therapists, in the same way that they may be very poorly dealt with by significant others in the individual's life; indeed, there is evidence that the failure to deal adequately with negative emotions may lead to poor outcome in therapy (e.g. Henry, Schacht, & Strupp, 1986) irrespective of the framework that one is using (Beach & Power, 1996). The therapeutic relationship at its best may therefore provide an opportunity for the patient to learn how to express emotions in a non-destructive and contained way, in which the feared consequences do not occur. Only then can the patient test the expression of these emotions in other significant relationships, or, if these relationships are genuinely unhealthy and destructive, perhaps set about establishing newer, healthier relationships in their lives. This capacity to plan and develop healthy relationships has been dramatically demonstrated to be protective for individuals brought up in care (Quinton & Rutter, 1985) and for adults who had emotional and behavioural problems in childhood (Champion et al., 1995).

RESEARCH IMPLICATIONS OF
THE SPAARS APPROACH

If a theory doesn't butter any parsnips, then, however grand it may appear, it will be of little scientific value. We hope that we have demonstrated throughout this book that the SPAARS approach makes interesting empirical predictions and that it can be tested against rival theories. We believe that the SPAARS model provides a unique multi-level approach to emotion. The derivation of complex emotions and emotional disorders from the underlying basic emotions of Fear, Sadness, Anger, Disgust, and Happiness provides a fruitful analysis of these often puzzling phenomena. Whether or not you are persuaded by the arguments that we have mustered, we hope that you may at least have been led to reconsider some of your own assumptions about the emotions and their disorders. Our own views have certainly changed in the process of trying to articulate these ideas so that we are now beginning to understand the point from which we started. To quote from T.S. Eliot (*Little Gidding*):

> We shall not cease from exploration
> And the end of all our exploring
> Will be to arrive where we started
> And know the place for the first time.

References

Abramson, L.Y., Alloy, L.B., & Metalsky, G.I. (1988). The cognitive diathesis stress theories of depression: Toward an adequate evaluation of the theories' validities. In L.B. Alloy (Ed.), *Cognitive processes in depression*. New York: Guilford.

Abramson, L.Y., Metalsky, G.I., & Alloy, L.B. (1989). Hopelessness depression: A theory-based sub-type of depression. *Psychological Review, 96*, 358–372.

Abramson, L.Y., Seligman, M.E.P., & Teasdale, J.D. (1978). Learned helplessness in humans: Critique and reformulation. *Journal of Abnormal Psychology, 87*, 49–74.

Agras, W.S., Sylvester, D., & Oliveau, D. (1969). The epidemiology of common fears and phobias. *Comprehensive Psychiatry, 10*, 151–156.

Ainsworth, M.D.S., Blehar, M.C., Waters, E., & Wall, S. (1978). *Patterns of attachment: A psychological study of the strange situation*. Hillsdale, NJ: Lawrence Erlbaum Associates Inc.

Akhtar, S., Wig, N.N., Varma, V.K., Pershad, D., & Verma, S.K. (1975). A phenomenological analysis of symptoms in obsessive-compulsive neurosis. *British Journal of Psychiatry, 127*, 342–348.

Alloy, L.B. (Ed.)(1988). *Cognitive processes in depression*. New York: Guildford Press.

Alloy, L.B., & Abramson, L.Y. (1979). Judgment of contingency in depressed and nondepressed students: Sadder but wiser? *Journal of Experimental Psychology: General, 108*, 441–485.

Alloy, L.B., & Abramson, L.Y. (1988). Depressive realism: Four theoretical perspectives. In L.B. Alloy (Ed.), *Cognitive processes in depression*. New York: Guilford Press.

Alloy, L.B., & Ahrens, A.H. (1987). Depression and pessimism for the future: Biased use of statistically relevant information in predictions for self versus others. *Journal of Personality and Social Psychology, 52*, 366–378.

American Psychiatric Association. (1980). *Diagnostic and statistical manual of mental disorders* (3rd edn.). Washington, DC: Author.

American Psychiatric Association. (1994). *Diagnostic and statistical manual of mental disorders* (4th edn.). Washington, DC: Author.

Amis, M. (1981). *Other people: A mystery story.* London: Cape.

Anastasi, A., Cohen, N., & Spatz, D. (1948). A study of fear and anger in college students through the controlled diary method. *Journal of Genetic Psychology, 73,* 243–249.

Anderson, J.R. (1982). Acquisition of cognitive skill. *Psychological Review, 89,* 396–406.

Anderson, J.R. (1987). Skill acquisition: Compilation of weak-method problem solutions. *Psychological Review, 94,* 192–210.

Anderson, J.R., & Bower, G.M. (1973). *Human associative memory.* Washington, DC: Winston.

Anderson, R.C., Pichert, J.W., Goetz, E.T., Schallert, D.L., Stevens, K.V., & Trollip, S.R. (1976). Instantiation of general terms. *Journal of Verbal Learning and Verbal Behavior, 15,* 667–679.

Andrews, B. (1995). Bodily shame as a mediator between abusive experiences and depression. *Journal of Abnormal Psychology, 104,* 277–285.

Andrews, F.M., & Withey, S.B. (1976). *Social indicators of well-being: America's perception of life quality.* New York: Plenum.

Andrews, F.M., & Robinson J.P. (1991). Measures of subjective well-being. In J.P. Robinson, P.R. Shaver, & L.S. Wrightsman (Eds.), *Measures of personality and social psychological attitudes.* San Diego, CA: Academic Press.

Angyal, A. (1941). Disgust and related aversions. *Journal of Abnormal and Social Psychology, 36,* 393–412.

Aquinas, T. (1993). *Selected philosophical writings.* Oxford: Oxford University Press. (Original work published 1266–1273).

Argyle, M. (1987). *The psychology of happiness.* London: Methuen.

Arieti, S., & Bemporad, J. (1978). *Severe and mild depression: The psychotherapeutic approach.* London: Tavistock.

Aristotle. (1941). De Anima. In R.P. McKeon (Ed.), *Basic works of Aristotle.* New York: Random House.

Aristotle. (1947). Nicomachean ethics (W.D. Ross, Trans.). In R. McKeon (Ed.), *Introduction to Aristotle* (pp.300–543). New York: Modern Library.

Aristotle. (1991). *The art of rhetoric.* London: Penguin.

Arnold, M. (1960). *Emotion and personality* (2 vols.) New York: Columbia University Press.

Asendorpf, J.A., & Scherer, K.R. (1983). The discrepant repressor: Differentiation between low anxiety, high anxiety, and repression of anxiety by autonomic-facial-verbal patterns of behaviour. *Journal of Personality and Social Psychology, 45,* 1334–1346.

Asmundsen, G.J.G., Sandler, L.S., Wilson, K.G., & Walker, J.R. (1992). Selective attention toward physical threat in patients with panic disorder. *Journal of Anxiety Disorders, 6,* 295–303

Atkeson, B., Calhoun, K., Resick, P., & Ellis, E. (1982). Victims of rape: Repeated assessment of depressive symptoms. *Journal of Consulting and Clinical Psychology, 50,* 96–102.

Averill, J.R. (1979). Anger. In H. Howe & R. Dienstbier (Eds.), *Nebraska Symposium on Motivation 1978* (Vol. 26). Lincoln, NB: University of Nebraska Press.

Averill, J.R. (1982). *Anger and aggression: An essay on emotion*. New York: Springer-Verlag.

Averill, J.R. (1983). Studies on anger and aggression: Implications for theories of emotion. *American Psychologist, 38*, 1145–1160.

Averill, J.R. (1985). The social construction of emotion: With special reference to love. In K.J. Gergen & K.E. Davis (Eds.), *The social construction of the person*. New York: Springer.

Averill, J.R. (1990). Emotions as related to systems of behavior. In N.L. Stein, B. Leventhal, & T. Trabasso (Eds.), *Psychological and biological approaches to emotion* (pp.385–404). Hillsdale, NJ: Lawrence Erlbaum Associates Inc.

Averill, J.R., & Moore, T.A. (1993). Happiness. In M. Lewis & J.M. Haviland (Eds.), *Handbook of emotions*. New York: Guilford.

Baddeley, A.D. (1990). *Human memory: Theory and practice*. Hove, UK: Lawrence Erlbaum Associates Ltd.

Balatsky, G., & Diener, E. (1991). Subjective well-being among Russian students. *Social Indicators Research, 28*, 21–39.

Bargh, J.A., & Gollwitzer, P.M. (1995). Environmental control of goal-directed action: Automatic and strategic contingencies between situations and behaviour. In W.D. Spaulding (Ed.), *Integrative views of motivation, cognition and emotion*. Nebraska: University of Nebraska Press.

Barlow, D.H. (1988). *Anxiety and its disorders*. New York: Guilford.

Barlow, D.H., Vermilyea, J., Blanchard, E.B., Vermilyea, B.B., Di Nardo, P.A., & Cerny, J.A. (1985). The phenomenon of panic. *Journal of Abnormal Psychology, 94*, 320–328.

Barnard, P. (1985). Interacting cognitive subsystems: A psycholinguistic approach to short-term memory. In A. Ellis (Ed.), *Progress in the psychology of language* (Vol. 2). Hove, UK: Lawrence Erlbaum Associates Ltd.

Barnard, P.J., & Teasdale, J.D. (1991). Interacting cognitive subsystems: A systemic approach to cognitive-affective interaction and change. *Cognition and Emotion, 5*, 1–39.

Barrett, K.C. (1995). A functionalist approach to shame and guilt. In J.P. Tangney & K.W. Fischer (Eds.), *Self-conscious emotions: The psychology of shame, guilt, embarrassment, and pride*. New York: Guilford.

Barrett, K.C., Zahn-Waxler, C., & Cole, P.M. (1993). Avoiders versus amenders: Implications for the investigation of guilt and shame during toddlerhood? *Cognition and Emotion, 7*, 481–505.

Bartholomew, K. (1990). Avoidance of intimacy: An attachment perspective. *Journal of Social and Personal Relationships, 7*, 147–178.

Bartlett, F.C. (1932). *Remembering: A study in experimental and social psychology*. Cambridge, UK: Cambridge University Press.

Bateson, G., Jackson, D.D., Haley, J., & Weakland, J.H. (1956). Towards a theory of schizophrenia. *Behavioural Science, 1*, 251–264.

Baumeister, R.F., & Cairns, K.J. (1992). Repression and self-presentation: When audiences interfere with self-deceptive strategies. *Journal of Personality and Social Psychology, 62*, 51–862.

Beach, K., & Power, M.J. (1996). Transference: An empirical investigation across a range of cognitive-behavioural and psychoanalytic therapies. *Clinical Psychology and Psychotherapy, 3*, 1–14.

Bechtel, W., & Abrahamsen, A. (1991). *Connectionism and the mind: An introduction to parallel processing in networks*. Oxford: Blackwell.

Beck, A.T. (1976). *Cognitive therapy and the emotional disorders*. New York: Meridian.

Beck, A.T. (1983). Cognitive therapy of depression: New perspectives. In P.J. Clayton & J.E. Barrett (Eds.), *Treatment of depression: Old controversies and new approaches*. New York: Raven Press.

Beck, A.T. (1987). Cognitive models of depression. *Journal of Cognitive Psychotherapy: An International Quarterly, 1,* 5–37.

Beck, A.T., Brown, G., & Steer, R.A. (1989). Prediction of eventual suicide in psychiatric inpatients by clinical ratings of hopelessness. *Journal of Consulting and Clinical Psychology, 57,* 309–310.

Beck, A.T., & Emery, G. (1985). *Anxiety disorders and phobias: A cognitive perspective*. New York: Basic Books.

Beck, A.T., Epstein, N., & Harrison, R. (1983). Cognitions, attitudes and personality dimensions in depression. *British Journal of Cognitive Psychotherapy, 1,* 1–16.

Beck, A.T., & Freeman, A. (1990). *Cognitive therapy of personality disorders*. New York: Guilford Press.

Beck, A.T., Laude, R., & Bohnert, M. (1974). Ideational components of anxiety neurosis. *Archives of General Psychiatry, 31,* 319–325.

Beck, A.T., Rush, A.J., Shaw, B.F., & Emery, G. (1979). *Cognitive therapy of depression: A treatment manual*. New York: Guilford Press.

Becker, E. (1964). *The revolution in psychiatry*. New York: Free Press.

Becker, E. (1971). *The birth and death of meaning*. Harmondsworth, UK: Penguin.

Bedford, E. (1964). Emotions. In D.F. Gustafson (Ed.), *Essays in philosophical psychology*. London: Macmillan.

Bemis, K.M. (1978). Current approaches to the etiology and treatment of anorexia nervosa. *Psychological Bulletin, 85,* 593–617.

Ben-Zur, H., & Breznitz, S. (1991). What makes people angry: Dimensions of anger-evoking events. *Journal of Research in Personality, 25,* 1–22.

Berkowitz, L. (1962). *Aggression: A social psychological analysis*. New York: McGraw-Hill.

Berkowitz, L. (1974). Some determinants of impulsive aggression: Role of mediated associations with reinforcements for aggression. *Psychological Review, 81,* 165–176.

Berkowitz, L. (1990). On the formation and regulation of anger and aggression: A cognitive neoassociationistic analysis. *American Psychologist, 45,* 494–503.

Berkowitz, L., & LePage, A. (1967). Weapons as aggression-eliciting stimuli. *Journal of Personality and Social Psychology, 7,* 202–207.

Bhugra, D., & Gregoire, A. (1993). Social factors in the genesis and management of postnatal psychiatric disorders. In D. Bhugra & J. Leff (Eds.), *Principles of social psychiatry*. Oxford: Blackwell Scientific Publications.

Bibring, E. (1953). The mechanism of depression. In P. Greenacre (Ed.), *Affective disorders*. New York: International Universities Press.

Bjork, R.A. (1989). Retrieval inhibition as an adaptive mechanism in human memory. In H.L. Roediger III & F.L.M. Craik (Eds.), *Varieties of memory and consciousness: Essays in memory of Endel Tulving*. Hillsdale, NJ: Lawrence Erlbaum Associates Inc.

Blaney, P.H. (1986). Affect and memory: A review. *Psychological Bulletin, 99,* 229–246.

Blank, A.S. (1993). The longitudinal course of posttraumatic stress disorder. In J.R.T. Davidson & E.B. Foa (Eds.), *Posttraumatic stress disorder: DSM-IV and beyond*. Washington, DC: American Psychiatric Press Inc.

Blatt, S.J., D'Affliti, J.P., & Quinlan, D.M. (1976). Experiences of depression in normal young adults. *Journal of Abnormal Psychology*, 85, 383–389.

Blehar, M.C., & Lewy, A.J. (1990). Seasonal mood disorders: Consensus and controversy. *Psychopharmacology Bulletin*, 26, 465–494.

Bodenhausen, G.V., Sheppard, L.A., & Kramer, G.P. (1994). Negative affect and social judgement: The differential impact of anger and sadness. *European Journal of Social Psychology*, 24, 45–62.

Bonnano, G.A., Davis, P.J., Singer, J.L., & Schwartz, G.E. (1991). The repressor personality and avoidant information processing: A dichotic listening study. *Journal of Research in Personality*, 25, 386–401.

Borkovec, T.D. (1994). The nature, function and origins of worry. In G.Davey & F. Tallis (Eds.), *Worrying: Perspectives on theory, assessment and treatment*. Chichester, UK: Wiley.

Borkovec, T.D., Metzger, R.L., & Pruzinsky, T. (1986). Anxiety, worry and the self. In L. Hartman & K.R. Blankstein (Eds.), *Perception of self in emotional disorders and psychotherapy*. New York: Plenum.

Borkovec, T.D., Robinson, E., Pruzinsky, T., & DePree, J.A. (1983). Preliminary exploration of worry: Some characteristics and processes. *Behaviour Research and Therapy*, 21, 9–16.

Borkovec, T.D., Shadick, R., & Hopkins, M. (1990). The nature of normal and pathological worry. In R. Rapee & D.H. Barlow (Eds.), *Chronic anxiety and generalized anxiety disorder*. New York: Guilford Press.

Bourdon, K.H., Boyd, J.H., Rae, D.S., Burns, B.J., Thompson, J.W., & Locke, B.Z. (1988). Gender differences in phobias: Results of the ECA community survey. *Journal of Anxiety Disorders*, 2, 227–241.

Bower, G.H. (1981). Mood and memory. *American Psychologist*, 36, 129–148.

Bower, G.H. (1986). Prime time in cognitive psychology. In P. Eelen & O. Fontaine (Eds.), *Behaviour therapy: Beyond the conditioning framework*. Leuven: Leuven University Press.

Bower, G.H. (1987). Commentary on mood and memory. *Behaviour Research and Therapy*, 25, 443–456.

Bower, G.H. (1990). Awareness, the unconscious, and repression: An experimental psychologist's perspective. In J.L. Singer (1990), *Repression and dissociation: Implications for personality theory, psychopathology, and health*. Chicago, IL: The University of Chicago Press.

Bower, G.H. (1992). How might emotions affect learning? In S.-A. Christianson (Ed.), *The handbook of emotion and memory*. Hillsdale, NJ: Lawrence Erlbaum Associates Inc.

Bower, G.H., & Cohen, P.R. (1982). Emotional influences on memory and thinking: Data and theory. In S. Fiske & M. Clark (Eds.), *Affect and cognition*. Hillsdale, NJ: Lawrence Erlbaum Associates Inc.

Bowlby, J. (1969). *Attachment and loss: Vol. 1. Attachment*. London: Hogarth Press.

Bowlby, J. (1973). *Attachment and loss: Vol. 2. Separation*. London: Hogarth Press.

Bowlby, J. (1980). *Attachment and loss: Vol. 3. Sadness and depression*. London: Hogarth Press.

Bowlby, J. (1988). *A secure base: Clinical applications of attachment theory*. London: Routledge.

Boyd, W. (1993). *The blue afternoon*. Harmondsworth, UK: Penguin.

Bradley, B., & Mathews, A. (1983). Negative self-schemata in clinical depression. *British Journal of Clinical Psychology, 22*, 173–181.

Bradley, B., & Mathews, A. (1988). Memory bias in recovered clinical depressives. *Cognition and Emotion, 2*, 235–245.

Bransford, J.D. (1979). *Human cognition*. Belmont, CA: Wadsworth.

Breier, A., Charney, D.S., & Heninger, G.R. (1986). Agoraphobia with panic attacks: Development, diagnostic stability, and course of illness. *Archives of General Psychiatry, 43*, 1029–1036.

Breslau, N., Davis, G.C., Andreski, P., & Peterson, E. (1991). Traumatic events and posttraumatic stress disorder in an urban population of young adults. *Archives of General Psychiatry, 48*, 216–222.

Breuer, J., & Freud, S. (1974). *Studies on hysteria*. (Pelican Freud Library, Vol. 3.) Harmondsworth, UK: Penguin. (Original work published 1895)

Brewin, C.R. (1985). Depression and causal attributions: What is their relation? *Psychological Bulletin, 98*, 297–309.

Brewin, C.R. (1989). Cognitive change processes in psychotherapy. *Psychological Review, 90*, 379–394.

Brewin, C.R., Dalgleish, T., & Joseph, S. (in press). A dual representation theory of post-traumatic stress disorder. *Psychological Review*.

Brewin, C.R., Smith, A.J., Power, M.J., & Furnham, A. (1992). State and trait differences in the depressive self-schema. *Behaviour Research and Therapy, 30*, 555–557.

Brickman. P., Coates, D., & Janoff-Bulman, R. (1978). Lottery winners and accident victims: Is happiness relative? *Journal of Personality and Social Psychology, 36*, 917–927.

Briggs, J.L. (1970). *Never in anger*. Cambridge, MA: Harvard University Press.

Brown, D.E. (1991). *Human universals*. Philadelphia, PA: Temple University Press.

Brown, G.W., Bifulco, A., & Harris, T.O. (1987). Life events, vulnerability and onset of depression—some refinements. *British Journal of Psychiatry, 150*, 30–42.

Brown, G.W., & Harris, T.O. (1978). *Social origins of depression: A study of psychiatric disorder in women*. London: Tavistock.

Brown, G.W., Harris, T.O., & Hepworth, C. (1995). Loss, humiliation and entrapment among women developing depression: A patient and non-patient comparison. *Psychological Medicine, 25*, 7–21.

Brown, G.W., Lemyre, L., & Bifulco, A. (1992). Social factors and recovery from anxiety and depressive disorders: A test of specificity. *British Journal of Psychiatry, 161*, 44–54.

Bruch, H. (1978). *The golden cage: The enigma of anorexia nervosa*. Shepton Mallet, UK: Open Books.

Brugha, T.S. (Ed.) (1995). *Social support and psychiatric disorder: Research findings and guidelines for clinical practice*. Cambridge, UK: Cambridge University Press.

Buck, R. (1988). *Human motivation and emotion* (2nd Edn.). New York: Wiley.

Burgess, A.W., & Holmstrom, L.L. (1974). Rape trauma syndrome. *American Journal of Psychiatry, 131*, 981–986.

Burgess, A.W., & Holmstrom, L.L. (1978). Recovery from rape and prior life stress. *Research in Nursing and Health, 1*, 165–174.

Burt, C.D.B. (1993). Concentration and academic ability following transition to university: An investigation of the effects of homesickness. *Journal of Environmental Psychology, 13*, 333–342.

Buss, A.H. (1962). Two anxiety factors in psychiatric patients. *Journal of Abnormal and Social Psychology, 65*, 426–427.

Butler, G. (1989). Phobic disorders. In K. Hawton, P.M. Salkovskis, J. Kirk, & D.M. Clark (Eds.), *Cognitive behaviour therapy for psychiatric problems: A practical guide*. Oxford: Oxford University Press.

Butler, G., & Mathews, A. (1983). Cognitive processes in anxiety. *Advances in Behavioural Research and Therapy, 5*, 51–62.

Byrne, D. (1964). Repression-sensitization as a dimension of personality. In B.A. Maher (Ed.), *Progress in experimental personality research*, (Vol. 1). 169–220. New York: Academic Press.

Camus, A. (1955). *The myth of Sisyphus: And other essays*. New York: Alfred A. Knopf.

Camus, A. (1958). *L'Etranger*. London: Methuen.

Cannon, W.B. (1927). The James–Lange theory of emotions: A critical examination and an alternative theory. *American Journal of Psychology, 39*, 106–124.

Carlson, J.G., & Hatfield, E. (1992). *Psychology of emotion*. Fort Worth, TX: Harcourt Brace Jovanovich.

Carver, C.S., & Scheier, M.F. (1990). Origins and functions of positive and negative affect: A control process view. *Psychological Review, 97*, 19–35.

Champion, L.A. (1990). The relationship between social vulnerability and the occurrence of severely threatening life events. *Psychological Medicine, 20*, 157–161.

Champion, L.A. (1992). Depression. In L.A. Champion & M.J. Power (Eds.), *Adult psychological problems: An introduction*. London: Falmer Press.

Champion, L.A., Goodall, G., & Rutter, M. (1995). Behavioural problems in childhood and stressors in early adult life: I. A 20 year follow-up of London school children. *Psychological Medicine, 25*, 231–246.

Champion, L.A., & Power, M.J. (1995). Social and cognitive approaches to depression: Towards a new synthesis. *British Journal of Clinical Psychology, 34*, 485–503.

Cherry, E.C. (1953). Some experiments on the recognition of speech, with one and with two ears. *Journal of the Acoustical Society of America, 25*, 975–979.

Clark, D.M. (1986). A cognitive approach to panic. *Behaviour Research and Therapy, 24*, 461–470.

Clark, D.M. (1988). A cognitive model of panic attacks. In S. Rachman & J.D.Maser (Eds.), *Panic: Psychological perspectives*. Hillsdale, NJ: Lawrence Erlbaum Associates Inc.

Clark, D.M. (1989). Anxiety states: Panic and generalised anxiety. In K. Hawton, P.M. Salkovskis, J. Kirk, & D.M. Clark (Eds.), *Cognitive behaviour therapy for psychiatric problems*. Oxford: Oxford University Press.

Clark, D.M., & Beck, A.T. (1988). Cognitive approaches. In C.G. Last & M. Hersen (Eds.), *Handbook of anxiety disorders*. Elmsford, NY: Pergamon Press.

Clark, D.M., Salkovskis, P.M., Gelder, M., Koehler, C., Martin, M., Anastasiades, P., Hackmann, A., Middleton, H., & Jeavons, A. (1988). Tests of a cognitive theory of panic. In I. Hand & H.U. Wittchen (Eds.), *Panic and phobias* (Vol. 2). Berlin, Germany: Springer-Verlag.

Clark, D.M., & Teasdale, J.D. (1982). Diurnal variation in clinical depression and accessibility of memories of positive and negative experiences. *Journal of Abnormal Psychology, 91*, 87–95.

Clark, D.M., Teasdale, J.D., Broadbent, D.E., & Martin, M. (1983). Effect of mood on lexical decisions. *Bulletin of the Psychonomic Society, 21*, 175–178.

Clark, H.H., & Clark, E.V. (1977). *Psychology and language: An introduction to psycholinguistics.* New York: Harcourt Brace Jovanovich.

Clark, L.A., & Watson, D. (1991). Tripartite model of anxiety and depression: Psychometric evidence and taxonomic implications. *Journal of Abnormal Psychology, 100*, 316–336.

Clayton, P.J. (1990). Bereavement and depression. *Journal of Clinical Psychiatry, 51* (Supp.), 34–40.

Cochrane, R. (1983). *Social creation of mental illness.* London: Longman.

Collins, A.M., & Loftus, E.F. (1975). A spreading-activation theory of semantic processing. *Psychological Review, 82*, 407–428.

Collins, A.M., & Quillian, M.R. (1969). Retrieval time from semantic memory. *Journal of Verbal Learning and Verbal Behavior, 8*, 240–248.

Collins, A.M., & Smith, E.E. (1988). *Readings in cognitive science.* San Mateo, CA: Morgan Kaufman.

Costa, P.T., & McCrae, R.R. (1980). Influence of extraversion and neuroticism on subjective well-being: Happy and unhappy people. *Journal of Personality and Social Psychology, 38*, 668–678.

Costello, C.G. (1982). Fears and phobias in women: A community study. *Journal of Abnormal Psychology, 91*, 280–286..

Coyne, J.C., & Gotlib, I.H. (1983). The role of cognition in depression: A critical appraisal. *Psychological Bulletin, 94*, 472–505.

Cramer, P. (1968). *Word association.* New York: Academic Press.

Creamer, M., Burgess, P., & Pattison, P. (1992). Reaction to trauma: A cognitive processing model. *Journal of Abnormal Psychology, 101*, 452–459.

Dalgleish, T. (1991). *The processing of emotional information in clinical and sub-clinical anxiety states.* Unpublished doctoral thesis. University of London.

Dalgleish, T. (1993). *The judgement of risk in traumatised and non-traumatised disaster survivors.* Unpublished master's thesis. University of London.

Dalgleish, T. (1994a). The appraisal of threat and the process of selective attention in clinical and sub-clinical anxiety states: Theoretical issues. *Clinical Psychology and Psychotherapy, 1*, 153–164.

Dalgleish, T. (1994b). The relationship between anxiety and memory biases for material that has been selectively processed in a prior task. *Behaviour Research and Therapy, 32*, 227–231.

Dalgleish, T., Cameron, C.M., Power, M.J., & Bond, A. (1995). The use of an emotional priming paradigm with clinically anxious subjects. *Cognitive Therapy and Research, 19*, 69–89.

Dalgleish, T., & Power, M.J. (1995). *Theoretical approaches to post-traumatic stress disorder: The SPAARS model.* Paper presented at the Second International Conference on Mental Health in the State of Kuwait, Kuwait.

Dalgleish, T., Rosen, K., & Marks, M. (1996). Rhythm and blues: The assessment and treatment of seasonal affective disorder. *British Journal of Clinical Psychology, 35*, 163–182.

Dalgleish, T., & Watts, F.N. (1990). Biases of attention and memory in disorders of anxiety and depression. *Clinical Psychology Review, 10,* 589–604.

Darwin, C. (1965). *The expression of the emotions in man and animals.* Chicago: Chicago University Press. (Original work published 1872)

Darwin, C. (1988). *Diaries of the Voyage of The Beagle.* (R.D. Keynes, Ed.). Cambridge: Cambridge University Press. (Original work published 1839)

Davey, G., & Tallis, F. (Eds.) (1994). *Worrying: Perspectives on theory, assessment and treatment.* Chichester, UK: Wiley.

Davey, G.C.L. (1994a). Disgust. In V.S. Ramachandran (Ed.), *Encyclopedia of human behaviour.* San Diego, CA: Academic Press.

Davey, G.C.L. (1994b). Self-reported fears to common indigenous animals in an adult UK population: The role of disgust sensitivity. *British Journal of Psychology, 85,* 541–554.

Davey, G.C.L., Forster, L., & Mayhew, G. (1993) Familial resemblances in disgust sensitivity and animal phobias. *Behaviour Research and Therapy, 31,* 41–50.

Davidson, J.R.T., & Foa, E.B. (1991). Diagnostic issues in posttraumatic stress disorder: Considerations for the DSMIV. *Journal of Abnormal Psychology, 100,* 346–355.

Davidson, J.R.T., Kudler, H.S., Saunders, W.B., & Smith, R.D. (1990). Symptom and comorbidity patterns in World War II and Vietnam veterans with posttraumatic stress disorder. *Comprehensive Psychiatry, 31,* 162–170.

Davidson, R.J. (1992). A prolegomenon to the structure of emotion: Gleanings from neuropsychology. *Cognition and Emotion, 6,* 245–268.

Davis, P.J. (1987). Repression and the inaccessibility of affective memories. *Journal of Personality and Social Psychology, 53,* 585–593.

Davis, P.J. (1990). Repression and the inaccessibility of emotional memories. In J.L. Singer (Ed.), *Repression and dissociation.* Chicago, IL: University of Chicago Press.

Davis, P.J., & Schwartz, G.E. (1987). Repression and the inaccessibility of affective memories. *Journal of Personality and Social Psychology, 52,* 155–162.

Davis, P.J., Singer, J.L., Bonnano, G.A., & Schwartz, G.E. (1988). Repression and reponse bias during an affective memory recognition task. *Australian Journal of Psychology, 40,* 147–157.

Davis, R. (1979). Black suicide in the seventies: Current trends. *Suicide and Life-threatening Behaviors, 9,* 131–140.

Dawkins, K., & Furnham, A. (1989). The colour naming of emotional words. *British Journal of Psychology, 80,* 383–389.

de Silva, P. (1994). Short-term interventions for morbid jealousy. *Clinical Psychology and Psychotherapy, 1,* 174–178.

de Sousa, R. (1987). *The rationality of emotion.* Cambridge, MA: MIT Press.

DeMonbreun, B.G., & Craighead, W.E. (1977). Distortion of perception and recall of positive and neutral feedback in depression. *Cognitive Therapy and Research, 1,* 311–329.

Denny, E.B., & Hunt, R.R. (1992). Affective valence and memory in depression: Dissociation of recall and fragment completion. *Journal of Abnormal Psychology, 101,* 575–580.

Derry, P.A., & Kuiper, N.A. (1981). Schematic processing and self-reference in clinical depression. *Journal of Abnormal Psychology, 90,* 286–297.

Descartes, R. (1989). *The passions of the soul.* Indianapolis, IN: Hackett. (Original work published 1649)

Dickinson, A. (1987). Animal conditioning and learning theory. In H.J. Eysenck & I. Martin (Eds.), *Theoretical foundations of behavior therapy.* New York: Plenum Press.

Diener, E. (1984). Subjective well-being. *Psychological Bulletin, 95,* 542–575.

Diener, E., Emmons, R.A., Larsen, R.J., & Griffin, S. (1985). The satisfaction with life scale. *Journal of Personality Assessment, 49,* 71–75.

Diener, E., & Larsen, R.J. (1993). The experience of emotional well-being. In M. Lewis & J. M. Haviland (Eds.), *Handbook of emotions.* New York: Guilford.

Diener, E., Sandvik, E., & Pavot, W. (1991). Happiness is the frequency, not the intensity, of positive versus negative affect. In F. Strack, M. Argyle, & N. Schwarz (Eds.), *Subjective well-being: An inter-disciplinary perspective.* Elmsford, NY: Pergamon Press.

Diener, E., Sandvik, E., Pavot, W., & Fujita, F. (1992). Extraversion and subjective well-being in a US national probability sample. *Journal of Research in Personality, 26,* 205–215.

Dienstbier, R.A. (1979). Emotion-attribution theory: Establishing roots and exploring future perspectives. In H.E. Howe, Jr., & R.A. Dienstbier (Eds.), *Nebraska symposium on motivation 1978* (Vol. 26). Lincoln, NB: University of Nebraska Press.

Digman, J.M. (1990). Personality structure: Emergence of the five-factor model. *Annual Review of Psychology, 41,* 417–440.

Dimsdale, J.E., Pierce, C., Schoenfeld, D., Brown, A., Zusman, R., & Graham, R. (1986). Suppressed anger and blood pressure: The effects of race, sex, social class, obesity and age. *Psychosomatic Medicine, 48,* 430–436.

Dixon, N. (1976). *On the psychology of military incompetence.* London: Futura.

Dobson, K. (1989). A meta-analysis of the efficacy of cognitive therapy for depression. *Journal of Consulting and Clinical Psychology, 57,* 414–419.

Dobson, K., & Shaw, B.F. (1987). Specificity and stability of self-referent encoding in clinical depression. *Journal of Abnormal Psychology, 96,* 34–40.

Dollard, J., Doob, L., Miller, N., Mowrer, O., & Sears, R. (1939*). Frustration and aggression.* New Haven, CT: Yale University Press.

Dollard, J., & Miller, N.E. (1950). *Personality and psychotherapy.* New York: McGraw-Hill.

Dring, G., & Kingston, B. (1992). Couple and sexual problems. In L.A. Champion & M.J. Power (Eds.), *Adult psychological problems: An introduction.* London: Falmer Press.

Duclos, S.E., Laird, J.D. Schneider, E., Sexter, M., Stern, L., & Van Lighten, O. (1989). Emotion-specific effects of facial expressions and postures on emotional experience. *Journal of Personality and Social Psychology, 57,* 100–108.

Dyer, M.G. (1983). *In-depth understanding: A model of integrative processing for narrative comprehension.* Cambridge, MA: MIT Press.

Dykman, B.M., Abramson, L.Y., Alloy, L.B., & Hartlage, S. (1989). Processing of ambiguous and unambiguous feedback by depressed and nondepressed college students: Schematic biases and their implications for depressive realism. *Journal of Personality and Social Psychology, 56,* 431–445.

Easterlin, R.A. (1974). Does economic growth improve the human lot? Some empirical evidence. In P.A. David & W.R. Melvin (Eds.*), Nations and households in economic growth.* Stanford, CA: Stanford University Press.

Eastman, C. (1976). Behavioural formulations of depression. *Psychological Review, 83,* 277–291.

Ehlers, A., & Breuer, P. (1992). Increased cardiac awareness in panic disorder. *Journal of Abnormal Psychology, 101,* 371–382.

Ehlers, A., Margraf, J., Davies, S., & Roth, W.T. (1988). Selective processing of threat cues in subjects with panic attacks. *Cognition and Emotion, 2,* 201–219.

Ehlers, A., Margraf, J., Roth, W. T., Taylor, C.B., & Birbaumer, N. (1988). Panic disorder. *Behaviour Research and Therapy, 26,* 1–11.

Ekman, P. (1973). Cross-cultural studies of facial expression. In P. Ekman (Ed.), *Darwin and facial expression: A century of research in review.* New York: Academic Press.

Ekman, P. (1980). *The face of man: Expressions of universal emotions in a New Guinea village.* New York: Garland SPTM Press.

Ekman, P. (Ed.) (1982). *Emotion in the human face* (2nd edn.). Cambridge, UK: Cambridge University Press.

Ekman, P. (1992). An argument for basic emotions. *Cognition and Emotion, 6,* 169–200.

Ekman, P. (1994). Strong evidence for universals in facial expressions: A reply to Russell's mistaken critique. *Psychological Bulletin, 115,* 268–287.

Ekman, P., & Friesen, W.V. (1978). *Facial action coding system: A technique for the measurement of facial movement.* Palo Alto, CA: Consulting Psychologists Press.

Ekman, P., Friesen, W.V., & Ellsworth, P. (1972). *Emotion in the human face: Guidelines for research and an integration of findings.* New York: Pergamon Press.

Ekman, P., Friesen, W.V., & Ellsworth, P. (1982). What emotion categories or dimensions can observers judge from facial behavior? In P. Ekman (Ed.), *Emotion in the human face* (2nd edn.). New York: Cambridge University Press.

Ekman, P., Friesen, W.V., O'Sullivan, M., Chan, A., Diacoyanni-Tarlatzis, I., Heider, K., Krause, R., LeCompte, W.A., Pitcairn, T., Ricci Bitti, P.E., Scherer, K.R., Tomita, M., & Tzavaras, A. (1987). Universals and cultural differences in the judgments of facial expressions of emotion. *Journal of Personality and Social Psychology, 53,* 712–717.

Ekman, P., Levenson, R.W., & Friesen, W.V. (1983). Autonomic nervous system activity distinguishes among emotions. *Science, 221,* 1208–1210.

Elliott, C.L., & Greene, R.L. (1992). Clinical depression and implicit memory. *Journal of Abnormal Psychology, 101,* 572–574.

Ellis, A. (1962). *Reason and emotion in psychotherapy.* New York: Lyle Stuart.

Ellis, A. (1977). *How to live with and without anger.* New York: Reader's Digest Press.

Ellis, A.W., & Young, A.W. (1988). *Human cognitive neuropsychology.* Hove, UK: Lawrence Erlbaum Associates Ltd.

Ellis, H.C., & Ashbrook, P.W. (1988). Resource allocation model of the effects of depressed mood states on memory. In K. Fiedler & J. Forgas (Eds.), *Affect, cognition, and social behavior.* Toronto, Canada: Hogrefe.

Ellsworth, P. (1991). Some implications of cognitive appraisal theories of emotion. In K.T. Strongman (Ed.), *International review of studies on emotion* (Vol. 1). Chichester, UK: Wiley.

Emmelkamp, P.M.G. (1994). Behavior therapy with adults. In A.E. Bergin & S.L. Garfield (Eds.), *Handbook of psychotherapy and behavior change* (4th edn.). New York: Wiley.

Emmons, R.A. (1986). Personal strivings: An approach to personality and subjective well-being. *Personality and Social Psychology, 51*, 1058–1068.

Emmons, R.A., & Diener, E. (1985). Personality correlates of subjective well-being. *Personality and Social Psychology Bulletin, 11*, 89–97.

Ennis, J., Barnes, R.A., Kennedy, S., & Trachtenberg, D.D. (1989). Depression in self-harm patients. *British Journal of Psychiatry, 154*, 41–47.

Epstein, S. (1972). The nature of anxiety with emphasis upon its relationship to expectancy. In C.D. Spielberger (Ed.), *Anxiety: Current trends in theory and research* (Vol.2.). New York: Academic Press.

Erber, R., & Erber, M.W. (1994). Beyond mood and social judgment: Mood incongruent recall and mood regulation. *European Journal of Social Psychology, 24*, 79–88.

Erdelyi, M.H. (1988). Issues in the study of unconscious and defence processes: Discussion of Horowitz's comments, with some elaborations. In M.J. Horowitz (Ed.), *Psychodynamics and cognition*. Chicago, IL: University of Chicago Press.

Erdelyi, M.H. (1990). Repression, reconstruction, and defense: History and integration of the psychoanalytic and experimental frameworks. In J.L. Singer (Ed.), *Repression and dissociation: Implications for personality theory, psychopathology, and health*. Chicago, IL: University of Chicago Press.

Evans, J. St. B.T. (1989). *Bias in human reasoning: Causes and consequences*. Hove, UK: Lawrence Erlbaum Associates Ltd.

Eysenck, M.W. (1990). *Happiness*. Hove, UK: Lawrence Erlbaum Associates Ltd.

Eysenck, M.W. (1992). *Anxiety: The cognitive perspective*. Hove, UK: Lawrence Erlbaum Associates Ltd.

Eysenck, M.W., & Keane, M.T. (1990). *Cognitive psychology: A student's handbook*. Hove, UK: Lawrence Erlbaum Associates Ltd.

Eysenck, M.W., Mogg, K., May, J., Richards, A., & Mathews, A. (1991). Bias in interpretation of ambiguous sentences related to threat in anxiety. *Journal of Abnormal Psychology, 100*, 144–150.

Fairbairn, W.R.D. (1952). *Psychoanalytic studies of the personality*. London: Tavistock.

Fava, M., Anderson, K., & Rosenbaum, J.F. (1993). Are thymoleptic-responsive "anger attacks" a discrete clinical syndrome? *Psychosomatics, 34*, 350–355.

Fenz, W.D., & Epstein, S. (1965). Manifest anxiety: Unifactorial or multifactorial composition. *Perceptual and Motor Skills, 20*, 773–780.

Finlay-Jones, R., & Brown, G.W. (1981). Types of stressful life event and the onset of anxiety and depressive disorders. *Psychological Medicine, 11*, 803–815.

Fischer, K.W., Shaver, P.R., & Carnochan, P. (1990). How emotions develop and how they organise development. *Cognition and Emotion, 4*, 81–127.

Fisher, S., & Hood, B. (1988). Vulnerability factors in the transition to university: Self-reported mobility history and sex differences as factors in psychological disturbance. *British Journal of Psychology, 79*, 309–320.

Fiske, S.T., & Taylor, S.E. (1991). *Social cognition* (2nd edn.). New York: McGraw-Hill.

Foa, E.B., Feske, U., Murdock, T.B., Kozak, M.J., & McCarthy, P.R. (1991). Processing of threat-related material in rape victims. *Journal of Abnormal Psychology, 100,* 156–162.

Foa, E.B., Ilai, D., McCarthy, P.R., Shoyer, B., & Murdock, T. (1993). Information processing in obsessive-compulsive disorder. *Cognitive Therapy and Research, 17,* 173–189.

Foa, E.B., & Kozak, M.J. (1986). Emotional processing of fear: Exposure to corrective information. *Psychological Bulletin, 99,* 20–35.

Foa, E.B., & McNally, R.J. (1986). Sensitivity to feared stimuli in obsessive-compulsives: A dichotic listening analysis. *Cognitive Therapy and Research, 10,* 477–486.

Foa, E.B., & Riggs, D.S. (1993). Post-traumatic stress disorder in rape victims. In J. Oldham, M.B. Riba, & A. Tasman (Eds.), *American Psychiatric Press review of psychiatry* (Vol. 12). Washington DC: American Psychiatric Press.

Foa, E.B., Steketee, G., & Rothbaum, B.O. (1989). Behavioral/cognitive conceptualisation of post-traumatic stress disorder. *Behavior Therapy, 20,* 155–176.

Foa, E.B., Steketee, G., & Young, M.C. (1984). Agoraphobia: Phenomemologic aspects, associated characteristics, and theoretical considerations. *Clinical Psychology Review, 4,* 431–457.

Foa, E.B., Zinbarg, R., & Rothbaum, B.O. (1992). Uncontrollability and unpredictability in post-traumatic stress disorder: An animal model. *Psychological Bulletin, 112,* 218–238.

Fodor, J.A. (1983). *The modularity of mind: An essay on faculty psychology.* Cambridge, MA: MIT Press.

Fodor, J.A. (1987). *Psychosemantics.* Cambridge, MA: MIT Bradford Books.

Fodor, J.A., & Pylyshyn, Z.W. (1988). Connectionism and cognitive architecture: A critical analysis. *Cognition, 28,* 3–71.

Fodor, J.D. (1977). *Semantics: Theories of meaning in generative grammar.* New York: Crowell.

Folkman, S., & Lazarus, R.S. (1980). An analysis of coping in a middle-aged community sample. *Journal of Health and Social Behavior, 21,* 219–239.

Folkman, S., & Lazarus, R.S. (1985). If it changes it must be a process: Study of emotion and coping during three stages of a college examination. *Journal of Personality and Social Psychology, 48,* 150–170.

Fontana, A., Rosenheck, R., & Brett, E. (1992). War zone traumas and posttraumatic stress disorder symptomatology. *Journal of Nervous and Mental Disease, 180,* 748–755.

Fordyce, M.W. (1981). *The psychology of happiness.* Fort Myers, FL: Cypress Lake Media.

Forgas, J.P. (1995). Mood and judgment: The affect infusion model (AIM). *Psychological Review, 117,* 39–66.

Forsterling, F. (1988). *Attribution theory in clinical psychology.* Chichester, UK: Wiley.

Fox, E. (1993). Allocation of visual attention and anxiety. *Cognition and Emotion, 7,* 207–215.

Fox, E. (1994). Attentional bias in anxiety: A defective inhibition hypothesis. *Cognition and Emotion, 8,* 165–195.

Fraczek, A., & Macaulay, J. R. (1971). Some personality factors in reaction to aggressive stimuli. *Journal of Personality, 39,* 163–177.

Frank, J.D. (1982). Therapeutic components shared by all psychotherapies. In J.H. Harvey & M.M. Parks (Eds.), *Psychotherapy research and behavior change*. Washington, DC: American Psychological Association.

Franzini, L.R., & Grossberg, J.M. (1995). *Eccentric and bizarre behaviors*. New York: Wiley.

Freedman, J.L. (1978). *Happy people*. New York: Harcourt Brace Jovanovich.

Freud, S. (1914). *On the history of the psychoanalytic movement* (Pelican Freud Library, Vol. 15). Harmondsworth, UK: Penguin.

Freud, S. (1919). *Introduction to the psychology of the war neuroses* (Standard edn., Vol. 18). London: Hogarth Press.

Freud, S. (1920). *Beyond the pleasure principle* (Standard edn., Vol. 18). London: Hogarth Press.

Freud, S. (1949). The unconscious. In J. Strachey (Ed. and Trans.) *The Standard Edition of the Complete Psychological works of Sigmund Freud* (Vol. 14). London: Hogarth Press. (Original work published 1915)

Freud, S. (1957). *Five lectures on psychoanalysis*. (J. Strachey, Ed.). (Standard edn., Vol. 11). London: Hogarth Press. (Original work published 1910)

Freud, S. (1958). Remembering, repeating and working-through. In J. Strachey (Ed.), *The Standard Edition* (Vol. 12). London: Hogarth.

Freud, S. (1971). *New introductory lectures on psychoanalysis* (Pelican Freud Library, Vol. 2). Harmondsworth, UK: Penguin. (Original work published 1933)

Freud, S. (1976). *Jokes and their relation to the unconscious* (Pelican Freud Library, Vol. 6). Harmondsworth, UK: Penguin. (Original work published 1905)

Freud, S. (1976). *The interpretation of dreams* (Pelican Freud Library, Vol. 4). Harmondsworth, UK: Penguin. (Original work published 1900)

Freud (1979). *Inhibitions, symptoms and anxiety* (Pelican Freud Library, Vol. 10). Harmondsworth, UK: Penguin. (Original work published 1926)

Freud, S. (1984). *Mourning and melancholia* (Pelican Freud Library, Vol. 11). Harmondsworth, UK: Penguin. (Original work published 1917)

Fridlund, A.J., Ekman, P., & Oster, H. (1987). Facial expressions of emotion: Review of the literature, 1970–1983. In A.W. Siegman & S. Feldstein (Eds.), *Nonverbal behavior and communication*. Hillsdale, NJ: Lawrence Erlbaum Associates Inc.

Frijda, N. (1986). *The emotions*. Cambridge, UK: Cambridge University Press.

Frijda, N. (1994). The lex talionis: On vengeance. In S.H.M. Van Goozen, N.E. Van de Poll, & J.A. Sergeant (Eds.), *Emotions: Essays on emotion theory*. Hillsdale, NJ: Lawrence Erlbaum Associates Inc.

Frijda, N.H. (1993) (Ed.). Appraisal and beyond: The issue of cognitive determinants of emotion. *Cognition and Emotion, 7*, 225–387.

Frodi, A. (1975). The effect of exposure to weapons on aggressive behaviour from a cross-cultural perspective. *International Journal of Psychology, 10*, 282–292.

Frye, J., & Stockton, R.A. (1982). Discriminant analysis of posttraumatic stress disorder among a group of Vietnam veterans. *American Journal of Psychiatry, 139*, 52–56.

Garcia, J., & Koelling, R.P. (1966). Relation of cue to consequence in avoidance learning. *Psychonomic Science, 4*, 123–124.

Garfinkel, P.E., & Garner, D.M. (1982). *Anorexia nervosa: A multidimensional perspective*. New York: Brunner Mazel.

Gates, G.S. (1926). An observational study of anger. *Journal of Experimental Psychology, 9*, 325–331.

Gazzaniga, M.S. (1988). Brain modularity: Towards a philosophy of conscious experience. In A. Marcel & E. Bisiach (Eds.), *Consciousness in contemporary science*. Oxford: Oxford University Press.

Geen, R.G. (1990). *Human aggression*. Milton Keynes, UK: Open University Press.

Geen, R.G., & Stonner, D. (1974). The meaning of observed violence: Effects on arousal and aggressive behaviour. *Journal of Research in Personality, 8*, 55–63.

Geiselman, R.E., Bjork, R.A., & Fishman, D.L. (1983). Disrupted retrieval in directed forgetting: A link with post-hypnotic amnesia. *Journal of Experimental Psychology: General, 112*, 58–72.

Gilbert, P. (1989). *Human nature and suffering*. Hove, UK: Lawrence Erlbaum Associates Ltd.

Gilbert, P. (1992). *Depression: The evolution of powerlessness*. Hove, UK: Lawrence Erlbaum Associates Ltd.

Gilbert, P., Allan, S., & Goss, K. (1996). Parental representations, shame, interpersonal problems, and vulnerability to psychopathology. *Clinical Psychology and Psychotherapy, 3*, 23–34.

Glick, I.O., Weiss, R.S., & Parkes, C.M. (1974). *The first year of bereavement*. New York: Wiley.

Goldberg, D., & Huxley, P. (1993). *Common mental disorders: A bio-social model*. London: Routledge.

Goldstein, A.J., & Chambless, D.L. (1978). A re-analysis of agoraphobia. *Behavior Therapy, 9*, 47–59.

Golin, S., Terrell, F., & Johnson, B. (1977). Depression and the illusion of control. *Journal of Abnormal Psychology, 86*, 440–442.

Gordon, R.M. (1987). *The structure of emotions: investigations in cognitive philosophy*. Cambridge, UK: Cambridge University Press.

Gotlib, I.H., & Cane, D.B. (1987). Construct accessibility and clinical depression: A longitudinal approach. *Journal of Abnormal Psychology, 96*, 199–204.

Gotlib, I.H., & Hammen, C.L. (1992). *Psychological aspects of depression: Toward a cognitive-interpersonal integration*. Chichester, UK: Wiley.

Gotlib, I.H., & McCann, C.D. (1984). Construct accessibility and depression: An examination of cognitive and affective factors. *Journal of Personalty and Social Psychology, 47*, 427–439.

Gotlib, I.H., McLachlan, A.L., & Katz, A.N. (1988). Biases in visual attention in depressed and nondepressed individuals. *Cognition and Emotion, 2*, 185–200.

Graf, P., & Mandler, G. (1984). Activation makes words more accessible, but not necessarily more retrievable. *Journal of Verbal Learning and Verbal Behavior, 23*, 553–568.

Gray, J.A. (1982). *The neuropsychology of anxiety*. Oxford: Oxford University Press.

Green, B.L. (1994). Psychosocial research in traumatic stress: An update. *Journal of Traumatic Stress, 7*, 341–362.

Greenberg, L.S., & Safran, J.D. (1987). *Emotion in psychotherapy*. New York: Guilford.

Gudjonsson, G.H. (1981). Self-reported emotional disturbance and its relation to electrodermal reactivity, defensiveness and trait anxiety. *Personality and Individual Differences, 2*, 47–52.

Gudykunst, W.B., & Ting-Toomey, S. (1988). *Culture and interpersonal communication*. Newbury Park, CA: Sage.

Haaga, D.A.F., Dyck, M.J., & Ernst, D. (1991). Empirical status of cognitive therapy of depression. *Psychological Bulletin, 110*, 215–236.

Haidt, J., McCauley, C., & Rozin, P. (1994). Individual differences in sensitivity to disgust: A scale sampling seven domains of disgust elicitors. *Personality and Individual Differences, 16*, 701–713.

Hammen, C., & Cochran (1981). Cognitive correlates of life stress and depression in college students. *Journal of Abnormal Psychology, 90*, 23–27.

Hammen, C., Krantz, S., & Cochran, S. (1981). Relationships between depression and causal attributions about stressful life events. *Cognitive Therapy and Research, 5*, 351–358.

Hampton, J.A. (1990). *Concepts*. Hove, UK: Lawrence Erlbaum Associates Ltd.

Hansen, C.H., Hansen, R.D., & Shantz, D.W. (1992). Repression at encoding: Discrete appraisals of emotional stimuli. *Journal of Personality and Social Psychology, 63*, 1026–1035.

Hansen, R.D., & Hansen, C.H. (1988). Repression of emotionally tagged memories: The architecture of less complex emotions. *Journal of Personality and Social Psychology, 55*, 811–818.

Harber, K.D., & Pennebaker, J.W. (1992). Overcoming traumatic memories. In S.-A. Christianson (Ed.), *The handbook of emotion and memory: Research and theory*. Hove, UK: Lawrence Erlbaum Associates Ltd.

Harder, D.W. (1995). Shame and guilt assessment, and relationships of shame- and guilt-proneness to psychopathology. In J.P. Tangney & K.W. Fischer (Eds.), *Self-conscious emotions: The psychology of shame, guilt, embarrassment, and pride*. New York: Guilford.

Harre, R. (1987). *The social construction of emotions*. Oxford: Blackwell.

Harris, P.L. (1989) *Children and emotion: The development of psychological understanding*. Oxford: Blackwell.

Harter, S. (1977). A cognitive-developmental approach to children's expression of conflicting feelings and a technique to facilitate such expression in play therapy. *Journal of Consulting and Clinical Psychology, 45*, 417–432.

Harter, S., & Buddin, B. (1987). Children's understanding of the simultaneity of two emotions: A five-stage developmental acquisition sequence. *Developmental Psychology, 23*, 388–399.

Hasher, L., & Zacks, R.T. (1988). Working memory, comprehension, and aging: A review and a new view. In G.H.Bower (Ed.), *The psychology of learning and motivation: Advances in research and theory* (Vol. 22). New York: Academic Press.

Hatfield, E., & Rapson, R.L. (1993). *Love, sex, and intimacy: Their psychology, biology, and history*. New York: Harper Collins.

Hatfield, E., & Sprecher, S. (1986). Measuring passionate love in intimate relations. *Journal of Adolescence, 9*, 383–410.

Hazan, C., & Shaver, P. (1987). Romantic love conceptualised as an attachment process. *Journal of Personality and Social Psychology, 52*, 511–524.

Hekmat, H. (1987). Origins and development of human fear reactions. *Journal of Anxiety Disorders, 1*, 197–218.

Henry, W.P., Schacht, T.E., & Strupp, H.H. (1986). Structural analysis of social behaviour: Application to a study of interpersonal process in differential psychotherapeutic outcome. *Journal of Consulting and Clinical Psychology, 54*, 27–31.

Herman, J.L. (1992). *Trauma and recovery*. New York: Basic Books.

Hertel, P.T., & Hardin, T.S. (1990). Remembering with and without awareness in a depressed mood: Evidence of deficits in initiative. *Journal of Experimental Psychology: General, 119*, 45–59.

Hibbert, G.A. (1984). Ideational components of anxiety: Their origin and content. *British Journal of Psychiatry, 144*, 618–624.

Hilgard, E.R. (1986). *Divided consciousness: Multiple controls in human thought and action*. New York: Wiley.

Hodgson, R.J., & Rachman, S. (1977). Obsessional compulsive complaints. *Behaviour Research and Therapy, 15*, 389–395.

Holland, J.G., & Skinner, B.F. (1961). *The analysis of behaviour: A program for self-instruction*. New York: McGraw-Hill.

Holt, R.R. (1967). Beyond vitalism and mechanism: Freud's concept of psychic energy. In J.H. Masserman (Ed.), *The ego*. New York: Grune & Stratton.

Holyoak, K.J., Koh, K., & Nisbett, R.E. (1989). A theory of conditioning: inductive learning within rule-based default hierarchies. *Psychological Review, 96*, 315–340.

Horowitz, M.J. (1973). Phase-oriented treatment of stress response syndromes. *American Journal of Psychotherapy, 27*, 506–515.

Horowitz, M.J. (1976). *Stress response syndromes*. New York: Jason Aronson.

Horowitz, M.J. (1979). Psychological response to serious life events. In V. Hamilton & D.M. Warburton (Eds.), *Human stress and cognition* (pp.235–263). New York: Wiley.

Horowitz , M.J. (1983). *Image formation and psychotherapy* (rev. edn.). New York: Jason Aronson.

Horowitz, M.J. (1986). *Stress response syndromes* (2nd edn.). Northvale, NJ: Jason Aronson.

Horowitz, M.J. (Ed.) (1988a). *Psychodynamics and cognition*. Chicago, IL: University of Chicago Press.

Horowitz, M.J. (1988b). Unconsciously determined defensive strategies. In M.J. Horowitz (Ed.), *Psychodynamics and cognition*. Chicago, IL: University of Chicago Press.

Horowitz, M.J. (1990). A model of mourning: Changes in schemas of self and others. *Journal of the American Psychoanalytic Association, 38*, 297–324.

Horowitz, M.J., & Reidbord, S.P. (1992). Memory, emotion, and response to trauma. In S.-A. Christianson (Ed.), *The handbook of emotion and memory: Research and theory*. Hillsdale, NJ: Lawrence Erlbaum Associates Inc.

Horowitz, M.J., Wilner, N., Kaltreider, N., & Alvarez, W. (1980). Signs and symptoms of post-traumatic stress disorder. *Archives of General Psychiatry, 37*, 85–92.

Hume, D. (1888). *A treatise of human nature*. Oxford: Oxford University Press. (Original work published 1739)

Ingram, R.E. (1984). Toward an information-processing analysis of depression. *Cognitive Therapy and Research, 8*, 443–478.

Isen, A.M. (1984). Toward understanding the role of affect in cognition. In R. Wyer & T. Srull (Eds.), *Handbook of social cognition* (Vol. 3). Hillsdale, NJ: Lawrence Erlbaum Associates Inc.

Isen, A.M. (1993). Positive affect and decision making. In M. Lewis & J.M. Haviland (Eds.), *Handbook of emotions*. New York: Guilford.

Isen, A.M., Johnson M.M.S., Mertz, E., & Robinson, G.F. (1985). The influence of positive affect on the unusualness of word associations. *Journal of Personality and Social Psychology, 48,* 1413–1426.

Isen, A.M., Niedenthal, P., & Cantor, N. (1992). An influence of positive affect on social categorization. *Motivation and Emotion, 16,* 65–78.

Isen, A.M., & Patrick, R. (1983). The effect of positive feelings on risk-taking: When the chips are down. *Organizational Behaviour and Human Performance, 31,* 194–202.

Isen, A.M., & Reeve, J.M. (1992). *The influence of positive affect on intrinsic motivation.* Unpublished manuscript. Cornell University.

Isen, A.M., Rosenzweig, A.S., & Young, M.J. (1991). The influence of positive affect on clinical problem solving. *Medical Decision Making, 11*(3), 221–227.

Isen, A.M., Shalker, T., Clark, M.S., & Karp, L. (1978). Affect, accessibility of material and behaviour: A cognition loop? *Journal of Personality and Social Psychology, 36,* 1–12.

Isen, A.M., & Simmonds, S.F. (1978). The effect of feeling good on a helping task is incompatible with good mood. *Social Psychology Quarterly, 41,* 345–349.

Izard, C.E. (1971). *The face of emotion.* New York: Appleton-Century-Crofts.

Izard, C.E. (1980). Cross-cultural perspectives on emotion and emotion communication. In H. Triandis & W. Lonner (Eds.), *Handbook of cross-cultural psychology: Basic processes* (Vol. 3). Boston, MA: Allyn & Bacon.

Izard, C.E. (1993). Four systems for emotion activation: Cognitive and noncognitive processes. *Psychological Review, 99,* 561–565.

Izard, C.E. (1994). What I should remember from my study of emotions, if I were to return to teaching and practicing psychotherapy. In N.H. Frijda (Ed.), *Proceedings of the VIIIth conference of the International Society for Research on Emotions.* Storrs, CT: ISRE Publications.

Izard, C.E., & Saxton, P.M. (1988). Emotions. In R.C. Atkinson, R.J. Herrnstein, G. Lindzey, & R.D. Luce (Eds.), *Stevens' handbook of experimental psychology* (2nd Edn.). New York: Wiley.

James, W. (1884). What is an emotion? *Mind, 9,* 188–205.

James, W. (1890). *The principles of psychology* (Vols. 1 & 2). New York: Holt.

Jamison, K.R. (1995). *An unquiet mind: A memoir of moods and madness.* London: Picador.

Jamner, L.D., & Schwartz, G.E. (1986). Integration of self-report and physiological indices of affect: Interactions with repressive coping strategies, *Psychophysiology, 23,* 444.

Janoff-Bulman, R. (1985). The aftermath of victimization: Rebuilding shattered assumptions. In C.R. Figley (Ed.), *Trauma and its wake: The study and treatment of posttraumatic stress disorder.* New York: Brunner Mazel.

Janoff-Bulman, R. (1989). Assumptive worlds and the stress of traumatic events: Applications of the schema construct. *Social Cognition, 7,* 113–136.

Janoff-Bulman, R. (1992). *Shattered asumptions: Towards a new psychology of trauma.* New York: Free Press.

Janoff-Bulman, R., & Frieze, I.H. (1983). A theoretical perspective for understanding reactions to victimisation. *Journal of Social Issues, 39,* 1–17.

Jehu, D. (1988). *Beyond sexual abuse: Therapy with women who were childhood victims.* Chichester, UK: Wiley.

Jenkins, J.H., Kleinman, A., & Good, B.J. (1991). Cross-cultural studies of depression. In J. Becker & A. Kleinman (Eds.), *Psychosocial aspects of depression.* Hillsdale, NJ: Lawrence Erlbaum Associates Inc.

Jensen, M.R. (1987). Psychobiological factors predicting the course of breast cancer, *Journal of Personality, 55*, 317–342.

Johnson, M.K., & Multhaup, K.S. (1992). Emotion and MEM. In S.-A. Christianson (Ed.), *The handbook of emotion and memory: Research and theory*. Hillsdale, NJ: Lawrence Erlbaum Associates Inc.

Johnson-Laird, P.N. (1983). *Mental models: Towards a cognitive science of language, inference and consciousness*. Cambridge, UK: Cambridge University Press.

Johnson-Laird, P.N. (1988). *The computer and the mind: An introduction to cognitive science*. London: Fontana.

Johnson-Laird, P.N., Herrmann, D.J., & Chaffin, R. (1984). Only connections: A critique of semantic networks. *Psychological Bulletin, 96*, 292–315.

Johnson-Laird, P.N., & Oatley, K. (1989). The language of emotions: An analysis of a semantic field. *Cognition and Emotion, 3*, 81–123.

Jones, G.V., & Martin, M. (1992). Conjunction in the language of emotions. *Cognition and Emotion, 6*, 369–386.

Jones, O.R. (Ed.) (1971). *The private language argument*. London: Macmillan.

Jonides, J., Naveh-Benjamin, M., & Palmer, J. (1985). Assessing automaticity. *Acta Psychologica, 60*, 157–171.

Joseph, S.A., Brewin, C.R., Yule, W., & Williams, R. (1991). Causal attributions and psychiatric symptoms in survivors of the Herald of Free Enterprise disaster. *British Journal of Psychiatry, 159*, 542–546.

Joseph, S.A., Brewin, C.R., Yule, W., & Williams, R. (1993). Causal attributions and post-traumatic stress in children. *Journal of Child Psychology and Psychiatry, 34*, 247–253.

Joseph, S.A., Dalgleish, T., Williams, R., Thrasher, S., Yule, W., & Hodgkinson, P. (in press). Attitudes towards emotional and post-traumatic stress at 5 years following the Herald of Free Enterprise disaster. *British Journal of Clinical Psychology*.

Joseph, S.A., Yule, W., Williams, R., & Hodgkinson, P. (1994). The Herald of Free Enterprise disaster: Correlates of distress at thirty months. *Behaviour Research and Therapy, 32*, 521–524.

Kahneman, D., & Miller, D.T. (1986). Norm theory: Comparing reality to its alternatives. *Psychological Review, 93*, 136–153.

Kahneman, D., & Tversky, A. (1979). Prospect theory: An analysis of decisions under risk. *Econometrica, 47*, 263–291

Kammann, R. (1982). *Personal circumstances and life events as poor predictors of happiness*. Paper presented at the annual convention of the American Psychological Association, Washington, DC.

Kaplan, H.B., & Pokorny, A.D. (1976). Self-attitudes and suicidal behavior. *Suicide and Life-threatening Behavior, 6*, 23–35.

Kaplan, H.S. (1979). *Disorders of sexual desire*. London: Ballière Tindall.

Kaufman, G. (1989). *The psychology of shame: Theory and treatment of shame-based syndromes*. New York: Springer.

Keane, T.M., Zimmering, R.T., & Caddell, R.T. (1985). A behavioural formulation of PTSD in Vietnam veterans. *Behaviour Therapist, 8*, 9–12.

Kekes, J. (1982). Happiness. *Mind, 91*, 358–376.

Keltner, D., Ellsworth, P.C., & Edwards, K. (1993). Beyond simple pessimism: Effects of sadness and anger on social perception. *Journal of Personality and Social Psychology, 64*, 740–752.

Kendell, R.E., Chalmers, J.C., & Platz, C. (1987). Epidemiology of puerperal psychoses. *British Journal of Psychiatry, 150*, 662–673.

Kennerley, H., & Gath, D. (1989). Maternity blues III: Associations with obstetric, psychological and psychiatric factors. *British Journal of Psychiatry, 155*, 367–373.

Kenny, A. (1963). *Action, emotion and will*. London: Routledge & Kegan Paul.

Kihlstrom, J.F. (1994). One hundred years of hysteria. In S.J. Lynn & J.W. Rhue (Eds.), *Dissociaion: Clinical and theoretical perspectives*. New York: Guilford.

Kilpatrick, D.G., Veronen, L.J., & Best, C.L. (1985). Factors predicting psychological distress among rape victims. In C. R. Figley (Ed.), *Trauma and its wake*. New York: Brunner/Mazel.

Kintsch, W. (1974). *The representation of meaning in memory*. Hillsdale, NJ: Lawrence Erlbaum Associates Inc.

Klein, D.F. (1981). Anxiety reconceptualized. In D.F. Klein & J.G. Rabkin (Eds.), *Anxiety: New research and changing concepts*. New York: Raven Press.

Klein, M. (1957). Envy and gratitude. In M. Klein, *The Writings of Melanie Klein*. London: Hogarth Press.

Kleinman, A., & Good, B. (Eds.) (1985). *Culture and depression: Studies in the anthropology and cross-cultural psychiatry of affect and disorder*. Berkeley, CA: University of California Press.

Konecni, V.J. (1975). The mediation of aggressive behaviour: Arousal level versus anger and cognitive labelling. *Journal of Personality and Social Psychology, 32*, 706–712.

Kovacs, M., & Beck, A.T. (1978). Maladaptive cognitive structures in depression. *American Journal of Psychiatry, 135*, 525–533.

Kozma, A., & Stones, M.J. (1980). The measurement of happiness: Development of the Memorial University of Newfoundland Scale of Happiness (MUNSCH). *Journal of Gerontology, 35*, 906–912.

Kraiger, K., Billings, R.S., & Isen, A. M. (1989). The influence of positive affective states on task perceptions and satisfaction. *Organizational Behaviour and Human Decision Processes, 44*, 12–25.

Kreitman, N. (1977). *Parasuicide*. Chichester, UK: Wiley.

Kreitman, N. (1990). Research issues in the epidemiological and public health aspects of parasuicide and suicide. In D. Goldberg & D. Tantam (Eds.), *The public health impact of mental disorder*. Stuttgart, Germany: Hogrefe & Huber.

Kuch, K., & Cox, B.J. (1992). Symptoms of PTSD in 124 survivors of the Holocaust. *American Journal of Psychiatry, 149*, 337–340.

Kumar, R., & Robson, K. (1984). A prospective study of emotional disorders in child bearing women. *British Journal of Psychiatry, 144*, 35–47.

Laird, J.D. (1974). Self-attribution of emotion: The effects of expressive behaviour on the quality of emotional experience. *Journal of Personality and Social Psychology, 29*, 475–486.

Lam, D.H. (1991). Psychosocial family interventions in schizophrenia: Review of empirical studies. *Psychological Medicine, 21*, 423–441.

Lam, D.H., Green, B., Power, M.J., & Checkley, S. (1994). The impact of social cognitive variables on the initial level of depression and recovery. *Journal of Affective Disorders, 32*, 75–83.

Lam, D.H., Green, B., Power, M.J., & Checkley, S. (1996). Dependency, matching adversities, length of survival and relapse in major depression. *Journal of Affective Disorders, 37*, 81–90.

Lam, D.H., & Power, M.J. (1991). A questionnaire designed to assess role and goals: A preliminary study. *British Journal of Medical Psychology, 64,* 359–373.

Lang, P.J. (1964). Experimental studies of desensitisation psychotherapy. In J. Wolpe (Ed.), *The conditioning therapies.* New York: Holt, Rhinehart, & Winston.

Lang, P.J. (1968). Fear reduction and fear behaviour: Problems in treating a construct. In J.M. Shlien (Ed.), *Research in psychotherapy* (Vol.3.). Washington, DC: American Psychological Association.

Lang, P.J. (1969). The mechanics of desensitization and the laboratory study of fear. In C.M. Franks (Ed.), *Behavior therapy: Appraisal and status.* New York: McGraw-Hill.

Lang, P.J. (1977). Fear imagery: An information processing analysis. *Behavior Therapy, 8,* 862–886.

Lang, P.J. (1979). A bio-informational theory of emotional imagery. *Psychophysiology, 16,* 495–512.

Lang, P.J. (1984). Cognition in emotion: Concept and action. In C.E. Izard, J. Kagan, & R.B. Zajonc (Eds.), *Emotions, cognition, and behaviour.* New York: Cambridge University Press.

Lang, P.J. (1985). The cognitive psychophysiology of emotion: Fear and anxiety. In A.H. Tuma & J.D. Maser (Eds.), *Anxiety and the anxiety disorders.* Hillsdale, NJ: Lawrence Erlbaum Associates Inc.

Larsen, R.J., & Diener, E. (1985). A multitrait-multimethod examination of affect structure: Hedonic level and emotional intensity. *Personality and Individual Differences, 6,* 631–636.

Larsen, R.J., & Diener, E. (1987). Affect intensity as an individual difference charactersitic: A review. *Journal of Research in Personality, 21,* 1–39.

Larsen, R.J., Diener, E., & Emmons, R.A. (1985). An eveluation of subjective well-being measures. *Social Indicators Research, 17,* 1–18.

Larsen, R.J., & Ketelaar, T. (1989). Extraversion, neuroticism, and susceptibility to positive and negative mood induction procedures. *Personality and Individual Differences, 10,* 1221–1228.

Larsen, R.J., & Ketelaar, T. (1991). Personality and susceptibility to positive and negative emotional states. *Journal of Personality and Social Psychology, 61,* 132–140.

Lavy, E., van Oppen, P., & van den Hout, M. (1994). Selective processing of emotional information in obsessive compulsive disorder. *Behaviour Research and Therapy, 32,* 243–246.

Lawler, K.A., Harralson, T.L., Armstead, C.A., & Schmied, L.A. (1993). Gender and cardiovascular responses: What is the role of hostility? *Journal of Psychosomatic Research, 37,* 603–613.

Lazarus, R.S. (1966). *Psychological stress and the coping process.* New York: McGraw-Hill.

Lazarus, R.S. (1982). Thoughts on the relationship between emotion and cognition. *American Psychologist, 37,* 1019–1024.

Lazarus, R.S. (1991). *Emotion and adaptation.* New York: Oxford University Press.

LeDoux, J.E. (1993). Emotional networks in the brain. In M. Lewis & J.M. Haviland (Eds.), *Handbook of emotions.* New York: The Guilford Press.

Lee, J.A. (1976). Forbidden colours of love: Patterns of gay love and gay liberation. *Journal of Homosexuality, 1,* 401–418.

Levenson, R.W. (1988). Emotion and the autonomic nervous system: A prospectus for research on autonomic specificity. In N.H.Wagner (Ed.), *Social psychophysiology: Theory and clinical applications*. Chichester, UK: Wiley.

Levenson, R.W., Cartenson, L.L., Friesen, W.V., & Ekman, P. (1991). Emotion, physiology, and expression in old age. *Psychology and Aging, 6*, 28–35.

Levenson, R.W., Ekman, P., & Friesen, W.V. (1990). Voluntary facial action generates emotion-specific autonomic nervous system activity. *Psychophysiology, 27*, 363–384.

Leventhal, H. (1980). Toward a comprehensive theory of emotion. In L. Berkowitz (Ed.), *Advances in experimental social psychology* (Vol. 13). New York: Academic Press.

Leventhal, H. (1984). A perceptual-motor theory of emotion. In L. Berkowitz (Ed.), *Advances in experimental social psychology* (Vol. 17). New York: Academic Press.

Leventhal, H., & Scherer, K. (1987). The relationship of emotion to cognition: A functional approach to a semantic controversy. *Cognition and Emotion, 1*, 3–28.

Lewin, B.D. (1951). *The psychoanalysis of elation*. London: Hogarth Press.

Lewinsohn, P.M., Mischel, W., Chaplin, C., & Barton, R. (1980). Social competence and depression: The role of illusory self-perceptions. *Journal of Abnormal Psychology, 89*, 203–217.

Lewis, M. (1993). The emergence of human emotions. In M. Lewis & J.M. Haviland (Eds.), *Handbook of emotions*. New York: Guilford.

Lewis, M.D. (1996). Self-organising cognitive appraisals. *Cognition and Emotion, 10*, 1–25.

Ley, R. (1985). Agoraphobia, the panic attack and the hyperventilation syndrome. *Behaviour Research and Therapy, 23*, 79–82.

Lichtenstein, S., Slovic, P., Fischoff, B., Layman, M., & Combs, B. (1978). Judged frequency of lethal events. *Journal of Experimental Psychology: Human Learning and Memory, 4*, 551–578.

Linehan, M.M. (1993). *Cognitive-behavioral treatment of borderline personality disorder*. New York: Guilford.

Litz, B.T., & Keane, T.M. (1989). Information processing in anxiety disorders: Application to the understanding of posttraumatic stress disorder. *Clinical Psychology Review, 9*, 243–257.

Lloyd, G.G., & Lishman, W.A. (1975). The effect of depression on the speed of recall of pleasant and unpleasant experiences. *Psychological Medicine, 5*, 173–180.

Locke, J. (1690/1977). An essay concerning human understanding. In S.M. Cahn (Ed.), *The classics of western philosophy* (3rd. edn.). Indianapolis, IN: Hackett.

Logan, G.D. (1980). Attention and automaticity in Stroop and priming tasks: Theory and data. *Cognitve Psychology, 12*, 523–553.

Logan, G.D. (1988). Toward an instance theory of automatisation. *Psychological Review, 95*, 492–527.

Lovestone, S., & Kumar, R. (1993). Postnatal psychiatric illness: The impact on partners. *British Journal of Psychiatry, 163*, 210–216.

Luria, A.R. (1976). *The neuropsychology of memory*. Washington, DC: Winston.

Lutz, C.A. (1985). Ethnopsychology compared to what? Explaining behavior and consciousness among the Ifaluk. In G. White & J.T. Kirkpatrick (Eds.), *Person, self, and experience: Exploring Pacific ethnopsychologies*. Berkeley, CA: University of California Press.

Lutz, C.A. (1988). *Unnatural emotions: Everyday sentiments on a Micronesian atoll and their challenge to Western theory*. Chicago, IL: University of Chicago Press.

Lycan, W. (1987). The continuity of levels of nature. In W. Lycan (Ed.), *Mind and cognition: A reader*. Oxford: Blackwell.

Lynn, S.J., & Rhue, J.W. (Eds.) (1994). *Dissociation: Clinical and theoretical perspectives*. New York: Guilford.

Lyons, W. (1980). *Emotion*. Cambridge, UK: Cambridge University Press.

Lyons, W. (1992). An introduction to the philosophy of emotions. In K.T. Strongman (Ed.), *International review of studies on emotion* (Vol. 2). Chichester, UK: Wiley.

MacLeod, A., Rose, G.S., & Williams, J.M.G. (1993). Components of hopelessness about the future in parasuicide. *Cognitive Therapy and Research, 17*, 441–455.

MacLeod, A., Williams, J.M.G., & Linehan, M.M. (1992). New developments in the understanding and treatment of suicidal behaviour. *Behavioural Psychotherapy, 20*, 193–218.

MacLeod, A.K., Andersen, A., & Davies, A. (1994). Self-ratings of positive and negative affect and retrieval of positive and negative affect memories. *Cognition and Emotion, 8*, 483–488.

MacLeod, C., & Hagan, R. (1992). Individual differences in the selective processing of threatening information, and emotional responses to a stressful life event. *Behaviour Research and Therapy, 30*, 151–161.

MacLeod, C., & Mathews, A. (1991). Biased cognitive operations in anxiety: Accessibility of information or assignment of processing priorities? *Behaviour Research and Therapy, 29*, 599–610.

MacLeod, C., Mathews, A., & Tata, P. (1986). Attentional biases in emotional disorders. *Journal of Abnormal Psychology, 95*, 15–20.

MacLeod, C., & Rutherford, E.M. (1992). Anxiety and the selective processing of emotional information: Mediating roles of awareness, trait and state variables, and personal relevance of stimulus materials. *Behaviour Research and Therapy, 30*, 479–491.

Maier, S.F., & Seligman, M.E.P. (1976). Learned helplessness: Theory and evidence. *Journal of Experimental Psychology: General, 105*, 3–46.

Main, M. (1991). Metacognitive knowledge, metacognitive monitoring, and singular (coherent) vs. multiple (incoherent) model of attachment: findings and directions for future research. In C.M. Parkes, J. Stevenson-Hinde, & P. Marris (Eds.), *Attachment across the life cycle*. London: Routledge.

Mallandain, I., & Davies, M.F. (1994). The colours of love: Personality correlates of love styles. *Personality and Individual Differences, 17*, 557–560.

Mandler, G. (1984). *Mind and body: Psychology of emotion and stress*. New York: Norton.

Mannuzza, S., Fyer, A.J., Liebowitz, M.R., & Klein, D.F. (1990). Delineating the boundaries of social phobia: Its relationship to panic disorder and agoraphobia. *Journal of Anxiety Disorders, 4*, 41–59.

Marks, I.M. (1969). *Fears and phobias*. New York: Academic Press.

Marquez, G. (1989). *Love in the time of cholera*. London: Penguin.

Marr, D. (1982). *Vision: A computational investigation into the human representation and processing of visual information*. San Francisco, CA: Freeman.

Maslow, A.H. (1968). *Toward a psychology of being* (2nd edn.). New York: Van Nostrand Reinhold.

Mathews, A., & MacLeod, C. (1985). Selective processing of threat cues in anxiety states. *Behaviour Research and Therapy*, *23*, 563–569.

Mathews, A., & MacLeod, C. (1986). Discrimination of threat cues without awareness in anxiety states. *Journal of Abnormal Psychology*, *95*, 131–138.

Mathews, A., May, J., Mogg, K., & Eysenck, M.W. (1990). Attentional bias in anxiety: Selective search or defective filtering? *Journal of Abnormal Psychology*, *99*, 166–173.

Mathews, A., Mogg, K., May, J., & Eysenck, M.W. (1988). Implicit and explicit memory biases in anxiety. *Journal of Abnormal Psychology*, *97*, 236–240.

Mathews, A., Richards, A., & Eysenck, M.W. (1989). Interpretation of homophones related to threat in anxiety states. *Journal of Abnormal Psychology*, *98*, 31–34.

Matthews, G.R., & Antes, J.R. (1992). Visual attention and depression: Cognitive biases in the eye fixations of the dysphoric and the nondepressed. *Cognitive Therapy and Research*, *16*, 359–371.

Maughan, B., & Champion, L.A. (1990). Risk and protective factors in the transition to young adulthood. In P.B. Baltes & M.M. Baltes (Eds.), *Successful aging: Perspectives from the behavioral sciences*. Cambridge, UK: Cambridge University Press.

McCabe, S.B., & Gotlib, I.H. (1993) Attentional processing in clinically depressed subjects: A longitudinal investigation. *Cognitive Therapy and Research*, *17*, 359–377.

McCrae, R.R. (Ed.). (1992). The five-factor model: Issues and application. *Journal of Personality*, *60*(2).

McCrae, R.R., & Costa, P.T., Jr. (1991). Adding Liebe und Arbeit: The full five-factor model and well-being. *Personality and Social Psychology Bulletin*, *17*, 227–232.

McDougall, W. (1926). *An introduction to social psychology*. Boston, MA: Luce.

McFarlane, A.C. (1988). The longitudinal course of posttraumatic morbidity: The range of outcomes and their predictors. *Journal of Nervous and Mental Disease*, *176*, 30–39.

McFarlane, A.C. (1989). The aetiology of post-traumatic morbidity: Predisposing, precipitating and perpetuating factors. *British Journal of Psychiatry*, *154*, 221–228.

McFarlane, A.C. (1992). Avoidance and intrusion in posttraumatic stress disorder. *Journal of Nervous and Mental Disease*, *180*, 439–445.

McGreal, R., & Joseph, S. (1993). The depression-happiness scale. *Psychological Reports*, *73*, 1279–1282.

McGuffin, P., & Katz, R. (1989). Nature, nurture and affective disorder. In J.F.W. Deakin & H. Freeman (Eds.), *Recent advances in the biology of affective disorder*. London: Royal College of Psychiatrists.

McIntosh, W.D., & Martin, L.L. (1991). The cybernetics of happiness: The relation of goal attainment, rumination and affect. In M.S. Clark (Ed.), *Review of personality and social psychology* (Vol. 13). Newbury Park, CA: Sage.

McKellar, P. (1949). The emotion of anger in the expression of human aggressiveness. *British Journal of Psychology*, *39*, 148–155.

McKellar, P. (1950). Provocation to anger and the development of attitudes of hostility. *British Journal of Psychology*, *40*, 104–114.

McNally, R.J. (1990). Psychological approaches to panic disorder: A review. *Psychological Bulletin*, *108*, 403–419.

McNally, R.J., & Foa, E.B. (1987). Cognition and agoraphobia: Bias in the interpretation of threat. *Cognitive Therapy and Research, 11*, 567–581.

McNally, R.J., Foa, E.B., & Donnell, C. (1989). Memory bias for anxiety information in patients with panic disorder. *Cognition and Emotion, 3*, 27–44.

McNally, R.J., Lasko, N.B. Macklin, M.L., & Pitman, R.K. (in press). Autobiographical memory disturbance in combat-related post-traumatic stress disorder. *Behaviour Research and Therapy*.

McNally, R.J., Litz, B.T., Prassas, A., Shin, L.M., & Weathers, F.W. (1994). Emotional priming of autobiographical memory in post-traumatic stress disorder. *Cognition and Emotion, 8*, 351–368.

McNally, R.J., & Lorenz, M. (1987). Anxiety sensitivity in agoraphobics. *Journal of Behaviour Therapy and Experimental Psychiatry, 18*, 3–11.

Meltzer, H. (1933). Students' adjustments in anger. *Journal of Social Psychology, 4*, 285–309.

Mesquita, B., & Frijda, N.H. (1992). Cultural variations in emotion: A review. *Psychological Bulletin, 112*, 179–204.

Metalsky, G.I., Joiner, T.E., Hardin, T.S., & Abramson, L.Y. (1993). Depressive reactions to failure in a naturalistic setting: A test of the hopelessness and self-esteem theories of depression. *Journal of Abnormal Psychology, 102*, 101–109.

Meyer, T.J., Miller, M.L., Metzger, R.L., & Borkovec, T.D. (1990). Development and validation of the Penn state worry questionnaire. *Behaviour Research and Therapy, 28*, 487–495.

Michalos, A.C. (1985). Multiple discrepancies theory (MDT). *Social Indicators Research, 16*, 347–413.

Michalos, A.C. (1986). Job satisfaction, marital satisfaction, and the quality of life. In F.M. Andrews (Ed.), *Research on the quality of life*. Ann Arbor, Michigan: University of Michigan, Institute for Social Research.

Mikulincer, M., & Solomon, Z. (1988). Attributional style and combat related posttraumatic stress disorder. *Journal of Abnormal Psychology, 97*, 308–313.

Mill, J.S. (1991). Autobiography. In R. Porter (Ed.), *The Faber Book of Madness*. London: Faber & Faber. (Original work published in 1853)

Miller, G.A., & Johnson-Laird, P.N. (1976). *Language and perception*. Cambridge, UK: Cambridge University Press.

Miller, I.W., & Norman, W.H. (1979). Learned helplessness in humans: A review and attribution theory model. *Psychological Bulletin, 86*, 93–118.

Mineka, S. (1985). Animal models of anxiety-based disorders. In A. Tuma & J. Maser (Eds.). *Anxiety and the anxiety disorders*. Hillsdale, NJ: Lawrence Erlbaum Associates Inc.

Mineka, S., & Kihlstrom, J. (1978). Unpredictable and uncontrollable aversive events. *Journal of Abnormal Psychology, 87*, 256–271.

Minichiello, W.E., Baer, L., Jenike, M.A., & Holland, A. (1990). Age of onset of major subtypes of obsessive-compulsive disorder. *Journal of Anxiety Disorders, 4*, 147–150.

Minsky, M. (1975). A framework for representing knowledge. In P.H. Winston (Ed.), *The psychology of computer vision*. New York: McGraw-Hill.

Mitchell, J., & Fensome, H. (1992). Eating disorders. In L.A. Champion & M.J. Power (Eds.), *Adult psychological problems: An introduction*. London: Falmer Press.

Mogg, K., Mathews, A., & Weinman, J. (1987). Memory bias in clinical anxiety. *Journal of Abnormal Psychology, 96*, 94–98.

Mogg, K., Mathews, A., May, J., Grove, M., Eysenck, M.W., & Weinman, J. (1991). Assessment of cognitive bias in anxiety and depression using a colour perception task. *Cognition and Emotion, 5*, 221–238.

Moscovici, S. (1976). *Social influence and social change.* London: Academic Press.

Mowrer, O.H. (1939). Stimulus response theory of anxiety. *Psychological Review, 46*, 553–565.

Mowrer, O.H. (1947). On the dual nature of learning—A re-interpretation of "conditioning" and "problem solving". *Harvard Educational Review, 17*, 102–148.

Mowrer, O.H. (1960). *Learning theory and behavior.* New York: Wiley.

Murphy, E. (1982). Social origins of depression in old age. *British Journal of Psychiatry, 141*, 135–142.

Murphy, S.T., & Zajonc, R.B. (1993). Affect, cognition, and awareness: Affective priming with optimal and suboptimal stimulus exposures. *Journal of Personality and Social Psychology, 64*, 723–739.

Myers, J.K., Weissman, M.M., & Tischler, G.L. (1984). Six-month prevalence of psychiatric disorders in three communities. *Archives of General Psychiatry, 41*, 959–967.

Myers, L.B. (1993). *Repression and autobiographical memory.* Unpublished doctoral dissertation. University of London.

Myers, L.B., & Brewin, C.R. (1994). Recall of early experience and the repressive coping style. *Journal of Abnormal Psychology, 103*, 288–292.

Myers, L.B., Brewin, C.R., & Power, M.J. (1992). Repression and autobiographical memory. In M.A. Conway, D.C. Rubin, H. Spinnler, & W.A. Wagenaar (Eds.), *Theoretical perspectives on autobiographical memory.* Dordrecht, The Netherlands: Kluwer.

Nasby, W., & Yando, R. (1982). Selective encoding and retrieval of affectively valenced information. *Journal of Personality and Social Psychology, 43*, 1244–1255.

Neely, J.R. (1977). Semantic priming and retrieval from lexical memory: Roles of spreading activation and limited-capacity attention. *Journal of Experimental Psychology: General, 106*, 226–254

Neisser, U. (1967). *Cognitive psychology.* New York: Appleton-Century-Crofts.

Neisser, U. (1976). *Cognition and reality.* San Francisco, CA: Freeman.

Neu, J. (1980). Jealous thoughts. In A.O. Rorty (Ed.), *Explaining emotions.* Berkeley, CA: University of California Press.

Newell, A. (1990). *Unified theories of cognition.* Harvard, MA: Harvard University Press.

Newell, A., Rosenbloom, P.S., & Laird, J.E. (1989). Symbolic architectures for cognition. In M.I. Posner (Ed.), *Foundations of cognitive science.* Cambridge, MA: MIT Press.

Newell, A., & Simon, H.A. (1972). *Human problem solving.* Englewood Cliffs, NJ: Prentice-Hall.

Newton, T.L., & Contrada, R.L. (1992). Repressive coping and verbal-autonomic dissociation: The influence of social context. *Journal of Personality and Social Psychology, 62*, 159–167.

Niedenthal, P., Tangney, J.P., & Gavanski, I. (1994). "If only I weren't" vs. "If only I hadn't": Distinguishing shame and guilt in counterfactual thinking. *Journal of Personality and Social Psychology, 67*, 585–595.

Nisbett, R.E., & Wilson, T.D. (1977). Telling more than we can know: Verbal reports on mental processes. *Psychological Review, 84*, 231–259.

Nolen-Hoeksema, S. (1987). Sex differences in unipolar depression: Evidence and theory. *Psychological Bulletin, 101,* 259–282.

Nolen-Hoeksema, S. (1990). *Sex differences in depression.* Stanford, CA: Stanford University Press.

Norman, D.A., & Shallice, T. (1980). *Attention to action: Willed and automatic control of behaviour* (CHIP Report 99). San Diego, CA: University of California.

Novaco, R.W. (1975). *Anger control: The development and evaluation of an experimental treatment.* Lexington, MA: Lexington Books/D.C. Heath.

Novaco, R.W. (1979). The cognitive regulation of anger and stress. In P.C. Kendall & S.D. Hollon (Eds.), *Cognitive-behavioural interventions: Theory, research, and procedures.* New York: Academic Press.

Nunn, J.D., Stevenson, R.J., & Whalan, G. (1984). Selective memory effects in agoraphobic patients. *British Journal of Clinical Psychology, 23,* 195–201.

Oakhill, J.V., & Johnson-Laird, P.N. (1985). The effect of belief on the spontaneous production of syllogistic conclusions. *Quarterly Journal of Experimental Psychology, 37A,* 553–569.

Oatley, K. (1992). *Best laid schemes: The psychology of emotion.* Cambridge, UK: Cambridge University Press.

Oatley, K., & Bolton, W. (1985). A social-cognitive theory of depression in reaction to life events. *Psychological Review, 92,* 373–388.

Oatley, K., & Duncan, E. (1992). Incidents of emotion in daily life. In K.T. Strongman (Ed.), *International review of studies on emotion* (Vol. 2). Chichester, UK: Wiley.

Oatley, K., & Jenkins, J.M. (1996). *Understanding emotions.* Oxford: Blackwell.

Oatley, K., & Johnson-Laird, P.N. (1987). Towards a cognitive theory of emotions. *Cognition and Emotion, 1,* 29–50.

Oatley, K., & Johnson-Laird, P.N. (1990). Semantic primitives for emotions: A reply to Ortony and Clore. *Cognition and Emotion, 4,* 129–143.

Ohman, A. (1993). Fear and anxiety as emotional phenomena: Clinical phenomenology, evolutionary perspectives, and information processing mechanisms. In M. Lewis & J.M. Haviland (Eds.), *The handbook of emotions.* New York: Guilford.

Ohman, A., Dimberg, U, & Ost, L.-G. (1985). Animal and social phobias: Biological constraints on learned fear responses. In S. Reiss & R. Bootzin (Eds.), *Theoretical issues in behaviour therapy.* New York: Academic Press.

Okun, M.A., & George, L.K. (1984). Physician and self-ratings of health, neuroticism and subjective well-being among men and women. *Personality and Individual Differences, 5,* 533–539.

Oppenheimer, R., Howells, K., Palmer, R.L., & Chaloner, D.A. (1985). Adverse sexual experience in childhood and clinical eating disorders: A preliminary description. *Journal of Psychiatric Research, 19,* 357–361.

Ortony, A., Clore, G.L., & Collins, A. (1988). *The cognitive structure of emotions.* New York: Cambridge University Press.

Ortony, A., & Turner, W. (1990). What's basic about "basic" emotions? *Psychological Review, 97,* 315–331.

Ost, L.G. (1987). Age of onset in different phobias. *Journal of Abnormal Psychology, 96,* 223–229.

Ost, L.G., Sterner, U., & Lindahl, I.L. (1984). Physiological responses in blood phobics. *Behaviour Research and Therapy, 22,* 109.

Oster, H., Daily, L., & Goldenthal, P. (1989). Processing facial affect. In A.W. Young & H.D. Ellis (Eds.), *Handbook of research on face processing.* Amsterdam: Elsevier.

Ottaviani, R., & Beck, A.T. (1987). Cognitive aspects of panic disorder. *Journal of Anxiety Disorders, 1,* 15–28.

Page, M.M., & Scheidt, R.J. (1971). The elusive weapons effect: Demand awareness, evaluation apprehension, and slightly sophisticated subjects. *Journal of Personality and Social Psychology, 20,* 304–318.

Paivio, A. (1971). *Imagery and verbal processes.* New York: Holt, Rinehart and Winston.

Paivio, A. (1986). *Mental representations: A dual coding approach.* Oxford: Oxford University Press.

Panksepp, J. (1982). Toward a general psychobiological theory of emotions. *Behavioral and Brain Sciences, 5,* 407–467.

Parducci, A. (1968). The relativism of absolute judgements. *Scientific American, 219,* 84–90.

Parkes, C.M. (1972). *Bereavement: Studies of grief in adult life.* New York: International Universities Press.

Parkes, C.M. (1993). Bereavement as a psychosocial transition: Processes of adaptation to change. In M.S. Stroebe, W. Stroebe, & R.O. Hansson (Eds.), *Handbook of bereavement: Theory, research, and intervention.* Cambridge, UK: Cambridge University Press.

Parrott, W.G., & Sabini, J. (1990). Mood and memory under natural conditions: Evidence for mood incongruent recall. *Journal of Personality and Social Psychology, 59,* 321–336.

Patton, G.C. (1988). Mortality in eating disorders. *Psychological Medicine, 18,* 947–951.

Pavot, W., Diener, E., & Fujita, F. (1990). Extraversion and happiness. *Personality and Individual Differences, 11,* 1299–1306.

Pennebaker, J.W. (1982). *The psychology of physical symptoms.* New York: Springer-Verlag.

Perry, C., & Laurence, J.R. (1984). Mental processing outside of awareness: The contributions of Freud and Janet. In K.S. Bowers & D. Meichenbaum (Eds.), *The unconscious reconsidered.* New York: Wiley.

Peters, R.S. (1960). *The concept of motivation.* London: Routledge & Kegan Paul.

Peterson, C. (1979). Uncontrollability and self-blame in depression: Investigation of the paradox in a college population. *Journal of Abnormal Psychology, 88,* 620–624.

Peterson, C., Maier, S.F., & Seligman, M.E.P. (1993). *Learned helplessness: A theory for the age of personal control.* New York: Oxford University Press.

Peterson, C., & Seligman, M.E.P. (1984). Causal explanations as a risk factor for depression: Theory and evidence. *Psychological Review, 91,* 347–374.

Peterson, C., Semmel, A., von Baeyer, C., Abramson, L.Y., Metalsky, G.I., & Seligman, M.E.P. (1982). The attributional style questionnaire. *Cognitive Therapy and Research, 6,* 287–300.

Pitcher, G. (1965). Emotion. *Mind, 74,* 326–346.

Plato. (1974). *Timaeus and Critias.* D. Lee (Trans.). Harmondsworth: Penguin.

Plato (1977). The Phaedo. In S.M. Cahn (Ed.), *The classics of Western philosophy* (3rd edn.). Indianapolis, IN: Hackett.

Plato (1977). The Republic. In S.M. Cahn (Ed.), *The classics of Western philosophy* (3rd edn.). Indianapolis, IN: Hackett.

Plutchik, R. (1980). *Emotion: A psychoevolutionary synthesis*. New York: Harper & Row.

Pollard, C.A., Pollard, H.J., & Corn, K.J. (1989). Panic onset and major events in the lives of agoraphobics: A test of contiguity. *Journal of Abnormal Psychology, 98*, 318–321.

Popper, K.R., & Eccles, J.C. (1977). *The self and its brain*. London: Routledge.

Posner, M.I. (Ed.) (1989). *Foundations of cognitive science*. Cambridge, MA: MIT Press.

Powell, J. (1992). Alcohol and drug dependence. In L.A. Champion & M.J. Power (Eds.), *Adult psychological problems: An introduction*. London: Falmer Press.

Power, M.J. (1986). A technique for measuring processing load during speech production. *Journal of Psycholinguistic Research, 15*, 371–382.

Power, M.J. (1987a). Cognitive theories of depression. In H.J. Eysenck & I. Martin (Eds.), *Theoretical foundations of behaviour therapy*. New York: Plenum Publishing Corporation.

Power, M.J. (1987b). The perception of life events in depressed inpatients and hospitalized controls. *Journal of Clinical Psychology, 43*, 206–211.

Power, M.J. (1990). A prime time for emotion: Cognitive vulnerability and the emotional disorders. In K.J. Gilhooly, M.T.G. Keane, R.H. Logie, & G. Erdos (Eds.), *Lines of thinking: Reflections on the psychology of thought* (Vol. 2). Chichester, UK: Wiley.

Power, M.J. (1991). Cognitive science and behavioural psychotherapy: Where behaviour was, there shall cognition be? *Behavioural Psychotherapy, 19*, 20–41.

Power, M.J. (1993). Social factors in phobias and obsessions. In D. Bhugra & J. Leff (Eds.), *Principles of social psychiatry*. Oxford: Blackwell.

Power, M.J., & Brewin, C.R. (1991). From Freud to cognitive science: A contemporary account of the unconscious. *British Journal of Clinical Psychology, 30*, 289–310.

Power, M.J., Cameron, C.M., & Dalgleish, T. (1996). Emotional priming in clinically depressed subjects. *Journal of Affective Disorders, 38*, 1–11.

Power, M.J., & Champion, L.A. (1986). Cognitive approaches to depression: A theoretical critique. *British Journal of Clinical Psychology, 25*, 201–212.

Power, M.J., Champion, L.A., & Aris, S.J. (1988). The development of a measure of social support: The significant others (SOS) scale. *British Journal of Clinical Psychology, 27*, 349–358.

Power, M.J., Dalgleish, T., Claudio, V., Tata, P., & Kentish, J. (submitted). *The directed forgetting task: Application to emotionally valent material*.

Power, M.J., Duggan, C.F., Lee, A.S., & Murray, R.M. (1995). Dysfunctional attitudes in depressed and recovered depressed patients and their first-degree relatives. *Psychological Medicine, 25*, 87–93.

Power, M.J., Katz, R., McGuffin, P., Duggan, C.F., Lam, D., & Beck, A.T. (1994). The dysfunctional attitude scale (DAS): A comparison of forms A and B and proposals for a new subscaled version. *Journal of Research in Personality, 28*, 263–276.

Quelhas, A.C., & Power, M.J. (1991). Raciocino dedutivo na depressao [Deductive reasoning in depression]. *Analise Psicologia, 9*, 43–52.

Quillian, M.R. (1968). Semantic memory. In M. Minsky (Ed.), *Semantic information processing*. Cambridge, MA: MIT Press.

Quinton, D., & Rutter, M. (1985). Parenting behaviour of mothers raised "in care". In A.R. Nicol (Ed.), *Longitudinal studies in child psychology and psychiatry.* New York: Wiley.

Rachman, S. (1976). The passing of the two-stage theory of fear and avoidance. *Behaviour Research and Therapy, 14,* 125–131.

Rachman, S. (1977). The conditioning theory of fear-acquisition: A critical examination. *Behaviour Research and Therapy, 15,* 375–387.

Rachman, S. (1980). Emotional processing. *Behaviour Research and Therapy, 18,* 51–60.

Rachman, S. (1993). Obsessions, responsibility and guilt. *Behaviour Research and Therapy, 31,* 149–154.

Rachman, S.J. (1990). *Fear and courage* (2nd edn.). New York: W.H.Freeman.

Rachman, S.J., & Hodgson, R.J. (1974). Synchrony and desynchrony in fear and avoidance. *Behaviour Research and Therapy, 12,* 311–318.

Rachman, S.J., & Hodgson, R.J. (1980). *Obsessions and compulsions.* Englewood Cliffs, NJ: Prentice-Hall.

Rachman, S., Lopatka, C., & Levitt, K. (1988). Experimental analyses of panic: II. Panic patients. *Behaviour Research and Therapy, 26,* 33–40.

Rapee, R.M. (1991). The conceptual overlap between cognition and conditioning in clinical psychology. *Clinical Psychology Review, 11,* 193–203.

Rapee, R.M., Ancis, J.R., & Barlow, D.H. (1988). Emotional reactions to physiological sensations: Panic disorder patients and non-clinical Ss. *Behaviour Research and Therapy, 26,* 265–269.

Rapee, R.M., & Barlow, D.H. (Eds.) (1991). *Chronic anxiety: Generalized anxiety disorder and mixed anxiety depression.* New York: Guilford.

Ravlin, S.B. (1987). *A computer model of affective reactions to goal-relevant events.* Unpublished Masters Thesis. University of Illinois, Urbana.

Reed, G.F. (1985). *Obsessional experience and compulsive behaviour: A cognitive-structural approach.* London: Academic Press.

Reisenzein, R. (1983). The Schachter theory of emotion: Two decades later. *Psychological Bulletin, 94,* 239–264.

Reiss, S., & McNally, R.J. (1985). Expectancy model of fear. In S. Reiss & R.R. Bootzin (Eds.), *Theoretical issues in behaviour therapy.* San Diego, CA: Academic Press.

Reiss, S., Peterson, R.A., Gursky, D.M., & McNally, R.J. (1986). Anxiety sensitivity, anxiety frequency and the prediction of fearfulness. *Behaviour Research and Therapy, 24,* 1–8.

Revusky, S.H., & Garcia, J. (1970). Learned associations over long delays. In G.H. Bower (Ed.), *The psychology of learning and motivation* (Vol. 4). New York: Academic Press.

Rheaume, J., Ladouceur, R., Freeston, M.H., & Letarte, H. (1995). Inflated responsibility in obsessive compulsive disorder: Validation of an operational definition. *Behaviour Research and Therapy, 33,* 159–169.

Rilke, R.M. (1986). *Letters to a younger poet.* (Trans. S. Mitchell). New York: Vintage Books.

Riskind, J.H. (1984). They stoop to conquer: Guiding and self-regulatory functions of physical posture after success and failure. *Journal of Personality and Social Psychology, 47,* 479–493.

Riskind, J.H., & Gotay, C.C. (1982). Physical posture: Could it have regulatory or feedback effects on motivation and emotion? *Motivation and Emotion, 6,* 273–298.

Rosaldo, M.Z. (1980). *Knowledge and passion: Ilongot notions of self and social life*. Cambridge, UK: Cambridge University Press.

Rosenbloom, P., & Newell, A. (1986). The chunking of goal hierarchies: A generalised model of practice. In R.S. Michalski, J.G. Carbonell, & J.M. Mitchell (Eds.), *Machine learning: An artificial intelligence approach*. Los Altos, CA: Kaufman.

Rosenstein, D., & Oster, H. (1988). Differential facial responses to four basic tastes in newborns. *Child Development, 59*, 1555–1568.

Rosenthal, N.E., Sack, D.A., Gillin, J.C., Lewy, A.J., Goodwin, F.K., Davenport, Y., Mueller, P.S., Newsome, D.A., & Wehr, T.A. (1984). Seasonal affective disorder: A description of the syndrome and preliminary findings with light therapy. *Archives of General Psychiatry, 41*, 72–80.

Rosenthal, N.E., & Wehr, T.A. (1992). Towards understanding the mechanism of action of light in seasonal affective disorder. *Pharmacopsychiatry, 25*, 56–60.

Ross, C.A., Joshi, S., & Currie, R. (1990). Dissociative experiences in the general population. *American Journal of Psychiatry, 147*, 1547–1552.

Rozensky, R.H., Rehm, L.P., Pry, G., & Roth, D. (1977). Depression and self-reinforcement behavior in hospitalized patients. *Journal of Behavior Therapy and Experimental Psychiatry, 8*, 35–38.

Rozin, P., & Fallon, A.E. (1987). A perspective on disgust. *Psychological Review, 94*, 23–41.

Rozin, P., Fallon, A.E., & Mandell, R. (1984). Family resemblance in attitudes to foods. *Developmental Psychology, 20*, 309–314.

Rozin, P., Haidt, J., & McCauley, C.R. (1993). Disgust. In M.Lewis & J.Haviland (Eds.), *Handbook of emotions*. New York: Guilford.

Rozin, P., Lowery, L., & Ebert, R. (1994). Varieties of disgust faces and the structure of disgust. *Journal of Personality and Social Psychology, 66*, 870–881.

Rubin, S.S. (1990). Death of the future: An outcome study of bereaved parents in Israel. *Omega, 20*, 323–339.

Ruiz-Caballero, J.A., & Gonzalez, P. (1994). Implicit and explicit memory bias in depressed and nondepressed subjects. *Cognition and Emotion, 8*, 555–569.

Rumelhart, D.E., & McClelland, J.L. (1986). *Parallel distributed processing: Explorations in the microstructure of cognition: Vol. 1. Foundations*. Cambridge, MA: MIT Press.

Rumelhart, D.E., & Ortony, A. (1977). The representation of knowledge in memory. In R.C. Anderson, R.J. Spiro, & W.E. Montague (Eds.), *Schooling and the acquisition of knowledge*. Hillsdale, NJ: Lawrence Erlbaum Associates Inc.

Russell, B. (1945). *A history of western philosophy*. New York: Simon & Schuster.

Russell, B. (1950). *The conquest of happiness*. New York: Liveright.

Russell, G.F.M. (1970). Anorexia nervosa: Its identity as an illness and its treatment. In J.H. Price (Ed.), *Modern trends in psychological medicine* (Vol. 2). London: Butterworth.

Russell, G.F.M. (1979). Bulimia nervosa: An ominous variant of anorexia nervosa. *Psychological Medicine, 9*, 429–448.

Russell, J. (1994). Is there universal recognition of emotion from facial expression? A review of the cross-cultural studies. *Psychological Bulletin, 115*, 102–141.

Rutter, M. (1984). Psychopathology and development: 1. Childhood antecedents of adult psychiatric disorder. *Australian and New Zealand Journal of Psychiatry, 18*, 225–234.

Ryff, C. D. (1989). Happiness is everything, or is it? Explorations on the meaning of psychological well-being. *Journal of Personality and Social Psychology, 57*, 1069–1081.

Ryle, G. (1949). *The concept of mind*. London: Penguin.

Sackheim, H.A., & Gur, R.C. (1978). Self-deception, self-confrontation and consciousness. In G.E. Schwartz & D. Shapiro (Eds.), *Consciousness and self-regulation: Advances in research* (Vol. 2). New York: Plenum.

Salkovskis, P.M. (1985). Obsessional-compulsive problems: A cognitive-behavioural analysis. *Behaviour Research and Therapy, 23*, 571–583.

Salkovskis, P.M., Clark, D.M., & Hackmann, A. (1991). Treatment of panic attacks using cognitive therapy without exposure or breathing retraining. *Behaviour Research and Therapy, 29*, 161–166.

Salovey, P. (Ed.). (1991). *The psychology of jealousy and envy*. New York: Guilford Press.

Sandvik, E., Diener, E., & Seidlitz, L. (1993). Subjective well-being: The convergence and stability of self-report and non-self-report measures. *Journal of Personality, 61*, 317–342.

Schachter, S. (1971). *Emotion, obesity, and crime*. New York: Academic Press.

Schachter, S., & Singer, J.E. (1962). Cognitive, social, and physiological determinants of emotional state. *Psychological Review, 69*, 379–399.

Schalling, D., Cronholm, B., & Asberg, M. (1975). Components of state and trait anxiety as related to personality and arousal. In L. Levi (Ed.), *Emotions: Their parameters and measurement*. New York: Raven Press.

Schank, R.C. (1982). *Dynamic memory*. Cambridge, UK: Cambridge University Press.

Schank, R.C. (1986). *Explanation patterns*. Hillsdale, NJ: Lawrence Erlbaum Associates Inc.

Schank, R.C., & Abelson, R.P. (1977). *Scripts, plans, goals and understanding*. Hillsdale, NJ: Lawrence Erlbaum Associates Inc.

Scheier, M.F., & Carver, C.S. (1987). Dispositional optimism and physical well-being: The influence of generalized outcome expectancies on health. *Journal of Personality, 55*, 169–210.

Scheler, M. (1972). *Ressentiment*. New York: Schocken Books.

Scherer, K.R. (1984). On the nature and function of emotion: A component process approach. In K.R. Scherer & P. Ekman (Ed.), *Approaches to emotion*. Hillsdale, NJ: Lawrence Erlbaum Associates Inc.

Scherer, K.R. (1993). Studying the emotion-antecedent appraisal process: An expert system approach. *Cognition and Emotion, 7*, 325–355.

Schwartz, G.E. (1982). Physiological patterning and emotion: Implications for the self-regulation of emotion. In K.R. Blankstein & J. Polivy (Eds.), *Self control and self-modification of emotional behaviour*. New York: Plenum.

Schwartz, G.E. (1990). Psychobiology of repression and health: A systems approach. In J.L. Singer (Ed.), *Repression and dissociation: Implications for personality theory, psychopathology, and health*. Chicago, IL: University of Chicago Press.

Scruton, R. (1986). *Spinoza*. Oxford: Oxford University Press.

Seligman, M. (1971). Phobias and preparedness. *Behavior Therapy, 2*, 307–320.

Seligman, M.E.P. (1975). *Helplessness: On depression, development and death*. San Francisco, CA: Freeman.

Seligman, M.E.P. (1988). Competing theories of panic. In S. Rachman & J.D. Maser (Eds.), *Panic: Psychological perspectives*. Hillsdale, NJ: Lawrence Erlbaum Associates Inc.

Seneca. (1963). De Ira. [On anger]. In J.W. Basore (Trans), *Moral essays*. Cambridge, MA: Harvard University Press.

Shands, H.C., & Schor, N. (1982). The modern syndrome of phobo-phobia and its management. In R.L. Dupont (Ed.), *Phobia: A comprehensive summary of modern treatments*. New York: Brunner/Mazel.

Shaver, P.R., & Hazan, C. (1988). A biased overview of the study of love. *Journal of Personal and Social Relationships, 5*, 474–501.

Shaver, P.R., Wu, S., & Schwartz, J.C. (1991). Cross-cultural similarities and differences in emotion and its representation: A prototype approach. In M.S. Clark (Ed.), *Review of personality and social psychology* (Vol 13). Newbury Park, CA: Sage.

Shepard, R.N. (1978). The mental image. *American Psychologist, 33*, 125–137.

Sheppard, L.C., & Teasdale, J.D. (1996). Depressive thinking: Changes in schematic mental models of self and world. *Psychological Medicine, 26*, 1043–1051.

Shiffrin, R.M., Dumais, S.T., & Schneider, W. (1981). Characteristics of automatism. In J. Long & A. Baddeley (Eds.), *Attention and performance* (Vol. IX). Hillsdale, NJ: Lawrence Erlbaum Associates Inc.

Shiffrin, R.M., & Schneider, W. (1977). Controlled and automatic human information processing: II. Perceptual learning, automatic attending and a general theory. *Psychological Review, 84*, 127–190.

Shore, J.H., Vollmer, W.M., & Tatum, E.L. (1989). Community patterns of posttraumatic stress disorder. *Journal of Nervous and Mental Disease, 177*, 681–685.

Shuchter, S.R., & Zisook, S. (1993). The course of normal grief. In M.S. Stroebe, W. Stroebe & R.O. Hansson (Eds.), *Handbook of bereavement: Theory, research, and intervention*. Cambridge, UK: Cambridge University Press

Siegman, A.W. (1993). Cardiovascular consequences of expressing, experiencing and repressing anger. *Journal of Behavioural Medicine, 16*, 539–569.

Siegman, A.W., & Wolfe, T.W. (Eds.) (1994). *Anger, hostility and the heart*. Hillsdale, NJ: Lawrence Erlbaum Associates Inc.

Simon, R.W. (1992). Parental role strains, salience of parental identity and gender differences in psychological distress. *Journal of Health and Social Behavior, 33*, 25–35.

Sincoff, J.B. (1992). Ambivalence and defense: Effects of a repressive style on normal adolescents' and young adults' mixed feelings. *Journal of Abnormal Psychology, 101*, 251–256.

Singer, J.L. (Ed.). (1990). *Repression and dissociation: Implications for personality theory, psychopathology and health*. Chicago, IL: University of Chicago Press.

Skinner, B.F. (1974). *About behaviourism*. New York: Alfred A. Knopf.

Slapion, J.J., & Carver, C.S. (1981). Self-directed attention and facilitation of intellectual performance among persons high in test anxiety. *Cognitive Therapy and Research, 5*, 115–121.

Smith, C.A., & Lazarus, R.S. (1990). Emotion and adaptation. In L.A. Pervin (Ed.), *Handbook of personality: Theory and research*. New York: Guilford.

Smith, P., & Jones, O.R. (1986). *The philosophy of mind: An introduction.* Cambridge, UK: Cambridge University Press.

Smith, R.H., Diener, E., & Wedell, D.H. (1989). Intrapersonal and social comparison determinants of happiness: A range-frequency analysis. *Journal of Personality and Social Psychology, 56,* 317–325.

Snell, W.E., McDonald, K., & Koch, W.R. (1991). Anger provoking experiences: A multidimensional scaling analysis. *Personality and Individual Differences, 12,* 1095–1104.

Solkoff, N., Gray, P., & Keill, S.N. (1986). Which Vietnam veterans develop posttraumatic stress disorders? Journal of *Clinical Psychology, 42,* 687–698.

Solomon, R.C. (1993). *The passions: Emotions and the meaning of life.* Indianapolis, IN: Hackett.

Solomon, R.C. (1994). Sympathy and vengeance: The role of the emotions in justice. In S.H.M. Van Goozen, N.E. Van de Poll, & J.A. Sergeant (Eds.), *Emotions: Essays on emotion theory.* Hillsdale, NJ: Lawrence Erlbaum Associates Inc.

Spiegel, D., & Cardena, E. (1990). Dissociative mechanisms in posttraumatic stress disorder. In M.E. Wolf & A.D. Mosnaim (Eds.), *Posttraumatic stress disorder: Etiology, phenomenology and treatment.* Washington DC: American Psychiatric Press.

Spielberger, C.D., Gorsuch, R.L., and Lushene, R. (1970). *Trait anxiety scale.* Palo Alto, CA: Consulting Psychologists Press.

Spielberger, C.D., Johnson, E.H., Russell, S.F., Crane, R.J., Jacobs, G.A., & Worden, T.J. (1985). The experience and expression of anger: Construction and validation of an anger expression scale. In M.A. Chesney & R.H. Rosenman (Eds.), *Anger and hostility in cardiovascular and behavioural disorders.* Washington, DC: Hemisphere.

Spinoza, B. (1955). *The ethics.* New York: Dover. (Original work published 1677)

Sprengelmeyer, R., Young, A.W., Calder, A.J., Karnat, A., Lange, H., Homberg, V., Perrett, D.I., & Rowland, D. (in press). Perception of faces and emotions: Loss of disgust in Huntington's disease. *Brain.*

Stearns, C.S. (1993). Sadness. In M. Lewis & J.M. Haviland (Eds.), *Handbook of emotions.* New York: Guilford.

Stein, N.L., & Trabasso, T. (1992). The organisation of emotional experience: Creating links among emotion, thinking, language, and intentional action. *Cognition and Emotion, 6,* 225–244.

Stemller, G. (1989). The autonomic differentiation of emotions revisited: Convergent and discriminant validation. *Psychophysiology, 26,* 617–632.

Storr, A. (1988). *Churchill's black dog, Kafka's mice, and other phenomena of the human mind.* New York: Grove Weidenfeld.

Stroebe, M.S., Stroebe, W., & Hansson, R.O. (1993). Bereavement research and theory: An introduction to the handbook. In M.S. Stroebe, W. Stroebe & R.O. Hansson (Eds.), *Handbook of bereavement: Theory, research, and intervention.* Cambridge, UK: Cambridge University Press.

Stroebe, W., & Stroebe, M.S. (1993). Determinants of adjustment to bereavement in younger widows and widowers. In M.S. Stroebe, W. Stroebe & R.O. Hansson (Eds.), *Handbook of bereavement: Theory, research, and intervention.* Cambridge, UK: Cambridge University Press.

Stroop, J.R. (1935). Studies of interference in serial verbal reaction. *Journal of Experimental Psychology, 18,* 643–662.

Sutherland, S. (1976). *Breakdown: A personal crisis and a medical dilemma.* London: Weidenfeld & Nicolson.

Sutherland, S. (1994). *Irrationality: The enemy within.* London: Penguin.

Sweeney, P.D., Anderson, K., & Bailey, S. (1986). Attributional style in depression: A meta-analytic review. *Journal of Personality and Social Psychology, 50,* 974–991.

Tallis, F. (1989). Experimental investigations of worry. Unpublished PhD thesis. University of London.

Tallis, F. (1995a). *Obsessive compulsive disorder: A cognitive and neuro-psychological perspective.* Chichester, UK: Wiley.

Tallis, F. (1995b). The characteristics of obsessional thinking: Difficulty demonstrating the obvious? *Clinical Psychology and Psychotherapy, 2,* 24–39.

Tallis, F., & Eysenck, M.W. (1994). Worry: Mechanisms and modulating influences. *Behavioural and Cognitive Psychotherapy, 22,* 37–56.

Tallis, F., Eysenck, M.W., & Mathews, A. (1991a). Elevated evidence requirements and worry. *Personality and Individual Differences, 12,* 21–27.

Tallis, F., Eysenck, M.W., & Mathews, A. (1991b). Worry: A critical analysis of some theoretical approaches. *Anxiety Research, 4,* 97–108.

Tallis, F., Eysenck, M.W., & Mathews, A. (1992). A questionnaire measure for the measurement of non-pathological worry. *Personality and Individual Differences, 13,* 161–168.

Tangney, J.P. (1992). Situational determinants of shame and guilt in young adulthood. *Personality and Social Psychology Bulletin, 18,* 199–206.

Tangney, J.P., & Fischer, K.W. (Eds.) (1995). *Self-conscious emotions: The psychology of shame, guilt, embarrassment, and pride.* New York: Guilford.

Tantam, D., & Whittaker, J. (1992). Personality disorder and self-wounding. *British Journal of Psychiatry, 161,* 451–464.

Tata, P.R., Leibowitz, J.A., Prunty, M.J., Cameron, M., & Pickering, A.D. (1996). Attentional bias in obsessional compulsive disorder. *Behaviour Research and Therapy, 34,* 53–60.

Teasdale, J.D. (1983). Negative thinking in depression: Cause, effect, or reciprocal relationship? *Advances in Behaviour Research and Therapy, 5,* 3–25.

Teasdale, J.D. (1988). Cognitive vulnerability to persistent depression. *Cognition and Emotion, 2,* 247–274.

Teasdale, J. (1993). Emotion and two kinds of meaning: Cognitive therapy and applied cognitive science. *Behaviour Research and Therapy, 31,* 339–354.

Teasdale, J., & Barnard, P. (1993). *Affect, cognition and change.* Hove, UK: Lawrence Erlbaum Associates Ltd.

Teasdale, J.D., & Fogarty S.J. (1979). Differential effects of induced mood on retrieval of pleasant and unpleasant events from episodic memory. *Journal of Abnormal Psychology, 88,* 248–257.

Teasdale, J.D., Taylor, M.J., Cooper, Z., Hayhurst, H., & Paykel, E.S. (1995). Depressive thinking: Shifts in construct accessibility or in schematic mental models? *Journal of Abnormal Psychology, 104,* 500–507.

Tennov, D. (1979). *Love and limerance.* New York: Stein & Day.

Terr, L.C. (1991). Childhood traumas: An outline and overview. *American Journal of Psychiatry, 148,* 10–20.

Thoits, P.A. (1985). Self-labeling processes in mental illness: The role of emotional deviance. *American Journal of Sociology, 91,* 221–249.

Thoits, P.A. (1986). Multiple identities: Examining gender and marital status differences in distress. *American Sociological Review, 51*, 259–272.

Thompson, C. (1989). The syndrome of seasonal affective disorder. In C. Thompson & T. Silverstone (Eds.), *Seasonal affective disorder*. London: CNS Publishers.

Thrasher, S.M., Dalgleish, T., & Yule, W. (1994). Information processing in posttraumatic stress disorder. *Behaviour Research and Therapy, 32*, 247–254.

Tillman, J.G., Nash, M.R., & Lerner, P.M. (1994). Does trauma cause dissociative pathology? In S.J. Lynn & J.W. Rhue (Eds.), *Dissociation: Clinical and theoretical perspectives*. New York: Guilford.

Tobias, B.A., Kihlstrom, J.F., & Schachter, D.L. (1992). Emotion and implicit memory. In S.-A. Christianson (Ed.), *The handbook of emotion and memory: Research and theory*. Hillsdale, NJ: Lawrence Erlbaum Associates Inc.

Tolstoy, L. (1980). *Anna Karenina*. Oxford: Oxford University Press. (Original work published 1877)

Tomkins, S.S. (1963). *Affect, imagery and consciousness: Vol. 2. The negative affects*. New York: Springer.

Tomkins, S.S. (1984). Affect theory. In K.R. Scherer & P. Ekman (Eds.), *Approaches to emotion*. Hillsdale, NJ: Lawrence Erlbaum Associates Inc.

Tov-Ruach, L. (1980). Jealousy, attention and loss. In A.O. Rorty (Ed.), *Explaining emotions*. Berkeley, CA: University of California Press.

Tran, T.V., Wright, R., & Chatters, L. (1991). Health, stress, psychological resources, and subjective well-being among older blacks. *Psychology and Aging, 6*, 100–108.

Trandel, D.V., & McNally, R.J. (1987). Perception of threat cues in post-traumatic stress disorder: Semantic processing without awareness? *Behaviour Research and Therapy, 25*, 469–476.

Trauer, H.C., & Pennebaker, J.W. (Eds.) (1993). *Emotion, inhibition and health*. Seattle, WA: Hogrefe & Huber.

Tuma, A.H., & Maser, J.D. (1985). Introduction and overview of selected issues. In A.H. Tuma & J.D. Maser (Eds.), *Anxiety and the anxiety disorders*. Hillsdale, NJ: Lawrence Erlbaum Associates Inc.

Turner, C.W., Layton, J.F., & Simons, L.S. (1975). Naturalistic studies of aggressive behaviour: Aggressive stimuli, victim visibility, and horn honking. *Journal of Personality and Social Psychology, 31*, 1098–1107.

Turner, T.J., & Ortony, A. (1992). Basic emotions: Can conflicting criteria converge? *Psychological Review, 99*, 566–571.

Turvey, C., & Salovey, P. (1994). Measures of repression: Converging on the same construct? Imagination. *Cognition and Personality, 13*, 279–289.

Tversky, A., & Kahneman, D. (1974). Judgement under uncertainty: Heuristics and biases. *Science, 125*, 1124–1131.

Vaillant, G.E. (1990). Repression in college men followed for half a century. In J.L. Singer (Ed.), *Repression and dissociation*. Chicago, IL: University of Chicago Press.

Van de Kolk, B.A., Perry, J.C., & Herman, J.L. (1991). Childhood origins of self-destructive behavior. *American Journal of Psychiatry, 148*, 1665–1671.

Van Egmond, M., & Jonker, D. (1988). Sexual abuse and physical assault: Risk factors for recurrent suicidal behaviour in women. *Tijdschraft die Psychiatrie, 30*, 21–38.

Van Oppen, P., Hoekstra, R.J., & Emmelkamp, P.M.G. (1995). The structure of obsessive-compulsive symptoms. *Behaviour Research and Therapy, 33*, 15–23.

Vargas, L.A., Loye, F., & Hodde-Vargas, J. (1989). Exploring the multi-dimensional aspects of grief reactions. *American Journal of Psychiatry, 146*, 1484–1488.

Vaughn, C.E., & Leff, J.P. (1976). The influence of family and social factors on the course of psychiatric illness: A comparison of schizophrenic and depressed neurotic patients. *British Journal of Psychiatry, 129*, 125–137.

Vazquez, C. (1987). Judgement of contingency: Cognitive biases in depressed and nondepressed subjects. *Journal of Personality and Social Psychology, 52*, 419–431.

Veenhoven, R. (1984). *Conditions of happiness*. Dordrecht, The Netherlands: D. Reidel.

Veenhoven, R. (1991). Is happiness relative? *Social Indicators Research, 24*, 1–34.

Velten, E. (1968). A laboratory task for induction of mood states. *Behaviour Research and Therapy, 6*, 473–482.

Vitousek, K.B., & Ewald, L.S. (1993). Self-representation in eating disorders: A cognitive perspective. In Z.V. Segal & S.J. Blatt (Eds.), *The self in emotional distress: Cognitive and psychodynamic perspectives*. New York: Guilford Press.

Waller, G. (1992). Sexual abuse and the severity of bulimic symptoms. *British Journal of Psychiatry, 161*, 90–93.

Ware, J., Jain, K., Burgess, I., & Davey, G.C.L. (1994). Factor analysis of common animal fears: Support for a disease-avoidance model. *Behaviour Research and Therapy, 32*, 57–63.

Wason, P.C., & Johnson-Laird, P.N. (Eds.) (1968). *Thinking and reasoning*. Harmondsworth: Penguin.

Watson, D., & Clark, L.A. (1992). Affects separable and inseparable: On the hierarchical arrangement of the negative affects. *Journal of Personality and Social Psychology, 62*, 489–505.

Watson, D., Clark, L.A., Weber, K., Assenheimer, J.S., Strauss, M.E., & McCormick, R.A. (1995). Testing a tripartite model: II. Exploring the symptom structure of anxiety and depression in student, adult, and patient samples. *Journal of Abnormal Psychology, 104*, 15–25.

Watson, D., Weber, K., Assenheimer, J.S., Clark, L.A., Strauss, M.E., & McCormick, R.A. (1995). Testing a tripartite model: 1. Evaluating the convergent and discriminant validity of anxiety and depression symptom scales. *Journal of Abnormal Psychology, 104*, 3–14.

Watson, J.B. (1913). Psychology as the behaviorist views it. *Psychological Review, 20*, 158–177.

Watson, J.B. (1919). *Psychology from the standpoint of a behaviourist*. Philadelphia, PA: Lippincott

Watson, J.B. (1930). *Behaviorism*. Chicago, IL: University of Chicago Press.

Watts, F.N. (1986). Cognitive processing in phobias. *Behavioural Psychotherapy, 14*, 295–301.

Watts, F.N. (1995). An information-processing approach to compulsive checking. *Clinical Psychology and Psychotherapy, 2*, 69–77.

Watts, F.N., Trezise, L., & Sharrock, R. (1986). Processing of phobic stimuli. *British Journal of Clinical Psychology, 25*, 253–259.

Webb, K., & Davey, G.C.L. (1992). Disgust sensitivity and fear of animals: Effect of exposure to violent or revulsive material. *Anxiety, Stress and Coping, 5*, 329–335.

Wegner, D.M. (1989). *White bears and other unwanted thoughts*. New York: Viking.

Wegner, D.M. (1994). Ironic processes of mental control. *Psychological Review, 101*, 34–52.

Weinberger, D.A., Schwartz, G.E., & Davidson. R.J. (1979). Low-anxious, high anxious and repressive coping styles: Psychometric patterns and behavioural responses to stress. *Journal of Abnormal Psychology, 88*, 369–380.

Weiner, B. (1972). *Theories of motivation: From mechanism to cognition*. Chicago, IL: Rand McNally.

Weiner, B. (1985). An attributional theory of achievement motivation and emotion. *Psychological Review, 92*, 548–573.

Weiner, B. (1986). *An attributional theory of motivation and emotion*. New York: Springer-Verlag.

Weiner, B., & Graham, S. (1984). An attributional approach to emotional development. In C. Izard, J. Kagan, & R. Zajonc (Eds.), *Emotions, cognition, and behaviour*. New York: Cambridge University Press.

Weiner, B., Russell, D., & Lerman, D. (1978). Affective consequences of causal ascriptions. In J.H. Harvey, W.J. Ickes, & R.F. Kidd (Eds.), *New directions in attribution research* (Vol. 2). Hillsdale, NJ: Lawrence Erlbaum Associates Inc.

Weishaar, M. (1993). *Aaron T. Beck*. London: Sage.

Weiskrantz , L. (1986). *Blindsight*. Oxford: Clarendon Press.

Weiss, J.M., Glazer, H.I., & Pohorecky, L.A. (1976). Coping behavior and neurochemical changes. An alternative explanation for the original "learned helplessness" experiments. In G. Serban & A. Kling (Eds.), *Animal models in human psychobiology*. New York: Plenum.

Weissman, M.M. (1974). The epidemiology of suicide attempts 1960 to 1974. *Archives of General Psychiatry, 30*, 737–746.

Weissman, M.M. (1986). The relationship between panic disorder and agoraphobia: An epidemiologic perspective. *Psychopharmacology Bulletin, 22*, 787–791.

Weissman, M.M. (1987). Advances in psychiatric epidemiology: Rates and risks for major depression. *American Journal of Public Health, 77*, 445–451.

Weissman, M.M., & Klerman, G.L. (1977). Sex difference and the epidemiology of depression. *Archives of General Psychiatry, 34,* 98–111.

Wells, A. (1987). Self-attentional processes in anxiety: an experimental study. Unpublished doctoral dissertation. Aston University, Birmingham, UK.

Wells, A. (1994). A multi-dimensional measure of worry: Development and preliminary validation of the Anxious Thoughts Inventory. *Anxiety, Stress, and Coping, 6*, 289–299.

Wells, A., & Matthews, G. (1994). *Attention and emotion: A clinical perspective*. Hove, UK: Lawrence Erlbaum Associates Ltd.

Wessman, A.E., & Ricks, D.F. (1966). *Mood and personality*. New York: Holt, Rinehart & Winston.

White, G.L., & Mullen, P.E. (1989). *Jealousy: Theory, research and clinical strategies*. New York: Guilford Press.

Williams, J.M.G. (1992). *The psychological treatment of depression* (2nd edn.). London: Routledge.

Williams, J.M.G., Watts, F.N., MacLeod, C., & Mathews, A. (1988). *Cognitive psychology and emotional disorders*. Chichester, UK: Wiley.

Wills, T.A. (1981). Downward comparison principles in social psychology. *Psychological Bulletin, 90*, 245–271.

Winters, K.C., & Neale, J.M. (1985). Mania and low self-esteem. *Journal of Abnormal Psychology, 94*, 282–290.

Winton, W. (1986). The role of facial response in self-reports of emotion: A critique of Laird. *Journal of Personality and Social Psychology, 50*, 808–812.

Wittgenstein, L. (1958). *Philosophical investigations*. Oxford: Blackwell.

Wolfgang, M.E. (1979). Aggression and violence: Crime and social control. In S. Feshback & A. Fraczek (Eds.), *Aggression and behavior change*. New York: Praeger.

Wolfgang. M.E., & Ferracuti, F. (1967). *The subculture of violence*. New York: Barnes & Noble.

Wolpe, J., & Rowan, V.C. (1988). Panic disorder: A product of classical conditioning. *Behaviour Research and Therapy, 26*, 441–450.

Woods, W.A. (1975). Syntax, semantics, and speech. In D. Raj Reddy (Ed.), *Speech recognition: Invited papers presented at the 1974 IEEE Symposium*. New York: Academic Press.

World Health Organization. (1992). *The ICD-10 classification of mental and behavioural disorders: Clinical descriptions and diagnostic guidelines*. Geneva: Author.

Wortman, C.B., Silver, R.C., & Kessler, R.C. (1993). The meaning of loss and adjustment to bereavement. In M.S. Stroebe, W. Stroebe & R.O. Hansson (Eds.), *Handbook of bereavement: Theory, research, and intervention*. Cambridge, UK: Cambridge University Press.

Wright, F.D., Beck, A.T., Newman, C.F., & Liese, B.S. (1993). Cognitive therapy of substance abuse: Theoretical rationale. *NIDA Research Monograph Series, 137*, 123–146.

Wycherley, R.J. (1995). Self-evaluation and self-reinforcement in depressed patients. *Clinical Psychology and Psychotherapy, 2*, 98–107.

Yates, J.L., & Nasby, W. (1993). Dissociation, affect, and network models of memory: An integrative proposal. *Journal of Traumatic Stress, 6*, 305–326.

Zajonc, R.B. (1980). Feeling and thinking: Preferences need no inferences. *American Psychologist, 35*, 151–175.

Zajonc, R.B., Murphy, S.T., & Inglehart, M. (1989). Feeling and facial efference: Implications of the vascular theory of emotion. *Psychological Review, 96*, 395–416.

Zaslow, R. (1950). A new approach to the problem of conceptual thinking in schizophrenia. *Journal of Consulting Psychology, 14*, 335–339.

Zeiss, R., & Dickman, H. (1989). PTSD 40 years later: Incidence and person-situation correlates in former POWs. *Journal of Clinical Psychology, 45*, 80–87.

Zillmann, D. (1971). Excitation transfer in communication-mediated aggressive behaviour. *Journal of Experimental Social Psychology, 7*, 419–434.

Zillmann, D. (1978). Attribution and misattribution of excitatory reactions. In J.H. Harvey, W.J. Ickes, & R.F. Kidd (Eds.), *New directions in attribution research* (Vol.2.). Hillsdale, NJ: Lawrence Erlbaum Associates Inc.

Zillmann, D. (1979). *Hostility and aggression*. Hillsdale, NJ: Lawrence Erlbaum Associates Inc.

Zillmann, D., Johnson, R.C., & Day, K.D. (1974). Attribution of apparent arousal and proficiency of recovery from sympathetic activation affecting excitation transfer to aggressive behaviour. *Journal of Experimental Social Psychology, 10*, 503–515.

Author index

Subject index